*Special Edition*

# Using
# JavaScript
# Second
# Edition

# USING
# JAVASCRIPT
# SECOND
# EDITION

*Written by Andrew Wooldridge and Mike Morgan with*

*Rick Darnell• Jerry Honeycutt• Mark C. Reynolds*

# Special Edition Using JavaScript, Second Edition

Library of Congress Catalog No.: 97-65024

ISBN: 0-7897-1138-9

99  98  97     6  5  4  3  2  1

Interpretation of the printing code: the rightmost double-digit number is the year of the book's printing; the rightmost single-digit number, the number of the book's printing. For example, a printing code of 97-1 shows that the first printing of the book occurred in 1997.

Screen reproductions in this book were created using Collage Plus from Inner Media, Inc., Hollis, NH.

# Credits

**PRESIDENT**
Roland Elgey

**SENIOR VICE PRESIDENT/PUBLISHING**
Don Fowley

**PUBLISHER**
Stacy Hiquet

**PUBLISHING MANAGER**
Jim Minatel

**GENERAL MANAGER**
Joseph Muldoon

**EDITORIAL SERVICES DIRECTOR**
Elizabeth Keaffaber

**ACQUISITIONS DIRECTOR**
Cheryl D. Willoughby

**ACQUISITIONS EDITOR**
Stephanie J. McComb

**PRODUCT DIRECTORS**
Mark Cierzniak
Stephen L. Miller

**SENIOR EDITOR**
Patrick Kanouse

**PRODUCTION EDITOR**
William McManus

**EDITORS**
Sean Dixon
Patricia Kinyon

**STRATEGIC MARKETING MANAGER**
Barry Pruett

**WEBMASTER**
Thomas H. Bennett

**PRODUCT MARKETING MANAGER**
Kristine R. Ankney

**ASSISTANT PRODUCT MARKETING MANAGER/ DESIGN**
Christy M. Miller

**ASSISTANT PRODUCT MARKETING MANAGER/ SALES**
Karen Hagen

**TECHNICAL EDITORS**
Russ Jacobs
Jim O'Donnell
Ernie Sanders

**MEDIA DEVELOPMENT SPECIALIST**
Brandon Penticuff

**TECHNICAL SUPPORT SPECIALIST**
Nadeem Muhammed

**ACQUISITIONS COORDINATOR**
Jane K. Brownlow

**SOFTWARE RELATIONS COORDINATOR**
Susan D. Gallagher

**EDITORIAL ASSISTANT**
Andrea Duvall

**BOOK DESIGNER**
Ruth Harvey

**COVER DESIGNER**
Dan Armstrong

**PRODUCTION TEAM**
Michael Beaty
Jenny Earhart
Maribeth Echard
Laura A. Knox
Staci Somers

**INDEXER**
Chris Barrick
Chris Wilcox

Composed in *Century Old Style* and *ITC Franklin Gothic* by Que Corporation.

*To my mother, Rosemarie, who teaches my family the value of fun*
*—Mike Morgan*

*To Jess*                                     *—Mark Reynolds*

# About the Authors

**Rick Darnell** is a native of the Midwestern plains, currently living in a place surrounded by mountains in Missoula, MT, with his wife and two daughters. He began his career in print after graduating from Kansas State University with a degree in broadcasting. While spending time as a freelance journalist and writer, Rick has seen the full gamut of personal computers since starting out with a Radio Shack Model I in the late 1970s. He has contributed to a variety of Que books, including *Web Programming Desktop Reference*, *Running a Perfect Web Site with Windows*, and *Intranet Publishing*. When not in front of his computer, Rick serves on a regional hazardous materials team.

**Jerry Honeycutt** provides business-oriented technical leadership to the Internet community and software development industry. He has served companies such as The Travelers, IBM, Nielsen North America, IRM, Howard Systems International, and NCR. Jerry has participated in the industry since before the days of Microsoft Windows 1.0, and is completely hooked on Windows and the Internet.

Jerry is the author of *Using Microsoft Plus!*; *Using the Internet with Windows 95*; *Windows 95 Registry & Customization Handbook*; *Special Edition Using the Windows 95 Registry*; *VBScript by Example*; *Special Edition Using the Internet, Third Edition*; *Using the Internet, Second Edition*; *Windows NT and Windows 95 Registry Customization Handbook*; and *Special Edition Using HTML 3.2, Third Edition*, all of which are published by Que. Many of his books are sold internationally and have been translated into a variety of foreign languages, including French, Italian, Korean, Japanese, Portuguese, Russian, Spanish, and Turkish.

Jerry is also a contributing author of *Special Edition Using Windows 95*; *Special Edition Using Netscape 2*; *Platinum Edition Using Windows 95*; *Visual Basic for Applications Database Solutions*; *Special Edition Using Netscape 3*; *Windows 95 Exam Guide*; *Netscape Navigator 3 Starter Kit*; *Using Java Workshop*; *Special Edition Using JScript*; *Internet Explorer Plug-In and ActiveX Companion*; and *Windows NT Server 4.0 Advanced Technical Reference*, all of which are published by Que. He has been published in *Computer Language* magazine and is a regular speaker at Windows World, Comdex, and other industry trade shows on topics related to software development, Windows, and the Internet.

Jerry graduated from the University of Texas at Dallas in 1992 with a B.S. degree in Computer Science. He currently lives in the Dallas suburb of Frisco, Texas, with two Westies, Corky and Turbo, and a bird called Opie. Jerry is an avid golfer, and has a passion for fine photography and international travel. Feel free to contact Jerry on the Internet at **jerry@honeycutt.com** or visit his Web site at **http://rampages.onramp.net/~jerry**.

**Mike Morgan** is founder and president of DSE, Inc., a full-service Web presence provider and software development shop. The DSE team has developed software for such companies as Intelect, Magnavox, DuPont, the American Biorobotics Company, and Satellite Systems Corporation, as well as for the Government of Iceland and the Royal Saudi Air Force. DSE's Web sites include the prestigious Nikka Galleria, an online art gallery. DSE's sites are noted for their effectiveness—one of the company's sites generated sales of over $100,000 within 30 days of being announced.

During Academic Year 1989-1990, Mike was invited by retired Navy Admiral Ron Hays to serve as the first Fellow of the Pacific International Center for High Technology Research (PICHTR) in Honolulu. PICHTR is a spin-off the University of Hawaii, and bridges the gap between academic research and industrial applications. Mike directed the first technology transfer initiatives at PICHTR, and helped PICHTR win its first industrial contract. Mike assisted Admiral Hays in presenting PICHTR and its mission to the Hawaii research community, the Hawaii legislature, and Hawaii's representatives to Congress.

Mike is a frequent speaker at seminars on information technology, and has taught computer science and software engineering at Chaminade University (the University of Honolulu) and in the graduate program of Hawaii Pacific University. He has given seminars for the IEEE, National Seminars, the University of Hawaii, Purdue University, and Notre Dame.

Mike is the co-manager of the CGI archives of the HTML Writers Guild, and is a member of the Help Team for Matt Wright's Script Archive. In those capacities, he works with programmers around the world helping set up advanced solutions on the Web.

He holds a Master of Science in Systems Management from the Florida Institute of Technology and a Bachelor of Science in Mathematics from Wheaton College, where he concentrated his studies on computer science. He has also taken numerous graduate courses in computer science through the National Technological University. Mike is a member of the IEEE Computer Society.

Mike can usually be found in his office at DSE, drinking Diet Pepsi and writing Perl and C++. He lives in Virginia Beach with his wife, Jean, and their six children.

**Mark C. Reynolds** has wide-ranging interests in network programming, Java, UNIX internals, and computer animation. He holds an M.S. degree in mathematics from M.I.T. He has edited and translated a number of works in the physical sciences and mathematics, including Stanislaus Ulam's posthumous collection of essays, *Science, Computers and People: From the Tree of Mathematics.*

He is a co-author of Que's highly successful titles *Special Edition Using JavaScript, Special Edition Using JScript*, and *Client/Server Programming with RPC and DCE*. He has also been a contributing editor to *Web Developer* magazine. Mark is an avid rock climber and mountaineer (no Everest yet, however). He can be reached at **MarkCReynolds@msn.com**.

**Andrew Wooldridge** is assistant Webmaster at Wells Fargo Bank, a pioneer in online banking and Internet services since 1989. Prior to joining Wells Fargo, he was a Webmaster of Global Village Communications. Andrew started the HTML Writer's Guild and has created the popular JavaScript Index at **http://www.c2.org/~andreww/javascript/**, which receives 40,000 hits per month.

# Acknowledgments

To my wife, who supported me through the whole thing.

*Andrew Wooldridge*

While my name appears on the cover of this book, many people worked together to produce the manuscript, and to turn the manuscript into the book you are now holding. If you find this book useful, you have them to thank.

As with all my books, I am indebted to my colleague, Christopher Kepilino, and to my wife, Jean. Chris and Jean attend to the myriad of details that are needed to turn an idea into a book. They produce the screen shots, review the manuscript, and make sure that files and e-mail move smoothly between my desk and the publisher's. Thank you both.

My daughter, Sarah, also took time to assist in the final preparation of the manuscript. She was of invaluable assistance in keeping us all organized.

The folks at Que have been capable and professional, as usual. Mark Cierzniak and Stephen Miller reviewed the entire manuscript, providing valuable insight into many aspects of JavaScript. Bill McManus and Patrick Kanouse edited the entire manuscript. Stephanie McComb helped all of us stay focused on the task. Thank you all.

I am also indebted to the readers of this and my previous books for your feedback. Please feel free to visit my Web site (**http://www.dse.com/General/2.MLM_Home.shtml**) and send me e-mail at **morganm@mail.dse.com**. I look forward to hearing from you.

*Michael Morgan*
*Virginia Beach*
*February 27, 1997*

# We'd Like to Hear from You!

As part of our continuing effort to produce books of the highest possible quality, Que would like to hear your comments. To stay competitive, we *really* want you, as a computer book reader and user, to let us know what you like or dislike most about this book or other Que products.

You can mail comments, ideas, or suggestions for improving future editions to the address below, or send us a fax at (317) 581-4663. For the online inclined, Macmillan Computer Publishing has a forum on CompuServe (type **GO QUEBOOKS** at any prompt) through which our staff and authors are available for questions and comments. The address of our Internet site is **http://www.quecorp.com** (World Wide Web).

In addition to exploring our forum, please feel free to contact me personally to discuss your opinions of this book: I'm **mcierzniak.que.mcp.com** on the Internet, and **76245,476** on CompuServe.

Thanks in advance—your comments will help us to continue publishing the best books available on computer topics in today's market.

Mark Cierzniak
Product Development Specialist
Que Corporation
201 W. 103rd Street
Indianapolis, Indiana 46290
USA

# Contents at a Glance

# Table of Contents

## I | Fundamentals of JavaScript

# V | Learning from the Pros

## VII | Appendixes

### A JavaScript Resources 745

# Introduction

Five years ago, the Internet was mostly the province of academics and programmers and the World Wide Web was an obscure idea in the minds of a few researchers. Today, both are experiencing explosive growth and unparalleled interest. Web pages are being created at an astonishing rate. The fundamental challenge of Web page development is that, while it is easy to create a Web page, it is more difficult to create an attractive and exciting one.

HTML, the markup language that describes the appearance of a page, is easy to learn and requires no background in programming. HTML has undergone several revisions in order to meet the expanding needs of Web page authors. However, there are limits to what can be achieved inside HTML. The Java programming language was introduced to dramatically extend the Web developer's set of tools, though it's more complex than HTML. The basics of Java are relatively easy to learn (especially if you have a background in C programming); however, like most programming languages, it isn't easy to master. JavaScript bridges this gap.

JavaScript offers Web page authors a new level of sophistication, without requiring that they become programmers. JavaScript brings dynamic and powerful capabilities to Web pages, yet JavaScript is no more difficult to learn than HTML. JavaScript can be used to solve common problems, such as validating forms input, and also can be used to create dramatic and visually appealing content, which would be impossible with HTML. The goal of this book is to completely explore JavaScript, from the mundane to the extraordinary. It is designed as an introduction, a reference, and a continuous source of ideas, so that you may continually improve the Web pages that you create. ▨

# Who Should Use This Book?

JavaScript is a very new language—even newer than Java. Despite its newness, it has attracted great attention because of its expressive power. This book is directed to anyone who wants to master that power in order to create more attractive, dynamic, and interesting Web pages.

No programming knowledge is required to benefit from this book, but some knowledge of HTML and Web page authoring is assumed. No prior experience with JavaScript is required, either. This book is designed to be inclusive and to provide information to all JavaScript users, from complete beginners to established experts. If you create Web pages and want to enliven and enhance them, this book adds JavaScript to your toolbox. If you have already learned JavaScript and want to go further by breaking through to complete mastery, this book gives you the information to do so.

# How This Book Is Organized

The organization of this book is based upon a modular approach to learning JavaScript. The intent is to provide material suitable for all levels of knowledge, from the complete beginner to the advanced JavaScript programmer. To this end the book has seven sections.

Part I, "Fundamentals of JavaScript," introduces the JavaScript language. The complete syntax and semantics of the language are thoroughly described, with particular attention paid to the close correspondence between HTML elements and JavaScript objects. Chapter 1, "What Is JavaScript?" discusses JavaScript's overall role in the development of Web pages. Chapter 2, "JavaScript: The Language," gives the syntax of JavaScript. This leads directly into a description of the relationship between events on a Web page and JavaScript in Chapter 3, "Events and JavaScript."

Part II, "JavaScript In-Depth," is a greatly expanded presentation of the JavaScript object model that begins with an introduction to the all-important topic of JavaScript objects in Chapter 4, "JavaScript Objects." JavaScript objects can be classified as built-in objects or HTML objects. Built-in objects are thoroughly described in Chapter 5, "JavaScript Strings," while Chapter 6 through Chapter 8 focus on HTML objects.

Properties and methods of the Math object are the subject of Chapter 6, "The *Math* Object"; date and time manipulation is described in Chapter 7, "The *Date* and *Array* Objects," while Chapter 8, "Interactive HTML Objects," presents validation of HTML forms. Chapter 9, "Advanced HTML Objects and Navigation," discusses navigation objects, such as links and anchors. Chapter 10, "Dynamic HTML and Netscape Objects," covers the top-level objects associated with the Web browser. Part II concludes with a thorough treatment of user-defined objects in Chapter 11, "Creating Your Own JavaScript Objects."

One of the tremendous advantages of a scripting language such as JavaScript is its ability to integrate diverse technologies on a single Web page. Part III, "JavaScript and Live Objects," is devoted to examining such technologies. The Java programming language has received massive attention and is quite similar to JavaScript in structure. Chapter 12, "A Java Tutorial," provides a thorough introduction to Java, while Chapter 13, "Advanced Applets," focuses on the critical topic of Web page animation using Java. The focus then shifts to Netscape's Live Connect and its relationship to JavaScript in Chapter 14, "LiveConnect and JavaScript." Chapter 15, "JScript and Internet Explorer," contrasts JavaScript with Internet Explorer's JScript. Chapter 16, "ActiveX Controls and VBScript," introduces the concept of embedded objects using Microsoft's ActiveX technology.

Part IV, "JavaScript Special Effects," brings the user the most advanced material available on creating special effects by using JavaScript. Chapter 17, "Development Tools for JavaScript," describes available tools for JavaScript programming. Controlling Web page appearance, producing spectacular visual effects, using frames, and fine-tuning user interaction are each subjects of an in-depth treatment in Chapters 18 through 21. Each chapter contains at least one fully worked example that can be used immediately. Part IV concludes with an in-depth look at server-side JavaScript (Chapter 22, "JavaScript on the Server"), advanced applications using cookies (Chapter 23, "Using Cookies in Advanced Applications"), and a discussion of methods for debugging JavaScript applications (Chapter 24, "Debugging JavaScript Applications").

Part V, "Learning from the Pros," contains chapters regarding site outlines (Chapter 25), adding frames and controlling navigation (Chapter 26), and an online ordering system (Chapter 27). These chapters contain useful tips from leading professionals in each subject area discussed.

Part VI introduces two advanced tools that are used for Web page style and enhancement. Chapter 28, "Creating Netscape Layers," provides guidance on how to add stylistic appeal to your Web site with layers. Chapter 29, "Style Sheets," explains how to make the Web pages at your site uniform throughout for ease of use by visitors.

Part VII rounds out the book with five Appendixes containing useful JavaScript resources that you can reference while creating your own Web pages.

# Web Site Information

As you can see, this book does not include a CD-ROM. Instead, source code from the listings in the book, as well as links to other JavaScript resources, can be found at **http://www.quecorp.com/javascript2ed/** for easy download.

# How to Use This Book

If you are completely new to JavaScript, then you should begin with a thorough study of the introductory language materials of Part I. This should be followed by the more in-depth treatment of JavaScript objects in Part II. From that point on, any chapter or section may be consulted, based on your own particular interest. It should be noted that later chapters are generally more advanced than earlier ones.

If you are already familiar with JavaScript, then you are encouraged to explore this book in a goal-oriented manner. The alternative technologies discussed in Part III may be new to you, even if you are an experienced Web professional. Finally, Parts IV and VI should have something new and informative for everyone, as they are intended to stretch the limits of JavaScript technology.

# Conventions Used in This Book

Que has more than a decade of experience writing and developing the most successful computer books available. With that experience, we've learned what special features help readers the most. Look for these special features throughout the book to enhance your learning experience.

The following font conventions are used in this book to help make reading it easier.

- *Italic type* is used to introduce new terms and to indicate code items when used in a chapter's headings.
- Screen messages, code listings, and command samples appear in `monospace type`.
- Code that you are instructed to type appears in **`monospace bold type`**.
- Shortcut keys are <u>underlined</u>. For example, "choose <u>F</u>ile, <u>E</u>dit" means that you can press Alt+F, then press E to perform the same steps as clicking the <u>F</u>ile menu and then clicking <u>E</u>dit.
- The ➥ symbol, found in listings, is used at the beginning of a line of code that is actually a continuation of the previous line of code that was too long to fit on one line.

 **TIP**   Tips present short advice on a quick or often overlooked procedure. These include shortcuts.

**N O T E**   Notes present interesting or useful information that isn't necessarily essential to the discussion. A note provides additional information that may help you avoid problems or offers advice that relates to the topic. ■

**CAUTION**

Cautions look like this and warn you about potential problems that a procedure may cause, unexpected results, or mistakes to avoid.

# Fundamentals of JavaScript

# CHAPTER 1

# What Is JavaScript?

Remember the thrill of creating your first Web page and clicking your first hyperlink to another site? The excitement of surfing from California to Maine, from Australia to Finland? This interactive nature of the Web attracts millions of people to the Web every day.

With JavaScript, new dynamic elements enable you to go beyond the simple click-and-wait. Users will not just read your pages, but will also interact with them. Your pages will come alive for any user, even with the slowest Internet connection. Users will get quick responses because the interaction does not need to involve the server, but can take place in the user's browser.

This interaction can change your pages into an application. Put together a few buttons, a text box, and some code to produce a calculator. Or an editor. Or a game. Or the "killer" JavaScript application that everyone wants. Users will save your JavaScript-enhanced pages to use your application again and again. We saved a Web page with a JavaScript calculator so we could have a calculator handy. We also have an HTML editor written in JavaScript saved on our hard drives. JavaScript is a programming language that allows scripting of events, objects, and actions to create Internet applications. ■

### JavaScript on the Web

See the various ways JavaScript is making Web sites more dynamic. Some are so good that you'll save them to use over and over.

### See how simple JavaScript pages can be

You will see easy-to-implement code that lets you add entirely new features to your Web site.

### JavaScript pages can also be complex

JavaScript provides interaction between frames and multiple windows. It's not just for gadgets.

### Learn the difference between JavaScript and Java

Though the two languages share a similar name, they are very different.

### Scripts make great applications

There is no firm definition of a scripting language. An examination of several scripting languages can provide some insights as to where you can go with JavaScript.

# Live Content on the World Wide Web

In building Web pages, you present information to your audience. The design and layout should entice them to explore your site. Your hyperlinks provide several different predefined paths to see your information.

With JavaScript, your pages come alive! Your pages respond to the requests of your audience, beyond a simple click here or there. Many more interactive elements are now available for exciting design and layout. Your users are no longer just readers. People will interact with your documents, not just read them. Your users can now interact with forms, change the look and feel of your Web documents, and use multiple windows.

## Forms Explode with Information

With JavaScript, forms are a consideration in nearly every page you design. Text fields and text areas can dynamically change in response to user responses. Your audience will look for buttons, selections, option buttons, and check boxes. Your pages will change at their touch. The following examples show you how JavaScript makes forms come alive:

- *Calculators*   Where is that calculator when you need it? It's on your page (see Figure 1.1). Beyond simple arithmetic, you can do conversions in hexadecimal, calories, metric, and more. Expand the form and you have the unlimited world of spreadsheets. For example, simple tax forms, grade-point averages, and survey analysis.

**FIG. 1.1**

This Web page has a calculator built in with JavaScript.

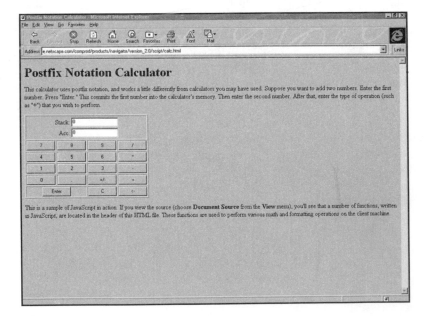

■ *Display the time*   What time is it? It's easy to show the time in a basic text box (see Figure 1.2). Or how about the time anywhere in the world? Add in a little math and show users the elapsed time. Different math produces a countdown time. A little different code and you have a population explosion or national debt counter.

**FIG. 1.2**
JavaScript time displays
can show you the local
time in any time zone.

■ *Feedback status*   As you build JavaScript applications, there will be a lot going on. Your code will have loops and increment variables, and will track user inputs.

■ *Let the users know what's happening*   Provide feedback with a numeric counter (see Figure 1.3). Say it "graphically" with a bar graph made of ASCII characters and show a status literally.

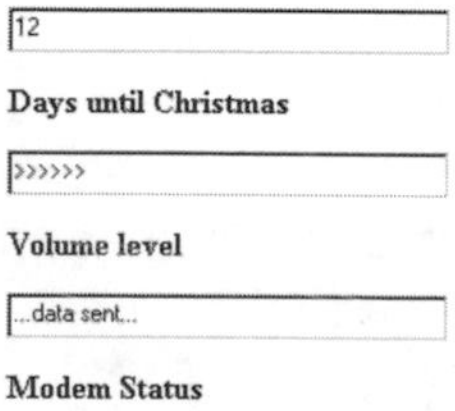

**FIG. 1.3**
Text boxes can show
feedback status of
applications numeri-
cally to users with ASCII
graphics, or verbally in
text boxes.

■ *Verification*   With user input, you usually want to verify the validity of the response. For example, if you want the response to be a number between 1 and 10, JavaScript can verify that the user's response falls in that range. If not, the code can notify the user and ask again for the input (see Figure 1.4). Once verified, the result is submitted to the server.

**FIG. 1.4**
Provide your users with
instant feedback,
without their waiting for
a response from the
server.

■ *Entertainment*   Everyone wants to have fun—even when learning. You can convey your information as an interactive game or even as a joke (see Figures 1.5 and Figure 1.6). The source code is very simple. It is given in Listing 1.1.

**FIG. 1.5**

Punchline: now you see the joke without the punchline revealed.

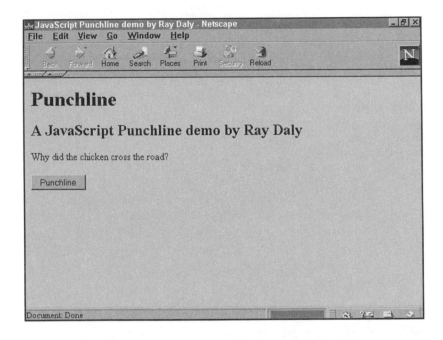

**FIG. 1.6**

Here's the punchline, hidden until you are ready to see it.

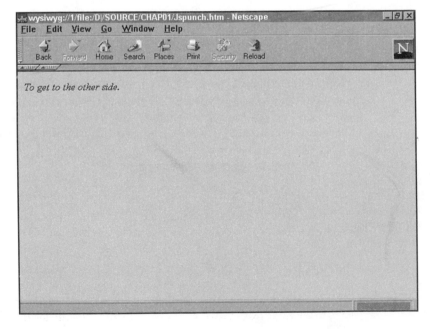

The source code in Listing 1.1 is easy to modify so that you can tell your own jokes on the Web, without giving away the punchline.

### Listing 1.1 Code for JavaScript Punchline

```
<HTML><HEAD><TITLE>JavaScript Punchline demo by Ray Daly</TITLE>
<SCRIPT LANGUAGE="JavaScript">
<!-- hide this script from some browsers
function Punchline () {
 document.open();
 document.write ("<BODY BGcolor=#00EE00><P><I>To get to the
➡other side.</P></I>") ;
 document.close();
}
// hidden ray.daly@mailcall.com 12/16/95-->
</SCRIPT>
</HEAD>
<BODY>
<H1>Punchline</H1>
<H2>A JavaScript Punchline demo by Ray Daly</H2>
<P>Why did the chicken cross the road?</P>
<FORM>
<P><INPUT TYPE="button" VALUE="Punchline" onClick="Punchline()">
</P></FORM></BODY></HTML>
```

## Look and Feel Is an Option

All of the elements inside the window of a browser are available in JavaScript. You can dynamically change some of these elements, or you can examine the elements of one document and use that information to create a different document. The following are some examples of changing the look and feel of documents:

- *Change colors*   Ever get to a page where the colors nearly make you go blind? Give your users a choice of several color combinations of backgrounds and text colors. As your application displays documents, use your users' colors.

**TIP**   There are too many colors from which users can choose. Don't make them experiment; let them select some good combinations you have already tested.

- *Change links*   Normally, users click hyperlinks and off they go to the site you specified as the URL for the chosen hyperlink. With JavaScript, this link can change based upon user responses. If a user indicates a preference for baseball over football, your code can change the hyperlink to point to the Yankees instead of the Cowboys.

- *Reformat Pages*   Since JavaScript can examine all of the elements of a document, you can read a document in one frame and completely reformat it in another. An example site is HTML Analysis by Ray Daly (see Figure 1.7). Listing 1.2 shows the frames of the top-level frame for HTML Analysis; Listing 1.3 shows the code for HTML Analysis.

### Listing 1.2    Frames for HTML Analysis

```
<HTML><HEAD><TITLE>HTML Analysis by Ray Daly</TITLE></HEAD>
<FRAMESET ROWS="80,300,*">
 <FRAME SRC="hanalys1.htm" NAME="control">
 <FRAME SRC="" NAME="displayhere">
 <FRAME SRC="" NAME="analysis">
 <FRAME SRC="guide.htm" NAME="guide">
</FRAMESET></HTML>
```

### Listing 1.3    Code for HTML Analysis

```
<HTML><HEAD><TITLE>hanalys1.htm: part of hanalysi.htm</TITLE>
<SCRIPT Lanuguage="JavaScript">
function doit() {
 for (i = 0; i <parent.displayhere.document.links.length; i++) {
 parent.analysis.document.write (parent.displayhere.document.links[i] + "<BR>")
 }
}</SCRIPT></HEAD>
<BODY>
<A HREF="http://www.cris.com/~raydaly/htmljive.html" TARGET="displayhere">
Get a page.</A>
<FORM><INPUT TYPE="button" VALUE="Probe it" onClick="doit()"></FORM>
</BODY></HTML>
```

**FIG. 1.7**

The URL specified in the top frame is displayed in the second frame. The third frame shows only the links from that page. Such tools are a great way to make certain pages on your site meet your standards.

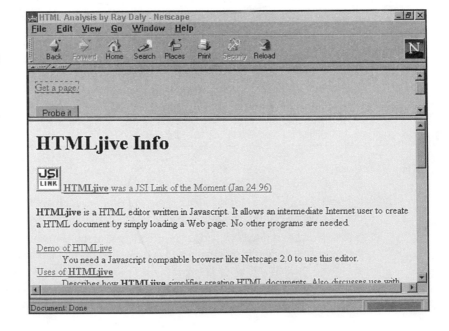

**CAUTION**

The HTML Analysis application is not stable on all platforms. Make sure the URL is completely loaded before you do the analysis.

 **T I P** You can reformat pages for dramatic results. Instead of showing the entire document in a large frame, bring the source document into an extremely small frame. Then display your reformatted document in the much larger frame. If the frame with your source is small enough, users won't even know what the original frame looked like.

■ *Analyzing tools*   Analyzing tools are a very interesting derivative of reformatting documents. Instead of displaying a reformatted document, analyzing tools provide an analysis of a document. Tools can check such simple things as word counts, link counts, or other statistics. Code can even be written to show the tree structure of all of the objects in a document. Or, you could write code to verify that pages meet the criteria for your corporate site.

## Multiple Windows and Frames

Netscape introduced frames and LiveScript with Navigator 2.0. Since then, LiveScript has evolved considerably. As a result of its convergence of features with the Java programming language, it has been renamed JavaScript. Internet Explorer (IE) now also supports JavaScript through Microsoft's implementation of JScript. Since their introduction, both JavaScript and JScript have grown explosively and are used in many Web sites. One of JavaScript's most popular features is the ability to open multiple windows for browsing the Web. Add some JavaScript behind these new features and the browser becomes a kaleidoscope on the World Wide Web. No longer are you limited to browsing one page at a time. Now you can view multiple documents and see a multifaceted view of the Internet world. The following list examines the use of multiple windows and frames:

■ *Alert, confirm, and prompt dialog boxes*   JavaScript has its own built-in windows that you can use in your design. Alert users to take caution (see Figure 1.8), confirm an action with an OK or Cancel response (see Figure 1.9), or prompt for a text input (see Figure 1.10).

**FIG. 1.8**
An Alert box notifies the user but provides no choices.

**FIG. 1.9**
A Confirm box notifies
users and allows them
to cancel the action.

**FIG. 1.10**
A Prompt box lets the
user type a response to
your code.

■ *Control windows*  You can create your own controls with custom windows. Populate
them with buttons, text boxes, or icons to control the results in your other windows.

■ *Navigation windows*  Have two, three, or more windows all opened simultaneously. As
the user navigates from one, the others display various screens of information. For
example, each window might pull in a live image from a different point around the globe,
as selected by the user. Internet Tri-Eye (see Figure 1.11) provides live views from
around the world.

**FIG. 1.11**
Internet Tri-Eye is
an example of a
multiwindow application
and a control panel.
Selections in one frame
produce results in other
frames.

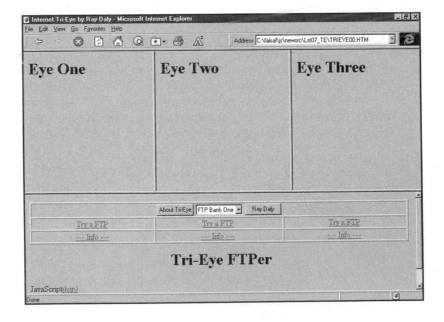

## Interacting with Other Live Objects

Sun Microsystems and Netscape Communications introduced JavaScript. Twenty-eight additional leading computer companies, including Microsoft, AOL, AT&T, Borland, Digital Equipment Corporation, Hewlett-Packard Corporation, and Oracle Corporation have endorsed JavaScript and/or its JScript implementation. These companies support JavaScript because it is an open-standard object language. Several companies will introduce products that incorporate JavaScript, which will allow even more interaction. Recently, Netscape submitted JavaScript to an open-standards body called the EMCA. The specification will now be open for third-party developers to use and embed in other software. This will truly transform JavaScript into the standard scripting language for the Internet.

Internet Explorer 3.0 supports a new functionality-enhancing feature that provides inline support for a huge range of Live Objects, known as ActiveX Controls. With Live Objects, developers can deliver rich multimedia content through Internet sites, allowing users seamlessly to view that content with ActiveX Controls, which will perform a wide variety of tasks without launching any external helper applications.

Netscape 3.0 brought about many new changes and improvements to JavaScript—including the ability to dynamically change inlined images on a page, and the ability to communicate directly with Java via LiveConnect. (LiveConnect is Netscape's technology for specifying the syntax by which Java applets can access JavaScript objects, and vice versa. It also contains an API for plug-ins to be accessible to JavaScript.)

# The Role of Scripting

There is no all-encompassing definition of a scripting language. Sometimes the term is used to make a distinction from compiled languages like C or C++. The term scripting is also used because a language will react to, control, or "script" a series of events. Even macro languages built into applications like spreadsheets, databases, word processors, and multimedia applications are now often called scripting languages.

The purpose of most scripting languages is to extend the capability of an application. Just as the authors of this book cannot imagine every creative use you will make of JavaScript, software authors cannot imagine every possible use of their applications. To make their products more versatile, they add a scripting language. With JavaScript, you have a scripting language that enables you to use your imagination on the Web.

Current uses of scripting languages may give you an insight into the potential of JavaScript. You probably know that macros are built into many applications. Apple's HyperCard contains a very powerful scripting feature. Perl is a scripting language used in many CGI scripts on the Web.

# Macros Become Scripts

Traditionally, a macro feature was added to application software to allow a simple series of commands to be executed with a single keystroke. With great fanfare, publishers introduced this feature as a way to reduce repetitive tasks and save time. For example, a word processor's simple macro might change the entire style of a document.

Over time, the macro feature of various applications became complex scripting languages. As scripts became longer and nontrivial, they extended the software beyond its normal purpose. New and creative combinations of commands made the software the basis for entirely new applications—for example, a set of word processing scripts for maintaining a small mailing list.

These scripting languages in software are so sophisticated that they are the subject of college courses. Many universities now require courses in spreadsheet scripting for accounting and business students; art majors are learning scripting procedures for high-end graphics and multimedia packages; legal courses include using scripts to create documents; computer science majors have a variety of courses involving scripting languages.

With the popularity of program suites like Microsoft Office, Lotus SmartSuite and Perfect Office, software publishers have started making the same scripting language work with more than one application. Not only is the same language used in each application, but the scripting language also helps the applications work together. Microsoft expanded the role of Visual Basic to work with Microsoft Access and Excel. Lotus has developed LiveBasic for its product suite. The same logic, when applied to the World Wide Web, led to the development of JavaScript.

Scripting gave these applications a competitive edge. First, it was a feature that could be used to sell the product. Second, people actually started to use the feature to create significant new capabilities for these products. Third, these scripts created a whole new market with magazine articles, books, third-party software publishers, and training. Fourth, the continuing use of these scripts became an investment in these products by the user: existing scripts often prevented users from switching to competitive products. And finally, even when a competitive product was introduced with new features, someone would introduce scripts that attempted to add these features into the existing products. Scripts allowed advancement by both publishers and users.

# Scripting in Macintosh Applications

The most notable use of scripting on the Macintosh is Apple's HyperCard program. This application lets you build a group of cards and hyperlink them together. The cards can contain both text and multimedia files. You can construct a stack of cards that respond to user input.

The scripting language is such a strong element of HyperCard that many people consider HyperCard itself to be a language. Many Mac owners were initially disappointed with HTML because it lacked many of the abilities of HyperCard. In many ways, JavaScript brings some of the HyperCard features to the Web.

## Perl Started as a UNIX Scripting Language

If you have used the Web, you have used Perl. It is the language that is used for the majority of CGI scripts. These are routines that run on Internet servers and respond to requests from browsers when a user completes a form. There are guestbooks, message boards, voting pages, surveys, and more, that use Perl scripts.

Perl is an interpreted language. While you should be able to find a version of Perl for almost any computer platform, it was created for UNIX systems. It is now platform-independent. The vast majority of Perl scripts will run on any system without modification. Take a script written on UNIX and it will run perfectly well on DOS.

CGI scripts are a type of script that responds to events. In this case, the event is a user submitting data from an HTML form. The attributes of a <FORM> include ACTION, which defines the script to process the data when it is submitted. For example:

```
<FORM ACTION="\cgi-bin\guestbook.pl">
```

will process the data from the form in a script called guestbook.pl. More than likely, this routine would store the data in a file and return an HTML page to the browser as feedback. It would probably say something like "Thanks for your entry into our guestbook."

Perl is freely distributed on the Internet, but please see its license for more details. You should be able to find a version for your system by using any of the Internet search services. Larry Wall created and maintains it. Find out more about Perl by visiting **http://www.perl.com** or by visiting the **comp.lang.perl** newsgroup.

Perl's strength as a language is in manipulating files and text to produce reports. This capability, along with its associative arrays, makes it a natural fit for creating CGI scripts. In a few lines, you can process data and return an HTML document in response to an HTML form.

If you are a Perl programmer, you rather quickly can learn JavaScript. Both have a similar control structure and both are interpreted languages. Unlike Perl, JavaScript is object-based, but it is not nearly as complex. You might miss the text-processing capabilities of Perl, but you will find that JavaScript is a delightful new language to learn.

There are some cases where JavaScript is not the appropriate solution, but using Perl for a CGI script would fit the requirement. Generally, if you need to store information, you are going to have to do that on the server, and Perl would be a good choice.

# JavaScript Extends the Capabilities of the HTML Page

Like other scripting languages that extend the capabilities of the application with which they work, JavaScript extends the standard Web page beyond its normal use. In this chapter, you have already seen numerous ways to make your Web site come alive. Given the flexibility of the language, the only limit is your imagination. We must now consider how JavaScript works within HTML pages.

# JavaScript Pages Work Differently from Standard HTML Pages

With a standard Web site, you can get more information by clicking a hypertext link, which prompts the server to send you another file. On a more interactive page, you complete a form, submit the results to the server, and wait for a response. In either case, you must wait for the server to send a new file. This information almost always is a new page, though it might be a multimedia file such as an audio clip or an animation.

With JavaScript-enhanced pages, there is JavaScript code embedded in the HTML code. The JavaScript can provide you with information instantly, without waiting for the server or your Internet connection (see Figure 1.12). This information can come from user input, from code "hidden" within the document, or from other documents in frames or other windows.

A JavaScript-enhanced page makes this new information visible by updating the contents of a form or by generating an entirely new document. In a JavaScript calculator (as seen earlier, in Figure 1.1), the form is updated when numbers are entered. In "Punchline" (see Figure 1.5), the user clicks the button and a new document is created from the joke's hidden punchline.

**FIG. 1.12**
With standard HTML pages, a Web site serves each page to the browser. With JavaScript-enhanced pages, the source for a page can be the existing page.

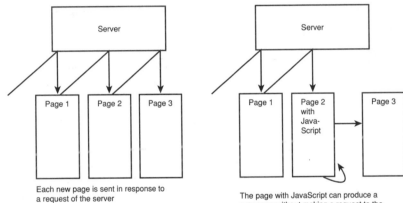

Each new page is sent in response to a request of the server

The page with JavaScript can produce a new page without making a request to the server

# JavaScript Meets the HTML Page

JavaScript works with browsers by embedding code directly into an HTML page. A new generic tag called <SCRIPT> has been added to HTML to recognize scripting languages. To inform the browser that your code is JavaScript, you must add the attribute of LANGUAGE="JavaScript" to the <SCRIPT> tag. Much of your JavaScript coding is enclosed within these tags, as you can see in the following example:

```
<SCRIPT LANGUAGE="JavaScript">
a = "Hello!"
//...set a variable called 'a' to a value of "Hello!"
</SCRIPT>
```

Like almost any other computer language, JavaScript allows you to place comments within your code. Single-line and multiple-line comments are possible. A multiple line starts with the following two characters: /*. It ends with the two characters: */.

Consider the following example:

```
/* This is the start of multiple lines of comments.
This is the end */
```

To make a comment at the end of a line or on a single line, just use the characters // and everything after that, until the end of the line, will be considered a comment.

Between <SCRIPT> tags, you can write two types of code: *direct statements* and *functions*. Direct statements are executed by the browser as they are loaded. For example, objects are initialized in direct statements. Functions are blocks of code that are executed only by other code or events. For example, mouse-click events usually trigger functions. Most of your programs will use both direct statements and functions.

▶ **See** "Events and JavaScript," **p. 59**

Many existing HTML tags now have additional attributes to support JavaScript. For example, all elements of a form now can be identified with the NAME element. You should be familiar with the NAME attribute because it long has been used in creating anchors. Using NAME to identify objects in your documents will generally simplify your coding and debugging.

Another addition to HTML is the ability to recognize events such as mouse clicks, changes in text boxes, and the loading or unloading of pages. This is how the document recognizes the user interaction. These events are used to trigger JavaScript actions. The code can be quite straightforward, as in the following:

```
<FORM>
<P>Click inside the box and then out to see change.
<INPUT TYPE="text" NAME="sample" onChange = "sample.value = a" >
<!-- ...after any change in this text box, put the value of a in the box -->
</FORM>
```

The JavaScript code that is triggered by an event can be simple or complex. With simple actions, the entire code can be placed in the event element. This is shown in the previous example with sample.value = a. Throughout this book, you will see more typical examples of where a function is called by the event.

# JavaScript Can Access Browser Objects

Like any language, JavaScript performs operations. These operations, or *methods*, manipulate information about objects. In addition to built-in objects,such as the String, Math, and Date objects, JavaScript can also operate on browser objects. This enables you to create new documents and modify your existing forms.

JavaScript works with browser objects in the same way that it manipulates user objects or built-in objects, which makes the language easier to learn. Most of the code manipulates HTML elements that you already know. For example, it will read properties of a LINK or write information into a TEXTAREA. Use elements you already know about to make pages come alive.

With Microsoft's ActiveX technology it is also possible to have JavaScript manipulate live objects. These operations can give you multimedia capability, such as sound or graphics, for example. Additional features can also be added by extending the capability of the browser with plug-ins or Java applets. These external entities can also be made to interact with JavaScript.

> **CAUTION**
>
> Plug-ins are written by software publishers to add capabilities to the browser. These publishers are not required to make these plug-ins work with JavaScript. So you must look at the specifications of a plug-in to see if it supports JavaScript.

# JavaScript and Java

Java and JavaScript are alike in more than just name. However, there are significant differences between these two languages. As you learn to understand the differences, you will also understand how they can work together. Each has its place, and neither does it all. Table 1.1 provides a quick overview of the differences.

▶ **See** "A Java Tutorial," **p. 317**

**Table 1.1  Comparing JavaScript and Java**

| JavaScript | Java |
|---|---|
| Interpreted by client | Compiled by the author, runs on client |
| Code integrated in HTML documents | Applets distinct from HTML document |
| Loose typing of data types | Strong typing of data types |
| Dynamic binding | Static binding |
| Script limited to browser functions | Stand-alone applications |
| Works with HTML elements | Goes beyond HTML (for example, multimedia) |
| Access browser objects and functionality | Limited access to browser objects or functionality |

## JavaScript and Java Work in the Same Environment

Both JavaScript and Java are languages for building Internet applications. These applications require browsers. The browsers run these applications by reading code embedded in an HTML page. In other words, they both work in the same environment.

Microsoft, Sun, and Netscape have mounted a high-profile campaign to ensure the security of these products. Neither product writes to the user's hard drive. Sensitive information about the user is also unavailable to these languages. So both products are limited by security and privacy concerns of their environment.

Because the two products have a similar name and work in the same environment, many people do not realize the distinction between JavaScript and Java.

# JavaScript Is NOT Java

In addition, it appears that more Internet browsers will support Java than JavaScript, though this is not certain. They display information differently in a browser window. Java applications can stand alone. One is compiled, the other is interpreted. The development tools are different and they have a surprisingly different audience.

**Java Displays Are Limited to a Graphic Area**  To display information on a Web page, Java is limited to painting its text and graphics within a defined area. Just as images on a page are drawn within a defined area of the page, so to with Java programs. Within these areas, the Java applets can create animations, paint, and use various fonts. However, an applet cannot affect anything outside its area.

JavaScript gives you access to the entire Web page. You can modify properties of the page or any element of the page. You can create new documents or update parts of a form. Unlike Java, JavaScript lets you change the appearance of any part of your Web documents, not just a limited area.

**Java Applications Can Stand Alone**  Java is a general-purpose language that can create stand-alone applications. Unlike the Java applets that run in Web pages, these applications may not even connect to the Internet, but may perform business functions such as accounting. This is an important aspect of Java that has many people excited.

JavaScript, like most other scripting languages, works only within an application. Currently, Javascript works with Microsoft's Internet Explorer, Netscape's Navigator, and the LiveWire server environment, as well as page-builder applications like Borland's Intrabuilder. But JavaScript applications will not function independently.

**Java Is a Compiled Language**  With Java, you write your code, compile it, and then run it. The person using your Java applet from a Web page cannot look at the source code. For many programmers, there is a sense of security here that they are not giving away their code.

JavaScript is interpreted. The code you write in JavaScript is the code that the browser executes. There is no intermediate step of creating executable code from the source code. People can look at the source code of the HTML page and read your JavaScript code and your comments. The exception to this is server-side JavaScript running on LiveWire.

**JavaScript and Java Development Tools**  The first generation of development tools for these languages has been introduced only recently. Since JavaScript and Java are very new languages, this is not surprising. However, looking at the nature of the products, some general distinctions can be made between the development tools.

Java is very much like the C++ language. It is object-oriented, it uses many of the same statements, it uses libraries, and it is compiled. Several companies that have strong C++ programming environments are developing similar environments for Java. This will allow the development of large-scale Java applications, but you will have to learn these programming environments.

JavaScript is tied to the HTML page. The code is embedded in it and it operates on HTML elements. Because the code is interpreted by a browser, the next generation of HTML editors will undoubtedly add features for creating JavaScript code.

**JavaScript and Java Have Different Audiences** Some significant features of Java require a multi-tasking operating system. So anyone operating on a UNIX platform, OS/2, Windows NT, and Windows 95 will be able to run Java applications and applets. This is a substantial part of the Internet audience.

JavaScript works in any version of Internet Explorer or Netscape Navigator on all of the operating systems to which it has been ported. Obviously, this is also a substantial part of the Internet audience. There are some big differences between these audiences. Because JavaScript is an interpreted language, there is a huge audience of potential JavaScript authors. All it takes to write a JavaScript program is a JavaScript-compatible browser and a text editor. Most HTML editors can also be used to write JavaScript code. So millions of people now have all the tools they need to create JavaScript applications. In a matter of a few months, Microsoft and Netscape have been able to distribute millions of JavaScript and JavaScript interpreters. It took Microsoft years to distribute nearly as many copies of Microsoft Basic.

Learning JavaScript is easy. By typing in just a few lines, you can run a JavaScript application. As you read through this book, you quickly will be incorporating many scripts into your pages. But, just as almost anyone can plant a seed, it does take some patience and skill to create a garden.

## Java and JavaScript Working Together

One of the more important aspects of the interplay between JavaScript and Java is the commitment to make the languages work together. They share a similar syntax and control structure, which makes it easier to write code for either language. But more importantly, a JavaScript page will be able to communicate with a Java applet referenced by the page. For instance, you might have a Java applet that displays a different animation, based on which link the user passes the mouse over, or you might have a scrolling Java ticker tape animation that can be changed dynamically on the page, based on a message that the visitor types in a form input field.

Another aspect of this sharing takes place not in the browser, but in the server. Both Microsoft and Netscape have server environments that support scripting, so the scripting language that works on the browser will also work on the server. Just as interactive scripts currently run as CGI scripts, JavaScript can handle such interaction on newer servers that support it.

## JavaScript and Other Live Content Tools

JavaScript will be incorporated into more Internet tools. While Netscape introduced JavaScript with Navigator 2.0, Microsoft has made it an open, cross-platform scripting language, which they call JScript. This means that any publisher can use it as their scripting language. This is the primary reason why JavaScript is gaining wide acceptance.

Several companies are expected either to incorporate JavaScript into their products or to provide an interface to JavaScript. The most visible products will be the ActiveX controls and plug-ins, as discussed previously. Work is also underway to provide other features, such as accessing high-end databases on the server. It will be interesting to see how this market develops.

All of this holds great potential for creating an exciting Web experience for your viewers. You will be able to use the same language to enhance your Web page, customize your server, create stunning effects with your controls and plug-ins, and communicate with specialized Java applets. JavaScript can make your Web page come alive; it can make your site an unforgettable experience that your users will want at the top of their favorites list. ●

# JavaScript: The Language

There are many, many different computer programming languages in use today. Each language has its own set of special features that are highly praised by its fans and vigorously panned by its detractors. If you have worked in more than one language, you are aware that there is a continuum of language styles, ranging from highly structured languages, such as Ada, to more freewheeling ones, such as LISP. Many are associated with specific settings or applications. Ada, for example, is often found in military projects, while LISP is often associated with artificial intelligence. Some languages such as HTML, the language used to describe the layout of World Wide Web pages, have a well-defined organizational structure but have very little in the way of traditional program structure (there are no data types, for example).

In trying to understand a new language, not only is it important to master its syntax, it is also vital to appreciate its style—the way in which that language can be used to accomplish specific goals. We have already reviewed the basic goals of JavaScript in Chapter 1, "What Is JavaScript?" and contrasted it to the more structured Java language. This chapter describes the JavaScript language from both perspectives.

## Use operators and expressions

*Operators* combine individual elements in some specific way; combinations of such elements are called *expressions*. Look here for a discussion of all JavaScript operators and the ways in which they form expressions.

## Manipulate data types and literals

Unlike most programming languages, JavaScript doesn't have explicit data types; however, it does treat different elements, such as integers and strings, differently.

## Manage the flow of control in several ways

JavaScript provides several ways to execute different sets of code based on prior conditions. Look here for details on flow control structures.

## Define JavaScript functions

Find out about JavaScript functions—the means by which Web page events are captured. The syntax for JavaScript functions and their various uses are illustrated.

A thorough description of its syntax is given and some initial concepts on how to structure a JavaScript program are introduced. Anyone who has programming experience in almost any modern declarative language, such as C, C++, Perl, or Pascal, will immediately feel at home. In addition, HTML authors who have never programmed will be able to acquire JavaScript proficiency rapidly. ■

# JavaScript Syntax

JavaScript is based on an action-oriented model of the World Wide Web. Elements of a Web page, such as a button or check box, may trigger actions or *events*. When one of these events occurs, a corresponding piece of JavaScript code, usually a JavaScript function, is executed. That function, in turn, is composed of various statements that perform calculations, examine or modify the contents of the Web page, or perform other tasks in order to respond in some way to that event. For example, pressing the Submit button on an online order form might invoke a JavaScript function that validates the contents of that form to ensure that the user entered all the required information.

In this section, we examine the syntax of JavaScript from the bottom up. We begin with the most basic concepts of how to write a JavaScript statement and what that statement does, and then progress upward through more-complex and powerful structures in subsequent sections, culminating in a detailed discussion of JavaScript functions and related concepts. Chapter 3, "Events and JavaScript," explores in greater detail how these elements are tied into Web pages through events.

In general, the elements of a JavaScript program can be divided into five categories, as follows:

- Variables and their values
- Expressions, which manipulate those values
- Control structures, which modify how statements are performed
- Functions, which execute a block of statements
- Objects and arrays, which are ways of grouping related pieces of data together

This set of categories is very similar to many other languages. As each of these elements is examined in subsequent sections, you will discover that JavaScript is somewhat minimalist in its approach. Many familiar elements, such as explicit data types (int, String, REAL), are missing or have been substantially simplified. However, JavaScript also provides a number of powerful object-oriented constructs that greatly simplify program organization. In this way, JavaScript has the expressive power of languages such as C or Java, while also having fewer rules to remember.

# Variables and Values

One of the main differences between JavaScript and most other languages is that JavaScript does not have explicit data types. There is no way to specify that a particular variable represents an integer, a string, or a floating-point (real) number. Any JavaScript variable can be any of these—in fact, the same variable can be interpreted differently in different contexts.

All JavaScript variables are declared by using the keyword var. A variable may be initialized, meaning that it is given a value when it is declared, or it may be uninitialized. In addition, multiple variables can be declared on the same line by separating their names with commas. For example, the statements:

```
var x = 7
var y,z = "19"
var lk = "lucky"
```

declare a variable named x with the initial value 7, an uninitialized variable y, and variables named z and lk whose initial values are "19" and "lucky", respectively. It might seem that x is an integer, z and lk are strings, and y is some undefined quantity. In fact, the real story is a little more complicated than this. The value of each variable depends on the context in which it is used. This context is related to the order in which the variables are seen. As you might guess, the expressions:

```
5 + x
lk + z
```

evaluate to 12 and "lucky19" — seemingly confirming our suspicions about what they really are. However, it is also possible to form the expressions:

```
lk + x
x + z
```

which evaluates to "lucky7" and 26, respectively. In the first expression, x has been interpreted as a string, while in the second, z has been interpreted as an integer.

**TIP**  JavaScript often attempts to treat all variables within a statement as if they had the same type as the first variable in the statement.

These examples illustrate two *critically* important points about the JavaScript language. First, while JavaScript does not have explicit data types, it does have implicit data types. Second, JavaScript has a set of conversion rules that allow it to decide how to treat a value based on the context in which it is used. The context is established by reading the expression from left to right. In the expression x + z, for example, x is implicitly a numerical value so that JavaScript also attempts to view z as a number and perform the sum numerically. It succeeds and the expected 26 results.

What would have happened if we had tried x + lk? The x variable occurs first on the left and is really a number at heart. JavaScript thus tries to interpret the variable lk as a number, too. This is extremely unlucky, in fact, because "lucky" cannot be converted to a number (while z, the string "19" can). JavaScript reports an error if asked to evaluate x + lk. To understand  JavaScript variables and values, therefore, it is necessary to understand its set of implicit types and how they may be converted between one another.

Before entering into these details, consider one final example. In all the preceding cases, the uninitialized variable y was never used. What would be the value of an expression such as

x = z + y?

Of course, as in all other programming languages, the result of using an uninitialized variable is never good. Because y has never been given a value, there is no way this expression can be evaluated. It may result in something seemingly innocent, such as x being assigned the value of z, as if y were zero. It may also result in something much more serious, such as the value of x becoming something strange, or, more likely, a JavaScript error occurring. This leads to the common sense rule stated in the TIP that follows.

**TIP**  Initialize all JavaScript variables to meaningful default values. If a variable has no meaningful default, initialize it to null.

## Implicit Data Types in JavaScript

There are five major implicit data types in JavaScript. A JavaScript value may be as follows:

- A number, such as -5, 0 or 3.3333
- A string, such as "Click Here" or "JavaScript"
- One of the logical values true or false
- A "nonatomic" JavaScript element, such as a function or object
- The special value null

Actually, it would be more accurate to say that there are five categories of data types because it is possible to distinguish two different types of numbers (integers and floating-point numbers), and many different types of JavaScript objects, functions, and other structured types. In fact, Part II of this book, "JavaScript In-Depth," is devoted entirely to explaining the many different JavaScript objects.

**Variables and Variable Names**   It is very important to distinguish between variables and their values. The statement x = 10 contains two components: the variable x and the literal value 10. A literal refers to anything that is referred to directly by its actual value. A variable is just an abstraction that provides a way of giving names to values. Thus, the statement x = 10 says, "I am going to refer to the concrete (literal) quantity 10 by the abstract (variable) name x," just as you might say, "I am going to call this lumpy thing I'm sitting on a chair." This leads to the important piece of advice contained in the following CAUTION.

> **CAUTION**
> It is bad practice to change the implicit data type of a variable. If a variable is initialized to have a certain type (such as string), it always should have that type.

Thus, because we have started out with x = 10, we should make sure that x always has some numeric value. There is no rule that prohibits later saying x = "Fortran" but this will generally lead to confusion or programming errors in most cases. No one will stop you from calling that lumpy thing you are sitting on "bacon and eggs," but many of your guests may become confused if you do so.

One final rule about variable names: A valid JavaScript variable name must begin with a letter or with the underscore character _. Case is important, so that norl, NoRl, NORL, and _NORL are all valid JavaScript variable names that refer to different variables.

**Numerical Values**   There are two numeric types in JavaScript: integers and floating-point numbers. The rules for specifying both types are almost identical to those of C, C++, or Java. Integers may be specified in base 10 (decimal), base 8 (octal), or base 16 (hexadecimal) formats. The three forms are distinguished as follows, based on the first one or two characters:

- 1-9 followed by any set of digits is a decimal integer.
- 0 followed by any set of the digits 0-7 is an octal integer.
- 0x or 0X followed by any of 0-9, a-f, or A-F is a hexadecimal integer.

Any three forms can also start with a plus (+) or minus (-) sign. Thus, -45 is a decimal integer, 017 is an octal integer, and 0x12EF5 is a hexadecimal integer. The minimum and maximum integers that can be used are implementation-dependent, but at least 32 bits should be expected.

Floating-point numbers can be specified in either the standard decimal point (.) format or the engineering E-notation. Typical floating-point numbers should contain a decimal point or an exponent, which may begin with either e or E. A floating-point number may also have a plus (+) or minus (-) sign. So 0.0, -1.4e12, and 3.14159 are all valid floating point numbers. The range of valid floats is, again, implementation-dependent, but you should expect that any valid, short, floating-point number, as defined by the IEEE standard, is acceptable. (The IEEE is the Institute of Electrical and Electronics Engineers, a professional and standards-making organization.)

Note that the original LiveScript language, as well as early versions of JavaScript, attempted to treat all the numeric types the same. Since it has become JavaScript, there has been a convergence toward the numerical types of the Java language and the distinction between integer values, such as 5, and floating-point (or real) values, such as 3.3333, has increased.

**CAUTION**

LiveScript is now completely obsolete. It has been replaced by its descendants, JavaScript and JScript (Internet Explorer). Avoid any code you encounter that is labeled as LiveScript, as it will almost certainly not work correctly.

**N O T E**   Watch out for changes in the way JavaScript handles numeric types. In the future, the distinction between integers, single-precision floating-point types (floats), and double-precision floating-point types (doubles) may become much sharper. ■

**Strings**  In JavaScript, strings may be specified by using either single quotes (`'stuff'`) or double quotes (`"otherstuff"`). If you begin a string with one type of quote, you must end it with that same form of quote—for example, `"badstuff'` is not a legal string in JavaScript. Strings also may be nested by alternating the types of quotes used. In fact, you must alternate single and double quotes if you want to put one string inside another. Here is an example of several nested strings:

```
"Oh, its 'Tommy this' and 'Tommy that' and 'throw im out, the brute'"
```

As in C and Java, JavaScript strings may contain special combinations of characters, known as *escape sequences*, to denote certain special characters. The rules for this are still emerging, but it is probably safe to assume that all the escape sequences defined in C will be supported. Because you will almost always be using formatting directives of HTML (such as `<BR>` for a line break), you probably will not use these directives very often. At the moment, the following sequences are supported:

| | |
|---|---|
| `\t` | tab |
| `\r` | line feed |
| `\n` | return |
| `\f` | form feed (vertical tab) |
| `\b` | backspace |

The special string `""` or `''` represents the zero-length string. This is a perfectly valid string whose length is zero. This is the shortest JavaScript string; the length of the longest is, as usual, implementation-dependent. It is reasonable to expect that most JavaScript environments will permit very long poems (or very short legislative measures) to be represented as single strings.

**Logical Values**  The logical, or Boolean, values `true` and `false` are typically used in expressions that test some condition to determine how to proceed. If that condition is met, one set of statements is executed; if it is not, another set is used instead. The first corresponds to the true condition, while the second represents the false condition. Not surprisingly, such expressions are known as conditional expressions. As you will see later in the section titled "Operators," there are several comparison operators, such as the equality test (`==`), which result in logical values.

It is possible to think of `true` as `1` and `false` as `0`. In fact, JavaScript often converts these logical values into `1` and `0`, respectively. JavaScript also accepts any non-zero integer in place of `true`, for example, so that `5` and `-3` both can be used as stand-ins for `true`. Many different programming languages follow this same convention. It should be avoided in JavaScript as it can lead to type confusion.

**The Value *null***  The value `null` has a very special role in the JavaScript language. It is the value of last resort, so to speak, for every variable. For the beginning JavaScript programmer, its primary role will be to initialize variables that do not have any more meaningful initial value. For example, in the set of variable declarations given in the section previous titled "Variables and Values," to initialize y to some value, we actually should have written:

```
var y = null
```

This prevents JavaScript errors that arise when an uninitialized variable is accidentally used in an expression that requires a value. It is important to realize that the value `null` does not give the variable y any implicit data type. `null` also has the property that enables it to be converted to a benign form of all the other types. When it is converted to a number, it becomes `0`; when it is converted to a string, it becomes the empty string `""`; and when it is converted to a Boolean value, it becomes `false`. This is the one case where it is permissible to change the implicit data type of a variable after it is declared.

Therefore, statements such as:

```
var lk2 = lk + y
var w = x + y
```

result in `lk2` having the value `"lucky"` (the same as `lk`) and w having the value `10` (the same as x). This is why the value `null` is an excellent way of initializing variables—it is guaranteed to be harmless.

## Type Conversion

Several of the examples in the previous section use the + operator to combine different types of things. You may recall that when a string is combined with a number in the form

```
stringthing + numberthing
```

the number is converted to a string and the + operator then glues the two strings together (known as *concatenation*). However, if they are combined in the opposite order

```
numberthing + stringthing
```

then JavaScript attempts to convert the `stringthing` to a number and add it, numerically, to `numberthing`. If the `stringthing` can be converted to a string such as `"-14"`, then all goes well; if it cannot, an error results. This illustrates the concept of implicit conversion in JavaScript.

We have already seen that some examples of implicit conversion are completely safe. `false` can be converted to `0`, `"5"` can be converted to `5`, and `null` can be converted to just about anything. However, some conversions are obviously invalid and others might be questionable. Questions such as: `"May the string '3.0' be legitimately converted to the integer 3?"` are actually very difficult to answer with complete generality.

There are two approaches to handling this complex issue: use explicit conversion whenever possible and use implicit conversion with great care. Some conversion techniques will be discussed later in this chapter.

▶ **See** "String Objects," **p. 105**, which discusses the rules for string-to-number and number-to-string conversion, the source of most conversion errors in JavaScript.

> **CAUTION**
>
> Use implicit conversion only when converting to a string form. Never use it to convert to numerical form. This is because attempts to convert a non-numerical quantity to a numeric form cause serious JavaScript errors, while conversion to string form generally does not.

You probably have already noticed that conversion to a string is always safe, at least for the data types encountered so far. In fact, this type of implicit conversion is a boon to the JavaScript programmer because it avoids the tedious formatting directives that are necessary in many languages such as C. In JavaScript you can say:

```
"This page has been accessed " + cnt + " times today"
```

without having to worry about the data type of the variable cnt. This construction will always give a valid string and never an error.

The preceding Caution is also based on standard principles of defensive programming. There are many things that cannot be sensibly converted to a numerical form, so the prudent approach is to try to never implicitly convert anything to a number. There are several more robust approaches that can be used in case you have a string that you want to convert to numerical form. These approaches are described in Chapter 5, "JavaScript Strings." You also will see other exceptions to this rule as your mastery of JavaScript increases.

# Statements and Operators

The basic unit of work in JavaScript is the *statement*, as is the case in most programming languages. A JavaScript statement accomplishes work by causing something to be evaluated. This can be the result of giving a value to a variable, by calling a function, by performing some sort of calculation, or by any combination of these. We have already seen variable declaration statements, which not only create (declare) a new variable, but also give it an initial value, such as the following statement:

```
var x = 10
```

JavaScript programs, as mentioned at the beginning of this chapter, are collections of statements, typically organized into functions, which manipulate variables and the HTML environment in which the script itself works in order to achieve some goal.

## The Structure of JavaScript Statements

Before plunging into a detailed description of the various types of statements and the operators they use, examine one simple statement in excruciating detail. Consider the statement:

```
y = x + 5
```

This statement contains three parts: the result y, the *operator* =, and the *expression* x + 5. The result always occurs on the left side because JavaScript always operates from left to right and is often called the *lvalue*. The result must always be something that can be modified. It would be erroneous to write `null` = `x` + `5`, for example, because `null` is a built-in, unchangeable component of JavaScript itself—it cannot be modified so it can never appear as a result.

The operator = is, of course, the assignment operator. It causes the expression on the right to be evaluated and its value given (assigned) to the result. The expression `x` + `5` contains another operator, the + operator, which acts to combine `x` and `5` in some context-specific way. Because `x` is a number in this case, the + operator performs ordinary addition and `y` gets the value 15. As we have already seen, if `x` had been a string, such as "`bleh`," then + would have acted as a string concatenation operator and `y` would be given the value "`bleh5`" instead. This is an example of *operator overloading*—the + operator can do different things in different situations. Several JavaScript operators are overloaded.

There is one final point to be made about this statement and about the structure of JavaScript programs in general. JavaScript has adopted a line-oriented approach to program flow. This means that it knows that a statement has ended when it reaches the end of a line. It is also possible to explicitly terminate a statement with a semicolon character (;). The statement `y` = `x` + `5`; is identical in effect to the statement `y` = `x` + `5`. This also means that you can, in fact, put multiple statements on a single line by separating each of them with a semicolon.

For those just starting out in JavaScript, it is often a good idea to terminate each statement with a semicolon and, also, to put only a single statement on each line. This might seem both redundant and extraneous, but it is well justified. The end of a line is often a purely visual concept. Anyone who has ever used a word processor has undoubtedly encountered the situation where a very long line looks like two lines. Different platforms (PC, Macintosh, UNIX) also have their own unique ideas as to what are the proper end-of-line characters. It is much safer to put in the extra semicolon character and be explicit about the end of the statement than it is to rely on one's eyesight.

## Operators

The set of operators that JavaScript uses is, once again, very similar to that of the C, C++, and Java languages. It provides a number of different ways of combining different values, both literals and variables, into expressions. Some operators require two elements to participate in the operation and are referred to as *binary* operators. The + operator is a binary operator. Other operators require only a single participant (`operand`), and are known as *unary* operators. The ++ operator, which adds 1 to its operand, is a unary operator. Operators also may join forces to form aggregate operators, as we shall see next.

JavaScript operators may be classified into the following groups:

- Computational operators
- Logical operators
- Bitwise operators
- Assignment and aggregate operators

This grouping is purely functional and is based on what the operators actually do. The next four subsections examine each type of operator in more detail. Table 2.1 summarizes the operators in each category and how they are used.

## Table 2.1    A Summary of JavaScript Operations

**Computational Operators**

| | |
|---|---|
| + | Addition, String Concatenation |
| - | Subtraction, Unary Negation |
| * | Multiplication |
| / | Division |
| % | Modulus |
| ++ | Preincrement, Postincrement |
| - - | Predecrement, Postdecrement |

**Logical Operators**

| | |
|---|---|
| ==, != | Equality, Inequality |
| <,<=,=>,> | Arithmetic and String Comparison |
| ! | Logical NOT |
| &&,¦¦ | Logical AND, Logical OR |
| ? | Conditional Selection (trinary) |
| , | Logical Concatenation |

**Bitwise Operators**

| | |
|---|---|
| &,¦ | Bitwise AND, Bitwise OR |
| ^ | Bitwise exclusive OR (XOR) |
| ~ | Bitwise NOT |
| <<,>>,>>> | Shift Left, Shift Right, Unsigned Shift Right |

**Assignment Operators**

| | |
|---|---|
| = | Assignment |
| *OP*= | Aggregate Assignment (+,-,*,/,%,&,¦,^,~,<<,>>,>>>) |

**Computational Operators**    The computational operators are addition (+), subtraction and negation (-), division (/), multiplication (*), modulus (%), increment (++), and decrement (--). These operators are often used in performing arithmetic computations, but do not forget that the + operator is overloaded; it also has the extremely important role of string concatenation.

The first five computational operators have their standard mathematical meanings. They add, subtract, divide, or multiply two numeric quantities. By combining two quantities using one of these operators, the result is made as precise as possible. If an integer is added to a floating-point number, the result is a floating-point number. The following four statements illustrate the use of these operators:

```
x = 4 + y;

y = 5.5 - z;

z = 10 / w;

w = 1.4e5 * v;
```

Note that division of integer quantities returns a result that is as precise as possible, so that if w had the value 4 in the third statement, z would get the floating-point value 2.5, not the integer value 2. Note also that the - operator may also be used as a unary operator to compute the negative of a numeric quantity:

```
n = -m;
```

This has exactly the same effect as if we had multiplied m by -1.

The modulus operator (%) is used to compute the remainder from a division. Although it can be used with floating-point numbers, it is typically used with integers, so that 21 % 4 evaluates to 1. The modulus operator always gives a remainder that has the same sign as the corresponding quotient, so that -21 % 4 evaluates to -1, not 3.

The increment and decrement operators are conveniences created to simplify the very common operations of adding or subtracting 1 from a number. Both these operators are unary and come in two forms: prefix and postfix. The expression ++x is the preincrement form of the ++ operator, while x++ is the postincrement form. This leads to a subtle and often misunderstood point about the increment and decrement operators.

Supposing that x has its usual value 10, consider the two statements:

```
y = ++x;

z = x++;
```

These look very similar, but are, in fact, very different. After both of these statements have been executed, x has the value 11. However, y ends up with the value 11, while z has the value 10. Why? The reason has to do with the complex issue of what order the operators ++ and = are evaluated in these two statements. In the first statement, the ++ is evaluated first so that x attains the value 11 and then the assignment = is evaluated so that this value is passed on to y. In the second statement, the assignment operator = is applied first so that z becomes 10, the current value of x, and then the ++ is applied to x so that it advances to 11. The same rule applies to the decrement operator (--).

This might seem like it is a violation of the rule of left-to-right evaluation, and it is. Even though the equal sign is to the left of the preincrement operator (++) in the first statement, the ++ operator takes effect first. This is an example of *operator precedence*, the order in which multiple operators are applied. This complex topic is discussed in more detail in the "Order of Evaluation" section, later in the chapter.

**Logical Operators**    Logical operators in JavaScript are used either to carry out some form of test or to combine the results of more than one such test. They are often referred to as conditional operators. The logical operators that perform a test of some sort are the equality/inequality operator (== and !=), the comparison operators (<, <=, >, and =>), and the logical negation operator (!). The operators that combine logical values are logical AND (&&) and logical OR (¦¦). Finally, the conditional operator (?) and the comma operator (,) are also combining operators, although they are only vaguely logical operators.

**Equality Operators**    The binary equality (==) and inequality (!=) operators are used to test if two quantities are the same or different. These operators are overloaded. On integers, they test for strict equality or inequality. On floating-point numbers, they test to see if the two quantities are equal within the precision of the underlying floating-point type. On strings, they test for exact equality—recall that case is significant in JavaScript strings. These operators all return a Boolean value, either true or false.

For example, if x has the value 10, y has the value 3.0, and z has the value "barney", then x == 10 is true, y != -5.0 is also true, and z =="fred" is false. Unfortunately, even operators as simple as these can be a source of error. It is regrettable that the logical operator == looks so much like the assignment operator =. Consider the following incorrect code fragment:

```
if ( x = 3 ) {
    stuff...
```

The purpose of this code is almost certainly to test the value of the variable x against the constant 3 and to execute the "stuff" if that test succeeded. This code fails to realize that purpose in two very dramatic ways, just by inappropriately using = instead of ==.

First of all, x = 3 always gives x the value 3, no matter what its previous value was. Instead of testing x using ==, we have altered it with =. Second, the value of the expression x = 3 is the value of its left side, namely 3. Even though 3 is not a true logical value, it is treated as true by the if statement (if is described in greater detail in the section "Control Structures," later in this chapter). This means that "stuff" will always be executed rather than only being executed when x has the prior value 3.

**N O T E**    Concerning the value of x being 3: this is true if it is a separate statement; for example, x = 3. But this is not the case when used with an 'if' statement. x will not be altered when coding a statement such as if x = 3. x will remain whatever 'x' was previously. This will, however, generate an equality check error, but the 'if' condition will process depending on the value of 'x' when compared to 3. ■

This type of error occurs in every programming language in which similar operators are used for very different purposes. In this case, we could have adopted another rule of defensive programming and said:

```
if ( 3 = x ) {
    stuff...
```

In this case, our typing mistake (= instead of ==) leads to an error rather than resulting in a subtle programming flaw. Since 3 is a constant, it can never appear on the left side of an assignment, but it is quite capable of appearing on the left side of a logical test. Said another way, because x == 3 and 3 == x are completely equivalent, the form 3 == x is preferable. If it is mistyped as an assignment statement (3 = x), it leads to an immediate error rather than one that might take hours of debugging to uncover.

---

**TIP** When testing for equality, always put constants on the left, especially null.

---

There is another subtle evil about the (in)equality operators when they are used with floating-point numbers. It is very tricky to make floating-point arithmetic completely independent of the underlying machine. This means that z == 3.0 might be true on one machine but false on another. It can also lead to seemingly absurd results such as 3. == 3.00 being false while 3.0 == 2.9999999 is true. A remedy for this problem is presented at the end of this section.

**Comparison Operators**   The comparison operators (<, <=, >, and >=) also operate on both numbers and strings. When they act on numbers, they perform the usual arithmetic comparisons, yielding Boolean values, as with the equality operators. When they act on strings, they perform comparisons based on dictionary order, also known as *lexicographic* order. If a string str1 occurs earlier in the dictionary than a second string str2, then the comparison str1 < str2 (and also str1 <= str2) will be true. For example, "barney" < "fred" is true, while "Franklin" < "Delano" is false.

**The Negation Operator**   The logical negation operator (!) is used to reverse the sense of a logical test. It converts true to false and false to true. If x < 15 is true then !(x < 15) is false, and vice versa. Note that ! may also be used with integer values, so that !0 is true, while !5 is false. As in other cases, this use of the ! operator violates type boundaries and should be avoided.

**Boolean Logical Operators**   The logical AND (&&) and OR (¦ ¦) operators are among the most powerful operators in JavaScript. Both may be used to combine two or more conditions into a composite test. The logical AND of a set of conditions is true only if all of its component conditions are true. The logical OR of a set of conditions is true if any one of its component conditions is true. Thus:

```
( x < 17 ) && buttonPressed && ( z == "Meta" )
```

is true precisely when x is less than 17 *and* the Boolean variable buttonPressed is true *and* z is exactly equal to the string "Meta." Similarly,

```
( x < 17 ) ¦ ¦ buttonPressed ¦ ¦ ( z == "Meta" )
```

is true if one or more of the three conditions is true.

**Lazy Evaluation**   JavaScript uses a lazy variant of its usual left-to-right evaluation rule with the && and ¦ ¦ operators. This *lazy evaluation* (or short-circuit evaluation) rule states that JavaScript stops trying to evaluate the expression as soon as its value is known.

To see how this works, suppose that x has the value 20, buttonPressed is true, and z is the string "Hyper". Because ( x < 17 ) is false, the second and third conditions in the logical AND statement are never evaluated. This is because false && anything is always false, so the value of the first expression must be `false`. Similarly, the second statement stops as soon as `buttonPressed` is evaluated. Because `true ¦¦ anything` is always `true`, the second expression must be `true`.

Lazy evaluation can be both a boon and a curse. Suppose that `"digofpi(1000000000)"` is a function that computes the billionth digit of *pi*. The expression:

```
( x < 25 ) ¦¦ ( digofpi(1000000000) == 3 )
```

does not actually try to compute the billionth digit of *pi* if x is `20` because the expression is already known to be `true` and `digofpi()` is never called. As an additional example, consider the following expression:

```
( x < 25 ) && beaupage()
```

Suppose that `beaupage()` is a function that displays a beautiful Web page. If x is `30`, this page will never be seen because the first part of the expression `( x < 25 )` is already known to be `false`. As a result, the function `beaupage()` is never called. We revisit this phenomenon in the "Functions and Objects" section at the end of this chapter. For the moment, it is wise to be aware of lazy evaluation.

***Fuzzy Comparison***   The logical AND and OR operators also provide one solution to the problem of floating-point comparison. While it may not ever be possible to determine if x is exactly equal to the constant `3.0`, you can be certain that it is close by using a combined test such as:

```
( x - 3.0 ) < epsilon ¦¦ ( 3.0 - x ) < epsilon
```

where `epsilon` is some suitably small value, such as `0.001`. This form of test is often referred to as a *fuzzy comparison*.

---

**CAUTION**

Floating-point arithmetic is not an exact science. Avoid exact comparison tests such as `==` and `!=`; use fuzzy comparisons instead.

---

***The Comma and Question Mark Operators***   The final two operators in the logical category are the conditional operator (?), often called the question mark operator, and the comma operator (,). These two operators are only vaguely logical but they don't readily fall into any of the other categories either.

The conditional operator is the only trinary (3-operand) operator in JavaScript. It is used to select one of two possible alternatives based on a conditional test. The following is the syntax for this operator:

```
( conditionthing ? truealt : falsealt )
```

If the `conditionthing` is `true`, the value of this expression is `truealt`; otherwise, it is `falsealt`. Note that the colon (:) separating the `true` alternative from the `false` alternative is mandatory. This can be used to select an appropriate alternative and to simplify code, as in this example:

```
printme = ( errorcode == 0 ? "OK" : "error" );
```

This expression makes the variable `printme` have the string value `"OK"` in case the variable `errorcode` is 0; otherwise, it is set to `"error"`. The question mark operator is often a fast way to select one of two choices when a control structure would be unnecessarily cumbersome.

Finally, the lowly comma operator can be used to force the evaluation of a set of expressions. All intermediate results are discarded and the value of the very last expression on the right is returned. For example, the expression:

```
b = (d = digofpi(1000000000)), beaupage(), (x < 17);
```

always computes the billionth digit of *pi* and assigns it to the variable d, always displays the beautiful page, always compares x against 17, and only returns the result of that comparison because x < 17 is the rightmost expression. The result of that comparison is assigned to the Boolean variable b. This might seem like a clever way to outwit JavaScript's lazy evaluation, but it would be clearer simply to write:

```
d = digofpi(1000000000);
```

```
beaupage();
```

```
b = ( x < 17 );
```

In general, the comma operator is useful only when it is inside a `for` loop (see "Control Structures," later in this chapter), and should otherwise be ignored.

**Bitwise Operators**   In many situations, you do not need to know, nor do you want to know, the precise binary representation of values in your program. There are some situations, however, in which it is absolutely essential to operate at the lowest possible level and deal with the individual bits of a particular value. This often arises in mathematical applications, for example, or when precisely manipulating color values. The bitwise operators are used for this purpose. Table 2.2 shows JavaScript's bitwise operators. Note that all are binary, except for bitwise NOT, which is unary. Each operates on its operands one bit at a time.

**Table 2.2   JavaScript's Bitwise Operators**

| Operator Name | Symbol |
| --- | --- |
| Bitwise AND | & |
| Bitwise OR | ¦ |
| Bitwise XOR | ^ |
| Bitwise Left Shift | << |
| Bitwise Signed Right Shift | >> |
| Bitwise Unsigned Right Shift | >>> |
| Bitwise NOT | ~ |

Bitwise AND (&) examines each bit position in each of its operands. If both operands have a 1 bit in a given position, then that bit will also be set to 1 in the result. In all other cases, the output bit position is zero. For example, suppose x = 0x00001234 and y = 0x8000ABCD. Then z = x & y will have the value 0x00000204. You can see this more easily by writing x and y in base 2 (binary) notation and by looking for those positions in which both x and y are 1, as shown in the first part of Figure 2.1.

**FIG. 2.1**

JavaScript's bitwise operators operate on each bit separately.

AND

| | | |
|---|---|---|
| x | 0000 0000 0000 0000 0001 0010 0011 0100 | 0x00001234 |
| y | 1000 0000 0000 0000 1010 1011 1100 1101 | 0x8000ABCD |
| z | 0000 0000 0000 0000 0000 0010 0000 0100 | 0x00000204 |

OR

| | | |
|---|---|---|
| x | 0000 0000 0000 0000 0001 0010 0011 0100 | 0x00001234 |
| y | 1000 0000 0000 0000 1010 1011 1100 1101 | 0x8000ABCD |
| z | 1000 0000 0000 0000 1011 1011 1111 1101 | 0x8000BBFD |

XOR

| | | |
|---|---|---|
| x | 0000 0000 0000 0000 0001 0010 0011 0100 | 0x00001234 |
| y | 1000 0000 0000 0000 1010 1011 1100 1101 | 0x8000ABCD |
| z | 1000 0000 0000 0000 1011 1001 1111 1001 | 0x8000B9F9 |

Note that x and y have the same bits set only in highlighted positions so that those are the only bits set in their logical AND z. In this way, bitwise AND is the bit level analog of the logical AND. Bitwise OR ( ¦ ) is similar. If either bit is 1 in any bit position, then that bit will be 1 in the result. Thus, the value of w = x ¦ y will be 0x8000BBFD, as you see in the middle part of Figure 2.1.

Each bit is set in w if either or both of the corresponding bits in x and y is set. The bitwise XOR (exclusive OR) (^) operator is a variation on the bitwise OR operator. It sets a bit in the result if either bit in the operand is set, but not both. The value of v = x ^ y is 0x8000B9F9, as shown at the bottom of Figure 2.1.

These three operators may also take more than two operands so that it is possible to write a very long expression such as:

```
n = ( a & b & c & d & e );
```

which operates from left to right, as usual. This expression takes the bitwise AND of a and b, ANDs that result with c, ANDs that result with d, and finally, ANDs that result with e. The final result is saved in the variable n.

> **CAUTION**
>
> The bitwise AND (&) and OR ( ¦ ) operators bear a shocking similarity to their logical counterparts && and ¦¦. This can lead to painfully undetectable errors. The same care that is exercised with = and == should also be used with these operators.

The unary bitwise NOT operator (~) changes each 0 bit in its operand to a 1 bit and each 1 bit in its operand to a 0 bit. The bitwise NOT of x will have the value 0xFFFFEDCB:

```
x       0000 0000 0000 0000 0001 0010 0011 0100

~x      1111 1111 1111 1111 1110 1101 1100 1011
```

While &, ¦, ^, and ~ operate on bits in place, the shift operators <<, >>, and >>> are used to move bits around. The left shift operator (<<) shifts a set of bits to the left by a specified number of positions, while both >> and >>> move that set of bits to the right in two potentially different ways. For example, let us evaluate these three expressions:

```
xleft = x << 5;

ysright = y >> 3;

yusright = y >>> 3;
```

The first of these shifts each bit in x to the left by five positions. Zero bits are tacked on at the right, while the bits that are shifted out at the left are lost when they exceed the overall 32-bit length. So, the value of xleft must be 0x00024680. The signed right-shift operator acts in almost the same way. Each bit of y is shifted to the right by three positions. Bits on the right edge of y are lost as they are shifted out. However, rather than shifting in zeroes at the left side of y, the most significant bit of y, which happens to be 1 in this case, is shifted in. The resulting value of ysright is 0xF0001579.

This might seem counterintuitive but it makes good mathematical sense because it preserves the sign of the operand. If y is negative (most significant bit set, as in our example), then any signed right-shifted version of y will also be negative. Similarly, if y had been positive (most significant bit equal to 0), then any right-shifted version of y would have been positive. The unsigned right shift operator (>>>) does not preserve the sign of its operand; it always shifts 0 bits in at the left edge. The value of yusright is therefore 0x10001579. The shift processes used to compute xleft, ysright, and yusright are shown in Figure 2.2.

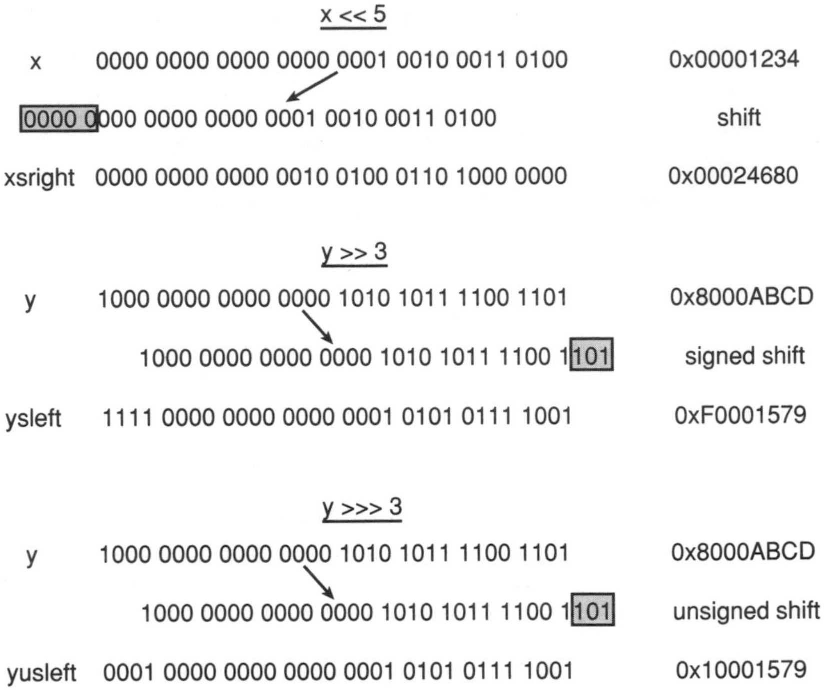

**FIG. 2.2**

JavaScript's shift operators move bits to the right or left and are equivalent to multiplication or division by a power of two.

x << 5

| x | 0000 0000 0000 0000 0001 0010 0011 0100 | 0x00001234 |
| | 0000 0000 0000 0000 0001 0010 0011 0100 | shift |
| xsright | 0000 0000 0000 0010 0100 0110 1000 0000 | 0x00024680 |

y >> 3

| y | 1000 0000 0000 0000 1010 1011 1100 1101 | 0x8000ABCD |
| | 1000 0000 0000 0000 1010 1011 1100 1101 | signed shift |
| ysleft | 1111 0000 0000 0000 0001 0101 0111 1001 | 0xF0001579 |

y >>> 3

| y | 1000 0000 0000 0000 1010 1011 1100 1101 | 0x8000ABCD |
| | 1000 0000 0000 0000 1010 1011 1100 1101 | unsigned shift |
| yusleft | 0001 0000 0000 0000 0001 0101 0111 1001 | 0x10001579 |

Because all the bitwise operators act at the bit level, chaos can result if they are applied to a variable that is not an integer. Floating-point numbers are particularly sensitive because an arbitrary bit pattern need not correspond to a valid floating-point number.

**CAUTION**

Never perform bitwise operations on floating-point numbers. Your code will be unportable and floating-point exceptions may result.

**Assignment and Aggregate Operators**   Our tour of JavaScript operators concludes with the assignment operator and its aggregates. You have already seen many examples of that most fundamental of all operators, the assignment operator (=). You are well aware that it is used to assign the result of an expression or value on the right side of the = sign to the variable or `lvalue` on the left side of the = sign.

In JavaScript, as in C, C++, and Java, you can also combine the assignment operator with any of the binary computational and logical operators. The expression:

```
Left OP= Right ;
```

is just shorthand for the expression:

```
Left = Left OP Right ;
```

where OP is any of the operators +, -, /, *, %, &, ¦, ^, <<, >>, or >>>. Therefore, to add 7 to x, multiply y by 19.5, or z with 0xAA7700, and to perform an unsigned right shift of 10 bits on w, you can write:

```
x += 7;

y *= 19.5;

z ¦= 0xAA7700;

w >>>= 10;
```

These compact expressions replace the wordier versions x = x + 7; y = y * 19.5, and so forth.

**Order of Evaluation**   In elementary school math, you were probably confronted with questions such as, "What is the value of 3 + 4 * 5? Is it 23 or is it 35?" This was your first exposure to the concept of order of evaluation or operator precedence. You probably remember that multiplication has a higher precedence than addition so that the correct answer is 23. The same issue arises in almost every programming language with the concept of operators—which comes first?

There are two approaches to this issue. The first involves learning, or attempting to learn, the operator precedence table. The more operators there are, the more rules there must be in this table. The second approach is to simply ignore the issue completely and explicitly group your expressions by using parentheses. Never write 3 + 4 * 5. Always write 3 + ( 4 * 5 ) or even ( 3 + 4 ) * 5, if that is what you want.

This recommendation is very much like several others in this chapter. It trades the effort (and perhaps some readability) of using the explicit parenthesized form against the promise that the order of evaluation will always be exactly as you wrote it. Incorrect order of evaluation is almost certainly the second most common source of programming error in JavaScript (confusing = and == is the first). For the daring, Figure 2.3 shows the operator precedence table for JavaScript. For everyone else, the following tip contains the recommended rule of thumb.

 **TIP**   Use parentheses to explicitly specify the order of evaluation in expressions containing more than one operator.

There is one case in which no amount of parentheses will help. When using the increment (++) and decrement (--) unary operators, you must simply know that preincrements and predecrements always happen before anything else.

Part
I

Ch
2

**FIG. 2.3**

Use the operator
precedence table to
determine the order of
evaluation.

Preincrement ++, Predecrement --
Function Call ()
!,`,Unary -, Postincrement ++, PostDecrement --
*,/,%
<<, >>, >>>
<, <=, =>, >
==, !=
&
^
|
&&
||
Conditional ?:
=, Aggregate Assignment OP=
,

Executed First

Executed Last

# Comments in JavaScript Code

All professional code should have comments that clearly indicate the purpose and logic behind each major section of the code. JavaScript offers two comment styles—the original comment style from C and the single line comment style from C++ and Java.

C style comments are typically used to document major functions or code blocks. Because a C comment may extend over multiple lines, it is ideal for detailed discussions of important parts of the code. C comments begin with /* and end with */. Our aesthetically pleasing function beaupage() might begin with a thorough description of just what makes it so beautiful, as follows:

```
/*
  The function beaupage() draws a stunningly beautiful
  Web page by performing the following nineteen steps.
  ... list of the 19 steps
*/
```

By contrast, C++ style comments are most suitable for short, pithy descriptions that will fit on a single line. A C++ style comment begins with // and ends at the end of the current line. Critical variables, for example, might merit a C++ style comment indicating how they will be used, as follows:

```
var done = false; // set to true when we are all done
```

Both comment styles may be mixed freely in the same JavaScript program. However, such comments should never be nested, as this can lead to confusion. Also, the temptation to use HTML style comments (<!-- and -->) should be strongly resisted, for reasons which will become clear in the next chapter.

▶ **See** "The *SCRIPT* Tag," **p. 66**

## TROUBLESHOOTING

**I have just written my first JavaScript program. Everything looks just fine, but the code does nothing. What is wrong? Here is the code:**

```
/* My first Javascript program *?
...many lines of code not shown
/* End of my first Javascript program */
```

Your comments are well thought out and informative. Unfortunately, your very first comment begins with /* but does not end with */. You have inadvertently typed *? instead of */, so that the comment does not end until very far down in your program. When you use C style comments, always make sure that they match.

# Control Structures

At this point, you have had just enough of the JavaScript language to declare variables, perform assignments, and do various types of arithmetic, string, and logical calculations. You are not yet able to write any meaningful code because you do not have any higher-level constructions. In this section, we will consider various methods of controlling the way in which statements are executed. The next section will expose the highest level of JavaScript—its functions and objects.

There are three types of control structure in JavaScript, as follows:

- if
- while
- for

These three control structures are very similar. Each is introduced by a keyword (while, for, and if, respectively) and each manipulates a *block* of JavaScript statements. A block is introduced by a left brace ({) and is terminated with a right brace (}). There can be as many JavaScript statements between { and } as you want, or as few. A block of code can even be empty, with nothing between the braces. In many ways, a block of statements is like a single gigantic statement. In particular, block-structured constructs are often all or nothing—either the entire contents of the block are executed or none of it is. Since blocks behave like single statements, it is also possible to put blocks inside other blocks in a nested fashion.

As you will see, each of the three control structures has its own specific format and its own special uses, although it is often possible to achieve the same results by using any of the three types, with varying degrees of elegance.

# The *if* Statement

The `if` statement is used to conditionally execute a single block of code. It has two forms, the simple `if` statement and the `if...else` statement. The simple `if` statement consists of a conditional expression, known as the `if` test, and a block of code that is executed if that expression evaluates to a Boolean `true`. An example of an `if` statement follows:

```
if ( condstmt ) {
    zero or more statements
    }
```

The block of code within the braces is often called the `if` block. The conditional statement `condstmt` can be any expression that yields a logical value. Note that numerical expressions also may be used; `0` is construed as `false`, and all other values are taken to be `true`. As stated earlier, an `if` statement should be considered a single statement. Code blocks are not traditionally terminated with a semicolon, although there is no harm in doing so. Listing 2.1 shows an example of a simple `if` statement.

### Listing 2.1   The *if* Control Structure

```
if ( ( x < 10 ) && ( -10 < x ) ) {       // if test
    y = ( x * x * x );                    // 1: cube of x
    ystr = "The cube of " + x + " is " + y;   // 2: informative string
}
```

In this example, the value of x is tested to see whether it is less than 10 and greater than -10. If the result of this test is `true`, then the variable y is set equal to the expression x * x * x, known mathematically as the cube of x, in the statement 1 (labeled 1:). The variable ystr is then set to a string that expresses this cubic relationship between x and y, in statement 2. If x fails either of the two tests in the `if` test, neither of the two statements in the `if` block is executed.

It is easy to see, even in this simple example, that it is often desirable to have a contingency plan in case the `if` test is `false`. This leads to the second form of the `if` statement, the `if...else` control structure. In this form, one block of code is executed if the `if` test passes, and a second block is executed if it fails. The format of this type of `if` statement is as follows:

```
if ( condstmt ) {
    ifblock of statements
} else {
    elseblock of statements
}
```

**N O T E**   In the current version of JavaScript, the placement of the braces is not important. The opening brace ({) may be on the same line as the if keyword or on the line immediately following it. Earlier versions, such as the JavaScript release bundled with Netscape Navigator 2.0, enforced much stricter rules on where { and } could be placed. ■

In this form of the `if` statement, the `if` block is still executed if `condstmt` is `true`. However, in this case, the block of code following the `else` is executed if `condstmt` is `false`. Listing 2.2 shows an enhanced version of the code from Listing 2.1 using the `if...else` form.

### Listing 2.2   The *if...else* Control Structure

```
if ( ( x < 10 ) && ( -10 < x ) ) {      // if test
    y = ( x * x * x );                   // 1: cube of x
    ystr = "The cube of " + x + " is " + y;  // 2: informative string
} else {                                 // false case
    y = null;                            // 3: be paranoid; give y a
value
    ystr = "Cannot compute the cube of " + x;  // 4: explain the failure
}
```

In this example, statements 1 and 2 are still executed if x meets both tests in the `if` test. If either test fails, statements 3 and 4 in the `else` block are executed instead. Statement 3 is another example of defensive programming. The variable y is given a value, albeit a meaningless value. This is done so that if y is used later, it will be guaranteed to have some value (even if we forgot to initialize it), regardless of whether the code flowed through the `true` part of the `if` (the `if` block) or the `false` part of the `if` (the `else` block).

Observe that `ystr` also gets a value no matter which of the two blocks is used. In the `true` case, it has the informative string documenting the cube of x; in the `false` case, it has a string indicating that the cube of x could not be computed. Because `ystr` will presumably be displayed to the user at some point, it is worthwhile to provide an error message. This is an example of *parallel code design*. Each conditional path modifies the same set of variables. For a simple case, such as Listing 2.2, it is easy to ensure that this happens. There are only two variables, y and `ystr`, and we can see exactly where they are set in every case. For more complicated, nested conditional expressions, it can become almost impossible to observe every variable in every case. Parallel code design is a good goal to strive for nonetheless.

## The *while* Statement

The `while` statement is used to execute a block of code while a certain condition is `true`. The format of the `while` statement is as follows:

```
while ( condstmt ) {
    zero of more statements
    }
```

The condition clause `condstmt` is evaluated as a logical expression. If it is `true`, the block of statements between the braces is executed. The flow of control then loops back to the top of the `while` statement and `condstmt` is evaluated again. This process continues until the `condstmt` becomes `false` or until some statement within the block forces it to terminate. Each pass through the block of code is called an *iteration*. Figure 2.4 illustrates the basic structure of a `while` statement.

**FIG. 2.4**

JavaScript's `while` control structure executes a block of statements conditionally.

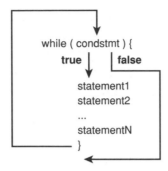

```
while ( condstmt ) {
   true │    │ false
         ▼
      statement1
      statement2
         ...
      statementN
      }
```

The first fundamental difference between a `while` statement and an `if` statement is that th `while` block may be executed many times, while the `if` or `else` blocks are executed once a most. You might well wonder how a `while` statement ever terminates. The code shown in Listing 2.3 illustrates a simple situation in which the `while` block eventually leads to the `condstm` becoming `false`

**Listing 2.3  A *while* Loop that Adds a Sequence of Number**

```
var x = 1
var xsum = 0

while ( x <= 10 ) {          // loop until x is greater than 1
    xsum += x;               // add x to the running sum xsu
    x++;                     // increment
```

This code accumulates the sum of all the integers between 1 and 10, inclusive, in a variabl called `xsum`. `x` starts out as 1, so that `xsum` initially becomes 1 as well. `x` is then incremented to by the `x++` statement. That value is then added to `xsum` so that it becomes 1 + 2 = 3. Thi process continues until `x` finally becomes 11 and the `x <= 10` condition is `false`. At this point `xsum` has the value 1 + 2 +...+ 9 + 10 = 55. Thus, the loop terminates. Note that it i critically important to initialize `xsum` to 0. If `xsum` is not initialized at all, then the statemen `xsum += x`, which is just shorthand for `xsum = xsum + x`, gives an error. If `xsum` is initialized t something other than 0, the final result contains that initial value and is not just the sum of th integers from 1 through 10

Listing 2.3 shows one way in which a `while` loop can terminate. Statements within the bloc may cause the conditional statement to become `false`. It could also happen that the conditiona statement at the top of the `while` was never `true`, so that the statements within the block ar not executed even once. If `x` had started with the value 20 in this example, the `while` test woul have been immediately `false`, and the statements `xsum += x` and `x++` would never have bee executed. In this event, `xsum` would retain its initial value of 0

**Using the *break* Statement**    There is a third way for a `while` loop to terminate. If th special statement `break` is encountered inside the `while` block, the loop is forced t terminate immediately. No further statements are executed and the `condstmt` is not retested. Execution continues with the first statement after the end of the `while` block. Listing 2.4 gives an example of the use of the `break` statement.

**Listing 2.4    A *while* Loop with an Internal *break* Statement**

```
var x = 1;
var xoddsum = 0;
var xtmp = 0;
var lastx = 0;

while ( true ) {                  // 1: loop forever (well, almost)
    xtmp = xoddsum + x;           // 2: compute a trial sum
    if ( xtmp > 100 )             // 3: if it is too large, then...
        break;                    // 4: we are done
    xoddsum += x;                 // 5: add x to the running sum xoddsum
    x += 2;                       // 6: increment x by 2
}
lastx = x;                        // 7: save the final value of x in the variable lastx
```

The test clause of this `while` (statement 1) is `true`, which, you might well suspect, is always `true`. This means that there is no way for this loop to terminate unless it is forced to do so by a `break` statement. In statement 2, a temporary sum is formed in the variable `xtmp`. This sum is tested against the limit `100` in statement 3; if `xtmp` exceeds it, then statement 4, the `break` statement, is executed and the loop terminates. If the test fails (`xtmp` is still less than `100`), then the real sum is formed in statement 5. (Note that it would have been equivalent and slightly more efficient if I had written statement 5 as `xoddsum = xtmp`.) In statement 6, `x` is incremented by 2.

What does this `while` loop do? It keeps adding up numbers, odd numbers in fact, until the sum is less than `100`. When the next sum would have exceeded `100`, the `if` test succeeds, the `break` is executed, and the flow of control of the program reaches the first statement after the entire `while` block, namely statement 7. This statement saves the last value of `x` in a different variable, `lastx`. This construction computes the largest sequence of odd numbers that can be added without having the sum exceed `100`. You can easily determine that the value of `lastx` must be 21 because 1 + 3 + ... + 21 = 100 exactly, while 1 + 3 + ... + 21 + 23 = 123 > 100.

**The Perils of Infinite Loops**    Listing 2.4 not only illustrates the use of `break`, it also shows two other elements worth noting. First, Listing 2.4 contains a nested conditional: there is an `if` statement inside the `while` block. This sort of construct is extremely common and many levels of nesting are not at all unusual. Second, this example has another very common but somewhat troublesome feature. Since the `while` test is always `true`, there is no way for the `while` to terminate unless the `break` statement is executed. In the preceding example, the loop terminated quite quickly. Suppose, however, that statement 6 had been incorrectly entered as `x -= 2`. In this case, `xoddsum` would constantly get smaller and `xtmp` would never exceed `100`. This type of error is known as an `infinite loop`. Listing 2.3 is not immune either, even though it has a conditional test rather than a blanket `true`. If the final statement of that example had been mistyped as `x--`, it would never terminate, either.

Naturally, infinite loops must be vigorously avoided. They will terminate only when some kind of internal error happens (such as an arithmetic overflow when something becomes too large) or as a result of user intervention. Unfortunately, there is no foolproof way to write a `while` statement (or a `for` statement, as we shall see shortly) that is guaranteed to be correct. JavaScript is no different from any other programming language in this respect. However, the following general principles will reduce the opportunity for error:

- Avoid `while ( true )` whenever possible.
- Have at least one way of exiting the loop body.

If the `while ( true )` construction is used, then the logic that exercises the `break` statement must be correct. If this logic isn't correct, the loop will never terminate. If you restrict your use of `while ( true )`, you will have fewer infinite loops. The second suggestion is based on the observation that the more chances there are to exit the loop, the less likely it is that the loop will last forever. Listing 2.5 shows a modified version of Listing 2.4 in which we have moved the test on the sum to the `while` clause itself, and have also added a very paranoid test on the number of times through the loop (the variable `loopcount`).

### Listing 2.5   An Improved Form of Listing 2.4

```
var x = 1;
var xoddsum = 0;
var lastx = 0;
var loopcount = 0;

while ( ( xoddsum + x ) < 100 ) {    // 1: loop while sum is < 100
    xoddsum += x;                    // 2: add x to the sum xoddsum
    x += 2;                          // 3: increment x by 2
    if ( ++loopcount > 1000 )        // 4: if we're working too late..
        break;                       // 5: quit
}
lastx = x;                           // 6: save the final value of x in lastx
```

This version satisfies both rules. Of course, the test in statement 4 is completely unnecessary. The code is simple enough that we can reassure ourselves that it is correct and will not go into an infinite loop. Once you are writing slightly more complicated `while` loops, you will find that there are usually multiple possible error conditions that arise. Every time you test for an error, you should consider using a `break` statement.

You will often see `while ( true )` written as `while ( 1 )`. These are equivalent, because `true` has the numerical value 1, but the latter form is sloppy. The conditional portion of a `while`, `if`, or `for` statement should always be a true logical expression.

**Using the _continue_ Statement**   There is another special statement that may be used inside `while` loops: the `continue` statement. The `continue` statement is used to force the flow of control back to the top of the `while` loop. When a `continue` statement is seen, all statements between it and the end of the `while` block are skipped and execution continues at the top of the `while`. Listing 2.6 shows a simple use for the `continue` statement.

**Listing 2.6   A *continue* Statement Returns to the Top of a *while***

```
var x = 0;
var xsum = 0;
var loopcount = 0;

while ( loopcount++ < 100 ) {     // 1: loop 100 times
    x++;                          // 2: increment x
    if ( ( x % 5 ) == 0 )         // 3: if x is divisible by 5
        continue;                 // 4: skip it
    xsum += x;                    // 5: otherwise, add x to xsum
}
```

This example adds up every number between 1 and 100 that is not divisible by 5. The numbers that are divisible by 5 are skipped by virtue of statements 3 and 4. Statement 3 computes the remainder when x is divided by 5. If that remainder is 0, then x must be evenly divisible by 5. In that case, the conditional in statement 3 is true, and statement 4 is executed. The continue statement causes execution to continue back to the top of the loop at statement 1. This means that statement 5 is not executed, so the sum always misses those values of x that are divisible by 5, and only those values.

Many programmers would write line 3 as if ( ! ( x%5 ) ). While this style is very common, it is also confusing and a potential source of error. One problem with this form is that it confuses JavaScript types by using the numerical value x%5 as if it were a logical value. This form also hides the explicit test for zero of Listing 2.6. While this ! form is more compact, it is also more error-prone and should be avoided.

One striking difference between this listing and previous ones is that x is initialized to 0, not 1, and x is incremented at the top of the loop, not at the bottom. If the x++ were at the bottom, what would happen? The values 1, 2, 3, and 4 would all be added into xsum. When x reached 5, however, statement 3 would be true, the continue in statement 4 would be executed, and both xsum += x and x++ would be skipped. x would stay equal to 5 forever! Because the x++ statement is critical to the correct functioning of the loop, it must occur before the continue. If it occurs after the continue, it will be skipped.

**CAUTION**

Any statement that must be executed on every pass through a loop must be placed before any continue statements.

# The *for* Statement

The for statement is the most powerful and complex of the three flow control constructions in JavaScript. The primary purpose of the for statement is to iterate over a block of statements for some particular range of values. The for statement has the following format:

```
for ( initstmt; condstmt; updstmt ) {
    forblock
}
```

The `for` clause, as shown, has three parts, separated by two mandatory semicolons. The `initstmt` is typically used to initialize a variable, although any valid statement may be used in this position. The `initstmt` is always executed exactly once, when the `for` statement is first encountered. The `condstmt` is a conditional test and serves exactly the same function as in the `while` statement. It is tested at the top of each loop. The `for` statement terminates when this condition evaluates to `false`. The `updstmt` is executed at the bottom of each loop as if it were placed immediately after the last statement in the `for` block. It is typically used to update the variable that is initialized by the `initstmt`.

Listing 2.7 shows a simple example of a `for` statement. In fact, the code in this listing accomplishes exactly the same task as the code in Listing 2.3. Note that this code does not bother to initialize x when it is declared. This is because the `initstmt` part of the `for` loop sets it equal to 1 immediately.

### Listing 2.7  Adding Up a Sequence of Numbers Using *for*

```
var xsum = 0;
var x;

for ( x = 1; x <= 10; x++ ) {      // 1: loop while x is <= 10
    xsum += x;                     // 2: add x to xsum
}
```

In many ways, the `for` statement is very much like a fancy version of the `while` statement. Many of the observations that were made for `while` also hold true for the `for` statement. In particular, it is possible to use the `break` and `continue` statements within a `for` loop. One of the advantages of a `for` loop is that its update statement is executed on every pass through the loop, even those passes that are cut short by a `continue`. The `continue` skips every statement in the block, but it does not cause the update statement to be skipped. The `for` statement may also be used unwisely, just like the `while` statement. If the `condstmt` portion of the `for` clause is omitted, it is as if a `true` conditional had been used, so that something within the `for` block must force looping to terminate. You will occasionally see the construction `for(;;)`, which is identical in meaning to `while ( true )`. The two semicolons are mandatory.

The `for` statement also has some unique features that are not shared by `while`. The first feature is that variables may actually be declared and initialized within the `initstmt` portion. In Listing 2.7, we could have dispensed with the external declaration of x and put `var x = 1;` as the initialization portion of the `for` loop. This is frequently very convenient because the loop variable (x in this case) is often used only within the loop itself, making an external declaration pointless.

> **N O T E** If a variable is used only inside a block of statements, it should be declared at the top of that block. This clarifies your code because it shows which sections of code use which variables (known as variable *scope*). ■

A second useful feature of the `for` statement is that both the initialization portion and the update portion of the `for` clause may contain multiple statements separated by the comma operator (,). Listing 2.8 shows another version of the code in Listing 2.6, rewritten so that both `x` and `lcnt` become loop variables.

**Part**
**I**

**Ch**
**2**

### Listing 2.8  A *for* Loop with Multiple Initialization and Update Statements

```
var xsum = 0;

for ( var x = 1, lcnt = 0; lcnt < 100; x++, lcnt++ ) {
    if ( ( x % 5 ) == 0 )          // if x is divisible by 5
        continue;                  // skip it
    xsum += x;                     // otherwise, add x to xsum
}
```

This usage underlines the fact that both `x` and `lcnt` are used only within the body of the `for` loop. It is also much more compact than its counterpart in Listing 2.6. In this example, we need not worry about the logical effect of the `continue`; because we know that both `x++` and `lcnt++` will always be executed. This is also the most common and useful way to use the comma operator.

Finally, there is another form of the `for` statement that is used exclusively with objects and arrays in JavaScript: the `for...in` statement. We will see how this is used in Chapter 4, "JavaScript Objects." Figure 2.5 shows the basic structure of the `for`, `while`, and `if` statements, and the use of the `break` and `continue` statements within them.

▶ **See** "Objects, Properties, and Methods in JavaScript," **p. 88**

### CAUTION

The control statements `if`, `for`, and `while` are examples of *keywords*. Keywords are words that have a special meaning to JavaScript itself. Keywords may never be used as variable names, so the statement `var if = 0;` is extremely illegal.

**FIG. 2.5**

Control statements
determine the flow of
execution in JavaScript.

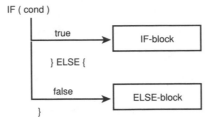

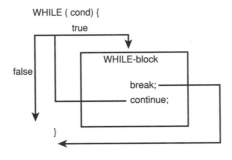

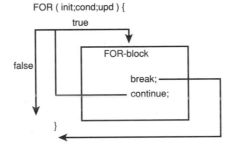

# Functions and Objects

The basic statements, expressions, and operators that were discussed at the beginning of this chapter are what computer scientists usually call *primitives*. Primitives are the building blocks from which more complex elements of a program are constructed. The for, while, and if control structures represent the next higher level of organization in JavaScript. Each of these control structures deals with blocks of code whose execution is controlled by the various conditional tests and other clauses. The for, while, and if statements are all block-structured.

Functions and objects represent the highest level of organization within the JavaScript language. We will spend many chapters learning how to make effective use of these concepts. The purpose of this section is to introduce them and describe their basic features.

# Functions

A *function* is a block of code that has a name. Whenever that name is used, the function is called, which means that the code within that function is executed. Functions may also be called with values, known as *parameters*, which may be used inside the body of the function. Functions serve two purposes. First, a function is an organizational tool, in the sense that it permits you to perform the same operation without simply copying the same code.

The second purpose of JavaScript functions is to link actions on a Web page with JavaScript code. Mouse clicks, button presses, text selections, and other user actions can call JavaScript functions by including suitable tags in the HTML source for the page.

▶ **See** "Events and Actions," **p. 60**

The syntax for a `function` statement in JavaScript is as follows:

```
function Name ( listofparams ) {
     body
}
```

The function's `Name` is given immediately after the `function` keyword. All function names should be unique and should not conflict with any of the statement names that JavaScript itself uses. You cannot have a function named `while`, for example, and you should not have two functions that are both named `UserHelp`. The `listofparams` is a comma-separated list of the values that are passed into the function. These are referred to as the function's *parameters* or *arguments*. This list may be empty, indicating that the function does not use any arguments (often called a *void function*). The function's body is the set of statements that make up the function. Listing 2.9 shows a function that adds up all the integers, starting at `1`, and ending at a value given as the sole argument.

## Listing 2.9   A *summation* Function

```
function summation ( endval ) {

    var thesum = 0;              // this variable will hold the sum

    for ( var iter = 1; iter <= endval; iter++ ) {
        thesum += iter;          // add the integer into the sum
    }                            // end of the for loop
    return( thesum );            // return the sum
}
```

This function does the same task that came up in the discussions of the `while` and `for` statements, earlier in this chapter. Now that it has been written as a function, this code never needs to be repeated. Any time you want to form the sum `1 + 2 + ... + N`, you can simply call the function, as `summation(N)`, and it will perform the task. Notice that the `endval` parameter is used as the argument to the function.

When the function is called, as `summation(14)`, for example, the actual value `14` is used for `endval` within the function. The function then executes the `for` statement, with `iter <= 14` as its termination condition, adding in each successive value into the variable `thesum`. When the `for` loop is finished, the function executes the `return` statement. This causes the function to give the value inside the `return` statement back to the caller. This means that if we write:

```
var sum14;

sum14 = summation(14);
```

the variable `sum14` is set to the value returned by the summation function when `endval` is given the value `14`, namely `105`. Functions can return any type of value and are not restricted to returning integers.

There are several things to notice about this example. First of all, the variables `thesum` and `iter`, which are declared within the body of this function, are local variables. This means that they are known only within the body of this function and are therefore completely unknown outside it. It is quite possible, even likely, that there are many functions, all of which have a local variable named `iter`. All these various `iter`s are unrelated. Changing the value of one of these `iter`s would not affect any of the others. This is why the `return` statement is necessary; it is the only way to communicate the work of the function back to the caller.

This same restriction applies to the parameter `endval`. The arguments to a function may *not* be changed within that function. We could well have written `endval = 15` just before the `return` statement in Listing 2.9. This statement would do nothing; it certainly would not change the caller's `14` into a `15`. It might seem that every function would always have a `return` statement. This is not the case, however, since it is possible for a function to have side effects without actually returning a value. This happens by referencing external *objects*, our next topic.

# Objects

Functions are used to provide a uniform method for organizing code. Objects serve the same purpose for data. Up to this point, the only data items we have seen are simple variables declared with `var`. Each of these typeless quantities can hold only a single value of some sort at a time. Objects provide the ability to hold multiple values so that a group of related data elements can be associated with one another.

What JavaScript calls an object is called a data structure (or class) in many other languages. As with JavaScript functions, there are two aspects to JavaScript objects: creating them and using them. For the moment, we will defer the question of how to create objects and instead concentrate on how they are used. We will also see that a JavaScript-capable browser will provide a number of its own *built-in objects*.

A JavaScript object is made up of a set of component parts, which are called its *properties*, or *members*. Suppose you have an object named `appt` which you are using to organize your appointments. The `appointment` object might have properties that specify the date and time of the appointment, as well as the name of the person with whom the appointment will take place. It might also have a general-description field to remind you of the purpose of this meeting. Thus, you can imagine that the appt object will have the following properties:

- day
- month
- time
- who
- why

Each of the properties of the appt object is referenced by using the dot operator (.). Thus, appt.month refers to the month property and appt.why gives us the reason for the appointment. These references may appear on both the right and left sides of an expression; we may get their values and also set them. Listing 2.10 shows a code fragment that tests the value of appt and displays a message about a current appointment.

### Listing 2.10   Using the *appt* Object

```
if ( appt.day == Today ) {
    document.write('<BR>You have an appointment today<BR>');
    document.write('See ' + appt.who + ' at ' + appt.time + '<BR>');
    document.write(appt.why + '<BR>');
}
```

This example assumes that the variable Today has somehow been initialized with today's date so that the equality test with appt.day is true only for today's appointments. If the test does succeed, then the three statements in the if block are executed. Each of these statements references document.write. The document object is a built-in object of the browser. This object has a member known as write, which is actually a function. Functional members of JavaScript objects are known as *methods*. This particular method takes a string and displays it on the current Web page.

Each of the three strings that is passed to document.write is constructed using + as a string concatenation operator. Each of them references one or more properties of the appt object in order to provide meaningful messages to the user. Each also includes <BR>, the HTML construction for a line break. This ability to directly issue HTML directives is one of the most powerful aspects of JavaScript, as it enables the programmer to modify dynamically the contents of Web pages by using JavaScript functions and objects.

Once you learn more about the Date object, in Chapter 7, "The *Date* and *Array* Objects," you will be able to construct a much more satisfying version of this example. Even at this stage, however, the advantage of object-based programming should be apparent. Rather than carrying about many variables, you can use objects instead. Each object can contain all the variables of interest to a particular idea. It can also contain method functions that perform related work. Objects can even contain other objects so that you can organize your data in a hierarchical structure. Subsequent chapters explore these ideas in much greater detail. ●

# CHAPTER 3

# Events and JavaScript

Although HTML pages can be difficult to develop, they are usually very simple to use. The number of things you can do with an HTML page is quite limited. For the most part, you simply look at it and read its text, admire its graphics, and, perhaps, listen to the sounds it can play. For many, the Web experience consists of visiting a series of pages without interacting with them. The only interaction occurs when the user selects a link or clicks an image map.

HTML forms have gradually changed that model to increase the level of interaction. A form can have a variety of ways of accepting input, including text boxes, buttons, check boxes, and multiple choice selections. In this way, HTML forms are a lot like paper forms. The user fills in the form, perhaps to purchase some item, and then submits the form. This submission process also mimics real life: It is difficult to tell whether the form has been properly filled in, and the time taken for processing the form is often quite lengthy. In the case of HTML, this processing delay occurs because the contents of the form must be sent across the network to some URL, processed there, and then returned to the user. Even the slightest error causes the form to be rejected so that the user must resubmit the form (with the possibility of having to enter all of the information again). ■

## Use the HTML *SCRIPT* tag

This tag is used to incorporate JavaScript code into an HTML document.

## Attach event handlers to HTML elements

Most user actions on a Web page can be linked to JavaScript functions.

## Intercept button clicks, text entry, and form submission

One of the most useful aspects of JavaScript is its ability to monitor and respond to user actions on-the-fly.

## Accept user input, validate it, and provide feedback

JavaScript's interactive power allows the browser client to perform many functions that are traditionally done on the server by using CGI.

One of the primary goals of JavaScript is to localize most of this process and perform the form validation within the user's browser. It won't actually be possible to locally submit an order, but it will be possible to locally make sure that the form is properly filled out and thereby avoid forcing the user to redo the form. JavaScript realizes this goal through *event handlers*. Event handlers are JavaScript statements (usually functions) that are called whenever something happens. JavaScript functions can be called when a form is submitted, or they can be called whenever the user does anything to the form. If your form requires that a certain field correspond to a number between 2 and 10, for example, you can write a JavaScript function that validates that field when the user changes it, and complains if the value is out of range.

This chapter describes event handling in JavaScript. We discuss all the events that can be handled, as well as the contexts in which these events may arise. In addition, you learn how JavaScript can be included within Web pages and how JavaScript functions are connected with different components of that page.

# Events and Actions

To understand JavaScript's event handling model, you must first think about the set of things that can actually happen on a Web page. Although there are many different things you can do with the browser, most of these have nothing to do with Web navigation. When you save a page as text, print a page, or edit your favorites list, you are not actually navigating the Web. In these cases, you are using some of the graphical capabilities of the browser, which are independent of the Web.

To understand which browser actions correspond to JavaScript events and which do not, it is important to distinguish those actions that actually cause (or might cause) some change in the Web page being displayed. From the user's standpoint, the number of such actions is actually quite limited. In fact, there are really only two types of top-level actions: The user can navigate, or the user can interact with an element of an HTML form. Navigation means to change from one Web page to another or, perhaps, to open a completely new page in a new window. Interaction with the contents of an HTML form means activating one of the elements in that form (clicking a button) or changing one or more of the elements in such a form that can be changed (editing a text field.)

## Navigation Actions and Events

In the navigation category, you can distinguish the following actions:

- Selecting a hypertext link
- Moving forward or backward in the history list
- Opening a new URL (possibly in a new window)
- Quitting the browser

In most of these cases, the current page is *unloaded*, which means it is no longer visible in any browser window. In several of these cases a new page is *loaded*, which means its contents appear in a browser window, perhaps a new one created specifically to display this particular page. Anyone who has used the World Wide Web realizes that selecting a hypertext link may not successfully take you to another site. The machine to which that link points may be down or simply inaccessible. The link may even be dead, meaning that it does not point to a valid destination. Selecting an inaccessible or dead link may unload the current page without loading a new page. Most browsers typically display a blank page or post an error message. You may or may not be left on the current page, depending on the type of error. A sample error alert from MSIE is shown in Figure 3.1.

**FIG. 3.1**

Attempting to access a nonexistent URL results in an error message in Internet Explorer.

These events, loading and unloading a page, are the two document-level events that can be handled by JavaScript. This means that it is possible to write JavaScript code, contained within the HTML definition of a page, that executes whenever that page is loaded. You can also have code that executes whenever that page is unloaded. It is important to realize that loading and unloading are two separate, unrelated events. For example, when you attempt to activate a link that leads to a nonexistent or blank page, the current page is unloaded, but nothing is loaded in its place. To return to the last valid Web page, you must use one of the navigation controls. For example, if you select Back in Netscape Navigator, the last page you visited is reloaded.

The following two additional events are vaguely related to navigation:

- mouseOver
- mouseOut

When you move the mouse over a hypertext link, a mouseOver event is generated. This event is not associated with clicking the link, it is associated with being *poised* to click it. This event can be used to give the user feedback, such as changing the color of the link or flashing it. The second event, mouseOut, occurs when you move the mouse away from the hyperlink (or client-side image map). This is useful when you have changed some aspect of the page because of a mouseOver event and want to restore the page to its previous state. For example, you might have a green graphical button that turns blue when someone passes their mouse over it (triggering the mouseOver), and then turns back to green when the mouse is moved away.

# Form Input and Events

We have now discussed the events that arise if you are using the browser to navigate the Web. Of course, you can also interact with your browser through the elements of an HTML form.

Every form element that permits input is associated with one or more JavaScript events. We can broadly characterize the possible components of an HTML form as follows:

- Buttons
- Text fields
- Selection lists
- Embedded objects

The first three components are standard parts of HTML. The final component, an embedded object created using the OBJECT tag, is a more recent addition that enables the Web page designer to embed a variety of active elements into an HTML page. For the moment we will concentrate on the first three items on this list.

▶ **See** "Embedded Objects: ActiveX," **p. 434**, for more information on embedded objects and the ActiveX technology.

**Button Elements in Forms**   Buttons come in five varieties, as follows:

- Simple buttons
- Yes/No check boxes
- Option buttons
- Submit buttons
- Reset buttons

Simple buttons are defined using the HTML <INPUT TYPE="button">. Check boxes define options, which are either off (not checked) or on (checked). These are created by using an <INPUT TYPE="checkbox"> directive. Option buttons use the <INPUT TYPE="radio"> directive, and permit the user to select exactly one of a set of choices. Submit buttons and Reset buttons are very special. Submit buttons, created by <INPUT TYPE="submit">, are used to end input operations on a form. When the Submit button is clicked, the contents of the form are packaged and sent to the URL target specified in the ACTION attribute of the FORM definition. Reset buttons bring the form back to its initial state, wiping out any input the user has performed; they are specified as <INPUT TYPE="reset">. Figure 3.2 shows a simple HTML form with all five button types.

**TIP**   Hidden fields on HTML forms do not generate JavaScript events.

The one thing the five types of buttons have in common is that you click the button to achieve its effect. Because this is an extremely common action, the JavaScript event model defines click as one of its HTML form events. This event is generated by each of the five button types. In addition, when a form is actually submitted, a submit event is generated. The submit event is really owned by the form being submitted and not the Submit button that causes it. You can also trigger an event when you click the reset button on the form, if it is available.

**FIG. 3.2**
All five types of HTML buttons have corresponding JavaScript events.

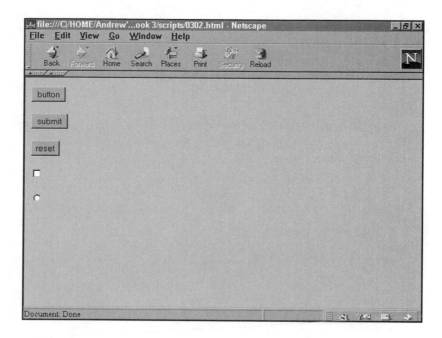

**Text Elements in Forms**   There are three types of text items possible within an HTML form, as follows:

- Text fields
- Text areas
- Password fields

Single-line text fields are created with an `<INPUT TYPE="text">` directive. Any text you type in a text field is displayed as you type it. This behavior is known as *echoing* the input. Single-line text fields that are created using `<INPUT TYPE="password">` do not echo their input. Multiline text fields are created with the `TEXTAREA` tag, and are usually called text areas. An HTML form showing all three types of text elements is shown in Figure 3.3. Interacting with text is more complex than interacting with a button because there are more things you can do with text: You can click in the text field, enter text, edit text, select text, and decide you are finished with the text and move on.

What are the events JavaScript generates in response to these various actions? JavaScript uses a text manipulation model that is familiar to anyone who has ever used a windowing system. It defines four events that are associated with text fields and text areas but not passwords fields—`change`, `select`, `focus`, and `blur`. The first two should be self-explanatory. The `change` event is generated whenever any text is changed, and the `select` event is generated whenever text is selected. Selecting text is more than simply clicking the editable text field or text area. It means actually highlighting a portion of the text with the mouse or arrow keys.

**FIG. 3.3**
HTML text elements generate several different JavaScript events.

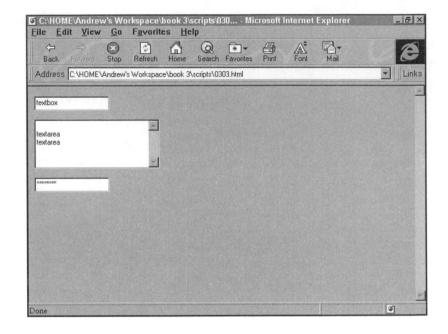

**N O T E**  Password fields do not generate JavaScript events. This was a conscious design decision to prevent malicious script code from diverting password text.

The `focus` and `blur` events are a little more involved. A text field or text area is said to have focus when it is currently accepting input typed at the keyboard. Clicking anywhere inside a text item is certain to give it focus, and simply moving the mouse over the text field may do so as well. The `blur` event is the opposite of `focus`. The `blur` event occurs when the text item no longer has focus. This may happen because some other item now has the focus or because the focus has simply been lost. You will notice that if you position the mouse over a graphic (other than an image map), you can type until your fingers are sore, but nothing happens. This is a case where nothing has focus.

**Selection Elements in Forms**    Selection lists are defined by the SELECT tag; their options are enumerated using the OPTION tag. They operate almost the same as text items; they are capable of generating `focus`, `blur`, and `change` events. Paradoxically, selection lists do not generate `select` events. You might well wonder why four event types are needed for text and three for lists. This is clarified later in this chapter under "Using JavaScript Event Handlers." Figure 3.4 summarizes the events understood by JavaScript and the HTML elements that generate them.

# Actions that Are Not Events

Anything not mentioned in the previous two sections should be considered an action, not a JavaScript event. Scrolling a window, reading newsgroups, or answering mail are certainly actions, but they are not events. Using the Back, Forward, or Home buttons on Netscape

Navigator's toolbar are not really JavaScript events, but they ultimately result in JavaScript events being delivered to the current page because they unload the current document. Creating an entry in the bookmarks list (hot list) is not even remotely related to JavaScript events because it does not affect the current page at all. How does one distinguish actions that might possibly be events from those that are not? The rule is that if an action affects or changes the current page, it is associated with one or more JavaScript events.

**FIG. 3.4**

JavaScript events model different types of user interaction with a Web page.

| Events / HTML Elements | Blur | Click | Change | Focus | Load | Mouseover | Select | Submit | Unload |
|---|---|---|---|---|---|---|---|---|---|
| Button | | X | | | | | | | |
| Checkbox | | X | | | | | | | |
| Document | | | | | X | | | | X |
| Form | | | | | | | | X | |
| Link | | X | | | | X | | | |
| Radio | | X | | | | | | | |
| Reset | | X | | | | | | | |
| Selection | X | | X | X | | | | | |
| Submit | | X | | | | | | | |
| Text | X | | X | X | | | X | | |
| Textarea | X | | X | X | | | X | | |

It might be argued that scrolling or resizing a window affects the current page and should therefore result in some kind of event. Those of you who have programmed any kind of windowing system know these are often called *visibility*, or *window damage*, *events*. JavaScript takes a more literal definition of a page. No matter how much or how little of a Web page is visible, it is still the same page. Even if you read only the cartoons in *The New Yorker*, the articles are still there, unchanged.

# JavaScript Code in HTML

So far we have talked about JavaScript as a language, and we have talked a bit about HTML, but we have not talked about how JavaScript is used in HTML. Event handlers are the glue that link HTML elements with JavaScript code, but how is it done? This section addresses this question. The answer has two parts: How JavaScript is included or referenced in a Web page, and how event handlers are attached to HTML items.

# The *SCRIPT* Tag

In the most general sense, every Web page is constructed from HTML statements that divide the page into two parts: the HEAD and the BODY. The HTML directives within the context of the <HEAD> give information about the page, while those in the BODY make up the page itself. In most simple HTML documents, the HEAD usually contains only the TITLE. It can also contain a BASE tag that specifies a path name that should be used to resolve relative HREFs within the document, and one or more LINK tags, which indicate the relationship of this document to one or more other documents, such as the browser's home page.

The HEAD section of an HTML document can also be used to contain the JavaScript code for your event handlers. While it is not absolutely necessary for all JavaScript code to go with the <HEAD>...</HEAD> delimiters, it is an excellent idea because it ensures that all JavaScript code has been defined before any of the BODY of the document is seen. In particular, if the document has a handler for the load event and that event was triggered before the event handler code had been read, an error would result because the event handler function would be undefined.

**Syntax of the *SCRIPT* Tag**    JavaScript code is introduced with the SCRIPT tag. Everything between this tag and the closing </SCRIPT> is assumed to be some kind of client-side script code, such as JavaScript. The syntax for the SCRIPT tag is

```
<SCRIPT LANGUAGE="LangName" [SRC="URL"]>
```

The element *LangName* gives the language that is used in the subsequent script code; this should be JavaScript. Internet Explorer, another browser similar to Netscape Navigator, also accepts JScript and VBScript (for scripts written in the Visual Basic scripting language). For maximum portability, you should specify your script language as JavaScript. This gives it a fighting chance of running on other browsers that support some version of JavaScript, such as Internet Explorer. If you are using Netscape 3.0 or higher, you can be more specific as to which implementation of JavaScript you use. If you use LANGUAGE="JavaScript 1.1", it allows you to take advantage of advanced features of this version, while older browsers will not attempt to execute the code. You would also need another set of code that has LANGUAGE="Javascript" for non-Netscape 3.0 browsers.

If the SRC attribute is specified, it should reference an URL containing code in the script language. For JavaScript, this should be a valid URL for a file containing the JavaScript code. The file name should have the extension .JS. If the SRC attribute is given, then the <SCRIPT> can be immediately terminated by a </SCRIPT> directive. A <SCRIPT> block that loads JavaScript code from a file named Click.js in a folder Jscode relative to the document base looks like the following:

```
<SCRIPT LANGUAGE="JavaScript" SRC="jscode/click.js">
</SCRIPT>
```

**N O T E**    Remember that you do not include any regular HTML code in a .js file. It must be all JavaScript code. If you add HTML tags outside of a script context, you will get errors. ▪

If the SRC attribute is not given, it is expected that all the code between <SCRIPT> and </SCRIPT> is the script source itself. In the glorious future, when the overwhelming majority of browsers understand the SCRIPT tag, or at least benignly ignore it, the JavaScript source may be given literally. Until then, it is recommended that source included between <SCRIPT> and </SCRIPT> be enclosed within the HTML comment delimiters <!-- and -->. A simple example showing a single JavaScript function is shown in Listing 3.1.

---

**CAUTION**

Use the C-style comments // and /* */ inside JavaScript code. Never use HTML comments *inside* JavaScript.

---

**Listing 3.1    A JavaScript *<SCRIPT>* with a Single Function**

```
<SCRIPT LANGUAGE="JavaScript">
<!--
function dontclickme()        {              // an ominous button click handler
    alert("I told you not to click me");
    return( false );
}
<!-- end script -->
</SCRIPT>
```

**Use of HTML Comments**    The function in Listing 3.1 does not do much; it merely uses the alert() function to display a warning dialog box with its argument as the message. Presumably, this function is the click event handler for a button you don't want the user to click. The important thing to notice about this simple example is the paradoxical but important use of HTML comments. The entire script body is enclosed within a comment, and the comment close --> is also paired with a second, seemingly redundant, comment start <!-- on the last line. At present, you should structure your script according to the following rules:

- Place the comment start (<!--) on a line of its own.
- Follow it with your JavaScript code.
- Terminate the code with <!-- and --> on its own line.

It is also possible to terminate the script code with a line like //, but the previously suggested method is a bit more general. You should use this magic incantation not because it makes sense but because it works. Note that JavaScript code referenced through an SRC URL should also follow these rules, as if it had literally been included in the <SCRIPT> block. Note also that you may have both a JavaScript SRC URL and literal JavaScript between <SCRIPT> and </SCRIPT>. In this case, the URL referenced by the SRC attribute is read and processed before the literal JavaScript.

> **CAUTION**
>
> HTML comments are one of the least conforming areas of HTML. Most browsers deviate a little from the HTML standards; some deviate a lot. The preceding comment rules may change in the future and may be implemented differently in different browsers.

**Processing <*SCRIPT*> Code**   There are two important aspects to JavaScript code defined by, or within, a SCRIPT block. The first important principle is that this JavaScript code does not execute; it is merely read and checked for syntax errors. When the browser sees the code shown in Listing 3.1, it does not execute the dontclickme() function; it merely recognizes that this function is a JavaScript function and saves the definition of that function for later use. This is precisely the opposite behavior of normal HTML. When you say <HR> in an HTML document, you get a horizontal rule. You don't get it immediately, but you do get it when the browser has finished laying out the page (assuming that there are no HTML errors, of course).

This is, however, the way that most interpreted languages work. If you create a Sub in the BASIC language, a defun in the LISP language, or a proc in the TCL scripting language, it does not execute when it is read. Instead, the interpreter *parses* it, which means that it scans through the function looking for obvious syntax errors, such as unbalanced parentheses, and records the function's definition for later use. The function is used only when it is called. In JavaScript, functions are most often called by events.

**Binding in JavaScript**   Another critically important aspect of JavaScript is that it carries out *dynamic binding*. Binding refers to the way in which names of things, such as variable names, function names, and object names, are associated with the things themselves. If you call the function dontclickme from Listing 3.1 by saying dontclickme(), you are not actually referring to the function itself, you are referring to the name of the function. "The Song of the Volga Boatmen" is really the name of that song; it is not the song itself. If you want the sheet music, you go to your favorite music store and ask for it by name; most people do not go in and begin singing "Eh-eh uxhnyot...."

There are two general approaches to binding: static binding and dynamic binding. Many languages, particularly compiled languages like C, C++, and Java, often insist on *static binding*. This means these compiled languages require that they be able to find all named references when a program is compiled. (Of course, with the advent of dynamically loaded libraries, this rule was relaxed a bit.) JavaScript uses the more liberal form, dynamic binding. JavaScript attempts to resolve named references only when they are used.

Dynamic binding has several consequences. In the first place, if the function dontclickme() is never called, it can contain all but the most hideous syntax errors that will never be found. If dontclickme is the event handler for a button, and no one ever clicks the button, its problems are never exposed. Even if dontclickme() is absolutely perfect, but the event handler is erroneously declared to be a function named noclickme(), this mismatch is not detected until someone finally chooses to click the button. Only then does JavaScript try to find a function named `noclickme()`. It fails, and an error results. Dynamic binding is often called *runtime binding* or *late binding* because the binding process takes place only when the JavaScript interpreter attempts to run the code.

 **T I P** Always check meticulously to ensure that the function, object, and variable names used in HTML match those in the JavaScript code. Test your code by trying out as many of the possible interactions, events, and conditions as you can.

Dynamic binding has its advantages and disadvantages. Dynamic binding is used by many interpreters because it simplifies the language and makes it very easy to add in new functions. Since there is no brooding and melancholy compiler to satisfy, it is possible to build up a complex JavaScript application incrementally. Even if you really need an event handler for every possible event, you can start out with one or two handlers, make them work, and then gradually add more complexity.

The disadvantage of dynamic binding should be clear from the previous discussion. There is very little error-checking. When the JavaScript interpreter is reading all the code in the SRC URL or processing the code between `<SCRIPT>` and `</SCRIPT>`, it is performing some checking but it is by no means performing an exhaustive analysis of the code. Errors, particularly mismatched names, are not found until the erroneous code executes. To see a more complete example of this, look at the HTML page defined in Listing 3.2.

**Listing 3.2   An Illustration of Dynamic Binding**

```
<HTML>
<HEAD>
<TITLE>A Potentially Dangerous JavaScript Page</TITLE>
<SCRIPT LANGUAGE="JavaScript">
<!--
function dontclickme() {           // button click handler
     alert("I told you not to click me");
}
<!-- end script -->
</SCRIPT>
</HEAD>
<BODY>
<FORM METHOD="POST" ACTION="mailto:me@myhost.com">
<INPUT TYPE="button" NAME="mycheck" VALUE="HA!" onClick="dontclickme()">
</FORM>
</BODY>
</HTML>
```

If you copy this code (found at this book's Web site) into a local file, change the e-mail address in the form's ACTION to your own e-mail address, and then read that file into your browser, everything will be fine. Notice that the `click` event handler for the button is declared using the HTML attribute `onClick="dontclickme()"`, which tells JavaScript that when this button is

Part
I

Ch
3

clicked, the function `dontclickme` should be called. (The exact syntax for declaring event handlers is discussed in the next section.) If you now click that button, you should see something like Figure 3.5.

**FIG. 3.5**

Clicking an HTML button invokes a JavaScript event handler that displays an alert.

So far so good. The name of the event handler in the HTML statement that created the button matches the name of a JavaScript function in the SCRIPT block. Now try the following experiment. Change the handler declaration from

```
onClick="dontclickme()"
```

to

```
onClick="noclickme()"
```

and then read that file into your browser. You will notice that the initial appearance of the HTML page is exactly as before. No errors have been reported. If you attempt to click the HA! button, your browser reports an error, and the alert dialog box shown in Figure 3.5 does not appear. This is dynamic binding at work. JavaScript did not know that the function named `noclickme` does not correspond to any currently defined function until the user action forced it to try to find one. Technically, the function name `noclickme` is said to be *unbound*.

It might seem that dynamic binding is a great potential source of error without providing many benefits as compensation. As you will see when we discuss objects in Chapter 4, "JavaScript Objects," objects may be defined and even modified on-the-fly. Dynamic binding allows you to refer to things that do not yet exist but will exist when the event handler that uses them is actually called. Dynamic binding, like the loose typing provided by JavaScript's `var`, is a two-edged sword. It must be used with care, but it is very powerful.

▶ **See** "Defining Your Own Objects: The *new* Statement," **p. 89**, for more information on creating and modifying JavaScript objects.

Let's summarize these two critical points about JavaScript parsing and execution since they will dominate our thinking for several chapters to come:

- JavaScript code is parsed when it is seen in a SCRIPT block; it is executed only when an event occurs.
- JavaScript names are resolved when they are executed, not when they are parsed.

# Declaring JavaScript Event Handlers

The previous section demonstrated that JavaScript functions execute only in response to events. We also know that events themselves occur only when some interaction with, or change to, the current HTML page occurs. There must be a way in which we can link events to JavaScript functions in HTML. In fact, we have already seen one such example of this in Listing 3.2. The mechanism is known as the event handler declaration.

Event handler declarations look exactly like ordinary HTML attributes. Each attribute name begins with the word on and is followed by the event name so that onClick is the attribute that is used to declare an event handler for the click event. The full declaration of an event handler looks like the following:

```
onEvent="JavaScriptcode"
```

Attribute names are not case-sensitive, following the usual HTML convention. It is good practice, however, to use the coding style shown in the preceding line of code, with on in lowercase and the event name with an initial capital. This helps to distinguish it from other attributes, which are often fully capitalized.

The value of the attribute is a set of JavaScript code. The code may be included literally (known as inline JavaScript) or it may reference a JavaScript function. We can completely remove the dontclickme() function of Listing 3.2 and write the button statement as

```
<INPUT TYPE="button" NAME="mycheck" VALUE="HA!"
 onClick="javascript:alert('I told you not to click me');">
```

This has two disadvantages. First, it tends to lead to very long HTML statements. There is very little you can accomplish in only a few characters. If you have hundreds of characters between the opening (<) and the closing (>) of an HTML statement, it is almost certainly very hard to read, and, if it is too long, may cause your browser to choke. It is also not modular. As you add event handlers for different HTML elements, you may well find that there is a lot of common code. Each of the button handlers might use a variation of the same code. Such common code should always be encapsulated in a JavaScript function, rather than being repeated in several places.

**TIP** Declare all event handlers as JavaScript functions. Avoid inline JavaScript code.

One thing to notice about this example is the fact that the value of the onClick attribute is a quoted string. This follows standard HTML convention. Therefore, to include a string within the value of the attribute, we must alternate ' ' quotes with " " quotes.

▶ **See** "Implicit Data Types in JavaScript," **p. 28**

If you modify the dontclickme function to accept a string argument, you must carefully use quotes when passing in literal strings. Listing 3.3 shows a modified version of dontclickme, called donteventme, and the HTML event handler declarations that reference it.

**Listing 3.3   A JavaScript Function Can Be Shared by Several Event Handlers**

```
<HTML>
<HEAD>
<TITLE>An Uncooperative JavaScript Page</TITLE>
<SCRIPT LANGUAGE="JavaScript">
<!--
function donteventme( str ) {          // generic diffident handler
     alert("I told you not to " + str + " me");
}
<!-- end script -->
</SCRIPT>
</HEAD>
<BODY>
<FORM METHOD="post" ACTION="mailto:me@myhost.com">
<BR>No<INPUT TYPE="checkbox" NAME="mycheck" VALUE="HA!"
     onClick="donteventme('click')">
<SELECT NAME="mysel" onChange="donteventme('change')">
<OPTION SELECTED>Nope</OPTION>
<OPTION>Not Me</OPTION>
<OPTION>No Way</OPTION>
</SELECT>
</FORM>
</BODY>
</HTML>
```

In this example, the function donteventme is called whenever the check box is checked or any selection is made on the selection list. The alert function within the donteventme constructs an uncooperative message based on the function's string argument str. Although this example accomplishes no useful work, it is a perfect template for a JavaScript page. In general, a JavaScript page has the following three components:

- JavaScript functions inside a <SCRIPT> block, usually within the <HEAD> of the document
- Noninteractive HTML within the document's <BODY>
- Interactive HTML with event handler attributes whose values are JavaScript functions

You now know how to declare event handlers in general. The next section shows exactly which handlers can be associated with specific HTML tags and gives various examples of how these event handlers are used.

**CAUTION**

If you use the HTML IMG directive without assigning values to its WIDTH and HEIGHT attributes, event handling may be compromised. This limitation exists in Internet Explorer and Netscape Navigator. Make certain that you always include these attributes if you are using images together with JavaScript.

# Using JavaScript Event Handlers

JavaScript events occur at three levels: At the level of the entire Web document, at the level of an individual <FORM> within the document, and at the level of an element of a <FORM> within that document. At the same time, any particular element at any of these three levels may result in more than one event. For example, you have already seen that text items can generate up to four different events, depending on how they are manipulated. In this section, we examine each level and see which handlers are appropriate for the HTML elements within that level. As you might suspect, most of the action is at the lowest level, within HTML forms.

## Document-Level Event Handlers

The HTML BODY tag is the container that holds the descriptive content of an HTML page. Just as the material in the HEAD section is about the page, the material between <BODY> and </BODY> is the page. The BODY tag can contain two event handler declarations using the onLoad and onUnload attributes. A JavaScript page might have a BODY declaration that looks like the following:

```
<BODY onLoad="loadfunc()" onUnload="unloadfunc()">
```

The onLoad="loadfunc()" attribute declares a JavaScript handler that handles the load event. The load event is generated after the entire contents of the page, namely the HTML between <BODY> and </BODY>, have been read but before they have been displayed. The onLoad event handler is an excellent place to perform any one-time initialization. It can also be used to display a splash screen containing company, product, or copyright information. It can even launch a security dialog box that permits only authorized users, with an appropriate password or key, to completely load the page.

The onUnload="unloadfunc()" attribute declares an event handler that is invoked whenever the page is unloaded. This happens when the user executes any action that brings up a new page in the same browser window. An unload event does not occur if a new page is opened in a new window. Even if a new page is not successfully loaded, the current page may still be unloaded, and the unloadfunc is called in that case. An onUnload event handler can be used to ensure that there are no loose ends and to perform any cleanup necessary. For example, if the user has filled out a form but has failed to click the Submit button, the onUnload handler should inform the user of that fact. It could even submit the form itself, based on the user's response. Note that both the onLoad and onUnload handlers are optional.

There are two final document-level event handlers, although they are not associated with the BODY tag. Any HTML link can declare an event handler for the mouseOver or mouseOut events, which occur when the user places the mouse over the HREF of that link or leaves that link. This can be used to achieve a visual effect or to perform some special processing before the user actually tries to access the link. Listing 3.4 shows a slightly fanciful example.

**CAUTION**

In the current implementation of JavaScript, links have event handlers, but anchors do not. This means that you must catch navigation events by attaching event handlers to links. If any of your links point to anchors in the same document, the event must be handled at the link, not at the anchor.

**Listing 3.4   Using the *mouseOver* Event to Mediate Access**

```
<HTML>
<HEAD>
<TITLE>A Nationalist JavaScript Page</TITLE>
<SCRIPT LANGUAGE="JavaScript">
<!--
function warnthem( lnk ) {               // mouseOver event handler
    var theirhost = lnk.hostname;        // Statement 2; get hostname of link
    var domain = "", lastdot = 0, len = 0;
    len = theirhost.length;              // 4; string length of hostname
    lastdot = theirhost.lastIndexOf(".");    // Statement 5; find last dot
    domain = theirhost.substring(lastdot+1, len); // Statement 6; last part of
hostname
    if ( domain == "zz" ) {              //Statement 7; warn about country "zz"
        alert("Country zz only has 1200 baud modems");
    }
}
<!-- end script -->
</SCRIPT>
</HEAD>
<BODY>
<HR>
Check out the new links to <A HREF="http://home.std.zz"
    onMouseOver="warnthem(this)">Zzland</A>
and its neighbor <A HREF="http://home.xyzzy.xy"
onMouseOver="warnthem(this)">XYville</A>
<HR>
</BODY>
</HTML>
```

This HTML creates a page with two elements: It has links to the fictitious home pages of the countries Zzland and XYville, and it sets up a mouseOver event handler for those links. Note that the event handler function warnthem is called with an argument this. The special keyword this is used to refer to the current JavaScript object. When the warnthem function is called, its parameter lnk is filled in with the object that represents the link over which the mouse just moved.

Statement 2 (see the comments in the Listing 3.4) extracts the hostname part of that object, which in this example could be either home.std.zz or home.xyzzy.xy, depending on where the mouse is located. The next three statements use some of the string object functions (see "String Content Methods," in Chapter 4) to tear off the last part of this fully qualified hostname, namely zz or xy, and save it in the variable domain. This variable is then tested against zz in statement 7. If the test passes, an alert is shown to warn the user that the connection to the zz home page takes longer due to slow modems. Links can also have click event handlers, so this code can be modified not only to warn the user but also to abort the connection, if necessary. The result of placing the mouse over the Zzland link is shown in Figure 3.6.

**FIG. 3.6**
JavaScript event handlers can be used with any hypertext links.

The mouseOut event is useful for performing some action when the mouse leaves a hyperlink or an area in an image map. If you used JavaScript to display a message in a text area of a form when you passed your mouse over an image, mouseOut could clear that message when the mouse moves elsewhere.

The onAbort event handler is new to Netscape Navigator 3.0 and is associated with the new Image object. (See Chapter 4, "JavaScript Objects.") When a page is being loaded, the Abort event is triggered if the user halts the loading of an image before it is complete. If this is the case, JavaScript can intercept this event and perhaps display an alert dialog box or some other activity. The syntax of an onAbort handler is the following:

```
<IMG SRC="someimage.gif" onAbort="somefunction()">
```

The onError event handler is another one that is new in Netscape Navigator 3.0. This event can be triggered either by a page or an image on a page not loading correctly (but not aborted by the user). You can use onError in one of three ways. If you set window.onerror=null, then all of the JavaScript errors that exist on the document loaded in that window are suppressed. You can create your own error-handling function to override the one built into JavaScript. You must set it up to return true and take three arguments: message text, URL, and the line number of the error location. This function—if it returns true—enables you to catch JavaScript errors on a page without the standard JavaScript error alert dialog boxes. If you simply want to catch the errors but allow the standard JavaScript error messages to appear, simply construct your function to not return true.

For example, if you want to suppress an error message for an image loading, you can write the following:

```
<IMG SRC="someimage.gif" name="somename" onError="null">
```

If you want to override the error checking in a window, you cannot express the onError in standard HTML because there is no WINDOW tag, so you must place it inside <SCRIPT>... </SCRIPT> tags, such as the following:

```
<SCRIPT>
window.onerror = null
</SCRIPT>
```

Part
I

Ch
3

## Submit and Reset Event Handlers in the *FORM* Tag

The FORM tag is used to begin the definition of an HTML form. It includes attributes from the METHOD to be used in submitting the form and the ACTION to be taken and may also include the event handler attributes onSubmit and onReset. The syntax for a FORM tag is the following:

```
<FORM NAME="formname" ... onSubmit="return submithandler()">
```

 **T I P**  Put event handler attributes last on the attribute list of an HTML tag. This makes them easy to find and modify during debugging.

The onSubmit handler is invoked when the form's contents are about to be submitted. This is a top-level action that applies to the entire form. It is also possible to specify an onClick action on the Submit button in a form, as you shall see in the section "Button Click Events" later in this chapter. The natural use for an onSubmit handler is to validate the contents of a form. The submission proceeds if the contents are valid and is canceled if they are not.

> **CAUTION**
>
> To use a submit handler to cancel a submission, it is essential to use the word "return" before the submit handler's name, as shown in the preceding code line. If "return" is omitted, the submit handler is called, but the form is always submitted.

Listing 3.5 shows a very simple form with a single element, an editable text field. The value of the field is supposed to be a number between 1 and 9. The submit handler function checkit is called when the form is submitted. It validates the user-entered quantity and acts accordingly.

**Listing 3.5    Form Content Can Be Validated Using an *onSubmit* Handler**

```
<HTML>
<HEAD>
<TITLE>A Simple Form Validation Example</TITLE>
<SCRIPT LANGUAGE="JavaScript">
<!--
function checkit() {                        // submit validation function
    var strval = document.myform.mytext.value;   // Statement  2; input text
➥value
    var intval = parseInt(strval);               //  Statement 3; convert to
➥integer
    if ( 0 < intval && intval < 10 ) {           // Statement 4; input ok
        return( true );                          // Statement 5; allow submit
    } else {                                     // Statement 6; input bad - tell
➥user
        alert("Input value " + strval + " is out of range");
        return( false );                         //  Statment 8; forbid submit
    }
}
<!-- end script -->
</SCRIPT>
</HEAD>
```

```
<BODY>
<HR>
<FORM NAME="myform" METHOD="post" ACTION="mailto:me@myhost.com"
    onSubmit="return checkit()">
<P>Enter a number between 1 and 9:
    <INPUT TYPE="text" NAME="mytext" VALUE="1" SIZE="10"></P>
<BR><INPUT TYPE="submit">
</FORM>
<HR>
</BODY>
</HTML>
```

It is worthwhile to examine this example in some detail, as it exposes a number of points that are more thoroughly discussed later in this chapter. Let us consider the HTML in the <BODY> first. The FORM statement creates a form named myform with our usual fictitious mailto destination. It also contains an onSubmit attribute that specifies checkit() as the JavaScript function to call when the form is about to be submitted. Like all of our previous event handlers, this one takes no arguments. You will see very shortly that it is not only possible to pass in arguments but it can also be very beneficial. For a document this simple, however, it is not necessary.

The first INPUT tag establishes an editable text field named mytext, which can hold up to 10 characters and which is initialized to the string "1". The second INPUT tag puts a Submit button just below the input text field. Neither of these INPUT statements has any handler attributes, although they could. What happens next?

If the user types in any text or does anything except click the Submit button, nothing special happens. This example does not process any events other than the submit event, so changes in the text field or navigation actions do not result in any JavaScript code executing. If the user does click the Submit button, then the myform form tries to submit itself. This triggers the submit action, which results in its event handler, checkit(), being called.

The checkit function does two somewhat obscure things. In statement 2 (see comments in Listing 3.5), it sets the local variable strval equal to the value of document.myform.mytext.value.

▶ **See** "Functions and Objects," **p. 54**, which explains that the right side of this expression must be an object reference—in fact, a reference to an object within an object within an object.

It is reasonable and correct to assume that the myform sub-object corresponds to the HTML form named myform within the current document, and that the mytext sub-object corresponds to the HTML editable text field named mytext inside myform. This windy construct transfers the value of that text field into the local variable strval. In statement 3, an attempt is made to convert this string to an integer using the built-in function parseInt. The putative integer is stored in intval.

In statement 4 from the code, our validation test is performed. If the string in the text field did represent an integer between 1 and 9 inclusive, this if test passes and the checkit function returns true in statement 5. This is a message from JavaScript to the browser that the submission may complete.

If the text field was out of range, the else pathway in statement 6 is taken. Note that parseInt returns 0 if its argument cannot be parsed as an integer. This means that if the user entered "five" in the text field rather than 5, the value of intval is 0, and the else clause executes. Statement 7 displays an alert dialog box telling the user that the value was out of range. It contains the string representation of the value. This is useful because the alert dialog box may be inadvertently positioned over the text input field. Finally, statement 8 returns false, indicating that the submit operation should not complete. The outcome of entering a value that is out of bounds is shown in Figure 3.7.

**FIG. 3.7**

JavaScript submit handlers are often used to validate form input.

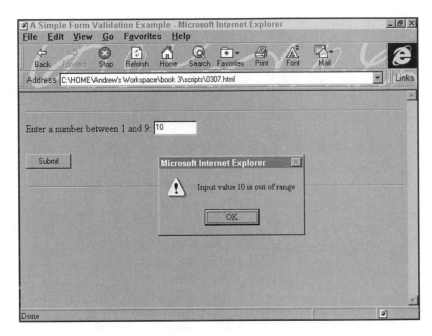

It should be stressed that if the event handler had been declared as onSubmit="checkit()" the function checkit() would still be called whenever the Submit button was clicked, but no validation would take place. The form would always be submitted in this case, even if the input value is out of range. In this case, the return code from the checkit() function is ignored. The version used in Listing 3.5, onSubmit="return checkit()", ensures that the submission is canceled if checkit() returns false.

In this particular case, it is important to give the mytext text field an initial value of 1. This ensures that if the user clicks the Submit button without altering that text field, it has an acceptable value, and the form is submitted. In many cases, just the opposite is true. The whole point of a catalog order form is to persuade the user to enter critical information, such as his or her name and e-mail address. In this case, it's a good idea to initialize the text field with a deliberately invalid value so that if the user clicks Submit without typing anything, the form is not submitted. Chapter 8, "Interactive HTML Objects," and Chapter 21, "Creative User Interaction," provide several more-sophisticated examples of customized user interaction using JavaScript.

**N O T E** Always give the user meaningful feedback on inappropriate input or other error conditions. Indicate why and where the error occurred, not just that an error occurred. Be brief but specific. ■

The onReset handler is invoked when you click the Reset button on a form. It, too, is a top-level event similar to onSubmit. A possible application of the onReset handler might be to ask the user if they really wanted to reset this form they've spent so much time filling out and cancel the event if they don't want to clear the form. Again, remember that if you set onReset to some function, make sure it returns false and that you set the onReset to "return *<functionname>*" if you want the Reset event to be canceled.

# Event Handlers in *<FORM>* Elements

Almost all form elements may have one or more event handlers. The type of event handlers permitted on a given element depends on the type of element itself. You have already seen the linkage between events and HTML entities in Figure 3.4. Broadly speaking, buttons can generate click events, and text and select items can generate focus, blur, select, and change events. The one potentially confusing aspect of this organization of events is that selection lists cannot generate the select event. This is because they have no editable text. We will not consider all possible events in this chapter, only a pithy subset.

There are two important exceptions to the rule that all form elements can have handlers. The first exception applies to hidden items, those with <INPUT TYPE="hidden">. Because they cannot be seen, they cannot be changed by the user and, therefore, cannot generate events. The second exception applies to individual OPTION elements within a SELECT selection list. The SELECT tag itself may have attributes declaring focus, blur, and change handlers, but the OPTIONs may not generate their own events. Any acquisition or loss of focus and any change in the item(s) that have been selected apply to the whole list, not to an individual element.

**Button Click Events**    All button types within an HTML form can have click event handlers by adding an onClick attribute to their <INPUT> declaration. Simple buttons with a TYPE attribute of "button", "reset", or "submit" merely signal that they have been clicked. (Recall that the act of submitting a form may also be caught by using an onSubmit handler attached to the <FORM> declaration as well as by catching the act of resetting with onReset.) Check boxes and option buttons also have values. Check boxes and individual option buttons can be asked if they are on or off. A group of option buttons can also be asked for the unique index of the button currently checked.

One very common problem in HTML form design is the issue of conflicting options. Users are often presented with a variety of different choices, which may even be spread out over more than one HTML form. Some combinations of choices may be invalid or dubious. Unfortunately, in standard HTML, there is no way to perform input validation of this kind without actually submitting the form and asking the ACTION URL if that particular combination is acceptable.

JavaScript event handlers are ideal for this kind of validation. As you will learn in Chapter 4, every HTML form element is also a JavaScript object. You have already seen some examples of this in Listings 3.4 and 3.5. Listing 3.6 shows two option buttons working together with a check box using a JavaScript onClick event handler.

---

**Listing 3.6   Values of Different Form Elements Can Be Accessed in JavaScript**

```
<HTML>
<HEAD>
<TITLE>Two Choices Work as One</TITLE>
<SCRIPT LANGUAGE="JavaScript">
<!--
function insok() {  // make sure payment & ins choices are compatible
    var isgold = document.myform.payment[1].checked; // Statement 2; gold
➥checked
    var isins = document.myform.insurance.checked; // Statement 3; insurance
➥selected?
    var ok = null;
// 5; if paying in gold without insurance then..
    if ( isgold == true && isins != true ) {
        ok = confirm("Do you want insurance?");     // Statement 6; ask for
➥insurance
        if ( ok == true ) {                         // Statement 7; yes, get
➥insurance
            document.myform.insurance.checked = true;    // Statement 8;
➥check it
        }
    }
}
<!-- end script -->
</SCRIPT>
</HEAD>
<BODY>
<HR>
<FORM NAME="myform" METHOD="POST" ACTION="mailto:me@myhost.com">
<STRONG>Payment Options</STRONG><BR>
<HR>
<INPUT TYPE="radio" NAME="payment" VALUE="1" CHECKED
    onClick="insok()"> Personal Check
<INPUT TYPE="radio" NAME="payment" VALUE="2"
    onClick="insok()"> Gold Bullion
<HR>
<INPUT TYPE="checkbox" NAME="insurance" VALUE="Ins"> Insurance?
</FORM>
<HR>
</BODY>
</HTML>
```

---

The <BODY> of this page sets up a two-choice option button named payment and a check box named insurance. The first button is selected, and the check box starts off unchecked. The option button group has the function insok as its click event handler. Whenever either of the buttons is clicked, the insok function is called.

In statements 2 and 3 (see comments in Listing 3.6), insok fetches the current value of the second option button named payment. Note that payment actually denotes the entire group of buttons, not any single option button, so that you must use the array reference payment[1] to refer to the second button (0-based indexing is used). That value is stored in the Boolean variable isgold. The variable insok gets the state of the insurance check box, which is also true if it is checked and false if it is not. A compatibility test is now performed in statement 5. If the option button group indicates payment in gold bullion, but the insurance button is not checked, a confirmation dialog box is appears using the confirm() function in statement 6.

The confirmation dialog box has OK and Cancel buttons. If the user clicks OK, the function returns true; otherwise, it returns false. The return value is tested in statement 7. If it was true, then the user does want insurance, and the method function value of the checked property of the myform.insurance object is set to true. Without worrying too much about what methods and properties really mean just yet, it is easy to infer that this assignment statement has the same effect as a click of the insurance button. That check box is now checked.

Part

I

Ch

3

## TROUBLESHOOTING

**I modified the code shown in Listing 3.6.** I added another group of option buttons to collect information about the user's income level, with its own event handler doinc(). I would like to force the insok() function to be called from the new event handler. Inside doinc() I have the following statement:

```
myform.insurance.click();
```

**This click() function is supposed to cause the insurance check box to be checked, but the handler is never called. Why?** JavaScript has many functions like click() that emulate user actions. These emulated actions do not generate events, however, so the corresponding event handler functions are never called. There is nothing mystical about the event handler function insok()—it is an ordinary JavaScript function that happens to be linked to an HTML event. If you want to call insok() in your doinc() event handler, just do the following:

```
insok();
```

**Text Edit and Selection Events**   HTML text <INPUT> fields with a TYPE attribute of "text" may declare event handlers for any combination of the four text events: focus, blur, change, and select. Multiline text input items created with a TEXTAREA tag may also have these handlers. Selection lists created with <SELECT> can generate all these events except select.

The focus event is generated when the text item gets the input focus, usually as a result of a mouse click. Tabbing through form fields also moves the input focus. The blur event is generated when an item that had focus loses it. The change event is generated whenever something changes. In a text item, this results when any new text is entered or existing text is deleted. In a selection list, it happens whenever a new selection is made, even in a list that permits MULTIPLE selections. The select event is generated when the user selects some text, usually by click-and-drag or double-click operations with the mouse. The select event is almost always accompanied by a visual cue, usually by the selected text becoming highlighted or changing color.

These events can be used to obtain very fine control over the content of text or selection list items. The most common application is to use the change or blur events to ensure that a text field has an appropriate value. If you ask the user to enter his or her birth date, for example, and provide separate fields for the month, day, and year, you will almost certainly want to make sure that the value of the day field is a number between 1 and 31. You might even go to greater lengths and limit the day field's value based on the value of the month field. In any case, you want to avoid erroneous input such as "bleen." Text events can also be used to coordinate the values coming from multiple form elements, as we saw in Listing 3.6.

Listing 3.7 shows a linguistic application of the blur event for a TEXTAREA. The user is inspired to enter a sentence without a single instance of the letter "e." If the user tries and fails, he or she is chided for his or her lack of creativity. Note that the blur event handler is only called if the user clicks outside the text area because blur is generated only when focus is lost. Parts II and IV of this book, "JavaScript In-Depth" and "JavaScript Special Effects," respectively, provide many more detailed examples of all the JavaScript events.

### Listing 3.7 An Example of JavaScript's Text Events

```
<HTML>
<HEAD>
<TITLE>A Literary Exercise</TITLE>
<SCRIPT LANGUAGE="JavaScript">
<!--
function hasE() {                       // complain if there is an e
    var thestr = document.myform.mytarea.value;    // Statement 2; get
➥textarea value
    var uthestr = thestr.toLowerCase();     // Statement 3; convert to
➥lowercase
    if ( uthestr == "" ) {              // Statement 4; no entry
        return;                         // Statement 5; just return
    }
    if ( uthestr.indexOf("e") >= 0 ) {      // Statement 7; found an 'e'
        alert("Alors! You've got an E in there!");     // Statement 8; failed
    } else {
        if ( uthestr.length <= 20 ) {
            alert("Nice try, but too brief");     // Statement 11; too short
        } else {
            alert("Congratulations!");            // Statement 13; succeeded
        }
    }
}
<!-- end script -->
</SCRIPT>
</HEAD>
<BODY>
<P>The novel <I>A Void</I> does not contain a single &quote&quot.<BR>
Can you create a sentence without one?</P>
```

```
<HR>
<FORM NAME="myform" METHOD="POST" ACTION="mailto:me@myhost.com">
<TEXTAREA NAME="mytarea" ROWS="5" COLUMNS="80" onBlur="hasE()">
</TEXTAREA>
</FORM>
<HR>
</BODY>
</HTML>
```

The modus operandi of this example should be familiar to you now. If the user types or clicks in the text area, nothing happens. When the user leaves the text area and clicks elsewhere, a blur event is generated and the handler function hasE is invoked. This function gets the contents of the text area into a local variable named thestr (in statement 2—see the comments in Listing 3.7) and then uses one of the string functions to convert it to lowercase (statement 3). This saves a little time, as the function won't have to test for the presence of both "e" and "E." The new lowercase string uthestr is tested against the empty string in statement 4. If there is no text, the function returns without complaint.

If there is some text, but it has an "e," the user is reprimanded in statement 8. If there is no "e," but the text has less than 20 characters, the user is encouraged to try a more ambitious work in statement 11. If the text is long enough and has no "e," the user is praised in statement 13. Of course, there is nothing preventing the user from entering gibberish such as zzzzzzzzzzzzzzzzzzzzzzzzzz and being congratulated anyway. Much more sophisticated checking would be necessary to ensure that the input was actually a sentence. ●

Part

I

Ch

3

# JavaScript In-Depth

# CHAPTER 4

# JavaScript Objects

The idea of object-oriented programming is not a new one. It actually dates back over 30 years and has gone through several phases of popularity in that time. Currently, object-oriented programming is considered by many to be an established concept that should be part of all modern programming languages. There are several different conflicting definitions of object-oriented programming. Fortunately, there are some key concepts that are shared by (almost) all versions of objected-oriented programming.

At its most basic level, object-oriented programming is a style of programming in which related concepts are grouped together. If you have five data elements and three functions that manipulate those elements, then you group those elements and functions together into a generic container known as an *object*. This is the common ground shared by (almost) all object-oriented programming languages. Differences arise in the details of how such containers are organized and in how their contents can be accessed and modified. ■

### Use the *Date*, *String*, *Math*, and *Array* objects

These objects are built into JavaScript and provide many commonly used functions for date and string manipulation, a large collection of mathematical operations, and array creation and manipulation.

### Create new objects with specific properties and methods

User-defined objects are an excellent way of grouping related data items and functions together, and they work well with JavaScript's object model.

### Build and use JavaScript arrays

JavaScript arrays can be accessed by using a numerical index or an element name; this dual capability simplifies many programming tasks.

### Understand the hierarchy of objects on a Web page

Almost every HTML element is associated with a JavaScript object. These objects are arranged in a logical hierarchy, much like a directory tree.

### Associate HTML tags with HTML objects

To access HTML objects from JavaScript, it is necessary to explore JavaScript's rules for HTML elements and their attributes.

# Objects, Properties, and Methods in JavaScript

Before we can delve into object-oriented programming in JavaScript, it is first necessary to review some of the basic concepts of object-oriented programming itself. You have already had a brief introduction in the "Functions and Objects" section of Chapter 2, "JavaScript: The Language." This section takes you farther, to explain several critical and often misunderstood ideas.

## Object-Oriented Programming Concepts

We already know that an object is basically a container for related items. Rather than carry around money and credit cards in many different pockets and folders, many people choose a more unified method: they keep their money in a wallet. Perhaps they even keep their change in a change purse. The wallet is a container for related items. This is not to say that all such items must be in that wallet; this is often a near-impossible goal for even the most organized individuals. As a flexible principle, however, it is of enormous utility. You might think of bills and change as "data."

Objects operate the same way. Objects collect related data items in a single place and make it simpler, or at least more logical, to access those items. As we have already seen, JavaScript refers to the items collected within an object as its *properties*. You may also recall that JavaScript objects not only store data, they also store functions. It is useful to keep functions that manipulate data items in a specific way with those data items themselves. These functions are known as the *methods* of an object. In the wallet analogy, you might think of credit cards as methods, because they are a way to spend or manipulate money.

The JavaScript Date object is a perfect example of the benefits of this kind of organization. As the name implies, a JavaScript Date object is used to store a date, as well as a time. The Date object also has a very particular set of methods that are useful in converting string representations of dates in Date objects. While these functions are vitally important when manipulating strings, such as Nov 23, 1990, they do not really have sweeping application elsewhere. In a word, they are date-specific. It makes good sense to keep these methods with Date objects, rather than making them generally available functions.

In addition to the concepts of object, property, and method, there is a fourth, somewhat more subtle concept that is also of great importance: the *instance*. The relationship between an object and an instance of an object is similar to how you might classify your pet dog. Your dog "Spot" is an instance of the breed "collie." Another way to think of this distinction is to think of an object as a set of shelves, some of which may be occupied while others are not. You convert that object into an instance when you completely fill in all the empty shelves.

While the Date object is an abstract thing that does not refer to any specific date, an instance of the Date object must refer to some specific date. The Date as an object simply indicates how data will be stored and possibly manipulated (if it has methods), while the Date as an instance exists only when specific data has been placed into variables. The Date instance's empty slots (variables), which specify the actual day, month, year, and so forth, have all been assigned specific values.

**N O T E**  Do not confuse the concept of a generic object with the much more specialized type of embedded object that is created with the HTML OBJECT tag. The latter is a considerably more-advanced topic, which will not be discussed until Part III, "JavaScript and Live Objects." ■

## Defining Your Own Objects: The *new* Statement

Now that we have presented the basic object foundation upon which JavaScript rests, it is time to consider how these concepts are implemented. How does one create objects and instances in JavaScript? In fact, you already know part of the answer to this question, as objects are created by defining a very special sort of function.

Let's pursue the home ownership analogy even further and define a house object. The fundamental properties of our house object will be as follows:

- Number of rooms
- Architectural style
- Year built
- Has a garage?

To define an object to hold this information, we write the function shown in Listing 4.1. Note that this function makes use of the extremely important keyword this, which always refers to the current object. In this case, it refers to the current object we are creating.

Part
II

Ch
4

**Listing 4.1   Defining a Function to Create a *house* Object**

```
function house( rms, stl, yr, garp ) {        // define a house object
     this[0] = rms;                  // number of rooms (integer)
     this[1] = stl;                  // style, e.g. Colonial,
[ic:ccc]Tudor, Ranch (string)
     this[2] = yr;                // year built, integer
     this[3] = garp;              // has a garage? (boolean)
     }
```

There are several things to notice about this object definition. First of all, the name of the function is the name of the object: house. Second, this function does not return anything. When functions were first introduced in Chapter 2, it might have seemed mysterious how a function could actually do useful work without a return statement because everything inside a function is local. Using a function to create an object works by modifying this so that it need not return anything. You can also have the function return(this). Using this explicit return statement has the same effect as the code shown in Listing 4.1.

This example shows how a house *object* is defined. It does not create a specific house *instance*. The hypothetical house object has four slots to hold the four properties: rooms, style, yearbuilt, and hasgarage (these property names are shortened in the actual code, but are longer here for readability). A specific house instance fills those slots with actual values. Instances are created by using the new statement combined with a function call. The keyword new is required because it tells JavaScript that we are creating an instance rather than just calling a function. We could create an instance of house, named myhouse, as follows:

```
var myhouse = new house( 10, "Colonial", 1989, true );
```

# Objects as Arrays

Many programming languages support array data types. An *array* is an indexed collection of items, all of which have the same underlying type. In C or Java, for example, we can say int iarr[10]; which defines a collection of 10 integers. These integers are referred to as iarr[0] through iarr[9]. These two languages use *zero-based indexing*, which means that the first element of the array is at location 0 and the last element of the array is at one less than the length of the array—9 in this case. Other languages, such as Basic, have *one-based indexing*, in which the elements range from 1 up to the length of the array. This might seem more intuitive, but zero-based indexing is actually the more common form.

In the previous example (Listing 4.1), we created a new instance of the house object named myhouse. The instance myhouse is treated just like any other variable. It must be declared by using var. Now that myhouse has been created, how do we refer to its properties? The [ ] notation in the house function looks suspiciously like an array reference. In fact, JavaScript also has arrays that use zero-based indexing. In JavaScript, however, arrays and objects are really two views of the same concept. Every object is an array of its property values, and every array is also an object. The myhouse instance, for example, is an array with the following four elements:

```
myhouse[0] = 10;              // rooms
myhouse[1] = "Colonial";      // style
myhouse[2] = 1989;            // yearbuilt
myhouse[3] = true;            // hasgarage
```

The various elements of the myhouse array contain its properties, which can be accessed by their numerical indexes. myhouse[0] has the value 10, myhouse[1] is the string "Colonial," myhouse[2] is 1989, and myhouse[3] is the Boolean value true. The fact that the number of rooms and yearbuilt are integers, the style property is a string, and hasgarage property is a Boolean is only implicit, of course. There is nothing stopping us from creating a house instance in which the hasgarage property has the string value yes rather than a Boolean value. Care must be taken to avoid this kind of type confusion.

**N O T E**    Object properties are typeless, just like all other variables in JavaScript. The new operator does not protect you against inadvertently assigning an inappropriate value to a property.

In this form of object, it is possible to access the properties sequentially, which is often very useful. If we know that house objects always have four members, we can write the function shown in Listing 4.2 to display the property values.

### Listing 4.2 A Function that Displays the Properties of a *house* Object

```
function showhouse( somehouse ) {
[ic:ccc]// display properties of a house instance
    for( var iter = 0; iter < 4; iter++) {      // four properties exactly
        document.write("<BR>Property " + iter + " is " + somehouse[iter]);
    }
    document.write("<BR>");
}
```

If we call this function showhouse( myhouse ), the four properties of the myhouse instance appear. This function must be called with an instance, not an object. It would be an error to try showhouse( house ). Since there are several alternative ways of writing it, we will revisit this function when we have learned more about methods and the for...in statement.

One deficiency of the showhouse function should strike you immediately. It relies on several pieces of implicit knowledge. We must remember that every house instance has exactly four properties, and we must remember which property is associated with each index. If we were to mistakenly use the myhouse[2] property as the hasgarage Boolean, rather than the yearbuilt integer, an error would no doubt result. In addition, if we augment the definition of a house object by adding a property known as taxrate (a floating-point number describing the current real estate taxation rate on the house), then the showhouse function needs to be modified to increase the loop count in the for statement from 4 to 5. If we neglect to do so, the showhouse function prints only the first four properties and would never print the tax rate.

An even more disastrous error occurs if we redefine the house object to have only three properties but forget to drop the loop count to 3; then the reference to somehouse[3] refers to a nonexistent array member. This type of error is known as an *out-of-bounds error* because it refers to an array element that was not within the boundaries of the array.

Fortunately, JavaScript provides a simple means to address these issues. In JavaScript, it is possible to create arrays that are indexed by names rather than numbers. We can rewrite the definition of the house object to reference its properties by name. This code for the new house object function is shown in Listing 4.3.

### Listing 4.3 A Better *house* Object that Knows Its Own Properties

```
/*
  This function creates a house instance whose first property
 contains the number of properties in the house
  instance. All properties are referenced by name.
*/

function house ( rms, stl, yr, garp ) {
    this.length = 5;              // four informative properties, and length
    this.rooms = rms;            // rooms
```

*continues*

Part II

Ch

4

**Listing 4.3   Continued**

```
    this.style = stl;        // architecture style
    this.yearbuilt = yr;     // year constructed
    this.hasgarge = garp;    // does it have a garage?
}
```

This `house` object function takes four parameters, as before. It sets its `length` property to this number plus 1 because there are four meaningful properties (`rooms`, `style`, `yearbuilt`, and `hasgarage`) and the `length` property itself. More importantly, each of the properties is now referenced by name. If we create a `myhouse` instance, as before, we can now refer to `myhouse.rooms`, whose value is `10`; `myhouse.style`, whose value is `"Colonial"`; `myhouse.yearbuilt`, whose value is `1989`; and `myhouse.hasgarage`, whose value is `true`. We can also use `myhouse.length`, whose value is `5`, to tell us the total number of properties. This method of accessing instance members using the dot operator (.) is known, naturally enough, as *dot notation*.

This use of the `length` property is a typical example of the true nature of object-oriented programming. One of the fundamental ideas in object-oriented programming is the idea of *encapsulation*, which is a long-winded way of saying keep related things in the same place. In the previous definitions of `house` (see Listings 4.1 and 4.2), the length of the `house` object was present in two places. It was implicitly present in the definition of `house` itself, and it was also present explicitly, as the upper limit in the `for` loop of the `showhouse` function. The doctrine of encapsulation says that this is bad. The length of an object should be stored only in one place—in the object itself. By the same token it might be argued that the `showhouse` function should really be part of the `house` object, too. The section "Method Functions and *this*," later in this chapter, describes how to do this.

 **TIP** Define all objects with a `length` property, which gives the number of properties in the object. Make the `length` property the first property.

It might seem that the two types of `house` objects, from Listings 4.1 and 4.3, are very different. In fact, JavaScript provides a powerful method by which objects created using the dot notation may be treated as arrays. Object properties may be referred to not only as indexed array elements but also as named array elements. This is why the JavaScript objects are also known as *associative arrays*. The set of properties of the `myhouse` instance created from Listing 4.3 could also be written as the following:

```
myhouse["length"] = 5;
myhouse["rooms"] = 10;
myhouse["style"] = "Colonial";
myhouse["yearbuilt"] = 1989;
myhouse["hasgarage"] = true;
```

Following the previously given advice, the first property of this object is its length, which we now know can be referred to as either `myhouse.length` or `myhouse["length"]`. We cannot refer to it as `myhouse[0]`, however, even though it is the first property. Earlier versions of the

JavaScript language, such as the original JavaScript that came with Netscape Navigator 2.0, did allow all three forms of access. The current implementation of JavaScript does not permit associative array elements to be accessed by using numerical indexes. This means that the showhouse function in Listing 4.2 cannot work with the myhouse object created by using Listing 4.3. The for...in statement, described in the next section ("The *for...in* statement"), allows us to rewrite showhouse to work with the associative array form of house instances.

---

**CAUTION**

JavaScript arrays can be accessed either by integer indexes or by property names, but not both. Property names are case-sensitive. Integer indexes are limited by the length of the array. If you refer to nonexistent array elements, by name or by index, this either generates a JavaScript error or gives you an invalid value (usually null).

---

# Using Variable Length Arrays and Extended Instances

There is one final point to be made about the difference between the house object and its various instances. Suppose we create another instance of house, named yourhouse, by using the following call to new:

```
yourhouse = new house( 26, "Tudor", 1922, true );
```

myhouse and yourhouse are both instances of the house object. Both result from filling in the four slots in the house template with four specific pieces of information that define myhouse and yourhouse (as well as the fifth, hidden piece of information, the length). It is possible to *dynamically extend* an instance by simply tacking on a new property. If you feel the need to also record the fact that your house has two tool sheds and a gazebo, you can write the following:

```
yourhouse.sheds = 2;
yourhouse.hasgazebo = true;
```

These two statements add two new properties to the end of the yourhouse array: the sheds (integer) property and the hasgazebo (Boolean) property. Dynamic extensions apply only to specific instances. The myhouse instance is not affected, nor is the house object changed in any way. If we execute showhouse( myhouse ), it prints out exactly the same as it did before. If we create a third house named pizza, as follows:

```
pizza = new house( 3, "Restaurant", 1993, false );
```

it will not have a sheds property, nor a hasgazebo property. Figure 4.1 illustrates the relationship between the house object and its various instances.

**N O T E**  Dynamic extensions are completely local to a particular instance. The underlying object and all other instances—past, present, and future—are not affected. ■

**FIG. 4.1**

Instances inherit their structure from the underlying object but can also be extended.

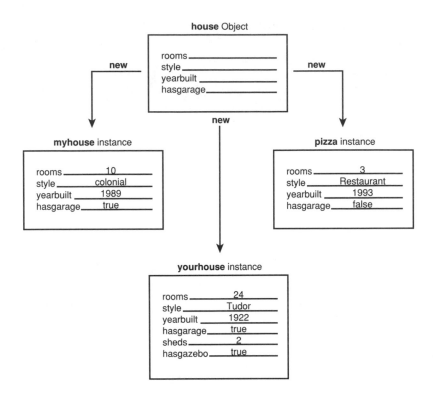

There are some situations in which dynamic extensions are absolutely essential and dramatically simplify programming. For the most part, however, dynamic extensions should be used with great care because they can be the source of numerous errors. In fact, we have already made one such error, which shows itself when we attempt to execute the function `showhouse( yourhouse )`. Since the `length` element of the `yourhouse` instance has not been modified, it still has the value `5`, so that only array elements 1 through 4 (properties `name` through `hasgarage`) appear. The two new properties do not appear. When we added `sheds` and `hasgazebo`, we should have also stated

```
yourhouse.length += 2;
```

to account for the two new properties in this instance. This is precisely the type of error that is easy to make. In general, it is much better for the `house` object always to have `sheds` and `hasgazebo` properties, which are seldom used, than to randomly glue them on. The most efficient way to do this is discussed later in the "Functions with a Variable Number of Arguments" section of this chapter.

The one common case where dynamic extension is extremely useful is in variable length arrays. Because object properties are just array elements, and because these elements can be referred to using a numerical index, it is easy to write an object-creation function that creates an array of arbitrary size and content. The function in Listing 4.4 can be used to define an object that is an array of strings. The number of strings in the array is the first argument and the initial value for each element is the second argument.

**Listing 4.4    A Variable Length Array-of-Strings Object**

```
function stringarr( howmany, initstr) {      // "howmany" strings
    this.length = howmany;
    for( var i = 1; i <= howmany; i++ ) {
        this[i] = initstr;                    // initial value "initstr"
    }
}
```

If we call this function as

```
mystringarr = new stringarr( 100, "spoon" );
```

it creates an instance with 101 properties. The first named property, `mystringarr.length`, is the all-important `length` property. The next 100, at numerical indexes 1 through 100 inclusive, are initialized to the string `spoon`. Presumably, at some point in the future, these 100 strings will be set to some other, less uniform values. It is important to initialize all the properties' values to something (the empty string `""` would do in this case). Note that we could print all the contents of this array by using a `for` statement, such as the following:

```
for(var oi = 1; oi <= mystringarr.length; oi++)
    document.write("Element " + oi + " is " + mystringarr[oi] + "<BR>");
```

If we later find that we need more than 100 strings, we do not need to create a new, even longer, `stringarr` instance. Instead, we can dynamically extend the array to include these new strings. It is essential that the `length` property be updated in this case, as there is no other way of determining how many elements are in the array, short of counting them with a `for...in` loop (see the following section). The following statements add three new strings and update the length:

```
mystringarr[101] = "I'm";
mystringarr[102] = "doing";
mystringarr[103] = "laundry";
mystringarr.length += 3;
```

# The *for...in* Statement

Chapter 2 introduced the extremely useful `for` statement. The standard form of the `for` statement begins with a clause that defines the initial state of the `for` loop, the condition under which it will terminate, and the way in which it is updated at the end of each iteration. There is also a variant of the `for` statement that may be used to iterate over the properties of an object. This statement, the `for...in` statement, has the following form:

```
for ( varname in objname ) {
    forbody
    }
```

Part
II

Ch
4

In the `for...in` statement, *varname* is the name of a variable that takes on the successive property names of the object *objname*. This form of the `for` statement also permits the *varname* to contain a `var` declaration. Using the `for...in` statement, we can write yet another form of the `showhouse` function that works with associative arrays and does not rely on the presence of a `length` property. This function is shown in Listing 4.5. This version actually works on any instance or object, not just on instances of `house`, so it has been renamed `showany`.

**Listing 4.5   A Function that Displays the Properties of Any Object**

```
function showany(anyobj) {        // display properties of an instance or object
    for( var iter in anyobj ){     // iterate over all properties
        document.write("<BR>Property " + iter + " is " + anyobj[iter]);
    }
    document.write("<BR>");
}
```

# Method Functions and *this*

One of the most powerful aspects of object-oriented programming in JavaScript is the ability to create objects with functional properties. You may recall that these functional properties are known as methods. Aside from being a convenient organizational principle, there are other distinct advantages to associating functions with objects. We have already seen the special keyword `this` that is used in object creation. It's also used in method functions to refer to the *current object*. To see how this works, consider one more variation on the `house` object and the `showhouse` function, shown in Listing 4.6.

**Listing 4.6   The *showhouse* Function as a Method of *house***

```
/*
  This function creates a house instance with a "show" method
*/

function house( rms, stl, yr, garp ) {
    this.length = 5;            // four info props and length itself
    this.rooms = rms           // rooms
    this.style = stl;          // style
    this.yearbuilt = yr;       // year built
    this.hasgarage = garp;     // garage?
    this.show = mshowhouse;    // the showhouse method
}

/*
  This function is the show method of the house object
*/

function mshowhouse() {         // note: no arguments!
    var nprops = this.length;  // len of property array not including show
    var idx = 0;
```

```
for ( var iter in this) { //iterate
    if ( idx < 1 || idx >= nprops ) {
        idx++;
        continue;          // skip "length" and "show"
        }
    document.write("<BR>Property " + idx + " is " + this[iter]);
    idx++;                 // increment numerical index}
document.write("<BR>");
}
```

This version of the instance-creation function house not only has the usual four pieces of house information (rooms, style, yearbuilt, and hasgarage) and the length property, which gives the number of properties, but it also has a final property named show, which is set equal to the function mshowhouse (it has been given a new name to emphasize that it is now a method function). Note that we deliberately did not count this method in the length of the property array: the value of the length property is 5, even though there are six properties.

The method version of the showhouse function is shown next. It does not have any arguments. Instead, it refers to its enclosing object as this. The usual for loop works as before. We have deliberately shortened the length property by one and used an auxiliary variable named idx so that we can display the numerical index of each property. Only the first four properties of the house instance are displayed. We have used both a dot-style reference and an array-style reference with this, which acts just like any normal instance. If we execute the show method on the myhouse object, a display something like Figure 4.2 appears.

**FIG. 4.2**

Method functions can be used to display the properties of their instances.

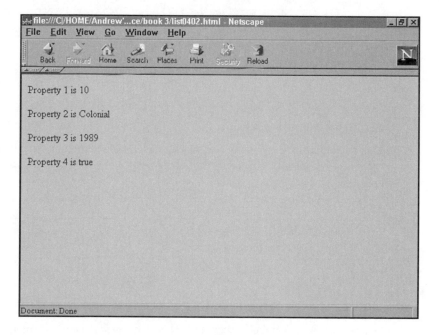

Property 1 is 10

Property 2 is Colonial

Property 3 is 1989

Property 4 is true

Since this function takes no arguments, you might wonder how it is used. The answer is that, because the show method is a property just like any other property, it may be accessed in the same way. The following statements:

```
myhouse.show();

yourhouse.show();

pizza.show();
```

all work in the same way as their non-method counterparts:

```
showhouse( myhouse );

showhouse( yourhouse );

showhouse( pizza );
```

This particular method function takes no arguments and is also void; it does not return any value. Method functions can take as many arguments as you want and can also return values. Listing 4.7 shows a very simple method function that takes the current year and an argument and returns the age of the house as its value. It checks the argument for validity and returns -1 if the current year is actually earlier than the yearbuilt property.

**Listing 4.7   A Method Function for Displaying the Age of a House**

```
function howold ( curyear ) {           // current year passed as arg
    if ( curyear < this.yearbuilt )     // invalid year: too early
        return(-1);                     // no time travel (yet)
    return( curyear - this.yearbuilt ); // return difference
}
```

This method must be added to the object-defining function house in order for it to work, of course. This function would be called by a standard property reference, such as the following:

```
myhouseage = myhouse.howold( 1996 );
```

This type of function call is not any different from a standard function call such as showhouse( myhouse ). The only difference between method functions and other functions is that method functions may use this as an indirect way of naming the object that contains them.

 **TIP** If you have special-purpose functions that operate only on instances of an object, then those functions should be methods of that object.

# Nested Objects

Object properties are typeless quantities. They may be ordinary variables of any implicit type. Our house object contains properties that are implicitly integers, strings, and Booleans. It also contains functional members (methods). In a very real sense, every new object is a new data type, and every instance of that object is a new variable with its object as the underlying, implicit type of that instance. Because JavaScript is typeless, does this mean that objects can contain other objects? In a word, yes.

Suppose we create a new object called desc that holds some common pieces of information about various items. In particular, the desc object has properties for length, width, height, and color, and a method for computing the volume. The definition of this object and its volume method are shown in Listing 4.8.

### Listing 4.8    A Description Object and Its Volume Method

```
/*
  The object creation function. The len, width and height
  properties will be specified in meters. The color will be
  a string.
*/

function desc( ln, wd, ht, col) {        // describe something
    this.length = 5;                     // four properties and length of the
array
    this.len = ln;                       // length of the thing
    this.width = wd;                     // width of the thing
    this.height = ht;                    // height of the thing
    this.color = col;                    // color
    this.findvolume = findvolume;        // volume computation method
    }

/*
  The volume computation method. If the ismetric argument is
 true then the metric volume will be returned; otherwise
  the volume in cubic feet will be returned
*/

function findvolume ( ismetric ) {
    var mylen, mywid, myht;
    var conv = ( 39.37 / 12.0 );         // conversion from metric to English
    if ( ismetric == true ) {
        mylen = this.len;                // metric by default
        mywid = this.width;              // ditto
        myht = this.height;              // ditto
    } else {
        mylen = this.len / conv;         // convert
        mywid = this.width / conv;
        myht = this.height / conv;
    }
    return( mylen * mywid * myht );       // return volume
}
```

Part
II

Ch

4

We can now add a desc object as a property of the house object. We could simply add length, width, height, and color properties directly to the definition of house, but this would go against another fundamental principle of object-oriented programming: *object reuse*. The desc object is very general. It can be used to describe a house, a car, a boat, or a teacozy. It makes good sense to encapsulate these common properties in the desc object and then reuse that object's definition over and over by including it within the house, car, boat, and teacozy objects. It would be serviceable, but wasteful, to repeat the same information in all these object definitions. Listing 4.9 shows the latest version of the house object creation function.

**Listing 4.9   The *house* Object with a *desc* Subobject**

```
/*
  This function creates a house instance with a "show" method
  and a "desc" subobject
*/

function house( rms, stl, yr, garp, desci ) {
      this.length = 5;                  // four info props and length itself
      this.rooms = rms;                  // rooms
      this.style = stl;                 // style
      this.yearbuilt = yr;              // year built
      this.hasgarage = garp;            // garage?
      this.descr = desci;               // description instance
      this.show = mshowhouse;           // the showhouse method
      this.howold = howold;             // the howold method
}
```

To properly create a house instance, we must first create a desc instance and pass it as the fifth argument to house. It would be an error to pass in a desc object. A house instance, even one with a subobject, must have all its slots filled in; this is what makes it an instance. This means that all the slots in the desc property of house must be filled in, as well, so that it, too, must be an instance. Once this has been done, it is possible to use all the properties and methods of the desc of the house. Listing 4.10 shows code that creates a desc instance, creates a house instance with that description, and then displays the color, age, and volume of the house, using the properties and methods of the desc (and myhouse itself). This type of structure, in which objects and instances can be contained within one another, is referred to as an *object hierarchy*. When this code executes, we obtain a page that looks like Figure 4.3.

**Listing 4.10   Creating and Using Subobjects**

```
/*
  Create a desc instance and use it to create a house instance
*/

var mydesc;
var myhouse;
var mycol, myvol;

mydesc = new desc( 20, 18, 15, "beige" );        // fairly big; ugly color
myhouse = new house( 10, "Colonial", 1989, true, mydesc );  // mine, though

/*
```

```
   Display the colorvolume and age of the house using a reference
   to the desc properties of myhouse.
*/

mycol = myhouse.descr.color;                  // property of property
myvol = myhouse.descr.findvolume(true);       // submethod
document.write("<BR>My house is " + mycol);
document.write("<BR>It is " + myhouse.howold( 1996 ) + " years old");
document.write("<BR>My house occupies " + myvol + " cubic meters");
document.write("<BR>");
```

**FIG. 4.3**

Objects can contain one another in an object hierarchy.

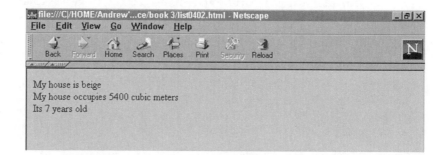

## The *with* Statement

Once you have become hooked on object-oriented programming, it often becomes a pervasive aspect of your coding style. Objects begin to show up everywhere. JavaScript has a convenient statement, borrowed from the Pascal language, that performs a set of object manipulations on the same object. Listing 4.10 may have impressed you with the power of its object manipulations. It may have also intimidated you a bit with the amount of typing that is required to get the color of the myhouse instance.

The purpose of the with statement is to permit a number of object references to be made to the same object (or instance) without having to repeat the name of that object. The format of the statement is

```
with ( objname ) {
     statements
     }
```

*objname* is the name of an object or instance. Inside the with block, any reference to properties of *objname* occurs as if they had been prefixed with *objname* and the dot operator. Listing 4.11 shows an expanded version of the second part of Listing 4.10, in which various aspects of myhouse are displayed. The mshowhouse method should now be extended not only to display the properties of its instance but also to call a similar show method within the desc object, which will also need to be created.

**Listing 4.11   Using the *with* Statement as an Implicit Object Reference**

```
/*
  Display the color and volume of the house using a reference
  to the desc properties of myhouse.
*/

var mycol, myvol, myage;

with ( myhouse ) {
    mycol = descr.color;           // 1: ref to myhouse.descr.color
    myvol = descr.findvolume(true); // 2: ref to myhouse.descr.findvolume
    myage = yearbuilt;              // 3: reference to myhouse.yearbuilt
    document.write("<BR>My house is " + mycol);                        // 4
    document.write("<BR>My house occupies " + myvol + " cubic meters"); // 5
// 6: explicit reference to another instance
    if ( myage > yourhouse.yearbuilt) {
        document.write("<BR>Its newer than yours!");                   // 7
        }
    document.write("<BR>");
    }
```

Each of the statements labeled 1, 2, and 3 makes an implicit reference to the myhouse object, which was established as the default object to use in the with statement. Note that not every statement within the with block need refer to myhouse. Statements 4, 5, and 7 make absolutely no reference to any house object. Also, statement 6 makes an explicit reference to a different house instance, namely yourhouse.

Statement 6 exposes one of the wrinkles of the with statement. When JavaScript proceeds through this with block, it must decide many times when the implicit myhouse is to be used and when it is to be skipped. It must examine every reference, in fact. So for mycol, it must decide if you meant the local variable mycol or if there is some property of myhouse named myhouse.mycol. Fortunately, there is an unambiguous choice in every case. There is no mycol property of the house object.

Statement 6 uses an explicit reference to yourhouse. If statement 6 had been written as the following:

```
if ( myage > yearbuilt ) {
```

JavaScript would have misinterpreted your intentions as to the meaning of yearbuilt and would have implicitly translated this statement to

```
if ( myage > myhouse.yearbuilt ) {
```

because there is a yearbuilt property of myhouse. This type of error is both common and pernicious. Since JavaScript is an interpreted language, there is no way to see that this inappropriate translation has taken place. There is no compiled output that can be examined. Such errors are very hard to debug. Even though with is very useful, its use should be strictly circumscribed.

▶ **See** "Debugging JavaScript Applications," **p. 637**, for more information about debugging code.

> **CAUTION**
>
> `with` blocks should be as short as possible. Check all statements within the `with` block to ensure that there are no ambiguous references to local variables or to properties of other objects.

# Functions with a Variable Number of Arguments

Our discussion of the object foundations of JavaScript is almost complete. We have learned that functions are used to define objects and create instances using the `new` operator. We have also learned that indexed arrays and associative arrays are both really objects. In fact, the unity between all these concepts goes even deeper. JavaScript functions, themselves, have properties that can be used to fine-tune their behavior.

This aspect of JavaScript is still evolving at the time of this writing. However, we can say for certain that all JavaScript functions have at least the following two properties:

- `caller`
- `arguments`

The `caller` property is a string containing the name of whoever called the function. The `arguments` property is an array of all the arguments that are not on the argument list of the function. The `caller` property permits a function to identify and respond to the environment in which it is called. The `arguments` property allows us to write functions that take a variable number of arguments. The arguments in the function's argument list are mandatory, while those in the `arguments` property are optional. Listing 4.12 shows a function that takes one mandatory argument and a potentially unlimited number of option arguments. It returns a string describing its invocation.

**Part**

**II**

**Ch**

**4**

---

**Listing 4.12  A Function with Mandatory and Optional Arguments**

```
/*
 . Demonstrate mandatory and optional
   arguments to a function. Add all optional argument, and return the sum
   as a string.
*/

function addem( str1 ) {                  // one mandatory argument
    var nopt = addem.arguments.length;    // # of arguments
    var sum = 0;                          // sum of optional arguments
    var strres;                           // string result

    for(  var i = 1; i < nopt; i++ ) {    // iterate over all optionals
        sum += addem.arguments[i];        // add them
    }
    strres = "Hello " + str1 +  ", sum is " + sum;
    return(strres);
}
```

To see how this works, suppose that this function is called from within another function named test1, with the following invocation:

```
var str = addem( "there", 1, 3, 5, 7 );
```

What happens? The mandatory argument "there" is assigned to the parameter str1 of the function addem. The complete argument list is also assigned to the variable length array addem.arguments. This has a length property (as do all well-behaved arrays), which has the value 5 because there are five arguments altogether: one mandatory argument and four optional arguments. This means that the local variable nopt is 5. Unlike the examples we have used, the length property is not at index 0 of the arguments array. The arguments begin at addem.arguments[0] and continue up to addem.arguments[4] (five elements total). This means that the optional arguments begin at addem.arguments[1]. The for loop in addem adds the optional arguments together and arrives at 1 + 3 + 5 + 7 = 16, which is assigned to the local variable sum. Finally, strres is constructed by concatenating various strings, among them the mandatory parameter str1, which is "there", and the value of the sum. The concatenated string is returned and assigned to str; its value is the string "Hello there, sum is 16."

Notice that both the mandatory argument str1 and the optional arguments are part of the argument list addem.arguments. Notice also that there need not be any optional arguments. The function call

```
var str = addem( "on a stick" );
```

returns the value "Hello on a stick, sum is 0."

# Built-In Objects

Now that we have covered the foundations of object-oriented programming in JavaScript, we can begin to look at the actual objects that JavaScript itself provides. These objects can be put into the following three categories:

- Built-in objects
- HTML objects
- Browser objects

Built-in objects include the String object, the Date object, the Math object, and the Array object. They are referred to as *built-in* because they really do not have anything to do with Web pages, HTML, URLs, the current browser environment, or anything visual. HTML objects, in turn, are directly associated with elements of Web pages. Every image, link, and anchor is a JavaScript object. Every form and every element within a form is an HTML object. The hierarchical organization of display elements on a Web page is reflected almost exactly in a hierarchical set of nested HTML objects. You've already gotten a taste of this hierarchy in the event-processing examples of Chapter 3.

▶ **See** "HTML Objects in JavaScript," **p. 189**, for more information on the relationship between HTML elements and JavaScript functions.

Browser objects are at the top of JavaScript's object hierarchy. These objects represent large-scale elements of the browser's current environment and include objects such as window (the current window), history (the list of previously visited pages), and location (the URL of the current page).

# *String* Objects

String objects are the most built-in of all the built-in JavaScript objects. You do not even need to use new when creating a String object. Any variable whose value is a string is actually a String object. Literal strings such as "HelloWorld" are also String objects. You can also use new on the string object to obtain a new string. The following statements both construct a string whose value is hiya:

```
var mystring = "hiya";
var mystring2 = new String("hiya");
```

String objects have two properties—length and prototype—and many methods. The length property gives the length of the string. The prototype property allows you to add properties to a String object. The methods fall into three categories: methods that manipulate the contents of the string, methods that manipulate the appearance of the string, and methods that convert the string into an HTML element.

**String Content Methods**   The following methods can be used on String objects to access, control, or modify their content:

- charAt( *idx* )
- indexOf( *chr* )
- lastIndexOf( *chr* )
- substring( *fromidx*, *toidx* )
- split(*separator*)
- toLowerCase()
- toUpperCase()

The toLowerCase and toUpperCase methods convert the contents of the string entirely to lower- and uppercase, respectively. So if we define the string variable as

```
var mystr = "Look At This"
```

then its length property, mystr.length, has the value 12 because there are 12 characters in the string. In addition, we can apply the two case-conversion methods and get:

```
mystr.toLowerCase() = "look at this"
mystr.toUpperCase() = "LOOK AT THIS"
```

These two functions do nothing to characters that have no case, so the two spaces in this string are unchanged. We could have also applied the methods directly to the literal form of this String object, so "Look At This".toLowerCase is also equal to "look at this."

The methods `charAt` and `substring` are used either to extract a single character from a string, at position *idx*, or to extract a range of characters from position *fromidx* up to, but not including, position *toidx*. Character positions are zero-based, as are all JavaScript arrays so that all indexes must fall between 0 and 1 less than the length of the array. For example, using `mystr`, we have:

```
mystr.charAt(5) = "A"
mystr.substring(5,7) = "At"
```

Like the method functions `toUpperCase()` and `toLowerCase()`, these methods both return strings. Care should be take to give these methods valid indexes that are actually within the string. The `substring` method forgives you if you accidentally specify a *toidx* that is less than or equal to the corresponding *fromidx*—; the method will return the empty string `""`.

The `split` method separates a string into an array of substrings, based on the optional separator argument passed to it. If you leave out the separator, then the `split` method returns an array of one element consisting of the whole string. The separator is treated as a string. This method is very useful to create an array of elements from a list, such as "`Mon, Tue, Wed, Thur, Fri, Sat, Sun`." If this list were called `weekDays`, and you used the method `weekDays.split(",")`, it would return an array whose first element is `Mon` and whose seventh element is `Sun`.

Finally, both the `indexOf` and `lastIndexOf` methods are used to search for *chr* with a string. `indexOf` searches from the beginning (left side) of the string and `lastIndexOf` searches from the end (right side). Both return an integer index if they find the character, and `-1` if they do not. Using `mystr` again, we can search for the character "o" from both sides:

```
mystr.indexOf("o") = 1
mystr.lastIndexOf("o") = 2
```

The first search finds the first "o" of the word "Look" at position 1 (second character), and the second search finds the second "o" of "Look" because that is the first "o" when searching from right to left. Both of these methods also take an optional second argument that specifies an initial index at which to start the search.

**String Appearance Methods**   The string appearance methods are used to control how a string appears when displayed on a Web page. If you are creating a page with standard HTML tags, you would achieve the same effects by using various tags. For example, to make the string `help` appear in italics, you would write `<I>help</I>`. The string appearance methods enable you to obtain the same effects in JavaScript without using the corresponding HTML elements. The string appearance methods are as follows:

- `big()`
- `blink()`
- `bold()`
- `fixed()`
- `fontcolor( `*colr*` )`

- fontsize( *sz* )
- italics()
- small()
- strike()
- sub()
- sup()

Most of these methods should be self-explanatory. The italics method, for example, performs exactly the same function as the I tag in HTML. The only two that take arguments are the fontcolor and fontsize methods. The fontcolor method changes the font color of the string, as if the <FONT COLOR=*colr*> attribute had been used. Similarly, the fontsize method changes the size of the font used for displaying a string as if the <FONT SIZE=*sz*> attribute had been used. *colr* should be a string; *sz* may be a number or a string. If it's a number, this specifies an absolute font size; if it's a string such as "+2", it specifies an increment relative to the current font size. Listing 4.13 shows several examples using the string appearance methods. The output of this code is shown in Figure 4.4.

**N O T E** Not all HTML style tags have corresponding string appearance methods. You can always directly embed an HTML tag in the string itself if there is no method with the same functionality. ▪

**Part**

**II**

**Ch**

**4**

### Listing 4.13 String Methods Can Be Used to Change How Strings Appear

```
var bstr = "big";
var sstr = "small";

/*
  This displays strings with both big and small text.
*/
document.write("<BR>This is " + bstr.big() + " text");
document.write("<BR>This is " + sstr.small() + "text");
/*
  The following two strings contain directly embedded HTML tags.
  They have exactly the same result as the two method calls above
*/
document.write("<BR>This is <BIG>big</BIG> text");
document.write("<BR>This is <SMALL>small</SMALL> text");
/*
  If your favorite tag does not have a method, just embed it
*/
document.write("<BR>This is <STRONG>strong</STRONG> text ");
document.write("<BR>");
```

**FIG. 4.4**

Many HTML style tags have equivalent JavaScript methods.

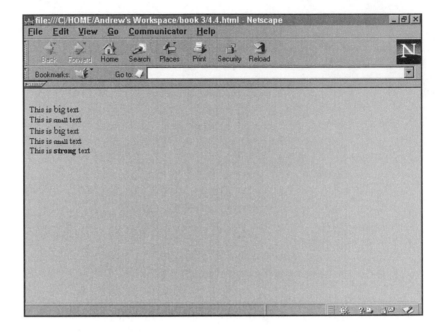

**HTML String Methods** JavaScript provides two string methods for converting strings into hypertext entities. These methods should be clearly distinguished from the HTML objects, such as forms, which are discussed in the section on "Browser and HTML Objects" later in this chapter. These two methods are used to create HTML, while the HTML objects already *are* HTML. The two methods in this category are as follows:

- anchor( *namestr* )
- link( *hrefstr* )

Both these methods are used to create some form of the anchor (<A>) HTML attribute. The difference between them is that the anchor method is used to create an anchor with *namestr* as the value of the NAME attribute, while link is used to create an anchor with the HREF attribute set to *hrefstr*. Said another way, anchor creates an anchor that is a target, while link creates an anchor that is a link. Both methods convert the string on which they operate into the text portion of that anchor. *namestr* may be any valid string that may be a NAME, so it should not have any embedded white space. *hrefstr* should be a valid URL because the user is being invited to click it. Listing 4.14 uses these methods and shows a simple example that sets up an anchor target and then links to it.

**N O T E** The anchor() string method uses the older but more common HTML NAME attribute rather than the newer ID tag. ▨

> **Listing 4.14    String Methods Can Be Used to Create HTML Anchors and Links**
>
> ```
> var sum4str = "Summary of Chapter 4";
> var sum4tar = "Summary4";
>
> /*
>   Create a summary target and a link to it. The following two
>   statements are completely equivalent to this HTML:
>
>   <A NAME="Summary4">Summary of Chapter 4</A><HR>
>   Click here for a <A HREF="#Summary4">Summary of Chapter 4</A>
> */
> document.write(sum4str.anchor(sum4tar));
> document.write("<HR>");
> document.write("Click here for a " + sum4str.link(location + "#" + sum4tar));
> document.write("<BR>");
> ```

# The *Math* Object

The Math object is used for various forms of mathematical calculations. It contains several properties that are standard constants, such as pi, which equals 3.14159..., as well as a large set of methods that represent common trigonometric and algebraic functions. All Math methods deal with floating-point numbers. Angles are expected to be given in radians, not degrees.

The Math object is our first example of a *static object*. A static object is one that does not change. All of the slots in the Math object already have values. This makes perfect sense because you cannot change the value of pi or invent a new meaning for the cos() function (not without creating chaos). The practical consequence of Math being static is that you never use new with Math; you always refer to the Math object directly. Static objects, such as the Math object, are different from ordinary objects, which have themselves as well as their instances. The Math object has only itself and no instances.

The Math object has the following properties:

- E
- LN10
- LN2
- PI
- SQRT1_2
- SQRT2

The Math object has the following methods:

- abs( *num* )
- acos( *num* )

- asin( *num* )
- atan( *num* )
- ceil( *num* )
- cos( *ang* )
- exp( *num* )
- floor( *num* )
- log( *num* )
- max( *num1, num2* )
- min( *num1, num2* )
- pow( *num1, num2* )
- random()
- round( *num* )
- sin( *ang* )
- sqrt( *num* )
- tan(*ang*)

These are all the functions and constants you find on any decent calculator. Remember that JavaScript is case-sensitive, so you must write Math.PI exactly to get the value of pi. The constants stand for the base of the natural logarithm (Napier's constant, or about 2.71828), the natural log of 10 (about 2.30259), the natural log of 2 (about 0.69315), everyone's favorite pi (about 3.141592653589793), the square root of 1/2 (about 0.7071), and the square root of 2 (about 1.4142).

The methods of the Math object include the common trigonometric functions, including sine (sin), cosine (cos), and tangent (tan), and their inverses, arcsin (asin), arccos (acos), and arctan (atan). Each of the trigonometric functions takes an angle in radians and produces a floating-point number. The values should be between -1 and 1 for the sin and cos methods. Each of the inverse trigonometric functions takes a number, which should be between -1 and 1 for the asin and acos methods, and returns an angle in radians.

The ceil, floor, and round methods all take floating-point numbers as inputs and return integers as outputs. The ceil method gives the smallest integer that is greater than or equal to its argument, while floor returns the largest integer that is less than or equal to its argument. (Except when the argument is negative; then ceil "rounds" away from zero, floor toward zero.) The round method gives the nearest integer.

The exp, log, pow, and sqrt methods all deal with exponentiation or its inverse. The exp method raises Math.E to the power given by its argument and is the inverse of the log method, which returns the natural logarithm of its argument, which should be positive. The pow method raises num1, its first argument, to the power num2, its second argument. The sqrt returns the square root of its argument. If you inadvertently give sqrt a negative number, it forgives you and returns 0.

Finally, the abs, min, max, and random methods perform various useful operations. The abs method returns the absolute value of its argument. min and max give the minimum and maximum value of their two arguments, respectively. The random method takes no arguments. It returns a random, floating-point number between 0 and 1. Although older releases of Internet Explorer did not support random(), all versions since 3.0 do. Listing 4.15 presents some simple uses of the Math object.

▶ **See** "The *Math* Object," **p. 145**, for more detailed examples using the Math object.

**Listing 4.15    Three Useful Functions Using the *Math* Object**

```
/*
  Compute the area of a circle given its diameter
*/

function areaofcir(diam) {
    var radius = diam / 2;
    return( Math.PI * radius * radius );      // pi times r squared
}

/*
  Given the coordinates of a point on a circle,
  determine how far around the circle we must rotate in order
  to reach that point. Return the angle in radians.
*/

function angoncircum( x, y ) {
    var epsilon = 0.00001;                // a very small number
    if ( Math.abs(x) < epsilon ) {        // if x is very close to zero
        if ( y > 0 ) {                    // positive x axis
            return(0.0);                  // 0 degrees = 0 radians
        } else {                          // negative x axis
            return( Math.PI );            // 180 degrees = pi radians
        }                                 // end of inner if-else
    }                                     // end of outer if
// division by zero avoided by the "if" test above
    return( Math.atan( y / x ) );
}

/*
  Given the diagonal size of a television, compute its width
  assuming that the screen is square
*/

function tvsize( diag ) {
    return( diag / Math.SQRT2 );
}
```

# The *Date* Object

Dealing with dates is one of the most tedious tasks in any language. This is because we like to represent dates and times in decidedly non-decimal systems. Months come in units of 12, hours in units of 24, and minutes and seconds in units of 60. All these variations are quite illogical from the computer's standpoint. It likes to deal with nice, round numbers, preferably powers of 2, or at least multiples of 10.

The Date object simplifies and automates a lot of the conversion woes associated with going back and forth between a human-readable representation, such as Nov. 23, 1990, and the internal representation. JavaScript's Date object follows the UNIX standard of storing date and time information internally as the number of milliseconds since January 1, 1970. This date is often called "The Epoch," since it is shortly after UNIX was first unleashed on an unsuspecting world.

> **CAUTION**
>
> The current version of JavaScript does not permit you to manipulate dates earlier than The Epoch. Attempting to do so gives unexpected and incorrect results.

The Date object has only one property (prototype, which allows you to add properties to the Date object), but many methods. To use the Date object, you must first understand how to construct instances of it. There are three basic methods of creating a Date instance, as follows:

- new Date()
- new Date( *datestring* )
- new Date( *yr*, *mon*, *day* )

The first form constructs a Date instance that represents the current date and time. This should be accurate to within a second and should also include information about your time zone and any corrections to it currently in effect (such as Daylight Savings Time). The second form takes a string of the form "Month Day, Year," such as "November 23, 1990," and converts it to a Date instance. This string may optionally have a time of the form HH:MM:SS at the end, which is used to set the time to hours, minutes, and seconds. Hours should be specified using a 24-hour clock, also known as military (or European) time, so that 10:15 P.M. is represented as 22:15:00. The third form takes three integers, representing the year, month, and day. Note that the month is always indexed from zero, so that November is month 10. The year can also be offset by 1900 so that you can use either of the following two forms:

```
var ndat = new Date(90, 10, 23);
```

```
var ndat = new Date(1990, 10, 23);
```

to create a Date instance named ndat for November 23, 1990. Note that for the year 2000 and beyond you must use the second form. This form may optionally take an additional three integer arguments for the time, so that 1:05 P.M. on November 23, 1990, is

```
var ndat2 = new Date(90, 10, 23, 13, 5, 0);
```

The Date object has a large set of methods for getting and setting the components of a date. These methods are as follows:

- getDate()
- getDay()
- getHours()
- getMinutes()
- getMonth()
- getSeconds()
- getTime()
- getTimeZoneOffset()
- getYear()
- setDate()
- setHours()
- setMinutes()
- setMonth()
- setSeconds()
- setTime()
- setYear()

Part

II

Ch

4

Most of these methods perform the obvious operation on their Date instance. nvar.getMonth() returns 10, representing November. It is 10, rather than 11, because months are zero-indexed so that the value of getMonth() is always between 0 and 11, inclusive. The confusingly named getDate, getDay, and getTime are worth a slightly closer look. The getDate method returns the day of the month (1–31), the getDay method returns the day of the week (0–6), and the getTime method returns JavaScript's internal representation of the date, namely, the number of milliseconds since The Epoch. This last method might seem to be of dubious utility, but it is useful for comparing two dates to see which is later. The set methods are, of course, used to set the various components of a Date instance. Listing 4.16 shows two simple date manipulation functions.

**Listing 4.16  Two Useful Functions Using the _Date_ Object**

```
/*
  Given a date as a string, return the day of the week
  as an integer between 1 and 7. Note Sunday = 1.
*/

function dayofweek( datestr ) {
    var dati;
    dati = new Date( datestr );          // make datestr into a Date instance
    return( 1 + dati.getDay() );         // get the day of the week and add 1
}
    // since getDay() returns a number between 0 and 6
```

*continues*

**Listing 4.16   Continued**

```
/*
   Compute the number of days to your birthday. Your birthday is specified
   as the day and month. Note that your birthday is assumed to occur at
   midnight, so that if today is your birthday it will be reported as a
   year away.*/

function tobday( dayi, moni ) {
    var today, todayy, todayms;
    var you, youms;
    var tdiff;
    today = new Date();                  // today's date
    todayy = today.getYear();            // current year
    you = new Date(todayy, moni-1, dayi);    // your birthday this year
// need to subtract 1 because months are zero-indexed
    todayms = today.getTime();                // convert today to ms since The Epoch
    youms = you.getTime();
  // convert your birthday to ms since The Epoch
    if ( youms < todayms ) {
    // if your birthday has already passed...
        you.setYear(1 + todayy);         // look forward to next year
        youms = you.getTime();           // recompute ms since The Epoch
        }
    tdiff = youms - todayms;
  // number of milliseconds until your next birthday
    tdiff /= 1000;                       // convert to seconds
    tdiff /= 60;                         // minutes
    tdiff /= 60;                         // hours
    tdiff /= 24;                         // convert to days
 return( Math.round( tdiff ) );       // round to nearest integer
 }
```

In addition to the get and set methods, the Date object also has methods for converting a Date instance to a string and two static methods for parsing dates. These methods are as follows:

- toGMTString()
- toLocaleString()
- toString()
- parse( *datestr* )
- UTC( *datestr* )

The first three of these methods convert a date instance into a string representing the date and time relative to Greenwich Mean Time (GMT, also called UTC for Universal Coordinated Time), relative to the current date-formatting conventions (which vary between Europe and the U.S., for example), and as just a plain, ordinary string, respectively. The last two methods are used for converting date strings in local time (parse method) or in UTC time (UTC method) into the number of milliseconds since The Epoch. These methods must be referenced as

`Date.parse()` and `Date.UTC()` because they are static; they may not be used with `Date` instances. Since they return the internal representation of dates, these values are often simply passed to `setTime`.

▶ **See** "Using the *Date* Methods," **p. 165,** where the methods of the `Date` object are explored more thoroughly.

### TROUBLESHOOTING

**I have modified your function `tobday` in Listing 4.16. My version accepts an arbitrary string as the input birthday. It works perfectly for my birthday, but it fails horribly for my father's birthday. What is wrong? The code looks like:**

```
function tobday2( bdaystr ) {
var bdayint = new Date( bdaystr );
... many lines of code not shown
```

Since your father was undoubtedly born before January 1, 1970, the very first line attempts to create a `Date` instance corresponding to a date before The Epoch. This is not currently permitted. Since it seems that you were born after The Epoch, the code works fine for your birthday. Until this restriction is lifted, you must convert the year to one after 1970 before you construct a `Date` instance, or simply omit the year entirely.

# The *Array* Object

The `Array` object is an extremely simple built-in object that is used to construct an array of empty slots. Any instance of the `Array` object always has a `length` property and also has as many elements as are specified in the constructor. For example, the statement

```
var myarr = new Array(10);
```

constructs an `Array` instance named `myarr`. The value of `myarr.length` is `10`, and the properties `myarr[0]` through `myarr[9]` are all NULL. The `Array` object can often be used as a simple object-creation function when the values in the array are going to be initialized later. One of the most convenient things about this built-in object is the fact that it always creates a `length` property.

Like all built-it objects, it also has the `prototype` property, which you may use to assign new properties to the `Array` object.

The `Array` object has been enhanced in Netscape Navigator 3.0 to include three new methods:

- ▪ `join`(*separator*)
- ▪ `reverse`()
- ▪ `sort`(*compareFunction*)

The join method is the complement to the String object's split method. You can convert an array of elements into a single string that contains all of the elements separated by the separator argument passed to join. If you omit the separator, a comma is used. For example,

```
roygbiv = new Array("Red","Orange","Yellow","Green","Blue","Indigo", "Violet");
colors = roygbiv.join(" : ");
return colors;
```

returns a string that looks like the following:

```
"Red : Orange : Yellow : Green : Blue : Indigo : Violet"
```

This method can be used to combine a series of elements into one string to display on the screen, or perhaps to be sent as an argument to another function.

The reverse method is useful when you have a sorted array that needs to have its order reversed. When you call the reverse method on an array, all of the elements in that array are reordered such that the first element is now the last, and the last element is the first. All of the elements between are also rearranged to the reverse order. For example, if an array contained the elements one, 2, three, green, and last, the array subsequently would be last, green, three, 2, and one. Note that this method does not return a new array with the order reversed; rather, it returns the same array with the new ordering.

The final method is sort. This one is highly useful because you can create your own sorting function to plug into this method and sort your array any way you would like. JavaScript defaults to a dictionary-style of sorting your array if you do not specify a sorting function. What this means is that each element is interpreted as a string and then sorted by the position it would take if you had sorted them as names. This method of sorting is akin to the way file names are displayed on both Macs and PCs. This means that if you had the elements 9, nine, 800, 09, and the Boolean TRUE, they are sorted in the array in the following order: 09, 800, 9, nine, TRUE.

If you want to construct your own sorting function, your function should take two arguments, for example, x and y.

- If your function is in the form of sortFunction(x,y) and returns a value less than zero, then y is sorted to a lower index (moved one step closer to the end of the array).
- If sortFunction(x,y) returns a zero, x and y are not changed in respect to each other but are still sorted with respect to the other elements.
- If the function returns a value greater than zero, then y is sorted to a higher index (moved one step toward the top of the array).

JavaScript uses a stable method of sorting. For example: if x and y are equal, and x has a lower index than y (meaning that it is closer to the bottom of the array), then no matter how x and y move about due to the sort, x will still have a lower index than y after the sort.

In general, your sorting function should look something like the following:

```
function sort(x,y) {
    if( x is less than y by some comparison)
        return -1
    if ( x is greater than y by some comparison)
        return 1
    //Otherwise, they are equal
    return 0
}
```

Another way of thinking about this is that the only time the order of x and y changes is if you return a positive value to the comparison. Here is a simple example that sorts numbers:

```
function compareNumbers(a, b) {
   return a - b
}
```

## The *Function* Object

The Function object is a very specialized object in JavaScript. Because functions are so basic to JavaScript, they behave similarly to objects and are, in fact, a kind of specialized object. Usually, you create functions in JavaScript with the function keyword. For example,

```
function rattle(sound, noise) {
    racket=sound+100/noise;
}
```

This declares a function for you that is compiled by JavaScript at the time it is declared, to be reused whenever you call it. There are occasions, though, when you want to explicitly describe some JavaScript code to be compiled as a Function object. To do this, use the following syntax:

```
functionLocation = new Function (arg1, arg2, ... argn, functionBody)
```

The functionLocation can be a variable, a property of an object, or it can be set to an event handler of an existing object. A Function object has the following properties:

- arguments[]  An array that contains the arguments passed to the function.
- arguments.length  The size of the arguments[] array.
- caller  A reference to the function that called this one.
- prototype  An object used to add properties and methods to all objects created with this function (if it is an object constructor function).

The Function object also has two methods: toString and valueOf. The toString method converts the function into a string, returning the JavaScript code that defines the function as a string. The valueOf method returns the primitive value of that object, if defined; otherwise, it returns the object itself.

## Built-In Functions

You have now had your first exposure to the built-in String, Math, and Date objects. Some of these objects are built in more than others. While Date acts like an actual object, with the exception of its two static methods, the String object is almost invisible. All normal JavaScript programs manipulate strings as if they are a separate data type. The essence of a string is part of the JavaScript language.

JavaScript has a small set of functions built into it. They are not methods and are never applied to an instance using the dot operator. However, they are on the same plane as functions that you create by using the `function` keyword. At present, the following are the five built-in functions:

- `escape( str )`
- `eval( str )`
- `parseFloat( str )`
- `parseInt( str, radix )`
- `unEscape( str )`

The `escape` and `unEscape` functions are used to convert to and from the escape code convention used by HTML. In HTML, a number of special characters, such as the HTML delimiters, < and >, must be represented in a special way to include them in ordinary text. For example, if you have written any HTML at all, you know that you sometimes need to use %20 to represent a space character. The `escape` built-in function takes a string representing one of these special characters and returns its escape code in the form %xx, where xx is a two-digit number. Thus, `escape(" ")` returns %20, the code for a space character. The `unEscape` function is the inverse of the `escape` function. It takes an escape code and returns the character which that code represents. Thus, `unEscape("%20")` returns the string " " (a single space character).

The `parseFloat` built-in function attempts to parse its string argument as a floating-point number. It continues parsing the *str* until it encounters a character that could not possibly be part of a valid floating-point number, such as "g." The `parseInt` built-in function performs a similar operation. It attempts to parse its *str* argument as an integer in base *radix*. Thus, we would obtain the following values:

```
parseFloat("+3.14williamtell5") = 3.14
```

```
parseInt(10111, 2) = 23
```

Note that everything after the first w is ignored because w cannot possibly be part of a floating-point number. The second value is obtained because 23 in binary (base 2) notation is 10111.

Finally, the `eval` function attempts to evaluate its string argument as a JavaScript expression and return its value. All the normal rules for evaluating expressions, including variable substitution, are performed by the `eval` function. This function is extremely powerful simply because it evaluates any JavaScript expression, no matter what that expression does. You will see a lot more of this function in several subsequent chapters. For the moment, we briefly look at a simple example in which we ask `eval` to do some arithmetic for us. If x is a var with the value of 10, then the following two expressions assign 146 to both y and z:

```
y = ( x * 14 ) - ( x / 2 ) + 11;
```

```
z = eval("( x * 14 ) - ( x / 2 ) + 11");
```

# Browser and HTML Objects

The JavaScript object model and its very interesting set of built-in objects, methods, and functions provide what we would expect from any modern programming language. They provide control structures, encapsulation, functions, mathematical operations, and so forth. Because JavaScript is designed to work with and on the World Wide Web, there must also be a linkage between it and the contents of HTML pages.

This linkage is provided by JavaScript's extremely rich set of browser and HTML objects. The browser objects are a reflection of the browser environment and include objects that can be used to reference the current page, the history list, and the current URL. There are also methods for opening new windows, displaying dialog boxes, and writing HTML directly. We have already been leaning heavily on one such method, the `write` method of the `document` object.

The browser (or navigator) objects are at the top of JavaScript's object hierarchy because they represent overall information and actions that are not necessarily associated with a particular Web page. Within a given Web page, however, each HTML element has a corresponding object, an HTML object, within the object hierarchy. In particular, every HTML form, and every HTML element within every form, has a corresponding object. Figure 4.5 gives an overview of the JavaScript object hierarchy.

**Part**

**II**

**Ch**

**4**

**FIG. 4.5**
JavaScript browser
and HTML objects refer
to all elements of
a Web page.

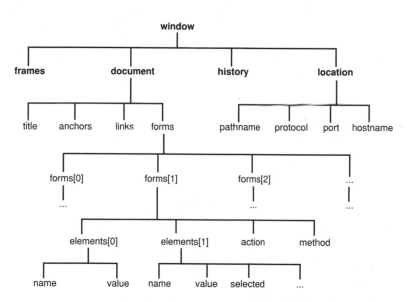

In this section, we briefly describe the key JavaScript browser and HTML objects and show how they relate to one another. Most of the subsequent chapters in this book are devoted to in-depth discussions of how you can make these objects work for you. Each chapter in Part II, "JavaScript In-Depth," in fact, is devoted to a particular category of JavaScript object (built-in, browser, or HTML). The purpose of this section, then, is to acquaint you with the structure of these objects without going into too much detail on how they are used.

# Browser Objects

The primary browser objects, in rough order of significance, are as follows:

- window
- document
- location
- history

**The *window* Object**    The window object, as Figure 4.5 shows, is the top object in the JavaScript object hierarchy. Every browser window that is currently open has a corresponding window object. All the other objects are children of one of the window objects. In particular, every window is associated with a particular Web page, and the HTML structure of this page is reflected in the window's document object. Every window corresponds to some URL; that URL is reflected in the location object. Every window has a history of the previous pages that have been displayed in that window, which are represented by the various properties of the history object.

There are several special window objects worth noting. The top window refers to the highest-level window on the current Web page. The self window refers to the current window, while parent refers to that window's parent, if any. JavaScript tries to keep track of the current window so that almost all references to subobjects of the current window do not need to refer to self explicitly. This is why all of our output has been done using document.write() rather than self.window.write() or window.document.write(). The window objects have the following interesting methods (among others):

- alert( *msgstr* )
- close()
- confirm( *msgstr* )
- open( *urlstr*, *wname* )
- prompt( *msgstr* )

All these methods are used to manipulate the window state of the browser itself. The alert and confirm methods are used to display their *msgstr* argument in a dialog box. The alert method is used to tell him or her something about which nothing can be done. An Alert dialog box contains a single OK button. The Confirm dialog box is more flexible and displays its message with both an OK and a Cancel button. If the user selects OK, the confirm method returns true; otherwise, it returns false. The prompt method is used to solicit user input in the form of a string. It displays a dialog box with the *msgstr* and an editable text field. This method also accepts a second optional argument that can be used to set a default value in the input field. This method returns whatever the user typed as a string.

You use the open method of the window object when you want to open a new browser window. The *urlstr* argument is a string representing the URL that will be loaded into that window. The *wname* argument is a string that gives the new window its name. This method returns an instance of the window object representing the new window created. This method also accepts a third argument that can be used to specify a wide variety of display options for the new window, such as whether or not it should display its toolbar. When the close method is invoked from a window instance, the underlying window is closed and the URL in it is unloaded.

▶ **See** "Dynamic Documents," **p. 264**, for several excellent examples of the open and close methods.

**The *document* Object**    Every window is associated with a document object. The document object contains properties for every anchor, link, and form on that page, as well as all of the subelements of those elements. It also contains properties for its title (the content of the <TITLE> field of the page), its foreground color (the fgColor property), its background color (the bgColor property), its various link colors, and other attributes of the page itself. The document object has the following methods:

- clear()
- close()
- open()
- write( *str* )
- writeln( *str* )

Part

II

Ch

4

The clear method is used to completely erase a document window. The entire contents are wiped out, regardless of how they got there. The clear method is particularly useful if you are constructing a Web page entirely within JavaScript and want to make sure it is empty before you start. The open and close methods are used to start and stop buffered output. If you call the open method, perform a series of writes or writelns, and then call the close method, the results of your write operations are laid out and appear on the page.

> **CAUTION**
>
> Do not confuse the open and close methods of the document object with the window methods of the same names. They perform very different functions and are not interchangeable. Use an explicit reference—document.open() or window.open()—to obtain the appropriate method.

Of course, we are intimately familiar with the write method by now. The write method is used to write any string expression, including one containing embedded HTML, to the current document. Note that the write method actually takes a variable number of arguments, rather than just one. If more than one argument is given, each of the arguments is interpreted as a string and written in turn. The writeln method is identical to the write method, except that it outputs a carriage return after it has completed writing its argument(s). Note that this carriage return is ignored by HTML, which really does not like embedded white space, unless the writeln is inside preformatted text (within <PRE>...</PRE> tags).

**N O T E**    Internet Explorer 3.0 has a bug in the implementation of document.write() and document.writeln(). The output of these functions is not appended at the end of the current document. A new document is always created, and the output written there. In addition, if no

*continues*

*continued*

document.close() is used after a write operation, it may be necessary to click the Stop button on the IE toolbar to close the document. This bug does seems to be fixed in 3.01. ■

**The *history* and *location* Objects**   The history object is used to refer to the history list of previously visited URLs. The history object has a length property, which indicates how many URLs are presently stored on the history list. It also has the following three methods:

- ■ back()
- ■ forward()
- ■ go( *where* )

The go method is used to navigate the history list. The where argument is a number that indicates how far we want to move in the history list. A positive number means that we want to move that many documents forward in this history list, while a negative number is used to move backward. Thus, go(5) has the same effect as using the Forward button five times, while go(-1) is the same as clicking the Back button once.

The location object describes the URL of a document. It has properties representing the various components of the URL, including its protocol part, its host name part, its path name part, and its port number part, among other properties. It also has a toString method that can be used to convert it to a string. We can use the following code to display a formatted message giving the current URL:

```
var loc = document.location;
document.write("<BR>URL is " + loc.toString());
document.write("<BR>");
```

# HTML Objects

To understand how HTML objects work in JavaScript, consider a simple piece of HTML that creates an anchor, a small form, and a link to that anchor. This is not intended to be HTML for a meaningful Web page, but it nevertheless illustrates the correspondence between HTML elements and JavaScript HTML objects. Our elementary HTML code is given in Listing 4.17.

### Listing 4.17   HTML Code for a Page with a Form, Anchor, and Link

```
<HTML>
<HEAD>
<TITLE>A very simple HTML page</TITLE>
</HEAD>
<BODY>
<IMG SRC=head.gif height=100 width=500><BR>
<A NAME="top">This is the top of the page</A>
<HR>
<FORM METHOD="post" ACTION="mailto:nobody@dev.null">
```

```
<P>Enter your name: <INPUT TYPE="text" NAME="me" SIZE="70">
</P>
<INPUT TYPE="reset" VALUE="Oops">
<INPUT TYPE="submit" VALUE="OK">
</FORM>
<HR>
Click here to go to the <A HREF="#top">top</A> of the page
</BODY>
</HTML>
```

This code creates an HTML page with an anchor at the top of the page and a link to that anchor at the bottom. In between is a simple form that allows users to enter their name. There is a Submit button for correct entries, and a Reset button for incorrect entries. If the user is successful, the form's contents are submitted via a post action to the fictitious e-mail address nobody@dev.null.

The important aspect of this example is not its primitive HTML, but the fact that the HTML elements in it are reflected in the JavaScript object hierarchy. We have already seen that we can access the title of this document through the `title` property of the `document` object. We can also access the other HTML elements of this document by using the following properties:

- anchors
- forms
- images
- links

Part

II

Ch

4

These properties of the `document` object are arrays representing every HTML element that is an anchor, form, image, or link on the page. In our particular example, there is only one of each, so we refer to the anchor at the top of the page as `document.anchors[0]`, the link at the bottom of the page as `document.links[0]`, the image at the top of the page as `document.images[0]`, and the form in the middle of the page as `document.forms[0]`. These are the top-level HTML objects represented by this document. Each of these elements, in turn, has properties and methods that can be used to describe and manipulate it.

In particular, the `form` object corresponding to `forms[0]` has subobjects for each of the three form elements (the Reset button, the Submit button, and the text-input field), as well as properties for the `submit` method and the submit target. `forms[0].elements[0]` corresponds to the text input field. `forms[0].elements[0].name` is the name of that field, as specified by the NAME field, which is "me" in this case. Figure 4.6 recapitulates this HTML code and shows how each element in the page is associated with an HTML object. We will have many more examples of this in subsequent chapters.

**FIG. 4.6**

Anchors, links, images, forms, and form elements are represented as objects in JavaScript.

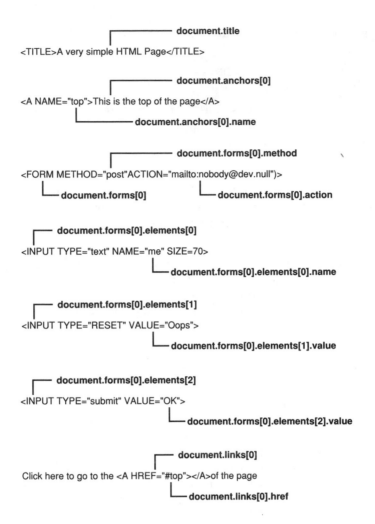

# CHAPTER 5

# JavaScript Strings

JavaScript is designed to be easy to learn and convenient to use by almost anyone who seeks to build dynamic Web pages and client-side checking of input forms (as well as many other uses discussed in this book). Because the authors of JavaScript have had this goal in mind, they have provided you, the programmer, with built-in objects that you will probably use often. These built-in objects are available through both the client-side JavaScript in the browser and on the server. In addition, JavaScript has four objects that you can use throughout your scripts without having to declare them.

The four built-in objects are the String, Math, Date, and Array objects. Each of these objects provides great functionality, and together, they give JavaScript its power as a scripting language. These built-in objects are discussed in-depth in this chapter and the two that follow. You will find many examples for use in your own projects. This chapter will discuss the first built-in object—the String—in detail.

Be sure to review Chapter 4, "JavaScript Objects," which introduced you to JavaScript's built-in objects. ■

**How to manipulate text with the *String* object**

Find out how to change the HTML formatting of strings, concatenate them with other strings, and find sub-elements inside strings.

**Learn the built-in methods of the *String* object**

This chapter shows you the capabilities already available to you by Netscape, Microsoft, and others who support JavaScript and its variants.

**Find out how to parse strings in JavaScript**

You can use JavaScript to take apart a String object and "decode" it according to a set of syntax rules.

**Learn JavaScript's new "tainting" capability**

You can ensure that strings entered by an end-user do not become a security hole in your scripts.

# HTML String Methods

As you saw in Chapter 4, you can make a new `String` object by assigning a string literal to a variable.

You call a string's methods by the same dot notation you would in other objects. For example, if `demostring` is `"Some text here!"` then `demostring.bold()` returns `"<B>Some text here!</B>"`. This string is rendered as bold text in most graphically oriented Web browsers.

You can also use string methods on literals, as follows:

```
"This is some text."italics()
```

This line of code returns "`<I>This is some text.</I>`", which is displayed as italicized text by your Web browser.

Table 5.1 shows the various methods that you can call with the `String` object to alter its HTML formatting.

**Table 5.1** *String* **Object Methods for HTML Formatting**

| Method Name | Example | Returned Value |
|---|---|---|
| anchor | `"quux".anchor("anchortext")` | `<A NAME="anchortext">quux</A>` |
| big | `"quux".big()` | `<BIG>quux</BIG>` |
| blink | `"quux".blink()` | `<BLINK>quux</BLINK>` |
| bold | `"quux".bold()` | `<B>quux</B>` |
| charAt | `"quux".charAt(3)` | x |
| fixed | `"quux".fixed()` | `<TT>quux</TT>` |
| fontcolor | `"quux".fontcolor("green")` | `<FONT COLOR="green">quux</FONT>` |
| fontsize | `"quux".fontsize(-1)` | `<FONT SIZE="-1">quux</FONT>` |
| indexOf | `"quux".indexOf("u")` | 1 |
| italics | `"quux".italics()` | `<I>quux</I>` |
| lastIndexOf | `"quux".lastIndexOf("u")` | 2 |
| link | `"quux".link("linktext")` | `<A HREF="linktext">quux</A>` |
| small | `"quux".small()` | `<SMALL>quux</SMALL>` |
| strike | `"quux".strike()` | `<STRIKE>quux</STRIKE>` |
| sub | `"quux".sub()` | `<SUB>quux</SUB>` |
| substring | `"quux".substring(1,3)` | uu |
| sup | `"quux".sup()` | `<SUP>quux</SUP>` |

| Method Name | Example | Returned Value |
|---|---|---|
| toLowerCase | "UPPERcase".toLowerCase() | uppercase |
| toUpperCase | "UPPERcase".toUpperCase() | UPPERCASE |

**CAUTION**

While JavaScript supports a string `blink()` method, many Webmasters believe that the `<BLINK>` tag is distracting and does not add to the quality of a Web page. Unless you have a specific reason (such as a safety warning), you should avoid using `blink()` and `<BLINK>`.

Listing 5.1 contains the code for this page and Figure 5.1 shows the effect of each of these `String` methods. Horizontal rules (`<HR>`) are placed between JavaScript lines to help you see how each method changes the appearance of the text. Note that all of the strings were called as literals—that is, not as variables as you might normally see them.

**Listing 5.1  This Page Demonstrates a Variety of String Styles**

```
<HTML>
<HEAD>
<TITLE></TITLE>
</HEAD>
<BODY>
<A NAME="anchortext">Anchor quux</A>
<HR>
<BIG>Big quux</BIG>
<HR>
<BLINK>Blink quux</BLINK>
<HR>
<B>Bold quux</B>
<HR>
charAt quux
<HR>
<TT>Fixed quux</TT>
<HR>
<FONT COLOR="green">Font color quux</FONT>
<HR>
<FONT SIZE="-1">Font size quux</FONT>
<HR>
<INDEX>indexOf quux</INDEX>
<HR>
<I>Italics quux</I>
<HR>
<INDEX>lastIndexOf quux</INDEX>
<HR>
<A HREF="linktext">Link quux</A>
<HR>
<SMALL>Small quux</SMALL>
<HR>
```

Part
II

Ch
5

*continues*

**Listing 5.1  Continued**

```
<STRIKE>Strike quux</STRIKE>
<HR>
<SUB>Sub quux</SUB>
<HR>
<SUB>substring quux</SUB>
<HR>
<SUP>Sup quux</SUP>
</BODY>
</HTML>
```

**FIG. 5.1**

String methods as rendered by Netscape Navigator.

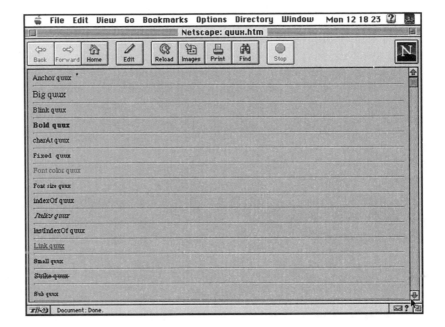

## Chaining Methods

Not only can you change the formatting of the text in one way at a time, you can "chain" the various methods together to mimic the behavior of nesting HTML tags around a piece of text. This technique can be particularly useful if you generate HTML automatically via a script. For example, the following displays a bold "**QUUX**" in fixed-point font:

```
document.write("quux".toUpperCase().fixed().bold())
```

Remember to include the parentheses after each of the methods even though they do not take any arguments. The preceding code appears to the browser as the following:

```
<B><TT>QUUX</TT></B>
```

You can see that the `<TT>` tag is nested inside the `<B>` tag, since the `fixed` method was called first. (JavaScript reads code from left to right and from top to bottom.) If you want to have a desired effect with nesting tags, remember that the order of nesting is the leftmost `string` method nested inside the next method called to the right. The reason you can nest these methods is that they all accept and return a `string` object, so it appears to the next method as a simple string—as if you had typed it in.

---

### Nesting Methods versus Chaining Methods

There are usually two ways you will see methods called in scripts you encounter. You might see something like this:

```
quux().bar().baz()  "Chaining"
```

or you might see:

```
quux(bar(baz()))  "Nesting"
```

The difference here can be subtle. With `quux().bar().baz()`, JavaScript will determine the result value of `quux()`, then treat that value as if it were the object called with `.bar()`. You must make sure that the value returned by the leftmost method is valid in order to have the second method "appended" to it to continue calculations. It is valid here if `quux()` and `bar()` return strings, because string literals (what each of these methods returns) can subsequently have other string methods. `quux(bar(baz()))` is different in that evaluation is conducted in right-to-left order. `baz()` is evaluated first and then is passed as a parameter to `bar()`, which must be able to accept a parameter of this type in order for this to work. For some methods, this difference in evaluation has no effect, but for others, you might get incorrect values.

---

## Anchors and Links

Anchors and links are often confused because they appear to have similar HTML representations. An anchor in HTML is a location for a link to point to, and is given a name so that subsequent links can identify that anchor. See Chapter 4, "JavaScript Objects," for more discussion of this difference.

If you want to make an anchor such as the following:

```
<A NAME="section2">Starting Up</A>
```

you can use the following JavaScript:

```
aVariable = "Starting Up"
```

```
aVariable.anchor("section2")
```

Or you can just use the following:

```
"Starting Up".anchor("section2")
```

It helps to read the string like this:

"Starting Up using an anchor of name 'section2.'"

Links are used in a similar fashion but, in this case, instead of giving an anchor a name, you are giving a link a Uniform Resource Locator, or URL. For example, to display a link to Yahoo!, you would write the code shown in Listing 5.2.

**Listing 5.2    A Link Displayed with the *link* Method**

```
var  linktext = "Yahoo!"
var URL = "http://www.yahoo.com"

document.open()
document.write("This is a link to" + linktext.link(URL))
document.close()
```

This is equivalent to writing the following:

```
This is a link to <A HREF="http://www.yahoo.com">Yahoo!</A>
```

In this case, you can read the string as:

"Yahoo's link is http://www.yahoo.com"

 **TIP**   You can quickly generate long strings from short ones by using the concatenation operator (+).

The expression `"Cat Fish "` + `"Sandwich"` yields `"Cat Fish Sandwich."` Also, you can use the += operator (called the `"plus-equal"` concatenator) to tack a string onto the end of another. If `string1 = "hello"`, then `string1+=" there"` would become `"hello there."`

---

**CAUTION**

A common mistake among beginning JavaScript programmers is to omit the space between concatenated strings. For example, a programmer might write `"Hello"` + `"World!"` expecting to get `"Hello World!"`, but will get `"HelloWorld!"` instead.

When you first start writing JavaScript, most of your strings will be written back to the browser, so you'll see errors immediately. As your JavaScript applications become more complex, many of your strings will be written to a CGI script, a LiveWire application, or a database. You may not see the incorrect string, but the program that reads the string won't work correctly.

---

# Substring Operations

In addition to changing the formatting of a `string` object in HTML, you can also return parts of the string without having to know the actual contents of that string. This technique is useful for parsing out different keywords or commands within some given input string.

This section introduces various methods for getting at the substrings of a string—the next section shows how to use these methods to parse a string into a series of symbols.

Table 5.2 lists the methods of the string object that pertain to displaying subsets of the string's contents.

**Table 5.2** *String* **Object Methods for Displaying Subsets of Strings**

| Method Name | Example(s) | Returned Value |
|---|---|---|
| charAt | `"Netscape Navigator"`<br>`.charAt(0)` | n |
|  | `"Netscape Navigator"`<br>`.charAt(10)` | a |
| indexOf | `"Internet Explorer"`<br>`.indexOf("net")` | 5 |
|  | `"Internet Explorer"`<br>`.indexOf("e",2)` | 3 |
| lastIndexOf | `"Netscape Navigator"`<br>`.lastIndexOf("a")` | 10 |
|  | `"Netscape Navigator"`<br>`.lastIndexOf("a", 9)` | 5 |
| substring | `"Internet Explorer"`<br>`.substring(0,8)` | Internet |
|  | `"Internet Explorer"`<br>`.substring(8,0)` | Internet |
|  | `"Internet Explorer"`<br>`.substring(0,50)` | Internet<br>Explorer |
| length | `"Netscape Navigator"`<br>`.length` | 18 |
|  | `"Netscape Navigator"`<br>`.substring(0,8).length` | b |

Note that `length` is a property of a string and receives its value indirectly based on the number of characters in a string. You cannot directly assign a value to the `length` property.

## charAt

The method `charAt` returns the character at the index specified. Characters are numbered from 0 to the length of the string minus 1.

Its syntax is:

```
stringName.charAt(index)
```

For example, the following code returns the character n:

```
thisstring = "Internet World"
```

```
thisstring.charAt(5)
```

## indexOf

This method can be used to search down a string (from left to right) until it finds a string fragment matching the specified value. It returns the index of the first character of the matching

Part

II

Ch

5

string. You can use this information with the method `substring` (described later in this section) to find keywords in a given string. This technique is useful when you allow the user to input some information and you want to place parts of that information into different variables. For example, the following code returns 9:

```
thisstring = "Internet World"

thisstring.indexOf("World")
```

If the keyword is not in the string, then `indexOf` returns a -1.

## lastIndexOf

This method is identical to `indexOf` except that the method searches from right to left down the string to find the given keyword. It also returns the index value of the first character of the keyword. For example, the following code returns 5:

```
"Internet World".lastIndexOf("n")
```

## substring

`substring` completes the suite of subset text methods. This method returns a substring when given beginning and ending index values. Note that the values do not have to be in numerical order. The string returned from `substring(1,9)` is identical to the one returned from `substring(9,1)`. Also, if you leave off the second index argument, `substring` assumes you want it to return everything from the first index to the end of the string. Leaving off both indices returns the entire string. For example, the code in Listing 5.3 returns `"World."`

---

**Listing 5.3    A String Dissected by Using *substring()***

```
thisstring = "Internet World"

thewordnum = thisstring.indexOf("World")

theword = thisstring.substring(thewordnum)

document.open()
document.write(theword)
document.close()
```

---

## Length

The `length` property appears in many types of objects across JavaScript and means different things depending upon the context in which it is used. In strings, this value is an integer that reflects the total number of characters in a string (counting white space). For a `null` string, this value is `zero`. You cannot directly alter this value except by adding or removing characters from a string. Because the value returned by `"quux".length()` is a number, you can perform mathematical operations on it, like any other number.

For instance:

```
"Hi There".length - 1
```

would return the following:

```
7
```

 **T I P** You may find yourself using many of the same functions over and over in many different scripts. It's good practice to keep a personal library of useful functions so you can find them (and use them!) again.

# String Parsing in JavaScript

When you read user input from a form with JavaScript, you often can ask the user to pigeon-hole information, using text fields and other input elements. But humans often prefer to enter strings of text, either in a natural language like English, or in a special-purpose language like those used in some adventure games (e.g., "Go North," "Pick up the keys").

▶ **See** "Global and Local Variables," **p. 276**, for a discussion of how you can use a function like `word()` to pull apart a delimited string.

Most serious work with strings and languages is done with a software component called a *parser*. A parser is the portion of a program responsible for taking the input apart (to its basic symbols). Along the way, it verifies that the input satisfies the rules of the grammar. Once the input is parsed and appears to be valid, the parser will pass the parsed input to other parts of the program, where the input is used. For example, the parser in a Java compiler reads the input and verifies that it is valid according to the rules of the Java language. The parser identifies which parts of the input are name variables, which are operators, and which are function calls. Then it passes the parsed input to a code generator, which writes the bytecodes that correspond to the Java input.

## Formal Languages and Parsers

In formal language theory, languages are defined by an alphabet and a grammar. For example, if the alphabet contains the symbols 0 and 1, the language might have strings like 101, 1111111, and 011101011011110111. *Terminal symbols* in the language consist of words in the language's alphabet. *Non-terminal symbols* do not appear in the actual sentences of the language, but are used as placeholders for concepts. For example, a language for simple arithmetic might include a rule that defines a term as

```
Number + Number
```

where `Number` is a non-terminal symbol. An actual term in the language might be

```
42 + 12
```

**A Sample Grammar** A key component of the grammar is a series of productions (sometimes called production rules), which describe how one string (of terminal or non-terminal symbols)

may be transformed into another. For example, a simple arithmetic language might have productions such as

```
Rule 1: S → E
Rule 2: E → T =
Rule 3: T → N + N
Rule 4: T → T + N
Rule 5: T → N - N
Rule 6: T → T - N
Rule 7: N → d
Rule 8: N → Nd
```

where S denotes the starting (non-terminal) symbol, E denotes an equation, T denotes a term, and N denotes a positive integer. The symbol $d$ denotes a member of the set of digits (0…9).

Suppose a parser with this grammar were given the following input:

```
42 + 12 - 21 =
```

Rule 7 allows the parser to replace the initial 4 with an N. Rule 8 allows the parser to replace N2 with N. By running the same pair of rules on 12, the parser now has N + N, which satisfies Rule 3, and allows the parser to write

```
T - 21 =
```

Again, Rule 7 and Rule 8 allow the parser to replace the number with N, giving the parser

```
T - N =
```

Rule 6 allows the parser to rewrite this string as

```
T =
```

By Rule 2, the parser replaces this string with E and, finally, by Rule 1, with the starting symbol S.

Since the parser can transform the original input into the starting symbol, the original input is valid according to the rules of this grammar. Along the way, the parser has built a representation of the input string. This representation, illustrated in Figure 5.2, can be passed to a simple calculator program, which generates the input.

**Language Classifications**   Computer scientists and other scholars of formal language theory classify grammars into four categories:

- **Type-3 languages (also called "regular languages")**

  In a type-3 language, each production has only a single, non-terminal symbol on its left side. Its right side has either a single terminal symbol or a terminal symbol followed by a non-terminal symbol.

- **Type-2 languages (also called "context-free languages")**

  The left side of each production has exactly one non-terminal symbol. (The calculator grammar described in the last section is a context-free grammar, and generates a context-free language.)

- **Type-1 languages (also called "context-sensitive languages")**

  The left side of each production cannot be longer than the right side.

- **Type-0 languages (also called "recursively enumerable languages")**

  There are no restrictions on the productions.

**FIG. 5.2**

As the parser reads the input string, it puts the components of the input into a data structure that represents the sentence.

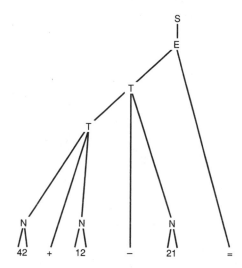

Natural languages and other complex problem domains are generally type-1 or type-0 languages. These languages are notoriously difficult to parse. Type-3 languages are much simpler—indeed, they are often too simple to be useful in real-world problems. Like the story of Goldilocks, one category of languages—the type-2 language—is "just right" for many practical needs.

**Designing a Parser for a Context-Free Grammar**    A *top-down* parser begins with the non-terminal starting symbol S and attempts to apply the production rules until it has generated the input string. A *bottom-up* parser starts with the input string and drives the production rules backwards, working toward the starting symbol. The parsing example given with the calculator language was bottom-up.

The following code contains a top-down parser for the calculator language used in the parsing example. The parser works in three steps. The basic document follows the template shown in Listing 5.4.

**Listing 5.4    Parser Template**

```
<HTML>
<HEAD>
...parsing functions...
// These functions are described later in this chapter.
</HEAD>
<BODY onLoad="init()">
```

*continues*

Part

II

Ch

5

**Listing 5.4    Continued**

```
<H1>Parser Demonstration</H1>
<FORM NAME="theForm">
Enter string to parse:
<INPUT TYPE="Text" NAME="stringToParse" SIZE=20>
<INPUT TYPE="Button" VALUE="Parse"
 onClick="parse(theForm.stringToParse.value)">
</FORM>
</BODY>
</HTML>
```

When the page is loaded, an onLoad event occurs, and the init() function runs. The init() function loads a multidimensional associative array that contains the production rules. Figure 5.3 illustrates the structure of the gProductions array.

▶ **See** "JavaScript's Associative Arrays," **p. 289**, for a discussion of the advanced topic of multi-dimensional associative arrays.

**FIG. 5.3**

The gProductions array is an associative array with the left side of the production rule on the left side of the array, and a list of the right sides of the rules on the right side of the array.

| S | E | | | |
|---|---|---|---|---|
| E | T= | | | |
| T | T+N | T–N | N+N | N–N |
| N | d | dN | | |

Once the page is loaded, the user enters a string in the text field and presses the Parse button.

▶ **See** "The *Button* Object," **p. 190**, and "Text Fields," **p. 191**, which discuss one of the major uses of JavaScript: to read and process the input a user places on a form (the connection between forms and JavaScript).

The Parse button is connected to the parse() function, shown in Listing 5.5.

**Listing 5.5    Top-Level Function to Actually Parse String**

```
function parse(aString)
{
  var inputString = stripBlanks(aString);
  var currentParse = "";
  treeWindow = self.open('', "ParseTree");
  treeWindow.document.write("<HTML><HEAD><TITLE>Parse Tree</TITLE>
  ➥</HEAD><BODY BGCOLOR=white><H1>Parse Tree</H1><TABLE BORDER=1>
  ➥<CAPTION>Read from bottom up</CAPTION><TR><TH>Rule</TH>
  ➥<TH>Left</TH><TH>Right</TH><TH>Matches</TH></TR>");
  var theResult = parse2("S", "", inputString);
  if (!theResult)
```

```
      treeWindow.document.write("</TABLE><P>" +
                            "Sorry, input string " +
       document.forms[0].elements[0].value.bold() +
                            " is not valid.</P>");
  else
    treeWindow.document.write("</TABLE>");
  treeWindow.document.write("<FORM NAME=aForm><INPUT TYPE=Hidden
NAME=dummy></FORM></BODY></HTML>");
  treeWindow.document.close();
  if (theResult)
    treeWindow.document.aForm.dummy.focus();
  else
    alert("Input string " +
            document.forms[0].elements[0].value +
          " is not valid.");

}
```

The parse function starts by calling stripBlanks(), described later in this section. Then the parse() function opens a second window (called treeWindow) where a representation of the parse tree will be written if the input string can be parsed.

The parser itself is in the function parse2(). That function takes a starting symbol, (S), a "right side" of symbols that are not yet matched (initially empty), and an input string. The parse2 function writes <TABLE> rows as it matches portions of the input string to symbols of the grammar.

Finally, the parse() function finishes off the table and writes a hidden field to the new window. By setting the focus to the hidden field, parse() brings the new window to the front.

Listing 5.6 is the source of parse2().

## Listing 5.6   Lower-Level Parsing Function

```
function parse2(x, right, unmatched)
{
  // x is leftmost nonterminal of the current sentential form.
  // right is the portion of the sentential form to the right of x
  // unmatched is the ummatched portion of the input

  var xProductions = "";
  var p = "";
  var beta = "";
  var currentParse = "";
  var theResult = false;

  xProductions = gProductions[x];
  for (var i=1; i<=xProductions.length; i++)
  {
    p = xProductions[i];
    currentParse = x + "->" + p;[']
    beta = p + right;
```

*continues*

Part
II

Ch
5

**Listing 5.6 Continued**

```
    if (compare (beta, unmatched))
      theResult = true;
    else
      theResult = false;
    if (theResult)
    {
      treeWindow.document.write("<TR><TD>" + x + "->" +
                                p + "</TD><TD>" +
                                p + "</TD><TD>" +
                                right + "</TD><TD>" +
                                unmatched +
                                "</TD></TR>");
      break;
    }
  }
  return theResult;
}
```

This function looks up the current non-terminal symbol (x) in the gProductions array. Then it attempts to match the right side of each production rule for that symbol with the current string by calling compare(). If compare() succeeds, the current production rule is added to the growing <TABLE>.

Compare(), in turn, is a two-step function. If the production rule and the unmatched string run out at the same time, the production rule is a match. If the unmatched string begins to grow in length while the unmatched string is being consumed, then the production cannot match, so compare() returns false. If the production rule starts with a terminal symbol, compare() attempts to match the terminal symbol against the first character of the unmatched string. If the terminal symbol matches the first character of the unmatched string, compare() calls itself recursively to attempt to match the rest of the rule with the rest of the string.

If the production rule begins with a non-terminal symbol, compare() calls parse2() to expand the non-terminal symbol and to attempt to match it with the remaining unmatched string.

Listing 5.7 shows the JavaScript for compare().

**Listing 5.7 Compare a String with Part of the Pattern**

```
function compare(beta, unmatched)
{
  // this function matches terminal symbols in the sentential
  // form with the input and continues the parsing if both
  // sides continue to match
  var theResult = false;
  if (beta == "")
    if (unmatched == "")
      theResult = true;
    else
      theResult = false;
```

```
    else if (beta.length > unmatched.length)
      theResult = false;
    else if (isTerminal(beta.charAt(0)))
      if (unmatched == "")
        theResult = false;
      else if (matchTerminals (beta.charAt(0),
                                unmatched.charAt(0)))
        // OK so far
        theResult =
          compare(beta.substring(1),
                  unmatched.substring(1));
      else
        theResult = false;
    else
      theResult = parse2(beta.charAt(0),
                         beta.substring(1),
                         unmatched)
    return theResult;
  }
```

The last function we'll examine in the parser is stripBlanks(). Here's the JavaScript for that function, in Listing 5.8.

**Listing 5.8   Use *stripBlanks* to Remove All Blanks from the String**

```
function stripBlanks(theString)
{
  var aString = theString;
  var newString = "";
  var kBlank = " ";
  if (aString.indexOf(kBlank) >= 0)
  {
    for (var i=0; i<aString.length; i++)
      if (aString.charAt(i) != kBlank)
        break;
    for (var j=aString.length-1; j>=0; j--)
      if (aString.charAt(j) != kBlank)
        break;
    if (i == aString.length && j == -1)
      // there are no non-blank characters
      newString = "";
    else
    if (i != 0 || j != aString.length - 1)
      newString = stripBlanks(aString.substring(i, j+1));
    else
      newString = aString.charAt(i) +
                  stripBlanks(aString.substring(i+1, j+1)) +
                  aString.charAt(j+1);
  }
  else
    newString = aString;
  return newString;
}
```

Part
II

Ch
5

This function makes heavy use of the `indexOf()` string method. If the input string has no blanks in it, `stripBlanks()` returns the input string (which has been copied into the variable `newString`). If the string has blanks, `stripBlanks()` searches from both ends of the string toward the middle in order to strip leading and trailing blanks.

Once `stripBlanks()` has a string with no leading and trailing blanks, it extracts and remembers the leading and trailing characters (which are guaranteed to be non-blank) and recursively calls `stripBlanks()` on the remaining characters. Figure 5.4 shows the data entry form and resulting parse tree for the complete parse example.

Figure 5.5 illustrates the parse tree generated by parse.htm, which appears on this book's companion Web site.

**FIG. 5.4**

When you enter a string in the text field and click Parse, the JavaScript writes out a representation of the parse tree in a new window.

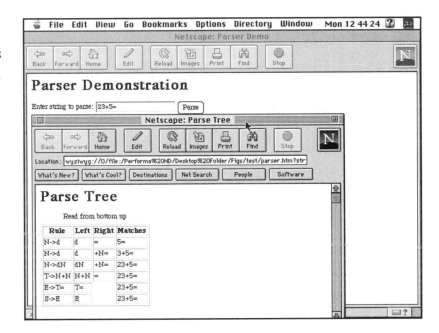

> **N O T E**  parse.htm contains several `alert()` statements that have been commented out.
>
> If you'd like to understand more about how the parser works, uncomment some of these `alert()` statements and reload the page. Be sure to start with short, simple input strings. The parser explores many paths while trying to match the production rules with the input string—you may have to click through many false paths before the parser finds the correct match. ■

**FIG. 5.5**
The parse.htm-
generated parse tree
can be expressed
graphically.

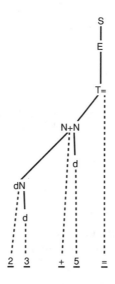

# Tainting and Security

The designers of JavaScript have been careful to restrict the amount of access a JavaScript programmer has to the client's machine. For example, you cannot read or write data files on the user's machine, and you cannot call non-JavaScript functions.

Some of these rules are bent in server-side JavaScript, since you, as the programmer, are (presumably) in control of your own server. You can read input from an HTML form and write it to a server disk file or pass it to the server's command interpreter.

One of the risks of giving end users access to input text fields and other strings in an HTML form is that you may want to pass the data from those fields directly to a different server. A malicious user could place a script on one machine that ran on the client and pass machine A's data on to machine B.

For years, Perl programmers have had a feature that enables them to keep track of which strings came from the outside world. Using this mechanism, Perl programmers can isolate strings that are suspect and cannot safely be passed to the command interpreter. The Perl mechanism is called *tainting*. A tainted variable is one which has been read from outside the program (for example, from an HTML form). Now Netscape has added tainting to JavaScript.

By default, without data tainting, a script residing on one server cannot access the properties of a script residing on another server. This protection acts as a global rule that not only obstructs hostile scripts from accessing information, but also blocks potentially helpful scripts. For example, a user might post a JavaScript syntax checker on the Web that you wish to use on a page existing on your own site. By default, you will not be able to use such a checker unless you copy it yourself and load it onto your own site.

Part
II

Ch
5

Tainting allows scripts from different servers to access properties and other information from one another. If some property is "tainted," however, the script from the other server will not be allowed to automatically send out the information it acquires from the first server. Instead, a dialog box appears to warn the user that this action is about to take place, which can effectively block that action.

Tainting is not yet widely used and presents a mystery to many script writers. You need to take special steps to enable tainting. In a UNIX environment, you have to use the setenv command. On Windows, you use set. On the Macintosh, use ResEdit, Apple's resource editor. By default, tainting in the browser is off—unlike other options, Netscape has not elected to allow the user to control tainting through the menu interface.

## Enabling Tainting

If you decide to use tainting, you first need to enable it. If you're on a UNIX or Windows machine, set the environment variable NS_ENABLE_TAINT. For example, a UNIX user who is using csh might add the line

```
setenv NS_ENABLE_TAINT 1
```

while one using ksh might say

```
NS_ENABLE_TAINT=1
export NS_ENABLE_TAINT
```

A Windows user would write

```
set NS_ENABLE_TAINT=1
```

in the autoexec.bat file. If you're a Mac user, use ResEdit to open Envi, resource number 128. Remove the two slashes in front of the string NS_ENABLE_TAINT. (It's at the bottom of the resource.)

## taint() and untaint()

Once tainting is enabled, it's easy to either add or remove taint from some property or variable. Suppose you wanted to allow any script to access the values of a form on your page. You would write:

```
newForm = untaint(document.forms[0])
```

This line does not modify the existing form, nor does it create a new untainted form. Rather, a new reference to that form has been created that does not contain the "identity" of that object.

Conversely, you can taint objects or properties with your own "taint-code." This code uniquely identifies objects as belonging to your domain. Such a code is useful if another script has marked some of its own information as "untainted" but your script wants to keep that data private. (Untainted data has a taint-code of NULL.)

# Taint-Codes

Objects, properties, whole scripts, and domains all can contain a "taint-code." Only when all of these codes are compatible (meaning there are either identical taint-codes or one is untainted) will a potentially unsecured operation take place.

Tainting can be inherited, as well. If some piece of data is untainted, and is added to some tainted data, the result will be tainted.

The tainting mechanism also prevents a programmer from using conditionals to bypass the taint. If you write an `if` statement, for example, that depends upon tainted data, then any data sent from the conditional has the same taint-code as the conditional data. This process works by keeping the taint-codes in "taint accumulators" associated with each script.

If you place `taint()` alone in a script, it will set the taint accumulator for that script, tainting the entire script with its own taint-code. Using `untaint()` alone will place a NULL in the taint accumulator, untainting the entire script—unless specifically tainted in another location in the script.

If you attempt to untaint data that does not contain your taint-code, the taint will remain unchanged and the new pointer to the data will contain the original taint-code.

# A *taint* Example

Suppose you have a form that downloads from your server, `www.xyz1.net`, and sends its data back to that same server. Listing 5.9 shows such a script:

### Listing 5.9   An Example of Data Tainting

Part
II

Ch
5

```
<HTML>
<HEAD><TITLE>Example</TITLE></HEAD>
<BODY>
<SCRIPT LANGUAGE=JavaScript>
<!--
if (navigator.tainted())
  alert("Taint is enabled.");
else
  alert("Taint is NOT enabled.");
// -->
</SCRIPT>
<FORM NAME=myForm METHOD=GET ACTION="http://www.xyz1.net/cgi-bin/test.cgi">
<INPUT TYPE=Text NAME=username VALUE=default>
<INPUT TYPE=Submit VALUE=Send>
</FORM>
<SCRIPT LANGUAGE=JavaScript>
document.write("<A HREF='http://www.xyz1.net/cgi-bin.test.cgi?username=" +
  document.myForm.username.value + "'>Send data</A>");
</SCRIPT>
</BODY>
</HTML>
```

When the page opens, you'll get a confirming alert telling you whether you successfully enabled tainting. This example assumes that you have enabled tainting.

> **CAUTION**
>
> Netscape's documentation says that if tainting is not enabled, no data may be passed from one server to another. At least one version (AIX) of Netscape Navigator Gold 3.01 does not observe this restriction. Do not assume that tainting will always be available to protect your sensitive data.

Since the data from the form is going back to the same server from which the form was downloaded, JavaScript has no problem allowing the form's `ACTION` to execute. You can also click the "Send data" link and send the user name back explicitly.

Now suppose you change the `ACTION` and the URL in the link from `www.xyz1.net` to `www.xyz2.net`. When you attempt to send the data, you'll get a dialog box telling you that potentially sensitive data will be sent to a different server. If you don't want the data to go there, you hit the Cancel button.

Finally, add the line

```
untaintedName = untaint(document.myForm.username.value);
```

at the beginning of the second script, and change the query `document.myForm.username.value` to `untaintedName`.

Now reload the form and select the `Send Data` link. The data is sent to `www.xyz2.net` without any warning to the user, because the programmer has explicitly untainted the data.

## Using *domain*

Some large organizations need to easily distribute their pages over many servers. For example, if you run a heavily visited site such as **www.yahoo.com**, you distribute the load across many machines. You may get the data from one server—www5.yahoo.com—and send it back to another—www17.yahoo.com. Rather than untaint everything, you are allowed to set the domain in your scripts *once*. You may set the domain to any value that matches the tail end of your real domain. Thus, both www5.yahoo.com and www17.yahoo.com may set their domains to `yahoo.com`, but may not set their domains to `yahoo1.com`. Once set, the domain may not be changed again.

Thus, a large user such as Yahoo! would be well-advised to set the domain in all scripts so that data tainting is not an issue at all. ●

# The *Math* Object

Chapter 5, "JavaScript Strings," began the exploration of the built-in objects that are available through both the client-side JavaScript in the browser and LiveWire on the server. This chapter continues that discussion by looking at the Math object.

The Math object is home to advanced functions such as sine, cosine, and tangent. Many JavaScript programmers will never need the capabilities of Math. If you do scientific or engineering computing, however, or if you need to build a simulator or a game, you may want to take advantage of these features. You'll learn some general JavaScript programming tips, too, from the examples included in this chapter. ■

**How to use JavaScript for math calculations**

Find out how you can do internal calculations within the script and avoid using CGI for math-intensive applications.

**Get details on each of the methods of the *Math* object**

JavaScript's Math object contains numerous functions, including a full set of trigonometric functions, utility functions, and a random number generator.

**Find out how to simplify repeated calls to the *Math* object**

JavaScript includes a with clause, which allows you to specify a default object.

**See how to build a special-purpose calculator**

The "Escape Velocity" calculator computes the escape velocity for any of the nine planets.

**Learn how to call unary and binary *Math* functions**

The "Desk Calculator" example shows how string and number objects can be transformed into one another. The advanced version of the calculator enables the user to call unary functions like sqrt() and binary functions like pow().

# Properties and Methods of the *Math* Object

As you saw in Chapter 4, "JavaScript Objects," the Math object provides built-in constants and methods for performing calculations within the script. The Math object's syntax is the following:

```
Math.propertyname
```

or

```
Math.methodname(parameters)
```

Table 6.1 summarizes the various methods and properties of the Math object.

### Table 6.1  *Math* Object Methods and Properties

| Method Name | Example | Returned Value |
|---|---|---|
| abs | Math.abs(-79) | 79 |
| acos | Math.acos(.5) | 1.047197551196597631 |
| asin | Math.asin(1) | 1.570796326794896558 |
| atan | Math.atan(.5) | 0.4636476090008060935 |
| ceil | Math.ceil(7.6) | 8 |
| cos | Math.cos(.4) | 0.9210609940028851028 |
| floor | Math.floor(8.9) | 8 |
| log | Math.log(5) | 1.609437912434100282 |
| max | Math.max(1, 700) | 700 |
| min | Math.min(1, 700) | 1 |
| pow | Math.pow(6,2) | 36 |
| random | Math.random() | .7877896 (varies) |
| round | Math.round(.567) | 1 |
| sin | Math.sin(Math.PI) | 0 |
| sqrt | Math.sqrt(9801) | 99 |
| tan | Math.tan(1.5*Math.PI) | INF (infinity) |

## *Math* Methods

Most of the methods used by Math are self-evident—such as using Math.sin to calculate the sine function of a number. They are summarized in the following sections, with reference examples.

***abs***    abs returns the absolute value of its numeric argument. For example, the following code returns 1:

```
Math.abs(-1)
```

***acos, asin, atan, cos, sin, tan***    These trigonometric functions work with angle measurements in radians. The a is short for arc. Thus, atan() is the arc tangent or $Tan^{-1}$ function.

For example, the following code returns 3.141592653589793116:

```
Math.acos(-1)
```

***ceil***    This function returns the smallest integer greater than or equal to the argument passed to it. This behavior is equivalent to always rounding up to the nearest integer. For example, the following code places 15 into the variable quux:

```
with (Math) {
quux = ceil(14.49999999);
}
```

See also floor.

***exp***    exp returns e to the power of its argument. If $x$ is the argument, exp returns $e^x$. (e is Euler's constant—the base of natural logarithms.) For example, the following code returns 148.4131591025765999:

```
Math.exp(5)
```

***floor***    This function returns the greatest integer less than or equal to the value passed to it. This procedure is equivalent to always rounding down to the nearest integer. For example, the following code returns 1:

```
numberone = Math.floor(1.9999999);
document.write(numberone);
```

See also ceil.

***log***    This function returns the natural log of the argument passed to it. The base is e. For example, the following returns the natural log of π, 1.144729885849400164:

```
pilog = Math.log(Math.PI);

document.write("The log (base e) of PI is: " + pilog + " .");
```

***max, min***    Given two numbers, max returns the greater of the two and min returns the lesser of the two. For example:

```
with (Math) {
document.write("Between Euler's constant and
PI, " + max(E,PI) + " is greater.")
}
```

Between Euler's constant (*e*) and π, 3.141592653589793 is greater.

***pow***    Given a base and an exponent, this function returns the base to the exponent power. For example, the following code returns 10000:

```
Math.pow(10,4)
```

Part
II
Ch
6

***random***    This method returns a pseudo-random number between 0 and 1. For example, the following line might return 0.09983341664682815475:

```
Math.random()
```

**N O T E**   The random() function was not implemented for all platforms in early releases of JavaScript, so some developers elected not to use it. random() is now supported on all platforms and is part of the JavaScript 1.1 specification. You can now use random() wherever you require it, with confidence that it is supported on any platform that supports JavaScript 1.1. ▪

***round***    This method returns the argument rounded to the nearest integer. It rounds up if the fractional part of the number is .5 or greater, and it rounds down otherwise. For example, the following code writes 1:

```
with(Math) {
tmp = round(1.4999999999);
document.write(tmp);
}
```

***sqrt***    This function computes the square root of its argument. Note: The argument must be non-negative; otherwise, the sqrt method returns 0. For example, the following returns 12:

```
Math.sqrt(144);
```

**Summary of *Math* Object Properties**    In addition to the Math methods, the designers of Java-Script include six constants, implemented as Math properties. These constants are listed in Table 6.2.

**Table 6.2  *Math* Object Properties Summary**

| Property Name | Description | Returned Value |
|---|---|---|
| E | Euler's constant, the base of natural logarithms | 2.718281828459045091 |
| LN10 | The natural log of 10 | 2.302585092994045901 |
| LN2 | The natural log of 2 | 0.69314718055994529 |
| LOG2E | The base 2 log of e | 1.442 |
| LOG10E | The base 10 log of e | 0.434 |
| PI | The ratio of the circumference of a circle to its diameter | 3.141592653589793116 |
| SQRT1_2 | The square root of 0.5 | 0.7071067811865474617 |
| SQRT2 | The square root of 2 | 1.4142135623730951 |

## Using *with* to Simplify Calls to the *Math* Object

Using the Math object is essentially identical to using other objects in JavaScript. However, you will frequently need to use several Math constants and methods together in a block of code. To avoid having to write Math.*this* and Math.*that* over and over, you can use the with statement.

For example, consider the following code:

```
beta = Math.E * 62;
gamma = Math.PI / beta;
delta = x * Math.sin(gamma);
```

becomes

```
with (Math) {
     beta  = E * 62;

     gamma = PI / beta;

     delta = x * sin(gamma);
}
```

Not only is this code easier to write, it is also clearer, making it easier to read and maintain. This practice reduces the likelihood of defects lurking in your code.

# An Example from Rocket Science

You certainly don't have to be a rocket scientist to use JavaScript. If you *are* interested in rocketry (or, for that matter, in the JavaScript Math object), you can use this example as a starting point.

In general, the equation that gives the velocity necessary to escape the gravity of a planet is

$$v_0 = \sqrt{2GM/R}$$

where

$v_0$ denotes escape velocity in feet per second,

G denotes the universal gravitational constant, $1.07 \times 10^{-9}$,

M denotes the mass of the planet in pounds, and

R denotes the radius of the planet in feet.

The escape velocity calculator is built on the template shown in Listing 6.1.

**Listing 6.1   An Escape Velocity Calculator**

```
<HTML>
<HEAD>
<TITLE>Escape Velocity Calculator</TITLE>
<SCRIPT LANGUAGE="JavaScript">
```

*continues*

Part
II

Ch
6

**Listing 6.1  Continued**

```
<!--
...functions to compute and format the escape velocity
// These functions are explained later in the text.
// -->
</SCRIPT>
</HEAD>
<BODY BGCOLOR="white" onLoad="init()">
<H1>Escape Velocity Calculator</H1>
<FORM NAME="theForm">
Choose a Planet:
<SELECT NAME="planet" SIZE=1 onChange=" theForm.escapeVelocity.value =
computeEscapeVelocity(theForm.planet.options[theForm.planet.selectedIndex].value)">
<OPTION VALUE="Mercury">Mercury
<OPTION VALUE="Venus">Venus
<OPTION VALUE="Earth" SELECTED>Earth
<OPTION VALUE="Mars">Mars
<OPTION VALUE="Jupiter">Jupiter
<OPTION VALUE="Saturn">Saturn
<OPTION VALUE="Uranus">Uranus
<OPTION VALUE="Neptune">Neptune
<OPTION VALUE="Pluto">Pluto
</SELECT><BR>
Escape velocity is
<INPUT TYPE="Text" NAME="escapeVelocity" SIZE=7>miles per hour.
</FORM>
<SCRIPT LANGUAGE="JavaScript">
<!--
...function init defined...
// This function is explained later in the text.
// -->
</SCRIPT>
</BODY>
</HTML>
```

Note that init() is called in the <BODY> tag's onLoad handler, but is defined at the end of the <BODY>, and not in the <HEAD> with the rest of the functions. This design allows all the time for the <FORM> to load. If you define init() in the <HEAD>, document.theForm is still undefined.

 **TIP**

Whenever you define functions in the <BODY>, there is a possibility that the user will attempt to use the function before it has loaded. In this example, init() is only called by the onLoad() handler, which runs at the end of the download sequence. The only user control on this page is <SELECT>, so the user would have to be very quick to change the <SELECT> option before the load was finished.

In pages with more content, however, the window of vulnerability grows larger. Listing 6.2 illustrates the use of a global Boolean gInitialized, which is initially set to false. When your <BODY> initialization routine completes, it sets Initialized to true. The user routine, computeEscapeVelocity(), checks gInitialized, and does not try to use the gPlanetaryMass or gPlanetaryRadius arrays before they are initialized. Instead, the escapeVelocity field is reset to the string "Initializing...." When init() completes, it reads the current setting on the <SELECT> element and initializes the escapeVelocity field with the correct numbers.

When init() runs, it populates two global arrays—gPlanetaryMass and gPlanetaryRadius. When the user changes the selected option in the <SELECT> element named planet, the onChange handler updates the escapeVelocity field by using computeEscapeVelocity(). Listing 6.2 shows the JavaScript for computeEscapeVelocity().

### Listing 6.2   Compute the Escape Velocity Based on a Planet's Mass

```
function computeEscapeVelocity(aPlanet)
{
  var theResult = "Initializing...";
  if (gInitialized)
  {
    var theVelocity = 0;
    var kG = 1.07E-9;
    var kFeetPerMile = 5280;
    var kSecondsPerHour = 3600;
    with (Math)
    {
      theVelocity = sqrt(2*kG*gPlanetaryMass[aPlanet]/
                    gPlanetaryRadius[aPlanet]);

      // normalize to miles per hour
      theVelocity = round((theVelocity / kFeetPerMile) *
                    kSecondsPerHour);
    }
    theResult = commas(theVelocity);
  }
  return theResult;
}
```

Since this routine is math-intensive, it has a

```
with (Math)
{
...
}
```

construct at its heart. Note, too, that the finished result is sent through the function commas() in order to make the number more readable. Listing 6.3 shows the source code for commas().

### Listing 6.3   Add Commas to Long Numbers to Make Them Attractive

```
function commas(aNumber)
{
  var theResult = "";
  if (aNumber < 1000)
```

*continues*

Part

II

Ch

6

**Listing 6.3    Continued**

```
      theResult = "" + aNumber;
  else
  {
     var leftPart = commas(Math.floor(aNumber/1000));
     var rightPart = aNumber % 1000;
     if (rightPart < 10)
       rightPart = "00" + rightPart;
     else if (rightPart < 100)
       rightPart = "0" + rightPart;
     theResult = "" + leftPart + "," + rightPart;
  }
  return theResult;
}
```

This function does its work recursively. If the number is under 1,000, then it does not need any commas added, so the function returns immediately. If the number is greater than 1,000, the function breaks the number into two parts—a right part that consists of the right three digits and a left part that consists of everything else. Note that this part of the code could have been written using the String object's substring() operator, instead of using mathematical operators.

The commas() function is called on the left part of the number, so that a number like 123456789 is split first into 123456 and 789. Then the left part is further split into 123 and 456. Commas are added between the left part and the right part. If the right part does not require all three digits, it is padded with zeroes on the left, so 24040 becomes 24,040 instead of 24,40.

Because floor is the only Math method called in commas, the Math object is referenced explicitly, rather than through a with statement.

The % operator is used in JavaScript as the module operator. Thus, aNumber % 1000 has the effect of repeatedly subtracting 1,000 from aNumber until the remainder is less than 1,000. Figure 6.1 shows the finished Escape Velocity Calculator.

**FIG. 6.1**
Whenever the user changes the value of the <SELECT> element, JavaScript updates the escapeVelocity field.

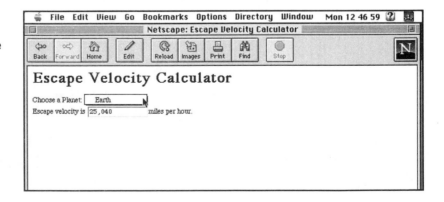

**NOTE** In general, if the number of options in a <SELECT> element is greater than about five, it's time to consider setting the SIZE attribute to something other than one. In this example, the SIZE attribute is left at one, even though there are nine planets. Since the <SELECT> element serves both as a control and as feedback for which planet was selected, this design seems clearer. ■

# A JavaScript Desk Calculator

The rich array of Math objects makes it easy to write a powerful JavaScript calculator. Listing 6.4 contains the foundation for a simple "four-banger:"

## Listing 6.4  A Simple Calculator

```
<!DOCTYPE HTML PUBLIC "-//W3C//DTD HTML 3.2//EN">
<HTML><HEAD>TITLE>Desk Calculator</TITLE>
<SCRIPT LANGUAGE="JavaScript">
<!--
var accumulator = 0;
var operator = "";
var clearRegister = false;
var operationPending = false;
function doKey(theForm)
{ // alert("Please use the mouse, not the keyboard.");
  theForm.register.blur();}
function doNumber(theForm, theNumber)
{  if (operator != "") { operationPending = true; }
   if (clearRegister) { doClear(theForm); clearRegister = false; }
   if (theForm.register.value.indexOf(".") == -1)
   if (parseInt(theForm.register.value) != 0)
   ➥theForm.register.value += theNumber;
   else
     theForm.register.value = theNumber;
   else
     theForm.register.value += theNumber;
}
function doDot(theForm)
{
  if (clearRegister)
  {
    doClear(theForm);
    clearRegister = false;
  }
  // only display one decimal point in the register
   if (theForm.register.value.indexOf(".") == -1)
     if (theForm.register.value.length == 0)
       theForm.register.value = "0.";
     else
       theForm.register.value += ".";
}
function doClear(theForm)
{
```

Part

II

Ch

6

*continues*

**Listing 6.4   Continued**

```
  theForm.register.value = "";
}
function doClearAll(theForm)
{
  accumulator = 0;
  operator = "";
  doClear(theForm);
}
function doDivide(theForm)
{
  if (operationPending)
  {
    doEquals(theForm);
    operationPending = false;
  }
  accumulator = theForm.register.value;
  operator = "/";
  clearRegister = true;
}
function doMultiply(theForm)
{
  if (operationPending)
  {
    doEquals(theForm);
    operationPending = false;
  }
  accumulator = theForm.register.value;
  operator = "*";
  clearRegister = true;
}
function doSubtract(theForm)
{
if (operationPending)
  {
    doEquals(theForm);
    operationPending = false;
  }
  accumulator = theForm.register.value;
  operator = "-";
  clearRegister = true;
}
function doAdd(theForm)
{
  if (operationPending)
  {
    doEquals(theForm);
    operationPending = false;
  }
  accumulator = theForm.register.value;
  operator = "+";
  clearRegister = true;
}
function doEquals(theForm)
{
```

```
      var register = parseFloat(theForm.register.value);
      var theAccumulator = parseFloat(accumulator);
      if (operator == "/")
        theForm.register.value =
          1 * theAccumulator / register;
      else if (operator == "*")
        theForm.register.value =
          1 * theAccumulator * register;
      else if (operator == "-")
        theForm.register.value =
          0 + theAccumulator - register;
      else if (operator == "+")
        theForm.register.value =
          0 + theAccumulator + register
      clearRegister = true;
      operator = "";
      accumulator = 0;
    }// -->
    </SCRIPT></HEAD><BODY BGCOLOR="#FFFFFF">
    <H1>Desk Calculator</H1>
    <TABLE BORDER=1 CELLSPACING=5 CELLPADDING=5 >
    <TR ALIGN=CENTER VALIGN=CENTER>
    <TD ALIGN=CENTER VALIGN=CENTER COLSPAN="2"><FORM NAME="theForm">
    ➥<INPUT TYPE="Text" NAME="register" VALUE=""
    onFocus="doKey(document.theForm)"></TD></TR>
    <TR ALIGN=CENTER VALIGN=CENTER>
    <TD><INPUT TYPE="Button" NAME="ClearAll" VALUE="CA" SIZE=5
    onClick="doClearAll(document.theForm)"></TD>
    <TD><INPUT TYPE="Button" NAME="Divide" VALUE="/" SIZE=5
    onClick="doDivide(document.theForm)"></TD></TR></TABLE><HR>
    <DT> </DT>
    <TABLE BORDER=1 CELLSPACING=5 CELLPADDING=5 >
    <TR ALIGN=CENTER VALIGN=CENTER>
    <TD><DT><INPUT TYPE="Button" SIZE="5" NAME="Seven" VALUE="7"
     onClick="doNumber(document.theForm,7)"></DT></TD>
    <TD><DT><INPUT TYPE="Button" NAME="Eight" VALUE="8" SIZE=5
      onClick="doNumber(document.theForm,8)"></DT></TD>
    <TD><DT><INPUT TYPE="Button" NAME="Nine" VALUE="9" SIZE=5
      onClick="doNumber(document.theForm,9)"></DT></TD>
    <TD><DT><INPUT TYPE="Button" NAME="Multiply" VALUE="*" SIZE=5
      onClick="doMultiply(document.theForm)"></DT></TD></TR>
    <TR ALIGN=CENTER VALIGN=CENTER>
    <TD><DT> <INPUT TYPE="Button" NAME="Four" VALUE="4" SIZE=5
      onClick="doNumber(document.theForm,4)"></DT></TD>
    <TD><DT> <INPUT TYPE="Button" NAME="Five" VALUE="5"
     onClick="doNumber(document.theForm,5)"></DT></TD>
    <TD><DT> <INPUT TYPE="Button" NAME="Six" VALUE="6" SIZE=5
      onClick="doNumber(document.theForm,6)"></DT></TD>
    <TD><DT> <INPUT TYPE="Button" NAME="Subtract" VALUE="-" SIZE="5"
     onClick="doSubtract(document.theForm)"></DT></TD></TR>
    <TR ALIGN=CENTER VALIGN=CENTER>
    <TD><DT> <INPUT TYPE="Button" NAME="One" VALUE="1" SIZE=5
     onClick="doNumber(document.theForm,1)"></DT></TD>
    <TD><DT> <INPUT TYPE="Button" NAME="Two" VALUE="2" SIZE=5
      onClick="doNumber(document.theForm,2)"></DT></TD>
```

Part

II

Ch

6

*continues*

**Listing 6.4   Continued**

```
<TD><DT> <INPUT TYPE="Button" NAME="Three" VALUE="3" SIZE=5
  onClick="doNumber(document.theForm,3)"></DT></TD>
<TD><DT> <INPUT TYPE="Button" NAME="Add" VALUE="+" SIZE=5
  onClick="doAdd(document.theForm)"></DT></TD></TR>
<TR ALIGN=CENTER VALIGN=CENTER><TD>
<DT><INPUT TYPE="Button" NAME="Zero" VALUE="0" SIZE=5
 onClick="doNumber(document.theForm,0)"> </DT></TD>
<TD><DT> <INPUT TYPE="Button" NAME="Dot" VALUE="." SIZE=5
  onClick="doDot(document.theForm)"></DT></TD>
<TD><DT> <INPUT TYPE="Button" NAME="Clear" VALUE="C" SIZE=5
 onClick="doClear(document.theForm)"></DT></TD>
<TD><DT> <INPUT TYPE="Button" NAME="Equals" VALUE="=" SIZE=5
onClick="doEquals(document.theForm)"></DT></TD></TR></TABLE>
</FORM></BODY></HTML>
```

Figure 6.2 shows the resulting calculator form.

**FIG. 6.2**

JavaScript lets you build a simple calculator with just a few buttons and functions.

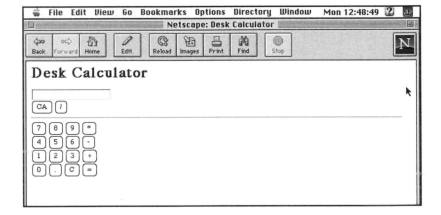

# Handling the Keyboard

The first function named in the calculator is doKey(). This function deals with the user's keyboard. While a good computerized calculator should handle the keyboard, JavaScript makes such a design difficult. JavaScript fields are not designed to handle individual keystrokes, only events such as onChange(). To discourage the user from attempting to type individual keys such as "*" and "+" into the register field, we hook doKey() to the onFocus event. doKey() simply calls

```
theForm.register.blur();
```

If the user clicks the register field (as though to enter a character from the keyboard), we take the focus away, forcing the user to use the buttons provided.

▶ **See** "Developing Java Applets," **p. 342**, to learn how to write a Java applet that will give you more fine-grained control over the keyboard than you get in JavaScript.

# Basic Calculator Operations

Our calculator design is based on the form's `register` field and four global variables:

- ▩ `accumulator`, a number
- ▩ `operator`, a string
- ▩ `clearRegister`, a Boolean
- ▩ `operationPending`, a Boolean

The most basic calculator operation is the one in which the user presses a series of digits to enter a number, then presses an operator key (such as +), then presses some more digits, and, finally, presses the = key.

**Entering the First Number**    Initially, `accumulator` and `operator` are empty and the two Booleans are `false`. When the operator clicks a number button, the form calls `doNumber()` and passes the form and the number to process. Listing 6.5 shows the relevant JavaScript for `doNumber()` when the first number is entered.

---

**Listing 6.5    The User Clicks a Number**

```
function doNumber(theForm, theNumber)
{
...
  if (theForm.register.value.indexOf(".") == -1)
    if (parseInt(theForm.register.value) != 0)
      theForm.register.value += theNumber;
    else
      theForm.register.value = theNumber;
  else
    theForm.register.value += theNumber;
}
```

---

If the user clicks, say, the 7 button, when the `register` field is empty, the string `"7"` is appended to the empty `register` field. A user could use this method to enter, say `"123."` With each click, a new digit is appended to the string in `register`.

Note the special processing if the `register` contains only a zero. If the user clicks the 0 button repeatedly in an otherwise empty `register`, only a single `"0"` is entered. If the user clicks a non-zero button, the non-zero digit replaces the zero (so we don't get `0123`). If the field already has non-zero digits in it, new zeroes get appended in the usual fashion.

If the field already has a decimal point, multiple zeroes *are* allowed, so the user can enter numbers like `0.000001`.

**Choosing an Operator**    After the first number is entered, the user clicks an operator button, which calls a function to process that operator. The code for `doAdd()` is in Listing 6.6.

Part
II

Ch
6

**Listing 6.6   The User Clicks the Plus Sign**

```
function doAdd(theForm)
{
  if (operationPending)
  {
    doEquals(theForm);
    operationPending = false;
  }
  accumulator = theForm.register.value;
  operator = "+";
  clearRegister = true;
}
```

Since operatorPending was initialized to false, this function simply copies the contents of the register field into the global accumulator, and loads the global operator with the symbol for addition. Finally, it sets clearRegister so that the next time a digit is entered, that digit *replaces* the existing number in the register rather than being appended to it.

**Entering the Second Number**   Now the user begins to enter the second number. Again, doNumber() is called. doNumber()is shown in Listing 6.7, this time showing the code that handles operationPending and clearRegister.

**Listing 6.7   A More Elaborate Handler for the Plus Sign**

```
function doNumber(theForm, theNumber)
{
  if (operator != "")
  {
    operationPending = true;
  }
  if (clearRegister)
  {
    doClear(theForm);
    clearRegister = false;
  }
  if (theForm.register.value.indexOf(".") == -1)
    if (parseInt(theForm.register.value) != 0)
      theForm.register.value += theNumber;
    else
      theForm.register.value = theNumber;
  else
    theForm.register.value += theNumber;
}
```

Because operator is no longer empty, doNumber() sets operationPending to true. Since clearRegister is set in doAdd() (and the other operator functions), doNumber() calls doClear() to empty the register, and then clears clearRegister. Now doNumber() proceeds to put the digits of the second number into the register in the usual manner.

**Getting the Result**   Finally, the user clicks the = button and doEquals() (shown in Listing 6.8) is called.

---

**Listing 6.8   Handle the Equals Sign**

```
function doEquals(theForm)
{
  var register = parseFloat(theForm.register.value);
  var theAccumulator = parseFloat(accumulator);
  if (operator == "/")
    theForm.register.value =
      1 * theAccumulator / register;
  else if (operator == "*")
    theForm.register.value =
      1 * theAccumulator * register;
  else if (operator == "-")
    theForm.register.value =
      0 + theAccumulator - register;
  else if (operator == "+")
    theForm.register.value =
      0 + theAccumulator + register
  clearRegister = true;
  operator = "";
  accumulator = 0;
}
```

---

First, doEquals() transforms the strings in register and accumulator into floating-point numbers. Then, it decodes operator back into an operation, making sure that the resulting value is stored as a number. Finally, it sets clearRegister so that the next digit will clear register, rather than being appended, and clears all traces of the operation that was just completed.

**Allowing Chains of Operators**   The preceding code is sufficient for sequences such as "12 + 13.6 = 25.6" series. But, sometimes the user wants to chain operators without explicitly using the = button. For example, the user might enter "12 + 13 + 14 + 15 =" and expect the running sums to be displayed after each click of the + button. The easiest way to add this behavior is to call doEquals() as part of each operator function. Listing 6.9 contains the full code for doAdd().

Part

II

Ch

6

---

**Listing 6.9   A More Elaborate Version of the Plus Sign Processor**

```
function doAdd(theForm)
{
  if (operationPending)
  {
    doEquals(theForm);
    operationPending = false;
  }
  accumulator = theForm.register.value;
  operator = "+";
  clearRegister = true;
}
```

---

Suppose the user presses "12 * 2 +". Since there's already an operation pending (the *), this function calls doEquals(), then clears operationPending. Then it goes on to process the "+" operator in the usual fashion.

**Adding Unary *Math* Operators**    Recall from the section "Properties and Methods of the *Math* Object," earlier in this chapter, that the Math object has three kinds of methods: those that require a single operand (such as sin()), those that require two operands (such as pow()), and those that require no operands. random() is the only example of this last category, although you can use the same mechanism to implement buttons for constants, such as π.

This section shows how to add a button that processes a unary operator—one that requires only a single operand.

First, add a button to the form that displays an appropriate label and calls a handler for the function. Here's the HTML to add an SQRT button:

```
<INPUT TYPE="Button" NAME="Sqrt" VALUE="SQRT"
  onClick="doSqrt(document.theForm)">
```

and here in Listing 6.10 is the JavaScript to implement doSqrt().

**Listing 6.10    Handle the Square Root Function**

```
function doSqrt(theForm)
{
  theForm.register.value =
    Math.sqrt(parseFloat(theForm.register.value));
  clearRegister = true;
}
```

To take the square root of, say, 144, enter 144 and click the SQRT button. The doSqrt() function does not disturb the operator chain; the user can enter "1 + 2 + 9 SQRT ="and the calculator will take the square root of 9 and replace the 9 with a 3. Upon pressing the = button, the user will see 6—the sum of 1, 2, and 3.

Some users prefer a design in which the user presses the unary operator button first and then enters the operand. You can implement such a button by using the binary operators (/, *, -, and +) as models. For example, you might write the function as shown in Listing 6.11.

**Listing 6.11    A Different Design for Processing *SQRT***

```
function doSqrt(theForm)
{
  accumulator = theForm.register.value;
  squareRootPending = true;
  clearRegister = true;
}
```

What *isn't* included from doAdd() and the other operator functions is more significant than what *is* included. Recall that the binary operator functions start with

```
if (operationPending)
{
    doEquals(theForm);
    operationPending = false;
}
```

In the case of a unary operator, we don't want to affect the operator chain, so we add a new global specific to that operator (in this case, squareRootPending). Now, at the top of doEquals(), right after the two calls to parseFloat(), we add the code shown in Listing 6.12.

### Listing 6.12 An Enhancement to *doEquals* to Handle *SQRT*

```
if (squareRootPending)
{
    theForm.register.value =
      Math.sqrt(0+register);
    register = parseFloat(theForm.register.value);
    squareRootPending = false;
}
```

Look at what happens now if the user enters "1 + 2 + SQRT 9 =". The processing proceeds as before until the user clicks the SQRT button. At this point, the register contains the sum of 1 and 2: 3. The doSqrt() function copies the 3 into the accumulator, then records two global facts: a square root operation is pending and the next digit entered should clear the register. Now the user enters "9" and "=". When doEquals() runs, it finds that squareRootPending is true, calls Math.sqrt, and writes the result back to the register field and the register local variable. Finally, it records the fact that the square root operation has been processed.

This design will support any of the unary operators. It does not support nested operators. For example, the sequence "1 + 2 + SQRT LN π =" works correctly only if the "LN" operator is above the "SQRT" operator in doEquals(). To build a calculator that supports nested unary operators, replace the squareRootPending global with a string or array that can simulate a stack. Then, push unary operators onto the stack as their operator functions are called and pop them off again in doEquals(). The pseudocode to add this mechanism to doEquals() is shown here:

```
while (stack is not empty)
{
  aUnaryOperator = stack.pop();
  process aUnaryOperator;
}
```

▶ **See** "JavaScript's Associative Arrays," **p. 289**, for more information about arrays.

**Adding Binary Operators**   A few of the methods in Math take two operands. Among them, Math.pow() is the most useful on a calculator. Use the operator functions of the "basic four" operators as a model for other binary operators.

Listing 6.13 shows the code for doPower().

**Listing 6.13  Handle the User's Request to Raise a Number to a Power**

```
function doPower(theForm)
{
  if (operationPending)
  {
    doEquals(theForm);
    operationPending = false;
  }
  accumulator = theForm.register.value;
  operator = "POW";
  clearRegister = true;
}
```

This code is almost identical to doAdd(). Now add a section to doEquals() to handle the POW operator:

```
else if (operator == "POW")
    theForm.register.value =
      0 + Math.pow(theAccumulator, register);
```

Note that this design does not accommodate operator precedence. If the user enters "1 + 2 + 2 POW 3 =", the calculator will run doEquals() at the beginning of doPower(), effectively making this calculation "(1 + 2 + 2) POW 3 =", or 125.

A commercial-grade calculator should include operator precedence; the POW operator is typically higher in precedence than division, multiplication, subtraction, or addition, so the preceding calculation would be computed as "1 + 2 + (2 POW 3) =", or 11. The easiest way to implement operator precedence is to keep an array of pending operators and values. Then each operator looks at the array of pending operators and runs doEquals() only if the top pending operator has a precedence equal to or higher than itself. The next paragraph explains how the previous example works in such a design.

When the user enters "1 + 2 +", the second call to the doAdd() operator sees that the pending operator has the same precedence as itself, so doEquals() is called to complete the first add. Now the arrays of operators and results contain "3 +". The user enters "2 POW". The POW operator has a higher precedence than "+" so doPower() does not call doEquals(). The user continues, entering "3 =". The final click on the "=" button triggers doEquals(), which works down the stack of operators. First, the POW operator is called with parameters 2 and 3. The result, 8, is stored back onto the end of the results array. Now the "+" operator is applied, resulting in "3 + 8", or 11.

As mentioned before, more information about arrays is available in Chapter 11, "Creating Your Own JavaScript Objects." ●

# The *Date* and *Array* Objects

**C**hapter 5, "JavaScript Strings," began the exploration of the built-in objects available through both the client-side JavaScript in the browser and LiveWire on the server. In this chapter, we continue that discussion by looking at the Date object. This chapter concludes with an introduction to JavaScript arrays. ■

■ **Find out how to use the date and time in JavaScript scripts**

Learn how to use the client's machine time to customize your Web pages so that they are based on the local time of day.

■ **Learn the *Date* object's methods**

The Date object is the largest and most complex of the built-in objects—there are many methods available to get and set the object's properties and to convert instances of Date to and from other objects, such as strings and integers.

■ **Learn how to add a clock to your pages**

The first example in this chapter shows how to display a continuously updating clock on the page or in the status bar.

■ **Learn about date and time calculations**

The second example in this chapter shows how to display customizable messages based on the time of day and day of the year. This example counts down to Christmas.

■ **Learn about JavaScript arrays**

You can use arrays to build objects and to build data structures of related objects.

# Building New *Date* Objects

As you saw in Chapter 4, "JavaScript Objects," the `Date` object provides information about the current date and time on the client's machine. The `Date` object is useful for designing sites that are sensitive to the time of day or that use time-based information to present new information to the user, without having to use a Common Gateway Interface (CGI) program to access the server's clock. Using the JavaScript `Date` object has another advantage of a CGI script—the date and time are local to the client's machine. Imagine the confusion caused to European users when they connect to a server late in the day and receive `"Good morning!"` because the server's clock is set to California time.

**N O T E**  You cannot work with dates prior to 1/1/70. This fact is due to the cross-platform nature of JavaScript—UNIX machines consider 00:00:00 GMT January 1, 1970, a date commonly known as "The Epoch," to be "zero" on their clocks. Other operating systems have earlier zero settings (like Macintosh's January 1, 1904), so the most recent of them is considered the baseline for time. ■

The `Date` object is similar to the `String` object in that you make new instances of the object when you assign it to a variable. It differs from the `String` object in that you must use the `new` statement to build it. Using the `new` statement, you generate a `Date` object that contains the specified time (with a resolution of one millisecond). By default, the `Date` object is set to the client machine's current time.

> **CAUTION**
>
> This value of the `Date` object is based on the time and date on the client's machine, not the time on the server. Therefore, if your server is located in New York and a user visits your site from California, the time reflects West Coast time, not Eastern Time. It is important to note this because you have no control over the time on users' machines. Their clocks may be wrong or not even running. If your script depends on having an accurate time on which to base its calculations, your script may fail due to the client's clock error.
>
> In general, try to avoid relying on the accuracy of the client's clock. If you do need accurate time, compare the client's clock against your server's clock—in most parts of the world, the minutes should agree fairly closely, even though you may be several time zones apart. If you just need to be sure that the client's clock is running, check it twice, with a short delay between the checks. You should see the clock advance by at least a few milliseconds.

To make a new `Date` object, you use the `new` operator. The `Date` object is predefined in JavaScript. Here is the syntax:

```
variableName = new Date(parameters)
```

For example:

```
today = new Date();
```

You have several optional parameters that you may specify when you construct the `Date` object:

- `variableName = new Date()`
- `variableName = new Date("month day, year hours:minutes:seconds")`
- `variableName = new Date(year, month, day)`
- `variableName = new Date(year, month, day, hours, minutes, seconds)`

 **TIP** Each of these forms has a few conventions of which you should be aware. The first form, in which you omit all parameters, automatically gives the current date and time in the standard format of:

*Day Month Date Hours:Minutes:Seconds Year*

For example,

`Sat   Dec  21  15:37:12  1996`

If you use the second or fourth form and omit the hours, minutes, or seconds, JavaScript automatically sets them to 0.

# Using the *Date* Methods

Once you have an instance of the `Date` object, you can then use the many `Date` methods to get or set the month, day, year, hours, minutes, or seconds of this instance.

**N O T E** You cannot set the day attribute independently—the day depends on the month, year, and date attributes. ▦

As with most object methods, you simply call a `Date` method as follows:

`variableName.methodname(parameters)`

For example:

`today.setHours(7);`

There are two exceptions to this rule with the `Date` object: The `UTC` and `parse` methods are *static* methods and are always called with just the generic `Date` object name. For example:

```
Date.UTC(parameters)
Date.parse(parameters)
```

Table 7.1 summarizes the different `Date` methods. This example assumes that the `Date` objects today and now are set to `Sat   Dec  21  15:37:12  1996` and that `yesterday` is set to `Fri Dec  20  00:00:00  1996`. The machine is located in Virginia, five hours behind Greenwich Mean Time.

**Table 7.1** *Date* Object Methods

| Method | Example | Returns |
|--------|---------|---------|
| getDate | today.getDate() | 21 |
| getDay | yesterday.getDay() | 5 |
| getHours | today.getHours() | 16 |
| getMinutes | today.getMinutes() | 37 |
| getMonth | year.getMonth() | 11 |
| getSeconds | time.getSeconds() | 12 |
| getTime | now.getTime() | 851197032000 |
| getTimeZoneoffset | today.getTimeZoneoffset | 300 |
| getYear | now.getYear | 96 (the years since 1900) |
| parse | Date.parse(July 1, 1996) | 851197032000 |
| setDate | now.setDate(6) | - |
| setHours | now.setHours(14) | - |
| setMinutes | now.setMinutes(50) | - |
| setMonth | today.setMonth(7) | - |
| setSeconds | today.setSeconds(7) | - |
| setTime | today.setTime(yesterday.getTime()) | - |
| setYear | today.setYear(88) | - |
| toGMTString | yesterday.toGMTString() | Fri, 20 Dec 1996 05:00:00 GMT |
| toLocaleString | today.toLocaleString() | Dec 21 16:37:12 1996 |
| UTC | Date.UTC(96, 11,3,0,0,0) | 849571200000 |

Using all these methods' strings and numbers may look like a daunting task, but if you approach the Date object with a few concepts in mind, it makes working with this object much easier.

**CAUTION**

Current versions of JavaScript do not always report the correct time zone. According to **http://www.arachnoid.com/lutusp/worldclock.htm**, this problem can be due to any one of several reasons—whether you get a correct result or not depends on where you live, when you ask, and what browser you're using. First, if Daylight Savings Time is in effect on the system, you can get a one-hour error in the reported time zone. Second, MSIE 3.0, Netscape 3.0 Beta, and Netscape 2.0 do three different things with this quantity. Netscape 2.0 always reports an incorrect value. Netscape browsers return a non-integer value for the number of minutes between GMT and the local zone—this is obviously impossible. The final release of Netscape Navigator (3.0p) reverses the sign of the time zone, so people who live in the Western Hemisphere appear to be living in the Eastern Hemisphere and vice versa. These problems appear to have been corrected in Navigator 4.0.

One test, conducted by using a generic JavaScript on a Compaq with Win95 using Netscape 4.0, gave 360 back for Dallas, Texas, which is correct. MSIE 3.0 returned a blank value; using MSIE 3.01 beta returned -360.

First, all of the methods can be grouped into four categories: get, set, to, and parse. The get methods simply return an integer corresponding to the attribute you requested. The set methods enable you to change an existing attribute in a Date object—again, by passing an integer—only this time, you are sending a number instead of receiving it. The to methods take the date and convert it into a string, which then allows you to use any of the string methods to further convert that string into a useful form. The two parse methods (parse and UTC) simply parse—or interpret—date strings.

Second, Date attributes such as month, day, or hours are all zero-based numbers. That is, the first month is 0, the second 1, and so on. The same goes for days, where Sunday is 0, Monday is 1, and so on. The reason why numbering starts at 0 instead of 1 is that JavaScript closely mirrors Java in many respects—such as always starting an array of "things" with 0. This is a convention followed by many languages, such as C, C++, and Perl. Table 7.2 lists the numeric conventions.

### Table 7.2  *Date* Object Number Conventions

| *Date* Attribute | Numeric Range |
| --- | --- |
| seconds, minutes | 0-59 |
| hours | 0-23 |
| day | 0-6  (0 = Sunday, 1 = Monday, and so on) |
| date | 1-31 |
| month | 0-11 (0 = January, 1 = February, and so on) |
| year | 0 + number of years since 1900 |

Part
II

Ch
7

Third, when a Date object is created, it takes the information from the browser's environment—usually right as the Web page is being loaded or sometime shortly after.

In the following sections, each Date method is described with a brief example.

## *get* Methods

These methods enable you to retrieve information from the current Date object. This information can be the seconds, minutes, hour, day of the month, day of the week, month, or year. Notice that there is a getDay method that will give you the day of the week, but you cannot set this value because the day of the week is dependent on the month, day, and year. See Figure 7.1 and Listing 7.1 for examples of the get methods.

**FIG. 7.1**

The get methods extract information from a Date object.

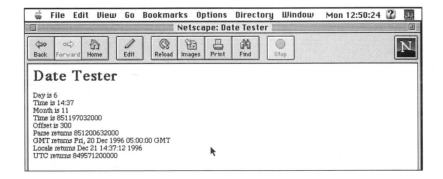

**Listing 7.1—This Date Tester Demonstrates the *Date* Object's *get* Methods**

```
<HTML>
<HEAD>
<TITLE>Date Tester</TITLE>
</HEAD>
<BODY BGCOLOR="white">
<H1>Date Tester</H1>
<SCRIPT LANGUAGE="JavaScript">
var today=new Date();
var yesterday=new Date("December 20, 1996");
today.setTime(851197032000);
document.write("Day is " + today.getDay() + "<BR>");
document.write("Time is " + today.getHours() + ":" + today.getMinutes() +
➥"<BR>");
document.write("Month is " + today.getMonth() + "<BR>");
document.write("Time is " + today.getTime() + "<BR>");
document.write("Offset is " + today.getTimezoneOffset() + "<BR>");
document.write("Parse returns " + Date.parse("December 21, 1996 15:37:12") +
➥"<BR>");
document.write("GMT returns " + yesterday.toGMTString()+ "<BR>");
document.write("Locale returns " + today.toLocaleString()+ "<BR>");
document.write("UTC returns " + Date.UTC(96, 11,3,0,0,0) + "<BR>");
</SCRIPT>
</BODY>
</HTML>
```

***getDate*** Given a Date object, this returns the day of the month as an integer between 1 and 31. For example, the following code returns 21:

```
today = new Date("December 21, 1996")
document.write(today.getdate())
```

***getDay*** This returns the day of the week. For example, the following code returns "Today is Saturday":

```
        today = new Date("December 21, 1996")

if (today.getDay() == 0) {document.write("Today is Sunday")}
if (today.getDay() == 1) {document.write("Today is Monday")}
if (today.getDay() == 2) {document.write("Today is Tuesday")}
if (today.getDay() == 3) {document.write("Today is Wednesday")}
if (today.getDay() == 4) {document.write("Today is Thursday")}
if (today.getDay() == 5) {document.write("Today is Friday")}
if (today.getDay() == 6) {document.write("Today is Saturday")}
```

***getHours*** This gives you the number of hours since midnight. For example, if it is 4 P.M., the following code returns, "It's been 16 hours since midnight here!":

```
today = new Date();
var howLong = today.getHours();
var hours = " hours";
if (howLong <= 1)
  hours=" hour";
document.write("It's been " + howLong + hours + " since midnight here!");
```

***getMonth*** getMonth returns the month attribute of a given Date object. For example, the following code returns 11 (if this month is December):

```
now = newDate()
nowmonth = now.getMonth();
document.write(nowmonth);
```

***getSeconds*** getSeconds returns the seconds of the given Date object. For example, the following code displays one image if the user loads the page during the first half of each minute, and a different image if the user loads the page during the second half:

```
now = newDate();
if (now.getSeconds() >30) {document.write("<img src = 'randimage1.gif'>")}
  else {document.write("<img src = 'randimage2.gif'>")}
```

***getTime*** getTime returns the number of milliseconds since January 1, 1970. This data is useful in setting the time of another Date object. For example:

```
thisDay = new Date("May 8, 1983");
RobertsBirthday = new Date();
RobertBirthday.setTime(thisDay.getTime());
```

See also setTime.

***getTimezoneOffset*** This function gives you the difference between the local time and GMT (Greenwich Mean Time) in minutes. For example:

```
now = new Date()
timeDifference = now.getTimezoneOffset();
```

***getYear*** getYear returns an integer representing the year of the twentieth century. Add 1900 to this number to get the current year. For example:

```
thisYear = new Date("January 1, 1997");
today = new Date();
var output = "Hi!";
if (today.getYear() >= thisYear.getYear()) { output +=" and Happy New Year!"};
document.write(output);
```

If the year is 1996, this code returns `"Hi!"` If it is 1997 or later, it returns `"Hi! and Happy New Year!"`

# *set* Methods

These methods enable you to add or change attributes of the Date object. You can change the date, month, year, hours, minutes, and seconds of the Date object. All of these methods require integers. Although you will probably use the get methods more often, these methods are handy when you want to build a date and time quickly—perhaps for display on a page as a modification date.

***setDate*** This function sets the day of the month of a Date object. For example, the following code returns 4:

```
today = new Date("July 1, 1996")
today.setDate(4);
document.write (today.getDate())
```

***setHours*** This function sets the hour to the specified time. For example, the following code sets the hours attribute of today ahead 3 hours:

```
today = new Date()
today.setHours=(today.getHours() + 3);
```

***setMinutes*** The setMinutes() function sets the minutes of the given time object from a number between 0 and 59. For example, the following code changes the current Date object (now) to set the minutes at 45:

```
now = new Date()
now.setMinutes(45)
```

***setMonth*** This function sets the month integer in the given Date object. For example, the following code sets today to have a month of May:

```
today = newDate()
today.setMonth(4)
```

**N O T E**  Remember that JavaScript counts months starting from 0. January is 0, February is 1,...,
May is 4. ■

***setSeconds***  This function sets the seconds of the given `Date` object. For example, the
following advances the seconds in `now` by five seconds:

```
now = new Date()
now.setSeconds(now.getSeconds()+5)
```

***setTime***  The function `setTime()` sets the time value by using an integer representing the
number of milliseconds since midnight on the morning of January 1, 1970. For example:

```
aDate = new Date();
aDate.setTime(26*365*24*60*60*1000);
alert(aDate);
```

would return:

```
Mon Dec 25 21:00:00 1995
```

Merry Christmas!

**T I P**  Instead of using a large integer as a parameter, you can pass the return value from `getTime()` on
another date, such as:

```
thisDay.setime(thatDay.getTime())
```

See also `getTime`.

***setYear***  `setYear` sets the year of the current date. For example, the following code sets the
year in `now` to 1998:

```
nowYear = new Date()
nowYear.setYear(98)
```

# *to* Methods

These methods convert date information into another format.

You can convert a date into a string (based on some set of conventions, as explained later).
Once you have converted the date into a string, it can be treated just like any other string, as
shown in Figure 7.2 and Listing 7.2. Note that the original `Date` object is not affected. These
methods simply parse the `Date` object and return a string based on the information it found.

**Listing 7.2  *Date to methods***

```
<HTML>
<SCRIPT language="javascript">
```

Part

II

Ch

7

*continues*

**Listing 7.2   Continued**

```
yesterday = new Date()
today = new Date()
document.write("<FONT SIZE=+2>")
document.write(yesterday.toGMTString())
document.write ("<P>")
document.write (today.toLocaleString())
document.write ("<P>")

</SCRIPT>
</HTML>
```

**FIG. 7.2**

The to methods of the Date object provide several different string output formats.

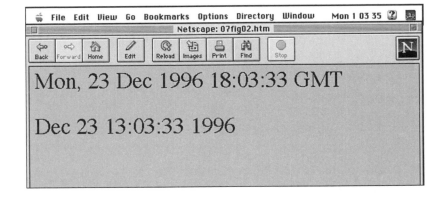

***toGMTString***   This method converts the date to a string that uses the GMT convention. For example:

```
today = new Date()
document.write((today.toGMTString).bold())
```

This code writes `<B>Sat, 21 December 1996 22:04:18 GMT</B>`. This line is rendered in bold text. Note that the bold method appended the `<B>` and the `</B>` to the string and is not a default action of the `toGMTString` method. This example illustrates how you can compact your code based on the knowledge that a method returns a known type that you can then use with other methods.

***toLocaleString***   This method converts a date to a string that uses the locale conventions. Locale conventions are specific to each area that will view this site—meaning that `toLocaleString` might return a different string in Europe than in the U.S. because in Europe the day is presented before the month. So 09/03/96 would mean September 3rd in the U.S. but March 9th in Europe.

For example, if the date were September 4th, 1996, the code

```
thisdate.toLocaleString()
```

would return the following string in the U.S:

```
09/04/96 08:06:40
```

In Europe, it would return

`04/09/96 08:06:40`

> **CAUTION**
>
> Locale strings are not only dependent upon the locale, but also upon the platform. For example, on the Macintosh the U.S. format is "`December 21 17:14:22 1995.`"

## *parse* Methods

parse methods take strings and convert them to a resulting Date object. These methods complement the to methods in that they perform the inverse of taking a date and converting it into a string. parse methods are handy for rapidly creating a Date object or for simplifying the process of passing a new value to a setTime() method (see Listing 7.3 and Figure 7.3).

---

**Listing 7.3   *parse* and *UTC* Each Produces a Time String**

```
<HTML>
<SCRIPT language="javascript">

yesterday = new Date()
today = new Date()
document.write("<FONT SIZE=+2>")
document.write(Date.parse("FEB 25, 1996"))
document.write ("<P>")
document.write (Date.UTC(96,11,3,0,0,0))
document.write ("<P>")

</SCRIPT>
</HTML>
```

---

**FIG. 7.3**

Examples of parse and UTC methods.

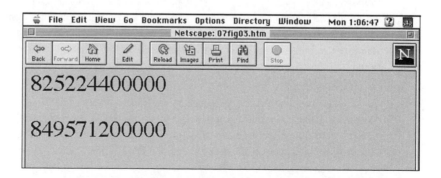

***parse***   This method returns the number of milliseconds since January 1, 1970 00:00:00. It takes a string such as Dec 21, 1996 and is useful for setting Date objects that already exist. It is acceptable to use the Internet Engineering Task Force (IETF) standard date syntax, such as Sat, 24 Feb 1996 18:15:11 GMT. parse() understands U.S. time zone abbreviations, but it is safer to use a time zone offset (thus the use for the `getTimezoneoffset` method). Note: The `parse` function is a static method of `Date`, so it is always called by using `Date.parse()`, not with the name of the specific `Date` object instance.

For example:

```
netTime = new Date()
timeString="Dec 21, 1996"
netTime.setTime(Date.parse(timeString));
```

sets `netTime` to the specified month, day, and year.

**UTC**   UTC stands for Coordinated Universal Time (but this time standard's abbreviation is always UTC, never CUT—see the sidebar in this section). For most purposes, UTC is equivalent to Greenwich Mean Time, or GMT. The `UTC()` method is static for `Date` and is always called via `Date.UTC()`. It is called by using the following syntax:

```
Date.UTC(year, month, day)
```

or:

```
Date.UTC(year, month, day, hours, minutes, seconds)
```

Remember that JavaScript is case-sensitive, so always use uppercase UTC. Also, remember that you use the same integer conventions listed in Table 7.2.

For example:

```
theDate = new Date(Date.UTC(96 ,  1 ,  24 ,  12 ,  45 ,  22));
```

---

### What Is Coordinated Universal Time?

Why is the abbreviation for Coordinated Universal Time UTC and not CUT? The answer lies in the way time is measured by astronomers, navigators, and others who require precision time measurement.

Beginning in 1884, the astronomers at the Royal Greenwich Observatory in England provided the world's most precise time standard—a standard based on their observations of the apparent position of the sun, with certain adjustments made to even out the measurements. The original name for their time standard was Greenwich Mean Time, or GMT. The meridian that passes through Greenwich, 0 degrees longitude, became the primary reference line for navigation and time zones around the world. Ships' chronometers were set to GMT, regardless of where the ships might be in the world.

As timekeeping became even more precise, a new series of time standards emerged. In 1928, the mean solar time at the Greenwich observatory was renamed Universal Time (UT) and later UT0 (to denote the fact that it was the first in a series). Some researchers made minor adjustments to UT0 that took into account the wobble of Earth's axis and other small effects. These adjusted time standards became known as UT1 and UT2. UT1 and UT2, the best astronomical standards available, have an accuracy of roughly 0.05 seconds, averaged over a nine-year period.

The rise of the atomic clock made it possible to measure time in billionths of a second, far more precisely than UT0 or even UT1 and UT2. Since about 1960, laboratories around the world have cooperated to establish a worldwide time standard. This effort is coordinated by the International

Time Bureau in Paris. The weighted average of their efforts is disseminated to the public under the name "Coordinated Universal Time." The acronym UTC was chosen so that the name would fit the UTO, UT1, UT2 series. By international agreement, "leap seconds" are occasionally added or subtracted in order to keep the value of UTC within 0.7 seconds of UT1.

Users who need a precise time can connect their computers to the U.S. National Institute of Standards and Technology (the former U.S. National Bureau of Standards) and set their system clock to UTC automatically.

# JavaScript Examples Using the *Date* Object

Now that you have survived learning all of the various methods, examples, and numerical conventions, it's time to begin doing some interesting things with your knowledge. The following sections show two examples of JavaScript scripts that use the Date object in very different ways. One gives you a straightforward clock to add to your Web page and the other provides a way of customizing your page based on the local date and time.

## A Simple Clock in JavaScript

This script, shown in Listing 7.4, samples the time every second, converts that information into a readable string, and displays that string in a small text box on the screen.

**Listing 7.4    A Simple Clock**

```
<HTML>
<HEAD>
<TITLE>JavaScript Clock</TITLE>
<SCRIPT LANGUAGE="JavaScript">
<!-- Hide me from other browsers

// This code was adapted from Netscape's clock, given in
// their JavaScript examples page

// Global variables
var timerID = null;
var timerRunning = false;

// stop the clock
function stopclock ()
{
  if (timerRunning)
    clearTimeout(timerID);
  timerRunning = false;
}

// start the clock
function startclock ()
```

Part

II

Ch

7

*continues*

**Listing 7.4   Continued**

```
{
  // Make sure the clock is stopped
  stopclock();
  showtime();
}

// actually display the time
function showtime ()
{
  var now = new Date();
  var hours = now.getHours();
  var minutes = now.getMinutes();
  var seconds = now.getSeconds();
  var timeValue = "" + ((hours >12) ? hours -12 :hours);
  timeValue += ((minutes < 10) ? ":0" : ":") + minutes;
  timeValue += ((seconds < 10) ? ":0" : ":") + seconds;
  timeValue += (hours >= 12) ? " P.M." : " A.M.";
  document.Clock.Face.value = timeValue;

  // you could replace the above with this code
  // and have a clock on the status bar:
  // window.status = timeValue;
  timerID = setTimeout("showtime()",1000);
  timerRunning = true;
}
-->

</SCRIPT>
</HEAD>
<BODY BGCOLOR="white" onLoad="startclock()">
<FORM NAME="Clock">
<DIV ALIGN=RIGHT>
<INPUT TYPE="Text" NAME="Face" SIZE=12 VALUE="">
</DIV>
</FORM>
<H1>Now you can add a clock to your pages!</H1>
</BODY>
</HTML>
```

Figure 7.4 shows how this code would appear on your page.

**The *showtime()* Function**   The heart of this script is the function showtime(). This function builds a Date object called now and pulls out (via getHours(), getMinutes(), and getSeconds()) the hour, minutes, and seconds values. It then makes a string variable called timeValue and assigns the hour to it. timeValue is interpreted by JavaScript as a string, even though hours is a number, because the first value assigned to timeValue was the empty string (""). Notice that if the hours value is greater than 12, it is reduced by 12 to account for conventional 12-hour time notation. Notice also that if the number of seconds or minutes is less than 10, the function appends a "0" before that number to keep the number of digits the same, and to avoid confusion between `03` and `30`. This script runs the function `showtime()` every 1,000 milliseconds (once a second) to display the current time in a format that is easy for the user to interpret.

**FIG. 7.4**

The `Date` object can be used to construct a simple Web page clock.

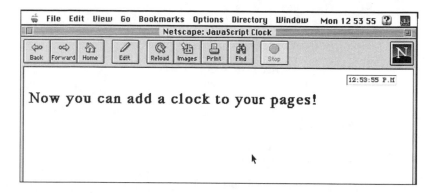

**An Alternative Design—Sending the Time to the Status Bar**   As the comments of Listing 7.4 indicate, you can direct the output of the function `showtime()` to the status bar on the bottom of your browser instead of displaying it in the text box field on the page. To make this change, comment out the following line:

```
document.Clock.Face.value = timeValue;
```

You also need to remove the comments (the `//`) from the following line:

```
// window.status = timeValue;
```

If you make this change, you can delete the form `Clock` and its text field `Face` in the `<BODY>` of the page.

It is advantageous to use the status line rather than displaying output in the text box field because the text is less likely to flicker when it updates, as many rapidly updated form fields tend to do. Also, you can easily modify this code—instead of displaying the current time on the screen—to send it to another function. This function might then use that changing information to reload a clock-face image (or almost anything your imagination comes up with).

## Customizing a Web Page

Some sites display different effects, depending upon the time of day that you visit them. For example, **http://www.whitehouse.gov/** displays a nighttime photo of the White House if you visit during the evening. Most pages of this sort use the server's clock, so a visitor to **http://www.whitehouse.gov/** will see whichever White House photo corresponds to the current time in Washington, DC, not the visitor's local time.

But, suppose you want to display different information based on the *local* time of day? You need to access the client's clock through a `Date` object. This section shows how to do that in Listing 7.5.

**Part**

**II**

**Ch**

**7**

## Listing 7.5   A Time-Based Customizer

```html
<HTML>
<HEAD>
<TITLE>Time-based Customizer</TITLE>
<SCRIPT LANGUAGE="JavaScript">
<!--
function getHours ()
{
  var now = new Date();
  var theHours = now.getHours();
  return theHours;
}
function tilChristmas()
{
  //var now = new Date("Dec 24, 1996 01:00:00");
  var now = new Date();

  // find the current year
  var theYear = now.getYear();
  var Christmas = new Date("Dec 25," + theYear +
    " 06:00:00");
  var nextYear = theYear + 1;
  if (now.getTime() > Christmas)
    Christmas.setYear(nextYear);
  var daysTilChristmas =
    Math.round((Christmas.getTime() -
    now.getTime())/(1000*3600*24));
  var daysTilChristmasMessage = ""
  var countDown = "";
  if (daysTilChristmas < 30)
    countDown = " just ";
  if (now.getMonth() == 11 && now.getDate() == 24 &&
      now.getHours() > 18)
    daysTilChristmasMessage = "Tonight is Christmas Eve!";
  else if (now.getMonth() == 11 && now.getDate() == 25)
    daysTilChristmasMessage = "Merry Christmas!";
  else if (daysTilChristmas > 1)
    daysTilChristmasMessage = "There are now " + countDown +
      daysTilChristmas + " days til Christmas.";
  else
    if (daysTilChristmas == 1)
      // cover "Christmas Eve Eve"
      daysTilChristmasMessage =
        "Only one day til Christmas!"
    else
      // belt-and-suspenders
      // we have already handled Dec 24 above.
      daysTilChristmasMessage = "Tomorrow is Christmas!";
  return daysTilChristmasMessage;
}
// -->
</SCRIPT>
</HEAD>
<BODY BGCOLOR="white">
```

```
<H1>Time-based Customizer</H1>
<SCRIPT LANGUAGE="JavaScript">
document.write("<H2>");
var theHours = getHours();
if (theHours > 18)
  document.write("Good evening.");
else if (theHours > 12)
 document.write("Good afternoon.");
else if (theHours > 6)
  document.write("Good morning.");
else
 document.write("Good grief, what are you doing up at this hour?");
document.write("</H2>");
document.write(tilChristmas());
</SCRIPT>
<NOSCRIPT>
<H2>Welcome to our site!</H2>
</NOSCRIPT>
</BODY>
</HTML>
```

Figure 7.5 shows how this page would appear at 9 A.M. local time on December 23.

**FIG. 7.5**

The customizer displays a different image, depending upon the client's time of day and date.

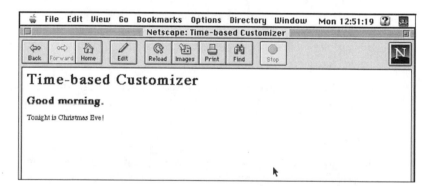

Note that the `tilChristmas()` function takes into account some of the inconsistencies in the ways in which people count down toward Christmas. If you ask the question, "How many days until Christmas?" midday on December 22, many people will answer, "3." On the evening of the same day, the answer changes to "2." During the day on December 24, people will tell you there's just one day until Christmas but, by evening, they're wishing you a merry Christmas Eve. Of course, all day on December 25 is Christmas, regardless of the time of day, but one second after midnight the countdown resumes again for another 364 days.

While the rules are complex (and subject to vigorous debate), the code is straightforward. Whatever rules you decide are appropriate for counting down toward Christmas or some other special event, just follow the template given in Listing 7.5

Part

II

Ch

7

**N O T E**   Listing 7.5 includes a <NOSCRIPT>...</NOSCRIPT> section. If the visitor's browser does not understand JavaScript, it will display the greeting in the <NOSCRIPT> section. You can test this code by turning off JavaScript in your browser; in Navigator, select Edit, Preferences, Network Preferences, then choose the Languages tab and turn JavaScript off. ■

# The *Array* Object

An *array* is an indexed variable—it can store many different values. In JavaScript, those values may be numbers, strings, objects, or even other arrays. In fact, JavaScript uses arrays to implement objects. This section introduces the basics of array setup and use.

▶ **See** "JavaScript's Associative Arrays," **p. 289**, for an advanced treatment of arrays in JavaScript.

Most programming languages, including JavaScript, begin counting array elements with the zeroth element. Thus, an array with ten elements will have an element 0, an element 1, and so on to element 9. The elements are represented by using square brackets—if the array's name is anArray, the third element is anArray[2]. (Remember, the first element is anArray[0].)

In most programming languages, the number of elements in an array is fixed. If you build a ten-element array, that array has ten elements from the time it comes into existence until it is destroyed. JavaScript is more flexible; you can add and delete elements while your program is running. With this flexibility comes a price—you, and not JavaScript, need to keep track of how many elements are currently in your array.

By convention, the first element in a JavaScript array is used to store the size of the array. Thus, if you had a ten-element array named myArray, myArray[0] would be set equal to 10.

> **CAUTION**
>
> Do not rely on JavaScript to update the length property in element zero for you. You should set this property yourself when you initially build the array and you should maintain it if you change the number of elements.
>
> If you attempt to refer to an array element that has not been initialized, you may get a JavaScript error or JavaScript may just respond with an invalid value.

## Uses of Arrays

You'll find arrays useful in two circumstances. First, if you want to build an object, use an associative array to store the names and values of each of the object's properties. This application of arrays is the subject of Chapter 11, "Creating Your Own JavaScript Objects."

A second use of arrays is to deal with a number of similar items or objects. Recall from the calculator example in Chapter 6, "The *Math* Object," that operator precedence could have been implemented if we had maintained the operators and values in an array. Many dynamic data structures, such as stacks, queues, and dequeues, can be implemented by using a JavaScript array.

Because JavaScript enables you to build arrays of arrays, you can build an array of similar objects and implement each object as an associative array. For example, suppose you are building a vehicle maintenance database. Each vehicle is an object with properties like lastLube and tuneupDue. You could then build an array called vehicle, so that vehicle[*n*] holds the data on vehicle *n*, and vehicle[0] holds the length of the array.

## The Vehicle Maintenance Database

Here's a function to build a vehicle object for the database introduced in the previous section:

```
function vehicle(theName,
                 theYear,
                 theVIN,
                 theMileage,
                 mtheLastLube,
                 mtheLubePeriod,
                 dtheLastTuneUp,
                 dtheTuneUpPeriod)
{
// NOTE: LastLube and LubePeriod are in miles, but
//       LastTuneUp is a date,and theTuneUpPeriod is in days.
//       We use "Hungarian notation" to remind ourselves of this difference
  this.length = 8;
  this.name = theName;
  this.year = theYear;
  this.VIN = theVin;
  this.mileage = theMileage;
  this.lastLube = theLastLube;
  this.lubePeriod = theLubePeriod;
  this.lastTuneUp = new Date(theLastTuneUp);
  this.tuneUpPeriod = theTuneUpPeriod;
}
```

You use a function like this by writing

```
var aVehicle = new vehicle("Chevy Pickup", 1995, 12345678,
➥34567, 20000, "July 1, 1996", 183);
```

This vehicle is a 1995 Chevy Pickup with Vehicle Identification Number (VIN) 12345678. The last lube was performed with the mileage reading 34567; a lube is due every 20,000 miles. The last tune-up was performed on July 1, 1996. A tune-up is due every six months (approximately 183 days).

You can build an array of vehicles by writing an array initialization function:

```
function fleet( howMany, initstr)
{
  this.length = howMany;
```

Part
II

Ch
7

```
  for (var i=1; i<=howMany; i++)
  {
    this[i] = initstr;
  }
}
```

If you write

```
var myFleet = new fleet(10, "-");
```

you'll get a fleet of 10 vehicles stored in an array with 11 elements. (Remember that element zero is used to store the length.) Now you can use the array elements to store vehicles:

```
var myFleet[1] = new vehicle("Ford Wagon", 1989, 23456789,
➡89012, 2000, "Nov 10, 1996", 183);
```

Over time, the size of the fleet may outgrow the ten elements initially allocated to `myFleet`. When that happens, you must remember to update the length property of the array:

```
var myFleet[11] = new vehicle("Dodge Van", 1993, 34567890,
➡56789, 2000, "Oct 12, 1996", 183);
myFleet.length += 1;
```

If you forget to update the `length` property, your script is likely to develop strange errors—eventually, the browser may exit unexpectedly. ●

# Interactive HTML Objects

**A**s we've seen in preceding chapters, JavaScript adds strings, dates, arrays, and other objects to the language of HTML. If these additions were all there was to JavaScript, JavaScript would be an interesting and useful addition to an HTML coder's tools. But there's much more to JavaScript—JavaScript allows you to download an interactive form that users can run on their computers, whether they use Windows 3.*x*, Windows 95 or NT, Macintosh, or UNIX.

To get the most out of JavaScript, place JavaScript functions in the <HEAD> section of your pages. Then, attach those functions to the elements of your HTML form by using event handlers such as onChange(), onClick(), and onSubmit(). The functions can be used to validate the contents of the form before sending it on to a host, or they can be used to turn your form into a sophisticated stand-alone calculator.

JavaScript is one of the first scripting languages to apply an object-oriented approach (via its roots in Java) to writing and modifying Web pages. JavaScript takes expressions in HTML, such as:

```
<A HREF="http://www.yahoo.com">Yahoo!</A>
```

and builds an object with methods and properties similar to the ones you read about in other chapters in Part II, "JavaScript In-Depth."

### Review the basics of HTML forms

Familiarize yourself with the standard HTML tags that make up a user input form and see how you can adapt them to other uses.

### Get to know JavaScript buttons, check boxes, and radio buttons

Learn how to integrate these elements of a form using JavaScript and how to trigger events through buttons.

### Find out how you can manipulate text fields

See how to use JavaScript to read and display information through text fields and text areas.

### Validate and submit a form under JavaScript control

Use Netscape JavaScript to check the information a visitor submits, without using a host-based program such as a CGI script or server-side JavaScript.

This and the next two chapters take you through the objects in JavaScript that are built and used when you write HTML code. This chapter concentrates on JavaScript objects that are related to HTML forms. Forms provide a key way for you to build a user interface with small, specific functions.

Before JavaScript, the process of validating information that a user entered via a form depended on sending and receiving information from a server-side Common Gateway Interface (CGI) script. A CGI script was often used for validating the information—checking that all of the fields were filled in correctly—and sending a response back to the user, confirming that the information had been sent successfully. The CGI script ran on the server so that all the information in the form had to be sent back to the server and then manipulated.

Using JavaScript, you can place much of the work on the client side, which can reduce dramatically the connection times between the client (the browser) and the server (your Web server). You can validate your form by allowing the JavaScript to inspect the contents of each field that the user has entered and to present an alert to the user if the information does not meet some specific requirements. For example, you can require that the user's name and address be non-blank, or that an account number be exactly twelve digits.

When you finish this chapter, you should be well on your way to building your first set of JavaScript scripts for your site. Most of the sites that you find today were built on the following concepts, which appear in this chapter:

- The ability to use forms to lay out input and output areas
- Buttons to accept questions, replies, or other input
- "Back end" JavaScript to interpret that input

Once you are using these capabilities, you have the beginnings of a full-fledged application. The ability to use the Web browser's GUI (Graphical User Interface) to develop small programs quickly, substantially reduces your development cost and time to market. ■

# Review of HTML Forms

Before we apply JavaScript to HTML forms, let's first review the various HTML tags that allow you to display a form. Table 8.1 summarizes these tags.

**Table 8.1   Use Standard HTML 3.2 Tags to Develop a Web Form**

| Tag Example | Meaning |
| --- | --- |
| `<FORM ACTION="URL" METHOD="GET"></FORM>` | Defines a form |
| `<FORM ENCTYPE="multipart/form-data"></FORM>` | Uploads a file via a form |
| `<INPUT TYPE="text">` | Input field |
| `<INPUT TYPE="text" NAME="somename">` | Field name |
| `<INPUT TYPE="text" VALUE="somevalue">` | Field value |

| Tag Example | Meaning |
| --- | --- |
| `<INPUT TYPE="checkbox" CHECKED>` | Checked check box |
| `<INPUT TYPE="text" SIZE=6>` | Field size in characters |
| `<INPUT MAXLENGTH="100">` | Maximum length of field |
| `<SELECT></SELECT>` | Selection list |
| `<SELECT NAME="somename">` | Selection list name |
| `<SELECT SIZE="6">` | Number of options in list |
| `<SELECT MULTIPLE>` | Allows multiple selections |
| `<OPTION>sometext` | Option |
| `<OPTION VALUE=10>sometext` | Option with specific value |
| `<OPTION SELECTED>` | Default option |
| `<TEXTAREA ROWS="5" COLS="5">...</TEXTAREA>` | Text area input box size |
| `<TEXTAREA NAME="somename">...</TEXTAREA>` | Text area name |
| `<TEXTAREA WRAP=OFF>` | Wraps the text |

**N O T E** The latest version of the HTML specification is available online at **http://www.w3.org/ pub/WWW/TR/WD-html32/**. This URL points to the draft specification of HTML 3.2. It may be replaced at any time—if it is replaced, look for links at **http://www.w3.org/pub/WWW/TR/** for a newer version. ▪

Information on forms and form elements is available in the HTML 3.2 specification, in the section, "The BODY element and its children." For more details on forms, you may also want to see Request For Comments (RFC) 1867.

# The *<FORM>* Tag

This tag must begin and end your form. In the `<FORM>` tag, you may specify attributes, including:

- ACTION is the URL of the program that processes the contents of the form. This URL may point to a server-side JavaScript program or a Common Gateway Interface (CGI) program.

- METHOD is the way in which the browser returns the form's information to the ACTION URL. The METHOD may be POST or GET and must match the method used by the ACTION program.

- ENCTYPE is the MIME type of the information you upload to a server. (File upload was first developed by Netscape, but is now part of the HTML 3.2 standard and is becoming available in many browsers.)

# The *<INPUT>* Tag

This tag adds an input field to the form. Each input field has a type—the default type is a text field. For example, the line

```
<INPUT NAME="Address">
```

adds a text input field within the form. When the contents of the form are submitted to the ACTION URL, the name Address will be associated with the data in the field.

You can add additional attributes to the <INPUT> tag:

- NAME is the name of this field.
- VALUE is the string or numeric value that is used to initialize this field.
- CHECKED applies to check boxes and radio boxes and determines whether they are checked when the page is loaded.
- TYPE determines which type of input this field is. The types include Text, Password (a text box that does not reveal its contents when you type into it), Checkbox, Radio, Image (used to implement client-side image maps), Hidden, SUBMIT, and RESET.
- SIZE is the size of the input field (in number of characters) for text or password types.
- MAXLENGTH sets the maximum number of characters to be allowed within a field of a text or password type.

**TIP** HTML is case-insensitive. JavaScript is case-sensitive. For example, <INPUT TYPE="text"> and <input type="TEXT"> are both treated the same because these tags are interpreted by the HTML browser, but TRUE is not the same as the Boolean literal true in JavaScript. When you're using tools such as case-sensitive editors, grep, or server-side JavaScript programs to write and maintain client-side JavaScript, you'll often find it convenient to have a standard for capitalization, even in your HTML. This chapter uses uppercase for tags and attributes, and mixed case for attribute values.

Figure 8.1 shows a form built up from various <INPUT> elements. Listing 8.1 shows the corresponding HTML.

### Listing 8.1 A Complete HTML Form

```
<!DOCTYPE HTML PUBLIC "-//W3C//DTD HTML 3.2//EN">
<HTML>
<HEAD>
<TITLE>A complete HTML form</TITLE>
<META NAME="Author" CONTENT="Michael Morgan">
<META NAME="GENERATOR" CONTENT="User-Agent: Mozilla/3.01Gold (Macintosh; I; PPC)">
</HEAD>
<BODY>
<H1>A Complete HTML Form</H1>
<FORM ACTION="http://www.dse.com/books/SEUJavaScript/complete.cgi">
<P>
Please enter some text:
```

```
<INPUT TYPE="Text" NAME="theTextField" VALUE="Enter text here." SIZE=20>
<BR>What's your password:
<INPUT TYPE="Password" NAME="thePassword" SIZE=8>
<BR>Please enter a number:
<INPUT TYPE="Text" NAME="aNumericField" SIZE=2>
</P>
<P>
<BR>Choose as many as you like:<BR>
<INPUT TYPE="Checkbox" NAME="Rudolph" CHECKED>Rudolph
<INPUT TYPE="Checkbox" NAME="Dasher">Dasher
<INPUT TYPE="Checkbox" NAME="Dancer">Dancer
<INPUT TYPE="Checkbox" NAME="Prancer">Prancer<BR>
<INPUT TYPE="Checkbox" NAME="Comet">Comet
<INPUT TYPE="Checkbox" NAME="Cupid">Cupid
<INPUT TYPE="Checkbox" NAME="Donner">Donner
<INPUT TYPE="Checkbox" NAME="Vixen">Vixen
</P>
<P>
Choose one of the following:<BR>
<INPUT TYPE="Radio" NAME="hero" CHECKED>David<BR>
<INPUT TYPE="Radio" NAME="hero">Goliath<BR>
</P>
<P>
<INPUT TYPE="Submit" VALUE="Send">
<INPUT TYPE="Reset" VALUE="Reset">
</P>
</FORM>
</BODY>
</HTML>
```

**FIG. 8.1**
You can build a complete form by using only the <FORM> and <INPUT> tags.

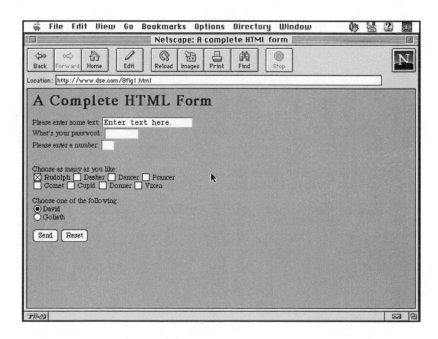

**TIP**  Many HTML writers set the value of their form's RESET button to Clear. This practice can lead to confusion. The RESET button does not clear the form—it resets the contents to the values they had before the user changed them. As you build increasingly sophisticated forms, you will have many occasions when you want to set the form's elements to initial, non-blank values. Get in the habit of using a word like RESET for the RESET button's value rather than Clear.

## The *<SELECT>* Tag

This tag presents either a scrolling list of choices or a pop-up menu. You can use <SELECT> to put up a single menu option that "pops open" to reveal all of the options, or you can see a scrolling list of options. Pop-up menus are best for those times when you want someone to choose a single option. As a practical matter, you should limit pop-up menus to those times when the number of options is smaller than five. As your site grows, you might choose to stick with a pop-up menu until the number of options is between seven and nine. Around that time, consider switching to a scrolling list—your users will find this design less confusing. When you put up a scrolling list with more than seven options, set the SIZE attribute to some number between five and seven and allow the user to scroll to get the rest of the options.

Here are the attributes you use with <SELECT>. Try out many variations on a test Web page to see how changing the attributes changes the way the list is shown:

- NAME is the name of the data.
- SIZE determines how many choices to show. If set to 1 or omitted, the <SELECT> is rendered as a pop-up menu. If set to 2 or more, the <SELECT> becomes a scrolling list.
- MULTIPLE allows you to select multiple options and always renders a scrolling list.

 **TIP**  The exact mechanism by which the scrolling list allows multiple selections depends upon the browser and is generally platform-specific. Avoid instructions in your site that tell the user, for example, to "shift-click," unless you also make your help files platform-specific.

## The *<OPTION>* Tag

Contained within the <SELECT> and </SELECT> tags, the <OPTION> tag designates a selectable item. The <OPTION> tag may have two attributes:

- VALUE is the value returned when the form is submitted if this option is selected.
- SELECTED means when the page is loaded, this option is selected by default.

For example, suppose you want a form that will submit a U.S. mailing address. You might write a <SELECT> tag like this one:

```
<SELECT NAME="theState" SIZE=5>
<OPTION VALUE="AR">Arkansas
<OPTION VALUE="AL">Alabama
<OPTION VALUE="AK">Alaska
...
<OPTION VALUE="WY">Wyoming
</SELECT>
```

With this design, the user sees the full name of the state, while the ACTION URL gets the two-letter abbreviation.

## The <TEXTAREA> Tag

Sometimes you need a larger space for text than a simple text input affords. For example, you may want to allow a visitor to your site to enter comments about your site's design and content. The <TEXTAREA> tag provides an area for a user to enter multiple lines of text. The following list describes each attribute you can use with a <TEXTAREA> tag:

- NAME defines the name for the information.

- ROWS is the number of rows in this field.

- COLS is the number of characters wide this field is.

- WRAP determines how text flows inside a text area. You have three options for this attribute:

    - OFF    No text wrap.

    - VIRTUAL    Text flows to the right border then wraps to the next line. It will be submitted as one line, without new lines. So, although the text appears to wrap, it will be one line when sent to the server (or script).

    - PHYSICAL    Text flows beyond the right border beyond the text area window. When it is submitted, the text will be wrapped based on any new lines.

**N O T E**    WRAP is not yet part of the HTML standard but is supported by popular browsers such as Netscape Navigator and Microsoft Internet Explorer. ▓

# HTML Objects in JavaScript

This section introduces JavaScript's HTML objects that relate to forms. With each of these objects, you will see further how to build a form that will be able to respond instantly to user input. You will learn about buttons, check boxes, and radio buttons. These form elements consist of all the "clickable" elements. Mouse clicks on these elements can be used to trigger JavaScript functions or to submit a form to either your home server or another JavaScript script running on the client's machine. You can get quite a bit of mileage out of these elements and Netscape has enhanced them with its ability to monitor their status (such as if a radio button is on or off).

When you begin to use JavaScript in your forms, you gain access to three new attributes in the `<FORM>` tag: NAME, TARGET, and onSubmit. Use TARGET to specify which window or frame gets the responses. Use onSubmit to specify a JavaScript function that gets called when the user attempts to submit the form. See the section "Form Validation" later in this chapter to learn more about onSubmit.

▶ **See** "Using Frames," **p. 469,** to learn more about specifying TARGETs.

JavaScript places each form on a page in an array called forms in the document object. You can access a form by its position in the array (e.g., document.forms[0]) or by its name. Thus, if your page contains the lines:

```
<FORM NAME="thisForm">
<INPUT TYPE="Text" NAME="Input1" VALUE="Hi, there!">
</FORM>
```

Your JavaScript functions can refer to this form as document.forms[0] or by the name: thisForm.

# The *Button* Object

The Button object is a new type of INPUT tag that enables you to create general-purpose buttons in a form. You can use these buttons to activate any function, to open a new URL, or to perform any other action that JavaScript can initiate. To define a Button object, use the following syntax:

```
<INPUT
  TYPE="Button"
  NAME="nameInside"
  VALUE="nameOnButton"
  [onClick="handlerText"]>
```

Listing 8.2 shows how to connect the onClick() event handler of a button to a JavaScript function. Recall from the section entitled "Functions and Objects" in Chapter 2, "JavaScript: The Language," that functions should be defined in the `<HEAD>` section of the page and should be protected from browsers that do not understand JavaScript with the comment characters (`<!--...//-->`).

**Listing 8.2   A Button in Action**

```
<HTML>
<HEAD>
<TITLE>Button Demo</TITLE>
<SCRIPT LANGUAGE="JavaScript">
<!-- hide script from other browsers
function hey()
{
  document.alert("Hey there! You pushed the button!")
}
// end hiding from other browsers -->
</SCRIPT>
</HEAD>
```

```
<BODY>
<H1>Button Demonstration</H1>
<FORM>
<h2>Click below for an alert!</h2>
<INPUT TYPE="Button" NAME="alertButton" VALUE="Click Me!" onClick="hey()">
</FORM>
</BODY>
</HTML>
```

You can access the properties of the button in Listing 8.2 by using either of the following lines of code:

```
document.forms[0].elements[0].name
```

or

```
alertButton.name
```

 **TIP** JavaScript is not case-sensitive—`alertButton` is the same as `alertbutton`. Like HTML, you should adopt a capitalization style for JavaScript that is easy to read and easy for you to remember when you *do* use case-sensitive tools (such as some editors).

If you want to retrieve the name of the button as a `string` object, you can use either of the following examples—which return `"Click Me!"`:

```
document.forms[0].elements[0].value
```

or

```
alertbutton.value
```

> **CAUTION**
>
> Once you have a `Button` object on your page, you can change its value, but the text on the button does not change to reflect this. This effect is caused by the fact that the button was written to the screen when the page was loaded and cannot be changed unless the page is reloaded. Reloading the page alone does not implement the change because the button reverts to its default value from the HTML code when it is reloaded.

▶ **See** "Advanced Applets," **p. 359**, for more information on how to use LiveConnect to hook JavaScript to Java.

▶ **See** "LiveConnect and JavaScript," **p. 383**

▶ **See** "JavaScript on the Server," **p. 589**, to learn more about server-side JavaScript (also known as LiveWire JavaScript).

# Text Fields

This section gives you experience working with the text-based input fields in an HTML form and shows how you can use JavaScript to enhance these input fields' usefulness to you as a script writer.

## The *Text* Object

The text input field in an HTML document is your workhorse for inputting many types of information. Most other types of input in forms are derivations of this kind of input.

The text input field is simply a small box of a fixed size that contains a cursor when you click it. It allows a user to type in information such as a name, a date, or any other kind of information. If the text a user types is too long for the box, the text scrolls to the left.

In JavaScript, this field serves a new purpose. Not only can a user using the form enter information into this field, but the script itself can also enter information. In Chapter 7, "The *Date* and *Array* Objects," you saw a script that used this field to display a constantly changing digital clock.

You add a JavaScript Text object by using this syntax:

```
<INPUT
  TYPE="text"
  NAME="textName"
  VALUE="textValue"
  SIZE=integer
  [onBlur="handlerText"]
  [onChange="handlerText"]
  [onFocus="handlerText"]
  [onSelect="handlerText"]>
```

Listing 8.3 shows an example of how to use a Text object.

### Listing 8.3 An Example with a *Text* Object

```
<HTML>
<HEAD>
<TITLE>Text Area Demo</TITLE>
</HEAD>
<BODY>
<FORM>
<INPUT TYPE="Text" NAME="todaysDate" VALUE="" SIZE="5"
  onBlur="getDate()" onChange="setDate()"
  onFocus="alert('Set the date')"
  onSelect="alert('Really change?')">
</FORM>
</BODY>
</HTML>
```

The Text object's properties reflect the information you provide in the tag when you create the object. Table 8.2 is a listing of those properties, with an example of how you access them.

### Table 8.2  Use a *Text* Object's Properties to Get and (in the Case of *VALUE*) Set Its Attributes

| Property | Example | Description |
| --- | --- | --- |
| defaultValue | myText.defaultValue | The value of the input tag at page load time |
| name | myText.name | The NAME argument |
| value | formName.elements[0].value | VALUE argument |

You can act on this object in a number of ways, either indirectly by another function, or directly by using the event handlers contained in the object. Tables 8.3 and 8.4 list the methods and event handlers associated with the Text object.

### Table 8.3  Use the *Text* Object's Methods from a Function to Simulate User Actions on the Field

| Method | Example | Description |
| --- | --- | --- |
| focus | myText.focus() | Equivalent to clicking this field |
| blur | myText.blur() | Equivalent to clicking another field after using this one |
| select | myText.select() | Equivalent to dragging the mouse across all the text in this field, selecting it |

### Table 8.4  The *Text* Object's Event Handlers Connect the User to the Field

| Event Handler | Example | Description |
| --- | --- | --- |
| onBlur | `<input type=text onBlur="alert ('blur!)">` | Runs "alert()" when focus leaves this field |
| onChange | `<input type=text onChange="alert ('changed')">` | Runs "alert()" if the text has changed when focus leaves this field |
| onFocus | `<input type=text onFocus="alert ('start typing!')">` | Runs "alert()" when user clicks in (or otherwise gives focus to) this field |
| onSelect | `<input type=text onSelect="alert ('text selected!')">` | Runs "alert()" once some text in this field is selected |

The script in Listing 8.4 places information about a link in a text field below a series of links when a user passes the mouse over each link. This program illustrates how you can use other event handlers to pass information to a text field.

**Listing 8.4    Event Handlers and Text Fields**

```
<HTML>
<HEAD>
<TITLE>JavaScript Text Object Demo</TITLE>
<SCRIPT LANGUAGE="JavaScript">
<!-- hide from other browsers
var description="";
function showLink(description)
{
    document.forms[0].elements[0].value=description;
}
// stop hiding -->
</SCRIPT>
</HEAD>
<BODY>
<H1>JavaScript Text Object Demo</H1>
<FORM>
<INPUT TYPE="Text" SIZE=60 >
</FORM>
<A HREF="http://www.yahoo.com/" onMouseOver="showLink('An important Web search
engine')">Yahoo</A><BR>
<A HREF ="http://www.mcp.com/" onMouseOver="showLink('The world\'s largest
➥publisher of computer books')">Macmillan Computer Publishing</A><BR>
<A HREF ="http://www.dse.com/" onMouseOver="showLink('A full-service Web service
provider')">DSE</A><BR>
</BODY>
</HTML>
```

As the user passes his or her cursor over each link, the text in the text field changes. You can easily modify this code to display helpful information about links on your own page, beyond the URL that displays at the bottom left of the Netscape Navigator (which is called the status area).

## The *TextArea* Object

When you need a user to input more than just one line of text in a form, use the TextArea input type. For example, if you are providing the user with an e-mail feedback form, you may want to allow space for the user to type in a note. The syntax for a text area is:

```
<TEXTAREA
  NAME="textAreaName"
  ROWS=integer
  COLS=integer
  WRAP=on¦off¦physical¦virtual
  [onBlur="handlerText"]
  [onChange="handerText"]
  [onFocus="handlerText"]
  [onSelect="handlerText"]>
```

```
textToDisplay
</TEXTAREA>
```

A `TextArea` object uses the same properties, methods, and events as does the `Text` object (see Tables 8.2, 8.3, and 8.4). You can provide default text to display in this field by adding text between the `<TEXTAREA>` and `</TEXTAREA>` tags.

Figure 8.2 shows the controls of an adventure game by Andrew Wooldridge, featuring the exploits of "Foobar the Bazbarian." The large field at the top of the page is a text area. As the game proceeds, the script changes the value of the text area, writing a description of the current location into that field.

**FIG. 8.2**
The "Foobar" adventure game uses text fields, buttons, and a text area as its principal controls.

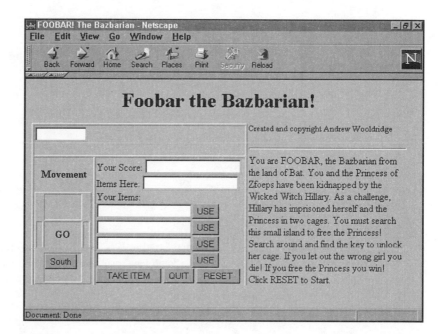

## The *Hidden* Object

Often when you build an interactive form, you want to keep some information hidden, yet still pass this information on to the server when the form is submitted. For example, you may want to associate an identifying string with the user in order to build multi-page forms. You also might want to allow the user to select some preference or option and remember that choice on a later page.

You can keep track of this information with a hidden field. This field is often used in place of the browser's cookies for compatibility with browsers that do not support the cookie specification. Hidden fields contain text information and are not displayed on the screen with the rest of the form.

**NOTE**   Cookies are small strings of text; they are stored either in a single file named COOKIES.TXT or in separate files in a folder named COOKIES. They are often used to store information about the end user or the end user's computer. The server writes this text to the end user's machine and will reread it when that end user visits again. Cookies can be set up so that they persist between a user's visits to the site, or they can expire when the user quits out of the browser. Although this feature is very useful, there are still some debates as to its security and validity of use. For more information on cookies, see Chapter 23, "Using Cookies in Advanced Applications." ▪

To add a `Hidden` object, use the following syntax:

```
<INPUT
  TYPE="Hidden"
  NAME="hiddenName"
  [VALUE = "textValue"]>
```

You can access the properties of this object by using the following:

- `hiddenName.propertyName`
- `formName.elements[index].propertyName`

For example, the following code returns `"Hi, there!"`:

```
<FORM>
<INPUT TYPE=Hidden NAME=hideme VALUE="Hi, there!">
</FORM>
...

document.write(hideme.value);
```

Using hidden fields adds a sense of "state" to the Web. The Hypertext Transfer Protocol (HTTP)—the protocol of the Web—is a "stateless" protocol. A Web site has no way of knowing if a visitor to that Web site was there just moments ago or if the visitor is visiting for the first time. Using the hidden field, you can place a hidden reminder to your software on the Web site and retrieve that reminder whenever the user submits that form to you.

## The *Password* Object

The password input field is useful for those times when you need to build a logon screen and keep the password hidden from view. Any time you want the information hidden from sight as a user types that information on the screen, use the password input field. To add this field to a form, use the following syntax:

```
<INPUT
  TYPE="Password"
  NAME="PasswordName"
  [SIZE=integer]
  [VALUE="textValue"]
  [onBlur="handlerText"]
  [onFocus="handlerText"]
  [onSelect="handlerText"]>
```

You can access the properties and methods of the Password object just as if it were a Text object.

The Password object uses the focus, blur, and select event handlers as methods. However, JScript imposes a certain security restriction on the use of the Password object. It is not possible to check the validity of a password before a user actually sends it back to the server for a login. This restriction was introduced to prevent authors of malicious script code from capturing passwords. For this reason, you cannot get at the Value field of a Password object.

**CAUTION**

Don't confuse the Password object with the Hidden object. The Password object conceals what a user types into a text entry field, while a Hidden object simply hides the whole field.

# Selection Elements

Sometimes you want to constrain the user to a short range of choices. You can use radio buttons and SELECT tags to allow the user to choose one of several options. You can use check boxes and SELECT tags (with the Multiple attribute set) to allow the user to specify more than one choice. This section shows how JavaScript enhances these elements.

## The *Checkbox* Object

The Checkbox object is displayed inside a form and appears as a small box with or without a mark (which usually resembles an 'X') inside it. Think of a check box as an On/Off switch. A user can flip this switch on or off by clicking inside this box.

Clicking here also triggers an onClick event in your script. You create a check box via the following syntax:

```
<INPUT
  TYPE="Checkbox"
  NAME="checkboxName"
  VALUE="checkboxValue"
  [CHECKED]
  [onClick="handlerText"]>
  textToDisplay
```

Accessing the properties of this object is very similar to accessing the properties of the Button object. The properties are as follows:

- ■ CHECKED indicates true or false to specify if the check box is currently checked.
- ■ DEFAULTCHECKED indicates whether or not the check box was marked checked when the page was initially loaded.
- ■ NAME indicates the name of the check box.
- ■ VALUE indicates the value that is returned by the form if the check box is checked. (The value defaults to the string, "On.")

Listing 8.5 shows an example of using the Checkbox object in a script.

### Listing 8.5   Using the *Checkbox* Object

```
<HTML>
<HEAD>
<TITLE>Checkbox Demo</TITLE>
<SCRIPT LANGUAGE="JavaScript">
function mystatus()
{
  (document.theForm.theCheckbox.checked) ?
    alert("The box is checked") :
    alert("The box is not checked! Oh no!")
}
</SCRIPT>
<FORM NAME="theForm">
<INPUT TYPE="checkbox" NAME="theCheckbox" VALUE="myValue" onClick="mystatus()">
</FORM>
</HTML>
```

# The *Radio* Object

Radio buttons allow a user to make a choice of a single selection from many—usually a list of related items from which you want the user to pick only one choice.

The Radio object is very similar to the Checkbox object, except that a series of Radio objects with the same NAME attribute toggle all of the radio buttons off except for the one that was picked. You create a Radio object by using the following syntax:

```
<INPUT
  TYPE="Radio"
  NAME="radioName"
  [CHECKED]
  [onClick = "handlerText"]>
  textToDisplay
```

Accessing information from the Radio object is done in a slightly different manner than accessing information from the Checkbox object. Since all of the radio buttons of a given group have the same NAME attribute, you access individual radio buttons by adding an index value to the NAME. You can use code like that in any of these lines:

```
radioName[index1].propertyName
radioName[index1].methodName
formname.elements[index2].propertyName
formname.elements[index2].methodName
```

You can simulate a click on a specific radio button in JavaScript by using the following:

```
radioName[index1].click
```

Listing 8.6 is an example of using radio buttons with JavaScript.

**Listing 8.6    Radio Button Example**

```
<HTML>
<HEAD>
</HEAD>
<BODY>
<FORM NAME="Game">
<INPUT TYPE="Text" NAME="Output" size=15>
<INPUT TYPE="Radio" NAME="Choice" VALUE="Rock"
  onClick="Game.Output.value='The Rock'">The rock
<INPUT TYPE="Radio" NAME="Choice" VALUE= "Scissors"
  onClick="Game.Output.value='The Scissors'">The scissors
<INPUT TYPE="Radio" NAME="Choice" VALUE="Paper"
  onClick="Game.Output.Value='The Paper'">The paper
</FORM>
</BODY>
</HTML>
```

This piece of code allows a user to pick one of the three choices—rock, paper, or scissors—which then shows up in the text field box. If the user wants to choose an alternative not listed on the radio buttons, then he or she just has to type it into the box. Radio buttons that enter data into an editable text field offer a quick way for you to offer both a series of preset choices as well as a customized choice.

# Using the *<SELECT>* Tag with JavaScript

The SELECT object is displayed inside a form and appears as a pop-up menu or a scrolling list, depending upon how you set the SIZE attribute.

If you, as the HTML coder, specify the MULTIPLE attribute, the end user can choose more than one option. If you specify MULTIPLE, the SELECT object is displayed as a scrolling list, even if you leave SIZE at its default of 1.

You add a SELECT object to your form by using the following syntax:

```
<SELECT
  NAME="selectName"
  [SIZE=integer]
  [MULTIPLE]
  [onBlur="handlerText"]
  [onChange="handlerText"]
  [onFocus="handlerText"]>
<OPTION VALUE="optionValue" [SELECTED]>testToDisplay
[<OPTION ...]
</SELECT>
```

Accessing the properties of this object is very similar to accessing the properties of the other object's object. The properties are as follows:

- NAME indicates the name of the SELECT object.
- LENGTH indicates the number of options in the SELECT object.

- SELECTEDINDEX indicates the index of the selected option. If the SELECT object supports multiple selections, SELECTEDINDEX reflects the first selected option.
- OPTIONS is an array of OPTION tags.

**N O T E** Unlike Text and Button objects, the SELECT object contains an array within its structure. To get all of the benefit from a SELECT object, your code should read the properties of the OPTIONs in the OPTIONS array as well as the code of the SELECT object itself.

Note that the OPTIONs' properties are read-only. You cannot change the options at runtime. ■

**Accessing the *OPTIONS* Array**    One member of the SELECT object is the OPTIONS array. The members of the OPTIONS array are OPTION objects. Here are the properties of the OPTION object:

- defaultSelected—reflects the SELECTED attribute
- index—returns the index of an option
- length—returns the number of options in a SELECT object
- name—returns the NAME attribute
- selected—lets you set the selected option from JavaScript
- selectedIndex—returns the index of the selected option
- text—returns the text that follows an OPTION tag
- value—returns the Value attribute

**Reading Multiple Selections**    If you set the Multiple attribute in the <SELECT> tag, the end user may choose more than one option, but selectedIndex returns the index of the first selected option only.

In client-side JavaScript, you should iterate through the options; use the selected property to determine which options have been selected.

**T I P** If you are using server-side JavaScript, you need to use a two-step process to read multiple options. First, determine the number of selected options by calling getOptionValueCount(); this function takes a parameter that is the name of the SELECT statement. Iterate through the selected options by using getOptionValue(). Again, the parameters are the name of the SELECT statement and the index value. You can find details and examples of both of these functions in the LiveWire Developer's Guide that comes with LiveWire

▶ **See** "HTML with JavaScript," **p. 596**, for more information on server-side JavaScript.

**Hands-On the *SELECT* Object**    Listing 8.7 shows an example of using the Checkbox object in a script.

**Listing 8.7    Using the *Checkbox* Object**

```
<HTML>
<HEAD>
<TITLE>Checkbox Demo</TITLE>
<SCRIPT LANGUAGE="JavaScript">
function mystatus()
{
  (document.theForm.theCheckbox.checked) ?
    alert("The box is checked") :
    alert("The box is not checked! Oh no!")
}
</SCRIPT>
<FORM NAME="theForm">
<INPUT TYPE="checkbox" NAME="theCheckbox" VALUE="myValue" onClick="mystatus()">
</FORM>
</HTML>
```

# Form Validation

This section covers the final pieces of information you need to complete your exploration of JavaScript and forms. The last two form-based objects, SUBMIT and RESET, are accompanied by an example of a simple mail-in form that checks the input before it is sent back to you.

## The *SUBMIT* Object

The SUBMIT button was originally intended in HTML to be the final button a user would click to send a form back to the server. It would submit information, send feedback, or present a structured request for new information (you see this in search engines such as Yahoo!). With JavaScript, you can now use this button to send all of the information collected in a form to another window on your browser, or to the same window itself, which causes the contents of the window to change in some way. For example, you might change the background color of the window based on the user's choice on a form. You add a SUBMIT object to your form by using the following syntax:

```
<INPUT
  TYPE="Submit"
  NAME="submitName"
  VALUE="buttonText"
  [onClick = "handlerText"]>
```

You access this object's properties and methods with lines of code like:

```
submitName.propertyName
submitName.methodName(parameters)
formName.elements[index].propertyName
```

or

```
formName.elements[index].methodName(parameters)
```

When you click a SUBMIT button, it always loads a new page—even if that page is the same page you were already on. This behavior is useful in that you can use a form to change attributes of the current page and see them change when you submit the form. The SUBMIT object uses the onClick() event handler to process the user's click. You can simulate a click event within your program by using the *submitName*.click method.

> **CAUTION**
>
> Many new JavaScript programmers attempt to validate a form by running a validate function from the SUBMIT button's onClick() handler. That design doesn't work—once the SUBMIT button has been clicked, onClick() is powerless to stop the submission process.
>
> A better design is to use the onSubmit() handler in the <FORM> tag. An example of form validation using this design is coming up later in this chapter in the section titled "A Simple Form Validation Example."

## The *RESET* Object

The RESET button allows a user to completely reset a form's input fields to their defaults. Note that it does not explicitly clear all fields, though many HTML coders have that misconception. You add a RESET object to your form in JavaScript by using the following syntax:

```
<INPUT
  TYPE="Reset"
  NAME="resetName"
  VALUE="buttonText"
  [onClick ="handlerText"]>
```

To access its methods and properties, you use the same familiar syntax, as follows:

```
resetName.propertyName
resetName.methodName(parameters)
formName.elements[index].propertyName
```

or

```
formName.elements[index].methodName(parameters)
```

The RESET button uses the same onClick event handler and Click method as the SUBMIT object.

## A Simple Form Validation Example

Listing 8.8 shows a simple script that checks all of your input to see that you have placed the correct information inside each field. It then submits the form.

### Listing 8.8   Form Input Validation Example

```
<HTML>
<HEAD>
<TITLE>Validation.htm</TITLE>
<SCRIPT LANGUAGE="JavaScript">
```

```
<!-- hide me
function testone()
{
  var theResult = true;
  if (document.forms[0].elements[0].value=="")
  {
    alert("Please put a name in the first field!");
    theResult = false;
    document.forms[0].elements[0].focus();
    document.forms[0].elements[0].select();
  }
  return  theResult;
}
function testtwo ()
{
  var theResult = true;
  if (document.forms[0].elements[2].value.length < 5)
  {
    alert("Please input at least 5 characters.");
    theResult = false;
    document.forms[0].elements[2].focus();
    document.forms[0].elements[2].select();
  }
  return theResult;
}
function testthree()
{
  var theResult = true;
  if (document.forms[0].elements[4].value=="No")
  {
    alert("Please change field three!");
    theResult - false;
    document.forms[0].elements[4].focus();
    document.forms[0].elements[4].select();
  }
  return theResult;
}
function validate()
{
  var theResult = true;
  theResult = testone() && testtwo() && testthree();
  return theResult;
}
// end hiding -->
</SCRIPT>
</HEAD>
<BODY>
<H1>Form Validation Example</H1>
<FORM ACTION="http://www.dse.com/books/validate.cgi" METHOD="POST"
  onSubmit="return validate()">
Here is a series of fields that you must set before you can send this form.<BR>
<INPUT TYPE="Text" NAME="one" VALUE="">
Input your name (any text)
<INPUT TYPE="Button" NAME="Check" VALUE="Check Me" onClick="testone()">
<BR>
```

*continues*

**Listing 8.8   Continued**

```
<INPUT TYPE="Text" NAME="two">
Input at least 5 characters
<INPUT TYPE="Button" NAME="checktwo" VALUE="Check Me" onClick="testtwo()">
<BR>
<INPUT TYPE="Text" NAME="three" VALUE="No">
Change this text to something else.
<INPUT TYPE="Button" NAME="three" VALUE="Check Me" onClick="testthree()">
<BR>
<INPUT TYPE="Submit" VALUE="Send">
<INPUT TYPE="Reset" VALUE="Reset">
</FORM>
</BODY>
</HTML>
```

Figure 8.3 shows this script in action.

**FIG. 8.3**

The form validation script checks the contents of the form before the browser sends it to the server.

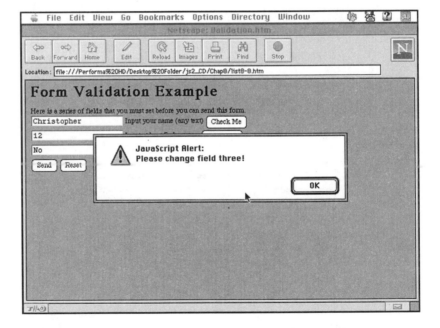

From the example in Listing 8.8, you can see how an input of type Button was used to check each field individually. In a real-world script, you could use either a Button input type (not a SUBMIT object) with an event handler, which would run a check on each field and then call the form's SUBMIT method, or you could keep the SUBMIT button and use the onSubmit event handler to run checks on all of the input fields at once.

You won't usually want to leave the "Check Me" buttons in production code, but you might want to add onChange() handlers to each field and call the field's validation routine from there. If you remove the "Check Me" buttons, be sure to change the indices on the elements array in the test functions (or, better still, use the field names).

One of the problems with form validation is that only JavaScript-aware browsers run the validation function. If you submit your form's contents to a CGI-script or LiveWire JavaScript on the server, your server-based program doesn't know whether the contents have been validated or not.

To solve this problem, add a new field,

```
<INPUT TYPE="Hidden" NAME="Validated" VALUE="false">
```

In validate(), set the value of Validated to true. On the server, check first for Validated == true. If Validated has been set to true, the validation function has run and the contents can be considered valid. If validate() never ran, the server should run its own validation routine on the contents and report any invalid fields back to the client. ●

# Advanced HTML Objects and Navigation

**Y**our users will demand quicker response time as you add more interactivity. Before JavaScript, most interactive features required that your Web page invoke a CGI script on the server. The more interactivity, the more the users have to wait for the server to deliver new documents. The response time improves dramatically as JavaScript handles interactivity on the browser side instead of waiting for CGI scripts.

Better response time has a tradeoff in that the size of your HTML files will increase when you add JavaScript. This occurs because your pages are more like applications and less like plain reading material. As your document gets larger, you will incorporate more navigational aids. You will create dynamic elements with JavaScript to let users quickly see the material they want and skip irrelevant information. And, you will do this without waiting for the server.

Controlling the flow of user interaction is critical to good design. You can confuse your users with the multiple windows and frames possible in the new browsers. The dynamic capability of JavaScript enables you to create new documents in response to your users' preferences. For example, if the viewer selects a favorite sport, the hyperlink named "Last Year's Champion" could vary based on the viewer's selection.

## Change the hyperlinks

Though you can't change the displayed text of a hyperlink, you can dynamically change where a link will take your user.

## Learn the importance of the *NAME* attribute

JavaScript puts document elements into arrays. You can reference them by the array index if you know which one to use, but you will find names easier to use.

## Select input verification

Multiple choice often leads to more accurate responses from users. JavaScript allows verification with the select element.

## Build a browser within a browser

With frames and dynamic hyperlinks, you can build a new type of browser. A complete example of this type of customization will be presented.

With JavaScript's features, you can transform the browser from static displays to interactive applications. There is a variety of examples in this chapter that let you try out the new dynamics of hyperlinks, anchors, and selection lists. The chapter concludes with a much larger application that shows you the possibilities of JavaScript. ▦

# Link In with JavaScript

Click and follow the designer's lead. That's how people navigate the Web: they follow the links chosen by the designer. Click the same link a hundred times and it takes you to the same page every time. Every user is different and has different expectations. For example, a link that's appropriate for an adult might be too complex for a young child.

This limitation of HTML drives many people to try to "build a better Web page." You probably looked at a few poorly designed Web pages and were frustrated by the hyperlinks designed into those pages. As a designer, you might have chosen other sites to link to. So people build other Web pages and try to make them perfect for their audiences. They still end up with pages in which the viewer follows the designer.

Your links are now dynamic with JavaScript. Based on the options a user can select, clicking the link takes the user to different places, without waiting for a CGI script to feed a page from the server. Also, by using the frames and windows, your existing page is not necessarily replaced by the new page. Your browser can be a kaleidoscope on the Web, simultaneously viewing multiple sites around the world. Or, you can pull in different publications based on the day of the week.

## Additions to the *LINK* Syntax

You are probably familiar with using a hyperlink in an HTML document. A very simple example is the following:

```
<A HREF="http://www.yoursite.com">Click here</A>
```

Your browser would display "Click here" as a hyperlink.

The reference of a LINK is an URL or a location. As seen in the preceding example, the World Wide Web protocol is http://. You also could have used the MailTo protocol (for example, **mailto:info@mailcall.com**). There are formats for FTP, Gopher, and File.

A new URL type is now defined for JavaScript. The protocol is simply javascript:. For example, you may specify JavaScript: history.go(-1) as the URL (Listing 9.1). When used as the URL for a LINK, the browser executes the statement following the colon. In the following example, it executes: history.go(-1). As a useful example, try adding the following line to any page:

```
<A HREF="JavaScript: history.go(-1)>Go back to previous page</A>
```

This is particularly useful on documents displayed in browser windows where you have disabled the toolbar.

When you click this hyperlink, the browser takes you back to the previous page in your history list. If you want to test this, open your browser and load your default home page. Then load a page that contains the HTML statement listed above, by itself. Clicking the hyperlink returns you to your default home page.

### Listing 9.1    Demo of *JavaScript* URL

```
<HTML><HEAD><TITLE>history.htm by Ray Daly</TITLE>
</HEAD><BODY>
<P>Juno said, "<A HREF="javascript:history.go(-1)">
History will repeat itself.</A>"<P>
</BODY></HTML>
```

The limitation on the `javascript:` protocol is that it evaluates its expression to a location. In other words, the result of the expression should be a string that represents a location. For example, earlier in your code you could have set a variable equal to an URL and then used the `javascript:` protocol in a link to jump to that location:

```
Var demoloc="http://www.microsoft.com"
<A HREF="javascript:demoloc">
```

**N O T E**   Internet Explorer 3.0 does not currently support the `about:` protocol or the `javascript:` protocol. Therefore, URLs such as "`about:plug-ins`" will not work at present. You will find that IE does not completely support JavaScript in other ways as well. ▨

## Properties of the *LINK* Object

Each object has properties. The properties of the `LINK` object tell you about the URL. There is also a property to tell you the target for the document. Listing 9.2 shows a small page that gives all of the `LINK` properties in action. When this page is loaded into Internet Explorer, Figure 9.1 results.

### Listing 9.2    Demo of *LINK* Object Properties

```
<HTML><HEAD><TITLE>linkprop.htm by Ray Daly</TITLE></HEAD><BODY><P>
<B>LINK[0]:   </B>
<A HREF="http://www.yoursite.com:80/mystuff/index.html?search=htmljive"
TARGET="parent.bottom">
http://www.yoursite.com:80/mystuff/index.html:80?search=htmljive</A>
<BR><B>LINK[1]:   </B>
<A HREF="http://www.yoursite.com:80/mystuff/index.html#anchorhere"
TARGET="parent.bottom">
http://www.yoursite.com:80/mystuff/index.html:80#anchorhere</A>
<BR><BR>>This demonstrates the properties of the LINK[0] object.
<SCRIPT LANGUAGE="JavaScript">
document.write( "<BR>hash = " + document.links[0].hash)
```

*continues*

**Listing 9.2 Continued**

```
document.write( "<BR>host = " + document.links[0].host)
document.write( "<BR>hostname = " + document.links[0].hostname)
document.write( "<BR>href = " + document.links[0].href)
document.write( "<BR>pathname = " + document.links[0].pathname)
document.write( "<BR>port = " + document.links[0].port)
document.write( "<BR>protocol = " + document.links[0].protocol)
document.write( "<BR>search = " + document.links[0].search)
document.write( "<BR>target = " + document.links[0].target)
document.write( "<P>>The LINK[0] has no hash. ")
document.write("However the LINK[1] has:<BR>")
document.write( "hash = " + document.links[1].hash)
document.write("<BR><BR>The number of links  = ")
document.write( document.links.length)
</SCRIPT></BODY></HTML>
```

**FIG. 9.1**

All of the properties, except TARGET, extract substrings from the HREF property.

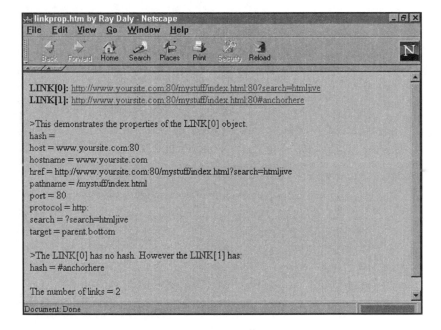

## The *NAME* Attribute Has New Significance

Prior to putting JavaScript into HTML pages, there was not much point in using the NAME attribute, so many tags remained nameless. NAME was used only for anchors and when sending form information to a CGI script.

As you use JavaScript to make your links dynamic, you need to distinguish between the various links on your page. The properties of the LINK object are accessible by using the following format:

```
document.links[index].propertyname
```

But, in using this format, you need to know the index number. The index number is assigned to each LINK object in sequence as it is loaded by the browser. The first link loaded has the index of 0, the second is 1, and so on. So you need to keep track of the order in which the LINK objects are loaded. This is the default method of accessing properties.

Often, a simpler means is to name the elements that are referenced by your JavaScript code. Therefore, using our first example, add the NAME attribute as follows:

```
<A NAME="myname" HREF="http://www.yoursite.com">Click here</A>
```

Now your JavaScript code can access the properties of this object without having to know the index number. Simply use the following format:

```
document.name.propertyName
```

Using the NAME attribute is probably familiar to you if you have used anchors in your HTML documents. It is the identical format and is still the manner by which you create anchors. So, when you use the NAME attribute for your JavaScript code, you are also adding a new Anchor.

## LINK Events: *onMouseOver* and *onClick*

JavaScript code executes when the browser recognizes certain events. The LINK object recognizes two events: onClick and onMouseOver. You probably will use onClick in most of your code and onMouseOver only occasionally. This will remind you of the format of these events used with the LINK tag.

▶ **See** "Events and JavaScript," **p. 59**

 **T I P** In debugging code involving the status bar, make sure you include the statement return true.

The format is the same as for other events. Use our example, as follows:

```
<A NAME="myname" HREF="http://www.yoursite.com"
onMouseOver="window.status='Please visit my site.'; return true">
Click here</A>
```

This places the message 'Please visit my site.' in the status bar when the viewer places the mouse pointer over the hyperlink. This overrides most browsers that would otherwise display the URL in the status bar in this event.

You can use this feature to change the look and feel of your pages. Instead of showing the URL, which is irrelevant to many, change your links to tell people verbally where the links will take them. So, instead of displaying something like

```
http://www.cris.com/~raydaly/sponsors.html
```

you can display an easier-to-understand message in the status bar, such as

```
Hyperlink to "Sponsor of the Day"
```

The onClick event uses the same format. Also, the example application for this chapter makes frequent use of the onClick event. The following is a short example:

```
<A NAME="mymessage" HREF="http://www.newsite.com"
onClick="alert('Thanks for visiting.  Enjoy the new site.')">
Visit Newsite</A>
```

This code displays an Alert dialog box prior to jumping to the new site (see Figure 9.2). Only after the user clicks OK in the dialog box does the browser hyperlink to **www.newsite.com**.

**FIG. 9.2**

You can display a dialog box prior to hyperlinking to a new site.

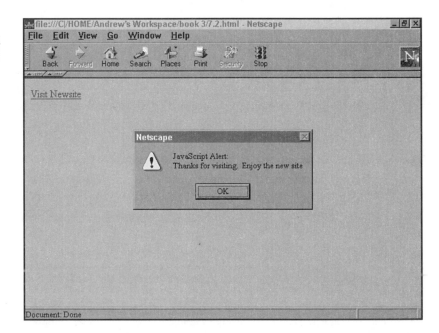

**CAUTION**

You can confuse your users by changing the HREF using onClick. Users often look to the status bar to see the URL to which the hyperlink will take them. When you assign the HREF attribute of the LINK, it is displayed in the status bar. When using the onClick event, you can set the HREF to a different URL. By reading the status bar, the user may assume he is going to the first URL, but instead, your JavaScript code takes him to the URL specified by the onClick statement.

In the following example, the status bar makes it appear that the link is to Yahoo!'s site, but the code takes you to InfoSeek. It goes to show that you cannot even trust links anymore.

```
<A NAME="searchme" HREF="http://www.yahoo.com"
onClick="this.href='http://www.infoseek.com'">
Search Internet for a Topic</A>
```

To avoid such a discrepancy in the status bar, just add `onMouseOver` to change the contents of status bar. For the preceding example, simply insert the following before the second line:

```
onMouseOver="window.status='Will take you to a search engine.'; return true"
```

## Change Link URLs, Not the Text Displayed

Unlike text boxes, JavaScript cannot change the hyperlink text displayed by the browser. In Listing 9.3, the hyperlink text is `Yahoo!` Regardless of the changes you make to this object, this text stays on the screen.

As you design your dynamic links, consider the words and images that reflect the new nature of your hyperlinks. For example, you can write a simple random URL function. When you click the link, it takes you to a random search site. You might use the words, `"Spin the wheel to a random search site"` or add a graphic image of a roulette wheel.

Listing 9.3 is an example showing how to make a dynamic link to Yahoo! The browser simply displays the hyperlink text `Yahoo!` When you click this link before 6:00 P.M., you link to the text-only version of Yahoo! But after 6:00 P.M., you link to the regular graphic version of Yahoo! So the `HREF` changes, but the displayed text stays the same.

**Listing 9.3    Page with Alternative Yahoo! Links**

```
<HTML>
<HEAD><SCRIPT Language="JavaScript">
function timeText () {
   today=new Date()
   hour = today.getHours()    //...get hour of the date
   if (hour>18 ) {
        //...after 6:00 p.m use graphics
        yahooURL= "http://www.yahoo.com/"
   } else {
      //...all other times use test mode
       yahooURL = "http://www.yahoo.com/text/"
   }
   return yahooURL    //...result of function is a URL
}
</SCRIPT></HEAD>
<BODY>
<A NAME="yahooLink" HREF=""
onClick="location.href=timeText()"   //...get the right URL
onMouseOver="window.status='Hyperlink to Yahoo!'; return true">
Yahoo!</A>
</BODY></HTML>
```

The URLs are not just for the Web. For example, suppose you have a fairly lengthy form to be completed by a customer and one of the first entries asks about the customer's location. Based on that entry, you might dynamically change the mailto address. Then any e-mail the customer might send is directed to the proper salesperson. Listing 9.4 asks the user where he is located. Based on his selection, e-mail goes to a different address. Figure 9.3 shows the result of Listing 9.4.

**Listing 9.4    Page that Switches *Mailto:* Addresses**

```
<HTML>
<HEAD>
<SCRIPT Language="JavaScript">
var salespersonMailto;
</SCRIPT>
</HEAD>
<BODY>
<FORM>
<B>Where are you located?</B><BR>
<INPUT TYPE="radio" NAME="country" onClick="salespersonMailto=
     'mailto:worldsales@company.com'"> Outside North America<BR>
<INPUT TYPE="radio" NAME="country" onClick="salespersonMailto=
     'mailto:nasales@company.com'"> North America<BR>
</FORM>
<A NAME="salesperson" HREF="mailto:info@yoursite.com"
onClick="location.href=salespersonMailto">
Email your salesperson.</A>
</BODY></HTML>
```

**FIG. 9.3**

Depending on the selection, e-mail goes to a different address. Remember to include a default address or use a dialog box to ask the user to make a choice before trying to send e-mail.

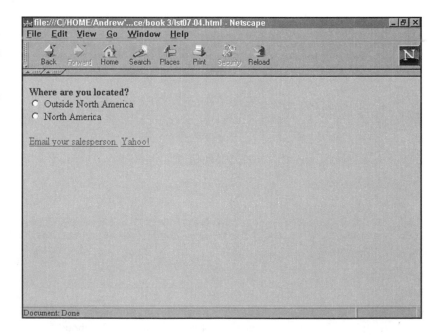

# Create Documents in Frames and Windows

The LINK tag now enables the designer to specify the TARGET for the URL. This is an optional attribute. If it is not used, the new page simply replaces the previous page as before. But JavaScript enables you to display these new pages in frames or new windows.

One target for your link can be a new browser window. The windows will generally look and function as if you opened a second browser. Therefore, the original page is still displayed in your first window and the new page is displayed in the second. You can reduce the functionality of these windows by changing their features when the windows are open.

A frame is the other possible target for your link. Frames divide your browser window into two or more areas. Inside these frames, you can display standard Web pages or create your own documents. The applications constructed in this chapter use frames. A review of frames is found in Chapter 18, "Using Frames."

Windows and frames are often a vital part of a design that includes dynamic links. By using JavaScript code behind a link, you can build new types of browsers. You also can build new tools. For example, you might bring a page into a frame, analyze it, and display the results in another frame.

Often, when using frames, one area is like a control panel that can control the display in another. For example, researchers constantly use different search engines on the Web, and these sites are bookmarked. But it would be handier if these sites were always available, as are the toolbar buttons in Internet Explorer. Listings 9.5, 9.6, and 9.7 show how the top frame contains one line with hyperlinks to eight different search engines. This frame is similar to a control panel with the documents targeted at the lower frame. Figure 9.4 shows the result of these listings.

**Part**

**II**

**Ch**

**9**

### Listing 9.5    Top Page for *SearchDr*

```
<HTML><HEAD><TITLE> searchdr.htm </TITLE></HEAD>
<FRAMESET ROWS="60,*">
    <FRAME SRC="searc".htm" NAME="buttons">
    <FRAME SRC="display9.htm" NAME="display">
  </FRAMESET>
  </HTML>
```

### Listing 9.6    Initial Screen in Display Frame

```
<HTML><HEAD><TITLE>Part of searchdr.htm: display9.htm</TITLE></HEAD>
<BODY><H1>Display Area</H1>
<P>Click on any hyperlink above to display a search engine here.
</BODY></HTML>
```

**Listing 9.7 Frame for *SearchDr* with Hyperlinks**

```
<HTML><HEAD><TITLE>Part of searchdr.htm:  searc".htm</TITLE></HEAD>
<BODY>
<A HREF="http://www.altavista.digital.com/" TARGET="display"> Alta Vista</A>  --
<A HREF="http://www.excite.com" TARGET="display">Excite</A>  --
<A HREF="http://www.lycos.com/" TARGET="display">Lycos</A>  --
<A HREF="http://www.mckinley.com/" TARGET="display">Magellan</A>  --
<A HREF="http://www.nlightn.com/" TARGET="display">NlightN</A>  --
<A HREF="http://www.opentext.com:8080/" TARGET="display">Open Text</A>  --
<A HREF="http://www.webcrawler.com" TARGET="display">WebCrawler</A>  --
<A HREF="http://www.yahoo.com" TARGET="display">Yahoo!</A>
</BODY>
</HTML>
```

**FIG. 9.4**

SearchDr puts any of the listed search engines in the frame marked Display Area. When you create frames, let the default frames provide instructions to the new users.

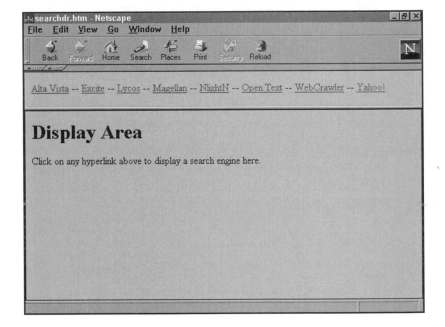

For a more substantial example, we will construct an application called Internet Tri-Eye later in this chapter. It truly will give you a different view of the world. In Listing 9.8 and its corresponding Figure 9.5, you see the frames used in creating Internet Tri-Eye.

Although this will be displayed using your browser, it is not the same old browser anymore. Frames and dynamic hyperlinks let you reshape the browser.

---

**Listing 9.8    Frame Document for Internet Tri-Eye**

```
<HTML><HEAD><TITLE>Internet Tri-Eye</TITLE></HEAD>
<FRAMESET ROWS="*,200">
   <FRAMESET COLS="33%,34%, 33%">
      <FRAME SRC="one.htm" NAME="one">
      <FRAME SRC="two.htm" NAME="two">
      <FRAME SRC="three.htm" NAME="three">
   </FRAMESET>
   <FRAME SRC="guide.htm" NAME="guide">

<NOFRAMES>
<H1>Internet Tri-Eye</H1>
<P><B>Internet Tri-Eye</B> is a demonstration of several features of
JavaScript.  To view and use this program you need a JavaScript or
Javascript compatible browser.
</NOFRAMES>

</FRAMESET></HTML>
```

---

Part
II

Ch
9

**FIG. 9.5**

The frames used to create Internet Tri-Eye will contain the control panel at the bottom and display Internet camera pictures from around the world.

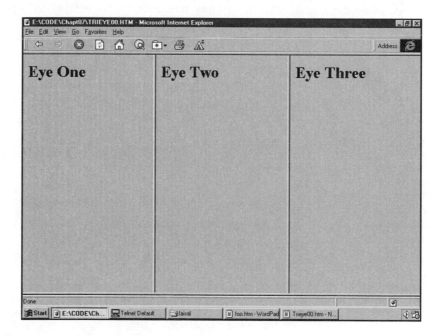

# Creating and Using Anchors

Anchors are not commonly used on most Web pages. If you have an alphabetical listing, an anchor might take you to a particular section. However, most sites have tended to use rather short pages. These pages might be one or two screens in length and often do not need anchors.

# Your HTML Elements

The pages you design with JavaScript are fundamentally different from most other HTML pages. Because these pages are so interactive, your viewers will most likely spend more time on your pages than on the average HTML page. They may also save the page because it is not just a page of text anymore, but an application.

These differences should make you consider making your pages bigger than before. The user may be willing to wait a little longer for a page to load if that means the page will be richer.

Since your pages are now applications, users will expect quick responses to their inputs; you cannot deliver that promise if you have to keep requesting documents from the server. Instead, take what you might have normally put on several different pages and build it into one big page. This can also benefit users because when they save the page, they can have the complete application.

For example, with your Great JavaScript Application, you might have a page of help and documentation. Given the sophistication of your application, this may be fairly lengthy, and normally you might consider separating it from the application page. However, if you follow that course, when users save the application they will not have the help when loading it from their hard drives. Instead, consider making a bigger page that includes all of the help information and documentation. Then set up anchors to the help topics so people can easily refer to them. This concept is illustrated in Figure 9.6.

**FIG. 9.6**
By combining multiple pages into one, your JavaScript application becomes more responsive. The fewer the requests to the server, the more responsive your application will be.

Regular HTML Page

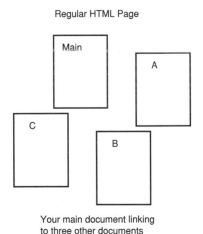

Your main document linking to three other documents

Longer Java Script Page

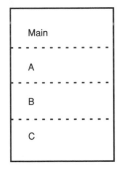

All documents combined into one document with hyperlinks now going to anchors

When you have longer documents, anchors become crucial for navigating around the document. Instead of scrolling through screen after screen, click the keyword and you will find your place. Use this technique for documentation, help, or other reference material.

# Anchor Any Text or Element

Use anchors in the standard way, and in new ways with JavaScript. Anchors enable you to specify a destination for a hyperlink within a document. For example, suppose you want the capability to jump to the words, "Part Two." The following code would be used in your document to do this:

```
<A NAME="jumphere">Part Two</A>
```

Note that the name does not have to be the same as the text. In this example, the name is jumphere, and the text displayed by the browser is "Part Two." To create the hyperlink to this section, use the following code:

```
<A HREF="#jumphere"> Go To Part Two</A>
```

This is useful not only within the current document, but also when pulling up information within frames or in other windows. For example, take the case of a form in which you are verifying the input. You would probably use a dialog box to notify the viewer that the input is out of range; then use an anchor at the description of the text box and link the browser to it with hypertext. Now the text box is right at the top of the screen, awaiting new input.

> **N O T E** You can use the anchor to scroll the page for the place you want. The FOCUS and the SELECT methods can do the same thing with form elements. However, if your form elements have labels, these methods will move the element to the top of the screen, cutting off your label. If you want your users to be able to read the labels, anchor the labels and jump to them. Both techniques are illustrated next. ▪

Anchors can also provide a new way to control the flow in completing a form, as shown in Listing 9.9 and Figure 9.7. Often, in completing paper forms, you see such instructions as "If you answered NO to question 6, skip to question 9." With JavaScript and anchors, you can look at the response to a question and then, depending on the answer, automatically jump to the anchor for the next appropriate question.

**Listing 9.9    Anchors in Form Verification**

```
<HTML><HEAD><TITLE>verfname.htm by Ray Daly</TITLE>
<SCRIPT LANGUAGE="JavaScript">
function skip2 (form) {
    if (form.q1.value>11) {
        alert ('You get FREE Overnite Shipping.  Skip to question 12.')
         form.q2.value="FREE Overnight"
         window.location="#a12"
         //...jump to anchor a12
    }
    if (form.q1.value<0) {
        alert ('You cannot return these items')
        form.q1.value=""
        form.q1.focus()
        form.q1.select()
```

*continues*

**Part**
**II**

**Ch**

**9**

**Listing 9.9   Continued**

```
        //...instead of jumping to an anchor, this uses focus and select method
    }
  }
</SCRIPT></HEAD><BODY><FORM>
<P>Try filling in quantities of 16, 8 and -3.  </P>
<B>1.)  How many do you want?</B><BR>
FREE Overnite shipping when ordering 12 or more.<BR>
<INPUT NAME="q1" TYPE="Text" onBlur="skip2(this.form)"><BR>
<a NAME="a2">
<B>2.)  How do you want it shipped?</B><BR>
<INPUT NAME="q2" TYPE="Text" ><BR>
<BR><BR><BR><BR><BR><BR>
<I>(more questions are listed here)
<BR><BR><BR><BR><BR><BR>
<BR><BR><BR><BR><BR><BR>
<B>12.)  What color do you want?</B><BR>
<A NAME="a12"><INPUT NAME="q12" TYPE="Text" ><BR>
<BR><BR><BR><BR><BR><BR>
<I>(more questions are listed here)
<BR><BR><BR><BR><BR><BR>
<BR><BR><BR><BR><BR><BR>
</FORM>
</BODY></HTML>
```

**FIG. 9.7**
You will see a visual difference in comparing the use of anchors to control the flow and the use of the FOCUS and SELECT methods.

 In debugging your JavaScript, check your quotes. While double quotes and single quotes work in the same way, you cannot start with a double quote and end with a single quote, or vice versa. Your quotes must match or you will end up with errors, perhaps several lines later.

# Using Selection or Scrolling—Your Option

What kind of test did you prefer in school: multiple choice or essay? You probably found multiple choice easier. Certainly, your teacher found multiple choice easier to grade.

When you design interactive forms, your viewers probably also find your requests easier to understand in a multiple choice format. Understanding this aspect of form design, you probably have used option buttons and check boxes. These are excellent devices for presenting a limited number of choices.

When you present the viewer with a large number of choices, use the SELECT element. This enables you to present a large list without cluttering up your page. A good use would be geographical lists, such as states or countries in address forms.

## Syntax in Review

Although using the SELECT element makes it easier for visitors to use your site, you have to do more work. Remember, SELECT is an element within a form, so it must be between the <FORM>...</FORM> tags. The syntax of SELECT is one of the most complicated of all the HTML elements. You should be familiar with most of this specification. Listing 9.10 shows the syntax for this element.

**Listing 9.10    Elements of the HTML *SELECT* Statement**

```
<SELECT
    NAME="selectName"
    [SIZE="integer"]
    [MULTIPLE]
    [onBlur="handlerText"]
    [onChange="handlerText"]
    [onFocus="handlerText"]>
    <OPTION VALUE="optionValue" [SELECTED]> textToDisplay
        [ ... <OPTION> textToDisplay]
</SELECT>
```

The SELECT tag has one required attribute: NAME. This name, and a value associated with the selected OPTION element, are sent to the server when a form is submitted. The NAME attribute also can be used as an anchor. An optional attribute is SIZE, which tells the browser how many options to display.

MULTIPLE is an optional attribute of SELECT, which changes the list so that one or multiple items can be selected by the user. This type of list is called a *scrolling list*.

The SELECT tag always contains two or more OPTION elements. This is where you list the items for the user to select. Each OPTION has a text property that is displayed in the select box. There is also an associated VALUE property that is sent to the server when the form is submitted, along with the name of the SELECT tag. The last attribute of OPTION is itself optional. The SELECTED attribute is a means to have one of the items in your selection list be the default when the page is displayed. The only addition to this specification for JavaScript are the events discussed in the next section.

## onChange, onBlur, and onFocus Events for *SELECT*

Like other objects in JavaScript, the SELECT object responds to events. Here you will learn specific uses of onFocus, onChange, and onBlur with SELECT objects.

▶ **See** "Events and JavaScript," **p. 59**

***onChange***   onChange is the most common event that you monitor in SELECT. It looks for change from one selection to another. When the event is triggered, your code executes. An example of using onChange, by selecting a country, is shown in Listing 9.11 and Figure 9.8. Suppose you change a country selection from the United States to Mexico. onChange then triggers a JavaScript function that changes the currency type from U.S. dollars to pesos. However, if you did not change the selection, the event does not trigger.

 **TIP**   When using SELECT, you have a built-in associative array. Each OPTION value relates to a selection.

**Listing 9.11   Currency by Country Using *onChange***

```
<HTML><HEAD><TITLE>money.htm by Ray Daly</TITLE>
<SCRIPT LANGUAGE="JavaScript">
function changeCurrency(form) {
      form.currency.value=form.country.options[form.country.selectedIndex].value
}
</SCRIPT></HEAD>
<BODY><FORM>
<P>This page demonstrates the <I>onChange</I> event.</P>
<B>Select your country</B><BR>
<SELECT NAME="country" onChange="changeCurrency(this.form)">
<OPTION VALUE="US Dollars">USA
<OPTION VALUE="Canadian Dollars">Canada
<OPTION VALUE="Peso">Mexico
</SELECT>
<P><B>Prices are displayed in:</B><BR>
<INPUT TYPE="text" NAME="currency">
</FORM></BODY>
</HTML>
```

***onBlur***   onBlur is a good way to verify proper selections. This event occurs when the focus is no longer on the SELECT object. In other words, it looks for when you click somewhere other than on the current element. When the event is triggered, you can execute a verification function. Although you can use the onChange event to verify selections, using onBlur might ensure your site visitor's choice. This is because the onBlur event triggers JavaScript code even if a change has not occurred.

**FIG. 9.8**
The onChange event is triggered when the selection changes.

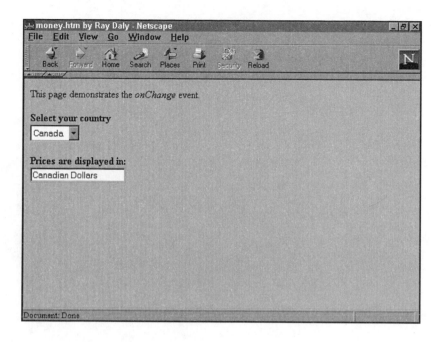

Verification is not always simply an either/or choice. For example, you might have a selection with some uncommon but acceptable answers. This might be an unusual color for a piece of merchandise. For this circumstance, you might verify that this is indeed the correct selection, even if the user made no change in his selection. In Listing 9.12, the user is simply notified with an Alert box if he or she wants to buy fewer than a dozen eggs. The result of executing this page is shown in Figure 9.9.

**Listing 9.12    Eggs Come by the Dozen Using *onBlur***

```
<HTML><HEAD><TITLE>eggs.htm by Ray Daly</TITLE>
<SCRIPT LANGUAGE="JavaScript">
function checkEggs(form) {
    form.eggs.value=form.quantity.options[form.quantity.selectedIndex].value
    if (form.quantity.selectedIndex==0) {
        alert ('People usually order eggs by the dozen.')
     }
}
</SCRIPT></HEAD>
<BODY><FORM>
<P>Demonstrates <I>onBlur</I> event.  After you select a quantity,
the number on-hold is not updated until you click somewhere else.</P>
<B>How many eggs do you want:</B><BR>
<SELECT NAME="quantity" onBlur="checkEggs(this.form)">
   <OPTION VALUE="6">Half dozen
   <OPTION VALUE="12">Dozen
```

*continues*

**Listing 9.12     Continued**

```
    <OPTION VALUE="24">Two dozen
</SELECT>
<P><B>We are holding this many eggs for you:</B><BR>
<INPUT TYPE="text" NAME="eggs">
</FORM></BODY>
</HTML>
```

**FIG. 9.9**

The event onBlur works almost exactly like onChange, except the JavaScript code is executed even if the selection does not change.

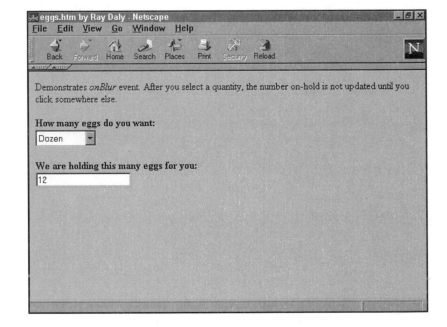

**onFocus**   onFocus is an excellent way to assist your site visitor in completing your form. It looks for the visitor to move the cursor to the SELECT element and then triggers code prior to any entry by the visitor.

For example, each question in your form can include particular instructions that assist the visitor in making a proper selection. When onFocus is triggered, your code can display, in a separate window or frame, the instructions related to that question. Or, if you require a numeric answer to be calculated, why not pop up a calculator in a new window? That's what happens in the math word problem presented in Listing 9.13. The results are shown in Figure 9.10.

**TIP** It is possible to create an endless loop by using the onFocus event. To avoid this trap, create a flag variable. Initially, set it to zero. Every time you call the routine, check the value of the flag. If the flag is zero, then execute the rest of the routine and set the flag to one. If the flag is not zero, then the routine has already been executed once, so you don't need to execute it again.

### Listing 9.13    Tricky Math Word Problem Using *onFocus*

```html
<HTML><HEAD><TITLE>wordprob.htm by Dr. Ray Daly III </TITLE>
<SCRIPT LANGUAGE="JavaScript">
function giveAnswer(form) {
    if (form.answer.selectedIndex==2) {
        alert ('People usually forget trains run on two tracks.')
     }
}
already=0
function callCalculator(form) {
if (already==0) {
   already = 1   //...only need to open this window once
newWindow=window.open("http://www.netscape.com/comprod/products/navigator/
version_2.0/script/calc.html")
}
}
</SCRIPT></HEAD>
<BODY><FORM>
<P>Demonstrates <I>onFocus</I> event.  As soon as you click on the SELECT
element, then a calculator pops up.</P>
<P><B>Railroad track is ordered for three sections of track.  The first is 15
miles long.  The second is 23 miles long and the third is 6 miles long.  How
many  miles of track needs to be ordered to complete construction?
</B></P>
<P><B>What is your answer:</B><BR>
<SELECT NAME="answer" onFocus="callCalculator(this.form)"
    onBlur="giveAnswer(this.form)">
   <OPTION VALUE="21">21
   <OPTION VALUE="29">29
   <OPTION VALUE="88">88
</SELECT>
</FORM></BODY>
</HTML>
```

**FIG. 9.10**
When you design your
JavaScript applications,
remember that you can
call up other people's
applications.

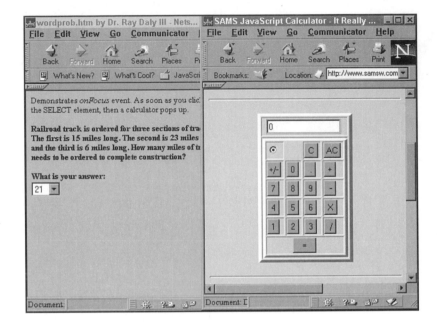

## Dynamically Change the Selection, Not the Text

Unlike its text box cousins, TEXT and TEXTAREA, your code cannot change the text displayed in the SELECT list if you are using Netscape 2.0. Although your viewer may have chosen Canada as the country, your code cannot substitute the name of the provinces for the names of the states as the text displayed by the options. In Netscape 3.0, you can change the text.

However, your code can dynamically change the selection made. The selected property reflects the selection status of an option. You can set selected, which immediately changes the selection displayed on the browser display. You can see how this works by using option buttons to change a SELECT list dynamically. Listing 9.14 illustrates how this works, with the resulting output shown in Figure 9.11.

---

**Listing 9.14    Pizza for Dinner Using the *SELECTED* Property**

```
<HTML><HEAD><TITLE>dinner.htm by Red Daly</TITLE></HEAD>
<BODY><FORM>
<P>Demonstrates <I>selected</I> property.  See what you can afford for dinner.
Click on the radio button for a dollar amount and show your dinner in the select
box..</P>
<P><B>How much money do you have for dinner?</B><BR>
<INPUT TYPE="radio" NAME="a"
onClick="this.form.meal.options[0].selected=1">$10<BR>
<INPUT TYPE="radio"
NAME="a"onClick="this.form.meal.options[1].selected=1">$15<BR>
<INPUT TYPE="radio"
```

```
NAME="a"onClick="this.form.meal.options[2].selected=1">$20<BR></P>
<B>Your dinner tonite is:</B><BR>
<SELECT NAME="meal" >
<OPTION VALUE="$10">Pizza
<OPTION VALUE="$15">Extra Cheese Pizza
<OPTION VALUE="$20">Extra Veggies Pizza
</SELECT>
</FORM></BODY>
</HTML>
```

**FIG. 9.11**
You can really confuse your users by having one form element change another. Be sure to think through your design.

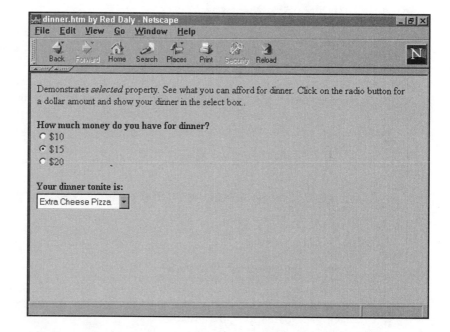

---

**CAUTION**

With text boxes, the information displayed in the box is the `value` property. With `select`, the value property is not displayed. This is like option buttons and check boxes. So don't change the `value` property of `select` and expect the display to change.

# Example: An Application Using Advanced Navigation

This example is designed to explain the concepts discussed in this chapter. There are several suggestions on how you can make them more robust, but the key is the explanation. You will see how links, as well as anchors, can be dynamic. The `select` element is also used.

Internet Tri-Eye is truly a kaleidoscope on the Web. With a few clicks, you can see New York, Hollywood, and Pike's Peak; Hong Kong, the Antarctic, and the Netherlands; or a school of fish, a cat, and some ants. It is a great way to demonstrate not only JavaScript, but also the Web.

The purpose of Internet Tri-Eye is to simultaneously display pictures from multiple cameras connected to the Internet. You select a set—for example, the U.S., International, or Animals. Then you click Show picture to display one view of the world. Further information about each camera is also available.

## Expand the View with Frames

Listing 9.15 shows the basic layout for the browser window. This layout is defined by the HTML page. The window is divided into two frames, with the top frame divided into three additional frames.

> **N O T E**  Internet Tri-Eye is a JavaScript application that uses frames. The entire application consists of five files: TRIEYE.HTM, ONE.HTM, TWO.HTM, THREE.HTM, and GUIDE.HTM. These files are available on this book's companion Web site. You start the application by loading the file TRIEYE.HTM. ▓

### Listing 9.15    Frameset for Internet Tri-Eye Application

```
<HTML><HEAD><TITLE>Internet Tri-Eye</TITLE></HEAD>

<FRAMESET ROWS="*,200">
   <FRAMESET COLS="33%,34%, 33%">
      <FRAME SRC="one.htm" NAME="one">
      <FRAME SRC="two.htm" NAME="two">
      <FRAME SRC="three.htm" NAME="three">
   </FRAMESET>
   <FRAME SRC="guide.htm" NAME="guide">

<NOFRAMES>
<H1>Internet Tri-Eye</H1>
<P><B>Internet Tri-Eye</B> is a demonstration of several features of
JavaScript.  To view and use this program you need a JavaScript or
Javascript compatible browser.
</NOFRAMES>

</FRAMESET>
</HTML>
```

The content of the top three frames, the eyes, are files ONE.HTM, TWO.HTM, and THREE.HTM (see Listings 9.16, 9.17, and 9.18). These are extremely small files that are used only when the application is first loaded. They can also be found on the companion Web site for this book.

### Listing 9.16    Initial Contents of Frame One for Tri-Eye

```
<HTML><HEAD></HEAD><BODY>
<H1>Eye One</H2>
</BODY></HTML>
```

### Listing 9.17    Initial Contents of Frame Two for Tri-Eye

```
<HTML><HEAD></HEAD><BODY>
<H1>Eye Two</H2>
</BODY></HTML>
```

### Listing 9.18    Initial Contents of Frame Three for Tri-Eye

```
<HTML><HEAD></HEAD><BODY>
<H1>Eye Three</H2>
</BODY></HTML>
```

The second two frames are identical to the first frame except that the headline is changed to Eye Two and Eye Three, respectively. The guts of Tri-Eye and all of the JavaScript code are found in the lower frame. As we progress in building the application, all of the changes are made to this frame. So far, these four frames are complete.

 **TIP** Most people find it easier to write JavaScript after doing the layout. Do your frames, your tables, your controls, and even some windows; then write the code to pull it all together.

## Objects for Tri-Eye

Now that we have the framework, the next step is to set up objects for each "eye," or camera. We start by defining an object called cam. The object has three properties: the description of the camera, the name for the anchor (more later), and the URL for the image. The code in GUIDE.HTM starts with the standard header, the SCRIPT tag, and then defines the cam object. Listing 9.19 shows the first part of the GUIDE.HTM file

### Listing 9.19    Start of the Coding for Tri-Eye

```
<HTML><HEAD><TITLE>Internet Tri-Eye by Ray Daly</HEAD>
<SCRIPT LANGUAGE="JavaScript">
<!--
function cam (name, anchor, rul) {
     this.name = name
     this. anchor = anchor
     this.url = url
}
```

Then for each camera, a new object is established. In this example, there are nine different cameras, so you create nine different objects labeled cam1 to cam9. Listing 9.20 shows this portion of the code. You can add more if you like.

**Listing 9.20    Setting Properties for *Cam* Objects for Tri-Eye**

```
     cam1 = new cam ("Hollywood, CA", "#Hollywood", "http://
hollywood.bhi.hollywood.ca.us:8000/pictures/image01.gif")
     cam2 = new cam ("Pikes Pike, CO",  "#Pikes",
"http://www.softronics.com/peak_cam/cam.jpg")
     cam3 = new cam ("New York City, NY", "#New York City",
"http://www.metaverse.com/gate/images/empire.jpg")
     cam4 = new cam ("Zandvoort, NE", "#Zandvoort",
"http://www.dataplace.nl//images/zandv-gr.jpg")
     cam5 = new cam ("Hong Kong",  "#Hong Kong",
"http://www.hkstar.com/images/capture1.jpg")
     cam6 = new cam (" Australian Antarctic",  "#Antarctic",
"http://www.antdiv.gov.au/aad/exop/sfo/mawson/video.gif")
     cam7 = new cam ("Fishcam", "#Fishcam",
"http://www.netscape.com/fishcam/fishcam.gif")
     cam8 = new cam ("Mojo - Cat", "#Mojo",
"http://www.lowcomdom.com/mojo.gif")
     cam9 = new cam ("Steve's Ant Farm", "#Ant Farm",
"http://sec.dgsys.com/images/zANTPIX/Untitled.jpeg")
```

We now have nine different objects. In order to make it easier to reference these objects, create another object called camset (see Listing 9.21). From this object, an object called camindex is created. The first property in camindex is cam1, the second is cam2, and so on. Thus, to get the contents of cam5, you reference the fifth element in camindex.

**Listing 9.21    Putting Nine Objects into One for Tri-Eye**

```
function camset (eye1, eye2, eye3, eye4, eye5, eye6, eye7, eye8, eye9 ) {
    this.eye1 = eye1
    this.eye2 = eye2
    this.eye3 = eye3
    this.eye4 = eye4
    this.eye5 = eye5
    this.eye6 = eye6
    this.eye7 = eye7
    this.eye8 = eye8
    this.eye9 = eye9
}
camindex = new camset (cam1, cam2, cam3, cam4, cam5, cam6, cam7, cam8, cam9)
```

We do not need to create so many different objects, but this method seems more straightforward than the other options. If you are good with objects, have fun minimizing.

The final two lines of the JavaScript for this section initialize two variables to one, as follows:

```
    var setnumber=1
    var camnumber=1
//-->
</SCRIPT>
</HEAD>
```

**Controls** To make anything happen with Internet Tri-Eye, controls need to be added. So far, all we have in GUIDE.HTM is the JavaScript defining the objects. Now the HTML code is added for the controls (see Listing 9.22).

To hold the controls, there is a table of three rows and three columns. Across the entire first row is a button and a select element. The button is very simple and labeled About. When you click it, an Alert window tells you about Internet Tri-Eye.

The next element in the top row is a SELECT box. Here you select which set of cameras you want to look at. The first three cameras are locations in the United States, the next three are international, and the last three are pets. When you make a selection, it sets the variable setnumber to 1 or 2 or 3.

Part II Ch 9

**Listing 9.22    Laying Out the Control Table for Tri-Eye**

```
<BODY><FORM>
<TABLE BORDER="1" WIDTH="100%">
<TR>
   <TD ALIGN=CENTER COLSPAN=3>
      <A NAME="top">
      <INPUT TYPE="button" NAME="aboutTE"  VALUE="About Tri-Eye"
 onClick="alert('Tri-Eye is a demo from the book:  JavaScript Special Edition')">
      <SELECT
         NAME="setselect"
          onBlur="setnumber=setselect.selectedIndex+1">
         <OPTION VALUE="US" SELECTED> U.S.
         <OPTION VALUE="World">World
         <OPTION VALUE="Pets">Pets
      </SELECT>
   </TD>
</TR><TR>
   <TD ALIGN=CENTER VALIGN=TOP WIDTH="33%">
<A HREF=" "onClick="this.href=findHREF(1)" " TARGET="one">Show picture One </A>
      </TD>
         <TD ALIGN=CENTER VALIGN=TOP WIDTH="34%">
<A HREF=" "onClick="this.href=findHREF(2)" " TARGET="two">Show picture Two</A>
   </TD>
   <TD ALIGN=CENTER VALIGN=TOP WIDTH="33%">
<A HREF=" "onClick="this.href=findHREF(3)" " TARGET="three">Show picture Tri</A>
   </TD>
</TR><TR>
   <TD ALIGN=CENTER>
     <A HREF=" "onClick="this.href=findHASH(1)" " NAME="Info1">-- Info --</A>
```

*continues*

**Listing 9.22    Continued**

```
      </TD>
      <TD ALIGN=CENTER>
       <A HREF=" "onClick="this.href=findHASH(2)" " NAME="Info1">-- Info --</A>
      </TD>
      <TD ALIGN=CENTER>
       <A HREF=" "onClick="this.href=findHASH(2)" " NAME="Info1">-- Info --</A>
      </TD></TR>
   </TABLE>
```

The final two rows of controls are for demonstrating dynamic links and anchors.

## Dynamic Links

The middle row of controls is for the dynamic links. When you click these links, one picture from one camera is displayed. There is one control for each of the "eyes." The code needed pulls in the proper URL, given "eye" 1, 2, or 3, and is based on the set chosen with the SELECT box (see Listing 9.23). These variables are `camnumber` and `setnumber`.

**Listing 9.23    *findHREF* Function for Tri-Eye**

```
function findHREF (eye) {
      // ...eye is 1, 2 or 3  -- the target frame
      indexnumber = (eye-1) +( 3 * (setnumber -1)
      //the value of indexnumber is between 0 and 8
      return camindex[indexnumber].url
}      //returns the url of the camera
```

This code is added between the <SCRIPT> tags. Once you have the URL, the code is fairly simple. When the hyperlink is clicked, the `findHREF` function is called. It returns the URL and the `href` property is changed. The target for the URL is the appropriate "eye" frame. Change the `href` property to the URL. For "eye" 3, the code is:

```
<A HREF=" "onClick="this.href=findHREF(3)" " TARGET="three">Show picture Tri</A>
```

For simplicity, the hyperlink text is "`Show picture One`" or "Two" or "Tri." To polish up the application, an icon can be used here.

## Anchors to Complete the Story

So far, Internet Tri-Eye is already spectacular. It is a true kaleidoscope of the world. However, it does not tell us anything about these pictures. Anchors are used two different ways to complete the story.

**Anchors to the Reference Information**    The final row of the controls is for information links. Click the text "---Info---" and the frame scrolls down to a description of the site. For this example, there is a short, three-line description with a link to the host site, if you want more information.

When the objects were created for this page, anchors were included. So the same technique that was previously used for links is now used for anchors. The function has only a minor difference: it returns the anchor property.

```
function findHASH (eye) {
        // ...eye is 1, 2 or 3 -- the target frame
        indexnumber = (eye-1) + ( 3 * (setnumber -1))
        return camindex[indexnumber].anchor
}
```

The control itself is also similar:

```
<A HREF=" "onClick="this.href=findHASH(3)" " NAME="Info1">---Info---</A>
```

**Anchors to Take Me Back**   Once you read the information on the picture, you will probably want to go back to the controls. Notice that the title of each description is followed by a hyperlink labeled (*top*). What you may not have noticed is that there is no anchor with the name top. Instead, (*top*) is the name of the About button. So click (*top*), and the About button will return to the top of the page. Listing 9.24 completes the file GUIDE.HTM.

```
<A HREF="#top">(top)</A>
```

**N O T E**   This code completes the GUIDE.HTM file (see Listing 9.24). You start the application by loading a file containing Listing 9.24 and calling it trieye.htm. ▧

**Listing 9.24   Anchor Section for Tri-Eye**

```
<CENTER><H1>Tri-Eye Guide</H1></CENTER>
<DL>
<DT><A NAME="Hollywood">Hollywood, CA</A>   <I><A HREF="#top">(top)</A></I></DT>
<DD>Not your typical American street corner, this is
<A HREF="http://www.geocities.com/cgi-bin/main/BHI/look.html">Hollywood and
Vine from GeoCities</A>.  Just remember that &quot;nobody walks in L.A.&quot;</DD>

<DT><A NAME="Pikes">Pikes Pike, CO</A>   <I><A HREF="#top">(top)</A></I></DT>

<DD>One of America's most famous mountains.
<A HREF="http://www.softronics.com/peak_cam.html">Pikes Peak Cam from
Softronics</A> gives you the view from Colorado Springs.</DD>

<DT><A NAME="NYC">New York City, NY</A>   <I><A HREF="#top">(top)</A></I></DT>

<DD>New York City's most famous building.
<A HREF="http://www.metaverse.com/empire.html">Empire Cam from Metaverse</A>
has a view across part of the skyline.  Check the weather.</DD>

<DT><A NAME="Zandvoort">Zandvoort, the Netherlands</A>   <I><A
HREF="#top">(top)</A></I></DT>
```

*continues*

**Listing 9.24   Continued**

```
<DD>No close ups of the people on the beach.  This
<A HREF="http://www.dataplace.nl/dp/pages/foto.htm">Livecam from Dataplace</A>
points northwest across a traffic circle and up the beach.</DD>

<DT><A NAME="Hong">Hong Kong</A>    <I><A HREF="#top">(top)</A></I></DT>

<DD>Street scene that is colorful almost anytime.  The
<A HREF="http://www.hkstar.com/starcam.html">STARcam from HK Star Internet Ltd.</A>
shows more cars than people.</DD>

<DT><A NAME="Antartic">Australian Antarctic</A>    <I><A HREF="#top">(top)</A>
➥</I></DT>

<DD>While often black, some previous pictures are available.  The
<A HREF="http://www.antdiv.gov.au/aad/exop/sfo/mawson/video.html">camera at
Mawson Station</A> captures the pictures and though a variety of technology gets
it to your desk.</DD>

<DT><A NAME="Fishcam">Fishcam</A>    <I><A HREF="#top">(top)</A></I></DT>

<DD>Perhaps the most famous fish in the world.
<A HREF="http://www.netscape.com/fishcam/fishcam.html">Fishcam from Netscape</A>
now has multiple cameras and formats.  Who ever imagined an aquarium as a
revenue source?</DD>

<DT><A NAME="Mojo">Mojo</A>    <I><A HREF="#top">(top)</A></I></DT>

<DD>You won't believe the technology used to bring you these images.
<A HREF="http://www.lowcomdom.com/mojo_cam.html">Mojo-Cam</A> isn't from a
fixed view so it worth following.</DD>

<DT><A NAME="Ant">Ant Farm</A>    <I><A HREF="#top">(top)</A></I></DT>

<DD>Some people won't even think that this is a safe distance away.
<A HREF="http://sec.dgsys.com/AntFarm.html">Steve's Ant Farm</A> also has a
movie available.</DD>
</DL>
</FORM>
</BODY></HTML>
```

Now Internet Tri-Eye is complete. Figure 9.12 shows its top-level display.

**FIG. 9.12**
The Tri-Eye Web page is
your window to the
world.

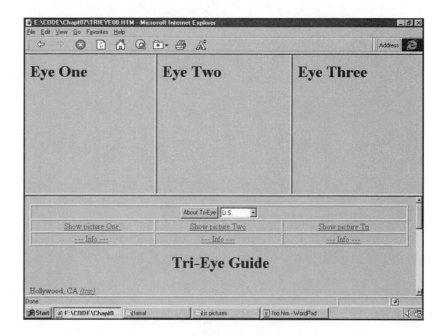

# Example: Tri-Eye FTP Auto Dialer

Trying to FTP a popular new piece of Internet software can be frustrating. You press a link and it seems like minutes before you're asked to try again later because the site is busy. We will modify the Internet Tri-Eye application to create a Tri-Eye Auto Dialer. To do this, we will replace the file GUIDE.HTM with a new file, GUIDEFTP.HTM.

You can create the Tri-Eye FTP Auto Dialer with a simple modification to one file of the Internet Tri-Eye application. Simply change the values of the properties for each cam object in the GUIDE.HTM file. These properties are the URLs for the information displayed in each of the upper frames. For example, to get the Windows NT version of Navigator 4.0 from Netscape's FTP site, you would use an URL such as:

```
ftp://ftp2.netscape.com/4.0/windows/n32e40.exe
```

Do the same for each FTP location simply by changing the host from **ftp2** to **ftp3**, and so on; the last one is **ftp10**. The function looks nearly the same; only the contents of the properties have changed (see Listing 9.25). The top-level FTP Auto Dialer window is shown in Figure 9.13.

**Listing 9.25    Redefined *cam* Object for Tri-Eye FTP Auto Dialer**

```
function cam (name, anchor, url) {
   this.name = name
   this.anchor = anchor
   this.url = url
}
cam1 = new cam ("FTP2", "#Netscape FTP",
"ftp://ftp2.netscape.com/2.0/windows/n32e20.exe")
cam2 = new cam ("FTP3", "#Netscape FTP",
"ftp://ftp3.netscape.com/2.0/windows/n32e20.exe")
cam3 = new cam ("FTP4", "#Netscape FTP",
"ftp://ftp4.netscape.com/2.0/windows/n32e20.exe")
cam4 = new cam ("FTP5", "#Netscape FTP",
"ftp://ftp5.netscape.com/2.0/windows/n32e20.exe")
cam5 = new cam ("FTP6", "#Netscape FTP",
"ftp://ftp6.netscape.com/2.0/windows/n32e20.exe")
cam6 = new cam ("FTP7", "#Netscape FTP",
"ftp://ftp9.netscape.com/2.0/windows/n32e20.exe")
cam7 = new cam ("FTP8", "#Netscape FTP",
"ftp://ftp8.netscape.com/2.0/windows/n32e20.exe")
cam8 = new cam ("FTP9", "#Netscape FTP",
"ftp://ftp9.netscape.com/2.0/windows/n32e20.exe")
cam9 = new cam ("FTP10", "#Netscape FTP",
"ftp://ftp10.netscape.com/2.0/windows/n32e20.exe")
```

**FIG. 9.13**

Tri-Eye FTP Auto Dialer will make multiple attempts to make an FTP connection. This should increase your chances for success.

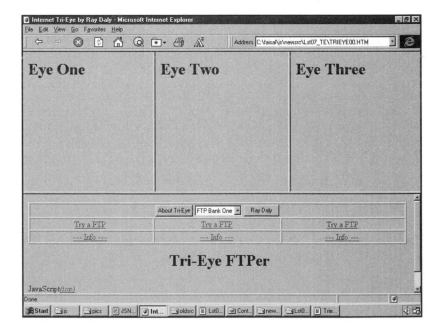

## Other Possible Improvements to and Uses of Internet Tri-Eye

Internet Tri-Eye was written with the goal of keeping the code simple to explain, not to dazzle you with graphics. The following are several suggestions for improving Tri-Eye or expanding its use:

- When you press `---Info---`, the control scrolls off the frame. Add one frame just for the table of controls. Show the information in another frame.

- Don't use any frames, but put everything in its own window. Press the control to show a picture and it pops up as a new window. Then every "eye" can be free-floating.

- Replace the text links with icons. Although `---Info---` is easy to explain in a book, the page will look better with graphics.

- Add more cameras. People are hooking up cameras all the time: some silly, some beautiful, and some scenic. Grab your favorite, and create some more objects.

- Instead of adding cameras, add magazines or other publications. Take a collection of magazines and put them in as objects. This would obviously work much better with windows instead of frames.

Part

II

Ch

9

# Dynamic HTML and Netscape Objects

This chapter describes the creation of dynamic documents and windows, as well as the interaction between windows and their components. This chapter presumes that you now have a working knowledge of JavaScript syntax; the material covered is somewhat more complex than in earlier chapters.

The first theme of this chapter is the creation of pop-up windows. These are small windows that you create via JavaScript, which appear and disappear in the browser, based on your script. The entire content of those windows is defined by a creation function, rather than an URL. We will examine various examples, including pop-up windows with text, pop-ups with buttons, and editable pop-ups.

We will next examine the history, status, and location objects. You will see how to send the user to a specific URL on the history list, how to examine the various parts of the location object, and how to store and retrieve information by using the search property of the location object. Finally, you will learn how to create dynamic documents. In fact, you will create a page entirely from JavaScript. You will also learn how to rewrite pages on-the-fly. ▪

**Write JavaScript statements that can access objects in windows and documents**

Almost every HTML element, as well as a large number of browser components, may be accessed from JavaScript.

**Create and format new browser windows**

The open() method is a very powerful statement that JavaScript programmers can use to open new browser windows.

**Add new elements by rewriting documents dynamically**

The HTML code for existing documents may be modified to change the appearance of a Web page.

**Create entirely new documents for JavaScript**

It is also possible to construct the entire HTML for a new page in JavaScript.

**Manipulate the history list and the *location* object**

These browser components describe the page currently being visited, as well as those that have been visited previously.

# JavaScript Object Hierarchy

You have already learned a lot about objects in JavaScript. In fact, the previous five chapters have been devoted to exploring the various JavaScript objects and their uses. You have already been exposed to the various built-in objects and HTML objects that JavaScript provides. To go further and explore dynamic HTML creation, we must first take a closer look at the hierarchy of objects in JavaScript.

If you are familiar with any object-oriented languages, you expect an object hierarchy to begin with a generic object from which all other objects are descendants or children. Unfortunately, the JavaScript object hierarchy does not really follow this model. It might be best described as a system of ownership, and, even then, the analogy is not really exact. For example, a window that creates another window could be thought of as the parent of the new window. However, if you try to refer to the original window from the child by saying `parent.someobject`, it may not work.

On the other hand, frames within a frameset have a parent-child relationship with the original window and asking for `parent.someobject` likely yields the object. Other ownership relationships are not characterized by a parent-child relationship at all. For example, form elements belong to a form, but to obtain the form, you use `this.form`, not `this.parent`. With these disconcerting thoughts in mind, let's attempt to sort out the dependencies among browser objects.

The browser is, in a way, the parent of all other JavaScript objects. It is the executable that runs the browser. The browser is responsible for the creation of all browser windows (see Figure 10.1). It is also responsible for responding to general window events. The browser is *not* a visual object. You cannot see it. You only interact with it through its visual constructs: its windows.

**FIG. 10.1**

JavaScript's Object Hierarchy.

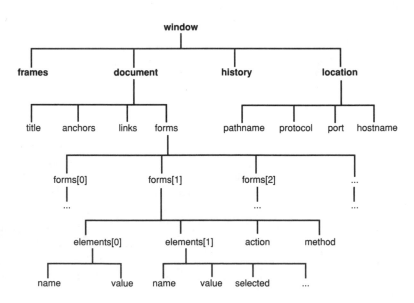

# Browser Windows

Most browser window components can be manipulated only in a yes/no fashion at the time of window creation. These include the menu, the button bar, the location display, the status display, the history list, and scroll bars. At the time of window creation, you can also determine whether the window can be resized, and you can find its dimensions.

This might seem like a significant restriction. By rewriting the document, however, you can change the contents of a window. This technique enables you to change the values of form elements, the content of the status bar, the position of the pointer in the history list, and the location (the URL that the window contains) at any time. Table 10.1 lists these various elements, when they can be modified, and how they can be modified. (Yes/No pertains to the fact that you specify YES or NO when you set these parameters in the window.open command, like MENU=NO. Complete pertains to the fact that the parameter is changed by assigning a completely new value to it.) Note that the last two items in this table are not really window elements: They control what appears, but do not explicitly appear themselves.

**Table 10.1 Modification Rules for JavaScript Controls**

| Object | When | How | Rewrite? |
|---|---|---|---|
| Button Bar | Window creation | Yes/No | NA |
| Menu | Window creation | Yes/No | NA |
| Location Display | Window creation | Yes/No | NA |
| Status Bar | Window creation | Yes/No | NA |
| History | Window creation | Yes/No | NA |
| Document | During rewrite | Complete | NA |
| Many Form Element Properties | Any time | Complete | No |
| Images | Any time | Complete | Yes |
| Status Bar Content | Any time | Complete | No |
| Location | Any time | Complete | Yes |
| History List | Any time | Complete | Yes |

# Dynamic Window Creation

One of the more advanced projects later in this book is the creation of a *sticky notes* application (in the "Dynamic Documents" section). To do that, you need to have a small note window in which to present the note. Let's create a primordial note window now. To do that, you must already have a window open with an element that enables you to call a JavaScript function, such as a button with an onClick handler. This base window is the parent of the child-note window.

The child can always find its parent with `self.parent`, but the parent can refer to the child only by its name. There is no `self.child[]` reference, nor is there a `windows` array available to JavaScript because of security concerns. You can also refer to a parent window with the `window.opener` property. This specifies the window of the parent document if the window was created by using the `open` method.

> **CAUTION**
>
> Netscape and Internet Explorer are mimics. If you create a window under a JavaScript control, the next window created by the browser will have the same dimensions as the last window created by JavaScript.

The element that we will use is an image that behaves as a button, which is triggered by an `HREF=javascript: :myfunc` included in the `LINK` tag. This works very well if you need to call only one function and you need no return value. When you try to use this mechanism in a window constructed on-the-fly, however, the image refuses to appear. In fact, any image that uses relative addressing refuses to appear in a dynamic window. This is due to security safe-guards in JavaScript.

The solution is either to use a completely static reference for the image or to set the base direc-tory of your page with `<BASE>path</BASE>` in the header. This latter approach helps JavaScript find the image. If you need an object that will be accessed later, you might want to use a form-input element, rather than one of the button images. JavaScript will have less trouble finding it.

The following three steps are necessary to use an image as a button for executing a JavaScript function:

1. Write an appropriate HTML declaration for the desired image.
2. Enclose this HTML declaration within reference tags.
3. Resolve the `HREF` to a JavaScript function declaration.

These three steps are shown in Listing 10.1.

**Listing 10.1   Creating a Button Image**

```
<IMG WIDTH=23 HEIGHT=22 VSPACE=2 HSPACE= 2 ALIGN=LEFT
    SRC="Images/gobtn.gif" BORDER=0>
<A HREF='xxxxxx'><IMG WIDTH=23 HEIGHT=22 VSPACE=2 HSPACE=2 ALIGN=LEFT
    SRC="Images/gobtn.gif" BORDER=0><A>
<A HREF='javascript: openNote'><IMG WIDTH=23 HEIGHT=22
    VSPACE=2 HSPACE= 2 ALIGN=LEFT SRC="Images/gobtn.gif"
    BORDER=0><A>
```

The function used in this example is the `openNote()` function, the source for which is given in Listing 10.2. Before we plunge into this code, it is worthwhile to notice that the border has been explicitly set to zero. This is the only way you can keep the browser from drawing a border around your image if it is within a reference statement. Listing 10.2 contains the HTML for the base window with the button that creates a note. It includes the openNotes() function in a header script. Once you open a note window, make sure you close it before it gets lost. Netscape does not open a second window by the same name; it just updates the first one. When this code executes by clicking the Make Note button, you see something like Figure 10.2.

### Listing 10.2 Creating a New Window in JavaScript

```
<HTML>
<HEAD>
<TITLE>Opening a Window with Javascript</TITLE>
<SCRIPT>

//window globals
    var aNoteWin

function openNote(topic)
{
    aPopUp= window.open('','Note','toobar=no,location=no,
        directories=no,status=no,scrollbars=yes,resizable=yes,
        copyhistory=no,width=300,height=200')
    ndoc= aPopUp.document
    astr ='<HTML><HEAD><BR><TITLE>' + topic + '</TITLE>'
    astr +='</HEAD>'
    astr +='<BODY>'
    astr +=topic +   '<BR>'
    astr +='</BODY></HTML>'
    ndoc.write(astr)
    ndoc.close()
    self.aNoteWin = aPopUp
}

function closeNote(which)
{
    self.aNoteWin.close()
}

</SCRIPT>
</HEAD>
<BODY>
<H3><BR><HR><BR></H3>
<CENTER>
<FONT SIZE=5 COLOR='darkred'><B>Example 1</B></FONT>:  <FONT SIZE=5
    COLOR='darkblue'><B>Opening a New Window</B></FONT>
<FORM NAME='noteForm'>
<INPUT TYPE='button' NAME='makeBtn' VALUE='Make Note'
    onclick='openNote("JoAnn Murphy at 7:00; bring salad")'>
<INPUT TYPE='button' NAME='closeBtn' VALUE='Close note'
    onclick='closeNote()'>
</FORM>
</CENTER>
<H3><BR><HR><BR></H3>
</BODY>
</HTML>
```

**CAUTION**

In a `windows.open` statement, there are three things to bear in mind:

1. You need only the first two parameters (the URL, which can be empty, and the window name) to open a window. If you do not include the third parameter, the window attributes will list and then the window will have all of its window attributes set to yes (present).

2. If you specify any of the windows attributes, then you must include the whole list of attributes. Otherwise, the results will be unpredictable.

3. Enclose the attributes list in quotation marks, separate the items with commas, and do not leave spaces.

**FIG. 10.2**
Dynamically created windows may be tied to button events in JavaScript.

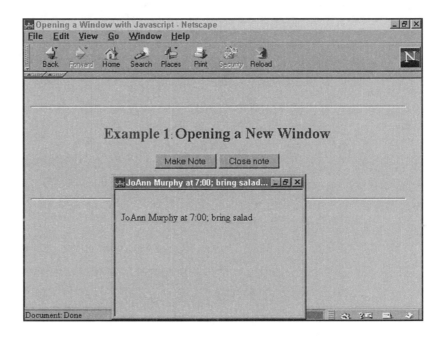

This small script illustrates several points. First, you can set a global window variable by defining it outside of any function and preceding it with `var`. Here, we set the window global `aNoteWin` with `var aNoteWin`. This variable is global, so you could use it to refer to `aNoteWin` in other functions. Although we did not do so here, you might want to save a number of notes in an `array`. Second, when you create a new window via a script and no URL is specified, the window document is still open, and you can write to it. Here, we wrote the note topic and then closed the document.

A window that you create can be as simple as the note window. However, you can also make this window quite complex. To do so, you must write everything to the document, including form elements, images, and JavaScript functions, before you close it. Listing 10.3 shows a second version of the openNote() function. This more elaborate version furnishes the note window with two buttons, including onClick handlers, the topic text, a warning message, and two JavaScript functions. Note that the save function is stubbed. All the display elements are neatly wrapped in a table.

**Listing 10.3   A More Sophisticated Notes Window**

```
function openNote(topic)
{
     aPopUp= window.open('','Note','toobar=no,location=no,
     directories=no,status=no,scrollbars=yes,resizable=yes,
   copyhistory=no,width=300,height=200')
     ndoc= aPopUp.document
astr ='<HTML><HEAD><TITLE>' + topic + '</TITLE>'
astr +='<SCRIPT>'
     astr +='function closeNote(aName){'
     astr +='self.close()'
     astr +='}'
     astr +='function saveNote(aName){'
     astr +='}'
     astr +='<\/SCRIPT>'
     astr +='</HEAD>'
     astr +='<BODY>'
     astr +='<FORM>'
     astr +='<TABLE ALIGN=LEFT BORDER><TR ALIGN=CENTER><TD>'
     astr +='<INPUT TYPE=button NAME=saveBtn VALUE="Save"
         ONCLICK="saveNote()">'
     astr +='</TD>'
     astr +='<TD ROWSPAN=4>' + topic
     astr +='</TD>'
     astr +='</TR><TR ALIGN=CENTER><TD>'
     astr +='<INPUT TYPE=button NAME=closeBtn VALUE="Close"
         ONCLICK="closeNote()">'
     astr +='</TD></TR>'
     astr +='<TR><TD><BR></TD></TR>'
     astr +='<TR><TD><BR></TD></TR>'
     astr +='</TABLE>'
     astr +='</FORM>'
     astr +='<BR CLEAR=ALL><H3><BR></H3>'
     astr +='Note:  Save button is not active yet'
     astr +='</BODY></HTML>'
     ndoc.write(astr)
     ndoc.close()
     self.aNoteWin = aPopUp
}
```

# Window Status

Netscape Navigator keeps you apprised via the status bar of which link or button your mouse pointer is over. Occasionally, it sends you other messages via that method, too. Perhaps you have seen it busily scrolling text to catch your attention. The *status* (not the status bar itself) is a property of a window and is accessible to you as `self.status = 'Some message'`. When you change the status, the browser immediately displays it in the status bar. You can also set a property called `defaultStatus`, which is the default message that appears in the status bar. Listing 10.4 provides code for using the `status` property in Netscape Navigator, the result of which is shown in Figure 10.3.

**Listing 10.4  Manipulating the Status Bar**

```
<HTML>
<HEAD>
<TITLE>Manipulating the Status Bar</TITLE>
<SCRIPT>
// set up a window global so that the new window can be accessed
// from all functions.
var aStatWin = null

function openStatus(defmsg,msg)
{
    aStatWin=window.open('','statWin','toobar=no,location=no,
        directories=no,status=yes,scrollbars=no,resizable=yes,
        copyhistory=no,width=550,height=2')
    if (aStatWin != null)
        {
            aStatWin.document.write('<FORM NAME="dform">
                <INPUT TYPE=TEXT NAME="dummy"></FORM>')
            aStatWin.document.close()
            aStatWin.defaultStatus = defmsg
            aStatWin.status = msg
            setFocus()
        }
}

function setStatus()
{
    if ( self.aStatWin == null )
        alert('Status window is closed!')
    else
        {
            self.aStatWin.status = document.statForm.statMsg.value
            setFocus()
        }
}

function setFocus()
{
    self.aStatWin.document.dform.dummy.focus()
}
```

```
function myclose()
{
    self.aStatWin.close()
    aStatWin = null
}

//This function is a work-around to make sure that the table
//    overlay is drawn correctly.
function fixup()
{
    blankWin=window.open('','blankWin','toobar=no,location=no, ¬
        directories=no,status=yes,scrollbars=no,resizable=no, ¬
        copyhistory=no,width=600,height=450')
    blankWin.close()
}

</SCRIPT>
</HEAD>
<!-- fixup forces redraw of window after everything, including images,
  has loaded.  The redraw is necessary to enforce correct drawing
  of table overlays.  -->
<BODY onLoad='fixup()'>
<H3><BR><HR><BR></H3>
<CENTER>
<FONT SIZE=5 COLOR='darkred'><B>Example : </B></FONT>
    <FONT SIZE=5 COLOR='darkblue'><B>Setting the Contents of the
     Status Bar</B></FONT>
<H3><BR><HR><BR></H3>
<H3><BR></H3>
</CENTER>
<CENTER>
<FORM NAME='statForm'>
<TABLE WIDTH=520 ALIGN=CENTER BORDER><TR ALIGN=CENTER><TD>
<TABLE WIDTH=500 ALIGN=CENTER>
<TR ALIGN=CENTER>
<TD WIDTH=35 ALIGN=CENTER>
<IMG WIDTH=48 HEIGHT=50 VSPACE=2 HSPACE= 2
    ALIGN=CENTER SRC="Images/gotray2.gif">
</TD>
<TD>
<!-- <INPUT TYPE=button VALUE='Make Status Window'
    onClick='openStatus("Status is GO!",
    document.statForm.statMsg.value)'> -->
<A HREF='javascript: openStatus("Status is GO!",
    document.statForm.statMsg.value)'>
<IMG WIDTH=23 HEIGHT=22 VSPACE=2 HSPACE=2  ALIGN=absMiddle
    SRC="Images/gobtn1.gif" BORDER=0>
Open Status Window</A>
</TD>
<TD ALIGN=LEFT >
<A HREF='javascript: setStatus()'>
<IMG WIDTH=23 HEIGHT=22 VSPACE=2 HSPACE=2  ALIGN=absMiddle
    SRC="Images/gobtn2.gif" BORDER=0>
Set Status</A>
```

Part

II

Ch

10

*continues*

**Listing 10.4   Continued**

```
</TD>
<TD ALIGN=CENTER >
<A HREF= 'javascript: myclose()'>
<IMG WIDTH=31 HEIGHT=30 VSPACE=2 HSPACE= 2 ALIGN=absMiddle BORDER=0
    SRC="Images/okbtn.gif">
Close Status
</A>
</TD>
</TR>

<TR ALIGN=CENTER>
<TD ALIGN=CENTER COLSPAN=4>
Msg <INPUT TYPE=text NAME='statMsg' VALUE='Howdy!'
    SIZE= 50 MAXLENGTH=80>
</TD>
</TR>
</TABLE>
</TD></TR></TABLE>
</FORM>
</CENTER>
<H3><BR></H3>
</BODY>
</HTML>
```

**FIG. 10.3**

The results of Listing 10.4; using the `Status` property in Netscape Navigator.

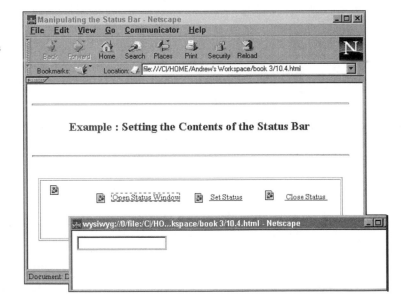

This example builds a window with a status bar included. Just to make things interesting, we'll set the content of the status bar from the parent window. In addition, this script provides an example of the advanced HTML concept of *table overlays* and an onLoad() handler, which provides a workaround for the browser's unpredictable order of drawing images. A bit more about table overlays will be provided in this section under the discussion of the fixup() function.

The status window is created with a 'javascript: openStatus(defMsg,msg)' link attached to an image. This function, openStatus(defMsg, msg), performs the following tasks:

- It creates a new window with everything turned off but the status bar.

- It checks that the window was actually created by examining aStatWin for a null value. It is important to perform this because attempts to access objects in a nonexistent window result in errors. The usual reason why a window fails to be created is lack of memory. This routine aborts with a message if the window was not created.

- It places a dummy text field in aStatWin. This button is just used as an object to set the focus so that we can bring the window to the front. Otherwise, small windows can get lost.

- It sets the initial and default status. Netscape Navigator immediately makes its presence known by writing to your status bar.

We will set the status of the status window with a call to setStatus(). This call is made from a 'javascript: setStatus(document.statForm.statMsg.value)' link attached to an image.

The setStatus() function also checks to see if aStatWin exists before it tries to address one of its objects. If aStatWin does exist, setStatus changes the content of its status bar. setStatus() then sets the focus on the dummy button in aStatWin to bring the window to the front. This is done by a call to the setFocus() method. The resulting window is shown in Figure 10.4. When you are done with the window, you can close it by using an Image button linked with a call to close function myclose(). The myclose() function simply closes aStatWin and makes sure that its value is reset to null. Note that it would have been unpleasant if we had named the close function simply close(). This is because there is a built-in window function called close(). If we had named our function close(), JavaScript would not have complained, but when we clicked the Close button, the built-in close() function would have been called, not ours.

The function fixup() is worth looking at in more detail. The order in which the browser draws images depends on where the images are coming from, whether they are in the cache, and whether their height and width are given explicitly. It can also depend on the size of the images. Extremely attractive presentations can be made by overlaying text and graphics on other graphics via the overlay feature of HTML tables.

However, Netscape Navigator often draws your bottom image last when the page first loads. Scrolling the screen causes the correct redraw, but you cannot expect or require your users to do that. One way to force the redraw is to open and quickly close another window over your page. You need to do this after all of the page elements have been loaded. When this occurs, the browser sends an onLoad event, which you can capture in the <BODY> tag. The fixup() function ensures that all of the image buttons are visible. Although this is far from an ideal solution, it is effective.

**FIG. 10.4**
A Status Bar window may be created dynamically by the parent window.

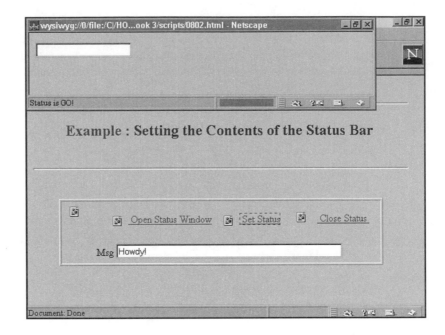

---

**T I P** Always check that a newly created window exists before you try to address its properties or methods. Do this by checking to see if the window is `null`. If it is `null`, use an alert to inform the user.

---

# The *location* Object

The `location` object essentially holds information about the URL to which the browser points. The browser reads this marked-up text from the server's disk and interprets it just as Microsoft Word reads and interprets a file on your disk. In addition to the URL, the `location` object also contains any post parameters of an HTML form submitted via a Submit button or your call to `submit()`. Because of this, you can use the `location` object for temporary storage. In Netscape Navigator and Internet Explorer, the location consists of the following parts:

`protocol://hostname: (port) pathname search hash`

*protocol* is the type of protocol used for this file. Examples are `http`, `ftp`, `gopher`, `telnet`, and `file` (for files on the local disk). *hostname* and *port* are valid only when the document is on a remote server. They contain the domain name/IP address of the server and the server port, respectively. The Web *port* is a number denoting the type of service, and is usually `80` for `http`. The *pathname* is the path to the file that the browser displays. *search* includes any post parameters that are compiled when a form is submitted. *hash* is usually a link to a local anchor.

The `location` object also has a `host` property, which consists of the combination of *hostname* and *port*, as well as an extremely important property, known as `href`, which contains the entire URL.

**Finding Out Where You Are** This next example is a page that has no body. It is written entirely by the header script. As the page is written, it dissects the location object and lists all of its properties in a table. The host, port, and hostname properties will be non-empty only if you have loaded some page from a server. Listing 10.5 provides the code for the Location Display script, shown in Figure 10.5.

**Listing 10.5 Displaying the Properties of the *location* Object**

```
<HTML>
<HEAD>
<TITLE>Parts of the Location Object</TITLE>
<SCRIPT>

var aline = '<H3><BR></H3><HR><H3><BR></H3>'
var skip='<H3><BR></H3>'

document.write('<CENTER>')
document.write('<FONT SIZE=5 COLOR="darkred"><B>Example : </B></FONT>
  <FONT SIZE=5 COLOR="darkblue"> ¬
  <B>What\'s in the Location      Object?</B></FONT>')
document.write('<BR>')
document.write('<BLOCKQUOTE><BLOCKQUOTE>If you are viewing this
     document from your hard disk, host, hostname, and port will
     be empty.</BLOCKQUOTE></BLOCKQUOTE>')
document.write('<BR>')

document.write('<CENTER><TABLE ALIGN= CENTER BORDER CELLPADDING=3>')
document.write('<TR><TD><B>Property</B></TD><TD ALIGN=CENTER>
     <B>Value</B></TD></TR>')
document.write('<TR><TD>href</TD><TD>' + location.href + '</TD></TR>')
document.write('<TR><TD>protocol</TD><TD>' + location.protocol
     + '</TD></TR>')
document.write('<TR><TD>hostname</TD><TD>' + location.hostname
     + '</TD></TR>')
document.write('<TR><TD>host</TD><TD>' + location.host + '</TD></TR>')
document.write('<TR><TD>port</TD><TD>' + location.port + '</TD></TR>')
document.write('<TR><TD>pathname</TD><TD>' + location.pathname
     + '</TD></TR>')
document.write('<TR><TD>search</TD><TD>' + location.search
     + '</TD></TR>')
document.write('<TR><TD>hash</TD><TD>' + location.hash + '</TD></TR>')
document.write('</TABLE></CENTER>')
document.write(aline)
document.write('<CENTER>')
document.write(aline)
</SCRIPT>
</HEAD>
</HTML>
```

Part

II

Ch

10

**FIG. 10.5**

An example of Listing 10.5: A display of the `location` object's properties.

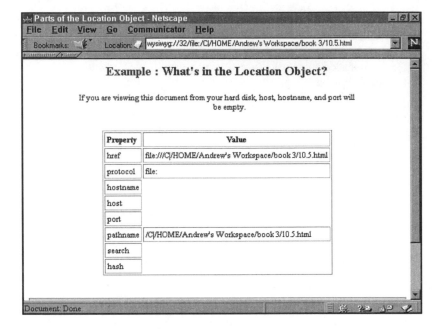

**Sending the User Elsewhere**    Not only can you obtain useful information by examining the `location` object, you can also modify it and send the user elsewhere. This is useful if you should want to dynamically generate an URL or a reference to an anchor. The example shown in Listing 10.6 builds an URL dynamically and sends the current browser to that URL. This code implements a "Message Center," which retrieves messages from URLs created via button clicks. Four users have been created to demonstrate this aspect of the `location` object (see Figure 10.6).

**Listing 10.6    Modifying the Current URL Dynamically**

```
<HEAD>
<TITLE>Message Center</TITLE>
<SCRIPT>
function getMessage(who)
{
    loc = self.location
    nloc = "" + lock = nloc.lastIndexOf('\\')
nnloc = nloc.substring(0,k+1) + who.value + '.htm'
    self.location = nnloc
}
</SCRIPT>
</HEAD>
<BODY>
<CENTER><HR>
<FONT SIZE=5 COLOR='darkred'><B>Example 4</B></FONT>:  <FONT SIZE=5
    COLOR='darkblue'><B>Moving Around Dynamically</B></FONT><BR>
<HR><FONT SIZE=6 COLOR='darkslateblue'><B>Message Center</B></FONT><BR>
</CENTER>
```

```
<CENTER>
<FORM>
<TABLE BORDER ALIGN=CENTER><TR><TD>
<INPUT TYPE=radio NAME='getMsgR' VALUE='John'
     onClick='getMessage(this)'>John
<INPUT TYPE=radio NAME='getMsgR' VALUE='George'
     onClick='getMessage(this)'>George
<INPUT TYPE=radio NAME='getMsgR' VALUE='Ken'
     onClick='getMessage(this)'>Ken
<INPUT TYPE=radio NAME='getMsgR' VALUE='Julie'
     onClick='getMessage(this)'>Julie
<INPUT TYPE=hidden NAME='translate' VALUE=''>
</TD></TR></TABLE>
</FORM>
</CENTER>

<H3><BR><HR><BR></H3>
<H3><BR><HR SIZE=5 WIDTH=80%><BR></H3>
</BODY>
</HTML>
```

Part
II

Ch
10

**FIG. 10.6**

A message center for mail retrieval.

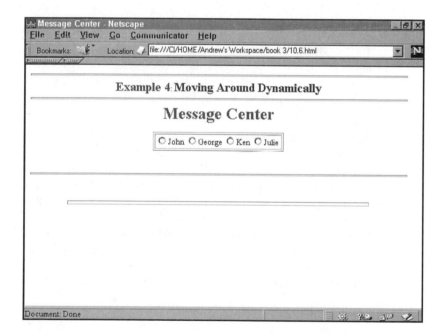

The script works by first obtaining the current location. It then strips off the file name and replaces it with the value of the option button clicked. The script also makes sure to tack on the suffix .htm. This presumes that the message HTML files are in the same directory as the current page. However, it would be easy enough to build in a subdirectory name just for the messages, or even have a separate subdirectory for each person. The location object is then set to the newly constructed URL. Setting the `location` object retrieves the file at that location. In our example, this file represents the set of messages for the particular user whose button was pressed.

**TIP**   You can force a page to be reloaded by setting the `location` object to the URL corresponding to that page.

**Using the *reload()* Method**   Another way to reload a page is to use the new `location.reload()` method. Implemented in Netscape Navigator 3.0, this method allows you to force a reload of the current document in a window. The `reload()` method can behave just like the client's Reload button, meaning that the page reloads by using the client browser's reload settings (verify the page every time, once per session, or never). This way, the page can either be reloaded from the cache, if it has not changed, or downloaded again from the server. However, you can also force the browser to reload the page from the server, regardless of the time the page was last modified. To do this, you pass a parameter that evaluates to TRUE. If the parameter evaluates to anything else but TRUE, then the client-browser reload settings apply. An example of the syntax follows:

```
location.reload(true)
```

When you use this in an event handler, remember to use `window.location.reload()`. Due to JavaScript's scoping rules for static objects, calling `location` by itself is equivalent to calling `document.location`, which itself is another way of saying `document.URL`. If you just call `location.reload()`, you will actually be telling JavaScript to call `document.location.reload()`, which is invalid.

**Using the *replace()* Method**   Sometimes, when you visit Web sites that ask you to input your name and address, perhaps to receive some beta software or to be placed on a mailing list, you often end up at a "dead end" once you have submitted your information. You have to click the Back button a few times to get to a more useful page on that site and navigate from there. The `location.replace()` method lets you avoid this. Normally, when you access Web pages, the browser places a new entry in your history list, which your browser uses to enable you to go back to locations you have visited before during the course of a session. When you use the `replace()` method, you instead are erasing the current location in the history list and replacing it with the one you set. The user cannot click the Back button to go to the page replaced because it is no longer recorded in the browser's history.

The syntax of the replace method is as follows:

```
location.replace("URL")
```

You can use this method when you want to make sure users can't go back to a given page once they have left it. Listing 10.7 presents users with a list of possible actions in a Web-based adventure game. Since the decisions can be undone, the `location.replace()` is used. As with the `reload()` method, you must use `window.location.replace()` because of JavaScript's scoping rules for static objects.

**Listing 10.7   Using *location.replace()* to Modify the Browser's History List**

```
<HTML>
<HEAD>
<TITLE>The Dark Pass</TITLE>
</HEAD>
<BODY BGCOLOR=black TEXT=white>
<H3>The Dark Pass</H3>
<B>You stand on a long stretch of stone across a deep chasm. Before you
roars a huge green dragon. Behind you the Ice Wraith is running
toward you at a rapid pace.   <BR>
What will you do?<BR>
<UL>
<LI><A HREF="javascript://"
onClick="window.location.replace('fall.html');return false">Jump off
➥the bridge</A>
<LI><A HREF="javascript://"
onClick="window.location.replace('dragon.html');return false">Attack the
➥dragon</A>
<LI><A HREF="javascript://"
onClick="window.location.replace('wraith.html');return false">Attack the
➥wraith</a>
</UL>
</BODY>
```

Notice that the onClick returns FALSE. This is done to override the href location and to instead instruct the browser to load the new page. javascript:// is used as a way to include an href location that has no effect because // is the indicator of a comment in JavaScript. Try this script out on your own (adding the three other HTML files) and see how the browser goes to the new location, but forgets your previous location.

**Using the *search* Property**   When you submit a form, all the values of the various form elements are retrieved, parsed, and concatenated with the location object; they are placed after the path and preceded by question marks. The value of location.search is precisely that string, including the question mark.

This string is not just a simple list of element contents, however. Each element value is placed in the string in the form 'elementName=elementValue' and followed by an ampersand (&). Any nonalphanumeric characters are coded or escaped. The ASCII value of any such character is changed into a two-digit hexadecimal number preceded by a percent sign. If text field or text area elements have multiple words, these words are separated by a plus sign. Consequently, when you get the location.search string, you have to decode it to get the various form elements that it contains.

▶ **See** "Global and Local Variables," **p. 276**, for more information about character encoding.

You can place your own form element values, or anything else, in the location's search property. As long as you precede it with a question mark, location.search retrieves it. However, not all nonalphanumeric characters can be placed in the string or retrieved intact. If you are going to concoct a homegrown search string, you may need to either encode the parameters yourself or not allow nonalphanumeric characters. Listing 10.8 is a simple page that shows you how to manipulate location.search. The results are demonstrated in Figure 10.7.

**Listing 10.8   Using the *search* Property of the *Location* Object**

```
<HTML>
<HEAD>
<TITLE>Forcing a Reload with Location</TITLE>
<SCRIPT>
function reloadMe()
{
     astr = document.nameForm.myName.value
     nastr= self.location.pathname  + '?' + astr
     self.location = nastr
}

function clearUp()
{
  self.location = self.location.pathname
}

if (self.location.search != null && self.location.search !='')
    {
         document.write('<CENTER><FONT SIZE=4 COLOR="darkslategray"><B>
             Form Entry Data: </B></FONT></CENTER>')
         document.write('<CENTER><FONT SIZE=4 COLOR="red"><B>' +
             self.location.search + '</B></FONT></CENTER>')
    }
</SCRIPT>
</HEAD>
<H3><HR></H3>
<CENTER><FONT SIZE=6 COLOR="blue"><B>Forcing a Reload with ¬
     Location</B></FONT></CENTER>
<H3><BR><HR><BR></H3>

<CENTER>

<FORM NAME=nameForm>
<INPUT TYPE=text NAME=myName VALUE='abracadabra&#^$()'>
<INPUT TYPE=button NAME=reloadBtn VALUE='Reload Page'
     onClick='reloadMe()'>
<INPUT TYPE=button NAME=submitBtn VALUE= 'Submit Form'
     onClick='this.form.submit()'>
<INPUT TYPE=button NAME=clearBtn VALUE= 'Clear' onClick='clearUp()'>
<INPUT TYPE=hidden NAME=hideFld>
</FORM>
</CENTER>
<H3><BR><HR><BR></H3>
<H3><BR><HR SIZE=5 WIDTH=80%><BR></H3>
</BODY>
</HTML>
```

**N O T E**  Internet Explorer 3.0 severely limits the use of the `location.search` property. In most cases, it will be empty on document reload. ■

**FIG. 10.7**

Forcing a reload with `Location` in Netscape Navigator.

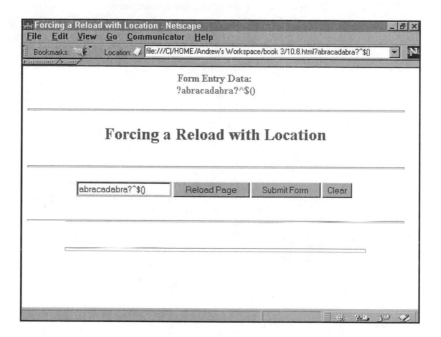

A script in the `<HEAD>` part of an HTML document can pick up the command-line parameters with `location.search` and write something to the document being loaded based on what it finds. This example just reads the parameter string and writes it for you at the head of the page. Note that this writing is guarded by a test to see if `location.search` is `null` or empty. If `location.search` is not a valid string and you attempt to parse it into variables that are used later, you will encounter error after error. Always test for a `null` string or an empty string.

The code in Listing 10.8 has two useful functions: `ClearUp()` simply strips the search string from the location by setting the `location` object to `location.path`, and the `reloadMe()` function takes the value from the text box and adds it to `location.path`. It then sets the location to that result.

## The *history* Object

The `history` object is a list that contains the locations of all the URLs that you have visited. You can move backward and forward through the history list with `history.back` and `history.forward`. You can also move around in the list in a relative fashion with `history.go()`. This function takes a positive or negative integer argument and moves you that many URLs forward or backward in the history list. The only property of a history list you can access is its `length`, which is the number of items in the list. You can neither set nor retrieve history list items.

To show how to manipulate the history list, we'll build another pop-up window that boasts only a Close button and four directional buttons. The buttons enable you to manipulate the history list of the parent window. You can move backward and forward by one step or five. Listing 10.9 illustrates this—but note: This listing is not complete.

**Listing 10.9   Using the *history* Object in a Pop-Up Window**

```
<HTML>
<HEAD>
<TITLE>Running through the History List</TITLE>
<SCRIPT>
var aNoteWin
var creat

function openPopUp()

{
     aPopUp= window.open('','Note','toobar=no,location=no,
          directories=no,status=no,scrollbars=no,resizable=no,
          copyhistory=no,width=110,height=150')
     ndoc= aPopUp.document
astr ='<HTML><HEAD><TITLE>Window Scroller</TITLE>'
     astr +='<SCRIPT>'
     astr +='var creat\n'
     astr +='function closeNote(aName){'
     astr +='self.close()'
     astr +='}\n'
     astr +='function saveNote(aName){'
     astr +='}\n'
     astr +='function goNext(){'
     astr +='creat.window.history.forward()\n'
     astr +='}\n'
     astr +='function goBack(){'
     astr +='creat.window.history.back()\n'
     astr +='}\n'
     astr +='function goBackFive(){'
     astr += 'creat.window.history.go(-5)\n'
     astr +='}\n'
     astr +='function goNextFive(){'
     astr +='creat.window.history.go(5)\n'
     astr +='}\n'
     astr +='<\/SCRIPT>'
     astr +='</HEAD>'
  astr ='<BODY>'
     astr +='<FORM NAME="popForm">'
     astr +='<TABLE ALIGN=LEFT BORDER>'
     astr +='</TR><TR ALIGN=CENTER><TD>'
     astr +='<INPUT TYPE=button NAME="closeBtn" VALUE="Close"
         ONCLICK="closePopUp()">'
     astr +='</TD>'
     astr +='</TR>'
     astr +='<TR ALIGN=CENTER><TD>'
```

```
            astr +='<INPUT TYPE="button" NAME="startBtn" VALUE="<<"
                  onclick="goBackFive()">'
            astr +='<INPUT TYPE="button" NAME="backBtn" VALUE="<"
                  onclick="goBack()">'
            astr +='<INPUT TYPE="button" NAME="nextBtn" VALUE=">"
                  onclick="goNext()">'
            astr +='<INPUT TYPE="button" NAME="endBtn" VALUE=">>"
                  onclick="goNextFive()">'
            astr +='</TD></TR>'
            astr +='<TR><TD>'
            astr +='<INPUT TYPE="hidden" NAME="IAm" VALUE="0">'
            astr +='</TD></TR>'
            astr +='</TABLE>'
            astr +='</FORM>'
            astr +='<BR CLEAR=ALL><H3><BR></H3>'
            astr +='</BODY></HTML>'
            ndoc.write(astr)
            ndoc.close()
            self.aNoteWin = aPopUp
            aPopUp.creat = self
}

function closePopUp()
{
    if ( self.aNoteWin != null )
        self.aNoteWin.close()
}

</SCRIPT>
</HEAD>
<BODY >
<CENTER>
<FONT SIZE=5 COLOR='darkred'><B>Example 5</B></FONT>:
    <FONT SIZE=5 COLOR='darkblue'><B>Running through the History List
        </B></FONT>
</CENTER>
<H3><BR><HR><BR></H3>


<H3><BR><HR><BR></H3>


<CENTER>
<FORM NAME='noteForm'>
<INPUT TYPE='button' NAME='makeBtn' VALUE='Make Popup'
    onClick='openPopUp()'>
<INPUT TYPE='button' NAME='closeBtn' VALUE='Close Popup'
    onclick='closePopUp()'>
</FORM>
</CENTER>
<H3><BR><HR><BR></H3>

<H3><BR><HR><BR></H3>
<H3><BR><HR SIZE=5 WIDTH=80%><BR></H3>
</BODY>
</HTML>
```

This pop-up is a variation on our old friend, aNoteWin. It can access its parent's variables through an artificial property of aNoteWin, the creat property, which we carefully write into the child's window as a var by using the astr += 'var creat\n' statement. At the end of the openNote() function, which creates and draws the window, aNoteWin.creat is set to self. This enables you to have ready access to the parent window's variables, functions, and objects.

# Security Aspects of JavaScript Objects

Although it would be useful to retrieve history list items, this functionality has been removed from JavaScript. Unfortunately, each history list entry contains the entire location, including the search string. If this information could be retrieved, the possibility exists that credit card or other personal information might be gleaned by malicious individuals.

You may have wondered why there is no windows array. This also does not exist in JavaScript for security reasons. If it did, a script from one window might reach into another, unrelated window and scavenge information from its form elements or its location object. Again, what might be perceived as a limitation in JavaScript has been imposed to protect you.

# The *document* Object

The document object encapsulates all JavaScript objects that correspond to the HTML elements. It is the parent of forms, links, images, and anchors. These objects occur as arrays and are accessed as document.forms[*xx*], document.links[*xx*], document.images[*xx*], and document.anchors[*xx*], where *xx* is an array index. The document object has several other useful properties. It has a property, for example, for all of the standard object colors, such as the background color, text color, and link colors. You cannot change the property of a static closed document, however, so these properties are useful only when building a document.

Four properties that are useful in keeping your documents up-to-date are the location, title, lastModified, and referrer properties. These are used to dynamically write a header or a footer for your documents. Listing 10.10 shows a typical example of how you could use the document object in this way. Note that the properties of the document object are read-only. The attempt to set document.title in this listing will fail. If you want to load this example, you must comment out that line.

**Listing 10.10   Writing the Document Header**

```
<HTML>
<HEAD>
<TITLE>Writing a Document Header</TITLE>
<SCRIPT>
document.bgcolor = 'linen'
document.text = 'darkslateblue'
document.link = 'coral'
document.vlink='peach'
document.alink='red'
document.title='Dynamic Headers'    // comment me out
document.write('<TABLE ALIGN=RIGHT WIDTH=300 BORDER=1>')
```

```
document.write('<TR><TD>')
document.write('<FONT SIZE=7 COLOR= "navy">')
document.write('<CENTER>' +document.title + '</CENTER>')
document.write('</TD></TR></TABLE>')
document.write('<CENTER><B>')
document.write('<HR>')
document.write('This document was last modified on<BR>
     <FONT COLOR="red">' + document.lastmodified + '</FONT><BR>')
document.write('Save this URL: <BR><FONT COLOR="red">'
     + document.location + '</FONT><BR>')
document.write('You arrived here from <BR><FONT COLOR="red">'
     + document.referrer + '</FONT><BR>')
document.write('<BR><HR><BR>')
document.write('</B></CENTER>')
document.write('')
</SCRIPT>
</HEAD>
<BODY>
<H3><BR><HR><BR></H3>
<H3><BR><HR SIZE=5 WIDTH=80%><BR></H3>
</BODY>
</HTML>
```

**Forms**   You can get input from your users via HTML form elements (sometimes known as widgets). You can have many forms on a page. If they are named (by an HTML NAME directive), you can refer to them by name. You can also refer to a form by its index in the zero-based `forms` array. Each form can have any one of the standard HTML form elements. These include single-line `text`, `radio`, `checkbox`, `hidden`, `password`, `reset`, and `submit`. There is also a `select` widget, which can be either a drop-down list or a plain list, and a `textarea` widget, which can be used to collect large amounts of text that spans multiple lines.

▶ **See** "Using JavaScript Event Handlers," **p. 73**, for more information about the correspondence between HTML form elements, the events they generate, and their JavaScript counterparts.

 **T I P**   A script can access only elements that have already been created. They cannot be accessed in a document <HEAD> because the forms and their elements do not yet exist.

**Links**   Links are the bread and butter of any hypertext system, especially HTML. In Java-Script, the `links` array can be canvassed to provide a list of links in a document. Links have only one property, the `target`. The `target` is not the URL pointed to by the link; rather, it is the window into which that URL will be loaded. Any link is also a `location` object so that you can dissect the link in the same way you dissect a `location` object.

Links can have an `onClick` handler just as buttons do. However, when the `onClick` handler finishes, the URL specified by the link loads. If you do not want the link to go anywhere, just specify the current URL as its destination. If you want to use a link to execute a function, use `HREF= 'javascript: myfunc()'`. Myfunc() can either call a function or contain JavaScript code. For example, `HREF='javascript: self.close()'` immediately closes the current window.

> **CAUTION**
>
> A `javascript:`*`xxx`*`()` call replaces an URL. The browser tries to interpret any return from a function call as if it were an URL. If the browser does not understand the return value, it reloads the current page. When that occurs, any window globals that you set during the *`xxx`*`()` function call are lost.

Both text and images can be links. You can include both in the same link, if you want, so that clicking either the text or the image activates the link's events. Because images can be links, you can use them as buttons to call functions if you use `javascript:`*`xxx`*`()` as the HREF instead of an URL. Also, you can now (in Netscape Navigator 3.0) use the AREA object contained in the links array to control image maps.

Links can also trap the `onMouseOver` and `onMouseOut` events. When you pass your mouse into a link area, it triggers an `onMouseOver` event, and when your mouse leaves that area, it triggers an `onMouseOut` event.

If you use the `onMouseOver` event to write to the status bar, you find that if you move your mouse too quickly you miss the status write. This is because it is rapidly replaced by the browser's own response to the event. When you exit, the status written stays there until you encounter another link. If you want to use the content of your link in a function called from an `onMouseOver` handler, you can pass the function the keyword `this`. Links are treated like any other JavaScript object.

Figure 10.8 shows an `onMouseOver` event being triggered just as the mouse moves over the link. This figure is the result of the code in Listing 10.11, which also includes examples of trapping `Click` and `MouseOver` events from links, as well as a script that uses the `document.links` array to write the number of links on the page. Examples of using a `javascript:`*`xxx`* replacement for an URL in a link can be found in a previous listing, Listing 10.4, which uses linked images as buttons.

### Listing 10.11   Event Processing for the *Link* Object

```
<HTML>
<HEAD>
<TITLE>What's Your Link</TITLE>
<SCRIPT>
function checkOut()
{
    a = (confirm("This file is 10 megs in size.  It will take 2 hours
    to download it.  Are you sure you want to do that at
        this time?"))
    if (a == true)
        {
            alert ('loading file...')
        }
    else
        {
```

```
                        alert('NOT loading file!')
        }
        }

        function enhance(what)
        {
             astr = what.href

             self.status = 'Example 4 from this chapter: ' + astr}

</SCRIPT>
</HEAD>
<BODY>
<TABLE ALIGN=RIGHT WIDTH=250 BORDER=1>
<TR><TD>
<FONT SIZE=7 COLOR="darkcorel">
<CENTER>What's Your Link</CENTER>
</TD></TR></TABLE>
<FONT SIZE=5 >Link Example</FONT><BR>
This page demonstrates onClick and mouseOver events for links
<HR>
<H3><BR><HR><BR></H3>
<TABLE ALIGN=LEFT BORDER WIDTH=250>
<TR><TD>
<A HREF='C8-4.HTM' onMouseOver='enhance(this)'>
<IMG WIDTH=100 HEIGHT=100  VSPACE=2 HSPACE= 2 ALIGN=Left
     SRC="Images/grkaleid.jpg">
<CENTER><FONT SIZE=5>Enhanced Status</FONT></CENTER></A>
</TD></TR></TABLE>
This Linked image has an onMouseOver event in its Link tag.
This event appears to be fired twice, once when the mouse passes
into the boundary of the image and once when it passes out.
Move the mouse SLOWLY to see the effect of the event handler.
<BR CLEAR ALL>
<H3><BR></H3>

<TABLE ALIGN=LEFT BORDER WIDTH=250>
<TR><TD>
<A HREF='C8-3.HTM' onClick='checkOut()'>
<IMG WIDTH=32 HEIGHT= 50 VSPACE=2 HSPACE=2 BORDER=2 ALIGN=Left
     SRC="Images/answer_u.gif">
<CENTER><FONT SIZE=5>File Information</FONT></CENTER></A>
</TD></TR></TABLE>
This onClick routine asks you if you want to load a very large file.
     <FONT SIZE=4 COLOR='red'> </FONT>
<BR CLEAR ALL>
<H3><BR><HR><BR></H3>
<H3><BR><HR SIZE=5 WIDTH=80%><BR></H3>
</BODY>
<SCRIPT>
k = document.links.length
document.write('This page has ' + k + ' links.  They are: <BR>')
</SCRIPT>
</HTML>
```

**FIG. 10.8**
MouseOver is fired
only when the mouse
pointer enters or leaves
the linked object.

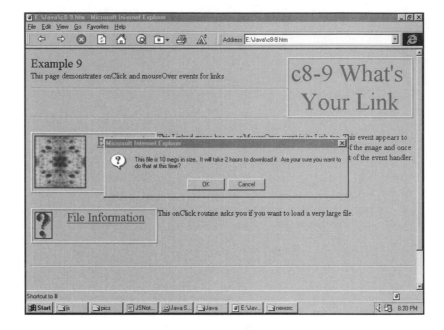

**Images**    One of the most exciting new features of JavaScript is the Images object. Every image displayed on a page is reflected in an Images[] array and actually can now be replaced dynamically based on the src attribute. The image object enables you to access many properties of each image displayed on the screen. These properties are: border (reflects the border attribute), complete (TRUE or FALSE based on whether the image has completed loading), height, hspace, lowsrc, name, src, vspace, and width.

Once an image is defined on a page, that image can be replaced by another image simply by setting the images[n].src attribute. The uses for this are wide, including animating an image when a mouse passes over it, simulating button clicks, and more. Any JavaScript event can be used to trigger a change in an image on a page.

**Anchors**    Anchors consist of text or images in your document that are marked, usually named, and can be referenced by a link within the same document (known as a *local* link). The document object has an anchors array, but at this time, its use is quite limited. You can find out how many anchors are on the page by using the length property.

# Dynamic Documents

Dynamic documents created by using JavaScript provide all the functionality of static documents written in HTML. If you can write it in HTML, you can write it on-the-fly in a document script. In fact, you can write your whole document in a script. You have already seen several examples of this, such as Listing 10.9, which creates a small window that can be used to manipulate the history list of the top-level window. You can also have a script after the </BODY> tag that writes a document footer in a similar fashion.

## Restrictions on *document.write*

Unfortunately, you cannot change anything on your current page once the document is finished. If you want to write to the current document, you have to open it and write to it via scripts placed at the beginning and end of the document. You can also choose to rewrite the entire document.

Using the `document.write` method is like printing on a dot-matrix printer: it is top-down only. This makes it particularly hard to do graphing or other innovative work that requires accurate positioning of objects on the page because you cannot know in advance where they will end up.

You must also be careful when enclosing an HTML statement within a `document.write` clause. The following seemingly innocent statement gives you at least one error:

```
document.write('<FONT SIZE=5 COLOR='red'>Javascript is GREAT!</FONT>')
```

Many HTML parameters need to be quoted, and it is much easier to use single quotes than double quotes. Unfortunately, the `write` statement terminates with the leading quote of `'red'`. The closing parenthesis of the `write` statement is not found, and an error occurs. The problem is easily fixed in this case: just use double quotes around `red`.

But what do you do if there is a need for a third level of nested quotes? Take the following HTML statement for example:

```
<INPUT TYPE='radio' NAME='mycolor' VALUE='red'
➥onClick='Alert("You chose red!")'>
```

This statement already has nested quotes. If you want to enclose this within a `document.write` clause, you have two choices:

- Escape one set of quotes, usually the ones most deeply nested:

  ```
  document.write("<INPUT TYPE='radio' NAME='mycolor' VALUE='red'
  ➥onClick='Alert(\"You chose red!\")'>")
  ```

- Put the contents of the deepest quotes into a variable:

  ```
  astr = "You chose red!"
  document.write("<INPUT TYPE='radio' NAME='mycolor'
  ➥VALUE='red' onClick='Alert(astr)'>")
  ```

If you have more than three levels of quotes, you must use the second option.

▶ **See** "Variables and Values," **p. 26**, for more information about the basic rules for string quoting.

## Using Nascent Documents

To provide a canvas for yourself to write on, use the `document.open` command. It is often a good idea to precede this with a `document.close` command as a safety precaution, in case there is already a document open. You can open or reopen a document in the current window or any window for which you have a reference. Opening a document in that window clears anything that is already there. Once the document is open, you can write to it.

> **CAUTION**
>
> If you issue a `document.open` command from within a script in the current page and it is not preceded by a window reference, the current page will be opened. Whatever is on the page is gone! This can be quite a surprise. Don't worry. You can recover the page with a reload, but your users might not know that. Check all `document.open` references carefully.

A document is open until you specifically close it or until the browser runs out of things to write on it. When you first open a window, the document associated with that window is also opened. You can then write to it with a header script. Then, the browser writes all of the body, if there is one, and anything it finds in the footer script, if there is one. When it reaches the end of the HTML text, it automatically closes the document. Note that if you open a new window with myNewWin = self.open('', 'NewWin'), you do not have to issue a document.open. Just start writing on the blank page.

We have already noted some items to be careful of in using `document.write` statements. If you try to write to a document that is not open, nothing happens. No error occurs—the command simply fails. You can write anything to a nascent document, including scripts. If you are creating a window from scratch, you have to write everything. Listings 10.4 and 10.9, earlier in this chapter, illustrate this approach.

## TROUBLESHOOTING

**I opened a fresh document using `document.open()` and wrote to it for quite a long time using `document.write()`, but nothing happened. Where did I go wrong?** document.write() places all of its output into an ASCII stream. Think of it as one big string that exists somewhere in memory. The browser does not get to interpret the stream until you specifically say, "That's all, folks!" with a `document.close()`. Once you close the document, everything that you have written (hopefully) is rendered in the browser window. This also means that any script errors are noticed until the document is actually closed.

# A Page Generated Entirely by JavaScript

If you examine Listing 10.10, you see that this document is written totally within the header. Let's revisit this document and add a little to it. Suppose that you have a number of images that have the same prefix and differ only in a final numerical suffix. Let us also suppose that these numbers are sequential. With very little JavaScript, you can dynamically generate the image citations and write them to the page.

Listing 10.12 takes this approach. The `for` loop is particularly worthy of close examination. It keeps adding citation information to a continuously growing string. When it is finished, it uses one document.write() statement to put the string on the document stream. There are several reasons to use this type of an iterative construct:

- It is easier to debug. You can use a separate string for each individual citation and pop it up in an alert so that you can check its syntax.

- It gets rid of some of the nested quote problems.

- You can save the resulting output string. This is particularly useful if you want to actually write the HTML for the citations as text, rather than have the browser interpret what you write. To do that, you need to replace all < with &lt; and all > with &gt;.

**Listing 10.12   Generating an Entire Document in JavaScript**

```
<HTML>
<HEAD>
<TITLE>Writing a Document with Javascript</TITLE>
<SCRIPT>
document.bgcolor = 'linen'
document.text = 'darkslateblue'
document.link = 'coral'
document.vlink='peach'
document.alink='red'
document.write("<TABLE ALIGN=RIGHT WIDTH=350 BORDER=1>")
document.write("<TR><TD>")
document.write("<FONT SIZE=7 COLOR=indianred>")
document.write("<CENTER>" + document.title + "</CENTER>")
document.write("</TD></TR></TABLE>")
document.write("<BR>")
document.write("<LEFT>")
document.write("This page is an example of a document written
      completely within a script. The reference for each image is
      generated dynamically")
document.write("</LEFT>")
document.write("<BR CLEAR ALL>")
document.write("<HR>")
bstr = 'DBLACE'
kstr = ''
for (i = 1 ; i <= 6 ; i++)
{
    var xstr = bstr + i + '.jpg'
    kstr += '<IMG SRC=\"Images\/' + xstr + '" '
    kstr += 'HEIGHT=100 WIDTH=100 VSPACE=5 HSPACE=5 BORDER=2 ALIGN=LEFT>'
    kstr += '<H3><BR><H3>'
    kstr += '<CENTER><FONT SIZE=4 COLOR="coral">' + xstr
          + '</FONT></CENTER>'
    kstr += '<HR><BR CLEAR ALL>'
}
document.write(kstr)
document.write("<BR><HR><BR>")
document.write("This document was last modified on<BR>
    <FONT COLOR=red><B>")
document.write(document.lastModified)
document.write("</FONT><BR>")
document.write("<BR><HR><BR>")
document.write("</B></CENTER>")
```

Part

II

Ch

10

*continues*

---

**Listing 10.12   Continued**

```
document.write("")
</SCRIPT>
</HEAD>
<BODY>
<H3><BR><HR SIZE=5 WIDTH=80%><BR></H3>
</BODY>
</HTML>
```

---

# Dynamically Rewriting Your Page

There are many reasons why you might want to rewrite your page dynamically. You may want to try out various background images and colors, for example. There are two steps to this process: obtaining (or generating) the current information that you will modify, and applying that information to the current page. If you use Internet Explorer's current release (3.0), it insists upon sending document.write() calls to a new page, and the best you can do is to generate as much information as possible when constructing that new page. Listing 10.13 shows an example of this. It can be easily extended to include a number of different items. In fact, you can build a simple page with it.

---

**Listing 10.13   Using JavaScript to Dynamically Rewrite a Document**

```
<HTML>
<HEAD>
<TITLE>Dynamic Modification of Documents</TITLE>
<SCRIPT>

function createArray(n)
{
    this.length = n
    return this
}

var parms = new createArray(6)

function reloadMe()
{
parms[1] = document.forms[0].aname.value
    parms[2] = document.forms[0].mytext.value
    parms[3] = document.forms[0].mylink.value
    parms[4]  += document.forms[0].myvlink.value
    parms[5]  += document.forms[0].myimage.value

    var astr
astr = '<BODY BACKGROUND = "Images/' + parms[5] + '" '
    astr += 'TEXT="'+ parms[2] + '" '
    astr += 'LINK="'+ parms[3] + '" '
    astr += 'VLINK="'+ parms[4] + '" '
    astr += 'ALINK="red" '
    astr += '>\n'
```

```
        document.write(astr)
        document.write('<TABLE ALIGN=RIGHT WIDTH=350 BORDER=1>')
        document.write('<TR><TD>')
        document.write('<FONT SIZE=7 COLOR= "indianred">')
        document.write('<CENTER>' + document.title + '</CENTER>')
        document.write('</TD></TR></TABLE>')
        document.write('<LEFT><B>')
        document.write('This page is an example of dynamically revised' +
        ➥' by a header script which acts on user\' choices.')
        document.write('</B></LEFT>')
        document.write('<BR CLEAR ALL>')
        document.write('<HR>')
        astr ='<CENTER><FONT SIZE=7 COLOR="' + parms[3] + '"><B> '
        astr += parms[1] + '</B></FONT></CENTER>'
        document.write(astr)
        document.write('<HR><BR>')
        document.close();
}

function clearUp()
{
  self.location = self.location.pathname
}

function doTC(what)
{
    what.form.mytext.value = what.value
}

function doLC(what)
{
    what.form.mylink.value = what.value
}

function doVC(what)
{
    what.form.myvlink.value = what.value
}

function doImage(what)
{
    document.forms[0].myimage.value = 'DBLACE' + what + '.jpg'
}

function doname(what)
{
    what.form.aname.value = what.value
}


</SCRIPT>
</HEAD>
<BODY>
<CENTER>
```

*continues*

**Listing 10.13 Continued**

```
<FORM NAME=nameForm>
Enter your first name here:<BR>
<INPUT TYPE=text NAME=myname  SIZE= 20
       onChange='doname(this)'><H3><BR></H3>
<CENTER>
<TABLE ALIGN=LEFT WIDTH=100 BORDER CELLPADDING=5>
<TR ALIGN=LEFT><TD>
<CENTER><B>Text</B></CENTER>
<INPUT TYPE="RADIO" NAME="tc" VALUE='white' ONCLICK='doTC(this)'>white<BR>
<INPUT TYPE="RADIO" NAME="tc" VALUE='yellow' ONCLICK='doTC(this)'>yellow<BR>
<INPUT TYPE="RADIO" NAME="tc" VALUE='navy' ONCLICK='doTC(this)'>navy<BR>
<INPUT TYPE="RADIO" NAME="tc" VALUE='blue' ONCLICK='doTC(this)'>blue<BR>
<INPUT TYPE="RADIO" NAME="tc" VALUE='orange' ONCLICK='doTC(this)'>orange<BR>
<INPUT TYPE="RADIO" NAME="tc" VALUE='red' ONCLICK='doTC(this)'>red<BR>
<INPUT TYPE="RADIO" NAME="tc" VALUE='black' ONCLICK='doTC(this)'>black<BR>
</TD></TR></TABLE>

<TABLE ALIGN=LEFT WIDTH=100 BORDER CELLPADDING=5>
<TR ALIGN=LEFT><TD>
<CENTER><B>Link</B></CENTER>
<INPUT TYPE="RADIO" NAME="lc" VALUE='white' ONCLICK='doLC(this)'>white<BR>
<INPUT TYPE="RADIO" NAME="lc" VALUE='yellow' ONCLICK='doLC(this)'>yellow<BR>
<INPUT TYPE="RADIO" NAME="lc" VALUE='navy' ONCLICK='doLC(this)'>navy<BR>
<INPUT TYPE="RADIO" NAME="lc" VALUE='blue' ONCLICK='doLC(this)'>blue<BR>
<INPUT TYPE="RADIO" NAME="lc" VALUE='orange' ONCLICK='doLC(this)'>orange<BR>
<INPUT TYPE="RADIO" NAME="lc" VALUE='red' ONCLICK='doLC(this)'>red<BR>
<INPUT TYPE="RADIO" NAME="lc" VALUE='black' ONCLICK='doLC(this)'>black<BR>
</TD></TR></TABLE>

<TABLE ALIGN=LEFT WIDTH=100 BORDER CELLPADDING=5>
<TR ALIGN=LEFT><TD>
<CENTER><B>VLink</B></CENTER>
<INPUT TYPE="RADIO" NAME="vc" VALUE='white' ONCLICK='doVC(this)'>white<BR>
<INPUT TYPE="RADIO" NAME="vc" VALUE='yellow' ONCLICK='doVC(this)'>yellow<BR>
<INPUT TYPE="RADIO" NAME="vc" VALUE='navy' ONCLICK='doVC(this)'>navy<BR>
<INPUT TYPE="RADIO" NAME="vc" VALUE='blue' ONCLICK='doVC(this)'>blue<BR>
<INPUT TYPE="RADIO" NAME="vc" VALUE='orange' ONCLICK='doVC(this)'>orange<BR>
<INPUT TYPE="RADIO" NAME="vc" VALUE='red' ONCLICK='doVC(this)'>red<BR>
<INPUT TYPE="RADIO" NAME="vc" VALUE='black' ONCLICK='doVC(this)'>black<BR>
</TD></TR></TABLE>
</CENTER>

<BR CLEAR ALL>
<HR>
<CENTER><FONT SIZE=4>Click on the image that you want for a
       background.</FONT></CENTER>
<H3><BR></H3>
```

```
<A HREF='javascript:doImage(1)'>
<IMG WIDTH=100 HEIGHT= 100 VSPACE=5 HSPACE=5 BORDER=2 ALIGN=Left
SRC="Images/DBLACE1.jpg"></A>

<A HREF='javascript:doImage(2)'>
<IMG WIDTH=100 HEIGHT= 100 VSPACE=5 HSPACE=5 BORDER=2 ALIGN=Left
SRC="Images/DBLACE2.jpg"></A>

<A HREF='javascript:doImage(3)'>
<IMG WIDTH=100 HEIGHT= 100 VSPACE=5 HSPACE=5 BORDER=2 ALIGN=Left
SRC="Images/DBLACE3.jpg"></A>

<A HREF='javascript:doImage(4)'>
<IMG WIDTH=100 HEIGHT= 100 VSPACE=5 HSPACE=5 BORDER=2 ALIGN=Left
SRC="Images/DBLACE4.jpg"></A>

<A HREF='javascript:doImage(5)'>
<IMG WIDTH=100 HEIGHT= 100 VSPACE=5 HSPACE=5 BORDER=2 ALIGN=Left
SRC="Images/DBLACE5.jpg"></A>
<BR CLEAR ALL>
<HR>
</CENTER>
<TABLE ALIGN= RIGHT WIDTH=300><TR ALIGN=RIGHT><TD>
Name: <INPUT TYPE=text NAME=aname><BR>
My Image: <INPUT TYPE=text NAME=myimage><BR>
My Text: <INPUT TYPE=text NAME=mytext><BR>
My Link: <INPUT TYPE=text NAME=mylink><BR>
My VLink: <INPUT TYPE=text NAME=myvlink><BR>
</TD></TR></TABLE>

<INPUT TYPE=button NAME=reloadBtn VALUE='Rewrite Page'
       onClick='reloadMe()'>
<INPUT TYPE=button NAME=clearBtn VALUE= 'Clear' onClick='clearUp()'>
<INPUT TYPE=hidden NAME=hideFld>
</FORM>
<HR>

<H3><BR><HR><BR></H3>
<H3><BR><HR SIZE=5 WIDTH=80%><BR></H3>
</BODY>
</HTML>
```

Figure 10.9 shows the result of loading this page. The page starts out in the default Netscape colors. It gives the user the opportunity to select text and link colors and a background tile. The user is in the process of selecting a tile.

**FIG. 10.9**

A dynamically rewritten page stores information for use in the next rewrite operation.

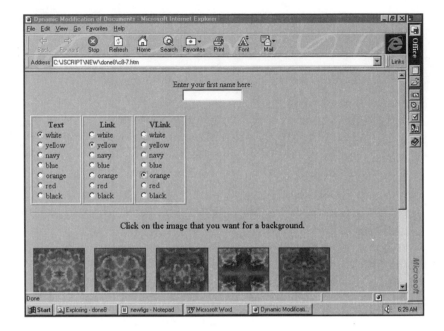

This script does several things that are worth noting, as follows:

- It creates a global array named parms. It does not bother to initialize the array because the program knows which parts of the array it is going to use later.
- It has a simple routine named reloadMe() to gather all of the form elements and write them to the location object.
- Its header script acts on the information provided by the user to dynamically reconstruct the page.

Figure 10.10 shows all the choices being placed in the summary form as the user clicks and enters text. Figure 10.11 shows the browser window after it has been rewritten dynamically to use the colors and tiles chosen by the user.

You can write to any page that appears in your window hierarchy. You cannot write to a page that is not a part of that hierarchy. Consequently, a parent can write to a child window and a child can write to its parent. If you want a parent window to write to a newly created child window, then you need to keep a handle to that window. The window.open() method returns such a handle; you should store this value as a global variable. It can then be used subsequently to access the child. If you do not use a global variable, you cannot access the child window from any function other than the one that created it.

**FIG. 10.10**
Dynamic documents can modify their own appearance under user control.

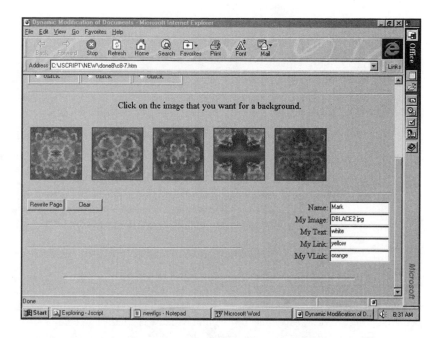

**FIG. 10.11**
Dynamic documents can rewrite their own background.

# The *openNote()* Script Revisited

Let's reexamine the very first complete example in this chapter (refer to Listing 10.3) now that you have more knowledge and experience. The parent window has two buttons: one to open the window and one to close it. These buttons call the parent window's functions, `openNote()` and `closeNote()`, respectively. The parent stores the handle to the `openNote` window in the global variable, `aNoteWin`. The responsibilities of the `open` routine are as follows:

- It defines the appearance of the window using the `open(...)` parameters.

- It writes the script of the window, including any event handle functions that are called by window objects and any initialization for the window.

- It writes the HTML for all of the objects in the window. In this case, the objects are a table with two buttons and the note text. The Close button includes the `onClick` handler that calls the `closeNote()` function of the child window.

The `open` routine also exemplifies a common and quite useful time-saving practice, known as *aliasing*. The full hierarchical representation of `aNoteWin`'s document (`self.aNoteWin.document`) is collected in the short and easy-to-write variable known as `ndoc`.

Finally, it is worth pointing out the utility of having the child window's Close button in the parent window, especially if the child window is small. The `open()` method does not create a second window of the same name, although it can do some updating if you make a second `open()` call with different parameters. If you click the Make Note button and nothing happens, it is possible that you did not get rid of the last window you made.

Murphy's Law dictates that the forgotten child will be at the very bottom of the eight other large windows on your screen. Being able to close the window from the parent is a great time-saver and an excellent debugging tool. ●

# CHAPTER 11

# Creating Your Own JavaScript Objects

In Chapter 4, "JavaScript Objects," you learned about JavaScript arrays and their close relationship with JavaScript objects. That same chapter also explained how to use functions to do meaningful work. This chapter builds upon that foundation and describes how to use complex arrays, functions, and objects. In the process of this exploration, some of the hidden powers of JavaScript will be revealed.

We begin with a discussion of variable declarations and their relationship to the critical topic of function parameters and their validation. We also build up a function, known as word(), which is used in several later examples.

Associative arrays are one of JavaScript's most powerful features, but many users find them confusing. The second part of this chapter revisits the topic of associative arrays and examines extensions to them. Since arrays are the only way to store and access information in a database-like manner, we also learn how to fill arrays from lists and how to use extended arrays.

The final section of this chapter develops two important objects—the Image object and the Text object. The Image object stores a great deal of information about an image and can draw that image as a plain image, a framed image, or a linked image. The Text object stores text as

**How to build a reusable function library**

JavaScript's object-oriented model makes it particularly easy to write modular and reusable functions.

**Learn about parameter checking and validation**

A function can be called from many different contexts, so it is important that functions validate their arguments before using them.

**Using *eval* to execute functions written as strings**

Building functions dynamically in the form of strings is a very powerful technique in JavaScript. The eval function makes it possible to execute such functions.

**Look here for information on array initialization and storage**

Arrays must be properly initialized or they will cause runtime errors.

**Build extended arrays and multidimensional arrays**

JavaScript arrays are very flexible. Within limitations, array elements can be added at will; arrays may even contain other arrays.

well as information about how the text is to be formatted. Both of these objects are developed as arrays of objects, similar to a small database. Both can also be easily extended for your own purposes.

Many of the examples in this chapter are too large to be listed in their entirety within the chapter. All the source code can be found on this book's Web site in the source/chap11 directory. ■

# Global and Local Variables

We have already explored the distinction between global variables, which are visible in every function, and local variables, which are visible only in the function in which they are declared. If you want to declare variables global to the whole window, define them outside of any function. Whether you precede the declaration with var or not, it is still global. However, any declarations that you make inside functions should be preceded with var if you want them to remain local. As you know, it is not strictly necessary to declare variables within functions. JavaScript treats any unknown variable it sees as a new variable, as if you had declared it. If you do not explicitly declare such a variable, or do not precede it with var, it becomes a window-global variable. Check your functions very carefully for variable declarations. If you accidentally make a variable a global variable by not using var, it can cause endless trouble.

**TIP** Particular care should be taken with variables having common names, such as i, j, or iter. Always check the declaration of these variables carefully.

It is unfortunate that the rules for the use of var are confusing. Remember that placing var in front of a variable declaration restricts it to the *scope* in which it is declared. The scope of a variable is the context in which that variable can be used. In the case of a local variable declared in a function, the scope of that variable is the function itself. In the case of a window script, the scope is the window. If you do not use var in a function or a window script, the variable's scope is global—it can be used anywhere in the window.

Some languages, such as C and Pascal, require the programmer to declare or initialize variables before they can be used. Although JavaScript does not force you to do this, it's a good habit to get into. First, this step allows you to document the purpose of each variable. When you return to a function six months after you wrote it, you may not remember what the variable countme does, unless you explicitly document it as // array index variable. Second, if you explicitly declare each variable, you have the opportunity to initialize each one to some meaningful default value.

▶ **See** "Objects, Properties, and Methods in JavaScript," **p. 88**, for a description of the basic rules for JavaScript functions and their parameters and variables.

**CAUTION**

If you declare global variables *within* a function, you must execute the function first for the variables to be defined. This approach is generally considered poor design—you should declare your global variables *outside* of any function definition.

Listing 11.1 illustrates the lesson of this caution.

**Listing 11.1** *nor1* **Uses a Global Variable**

```
function nor1()
{
  myFuncVar = 5
}
nor1()
newval = myFuncVar + 3
```

This code uses the variable myFuncVar inside the function nor1. Since there is no var statement preceding the first use of myFuncVar, this variable will become a global variable, but only *after* the function nor1 is first executed. As written, the code will operate correctly, and newval will have the value 8. If we modify the third line to read var myFuncVar = 5 and then attempt to execute this code, the alert shown in Figure 11.1 will result. Since the variable was declared with var inside a function, it is local and "out of scope" to anything outside the function. Similarly, if you comment out the call to the function nor1() on line 5, this code will also generate the same error.

**FIG. 11.1**
JavaScript alerts you when you have used an undefined variable.

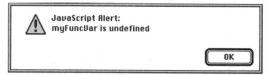

# Parameter Checking

Functions, particularly ones that carry out critical tasks such as opening windows, should always check to see if their parameters are valid. This check usually involves making sure that they are the correct type or are within some expected range.

This section describes several useful routines that determine whether parameters are valid. Strings are relatively safe as parameters, but numbers and Booleans are not. JavaScript can always convert a non-string, such as 5, to the corresponding string "5", but it may not be able to convert a string to a numerical or Boolean value. If a string parameter is specified as the number 5, no error occurs because the numerical value 5 and the string "5" may be freely converted to each other. If a numerical parameter is specified as the string "five", an error occurs because JavaScript does not know how to convert that string to a number.

If you discover a bad parameter, you have two choices: You can simply abandon all processing or you can change the bad parameter to some safe default. It is often preferable to do the latter and place an error message in a variable that calling routines can check. The library functions that we will develop later in this chapter use two of these; they are aWinErr() and aStringErr(). Of course, there is nothing you can do to keep the user from entering something totally unanticipated in a text field. The best you can do is to inform the user that their input did not meet your expectations and then decline to execute the function.

Now let's examine a few functions to see how they work. Three checking functions are shown in the next three sections: one for numbers or restricted characters, one for Booleans, and one for character encoding/decoding.

**Numbers or Restricted Character Sets**   The function isIn(), shown in Listing 11.2, serves two purposes. It can check to see if all of the characters in a parameter string are also found within a comparison string. If the comparison string is empty, it uses a string of digits (0-9) as the comparison string. This function returns a Boolean value to indicate if the comparison succeeded or failed. It can also strip unwanted characters from the parameter value and return a string that contains only acceptable characters.

**Listing 11.2   A Multipurpose Parameter-Checking Function**

```
function isIn(astr,nstr,strip)
// astr :  item in question
// nstr :  allowable character string; defaults to numbers
// strip:  determines whether return is true/false or only allowable characters.
Defaults to false.
{
    //declare and initialize variables to make sure they stay local
    var cc=''
    var dd=''
    var bstr = ''
    var isit
    var i = 0
    //force number to a string
    astr = '' + astr
    //default to checking for a number
    if (nstr== null |¦ nstr == '') nstr = '1234567890'
    //make sure that 'strip' is a boolean
    strip = (isBoolean(strip))
    //force to string; remember, this can return a boolean
     strip += ''
    //NOT a boolean--complain
    if (strip == 'false')
        {
                alert('"Value" must be (T/t)rue or (F/f)alse. It is neither. ')
                isit = null
                return isit
        }
    //just a check to make sure that it quits here
    //if (isit == null) alert('...but I went on anyway!')
```

```
        //now that everything is set up, let's get down to business
        isit=false
        // begin loop which cycles through all of the characters in astr
        for (i = 0 ; i < astr.length ; i++)
            {
                cc=astr.substring(i, i+1)
                // begin loop which cycles through
                // all of the characters in nstr
                for (j =0 ; j< nstr.length ; j++)
                    {
                        dd = nstr.substring(j, j + 1)
                        //alert('i = ' + i + '\n' + 'j = ' + j  +  '\n' + 'cc =
' + cc + '\n' + 'dd = ' +  dd + '\n' + isit)
                        isit = false
                        if (cc == dd)       // so far so good
                            {
                                isit = true
                                bstr += cc     // accumulate good characters
                                break          // no need to go further
                            }
                    }  // end of j loop
                //you found a mismatch; disqualify the item immediately
                //unless you are going to strip the string.
                if (isit == false && strip == 'F')
                        break;
                else continue
            }  // end of i loop
        if (strip=='T') return bstr  // return stripped string
        else return isit             // or return true/false (boolean)
}
```

The isIn() function takes three parameters. The parameter astr is the string to be checked. The parameter nstr contains the set of characters that are permissible in astr. By default, nstr will be "1234567890," which will have the effect of checking to see if astr is a positive integer. The Boolean parameter strip tells the function whether or not unacceptable characters (characters not in nstr) should be stripped out of astr.

The first portion of the isIn() function makes sure that astr and nstr are both strings and initializes nstr to its default value if it was given as the empty string. The parameter validation code also ensures that strip is a Boolean (the function isBoolean() is described under "Boolean Validation," in the next section). A for loop then examines every character in astr. The substring function extracts each character into the local variable cc and checks to see if that character may be found in nstr by using a second for loop. If any unacceptable characters are found, the isit variable is set to true. This for loop is also responsible for building a new string in the local variable bstr, which contains only acceptable characters.

If the strip parameter is true, the function will return the stripped string bstr at the end of its processing. (See Figure 11.2 for an example of isIn() in action.) The characters "1" and "v" are out of range and are removed. If strip had been false, the function would have returned a Boolean value that indicates whether the astr parameter contained any unacceptable characters.

**FIG. 11.2**

The isIn() function can convert unacceptable parameters to an acceptable form.

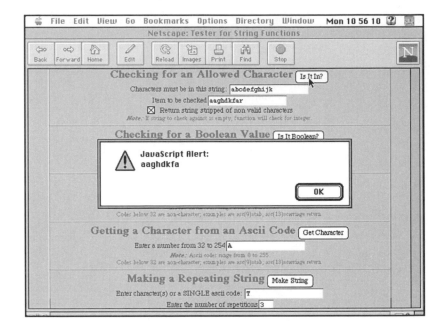

**Boolean Validation**   When you use JavaScript functions written by someone else, you may forget exactly how you are supposed to pass a variable. One of the characteristics of JavaScript is that it is relatively untyped when compared with strongly typed languages like Ada or Pascal. In JavaScript, the same function can return a Boolean, a string, or a number. The calling routine may have some trouble, though; it complains if you try to hand it a string when it thinks it should get a number. One way out of this dilemma is to forcibly convert the variable to the form you want. You can force an arbitrary value to be a string by concatenating it with an empty string. You can force an arbitrary value to be an integer with parseInt().

▶ **See** "HTML String Methods," **p. 126**, for a discussion of string conversion rules and methods.

This kind of type confusion occurs frequently with Boolean values. Should a function return true or "true" or "t" or "T" to indicate success? The code fragment in this section shows the isBoolean() routine. It takes the first character of a putative Boolean, changes it to uppercase, and checks to see if it is "T" or "F". If the resulting value is either "T" or "F", then the function returns true or false, respectively. If the resulting value is neither "T" nor "F", then isBoolean returns false. Note that only the first letter of the astr parameter is examined so that fear, Fortran, and felicity will all be interpreted as false, while tundra and TECO will be seen as true. The isBoolean() function in Listing 11.3 is used as part of the example from the previous section.

## Listing 11.3 A Boolean Validation Function

```
function isBoolean(astr)
//astr is the object to check
{
    var isit=''
    astr +=''
    if (astr == null ¦¦ astr == '') isit= false
    else
        {
                astr = astr.substring(0,1)   // just first letter
                astr = astr.toUpperCase()    // make it caps
                if (astr != "T" && astr != "F")
                    {
                            // unacceptable value entered
                            isit = false
                    }
                else
                {
//returns value which caller can test for true/false
//without having to do substrings, etc.
                            isit= astr
        }
//return is mixed:  can be either a Boolean or a string.
    return isit
}
```

**Character Validation and Conversion**   Most languages have a means of defining a character as a numeric ASCII code and, conversely, converting the code back to the character. In ASCII, for example, the space character has the decimal character code 32 (or 0x20 in hexadecimal), the letter "b" has the decimal code 98 (0x62), and the punctuation mark ampersand "&" has the decimal code 38 (0x26).

**N O T E**   There are many such character-encoding systems; one of the newest, Unicode, supports characters beyond the Roman character set used by English and other European languages. Unicode support is widely available in the newest versions of all major operating systems, such as Microsoft's Windows 95. ■

In fact, if we had functions to convert between the character representation and the numerical representation, many forms of parameter validation would become much easier. For example, an isNumber function, which attempts to determine if a parameter is a number, becomes extremely easy to write. One just examines each variable's numerical ASCII code to see if it is in the range represented by the numerical codes for the characters 0 through 9.

These two conversion functions are relatively easy to write. First, you need to construct a string that contains all of the printable ASCII characters. We will construct such a string (called the charset string) with a utility function called makeCharsetString(). To convert from the character representation to the numerical representation, we search for the character within the charset string. The numerical representation of that character is its index in the charset string, plus 32. The additional 32 is needed because that is the numerical code of the first printable ASCII character, the space character.

To convert from the numerical representation, we reverse the process. We subtract 32 from the numerical value and then extract the character in the charset string at that location. These two functions are shown here as the asc function, which converts from character to numeric code, and the chr function, which converts from numeric code to character. The asc() and chr() functions, along with the makeCharsetString() function, are shown in Listings 11.4, 11.5, and 11.6.

**N O T E** Case always matters in character encoding. The numerical code for an uppercase letter will always be different from that of the corresponding lowercase letter. For example, b is 98 (0x62) in ASCII, while B is 66 (0x42). ■

The asc() function is defined in Listing 11.4.

### Listing 11.4   A Function to Return the ASCII Code of a Character

```
function asc(achar)
//achar is a character whose ASCII code you want
{
     var n = 0
     var csstr = makeCharsetString()  //get ascii char string
     //alert(csstr)
     for (i = 0 ; i < csstr.length ; i++)
     {
//when you get a match, you have an index into the string
          if (achar == csstr.substring(i,i+1) )break
     }

//printable characters begin at 32 with [space]
     return n + 32
}
```

Listing 11.5 contains the definition of chr().

### Listing 11.5   A Function to Return a Character Given an ASCII Code

```
function chr(x)
{
     var ar = ''
     var astr = makeCharsetString()     //get ascii string
     //alert(astr)
     result = ''
     if (x >= 32 ¦¦ x < 126)            // printable
         {
               x = x - 32
                ar = astr.charAt(x)
               result = ar
         }
```

```
// non printable, return text representation
     else
          {
                if ( x == 9 ) result = '\t'
                if ( x == 13 ) result = '\r'
                if ( x == 10 ) result = '\n'
          }
     return result
}
```

**Listing 11.6** *makeCharsetString()* **Builds an Indexable String**

```
function makeCharsetString()
//returns a string with the entire ascii character set in it
{
     var astr
     astr=' !"#$%&\'()*+,-./0123456789:;<=>?@'
     astr += 'ABCDEFGHIJKLMNOPQRSTUVWXYZ'
     astr += '[\]^_`abcdefghijklmnopqrstuvwxyz'
     astr += '{¦}~□ÄÅÇÉÑÖÜáàâäãåçéèêëíìîïñóòôöõúùûü'
     astr += '†°¢£§•¶ß®©™´¨_±² ³¥µ___ªº½ æø'

     astr += '¿¡¬Äƒ̊Æ«»...°ÀÃÕŒœ---""''+×ÿŸ/¤‹›Þ_'
     astr += '‡·,„‰ÂÊÁ́ËÈÍÎ́ÏÌÓÔ̂ÒÚÛÙ¦´`'
     astr += '˜¯ù__˛ýþ'
     return astr
}
```

Note that there are some strategically placed `alert()` calls in these functions that are commented out. These alerts are for debugging purposes, to ensure that the functions are actually delivering what you want. Note also that the `chr()` function does not handle most of the non-printing characters, whose numeric codes are below 32 or above 126. The only control characters that it tells you about are the tab, return, and linefeed characters. This can be used in an ugly but useful way to insert a carriage return/linefeed combination into a string using the expression + `chr(13)` + `chr(10)`.

There is one additional function we will present: the `word()` function. The `word()` function extracts an indexed phrase from a delimited string. A delimited string is one containing one or more entries separated by a special character referred to as the delimiter or separator. For example, the string `"My:name:is:Hanover:Fiste"` contains five components—My, name, is, Hanover, and Fiste—separated by the delimiter colon (:).

**NOTE** Delimited strings are used frequently in JavaScript and other weakly-typed languages. Delimited strings are convenient because they allow multiple elements to be represented as a single string. Many spreadsheet and database programs, for example, can export their data as delimited strings. The comma (,) and colon (:) characters are frequently used as delimiters. ■

Part
**II**

Ch
**11**

The word() function takes three parameters: the delimited string inwhat, the delimiter sep, and the index which of the component required. The first component in inwhat is component which==1. The function returns the component requested. Thus, if you ask word() for the third component of the string "My:name:is:Hanover:Fiste", the function returns "is". Figure 11.3 shows some sample output from the word() function. In this case, we have used the '@' character as the delimiter and have asked for the second item in the string.

The source code for word() is in Listing 11.7.

**Listing 11.7 The Delimited String Processing Function *word()***

```
function word(sep,which,inwhat)
// separator character
// which word/pharase
// text in which to look
{
    //alert(inwhat)
    var n = 0              // start of a phrase
    var wstr = 0           // holds substring
    var i = 0              // loop counter
    var s = 0              // start of winning phrase
    var f = 0              // end of winning phrase
    for (i = 1 ; i < which ; i++)
        {
            n = inwhat.indexOf(sep,n)      // look for separator
            if (n < 0 )                     // if you do not find it
                {
                    return ''                // return empty string

                }
            n++                              // otherwise, loop again
        }

    // now we should be a the right place
    if ( n >= 0)                             // ... but do this only if we
    {                                        // found the separator
        //alert(n + '==' + wstr)
        var s = n                            // phrase starts with n, now s
        var f = inwhat.indexOf(sep,n)        // get next instance of sep
        if (f < 0 ) f = inwhat.length        // but if there is none ...
        wstr = inwhat.substring(n,f)         // must be last phrase in string
    }
    //alert(f + '--' + wstr)
    return wstr                              // return string; it will be
                                             // empty if sep was not found.

}
```

**FIG. 11.3**
The word() function extracts an indexed phrase from within a character-delimited string.

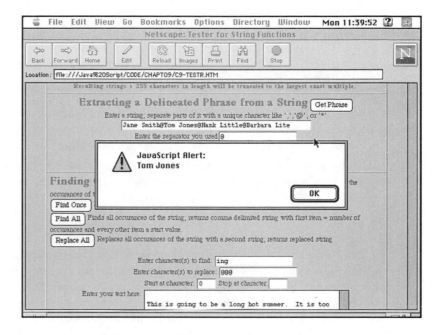

The word() function does its job by using a simple algorithm. The first for loop in this function uses the string method indexOf() to find each occurrence of the delimiter character sep in the input string inwhat. The local variable n is used to hold the current position of the delimiter, while the iteration variable i counts the number of such delimiters found so far. If fewer than the required number which are found, the word() function returns the empty string.

If the required number is present, the if test just after the for loop will succeed. At this point, n is positioned at the beginning of the element we want; it is now necessary to locate the end of that element. This will be either the next occurrence of the delimiter or the end of the inwhat string itself. The local variable f is used to hold the location of the end of the element. Once n and f have been computed, the word() function uses the substring() method to store the desired element in the local variable wstr, which is then returned as the value of the word() function.

# More on JavaScript Functions

Recall from Chapter 4, "JavaScript Objects," that functions are developed by declaring them within a script. This section briefly reviews some of the things to remember when writing functions, and then delves a little deeper into some of the fine points of functions in JavaScript. This material is developed further in the next section, "JavaScript's Associative Arrays."

Make sure that you declare your most elementary functions earliest in the <HEAD> of the page. This practice ensures that later functions are able to find them. The same rule applies to objects. Make sure that you do not reference any objects that have not yet been declared in any of your functions. Functions in the <HEAD> cannot see objects built by the HTML on your page,

Part

II

Ch

11

nor can they see objects built by code executing later in the script. If there is something that *must* be done with an HTML-generated object, place it in a script at the bottom of the page.

> **CAUTION**
>
> The <HEAD> of an HTML page is intended to convey information about the page; the <BODY> is intended to contain the elements that are displayed. When the body begins to download, the user can interact with the page—even before the download is complete. This fact means that a user could take some action that calls a function declared at the bottom of the page *before* the function has been downloaded to the browser.
>
> If you can, avoid declaring functions in the <BODY>. If you cannot avoid it, try to design your page so that the controls which call the <BODY> function are disabled until the page is completely downloaded.

Proper error-checking is also very important. If a function fails, provide a mechanism for the calling routine to detect the failure. Keep the damage to a minimum. It is a sign of very poor design when a browser dialog box comes up immediately after your page is loaded. One major problem with using functions has to do with passing the parameters in incorrect order. If some function expects three parameters that represent two numerical values and a string, but you give it a numerical value, a string, and then the second numerical value, an error will occur. A similar problem arises when a calling function misinterprets what should be passed in a parameter. If a function relies on unchecked input from a user, check that the parameter is at least of the right type. If you detect that it is incorrect, flag it and, if you can, fix it.

> **CAUTION**
>
> Make sure that all local variables within a function are preceded by var. If a function inadvertently declares a global variable that has the same name as a local variable in another function, inexplicable behavior will often result. In particular, function parameters may become garbled. This type of error is particularly difficult to diagnose, so special care should always be taken with variable declarations.

## Storing Your Functions

In most browsers, JavaScript cannot read (or write) local data files, but it can load and use HTML files. Therefore, even though you cannot generate a JavaScript function library in an ordinary file, you can write a function library in an HTML header and load that library inconspicuously when you want to use it. You can also specify a file of functions (known as a ".js" file) and add it to your page with a line like

```
<SCRIPT LANGAGE="JavaScript" SRC="pathToFunctionLibrary/filename.js">
</SCRIPT>
```

If you have enabled your browser's cache, the first page to reference this library will load it to the cache, where other pages can access the functions without a new download.

Function libraries can also be used with frames by designating one particular frame as the "owner" of the library. All of the other frame documents have a global variable called `funcs`, which refers to that special frame from the perspective of the calling frame. Consequently, you can call a function named `myfunction` in the function library by using the reference `funcs.myfunction` from anywhere in any of the nested frames. You can also make a function library in a frameset itself.

Note that the functions given here are meant to be introductory only. JavaScript lacks many of the functions that have become standard in most programming environments, so this chapter provides you with a library of some commonly used functions (due to its length, Listing 11.8, "A JavaScript Function Library," is located on this book's companion Web site). This library file not only contains the functions in the previous examples, it also writes a little test page that enables you to enter parameters and call a given function with them. It is also useful if you want to look up an ASCII code or convert some HTML text to a form in which it can be displayed by the browser, without being interpreted as HTML by the browser.

# The *eval* Function

In the early days of personal computers, most PCs came with a built-in BASIC interpreter; many end users (who did not consider themselves professional programmers) built sophisticated programs for their own use or shared them with others in their industry. The earliest PC-DOS and MS-DOS computers had a command-line interface—users could place a series of commands in a batch file to write simple programs.

Over time, the BASIC interpreters disappeared and machines with graphical user interfaces (GUIs) made the command line obsolete. Some users were frustrated that they could no longer write programs on their own. To address this need, Apple, manufacturer of the graphically oriented Macintosh, introduced a programming language and development environment "for the rest of us." This product was called HyperCard.

In HyperCard, one can write Hypertalk in a text field and then "do" the field, which executes the contents of that field. Because of this, HyperCard scripts can write and execute code on-the-fly. You can do something similar in JavaScript by using `eval()`. Although `eval()` sounds as if it should be used only to evaluate mathematical equations, this function can actually do much more. It can evaluate any string that is a JavaScript statement. Try this experiment. Build an HTML button and attach the following statement as its `onClick` event handler:

```
eval('alert("I did it!")')
```

When you click the button, the Alert box pops up. In the same way, you can pass the contents of an HTML text field or `textarea` to a JavaScript event handler. This approach is illustrated by the function `evaluate()`, which is found in Listing 11.9. This function consists of a single line of code, `eval(what)`. A single HTML button passes the contents of a textarea to this function, which tries to execute the contents of that textarea as JavaScript code. The `eval` statement can be placed directly in the button handler, of course. By placing it in the separate (but trivial) `evaluate` function, we make it easier to extend the function in the future.

**Listing 11.9    Perform Runtime Evaluation of Code**

```
<HTML>
<HEAD>
<!- Created 16 Feb 1996 a2:23 AM 02:23 AM -->
<TITLE>Javascript on the Fly</TITLE>
<SCRIPT>
document.bgcolor = 'linen'
document.text = 'darkslateblue'
document.link = 'coral'
document.vlink='peach'
document.alink='red'
document.write('<TABLE ALIGN=RIGHT WIDTH=250 BORDER=1>')
document.write('<TR><TD>')
document.write('<FONT SIZE=7 COLOR= "navy">')
document.write('<CENTER>' +document.title + '</CENTER>')
document.write('</TD></TR></TABLE>')
document.write('<HR>')
document.write('<CENTER>')
document.write('<FONT COLOR="steelblue"'>)
document.write('<FONT SIZE=5 ><B>A Javascript Scratch Pad</B></FONT><BR>')
document.write('</CENTER>')
document.write('This document has a single function, evaluate().  The function
➥simply hands off the contents of the text box to eval, which will try to
➥evaluate and run the code.')
document.write('</FONT><HR><BR>')
document.write('<CENTER>')
document.write('<B>This document was last modified on<BR><FONT COLOR="red">' +
document.lastModified + '</B></FONT><BR>')
document.write('<BR><HR><BR>')
document.write('</CENTER>')
document.write('')
function evaluate(what)
{
    eval(what)
}
</SCRIPT>
</HEAD>
<BODY>
<FORM NAME="test" >
<CENTER>
<TABLE WIDTH=95% CELLPADDING=5 CELLSPACING=0 BORDER=2 >
<TR ALIGN=CENTER VALIGN=MIDDLE>
<TD WIDTH=100%>Write some Javascript in the text area.  When you click on the
➥button, the program will try to evaluate it.
</TD>
</TR>
<TR ALIGN=CENTER VALIGN=MIDDLE>
<TD WIDTH=100%> <TEXTAREA NAME=atext ROWS=10 COLS=60 >
var astr = ''
for (i = 1 ; i < 10 ; i++)
 {
   astr = astr += 'color ' + i + '\n'
 }
alert(astr)
```

```
</TEXTAREA>
</TD>
</TR>
<TR ALIGN=CENTER VALIGN=MIDDLE>
<TD WIDTH=100%>
<INPUT TYPE="BUTTON" NAME="doeval" VALUE= "Run Code"
ONCLICK="evaluate(this.form.atext.value)" >
</TD>
</TR>
</TABLE>
</CENTER>
</FORM>
</BODY>
</HTML>
```

# JavaScript's Associative Arrays

Associative arrays were introduced in Chapter 4, "JavaScript Objects," and have been used in several previous chapters in this book. An associative array is a one-dimensional array of pairs. You access the left member of the pair with a numeric index. You access the right member of the pair with a string index equal to the value of the left member of the pair. For example, myArray[1] = "red" makes a direct assignment to the left side of the array, but myArray["red"]= "#FF0000" assigns both sides with a single statement. Arrays can be built in two ways: by using the new operator on the built-in Array object, or by writing a special-purpose function that takes a generic this object and gives it a size. If you use the former approach, you must specify the number of elements; you may also optionally specify a list of initializers. If you use the latter method, you can also add other properties to the array in the special-purpose function. To actually construct the array, you use the new operator together with your special array creation function. For example, if we use the myArray function, the statement:

```
myNewArray = new myArray(6,'')
```

constructs an array called myNewArray with 6 elements and initializes all of the left members to ''. Note that this is not being done for you by JavaScript in some magical way. You have to write the function (known as a *constructor*) and then invoke it with the appropriate parameters.

An array is a primitive JavaScript object. Its properties, which represent the array members, can be anything you choose. You must set the special property known as length, however, in your constructor. This property gives the length of the array (and is occasionally referred to as the size property). The length property is usually put in the zeroth element of the array during initialization. This fact means that your arrays will actually have $n+1$ elements: $n$ elements for data and one extra element at index zero to hold the array size. You need to be sure that your array access functions do not overwrite the zero element. Listing 11.10 shows a general-purpose myArray() function.

Part II

Ch 11

---

**Listing 11.10   A General-Purpose *createArray* Function**

```
function myArray(n, init)
{
  this.size = n  //This initialization is absolutely necessary
  for (i = 1 ; i <= n ; i++)
  {
    this[i] = init      //Initialize all of the left hand elements
  }
  return this          //Return the  array object to the caller
}
```

---

Notice that there is no initialization of the right members of the array. You can arrange to do this as well in the myArray function, but only with some effort. This is because the left element must be unique and we have initialized all the array elements to the same value, namely the value init. If you have two array members containing the same value, you are able to get to only the first one.

In addition to making arrays, you will sometimes want to reset or clear an array so that it may be reused. A special procedure, known as a *double replacement scheme*, must be used to clear or reset an existing array. (You can always build a completely new array.) This special approach is needed because you have no way of knowing which values are already stored in the array. In particular, you have no way of knowing that they are unique. The double replacement method uses the loop in Listing 11.11 to safely reset the array myArray.

---

**Listing 11.11   Loop to Initialize an Associative Array**

```
var i;
for(i=1; i< this.size; I++)
{
  myArray[i] = '@@@@@';
  myArray['@@@@@'] = '';
  myArray[i] = '';
}
```

---

This method uses a dummy replacement value to manipulate both the left and right sides of the pair. In the preceding example, the string '@@@@@' is used. To avoid the problem of non-unique indices, this dummy value must be chosen so that it is unlikely to appear in the array.

---

**CAUTION**

Do *not* try to initialize the right side of an array in the same loop in which you initialize the left side. JavaScript mixes left and right values for you. If you need to initialize the right side, do it in a separate loop.

---

# Using Associative Pairs

Associative arrays occur far more often than you might think. They occur in everyday life, although most people do not think of them that way. The picture on the top of a TV dinner box is related to what is in the box. You choose your dinner by looking at the picture because the picture is associated with the contents of the box. You would not open every box in the freezer and examine its actual contents in order to decide which one to put in the microwave. Programmers tend to think of an association in less colorful terms, such as a = b, x = $3y^2$, and so on. A Windows.INI file is an excellent example of the use of associative pairs. Every entry has a left element, such as *.DOC, and a right element, such as C:\WINWORD\WINWORD.EXE. In this case, the association is a relationship between a file suffix and the application that wrote it. Hypertext links are also associations; they are just ordered backward. The HTML

```
<A HREF='http://www.myfavoritelink.com'>My favorite link</A>
```

is actually an associative pair. If we were to place this into an array, most of us would place My favorite link on the left side, and http://www.myfavoritelink.com on the right. We often reference complicated or large objects with less complicated words or nicknames.

**An Enhanced Array Object**    A simple associative pair array may not be sufficient for your needs. Because an array is just an unstructured object, it can conveniently be made into a more complex object. For example, you can add a description property to an array. This addition is useful because the array may have a short name that is easy to use elsewhere in your code, but that name may not be very illustrative of the array's purpose.

Another property you might want to add is a property that reflects the "element of interest right this minute" or the "current" element. An example of this might be the strings in a list box. We want a property that refers to the currently selected item. That property might be called the currentIndex property, or, more tersely, the nDx property. (Remember that JavaScript is case-sensitive.) Finally, if we are using the list as some kind of a stack, or if we are keeping track of items that are constantly being added or deleted from the list, we might need to know where the next open slot is located. We will call this property the nextIndex property.

But where do we put these properties? Well, properties are just array elements, so the question is where in the element list they should be placed. If we put them at the beginning, the array elements proper do not start at index=1. If we put them at the end, the array elements are in the right place, but it is now more difficult to increase the size of the array. This is because there are referencing problems if you access the properties by their array index rather than by their names. We will examine the advantages and drawbacks of both approaches.

**Array Initialization and Storage**    While associative arrays are an extremely powerful programmer tool, there are some pitfalls in using arrays. Most of them stem from a lack of initialization or from incorrect initialization. Listing 11.12, located on the companion Web site, contains several array-initialization and array-manipulation functions, as well as array functions that present different approaches to the location of the enhanced array object properties, such as currentIndex and nextIndex, and how (or if) the array is initialized. You can explore these functions with the code in Listing 11.13.

**Listing 11.13   Testing Array Initialization**

```
<HTML>
<HEAD>
<TITLE>array</TITLE>
</HEAD>
<BODY>
<FORM NAME="test" >
<CENTER>
<TABLE WIDTH=95% CELLPADDING=5 CELLSPACING=0 BORDER=2 >
<TR ALIGN=CENTER VALIGN=MIDDLE>
<TD WIDTH=100% COLSPAN=5>
<FONT SIZE= 4 COLOR="corel">Adding Extra Array Parameters</FONT>
</TD></TR>
<TR><TD>
<INPUT TYPE="BUTTON" NAME="initBtn" VALUE= "Initialize" ONCLICK="initArrays()">
</TD>
<TD>
<INPUT TYPE="BUTTON" NAME="clearBtn" VALUE= "Clear" ONCLICK="clearAllArrays()">
</TD>
<TD>
<INPUT TYPE="BUTTON" NAME="clearXBtn" VALUE= "Clear to Null"
ONCLICK="clearAllArraysToNull()">
</TD>
<TD>
<INPUT TYPE="BUTTON" NAME="Fill1Btn" VALUE= "Fill Arrays"
➥ONCLICK="fillAllArrays()">
</TD>
<TD>
<INPUT TYPE="BUTTON" NAME="Fill1Btn" VALUE= "Enter One Value / Array"
ONCLICK="enter1Value()">
</TD>
</TR>
<TR ALIGN=LEFT VALIGN=MIDDLE>
<TD WIDTH=100% COLSPAN=5>
Arrays with Properties at the End:<BR>
<INPUT TYPE="BUTTON" NAME="ear1a" VALUE= "1a"
➥ONCLICK="alert(seeArray(array1_a))">
Initialized to '""'<BR>
<INPUT TYPE="BUTTON" NAME="ear1b" VALUE= "1b"
➥ONCLICK="alert(seeArray(array1_b))">
Initialized to property name<BR>
<INPUT TYPE="BUTTON" NAME="ear1c" VALUE= "1c"
➥ONCLICK="alert(seeArray(array1_c))">
Initialized to uniform init value<BR>
<INPUT TYPE="BUTTON" NAME="ear1d" VALUE= "1d"
➥ONCLICK="alert(seeArray(array1_d))">
Initialized to unique valuesBR>
</TD>
</TR>
<TR ALIGN=CENTER VALIGN=MIDDLE>
<TD WIDTH=100% COLSPAN=5>
<INPUT TYPE="BUTTON" NAME="bar1" VALUE= "Properties at Beginning: Not
➥Initialized" ONCLICK="alert(seeArray(beginArray1))">
</TD>
```

```
</TR>
<TR ALIGN=CENTER VALIGN=MIDDLE>
<TD WIDTH=100% COLSPAN=5>
<INPUT TYPE="BUTTON" NAME="bar2" VALUE= "Properties at Beginning: Whole Array
Initialized" ONCLICK="alert(seeArray(beginArray2))">
</TD>
</TR>
<TR ALIGN=CENTER VALIGN=MIDDLE>
<TD WIDTH=100% COLSPAN=5>
<INPUT TYPE="BUTTON" NAME="bar3" VALUE= "Properties at Beginning: Non-Property
➥Lines Initialized" ONCLICK="alert(seeArray(beginArray3))">
</TD>
</TR>
<TR ALIGN=CENTER VALIGN=MIDDLE>
<TD WIDTH=100% COLSPAN=5> <BR>
</TD>
</TR>
</TABLE>
</CENTER>
</FORM>
</BODY>
</HTML>
```

The page generated by this file has buttons to enable you to initialize various arrays, reset them, clear them to null, enter a single value, and fill the arrays. Each array is treated in the same fashion. After you have exercised one or more of these functions, you can then look at the contents of each array to see the effect. The array constructors are organized into two categories: those that place the enhanced properties at the end and those that place the enhanced properties at the beginning. The first four array constructors place the enhanced properties at the end of the array and initialize all empty slots to 0. They differ in how they handle the enhanced properties.

The final three constructors place the enhanced properties at the beginning of the array. This set of methods can be used to examine the consequences of not initializing the array or initializing all of the elements (including those of the special properties) to the same thing, and of initializing only the empty elements. These functions are obviously not the only possible ways in which such array functions can be written.

> **CAUTION**
>
> You cannot build an uninitialized array and still place the extended properties at the end of the array.

When you first load the page contained in Listing 11.13, as shown in Figure 11.4, all of its arrays have been constructed; those arrays that initialize themselves have done so. Initialization has been done only for the left elements. The viewing routine has been set to look at the first unused element. This will be the element at index n + 1, which is not yet processed or initialized in any way.

Part
II

Ch
11

**FIG. 11.4**

JavaScript's associative arrays can be accessed by using numerical or named indices.

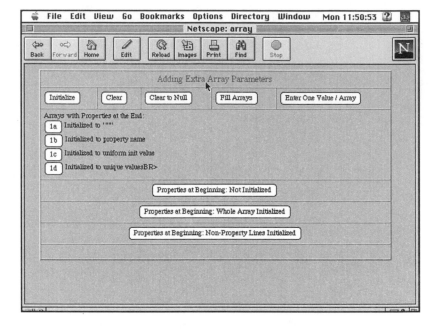

For purposes of this discussion, those array elements that are not directly related to a property are called the *empty* elements. Those that are associated with properties are called the *special* elements. Each element consists of a left and right element. The left element of the zeroth element of the array has the array size in it.

> **CAUTION**
>
> Platform dependencies have been reported in the current release of Netscape Navigator and Microsoft Internet Explorer. You may find array functionality to be different, depending on the platform on which you are running the browser. Try the code in Listing 11.13 (previously introduced) and Listing 11.14, which is located on the companion Web site, as test cases.

First, let's look at the those arrays that have the special elements at the end of the array. Click the 1a button. This constructor initializes all of the empty elements to `"@"` and the special elements to `""`. Did you expect to see the property names in the special elements? They do not appear here. They are properties associated with the array object, not values within the array object. This constructor design works as you would expect.

But look at the next array constructor (associated with button 1b). Because we could not tell which element was which, we decided to initialize the left side of each special element with the name of the property associated with it. We did not do anything to the right side of the properties…well, we didn't, but JavaScript did! Notice that the right element has also been filled in with the name of the property, as shown in Figure 11.5. This behavior should provide your first clue that JavaScript arrays seem to have a mind of their own. Further, the right side of anArray[0] has the last special property assignment in it.

**FIG. 11.5**
JavaScript fills uninitialized associative array values with null.

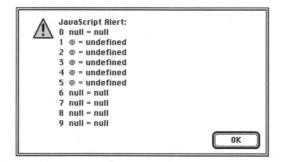

```
JavaScript Alert:
0  null = null
1  @ = undefined
2  @ = undefined
3  @ = undefined
4  @ = undefined
5  @ = undefined
6  null = null
7  null = null
8  null = null
9  null = null

                              OK
```

Button 1c manipulates an array in which all of the special elements have been initialized to the same value as the empty elements. There are no surprises here. The final constructor of the first series, method 1d, initializes the special elements to two unique characters for each related property. This constructor is the most well-behaved of all. The presence of the last special element assignment on the right side of anArray[0] is no longer a surprise.

The three creation methods in the second series put the special elements at the beginning of the array. Using the first of these three methods, it is possible to produce a completely uninitialized array. Still, nothing unusual happens; the empty elements are just null. The second of these creation methods initializes both the special elements and the empty elements. The very last creation method initializes only the empty elements; it also behaves properly.

Instead of clearing or reinitializing the arrays at this point, click the rightmost button named Enter One Value/Array. This button does exactly that. It enters a "red", "#FF0000" pair into anArray[2] for those arrays with special properties at the end and into anArray[6] for those arrays with special properties at the beginning.

The array generated by method 1a offers up no more surprises in this case. The value pair has been entered in the correct place. Notice that the array uses one-based indexing in terms of reference as well. The arrays built by the other methods with the special elements at the end (methods 1b2 through 1c) are also well behaved, as are the three methods with the special elements at the beginning.

To continue our array experimentation, let's reinitialize the arrays by reloading the file. Then click the Fill Arrays button. The JavaScript linked to this button fills the empty elements of the array with pairs in the form of name=month. Repeat your inspection process and you should uniformly see something like Figure 11.6.

Part
II

Ch
11

**FIG. 11.6**

Entering data into an uninitialized array fills in the values.

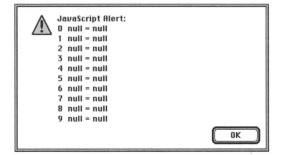

```
JavaScript Alert:
0  null = null
1  null = null
2  null = null
3  null = null
4  null = null
5  null = null
6  null = null
7  null = null
8  null = null
9  null = null

                                    OK
```

You can perform a variation on this experiment by reinitializing the arrays and then clearing them by using either method. Use the Initialize and Clear (or Clear to Null) buttons and then add a single value to all of the arrays or simply fill the arrays. The unused elements may be quirky, but the array elements themselves behave properly.

The code in Listing 11.14 (located on the Web site) provides a variation on the same theme. It is the same as the code in Listing 11.13, except that all of its arrays have an extra uninitialized element just after the original eight array elements. As before, a first unused element is displayed. It is worthwhile to go through the same procedures and see how the various arrays behave.

> **CAUTION**
>
> Initialize your arrays before you use them! Uninitialized arrays cannot be trusted to provide correct results when referenced. They cannot even be trusted to provide consistently incorrect results and can be a nightmare to debug.

**Filling Arrays from Paired Lists**   The `fillArrayFromLists()` function fills the associative pairs of an array from two parallel lists of delimited elements. It is a lot faster to write such lists than it is to specifically set each right and left element in an array. This function uses the library function `word()`, which was described earlier in this chapter. You may recall that this function uses a character delimiter to separate the elements in the list. The separator can be any character; the most common one is a comma (,). HyperCard enthusiasts will recognize this as an item list. The `fillArrayFromLists()` function is located in Listing 11.15.

**Listing 11.15   A Function to Load an Associative Array from Two Delimited Lists**

```
function fillArrayFromLists(anArray,aaList,bbList,sep,s,f)
{
    var lstr = ''              // left hand array element
    var rstr = ''              // right hand array element
    var i = 0                   // iteration variable
    var counter = 1
     for (i = s ; i <=f ; i++)
        {
```

```
            anArray[i] = word(sep,counter,aaList)
            anArray[anArray[i]] = word(sep,counter,bbList)
            counter++
        }
    }
```

This function takes six parameters: the array anArray, whose values are to be set, two delimited strings, aaList and bbList, which hold the right and left elements, the string delimiter
sep, and the first and last indices (s and f, respectively) in anArray that are to be set. The function executes a simple for loop over all the array indices from s to f inclusive. In each iteration,
it calls the word() function twice to extract the right and left elements from aaList and bbList.

As a demonstration of this function, let's invoke it by using two short lists. In this case, we use
the asterisk character (*) as the delimiter. The following code shows each person on the list
aList being associated with a particular month, as given in the list bList:

```
var aList = 'Mona*Jane*Barbara*Sandra*Maxine'
var bList = 'January*March*September*February*December'
fillArrayFromLists(array1,aList,bList,'*',1,5)
```

**Using the Enhanced Array Object**   Now that we have built our enhanced array object and
dissected it at great length, how can we use it and which version should we adopt? Although
each of the constructors we have tested works if the array is properly initialized, we use the
last constructor from the set of constructors that place their special properties at the beginning
of the array. This constructor is the one that did *not* overwrite our special properties. Most of
the time, only the left elements of the associative pair are used, but these lists can also hold an
associated object (right element).

 The enhanced array object can be used to implement a string list, object list, or a stack.

One array that arises frequently in JavaScript applications is an array of newly constructed
child windows because JavaScript does not provide such an array by default. This section describes the function winArrayAdd(), which can be used to add a window to such a window array.
This function uses global variables to keep track of the next available array slot (in nextWin) as
well as the current window (in curWin).

Listing 11.16 shows the source code for winArrayAdd():

**Listing 11.16   A Function to Add a Window to a Window-Tracking Array**

```
function winArrayAdd(aWinHdl)
{
    // set next open slot in winArray to hold this window handle
    // and that window's creator
    aWinArray[nextWin] = aNewWin
    aWinArray[aWinArray[nextWin]] = aNewWin.opener
    curWin = nextWin    // make this the current window
    nextWin++           // increment next available slot pointer
}
```

**Part**
**II**

**Ch**
**11**

Instead of using global variables, we can also use an array with special properties. The next version of `winArrayAdd()` illustrates this form of the window addition function. While this version does not look much different from the original version, the array-based version is preferred because it keeps essential window tracking information together. Other functions, therefore, may access all the relevant data by simply examining appropriate elements of the array, rather than having to look at the array and also consult some global variables.

Listing 11.17 is the array-based version of `winArrayAdd()`.

**Listing 11.17   A Better Version of the Window-Adding Function Using Special Properties**

```
function winArrayAdd(aWinHdl)
{
    // set next open slot in winArray to hold this window handle
    // and that window's creator
    aWinArray[aWinArray.nextIndex] = aNewWin
    aWinArray[aWinArray[nextWin]] = aNewWin.openerr
// make this the current window
    aWinArray.ndx = aWinArray.nextIndex
    nextWin++        // increment next available slot pointer
}
```

# Arrays of Arrays

One of the biggest criticisms of associative arrays is that they are one-dimensional. The argument can be made that the left and right sides constitute a second dimension, of size two, but this is not really a true multidimensional array. In fact, two-dimensional arrays are really just arrays of arrays. Because of the nature of associative arrays, one can develop such complex structures with relative ease.

**Simulating Multidimensional Arrays**   Imagine, if you will, an array of colors. In a simple implementation of such an array, the left element contains the name of the color, such as `"red"`, and the right member contains the hexadecimal value for the color. For red, this value is `0xFF0000`. There are many shades of red, however. Of course, we could add all of these variant names to the array. It would be much nicer to be able to go to an array, find `"red"`, and then access into a list of colors that were various shades of red. Let's construct an example in which we can do that. As usual, the left element is initialized to `"red"`. The right element, however, holds a handle to another array called `moreReds`. The array `moreReds` contains the typical `colorname=hexvalue` pair. Listing 11.18 shows a simple way of building such a multidimensional array.

**Listing 11.18   A First Approach to Creating a Multidimensional Array**

```
colors = new myArray(9,'')

moreRed = new myArray(20,'')
```

```
moreYellow = new myArray(20,'')
moreOrange = new myArray(20,'')
moreBrown = new myArray(20,'')
moreGreen = new myArray(20,'')
moreBlue = new myArray(20,'')
morePurple = new myArray(20,'')
moreGray = new myArray(20,'')
moreWhite = new myArray(20,'')

...
```

Not only is this approach tedious, but it's not even a complete solution. You have to put each of these secondary arrays into the right elements of the first array. There must be an easier way to do this. You need to develop an approach for getting the various values into the multidimensional array and getting them out again.

To improve the design of the multidimensional array constructor, we introduce three new functions. The myArray() function is very similar to the array constructor that we have already seen. The fillColorArray() function fills both the left and right elements of an associative array, which is passed in as a parameter. This means that if you execute the statement:

```
anArray = fillColorArray(anArray,'green','gr')
```

the left elements are filled with green1, green2,..., and the right elements are filled with gr1, gr2,.... The third function, lotsOfColors(), is used to orchestrate the allocation and initialization of this array. This function also uses our old friend, the word() function.

One might think of using eval() to change a constructed string into an array handle, as in the following statement:

```
dstr = eval(dstr = new myArray(20,''))
```

In fact, this approach is not necessary. Here we see another tribute to the flexibility of JavaScript variables because the following statement works just fine:

```
dstr = new myArray(20,'')
```

The resulting value of dstr is then passed to fillColorArray() to be stuffed with values. When this function returns, dstr is plugged into the right value of the current array pair.

Listing 11.19 holds the definitions of these three functions.

Part
II
Ch
11

### Listing 11.19 Three Functions Used to Create an Associative Array of Associative Arrays

```
function myArray(n,init)
//n           size of array
//init     what you want all values initialized to
{
        var i = 0
        this.length = n     // set the size of the array
```

*continues*

**Listing 11.19   Continued**

```
            for (i = 1 ; i < n ; i++)
                {
                      this[i] = init    // fill the array with "init"
                }
            return this           // return the newly constructed array
}

function fillColorArray(anArray,init,init2)
//  anArray is the array to be filled
//  init holds the values for the left side
//  init2 holds the values for the right side
{
            var i = 0
            var astr = ''
            var bstr = ''
            var n = anArray.length    // get array length
            for (i = 1 ; i <= n ; i++) // iterate over each element
                {
                      astr = init + i      // get left value
                      bstr = init2 + i     // get right value
                      anArray[i] = astr    // set left
                      anArray[astr] = bstr // set right
                }
            return anArray                 // return modified array
}

function lotsOfColors()
{
     var cstr
// colors will be an array of 9 colors
// colorstring will be the names of those colors, delimited by commas
     var colors = new myArray(9,'')
     var colorstring = 'red,yellow,orange,brown,green,blue,purple,gray,white'
     for (i = 1 ; i <= 9 ; i++ )    // iterate over array
            {
// extract the i-th element
                cstr = word(',', i , colorstring)
                colors[i] = cstr           // set left value
                dstr = 'more' + cstr
// allocate and initialize right value in next two statements
                dstr = eval(dstr = new myArray(20,''))
                dstr = fillColorArray(dstr,cstr,cstr.substring(0,2))
                colors[colors[i]] = dstr   // set right value
// next three statements are for debugging
// they display the values set in an alert
                astr = colors[cstr][3]
                bstr = colors[cstr][astr]
                alert( astr + '\n' + bstr)
            }
}
```

The function `lotsOfColors()` warrants close attention. It starts off by making the associative array named `colors`, as well as a comma-delimited string that lists the colors it uses. It then cycles through a loop for each color to be processed. It first extracts the color we want from `colorstring` (as a string) and then sets the left element of the current associative pair to that string. Thus, `colors[1]` yields "red." That's the easy part. How do we name the array handles that we place into the right member? We can construct an element named "moreRed," but "moreRed" is a string. Fortunately, JavaScript permits a string to be enough of a chameleon that it can be turned into an array handle.

**CAUTION**

Arrays should be initialized and filled in different routines. If you attempt to perform these operations in the same routine, strange substitutions, which are symptomatic of an uninitialized array, will result.

**Using a Multidimensional Array**     So far, we have not tried to access the secondary members of this construction. Surprisingly enough, that is not much harder than accessing the usual one-dimensional associative array. In fact, the debugging code at the end of `lotsOfColors()` shows how:

```
astr = colors[cstr][3]
    bstr = colors[cstr][astr]
    alert( astr + '\n' + bstr)
```

The variable `astr` holds the left element, and `bstr` the right element. If you attempt to do this in one step, it appears confusing. If you substitute the value of `astr` in the second expression, you get the following massive expression:

```
bstr = colors[cstr][colors[cstr][3]]
```

Note that we placed some convenient but arbitrary values into our subsidiary arrays. We could have had the `fillColorArray()` function generate successive, properly spaced hex values that were within the appropriate color range. In general, it is more likely that you will want to use these kinds of arrays to keep arbitrary data.

# Some JavaScript HTML Objects

This section reviews some of the fundamental concepts of HTML objects in JavaScript and then proceeds to the more complex `Image` and `Text` objects mentioned at the beginning of this chapter. By this point, you are well acquainted with the various HTML objects in JavaScript. The focus of this section is to explore some of their innovative uses. Many of the "tricks" of JavaScript revolve around the fact that integers and Booleans can be easily converted to strings.

Strings in JavaScript can be thought of as HTML objects, in addition to their usual meaning. JavaScript provides methods for giving strings many of the formatted characteristics of HTML text, such as bold (`<B>`), italics (`<I>`), big (`<BIG>`), and link (`<A>`). When you use a construction such as:

```
mystring = 'This is some text.'
mystring = mystring.bold,
```

mystring becomes `<B>This is some text.</B>`. We will use methods such as these in the `Text` object we produce.

▶ **See** "HTML String Methods," **p. 126,** for a detailed discussion of HTML string methods.

# Objects Revisited

By now, you are intimately aware that objects are just arrays of properties. However, properties are accessed somewhat differently from array elements, and they usually use only the left side of the array. New properties can be added to an object at any time. This is possible because *only* the left element of the array is used. Trying to add new array elements on-the-fly when you are using both sides of the array element is fraught with peril, as we have seen previously.

Objects can have both properties and methods. Methods are simply functions that have been declared as properties. For example, you might have a `color` object. Colors are cited in terms of their red, green, and blue components (at least in Web browsers; there are other color-mixing schemes). Many of the common colors also have common names. To declare a `color` object, we must make a constructor. This approach is no different from the type of construction methods we have seen for arrays. Listing 11.20 shows the code for such a constructor.

**Listing 11.20   Creating a Simple *color* Object**

```
function Color(name,red,green,blue)
{
     this.name       =    name
     this.red        =    red
     this.green      =    green
     this.blue       =    blue
     this.length     =     4
     return this
}

myGreenColorObject = new Color('green','22','DD','22')
```

**Property Taxes**   Object constructors really just reserve space for the property array elements. We can access the property values by their array indices, as well as by using the dot operator (.). This approach is useful for storing objects. To convert the `color` object into a string delimited with the @ character, you can use the function `storeColor()`, shown in Listing 11.21. This type of string is often useful for storing objects persistently, as we shall see in Chapter 23, "Using Cookies in Advanced Applications."

▶ **See** "Cookie Format Specification," **p. 626**, for a detailed description of how cookies may be used to store objects represented as delimited strings.

---

**Listing 11.21    Storing an Object's Properties as a Delimited String**

```
function storeColor(aColorObject)
{
    var k = aColorObject.length        // number of elements in object
    var astr = ''              // initialize to empty string
    var i = 0
    for(i = 1 ; i <= k ; i++)     // iterate over elements
        {
            astr += aColorObject[i] + '@'     // append to astr.
        }
    return astr              // return delimited string
}
```

---

You can easily reverse this process, as the function getColor() shows. The function getColor() tears apart the delimited string passed as its second argument astr, and sets the properties of aColorObject accordingly. Listing 11.22 displays getColor().

---

**Listing 11.22    Retrieving an Object's Properties from a Delimited String**

```
function getColor(aColorObject,astr)
{
    var lastloc = astr.lastIndexOf('@')     // final delimiter
    var n =0          // number of delimiters found
    var f = 0          // location of current delimited
    var i = 1          // current array index
    while ( n >= 0 )
        {
// find next delimiter, store in local variable f
            f = astr.indexOf(astr,n)
// set the i-th array element to the string between the last delimiter
// ( at location n ) and the current delimiter ( at location f )
            aColorObject[i] = astr.substring(n,f)
// if we are at the very last delimiter ( at location lastloc )
            if (f == lastloc)
                {
// then take the substring from the current position up to the end
// of the string and break out of the while loop
                    aColorObject[i+1] = astr.substring(f+1,astr.length)
                    break
                }
// if we are not at the very last delimiter then repeat the process
            else n = f  + 1
// update array index
        i++
        }
}
```

---

These examples are not the only ways to perform either one of these operations. The storage function `storeColor()` also could have been implemented, as shown in Listing 11.23.

### Listing 11.23 An Alternative Color-Storage Function Using the *for...in* Statement

```
function storeColor(aColorObject)
    {
        var astr = ""
        for (var i in aColorObject)
                astr += aColorObject[i] + '@'
        return astr
    }
```

We also could have used use the `word()` function to retrieve the properties of an object from a string in the `getColor()` function. However, this approach is slower than the approach shown in the first implementation of `getColor()`.

**Adding Your Own Methods**   It would be nice if the `color` object knew how to do its own conversion to and from the delimited string representation. Because we have already written the essential conversion functions, it's easy to make them methods of the `color` object: we just assign them as properties of the object itself. If we use this approach, our `color` object constructor is changed to the code shown in Listing 11.24.

### Listing 11.24 Creating a *color* Object with Methods and Properties

```
function betterColor(name,red,green,blue)
{
    this.name       =    name
    this.red        =    red
    this.green      =    green
    this.blue       =    blue
    this.toString   =    storeColor
    this.fromString =       getColor
    this.length     =    6
    return this
}

myGreenColorObject = new betterColor('green','22','DD','22')
```

**N O T E**   Always set the `length` property of an object in your constructor. Although JavaScript will automatically add a `length` property in the element at `index=0`, and keep that `length` property updated as new elements are added, this behavior is not guaranteed. ■

If you are going to convert a function into a method, you can (and should) alter it somewhat to exploit the fact that it is now a method function. If a function is not a method function of an object, then it may access that object only if the object is passed as a parameter to the function, or if the object has been declared globally. Once you make the function a method of the object, the function can reference the object that contains it via the keyword `this`. Consequently, we can rewrite the `storeColor` method as shown in Listing 11.25.

**Listing 11.25   String an Object's Properties by Using a Method Function**

```
function storeColor()
{
    var k = this.length
    var astr = ''
    var i = 0
    for(i = 1 ; i <= k ; i++)
        {
                astr += this[i] + '@'
        }
    return astr
}
```

**N O T E**   In order to change a function into a method function of an object, follow these three steps:

1. Make the method a property of the object, as in `aColor.toString = storeColor`.

2. Do not pass the object as a parameter to the function.

3. Change all explicit references to the object to the keyword `this`; for example, `l = aColorObject.length` becomes `l = this.length`. ∎

# Images as Objects

Drawing images is a complex affair. One of the most important things to remember about image manipulation, in terms of JavaScript, is that all images *must* be characterized by HEIGHT and WIDTH modifiers in their HTML tags. If you leave these modifiers out, JavaScript will misbehave or won't function at all. In this section, we develop an `Image` object that encapsulates all the important `Image` properties, including the `height` and `width`. The `Image` object will also know how to display itself in several contexts. The constructor for the `Image` object is shown in Listing 11.26.

**Listing 11.26   A Comprehensive Constructor for an *Image* Object**

```
function image(title, filename, height, width, vspace, hspace,
                    border, bordercolor, frame, framecolor, href, notes)
    {
        this.title      = title
        this.filename   = filename
        this.height     = height
        this.width      = width
        this.vspace     = vspace
        this.hspace     = hspace
```

*continues*

**Listing 11.26   Continued**

```
    this.border       = border
    this.bordercolor  = bordercolor
    this.frame        = frame
    this.framecolor   = framecolor
    this.href         = href
    this.notes        = notes
    this.draw         = drawImage
    this.frame        = frameImage
    this.reference    = referenceImage
    this.popup        = popImage
    return this
}
```

**Properties and Methods of the *Image* Object**    If you examine the constructor for the Image object shown in the previous section, you see that it not only encapsulates the usual HTML qualifiers for an image, but also has properties for a file name, a title, an associated URL, and notes. It can present itself as a plain image, a framed image, or a linked image. It can also pop itself up in a window of its own. The image "draws" itself by presenting you with a string that you can send to a nascent document by using document.write(). The functions drawImage(), referenceImage(), and frameImage() draw a plain image, a linked image, and a framed image, respectively.

▶ **See** "Using Nascent Documents," **p. 265**, which thoroughly covers documents generated on-the-fly, also known as *nascent* documents.

Listing 11.27 shows the definitions of those three functions.

**Listing 11.27   The *Image* Object's Plain Draw, Linked (reference), and Framed Method**

```
function drawImage(how,border)
{
     var astr = ''
// if the image does not use this modifier
// the parameter can be empty or '^'
     astr = '<IMG SRC="' + this.filename + '"'
     if (how != '') astr += ' ALIGN=' + how
     if (this.height != '') astr += ' HEIGHT=' + this.height
     if (this.width != '' && this.width != '^')
         astr += ' WIDTH=' + this.width
     if (this.vspace != '' && this.vspace != '^')
      astr += ' VSPACE=' + this.vspace
     if (this.hspace != '' && this.hspace != '^')
      astr += ' HSPACE=' + this.hspace
     if (this.border != '' && this.border != '^')
      astr += ' BORDER=' + this.border
     astr +='>'
     if (this.border != '' && this.border != '^')
         astr = '<FONT COLOR=' +
         this.bordercolor + '>' + astr + '</FONT>'
```

```
        return astr

}

function referenceImage(how,border,ref,atext)
{
        if (ref == '') ref=this.href
        if (ref == '') ref = location.href
        if (atext == '') atext = 'Your text here!'
        var astr = '<A HREF=' + ref + '>'
        astr += '<IMG SRC="' + this.filename + '"'
        if (how != '') astr += ' ALIGN=' + how
        if (this.height != '') astr += ' HEIGHT=' + this.height
        if (this.width != '' && this.width != '^')
      astr += ' WIDTH=' + this.width
        if (this.vspace != '' && this.width != '^')
      astr += ' VSPACE=' + this.vspace
        if (this.hspace != '' && this.width != '^')
      astr += ' WIDTH=' + this.hspace
        if ('' + border != '') astr += ' BORDER=' + this.border
        astr +='>'
        astr += atext
        astr += '</A>'
        return astr

}

function frameImage(how,border,leading)
{
        var astr = '<TABLE '
        if (how != '') astr += ' ALIGN=' + how
        if ('' + border != '') astr += ' BORDER=' + border
        if ('' + leading != '') astr += ' CELLSPACING=' + leading
        astr += '><TR><TD ALIGN=CENTER>'
        var bstr = '</TD></TR></TABLE>'
        astr += this.draw('',2)
        astr += bstr
        return astr
}
```

Part II
Ch
11

Notice that the frameImage method first draws the <TABLE>, which is used as a "frame," and then calls the drawImage method to draw the image. In all three cases, the image can have a border. In both the drawImage and frameImage methods, the border color is determined by the current font color. Since the Image object encapsulates the border color, it is as easy to include it as it is to include any other modifier. Referenced image borders, though, do not have such a choice; they will be the link color or vlink color specified for the page.

**Using the *Image* Object**   You can use the Image object to make a database of your images. A file name, notes (which can include a caption for the image), and an URL are included as part of the object, as we have seen. The example program in Listing 11.28—located on the companion Web site due to its length—arbitrarily sets up a trivial database of six Image objects held in an array. It can present these images as plain, framed, or referenced. It can also pop up any image in its own window.

Listing 11.29 shows the method that generates the pop-up.

---

**Listing 11.29   The Pop-Up Method of the *Image* Object**

```
function popImage(title)
{
    var w = 50 + parseInt(this.width)     // image width as displayed
    var h = parseInt(this.height) + 50    // image height as displayed
    scrl = 'no'                // do scrolling?
    if (w>640){w=640;scrl='yes'}    // if width too big then scroll
    if (h>480){h=480;scrl='yes'}    // if height too big then scroll
// specify HTML attributes for the image
    var whstr ='WIDTH=' + w + ',HEIGHT=' + h +
        'RESIZABLE=yes,SCROLLBARS=' + scrl
// open a new window
    aNewWin = self.open('',title,whstr)
// if the new window could not be allocated...
    if (!aNewWin)
        {
// notify the user that it failed, and try to indicate
// possible causes
        var alertstr = "Could not open a new window."
        alertstr += " A window of named " + title
        alertstr += " may already be open."
        alertstr += " You may also be out of memory"
        alert(alertstr)
        return;
    }
// if new window was allocated successfully...
// generate the HTML to display the image
    var astr = '<HTML><HEAD>'
    astr += '<BASE HREF="' + location.href + '">'
    astr += '<TITLE>' + this.title + '</TITLE>'
    astr += '</HEAD><BODY>'
// write out that HTML
    aNewWin.document.write(astr)
    var bstr = '<CENTER>' + this.draw('CENTER') + '</CENTER>'
    aNewWin.document.write(bstr)
    aNewWin.document.write('</BODY></HTML>')
// close the document
    aNewWin.document.close()
}
```

---

The resulting image display is shown in Figure 11.7. The page generated by the code in Listing 11.29 is covered with pop-up windows containing its tiny database of six images. The images were placed in the pages by hand; the page has no input interface. Any single image can be popped up by placing its number in the text box next to the Image button and by clicking the button.

**FIG. 11.8**
The Image object can be activated to pop up an image database.

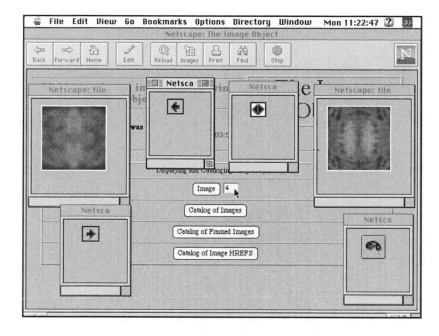

Figures 11.9 and 11.10 show the plain and framed versions of the image displayed in a catalog format. The image catalog is nothing more than a scrolling display of all the images in the database.

**FIG. 11.9**
The image database may be displayed as a scrolling window of plain images.

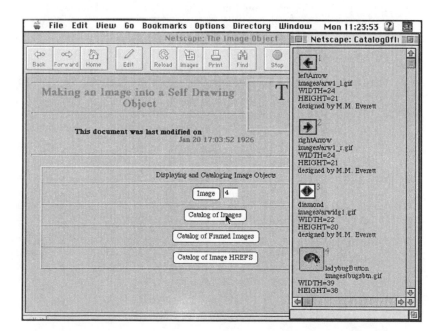

**FIG. 11.10**

The image database may be displayed as a scrolling catalog of framed images.

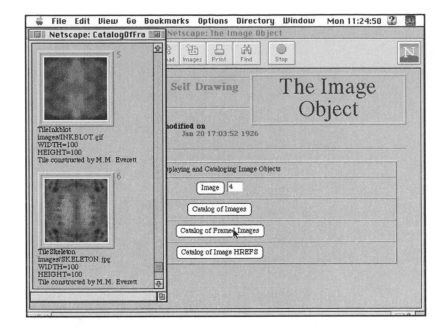

Most of the draw methods presented here accept a string terminator as a parameter and also return a string. The terminator is usually the linefeed character \n. This design results in a string with line breaks suitable for an alert. You can also use <BR> as the string terminator; this approach yields a string that can be nicely presented in a window. The utility function showInWindow pops up a window and tries to put anything you hand it into that window, as shown in Listing 11.30.

**Listing 11.30   A Function that Shows an Object in a Pop-Up Window**

```
function showInWindow(tstr,title)
{
    var w = 300
    var h = 300
    scrl = 'yes'
    if (w>640){w=640;scrl='yes'}
    if (h>480){h=480;scrl='yes'}
    var whstr ='SCROLLBARS=' + scrl + ',RESIZABLE=yes,WIDTH=' + w +
         ',HEIGHT=' + h
    aNewWin = self.open('',title,whstr)
    var astr = '<HTML><HEAD>'
    astr += '<BASE HREF="' + location.href + '">'
    astr += '<TITLE>' + title + '</TITLE>'
    astr += '</HEAD><BODY>'
    aNewWin.document.write(astr)
    aNewWin.document.write(tstr)
    aNewWin.document.write('</BODY></HTML>')
    aNewWin.document.close()
}
```

# The *Text* Object

The approach we employed for the Image object can be used for text manipulation as well. We will build a Text object that holds various important properties related to how the text is displayed. This Text object will be very similar to the Image object in terms of the type of draw methods that it supports. The constructor function for the Text object is shown here. All the code for the Text object can be found in Listing 11.31.

## Listing 11.31 The Constructor Function for the *Text* Object

```
function Text(type,title,text,size,color,bold,italic,
             supersub,frame,href,notes)
{
    this.type =        type
    this.title=        title
    this.text =        text
    this.size =        size
    this.color =       color
    this.bold =        bold
    this.italic   =    italic
    this.supersub =    supersub
    this.frame   =     frame
    this.href   =      href
    this.notes   =     notes
    this.draw =        drawText
    this.frame =       frameText
    this.reference =   referenceText
    this.popup =       popText
    this.lines =       stringToList
    this.word =        word
    return this
}
```

Notice that this function is very similar to the constructor for the Image object. It encapsulates some of JavaScript's own string properties. This object, too, knows how to present itself as plain, framed, or referenced text. It can also pop itself up in a window. Note that it has a type property; that is, the text can be a list, a paragraph, and so on. Its draw method accepts a parameter that enables you to draw the text according to a predefined type method or to draw the text using the properties you have set.

The Text object has some methods that can access the text as lines or words. Again, this is a crude emulation of HyperCard. These methods enable you to define the separator that separates one phrase from another. The stringToList method accepts a prefix and a suffix, as well as the list separator. It separates the string into phrases and then adds the prefix and suffix provided. Use the \n character as the separator to get logical lines. The word() function is used to return the word at the position you specify. The implementation of the stringToList method is shown in Listing 11.32.

**Listing 11.32  A Function to Separate Delimited Strings into Phrases**

```
function stringToList(sep, what, pref,suf)
// sep = separator (delimiter)
// what = object to use
// pref = prefix to prepend
// suf = suffix to append
{
        var n = 0           // location of current separator
        var f = 0           // location of next separator
        var astr = ''       // string being built
        var nstr = ''       // work string
        var finished = false
    if ( what == null ) what = this
        while (f >= 0 )
            {
// get position of next separator
                    f = what.indexOf(sep,n)
// if this the last one?
                    if (f == what.lastIndexOf(sep))
                        {
// if so then get the end of the string
                            f = what.length
// and set the finished flag
                            finished = true
                        }
// get the string, prepend the prefix and append the suffix
                    nstr = pref + what.substring(n,f) + suf
// add the current working string onto the final string
                    astr += nstr
// if all done then break out of the loop
                    if (finished ) break
// advance to the next separator
                    n = f + 1
            }
    return astr      // return the completed string
}
```

Note that this function uses an interesting trick to decide when it has come to the end of the string. It uses lastIndexOf() to get the character position of the last occurrence of the separator. As it walks the string, it checks to see if the character found equals the last instance of that character. If it does, it sets the phrase end to the end of the string, performs its usual string separation, and then exits.

Another useful routine, which can easily be modified for your own purpose, is the makeTitle method. MakeTitle goes through a string and eliminates spaces, but capitalizes the letter after the space. This is useful for catching two-word window names, such as "Hi there," that a user has entered. If you hand the open() command more than one word, it simply does not open the window, nor does it tell you why. The makeTitle method converts such strings into more acceptable titles, such as "HiThere" in this case. The makeTitle function is given in Listing 11.33. Figure 11.11 shows the result of exercising the pop-up capabilities of the Text object.

**Listing 11.33   A Function to Create Window Title Strings**

```
function makeTitle(what)
{
    var n = what.length      // length of string "what"
    var i = 0                // iteration variable
    var cc = ''              // current character
    var accstr=''            // output string being built
    for (i = 0 ; i < n ; i++)       // iterate over the whole string
        {
// get character at position "i"
            cc = what.substring(i,i+1)
// if that character is not a space, then add it to the output string
            if ( cc != ' ' )
                {
                    accstr += cc
                    continue
                }
            else
                {
// if that character is a space then skip it
                    i++
// grab the first character after the space
                    cc=what.substring(i,i + 1)
// convert it to uppercase
                    cc = cc.toUpperCase()
// add that uppercase letter onto the output string
                    accstr += cc
                }
        }
return accstr            // return the output string
}
```

Part

II

Ch

11

**FIG. 11.11**

The database of `text` objects can display itself in pop-up windows.

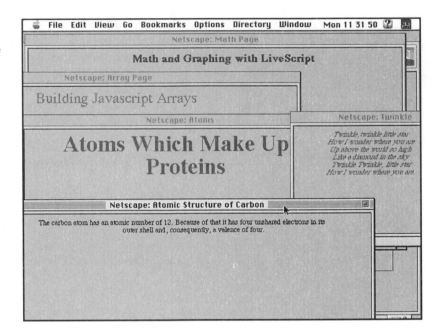

# JavaScript and Live Objects

# CHAPTER 12

# A Java Tutorial

JavaScript is an extremely powerful tool for developing Web pages. You have already seen in the preceding chapters a number of significant applications that use JavaScript. The complexity and power of applications that can be developed in JavaScript is almost unlimited. However, there are certain situations in which the Java programming language may be a better solution.

The difference between JavaScript and Java is very much like the difference between hand tools and power tools. Anything you can do with a lathe you can also do with a rasp, a hand saw, and sandpaper. It is quite possible to produce beautiful woodwork using only the simplest tools. One gains time, and perhaps uniformity, by using a lathe. To do this, however, one must know how to operate a lathe properly, without losing fingers. (In this analogy, JavaScript is the lathe.) JavaScript is a simpler language than Java, with fewer built-in functions, yet it is still extremely expressive. Java has a much larger set of capabilities, yet it is also a bit more difficult to use.

The correct approach, of course, is to use all the tools that are available. Nevertheless, it is very important to realize when to pick up the hand tools and when to fire up the power tools. This chapter introduces the Java language and describes the differences between it and JavaScript. The basic constructs of Java applets are explored and some simple examples are given. ■

**Define and use Java methods and classes**

Java classes are analogous to JavaScript's objects, while methods fulfill the same role in both languages.

**Create Java applets**

A Java applet is a small application that is embedded into a Web page. When the Web page is accessed, the applet can perform tasks that provide live content to that page.

**Use the Java Development Kit to compile applets**

The Java Development Kit (JDK) is a set of tools used to create the binary versions of Java applets, which are used in Web pages.

**Embed applets in a Web page**

The HTML APPLET tag is used to perform the actual embedding of Java applets. It has a number of attributes that can be used to influence the applet's behavior.

# The Java Language

If you have ever seen any Java code, you probably noticed that it bears a substantial resemblance to JavaScript. A large part of the Java language is identical to JavaScript. However, there are several significant differences between Java and JavaScript that are critical in learning how to effectively use both tools. These differences can be grouped into the following three categories:

- The object models
- Interactions with the browser environment
- Language differences

The way in which the two languages handle objects is fundamental to how they are each used. Their interactions with the Web browser are also fundamentally different—the concept of an event is completely different in Java. Finally, the Java language is much stricter in its usage than JavaScript. Before we plunge into a detailed description of Java code, it is useful to look at these differences in a little more detail. Java and JavaScript are very different "under the hood."

## Java and JavaScript Compared

In Part II of this book, "JavaScript In-Depth," we took a very close look at objects in JavaScript. JavaScript objects are used to access the built-in mathematical, string, and date functions. JavaScript objects also are used to access and manipulate HTML elements inside JavaScript code. Java takes this object-oriented approach even further. Everything in Java is based on objects (known as *classes* in Java), and their properties (*instance variables* in Java) and methods. In JavaScript, you often create functions that are methods of your own objects. You are also perfectly free to have functions that are not methods. Event handler functions usually are not method functions, for example. In Java, all functions must be methods of some object and all variables must be properties of some object.

In JavaScript, the focus is on responding to events. A user action produces an event that triggers a JavaScript event handler, which does something useful. In Java, user events are handled very differently. When the user loads a Web page containing Java code in the form of a Java *applet*, the browser tells the applet to start. When the user leaves that page, the applet is told to stop. While JavaScript code is ultimately event-driven, and intimately tied to its HTML environment, Java applets are much more independent. An applet may respond to a mouse click within its active area, but it won't be listening for the sound of a Submit button being pressed. An applet is a little application that lives in its own world, for the most part. JavaScript code is more like a *Dynamically Linked Library* (DLL), which is activated in response to something.

Finally, we know that JavaScript takes a very relaxed attitude toward variables and functions. Variables are typeless and the distinction between functions, objects, and arrays is blurry at best. By contrast, Java is an extremely strict language. All Java variables have an explicit data type. Types may be converted to one another only under very well-defined conditions and only by using explicit type-conversion functions. Java also enforces static name binding instead of JavaScript's dynamic binding. It is impossible (so they say) to reference an undefined function.

▶ **See** "Binding in JavaScript," **p. 68**, for a discussion of the name binding concept.

Java is actually a very small language when compared with other object-oriented programming languages such as C++. Nevertheless, it has a large number of capabilities. For example, the extensive set of built-in functions and objects, known as the *Java class hierarchy*, implements an extremely rich and powerful set of tools for image manipulation and network access, among other things. This Java tutorial focuses on the core part of Java that is necessary to create meaningful and interesting Web content.

# Data Types in Java

Java variables must be explicitly declared with a particular data type. Java is very similar to the C and C++ programming languages in terms of the types it supports. Java, however, rigidly specifies the size and representation of its various types so that there can be no confusion. If you have ever tried to port a C program from a DOS or Windows environment with 16-bit integers to a UNIX or Windows-NT environment with 32-bit integers, you know from firsthand experience how frustrating such low-level problems can be.

In addition to its primitive types, such as `int`, `float`, and `boolean`, Java also has object types, just like JavaScript. In Java, however, you must say which object was used to create a particular instance. The declarations that follow say that s is an instance of the `String` object and that d is an instance of the `Date` object.

```
String s;
Date d;
```

> **N O T E**   For the most part, Java statements are similar in form to their JavaScript counterparts.
> Every Java statement *must* end in a semicolon, however.  ■

As you might suspect, these are uninitialized instances. The variables s and d are of type `String` and `Date`, respectively, but have no values yet. They are unbound, just as the JavaScript declaration

```
var myvar;
```

creates an uninitialized (unbound) variable `myvar`. The only difference between the two languages is that in Java we at least know what the underlying type of s and d are, while in JavaScript `myvar` is a complete mystery until it is given some value.

There are several differences between the object models of Java and JavaScript, as well as the terminology they use. Note that Java refers to its objects as *classes*, unlike JavaScript. Java object members are referred to as *instance variables* rather than properties. Instances and methods have the same meaning in both languages. Note particularly that Java has no independent functions, only methods. These differences arise from the fact that Java is both explicitly typed and strongly typed. In Java, every piece of data must have a type. Every structured data type, such as `String`, is a class, while the data itself is an instance of that class. This concept of strong typing pervades all of Java and is even reflected in the differences in terminology with JavaScript.

In Java, almost all the built-in data types are numeric. This is a reflection of the fact that everything that is more complex than a number is represented by a Java class. The built-in data types in Java are as follows:

- `boolean`
- `byte`
- `char`
- `short`
- `int`
- `long`
- `float`
- `double`

The `boolean` data is a 1-bit type that may have the familiar values `true` and `false`. Java is more strict than JavaScript in that it does not allow you to use a numeric expression in a context in which a `Boolean` value is expected. You must say `while ( true )` rather than `while ( 1 )`, for example, because the clause of a `while` statement must be a logical (`Boolean`) value.

The `byte`, `short`, `int`, and `long` types are the basic fixed-point numeric types. All are signed quantities. They are represented by using 8, 16, 32, and 64 bits, respectively. If you are a C programmer from either the 16- or 32-bit worlds, this may seem a little confusing. In the 16-bit world, `int` and `short` are mostly the same, while in the 32-bit world, `int` and `long` are often the same. Java is actually more explicit. All the basic types are platform-independent. Their sizes are fixed as part of the language itself.

You may be wondering what the `char` data type is. Java has taken a very modern approach and adopted a standard known as the *Unicode* standard for character representation. Unicode is a way of representing almost any character in any language of the world by using a fixed Unicode sequence. Unicode sequences look like `\uNNNN`, where *NNNN* is a four-digit hexadecimal number. This is something like an extension to the escape sequences of the C programming language. In C, you can write `'\007'` to represent the character with ASCII code 7 (Ctrl+G, which usually makes the computer go 'ding'). In Unicode, you can write `'\u212B'` to represent the Angstrom symbol Å and `'\u1039'` for the Tibetan Rinchanphungshad.

**T I P**    With the exception of Unicode characters, Java has the same syntax for literals as does JavaScript.

> **CAUTION**
>
> What you see is not necessarily what you get with Unicode. Many browsers and most display devices are not able to properly handle most Unicode sequences. Avoid Unicode in your Java code unless you are sure your users have the appropriate fonts and software to display it.

The char data type is a Unicode character. It is 16 bits wide and is an unsigned quantity, unlike all the other Java data types. This can also lead to some confusion for programmers who are familiar with 8-bit characters because a char is twice as big as a byte in Java. One immediate consequence of the use of Unicode is that strings and arrays of bytes are not the same; some work must be done to convert from one to another. Another consequence is that if you ask a string such as "Hiya" how long it is, it will tell you 4. This means that it is 4 chars long, which is actually 8 bytes.

The float and double data types are standard single- and double-precision floating-point data types. The Java language mandates that these data types conform to the IEEE (Institute of Electrical and Electronics Engineers) 754 standard, so that a float will always be a 32-bit quantity and a double a 64-bit quantity, with very precisely defined notions of accuracy, precision, and permitted maximum and minimum values. Imposing a particular standard may be pushy, but at least it ensures that correct implementations will all work the same way.

On the surface, Java variables and JavaScript variables seem to behave in the same way. Because Java is a strongly typed language, unlike JavaScript, Java variables can be used only in much more restrictive ways. It is not possible to change the data type of a variable in Java, as it is in JavaScript. In order to convert between different data types, you must use explicit conversion routines. We will see several examples of this, particularly in the final section of this chapter, "An Accounting Applet in Java."

## Java Classes as Structured Data Types

Java would be very underpowered if it had only the built-in types listed in the previous section. Of course, it not only has these primitive types, it also has complex types that are built up from smaller components. These are classes in Java. They are very similar to JavaScript objects and to the classes of C++. In fact, the Java class model is a very simplified version of the one used by C++. Java has a very rich set of predefined classes, known as the Java class hierarchy. Some of the components of this hierarchy are described in the final section of this chapter. In this section, we discuss the basic concept of a class and show how classes are defined and used.

The Java concept of a class is quite close to the JavaScript concept of an object. The primary difference is that Java is much stricter about how instances may be used and has a more detailed set of rules that must be followed. For example, unlike JavaScript, it is not possible to dynamically extend a Java instance.

▶ **See** "Using Variable Length Arrays and Extended Instances," **p. 93**, which describes how to extend JavaScript instances.

A Java class is a collection of variables and methods. When a class is created, its variables and methods are defined as part of the class definition. Therefore, the shape of the class is fixed when it is created. Listing 12.1 shows a very simple Java class definition.

Part
III

Ch
12

### Listing 12.1   A Java Class for Keeping Track of Money

```
class Account {              // name of the class is "Account"
     int ivegot = 0;         // instance variable, initialized to zero

    void deposit ( int n ) {     // method for adding money
         ivegot += n;
    }
// method for determining how much is left
    int balance( ) {
         return(ivegot);
    }
// method for attempting to withdraw money
    boolean withdraw( int n ) {
         boolean result;     // local variable
         if ( n <= ivegot ) {
              ivegot -= n;
              result = true;
         } else {
              result = false;
         }
         return(result);
    }
}
```

 **TIP**  Java class names should begin with an uppercase letter. Instance names often begin with a lowercase letter and contain the class name of which they are an instance.

Listing 12.1 defines a class known as Account. It has a single instance variable, ivegot, which records the total amount of money stored in the Account. It is initialized to 0. It also has three method functions: deposit, balance, and withdraw. These method functions perform the operations specified by their names; they deposit money, get the account balance, and attempt to withdraw money.

There are several things to notice about this class definition. The first, and most obvious, thing about the class Account is that all its components are declared inside the class definition. In particular, all the class methods are given explicitly as part of the class itself. Methods and variables are not attached as they are in JavaScript—they are a required part of the definition itself.

The second important aspect of these methods is the fact that each of them is declared with its own data type. The balance method is declared to be an int method, which indicates that it returns an int value, the amount of money left in the account given by the int ivegot. The balance method is said to have a *return type* of int. Similarly, the withdraw method has a return type of boolean; it returns a boolean quantity.

**N O T E**  The return type of a method must match the value returned. It is a serious error to attempt to return something whose type is different than the return type. ▪

**The *void* Keyword**    The deposit method is interesting because it introduces a new keyword: void. The void keyword is used to indicate that nothing is returned. The deposit method simply takes its argument, adds it to the instance variable ivegot, and then falls off the end of its { } definition block. There is no return statement. void means what it says—there is nothing being returned.

The same rule applies for the empty argument list of the balance method. This indicates that the balance function accepts no arguments. This is in contrast to the deposit and withdraw methods, both of which accept a single argument, which we are told is an int. Just as it would be an error to pass a floating-point value to deposit, it would also be an error to pass any value to balance or to try to take the value of a method function declared to be void.

If we assume myacct is an instance of the Account class, then both of the following statements would be in error by virtue of misusing the void type:

```
int i = myacct.balance(0);  // bad: void args
int j = myacct.deposit(10); // bad: void return
```

**Declaring Java Classes**    With the example of Listing 12.1 in mind, you can see the general pattern for declaring both kinds of class members, namely instance variables and method functions. The general structure of a class declaration looks like the template shown in Listing 12.2.

**Listing 12.2    Declaring a Java Class and Its Members**

```
class Classname {        // a class named Classname
    Type1 Var1;          // instance variable Var1 of type Type1
    Type2 Var2;          // instance variable Var2 of type Type2
    ...                  // more instance variables
// Method Method1, return type RetType, arguments Arglist
    RetType Method1( Arglist ) {
        ...
        return( Thing );    // return statement if not void
        }                // end of Method1
    ...                  // more methods
}                        // end of class definition
```

This class declaration consists of three basic parts, as follows:

- The class declaration line
- The instance variable declarations
- The method declarations

The class declaration line declares the name of the class. It is Java tradition that this name begin with an uppercase letter, as noted earlier. This makes it easy to distinguish class names from variable names (and from the names' built-in types), which traditionally begin with a lowercase letter. In Listing 12.1, we declared a class named Account.

The instance variables are then declared immediately following the opening of the class definition, which is indicated by the opening bracket ({). It is possible in Java to declare instance variables anywhere outside a method definition, but it is simpler, and easier to understand, if they are all placed at the very top of the class definition. Our Account example had a single instance variable ivegot. Note that every instance variable must have a type and may be initialized. The Account variable ivegot was initialized to 0, for example. As usual, it is good programming practice to initialize all instance variables to reasonable defaults, if possible.

The method function should be placed after the instance variables have been declared. Each method function declaration is composed of the following four parts, all of which are mandatory for (almost) every method:

- The return type
- The method name
- The argument list
- The method body

The return type is given immediately before the name of the method itself. With one critical exception (constructor methods, which are described next), all methods must have a return type. If the method executes the return statement, then it must declare what type of quantity it is returning in its return type. If the method does not return anything, then it must declare its return type to be void. Java is very strict about mismatches of this form.

The method name is the name by which the method is invoked. This is exactly the same as the function and method names of JavaScript, with one exception. If the name of a method is exactly the same as the name of the class, then the method is known as a *constructor method*, or simply a *constructor*. Later in this section, you will see how these are used.

The argument list declares which arguments, if any, will be given to this method function. The argument list should contain the argument types, as well as the names of the arguments. In Listing 12.1, there is a method named deposit with a void return type and a single int argument named n; a balance method with int return type and no (void) arguments; and a boolean withdraw method, which also takes a single int argument named n, just like deposit. The argument list must match exactly the arguments used. We cannot call deposit with two arguments or with a string argument and we cannot call balance with any arguments at all.

Finally, the set of Java code between the opening and closing brackets ({}) constitutes the method *body*. The method body does the work of the method. In general, the method body may make use of its arguments and of the instance variables. The method function deposit is a perfect example of this. Its method body consists of a single statement

```
ivegot += n;
```

which adds the argument n, the amount being deposited, to the instance variable ivegot. Method functions can also call other method functions within the class.

Let's consider an example that makes use of the Account class. In this example, we will open an account, make a deposit of 100, and then make successive withdrawals of 40 and 70. The code to do this is shown in Listing 12.3. (Note that these deposits and withdrawals are not associated with any specific currency. The deposit of 100 could be 100 dollars, 100 Francs, or even 100 coconuts.)

### Listing 12.3 Using the *Account* Class

```
Account myacct;     // 1; declare an instance of the Account class
boolean gotit;                       // 2; got the money?

myacct = new Account();              // 3; initialize it
myacct.deposit(100);                 // 4; deposit 100
gotit = myacct.withdraw(40);         // 5; try to withdraw 40
if ( gotit == true ) {               // 6; got it
    System.out.println("Withdrawal ok");      // 7; print a message
} else {                             // 8; didn't get it
    System.out.println("Insufficient funds");
    System.out.println("Balance: " + myacct.balance()); // 10; print balance
}
gotit = myacct.withdraw(70);             // 12; try for 70 now
if ( gotit == true ) {                   // 13; got it
    System.out.println("Withdrawal ok");
} else {                             // 15; didn't get it
// 16; print failure message
    System.out.println("Insufficient funds");
// 17; print balance
    System.out.println("Balance: " + myacct.balance());
}
```

This code shows a typical sequence of operations in Java. Statement 1 declares an instance of the class Account. It is an uninitialized instance so it cannot be used until it is initialized. This initialization happens in statement 3 using the familiar new operator:

```
myacct = new Account();              // 3; initialize it
```

Note that the Account class is invoked as if it were a function (with no arguments). The variable myacct is now a fully initialized instance of the class Account, so we are free to use its methods.

### CAUTION

Do not confuse instances with instance variables. Instances are structured data items created from classes using the new operator. Instance variables are variables contained within a class definition.

In statement 4, we make a deposit of 100, so that the ivegot now has the value 100. Similarly, statement 5 withdraws 40, so that ivegot is then reduced to 60. Both these statements invoke methods of the myacct instance, as follows:

```
myacct.deposit(100);                 // 4; deposit 100
gotit = myacct.withdraw(40);         // 5; try to withdraw 40
```

This withdrawal succeeds so that the Boolean variable `gotit`, which holds the return value of the method function `withdraw`, is `true`. Therefore, the `if` test in statement 6 succeeds, and statement 7 is executed, as follows:

```
if ( gotit == true ) {                       // 6; got it
    System.out.println("Withdrawal ok");     // 7; print a message
}
```

We have enough experience to guess that `System.out.println()` calls the `println()` method of the sub-object `out`, of the system object `System`, and prints a message somehow.

> **N O T E**   The dot operator (.) works the same way in Java and JavaScript. It is used to reference an element (instance variable, property, or method) of an instance. ▪

We now grow bold and attempt to withdraw `70` from the account represented by the instance `myacct` by calling the method function `withdraw` again in statement 12, as follows:

```
gotit = myacct.withdraw(70);                 // 12; try for 70 now
```

This time it doesn't work, however, because the account holds only `60` at this time. If you examine the body of the method function `withdraw` in Listing 12.3, you see that it is quite careful to test and make sure that there are sufficient funds. In this case, therefore, `myacct.withdraw` returns `false`.

The `if` test of statement 13 fails and the `else` pathway of statement 15 takes us to statement 16, which prints out a discouraging but accurate assessment of our financial state. Statement 17 is also invoked to print our balance, as follows:

```
if ( gotit == true ) {                       // 13; got it
    System.out.println("Withdrawal ok");
} else {                                     // 15; didn't get it
// 16; print failure message
    System.out.println("Insufficient funds");
// 17; print balance
    System.out.println("Balance: " + myacct.balance());
}
```

Statement 17 uses the method function `balance` to get the value and also makes use of + as a string concatenation operator. This is one of the few cases in which Java relaxes its strict rules on data types. It is usually possible to use + to convert non-strings into strings, but there are certain exceptions. We learn more about this topic in the next chapter. For the moment, just know that converting any of Java's built-in numerical types to strings, as line 17 does, is safe. Figure 12.1 displays a time history of the code in Listing 12.3.

This example probably raises several questions. Based on your experience with JavaScript, you are probably wondering why we need any of the methods of the `Account` class. After all, can't we just refer to the instance variable `ivegot` as `myacct.ivegot` and use the following statements:

```
myacct.ivegot += n;

myacct.ivegot -= n;

int howmuch = myacct.ivegot;
```

to deposit n, withdraw n, and get the account balance into the variable howmuch? The example code in Listing 12.3 is also very unrealistic. Banks do not simply let you open an account; they want you to open an account with an initial balance. There should be some way of specifying that initial balance when we call new, just as we do in JavaScript. Finally, this example is insecure. We really do not want anyone to have access to our account balance, nor do we want people to withdraw our money. They should be able to deposit as much as they like.

**FIG. 12.1**
Java instance variables keep their value throughout the life of an instance.

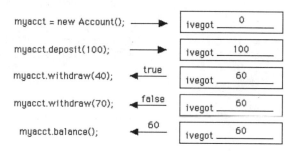

All three of these observations are valid. To make this example more meaningful, we must introduce two more Java constructions—private instance variables and constructor methods.

**Private Variables**   The basic deficiency of the class Account defined in Listing 12.3 is that the instance variable ivegot is completely wide open. After the account is opened (new is called to create an instance of Account), we can simply manipulate the balance directly. This makes the three methods of Account fairly useless and is also very insecure. We would like to hide ivegot from prying eyes, and also restrict the withdraw and balance methods. Listing 12.4 shows a revised definition of the Account class that does this.

Part
III

Ch
12

### Listing 12.4   A Safer Version of the *Account* Class

```
class Account {                 // new and improved Account
    private int ivegot = 0;      // 2; amount on deposit
    private int password = 29;   // 3; instance var for password
    boolean isopen = false;      // 4; account actually has money

    void deposit(int n) {        // 5; any one can deposit
        if ( n > 0 )             // 6; cannot deposit negative money
            ivegot += n;         // 7; do the deposit
/*
   Check account and make sure it is open
   Update the isopen variable
*/
        isopen = ( ivegot > 0 ? true : false ); // 8;
    }                                // end of deposit method
```

*continues*

**Listing 12.4 Continued**

```
// 10; password protected balance method
    int balance(int pword) {
        if ( pword == password )    // 11; correct password
            return( ivegot );       // 12; return accurate balance
        else                        // 13; incorrect password
            return( -1 );           // 14; return bogus balance
    }                               // 15; end of balance method
// 16; password protection here too
    boolean withdraw(int pword, int n) {
        boolean ok = true;          // 17; ok to withdraw?
        if ( pword != password )    // 18; bad password
            ok = false;             // 19; cannot withdraw
        if ( n > ivegot )           // 20; too much
            ok = false;             // 21; cannot withdraw
        if ( ok == true ) {         // 22; withdrawal allowed
            ivegot -= n;            // 23; update balance
// 24; update isopen variable
            isopen = ( ivegot > 0 ? true : false );
        }
        return(ok);                 // 26; return status
    }                               // end of withdraw method
}                                   // end of Account class
```

This version of the Account class has three instance variables: ivegot, password, and isopen. The first two are declared to be of type int and also have the special keyword private. A private variable is one that cannot be accessed outside the class. We can no longer refer to myacct.ivegot, nor can we refer to myacct.password, since both are declared private. We can, however, refer to the Boolean variable isopen by using myacct.isopen. This variable will be used to indicate whether the account has any money, so it is initialized to false. We can redundantly declare isopen as

```
public boolean isopen = false;
```

by using the public keyword. public is the opposite of private and it indicates that isopen may be accessed outside the class. By default, instance variables are public unless specified otherwise.

The methods deposit, withdraw, and balance are now essential. Because these methods are all within the Account class, they are permitted to access its private variables, as well as its public ones. The deposit method illustrates this in a very simple way. In statement 6, deposit tests its argument to ensure that it is positive so that no one can make a sneaky withdrawal by depositing a negative amount. If the test passes, then statement 7 is executed. It adds the argument n to the private variable ivegot. It also updates the public instance variable isopen in statement 8. If there is some money on deposit, the account is declared to be open (isopen is true); otherwise, it is closed (isopen is false). The following three statements constitute the body of the deposit method:

```
if ( n > 0 )            // 6; cannot deposit negative money
    ivegot += n;        // 7; do the deposit
isopen = ( ivegot > 0 ? true : false );     // 8; update isopen
```

The new version of the `balance` method now makes use of password protection. To successfully call this method function, a password must be supplied as the argument `pword`. This argument is tested against the private variable `password`. If the passwords match, then the actual balance is returned via the statement `return(ivegot)` on line 12. If they do not match, then -1 is returned in statement 14. Note that, because external access to a private variable is prohibited, it is not possible to steal the password by saying

```
int ha = myacct.password;
```

It also is not possible to gain access to the balance without supplying a password. The statement

```
int left = myacct.balance();
```

will be instantly rejected by Java because any call to `balance()` must have exactly one `int` argument. The `withdraw` method operates in a similar way. It now takes two arguments: the password argument `pword` and the amount to withdraw `n`. If the passwords do not match (`pword != password` on line 18) or the amount is too great (`n > ivegot` on line 20), then the local variable `ok` is set to `false`. If `ok` remains `true`, then both tests must have passed and the withdrawal takes place (statement 23). In this case, the status of the account is also updated in statement 24. If there is no money left, the account is automatically closed (`isopen` is set to `false`). Finally, the status of the transaction is returned using `return(ok)` on line 26.

**N O T E** Variables declared inside methods are known as *local variables*. They may only be accessed within the body of the method in which they are declared. ∎

This version of the `Account` class satisfies our security concerns. No one can tamper with our `myacct` instance and withdraw money, or even get our balance, without the proper password. The password and the account balance are hidden. However, we have allowed anyone to determine whether or not we have an active account by using the public instance variable `myacct.isopen`. Anyone may also deposit as much money as he or she likes.

We still do not have any way of simulating the real-life experience of opening an account because we must still execute two separate statements to open the account, as follows:

```
Account myacct = new Account();
```

```
myacct.deposit(100);
```

In addition, there is no way to set the account password. It is stuck at 29 forever. This means that any instance of the `Account` class will have this password. If you know the password on `youracct`, which is 29, then you also know the password on `myacct`, which is also 29. We can, of course, add a `newpassword()` method, which changes the password, but then we would have to execute three statements to open the account: a `new` statement to create the instance, a call to `deposit` to deposit some money, and a call to `newpassword()` to change the password. The solution to this inefficient situation is the use of constructor methods.

**Constructor Methods**    Constructor methods, or *constructors* as they are often called, are used to initialize instances. They are called when the new operator is used on a Java class. From your experience with JavaScript, this would seem to be the natural approach. In JavaScript, you call new on a function and pass it arguments, which become the properties and methods of that new instance. You use the special keyword this to denote the current instance.

In Java, constructors are used somewhat differently. For one thing, constructors are methods of the class itself. Constructors have two special aspects, as follows:

- The name of a constructor must be identical to the class name.
- A constructor has no return type.

The second aspect is the only case in which a method function does not have a return type. Other than these two special rules, a constructor is the same as any other method. Typically, you use a constructor to perform initialization, such as depositing money and setting the password to our Account class. Listing 12.5 shows the code for a constructor for Account that performs these two operations.

---

**Listing 12.5    A Constructor for the *Account* Class**

```
Account(int initdep, int newpword) {    // Constructor declaration
     ivegot = initdep;          // initialize amount on deposit
     password = newpword;       // set new password
     isopen = true;             // declare account open
}                               // end of constructor
```

---

This code must be inside the definition of the Account class, of course. This constructor meets both our requirements. It initializes the private variables ivegot and password with the two arguments to the constructor, and also sets the public instance variable isopen to true to declare to the world that the account is now open. We must now use the new operator with two integer arguments to create a new account

```
Account myacct = new Account(100, 12345);
```

This statement creates an instance myacct of the Java class Account, with an initial deposit of 100 and a new password of 12345. There is still a problem with this class definition because there is nothing stopping us from making the erroneous statement

```
Account badacct = new Account(-100, 12345);
```

This creates a perfectly valid instance, named badacct, with an initial balance of -100! The result here is simply nonsensical, but in other cases, spurious initialization can lead to disastrous results. There is, in fact, a way of providing error checking by using the isopen instance variable. Listing 12.6 shows a modified version of the Account constructor, which checks the initial deposit and makes sure that it is at least 100.

### Listing 12.6  A Constructor for the *Account* Class with Error Checking

```
Account(int initdep, int newpword) {  // Constructor
    if ( initdep >= 100 ) {  // 2; minimum deposit requirement met
        ivegot = initdep;
        password = newpword;
        isopen = true;
        }
    else                    // 7; minimum deposit requirement not met
        isopen = false;  // 8; declare failure
}
```

This constructor tests the argument `initdep`, in statement 2, to make sure that it passes the minimum deposit test. If it does pass, then the same three initialization statements of Listing 12.5 are executed. The constructor then sets the `isopen` variable to `true` to indicate that the instance was successfully constructed (line 6). If the initial deposit test failed, then the code branches to line 8 instead. This statement ensures that `isopen` is set to `false` to indicate that the instance construction failed.

**Method Signatures in Java**  At this point, our `Account` class has many of the features of a real bank account. We have password protection, all the methods that represent everyday transactions, and a reasonably accurate constructor. A little fine-tuning will give it even more verisimilitude, and will illustrate one of the most important aspects of Java methods.

In real life, many bank accounts are rarely this simple. Accounts often have several different pools of money (savings, checking, checking/NOW, CD), with different rules on how these pools must be handled. You might want to open a checking account and a savings account at the same time. We could accommodate this by rewriting the `Account` constructor to accept three arguments, representing the initial savings deposit, the initial checking deposit, and the new password. If either of the two initial deposit amounts is zero, then we would interpret this as meaning that no account of that type was to be opened.

There is a simpler way, however. In Java, we can have more than one method with the same name so long as all the argument lists are different. Suppose we assume that the default is to open only a checking account and we use the constructor shown in Listing 12.6 to perform that operation. We now need another constructor that will open both a checking and a savings account. Listing 12.7 shows this new constructor. Note that it references a new private instance variable named `ivegotsav`, which holds the savings account balance.

### Listing 12.7  An Alternate Constructor for the *Account* Class

```
Account(int initdep, int initsdep, int newpword) {
    if ( initdep >= 100 && initsdep >= 1 ) { // min balance tests
        ivegot = initdep;           // initialize checking
        ivegotsav = initsdep;       // initialize savings
        password = pword;           // reset password
        isopen = true;              // accounts are open
        }
    else
        isopen = false;   // below minima; don't open account
}
```

The constructor of Listings 12.6 and 12.7 can both be used in the same class. Java tells them apart by virtue of the fact that their argument lists are different. The constructor of Listing 12.6 takes two `int` arguments, while that of Listing 12.7 takes three. This is often referred to as the *method signature* or the *method shape*, and is written as `(int, int)` or `(int, int, int)`, respectively. The following statements open two new accounts (create two new instances of the `Account` class):

```
Account myacct = new Account(100, 12345);
Account wifesacct = new Account(500, 100, 54321);
```

The instance `myacct` represents a checking account with an initial deposit of `100` and a password of `12345`. The instance `wifesacct` has both a checking account and a savings account, with initial deposits of `500` and `100`, respectively, and a password of `54321`.

**NOTE** Multiple class methods can have the same name so long as they have different method signatures. This technique is known as *overloading*. While overloading is most useful for constructors, because the name of the constructor is fixed by the name of the class, it can be used for any class methods. ▨

**The *static* and *final* Keywords**   Now that we have introduced the concept of two pools of money within an `Account`, we must obviously modify the `deposit`, `balance`, and `withdraw` methods to make them aware of this fact. Let us suppose that we can withdraw money only from the checking account but we can deposit money to either account and query either account's balance. It would be nice to give the `deposit` and `balance` methods a tag indicating which pool of money to use.

If we were writing this code in C or C++ (or several other languages), we could make the tag be the member of an enumerated type. We could also use the `#define` construct to define symbolic constants to stand for the two types of account. Finally, we could create `constants` in C++ and use those for the two account types. How does one create a constant in Java? This question is answered as we dissect the code in Listing 12.8, which shows our final version of the `Account` class.

**Listing 12.8   A Fully Functional Version of the *Account* Class**

```
class Account {                       // Account Class
    private int ivegot = 0;       // 2; amount in checking account
    private int ivegotsav = 0;   // 3; amount in savings account
    private int password = 29;    // 4; account password
    public boolean isopen = false; // 5; account  has money?
// these constants refer to the checking and saving accounts
    public static final int CHECKING = 1;       // 6;
    public static final int SAVINGS = 2;        // 7;
// all accts at this bank have this id
    public static int Bankid = 2167;            // 8;
// Constructor: open checking acct only
    Account(int initdep, int newpword) {        // 9;
```

```
            if ( initdep >= 100 ) {     // 10; min deposit reqt met
                ivegot = initdep;        // 11; init checking acct
                password = newpword;     // 12; set acct password
                isopen = true;           // 13; the acct is open
                }
            else                         // 15; minimum deposit requirement not met
                isopen = false;          // 16; insure failure
        }                                // 17; end of first constructor
// 3 argument constructor
    Account(int initdep, int initsdep, int newpword) { // 18;
        if ( initdep >= 100 && initsdep >= 1 ) { // 19; min balance?
                ivegot = initdep;            // 20; initialize checking
                ivegotsav = initsdep;        // 21; initialize savings
                password = pword;            // 22; set password
                isopen = true;               // 23; accounts are open
                }
            else
                isopen = false;          // 26; below min; don't open
        }                                // 27; end of 3 arg constructor
// deposit method: any one can deposit anywhere ( no password )
    void deposit(int n, int which) {     // 28;
        if ( n <= 0 ) return;            // 29; no negative deposits
        if ( which == Account.CHECKING ) // 30; to checking
            ivegot += n;                 // 31; deposit to checking
        else if  ( which == Account.SAVINGS ) // 32; to savings
            ivegotsav += n;              // 33; deposit to savings
        }                                // 34; end of deposit method
// password protected balance method
    int balance(int pword, int which) {  // 35;
        if ( pword != password )         // 36; incorrect password
            return( -1 );                // 37; return bogus balance
// checking account balance wanted
        if ( which == Account.CHECKING ) // 38;
            return(ivegot);              // 39; return it
// savings account balance wanted
        else if ( which == Account.SAVINGS )     // 40;
            return(ivegotsav);           // 41; return it
        else                             // 42; some strange 'where'
            return( -2 );                // 43; return error code
        }                                // 44; end of balance method
// password protected checking acct withdrawal
    boolean withdraw(int pword, int n) {  // 45;
        if ( pword != password )         // 46; bad password
            return(false);               // 47; cannot withdraw
        if ( n > ivegot )                // 48; too much
            return(false);               // 49; cannot withdraw
        ivegot -= n; // 50; update checking acct balance
// update the isopen variable
        isopen = ( (ivegot+ivegotsav) > 0 ? true : false ); // 51;
        return(true);                    // 52; return status
        }                                // 53; end of withdraw method
}                                        // 54; end of Account class
```

Part
III

Ch

12

For the most part, this version of the Account class is an amalgamation of the two constructor methods we introduced in the previous sections together with updated versions of the deposit, withdraw, and balance methods from Listing 12.4. This version does introduce two new keywords, static and final, and one new concept, that of a *class variable*. We will examine in detail how this class now works.

There are seven variables declared, in lines 2 through 8. The first four have already been introduced: ivegot and ivegotsav hold the checking and savings account balances, password holds the account password, and isopen is the overall account status. The only change we have made is to declare explicitly isopen to be public. These four variables are instance variables; the first three are also private. The next three statements (lines 6 through 8) use the new keywords, as follows:

```
public static final int CHECKING = 1;        // 6
public static final int SAVINGS = 2;         // 7
public static int Bankid = 2167;             // 8
```

The final keyword simply states that this value may never be altered. A final variable must be initialized. final, in Java, serves the same purpose as const does in C++. The static keyword has a different purpose. It indicates that all instances refer to exactly the same shared variable. The static keyword makes a variable a *class variable* rather than an instance variable.

**T I P**   Declare class constants to be both final and static.

To understand the difference between a class (static) variable and an instance variable, consider the difference between the instance variable ivegot and the class variable Bankid, which we have just invented to hold an identifier associated with all accounts at this particular bank. Every instance of the Account class will have its own copy of the instance variable ivegot. The amount of money in my account, represented by the myacct instance, is unrelated to the amount of money in your account, represented by the youracct instance. You can conduct thousands of transactions and amass millions of dollars in the ivegot instance variable of youracct without it having any effect on the ivegot instance variable of myacct (unfortunately).

This is not the case with the class variable Bankid. There is exactly one such variable and it is shared among all instances of the Account class. This is what makes it a class variable: it belongs to the class and not to the individual instances of the class. This also means that we may refer to it as Account.Bankid, as well as myacct.Bankid and youracct.Bankid. Note that the static and final keywords may also be applied to methods. We have already seen examples of static methods in JavaScript, in the Date object.

▶ **See** "Building New *Date* Objects," **p. 164**, for a complete description of its static methods and how they are used.

The Account class has two constructors, which we have already seen. The two argument constructor is given in lines 9 through 17. It creates a checking account only. The three argument constructor, which allows us to open both checking and savings accounts simultaneously, is shown in lines 18 through 27. Both constructors check their arguments to ensure that minimum deposit requirements are met and set isopen to false if they are not.

We have rewritten the deposit method so that it takes a second mandatory argument, called which. This argument is used to indicate which account should receive the deposit of n. Error checking of n happens in statement 29, which refuses to make a deposit if the amount is negative, as follows:

```
if ( n <= 0 ) return;         // 29; negative deposit forbidden
```

If the test passes, then the value of which is examined. It is expected to refer to one of the class constants CHECKING or SAVINGS. Note that we refer to them as Account.CHECKING and Account.SAVINGS in statements 30 and 32. This is a class reference, which is permitted since they are static. We could just as well have used the instance references this.CHECKING and this.SAVINGS, since these constants are part of each instance, too.

If this is a checking account deposit, then the test in statement 30 passes and n is added to the checking account instance variable ivegot, in statement 31. If which is Account.SAVINGS instead, then n is added to ivegotsav in statement 33, as follows:

```
if ( which == Account.CHECKING )     // 30; checking account deposit
        ivegot += n;                 // 31; deposit to checking
else if  ( which == Account.SAVINGS )  // 32; saving acct deposit
        ivegotsav += n;              // 33; deposit to savings
```

If which is not equal to either constant, then nothing happens. We just fall off the end of the deposit method, which is quite acceptable because it is a void method.

The code for the balance method, on lines 35 to 44, operates in the same way as the deposit method. It performs its usual password test (line 36). If that test passes, then it tests the value of which and returns the corresponding balance. If which is neither CHECKING nor SAVINGS, the method returns an error code of -2. This value was deliberately chosen to be different from the bad password error return of -1 on line 37. The caller can distinguish the two error cases based on which bogus balance was returned.

The implementation of the withdraw method (lines 45 to 53) is almost unchanged from our previous version. We assume that we are permitted to withdraw only from the checking account, so no which parameter is needed. The test that updates the isopen variable has been updated to keep the account open so long as the total balance in both accounts (ivegot+ivegotsav) is greater than 0. This test is shown on line 51, as follows:

```
isopen = ( (ivegot+ivegotsav) > 0 ? true : false ); // 51; open?
```

**Arrays in Java**    There is one final piece of Java object machinery that we need before we can launch forward and actually make something appear on a Web page. We need Java *arrays*.

Part
III

Ch

12

It should come as absolutely no surprise that arrays are actually objects (classes) in Java. The similarity with JavaScript arrays ends there, however. There are no associative arrays in Java and there are no extensible arrays. Java's usual strictness is carried to fanatic extremes in dealing with arrays.

Java enforces the following five rules for all of its arrays:

- Arrays must be created with the new operator or by explicit initialization.
- Every array has a fixed length, given by its length instance variable.
- Every array element must have the same type.
- It is impossible to access memory before the beginning of an array.
- It is impossible to access memory beyond the end of an array.

This very restrictive approach is part of Java's security model. One of the most common ways of accessing memory that is not really yours is to declare an array, say int i[10], and then look at elements like i[-6]. Veteran FORTRAN and C programmers will recognize this as the famous "stack creep" technique for reaching into system memory. Of course, arrays are also a source of completely innocent but vicious errors, such as referring to i[10], even though only i[0] through i[9] really belong to us.

**TIP**  Java arrays are zero-indexed, as in C, C++, and JavaScript.

Let us briefly consider how to use arrays in Java. If we actually do want an array of 10 ints, we must declare a variable to hold this array and then allocate it by using the new operator. The following statements do the trick:

```
int iarr[]; // declare an int array variable
iarr = new int[10]; // allocate space
```

Before we call the new operator, the variable iarr is absolutely uninitialized, just as the statement Account myacct; declares an instance myacct of the Account class, but does not actually create such an instance. It is absolutely prohibited to attempt to make an array declaration such as

```
int badiarr[10];// hopelessly bad, awful, and wrong
```

The format used to allocate iarr is the pattern that should be followed to allocate an array of anything; do not attempt anything like the declaration of badiarr. In particular, we can use these two statements to allocate an array of Account instances:

```
Account acctarr[];
acctarr = new Account[10];
```

The variable iarr represents an array of 10 ints and the variable acctarr represents an array of 10 Account instances. None of these are initialized yet, however, so it is unwise to attempt to refer to iarr[5] or acctarr[3]. Each of the array slots must be initialized. Array creation is really a two-step process in which the memory is first allocated by using new and then the individual values are set. We could say

```
acctarr[0] = myacct;
acctarr[1] = youracct;
acctarr[2] = new Account(2000, 14141);
```

and so forth to fill in the various slots in the acctarr. We can also use explicit initialization, which creates an array and fills in its values at the same time. The following statement, for example, creates an array of four floating-point values:

```
float fltarr[] = { 3.14159, 2.71828, 1.4141, 0.7071 };
```

In each of these cases, we may get the length of the array by using the instance variable, so both iarr.length and acctarr.length are 10, while fltarr.length is 4. The valid elements of the array range from index 0 through index (length-1). An out-of-bounds error results if any other elements are accessed.

> **CAUTION**
>
> It is often worthwhile to check an array reference to make sure that it is in bounds. This can be accomplished by using an if test against the length member, as follows:
> ```
> if ( 0 <= idx && idx < arr.length )
>     ok to use arr[idx];
> ```

The other grievous mistake made in Java is to attempt to set an array element to any type other than its base type. Therefore, every member of iarr[] must be an int, every member of acctarr[] must be an instance of the Account class, and every member of fltarr must be a float. A statement such as fltarr[2] = "pi" generates a Java exception.

## Java Statements

So far we have said very little about statements in Java. You have no doubt noticed in each of the previous listings that Java statements greatly resemble JavaScript statements. Java has a few extra rules as well as a few new statement types that are not supported in JavaScript. There are also some JavaScript constructions that cannot be done, or can only be done very awkwardly, in Java. The reader is strongly encouraged to review Chapter 2, "JavaScript: The Language," particularly the section on "Control Structures" and the discussion of "Statements and Operators."

Since Java follows almost the same set of rules as JavaScript, we will not attempt an exhaustive discussion of those rules. Instead, we will focus on a few of the major differences. As mentioned quite early in this chapter, Java statements *must* be terminated with a semicolon. While this is a matter of style in JavaScript, it is mandatory in Java. If you omit the semicolons, Java attempts to interpret your program as a single, gigantic statement, to your eternal embarrassment.

It is already apparent that Java has the `if` statement; it also has the `while` and `for` statements of JavaScript. Java has three more very interesting control structures that are not present in JavaScript: the `do...while` statement, the `switch` statement, and a variant on the `break` and `continue` statements, which takes a label. In compensation, Java does not have the `for...in` statement of JavaScript. The reason for this latter omission has to do with the more circumscribed way that Java defines objects, as we have just seen.

**The *do...while* Statement** The `while` statement in Java and the `while` statement in JavaScript are identical. Both evaluate their `while` clause and then execute the `while` body only if the conditional in the `while` clause is `true`. This means that the `while` body may be executed an infinite number of times, once, or not at all. If we were foolish enough to write

```
while ( false ) {
find the meaning of life;
}
```

the `while` body would never be executed. The valid but meaningless `while ( false )` would never be used in practice, of course, but it is quite possible to have a `while` clause that does evaluate to `false` immediately. This is unfortunate in the case in which it is desirable to execute the `while` body at least once.

The `do...while` statement solves this problem. A `do...while` statement still contains a `while` body and a `while` test, but the `while` test is at the end, ensuring that the body of the `do...while` loop is executed at least once. The format of this statement is as follows:

```
do {
while-body;
} while ( conditional ) ;
```

**CAUTION**

The semicolon at the end of the `while` clause in a `do...while` statement is mandatory. The usual rule that the closing brace of a `{ }` code body terminates the body does not apply to the `do...while` statement because the `while` clause must occur after the closing brace.

**The *switch* Statement** The `switch` statement is used to select one alternative from a set of possible choices. It is designed to be a more compact form of the `if...else` construction, particularly in cases in which there are many possibilities. The format of the `switch` statement is shown in Listing 12.9.

**Listing 12.9 The Java *switch* Statement**

```
switch ( numberthing ) {
    case firstval:
        statements;
        break;
    case secondval:
        statements;
        break;
```

```
        ...
    default:
        statements;
    break;
}
```

Unlike the other conditional statements, the `numberthing` element inside the `switch` test is not a logical value; it is a numerical value. In particular, it must be a numerical value whose underlying type is `byte`, `short`, `char`, or `int`. The value of the `numberthing` is compared against each of the numerical values in the `case` statements. Note that each `case` statement ends with a colon (:). This is mandatory. If it finds a match, then it executes the statements after the `case` statement but before the first `break` statement. If none of the case clauses provide a match, then it looks for a clause of the form

```
default:
```

which matches anything that is not otherwise matched. In this situation, all the statements between the `default` and the next `break` statement are executed. As an example, consider the `balance` method that was shown in Listing 12.8. It does a three-way test on its argument `which`. This three-way test can be easily rewritten as a `switch` statement; the code is shown in Listing 12.10.

 **TIP** Default cases in `switch` statements are not required, but are recommended. They often catch otherwise mysterious errors.

### Listing 12.10 The *Account.balance* Method Rewritten Using the *switch* Statement

```
int balance(int pword, int which) {
    int retval;                    // 2; local variable for return
    if ( pword != password )       // 3; incorrect password
        return( -1 );              // 4; return bogus balance
    switch ( which ) {             // 5; switch on the value of "which"
        case Account.CHECKING:     // 6; which == Account.CHECKING
            retval = ivegot;       // 7; checking balance
            break;                 // 8; done with checking case
        case Account.SAVINGS:      // 9; which == Account.SAVINGS
            retval = ivegotsav;    // 10; savings balance
            break;                 // 11; done with savings case
        default:                   // 12; which has any other value
            retval = (-2);         // 13; return code indicates an error
            break;                 // 14; done with the default case
    }                              // 15; end of switch statement
    return(retval);                // 16; return the return code
}
```

This version of the balance method performs the usual password test and then immediately enters a switch in statement 5. The numerical value being tested is which, which is an int. If the value of which is Account.CHECKING, then the case Account.CHECKING: statement at line 6 matches, and statement 7 is executed:

```
case Account.CHECKING:     // 6; which == Account.CHECKING
      retval = ivegot;     // 7; return code is checking balance
      break;               // 8; done with checking case
```

This assigns the checking account balance ivegot to the local variable retval. The break statement at line 8 is then executed. Like any good break statement, it directs the flow of control to the first statement after the switch, namely statement 16, which returns retval.

If which has the other valid value Account.SAVINGS, then a similar block of code is executed, which instead gives retval the value of the savings account balance ivegotsav (lines 10 and 11). If which has any value other than Account.CHECKING or Account.SAVINGS, then the default case at line 12 matches and statements 13 and 14 execute, as follows:

```
default:                 // 12; which has any other value
    retval = (-2);       // 13; return code indicates an error
    break;               // 14; done with the default case
```

In any case, the code ends up at line 16 with retval having one of the two valid values, ivegot or ivegotsav, or the error value -2. In a situation such as this, where there are only three possible alternatives, the amount of code saved by using a switch statement versus using multiple if...else statements is minimal. However, if there had been a few more alternatives, the savings would have been dramatic.

## TROUBLESHOOTING

**I have a very simple switch statement, which examines an integer variable i. Based on the value of i, it sets a local variable j. For some reason, the two cases i==1 and i==2 always give the same result even though they have different code in their case blocks. What is wrong? The code looks like this:**

```
switch ( i ) {
    case 1:
        j = 2*i;
    case 2:
        j = 3*i;
        break;
    ...
}
```

You have made the most common error that occurs in using a switch statement. There is no break statement to conclude case 1. When i is equal to 2, the statement j = 3*i is executed, and j gets the value 6, as it should. However, when i is equal to 1, the statement j = 2*i is executed, and then the statement j = 3*i is executed also, so that j has the incorrect value 3 rather than the correct value 2.

The switch statement is more than happy to execute multiple blocks of code. The only way it knows to stop is when it encounters a break statement. The presence of another case statement, as you have included, won't even slow switch down. This is known as "falling through" a case statement. Sometimes this is desirable, but usually it is just an error.

**The Labeled *break* and *continue* Statements**   With the if, while, for, and the new switch statement, Java has a rich collection of techniques for controlling statement execution. Java also has one more trick up its sleeve, which can prove very valuable in cases where there are many nested conditionals. It might seem like overkill to add more and more new control structures, because this often leads to confusion. There is a school of thought that says everything can, and should, be reduced to just a single type control such as while. This may be accurate in a purely theoretical sense, but often, it is impractical.

On the other hand, it is also true that multiple control structures, particularly nested ones, can be hard to manage. If you have a for inside an if inside a while, and you say break, where do you go? You certainly know by now that the correct answer is that the break sends you to the first statement after the while block, wherever that is. This may be the correct answer, but it is often not the answer you want. If some kind of error or exceptional condition occurs, or if you have finally completed a calculation, you might just want to exit completely from the for, if, and while blocks. This is a situation in which many long for a goto statement.

Java does not have a goto statement. It does have a mechanism for going to an arbitrary location when a break or continue statement is executed. This is known as the *labeled break* or *labeled continue* statement, because the keyword is followed by a label that indicates the desired destination. Listing 12.11 shows a very peculiar set of Java code, which illustrates the labeled break.

**Listing 12.11   Using the Labeled *break* in Java**

```java
int i, j, k, w;
outtahere:                              // 2; label
for(i=0;i<200;i++) {
    if ( i%3 == 0 ) {
        j = 7*i; k = 0;
        while ( k++ < j ) {
            if ( k == 29 )          // eureka!
                break outtahere;    // 8; this gets us out of here
        }                           // end of while
    }                               // end of if
}                                   // end of for
w = j;                  // 12; this is where you will actually end up
```

Note that the label outtahere must come before the outermost loop, at statement 2. When the labeled break of statement 8 is executed, control actually flows to the first statement after the outermost (for) block, at statement 12 (which is w = j; in this example). This counterintuitive structure is necessary because the label must occur before any statement that uses it. Note also that the label must end with a colon (:).

Think of the label `outtahere` as a name for the next statement, which is the entire mass of the `for` statement in this case. A labeled `break` goes to the first statement after the labeled statement, while a labeled `continue` goes back to the labeled statement. If statement 8 had said `continue outtahere`, then the mathematical madness of Listing 12.11 would be started all over again.

# Developing Java Applets

We have now learned a considerable amount about the Java language itself. The next topic to consider is how it can be used on a Web page. The answer is surprisingly different from the JavaScript approach. Writing JavaScript is almost like writing HTML. You fire up your favorite text editor or HTML Wizard, create JavaScript event handlers and utility functions, link them to events on a Web page, and you are done. When you load the page, the JavaScript is executed when events arrive.

Java is fundamentally different. JavaScript is (almost) always interpreted, meaning that the Web browser analyzes the text content of the JavaScript code on-the-fly as it is needed. Java, on the other hand, is a compiled language. Java source is never included directly on a Web page. Instead, a special APPLET tag is used to reference Java code in a special binary format.

## The Java Development Cycle

Java is actually both compiled and interpreted, as contradictory as that seems. To understand how this is possible, we must examine the process used to develop Java code. The first step, of course, is to write Java source code. You have already seen a substantial amount of Java source in the various listings in this chapter. If you were writing JavaScript, you now would be almost done, because we could embed the code directly on a Web page. With Java, we must first convert the source in a binary format known as Java *bytecodes*.

One of the fundamental principles of Java is that it is architecture-neutral: it can run on any type of machine with a Java-capable Web browser. This goal could not be met if Java were compiled into Intel 486 binaries, or Sparc-5 binaries, or any specific machine's binary format. Instead, Java is compiled into the binary format for an abstract (or virtual) machine. For quite a while, this virtual machine did not have a physical counterpart—it was simply an abstract instruction set. In March 1996, however, Sun Microsystems announced that it would begin construction on a set of "Java microprocessors," which will actually run the Java instruction set directly. However, every other machine must still translate the Java instructions into its own native instructions.

When we write Java, we must therefore perform three steps, as follows:

- Create the Java source code
- Convert the Java source code to the abstract binary format
- Reference the Java binary code on a Web page

The second step of this process requires that we use a Java compiler to create Java binary code. There are several compilers available; the simplest, and one of the most widely used, is part of a set of tools from Sun known as the *Java Development Kit* (JDK). The third step makes use of the APPLET HTML tag. These two steps are discussed in the next two sections. First, the question of why Java is both interpreted and compiled is still open.

The answer is that we, the Java programmers, compile Java into its abstract binary format, but the Web browsers must then interpret that format. When a Web browser accesses a page that contains an APPLET tag specifying Java code, the Web browser fetches the binary version of that code (not the Java source). The Web browser must then interpret those abstract instructions to do real work on a real machine. After all, if you have Netscape Navigator running under Windows 95 on a Pentium, and Navigator tries to hand the Java bytecodes to the Pentium chip, the Pentium chip will spurn them.

## Java Compilers and the JDK

The Java Development Kit, or JDK, is a simple set of command line-driven tools for manipulating Java source and binary files. The JDK was the first such set of tools, but it is not the only such set. In fact, there are now many sophisticated, graphical development environments for Java. Since the JDK is the simplest, and still one of the most widely used, Java development environments, this section describes it in some detail.

It is also important to realize that there are several different versions of the JDK. The Macintosh version of the JDK has no command line interface, for example. It is beyond the scope of this book to provide a comprehensive description of all the tools in the JDK, or to discuss the differences between the various versions. However, we will at least mention all its major components, which are as follows:

- appletviewer
- java
- javac
- javadoc
- javah
- javap
- jdb

If you use the JDK, the appletviewer and javac tools are the two tools you will use most often, at least at the beginning of your Java career. The appletviewer is an application that can be used to view Java applets outside of any Web browser. Usually, you write a Java applet, compile it using the Java compiler javac, and then test it using the appletviewer. The appletviewer frees you from having to debug both your HTML and your Java code at the same time. It is also useful for tracking down browser-dependent bugs because appletviewer is not itself a browser. The appletviewer and the Java compiler javac are available on all platforms supported by the JDK.

The JDK can be downloaded free from Sun Microsystems' site at **http://www.javasoft.com**. The JDK is available for many popular platforms, including Windows 95, Windows NT, Solaris 2.4 and 2.5, Linux, and several other versions of UNIX, and the Macintosh. This list will no doubt continue to grow, so you are advised to check Javasoft's Web site regularly for the latest information.

**Components of the JDK**   The unfortunately-named java application is a Java interpreter. If you give the java application a Java binary file, it executes the contents of that file. This application is not really of interest to us because it is primarily used to test and execute stand-alone Java applications rather than applets. Java is a large enough language that it is possible to write full-blown applications in Java. java is then used to execute them.

The javadoc application automatically generates HTML documentation from Java source code. It searches for specially formatted comments with the source and uses those comments to construct the corresponding documentation. We will see a few simple examples of such comments in the next chapter.

The javah application is used when you want to mix Java code with C or C++ code. javah generates .h include files, which allow Java, C, and C++ to interoperate. At the moment, Java applets are forbidden to use modules written in any language other than Java (known as *native methods*), so javah is not of interest to us. Java enforces this prohibition for security reasons.

javap is the Java profiler. It enables you to instrument Java code to discover which portions of it are taking the most time. jdb is the Java debugger. It permits symbolic debugging of Java binaries. Once you are a bit further along the Java learning curve, you may well want to explore these tools further.

**The Java Compiler**   The javac tool is the Java compiler. It is invoked by giving it the name of one or more Java source files. If the files contain valid Java, then they will be converted to the binary format of the Java instruction set. Using the source code of Listing 12.8, you can make a very tiny change—modify the class declaration to say "public class Account" instead of "class Account." If we do this and then attempt to compile it by using the following statement:

```
javac ex13_8.java
```

the Java compiler complains with a message saying that "the public class Account must be defined in a file called 'Account.java'." Well, if it must, then it must. If we oblige and rename the file to Account.java and then try

```
javac Account.java
```

it succeeds, and the file Account.class is created. Files with the suffix .class are Java binary files. This seemingly peculiar restriction on the file name of the source code for a public class is something that must simply be tolerated in this revision of the JDK. In addition, we must make the Account class be a public class if we want to refer to it in other files. Finally, there is no flexibility in the name of the binary output file, either. The compiled version of the public Account class must be contained in a file named Account.class. The underlying reasons for these file name restrictions are complex and really cannot be explained without a long and painful discussion of Java internals. For our purposes, we will simply accept these rules, which are summarized in the note that follows.

**N O T E**  Public classes in Java should follow these rules:

- Put only one public class definition in a Java source file.

- The name of the source file must match the name of the public class.

- Do not rename the compiled output file. It must be the name of the public class, followed by the suffix `.class`. ▪

**Other Java Development Environments**   For a long time, the JDK was the only game in town. Since Java was developed by Sun, it is only natural to expect that its development environment would be the first and the most comprehensive. Because of Java's explosive popularity, a number of other environments have been created. Some are free, like the JDK, while others are commercial products.

One effect of Java's overwhelming growth rate is that any list or description of Java tools would be hopelessly out-of-date before it could be printed. No attempt will be made to present such a list in this book. Instead, the best way to learn about such tools is on the Web itself. There are two resources that can be used to obtain the most up-to-date information.

The Gamelan repository at **http://www.gamelan.com** contains a very large collection of information about Java, JavaScript, and many other Web-related topics. This site boasts several hundred Java entries. Some are simple applet demonstrations, while others are full-blown development tools. Both commercial offerings and public domain code are represented. Its Java page is well worth visiting.

After some initial reluctance, Microsoft (**http://www.microsoft.com**) also entered the Java arena. Its Java development environment is intended to be fully integrated with the Microsoft philosophy toward software products. This means that it has a visual development environment, J++, similar to Visual Basic and Visual C++. It also is designed to interface smoothly with Microsoft's object system (known as ActiveX and DCOM).

One of the most interesting features that Microsoft supports is the ability to compile Java directly to native machine code, in addition to producing standard `.class` output files. Of course, the native code will not be platform-independent, but significant performance improvements are obtained. If you will be developing Java on any of the Windows platforms, you should plan on regular visits to Microsoft's Web page for the latest information.

**Part**
**III**

**Ch**
**12**

# The *APPLET* Tag

Now that we have a compiled Java file, we are at last approaching the point at which we can actually create a fully functional Java applet. Since Java applets are binary files, there is no way we can literally include them in HTML, as we did by using the `<SCRIPT>...</SCRIPT>` block for JavaScript. Instead, we must use a new HTML tag, the APPLET tag, to reference the Java binaries for our applet.

An APPLET block consists of the following four parts:

- The `<APPLET>` declaration itself

- A set of parameters that may be given to the applet by using the PARAM tag

- Alternate text
- The closing `</APPLET>`

An example showing the basic HTML syntax for an APPLET block is shown in Listing 12.12.

### Listing 12.12   Example of an *APPLET* Block in HTML

```
<APPLET CODE="Something.class" WIDTH=100 HEIGHT=50>
<PARAM NAME="var1" VALUE="5">
<PARAM NAME="othervar" VALUE="somestring">
This alternate text is displayed on Java-impaired browsers
</APPLET>
```

**Mandatory Attributes**   The example in Listing 12.12 attempts to load and execute the Java binary code from a file named Something.class, which is given as the value of the mandatory CODE attribute. By default, a Java-capable browser searches for files referenced by CODE relative to the HTML document's BASE, although this search strategy can be changed by the optional attribute CODEBASE, described in the next section.

The mandatory WIDTH and HEIGHT describe the size of the box that is allocated for this applet. The applet may later attempt to change this size itself. The values of the WIDTH and HEIGHT attributes are in pixels. On a Java-enabled browser such as Netscape Navigator or Internet Explorer, the example of Listing 12.12 is drawn inside a box of 100×50 pixels. Other browsers instead display the alternate text This alternate text is displayed by Java-impaired browsers. The alignment of the applet's bounding box may be influenced by the optional ALIGN attribute.

**TIP**   APPLET tags may be enclosed in a heading (<H*n*>), paragraph (<P>), division (<DIV>) block, or some other block delimiter.

**Optional Attributes**   The APPLET tag also accepts the following optional attributes:

- ALIGN
- CODEBASE
- HSPACE
- NAME
- VSPACE

The ALIGN attribute is used to specify the alignment of the applet's bounding box with respect to other adjacent text and graphics. The values of the ALIGN attribute include BOTTOM, MIDDLE, and TOP, much like the IMG tag. They also include an additional set, ABSBOTTOM, ABSMIDDLE, BASELINE, LEFT, RIGHT, and TEXTTOP, for more precise control.

The CODEBASE attribute is used to specify an alternate location at which to find the Java binary specified in the CODE attribute. If the value of the CODEBASE attribute is an absolute path, then that path is searched for the Java code. If CODEBASE is specified as a relative path, such as `java\classes`, then that path is appended to the document's BASE and the code is sought in that relative location. This often is useful if you want to keep your HTML in one place and your Java binaries in another.

HSPACE and VSPACE are used to define the amount of horizontal and vertical space that should be created as a border for the applet. Both specify a numerical value in pixels. The NAME attribute is used to give the applet a name, which may be completely unrelated to any of the names of the classes it uses. Applet NAMEs are used for applet-to-applet communication, and also reserve a place for the applet in the JavaScript HTML hierarchy.

**N O T E**  The APPLET tag does not currently accept an ALT attribute to specify alternate text for Java-impaired browsers. Such text must be embedded in the <APPLET>...</APPLET> block itself. ▒

**The *PARAM* Tag**   The <APPLET>...</APPLET> block may contain any number of PARAM tags. Each PARAM tag takes two attributes: NAME and VALUE. The values of each of these attributes is an uninterpreted string. This is the standard mechanism for passing in initialization parameters from the Web page to a Java applet. Java applets have a special method, called getParameter(), to retrieve such values from their environment. Note that each PARAM tag specifies exactly one parameter.

# A Simple Applet

We are now ready to construct a simple Java applet. This applet doesn't do much. In fact, all it does is display a string in color. We will arrange to pass in a string to be displayed by using a PARAM tag. This applet shows us most of the fundamental components of Java applet design. The HTML code for a page containing the applet is shown in Listing 12.13, while the code for the applet itself is shown in Listing 12.14.

Part
III

Ch
12

---

**Listing 12.13   A Web Page Containing a Simple Applet**

```
<HTML>
<HEAD>
<TITLE>Displaying a String in Java</TITLE>
</HEAD>
<BODY>
<P>
<HR>
<APPLET CODE="PStr.class" WIDTH=400 HEIGHT=40 ALIGN="CENTER">
<PARAM NAME="mystring" VALUE="cocoanuts">
You will see this text if your browser does not understand Java.
</APPLET>
<HR>
The <A HREF="PStr.java">source</A>
</P>
</BODY>
</HTML>
```

**Listing 12.14   A Java Applet that Displays a String**

```
import java.lang.* ;              // 1; get Java language package
import java.awt.* ;               // 2; get Java AWT package

public class PStr extends java.applet.Applet { // 3; define applet type
    String userstring = null;                  // 4; instance variable

    public void init() {     // 5; called when applet is loaded
// get value of PARAM NAME="mystring"
        userstring = getParameter("mystring");      // 6;
    }
// override built-in paint()
    public void paint( Graphics g ) {       // 8;
        String outstr;
// string concatentation
        outstr = "I've got a lovely bunch of " + userstring;       // 10;
        g.setColor(Color.red);   // 11; set output color to red
// draw the string offset from the corner
        g.drawString(outstr, 10, 10);       // 12;
    }

}
```

The code in Listing 12.13 should be self-explanatory. An APPLET is declared to be implemented by the CODE at URL PStr.class, relative to the document's BASE. Its dimensions are 100×40 pixels and its alignment is CENTER. Some alternate text has been provided after the single PARAM tag, which gives the parameter mystring the value cocoanuts. A pointer is given to the source PStr.java in an HREF at the end of the <BODY>.

To run this applet, we must create the file PStr.class from the file PStr.java, which is shown in Listing 12.14. This is accomplished by using the javac tool, with the command

```
javac PStr.java
```

This command creates the java binary PStr.class. We can now view the results by pointing our favorite Java-capable browser at the file ex13_13.html, or by invoking the appletviewer on it by using the command "appletviewer ex13_13.html". The results of viewing this HTML are shown in Figure 12.2.

# Anatomy of an Applet

Just how does the PStr applet work? The code in Listing 12.14 contains a number of new concepts, which are described next. The PStr applet begins with two new statements, which are examples of the import directive, as follows:

```
import java.lang.*;
import java.awt.*;
```

This directive is used to inform the Java compiler that externally defined classes may be needed. Statement 1 says to import java.lang.* ;, where the * is a wildcard character.

The effect of this statement is to import all the classes within the `java.lang` package. A package is a related collection of classes.

**FIG. 12.2**

Java applets allow you to create text and graphics on-the-fly.

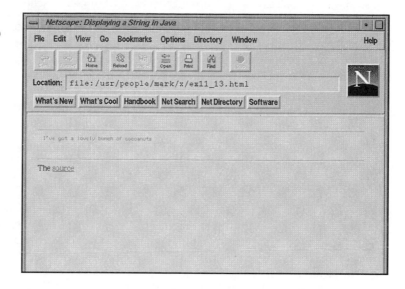

Of course, this applet does not use all the classes in the `java.lang` package, but it does not hurt to overspecify when using an `import` statement. Only those elements that are actually needed are used. Statement 2 makes a similar request for the `java.awt` package. The AWT is Java's Abstract Windowing Toolkit, a collection of graphics utilities.

▶ **See** "The Java Class Hierarchy," **p. 360**, which describes the classes in the AWT and shows how several of them are used to load and manage images.

Statement 3 declares the applet's class `PStr`. As indicated previously, this class name should be the same as the name of the file in which it is found. Rather than being a simple class declaration, however, statement 3 introduces one more new keyword, `extends`, as follows:

```
public class PStr extends java.applet.Applet {
```

Java supports the object-oriented notion of *inheritance*. This means that classes may be built on other classes and may inherit some of their properties and methods. In this case, the built-in applet class `java.applet.Applet` is being used as the *base class* (or *superclass*) and the customization `PStr` is the *derived class* (or *subclass*). This frees you from having to write a lot of code that would only duplicate the standard behavior of `java.applet.Applet`. All applets begin with a declaration of the form

```
public class Myclass extents java.applet.Applet {
```

The `PStr` class contains a single instance variable, `userstring`, declared in statement 4. This variable is of type `String`, the Java string class. It also contains two methods: `init()` and `paint()`. The `init()` method is one of four standard methods that are called during the life of an applet. The `init` method is called when an applet is first loaded and should be used to perform any one-time initialization. The `start` method is called when an applet begins running, generally right after init completes. The stop and destroy methods are called when an applet is stopped (when another page is visited, for example), and when the browser is completely finished with an applet (when it falls off the end of the browser's cache, for example).

This particular applet does not need to do anything when it is started, stopped, or destroyed, so these methods are not provided. In fact, the default java.applet.Applet class provides implementations of all of these methods so that an applet need not actually provide any of them. The PStr class *overrides* the init method of its parent java.applet.Applet. A method is overridden when a subclass implements a method that is also implemented in its superclass. When this happens, the method in the subclass is used. Thus, the PStr class uses the superclass implementations of start, stop, and destroy and its own implementation of init.

When the PStr.class file is loaded, the first thing that happens is that the init method is called. The init method executes a single statement (at line 6) as follows:

```
userstring = getParameter("mystring");
```

which uses the Java function getParameter(). This function is used to retrieve the value of a PARAM tag whose name is given as an argument. Therefore, if there is a PARAM whose NAME attribute is "mystring", the getParameter() call in statement 6 returns the VALUE of that PARAM. If not, it returns null. In our HTML code of Listing 12.13, there is such a parameter and its VALUE is the string "cocoanuts."

**N O T E**   PARAM values are always interpreted as strings in Java.

The initialization is now complete and the method function start, from the applet superclass, is called next. This method performs a variety of actions that need not concern us here. Most important from our perspective is that it eventually arranges to call the paint method, which forces the entire drawing area of the applet to be redrawn. In particular, it forces a call to our paint() method, which this PStr has also overridden. Unlike the init method, which has a void signature, the paint method accepts a single argument g, which is an instance of the Graphics class. The methods of the Graphics class are used to actually do graphics. The paint method looks like the following:

```
String outstr;
outstr = "I've got a lovely bunch of " + userstring;   // 10
g.setColor(Color.red);                 // 11
g.drawString(outstr, 10, 10);       // 12
```

Statement 10 constructs the output string outstr by concatenating a constant string with the value of userstring. Note that if userstring had been null, the value of outstr would be the string "I've got a lovely bunch of null" because the quantity null is converted to the string "null." Statement 11 sets the drawing color to red by using the red (static, final) class variable of the Color class. Finally, statement 12 draws the string outstr in that color. We place the string at relative coordinates (10,10), meaning that the string is offset 10 pixels from the top edge and 10 pixels from the left side of the applet's bounding box.

Even though this applet is extremely simple, it does illustrate all the major aspects of applet design. The more complex applet described in the next section has the same basic components, as do the applets of Chapter 13.

# An Accounting Applet in Java

In this section, we examine a slightly more sophisticated Java applet. This applet exercises the Account class, which we have meticulously built up in the previous sections of this chapter. Our Java applet uses the PARAM tag mechanism to process a set of transactions. When it is finished, it displays an account status in its applet window.

The PARAM mechanism we use is extremely simple. We specify the number of transactions by using a PARAM whose NAME is "ntrans". The VALUE of this parameter is the total number of transaction parameters to follow. Each one of those PARAMs has a name of the form trans#, followed by a number. Thus, the first transaction has PARAM NAME="trans#1", the second NAME="trans#2", and so forth. The VALUEs of these transaction parameters encode what we want. If the value is of the form "deposit:100", that indicates a deposit of 100, while if it is of the form "withdraw:150", that indicates a withdrawal of 150. The Java source for this applet is shown in Listing 12.15.

## Listing 12.15  A Java Applet that Processes Account Transactions

```
import java.lang.* ;
import java.awt.* ;

public class Acex extends java.applet.Applet {        // 3; class
        int ntrans = 0;                 // 4; number of transactions requested
        int ntransdone = 0;             // 5; number of transactions done
        int ndeposits = 0;              // 6; number of deposits done
        int nwithdrawals = 0;           // 7; number of withdrawals done
        int noverdrafts = 0;               // 8; number of overdrafts
        private Account myacct = null;    // 9; Account instance itself
        private static final int MyPass = 1492;       // 10; secret password

// private method to do 1 transaction
        private void do1trans(String thetrans) {       // 11;
                String numpart;         // 12; numerical part of a transaction
                int wherecolon;         // 13; location of colon separator
                int valu;               // 14; transaction' value
                int len;                // 15; length of string
                boolean ok;             // 16; withdrew ok?

                wherecolon = thetrans.indexOf(":");  // 17; find the sep
                if ( wherecolon <= 0 ) return;    // 18; bad transaction
                len = thetrans.length();          // 19; overall length
// get numerical part
                numpart = thetrans.substring(wherecolon+1, len);    // 20;
                valu = Integer.parseInt(numpart); // 21; convert to int
                if ( valu <= 0 ) return;          // 22; bad transaction
                switch ( thetrans.charAt(0) ) {   // 23; trans type?
```

*continues*

Part

**III**

Ch

**12**

**Listing 12.15   Continued**

```
// deposit ( 100 = numerical value of "d" )
            case 100:            // 24;
                myacct.deposit(valu, Account.CHECKING);   // 25;
                ndeposits++;            // 26; update counters
                ntransdone++;
                break;
            case 119:                  // 29; withdrawal ( 119 = "w" )
                ok = myacct.withdraw(MyPass, valu);      // 30;
                if ( ok == true ) {      // 31; success
                    nwithdrawals++, ntransdone++;        // 32;
} else {                  // 33; failure
                    noverdrafts++;       // 34; overdraft
                }
                break;
        }                              // 37; end of switch
    }                                  // 38; end of do1trans() method

    public void init() {               // 39; init method
        String tmp;
      String onetrans;
      int i;

        myacct = new Account(1000, 100, MyPass);      // 43;
        tmp = getParameter("ntrans");  // 44; get # of trans
// if not null then convert to integer and set ntrans
        if ( tmp != null )             // 45;
            ntrans = Integer.parseInt(tmp);   // 46;
for(i=1;i<=ntrans;i++) {  // 47; for all trans
// try to find the parameter
            onetrans = getParameter("trans#" + i);     // 48;
            if ( onetrans != null )        // 49; if found then..
                do1trans(onetrans);        // 50; do it
        }
}                                  // 52; end of init()

    public void paint( Graphics g ) {  // 53; paint method
        String msg1, msg2, msg3, msg4;  // 54; temp strings for messages
        int thebalance;                 // 55; final balance
        int loc = 15;                   // 56; drawing location

        thebalance = myacct.balance(MyPass, Account.CHECKING);
// msg1 contains a report on number of transactions requested and performed
        msg1 = "Transactions requested: " + ntrans;
        msg1 += "; transactions performed: " + ntransdone;
// msg2 contains a report on number of deposits and withdrawals done
        msg2 = "Deposits: " + ndeposits;
        msg2 += "; withdrawals: " + nwithdrawals;
        g.setColor(Color.black);        // 62; draw it in black
        g.drawString(msg1, 10, loc);    // 63; first message
        loc += 15;                      // 64; update y
        g.drawString(msg2, 10, loc);    // 65; second message
        loc += 15;                      // 66; update y again
        if ( noverdrafts > 0 ) {  // 67; oops, overdrafts...
            msg3 = "Overdrafts: " + noverdrafts;      // 68;
```

```
          g.setColor(Color.red);      // 69; draw it in panicky red
          g.drawString(10, loc);      // 70; overdraft message
          loc += 15;                  // 71; update y
          }
        msg4 = "Balance: " + thebalance;     // 73; balance message
// If the balance is nonzero then draw it in green, otherwise red
        g.setColor(thebalance > 0 ? Color.green : Color.red);
        g.drawString(msg4, 10, loc);          // 75; balance message
      }                               // 76; end of paint
  }                                   // 77; end of Acex
```

## The *init* Method

To understand how this applet works, approach it from a functional point of view. We know that the first thing in this applet that is executed is its init() method, which begins on line 39. The following extract shows the first part of the init() method:

```
String tmp;
String onetrans;
int i;
myacct = new Account(1000, 100, MyPass);      // 43; fire up account
tmp = getParameter("ntrans");    // 44; get # of transactions
// if not null then convert to integer and set ntrans
if ( tmp != null )                            // 45;
    ntrans = Integer.parseInt(tmp);           // 46;
```

The first thing the init() method does is to initialize our Account instance, myacct, with starting balances of 1000 in checking and 100 in savings. It also sets the account password to the private variable MyPass.

This illustrates one very important point about Java. The Account class is referenced indirectly through its Account constructor. It is not necessary for us to include the Account class code. When the Acex applet is loaded and the init() method is called, the Java interpreter within the browser detects that there is a reference to an external class on line 43. The interpreter knows that the name of that class must be the same as the name of the constructor. This tells the interpreter that it must load the file Account.class to actually call the Account constructor. This only works, however, now that we have made the Account class public.

This is the reason that we may not put the binary Java code for the Account class in a file named kickme.class, or in any file other than Account.class. If we do, the Java interpreter will not be able to find the class code. Even though the Java language has static binding, it also has dynamic loading. This keeps Java binary files as small as possible because external classes are loaded only when they are needed. This is very desirable because those binary files are being accessed across a potentially very slow network.

After the Account class code has been implicitly loaded and the constructor called, the init() method then calls the getParameter() function to retrieve the number of transactions from the parameter "ntrans." If the init() method can find such a parameter, it then attempts to convert that string value into an integer, on line 44. It uses the parseInt() method of the Integer class, which has exactly the same purpose as JavaScript's built-in function of the same name.

Part
III

Ch
12

**TIP** Many Java methods are the same in JavaScript.

After the `init()` method has completed the initialization of the new `Account` instance and has retrieved the number of transactions, it then executes a `for` loop, beginning on line 47. This code is as follows:

```
for(i=1;i<=ntrans;i++) {              // 47; for all transactions
// try to find the parameter
    onetrans = getParameter("trans#" + i);    // 48;
    if ( onetrans != null )                   // 49; if found then..
        do1trans(onetrans);                   // 50; do it
    }
```

It iterates for the number of transactions requested. For each iteration, an attempt is made to find a parameter whose NAME begins with `trans#`. These parameters contain the transaction requests as their VALUEs. If a parameter of this type is found, the `init()` method makes a call to the private method `do1trans()` to actually process the transaction.

## The *do1trans* Method

The `do1trans` method is the workhorse for transaction processing. It accepts a string argument that contains the requested transaction in the form `request:amount`. To process such a request, it must separate the request type (`deposit` or `withdraw`), which occurs before the colon (`:`), from the request amount, which occurs after the colon. Let's examine exactly how this works on a request such as `"deposit:400."` The first few lines of the `do1trans()` method handle this type of parsing, as follows:

```
wherecolon = thetrans.indexOf(":");   // 17; find the separator
if ( wherecolon <= 0 ) return;        // 18; bad transaction
len = thetrans.length();              // 19; overall length of string
// get numerical part
numpart = thetrans.substring(wherecolon+1, len);   // 20;
valu = Integer.parseInt(numpart);     // 21; convert it to an int
if ( valu <= 0 ) return;              // 22; bad transaction
```

In line 17, a call is made to the String method `indexOf()`. This call attempts to find the character index of the colon separator. In our case, that separator is the eighth character, so this method call returns 7 (since character indexing is zero-based). Line 20 uses the String method `substring()` to extract the portion of the transaction string beginning at character index 8 to the end of the string. This is just the string `"400"` in our case, which, of course, corresponds to the numerical part of the transaction. The result is saved in the local variable `numpart`. Line 21 uses the `parseInt()` method again to convert this value from a string to an integer. The next block of code in the `do1trans()` method is used to actually process the transaction, as follows:

```
switch ( thetrans.charAt(0) ) { // 23; type of transaction?
// deposit ( 100 = numerical value of "d" )
    case 100:                   // 24;
        myacct.deposit(valu, Account.CHECKING);     // 25; do it
```

```
            ndeposits++;          // 26; update counters
        ntransdone++;
        break;
    case 119:                     // 29; withdrawal ( 119 = "w" )
            ok = myacct.withdraw(MyPass, valu);    // 30;
            if ( ok == true ) { // 31; success; update counters
                nwithdrawals++, ntransdone++;      // 32;
            } else {              // 33; failure
                noverdrafts++;    // 34; flag an overdraft
            }
            break;
    }                             // 37; end of switch
```

The `switch` statement on line 23 now examines the first character of the transaction string `thetrans` by using the String method `charAt()`. This method returns numerical values, so that we must use the numerical codes for the characters `"d"` and `"w"` in the case statements. If the first character is `"d"` (line 24), then this must be a deposit transaction. Line 25 carries out the transaction, and lines 26 and 27 update the counting variables `ndeposits` and `ntransdone`, which record the number of deposits and successful transactions, respectively.

If the first character is `"w"` (line 29), then this is a withdrawal. We know that withdrawals may fail, so we record the result of calling the `withdraw` method of the `Account` class in the local variable `ok` on line 31. If the withdrawal succeeds, we again update counting variables (line 32). If it fails, we update a different counting variable, `noverdrafts`, which records the number of attempted overdrafts.

Note that the `doitrans()` method ignores any invalid input. If the input string were `"deposit:xxx"` or `"gag:45"`, both would be silently rejected. The former would fail the test on line 22, since `"xxx"` cannot be successfully parsed as an integer. The latter would simply fall off the end of the `switch` statement because the first letter `"g"` matches neither `"d"` nor `"w"`.

The `doitrans()` also accepts a string of the form `"deltatron:200"` as a deposit request (in the amount of 200) because it examines only the first character of the input. Most of the real syntax checking on deposits and withdrawals that you would find in a genuine accounting package has been eliminated from this example. This was done because the goal of this chapter is to introduce you to Java, not to teach you about string parsing or to bring you up-to-date on modern accounting practices. A fully robust version of the `doitrans()` method would have been many times longer, without any significant new Java content.

## The *paint* Method

Once the `init()` method has been executed, the applet's `start` method will be called. Once again, the `Acex` class does not provide its own `start` method so that the default applet `start` method is called. This default `start` method will attempt to repaint the applet's drawing area, which will ultimately call our `paint()` method. The `paint()` method draws a series of strings in various colors, summarizing the transactions. The following is the body of the `paint()` method:

```
thebalance = myacct.balance(MyPass, Account.CHECKING);  // 57;
msg1 = "Transactions requested: " + ntrans;
msg1 += "; transactions performed: " + ntransdone;
```

Part
III

Ch
12

```
msg2 = "Deposits: " + ndeposits;
msg2 += "; withdrawals: " + nwithdrawals;
g.setColor(Color.black);              // 62; draw it in neutral black
g.drawString(msg1, 10, loc);          // 63; first message
loc += 15;                            // 64; update y coordinate
g.drawString(msg2, 10, loc);          // 65; second message
loc += 15;                            // 66; update y again
if ( noverdrafts > 0 ) {              // 67; oops, overdrafts...
    msg3 = "Overdrafts: " + noverdrafts;      // 68; report how many
        g.setColor(Color.red);        // 69; draw it in panicky red
        g.drawString(10, loc);        // 70; overdraft message
        loc += 15;                    // 71; update y
    }
msg4 = "Balance: " + thebalance;      // 73; balance message
g.setColor(thebalance > 0 ? Color.green : Color.red);   // 74
g.drawString(msg4, 10, loc);          // 75; balance message
```

This code gets the current account balance (line 57) and then constructs two strings recording the number of transactions requested, the number actually processed, and the total number of deposits and withdrawals (lines 58 to 61). The code then displays these strings in basic black (lines 62 to 66). Note that the x coordinate of the strings is the same—it is always 10, while the y coordinate, stored in the variable loc, is incremented after each call to drawString(). This ensures that strings are not drawn on top of one another.

Having displayed this basic information, the paint() method next checks to see if any overdrafts occurred, on line 67. If they did, the paint() method constructs a message indicating how many overdrafts (line 68), sets the drawing color to red (line 69), and then draws that string (line 70). This method also updates the y coordinate for the next draw on line 71. Finally, the current balance is displayed. The color this string uses is determined by comparing the balance to 0. If the balance is greater than 0, then green is used; if the balance is 0, red is used (line 74). The final balance string is drawn in line 75.

# Executing the Account Example Applet

To execute the Account Example Java applet, we must do two things: we must compile it and place the code in the appropriate directory, and we must create some appropriate HTML that invokes it. The applet is compiled by using the command

```
javac Acex.java
```

which creates the binary file Acex.class. This must be placed in the same directory with the binary Account.class file because that file needs to be loaded to resolve the various references to methods in the Account class. Finally, we must have a small piece of HTML that issues some transactions. This is shown in Listing 12.16. The result of browsing this tiny Web page is shown in Figure 12.3.

## Listing 12.16   Executing the Accounting Applet on a Web Page

```
<HTML>
<HEAD>
<TITLE>Using the Accounting Applet</TITLE>
```

```
</HEAD>
<BODY>
<P>
<HR>
<APPLET CODE="Acex.class" WIDTH=400 HEIGHT=400 ALIGN="CENTER">
<PARAM NAME="ntrans" VALUE="5">
<PARAM NAME="trans#1" VALUE="withdraw:400">
<PARAM NAME="trans#2" VALUE="deposit:10">
<PARAM NAME="trans#3" VALUE="withdraw:900">
<PARAM NAME="trans#4" VALUE="withdraw:330">
<PARAM NAME="trans#5" VALUE="deposit:250">
You will see this text if your browser does not understand Java.
</APPLET>
<HR>
The Example <A HREF="Acex.java">source</A>.
<BR>
The <A HREF="Account.java">Account</A> base class.
</P>
</BODY>
</HTML>
```

**FIG. 12.3**

The Java Accounting
applet processes
transactions in vivid
color.

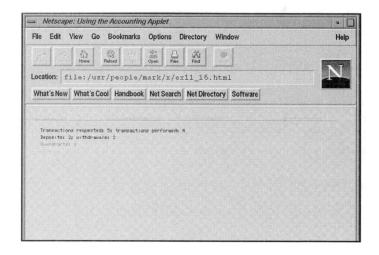

Part
**III**

Ch
**12**

# CHAPTER 13

# Advanced Applets

**O**ne of the major advantages of the Java language is its power and flexibility. Java is a full-featured programming language with all the constructs one needs to develop object-oriented applications. However, as you have already seen in Chapter 12, "A Java Tutorial," Java is not as directly connected with the environment of its Web page as JavaScript. Java cannot readily access HTML elements on a Web page in a direct manner. As compensation for this deficiency, Java provides some extremely powerful tools for manipulating images and URLs. Java also has a set of components, known as the *Advanced Windowing Toolkit* (AWT), which enable Java applets to create push buttons, text entry fields, and other HTML-like entities.

The term *Java* encompasses many things. In Chapter 12, we focused on gaining some initial understanding of Java as a programming language. In the process, you encountered some old familiar methods, such as parseInt() and charAt(), and also some new ones, such as paint(). This points to the fact that Java is more than a language. Java is also a set of methods, organized into a collection known as the Java Class Hierarchy, which enables us to do complex tasks. Much of the expressiveness of Java only becomes clear when we learn more about some of the components of the Java Class Hierarchy and what they can do for us.

## Use Java packages

All the major packages in the Java Class Hierarchy will be described, with special emphasis on the most important methods and classes.

## Load and display images in Java

The image package is a key component in Java's graphics system. This chapter examines several of its elements in detail.

## Layout components in the applet window

Layout is often the most challenging aspect in any windowing system. All of Java's built-in layout methods will be described and two of the most common will be used in detailed examples.

## Manipulate URLs

Java imposes certain rules for opening other Web pages. See what those rules are and examine how Java cooperates with the browser in handling URLs.

This chapter explores the Java Class Hierarchy with particular emphasis on image and URL manipulation. It presents the basic concepts necessary to explore Java further and enables you to write more complex and interesting Java applets. ■

# The Java Class Hierarchy

Chapter 12 introduced the concept of *inheritance* in Java. In particular, the section "An Accounting Applet in Java," described an applet that demonstrated three Java classes working together: the `Account` class, the `Acex` class, which drove the applet itself, and implicitly, the Java class `java.applet.Applet`. Chapter 12 also introduced the special keyword `extends` and explained that `Acex` is said to *extend* the built-in class `java.applet.Applet`. This idea of having one class extend another, also known as *subclassing*, is critical to understanding the Java Class Hierarchy.

▶ **See** "An Accounting Applet in Java," **p. 351**, for a detailed example of subclassing the `Applet` class.

## Classes and Subclasses

In Chapter 12, the `Account` class was built from the ground up and was gradually refined to perform a set of simple but useful operations. This process could have been continued *ad infinitum,* adding more and more methods for more and more specialized situations. This would make the `Account` class cover a larger number of situations but it would also lead to dramatic overkill in some cases. It would be nice to have the capability to handle escrow accounts, foreign currency transactions, and the like, but in many situations, you do not use these extra capabilities.

This leads to the notion that perhaps we do not want to extend a class by adding more and more to it but, rather, by creating specialized versions of that class. The specialized versions would have all the capabilities of the generalized class but would also have their own unique features. The specialized classes, such as `EscrowAccount` and `InternationalAccount`, have all the methods and instance variables of `Account` but also have their own methods, which `Account` does not have. The specialized classes *inherit* the attributes of their parent and are *subclasses* of their parent class, which is known as their *superclass.*

**N O T E**  There is no *multiple inheritance* in Java. Every Java class has exactly one parent class. ■

Naturally, this simple idea of inheritance acquires some twists and turns when it is actually implemented. The first such variation is the idea of having a subclass *override* a method in the superclass. The `Acex` applet, discussed at the end of Chapter 12, overrides the `paint()` method of its superclass.

As you can imagine, the international version of `Acex` would keep the `withdraw()` and `balance()` methods the same, and would add `convert()` and `transfer()` methods (to convert between different currencies and to transfer money). It also might override the `deposit()` method so that deposits could be made in foreign as well as local currency. A subclass not only extends its superclass, it also tends to modify its behavior for special situations.

Java has a special keyword, `super`, that is used to refer to the superclass of a class. Superclass instance variables can be accessed as `super.varname`, and superclass methods can be invoked as `super.methodname()`. This keyword is particularly useful if you want the subclass to use its own method named `NAME()` and also use its parent's method, also named `NAME()`.

For example, our internationalized version of the `deposit()` method might look something like Listing 13.1. This version of `deposit()` simply converts the `deposit()` amount, in any arbitrary currency, into the local equivalent (line 3) and then calls the `deposit()` method in the super-class (`Acex`) to perform the deposit. This procedure avoids the tedious approach of copying all the `deposit()` code in any subclass that overrides it.

### Listing 13.1 A Class Method Calls Its Superclass Method

```
// Assume that "currency" is a variable specifying the type of currency,
// and that convert is a method that converts between currencies
// this is the subclass deposit method
void deposit(int amount, int which, int currency) {        // 1;
    int localamount;
    localamount = convert(amount, currency);  // 3; convert to local
    super.deposit(localamount, which); // 4; invoke superclass method
}
```

What happens to instance variables of a class when a subclass is derived from it? As one might imagine, public instance variables remain public. Interestingly enough, private instance variables (and private methods) are completely private—they are unknown in the subclass just as they are unknown outside the class. This means that no subclass can reference private instance variables or make use of private methods of its superclass. Java also has a third category, known as protected variables and methods, which are known to the class and to all its subclasses, but remain invisible elsewhere. Figure 13.1 illustrates the relationship between the various types of class members and their subclass counterparts.

**FIG. 13.1**
Subclassing can be used in Java to create specialized classes.

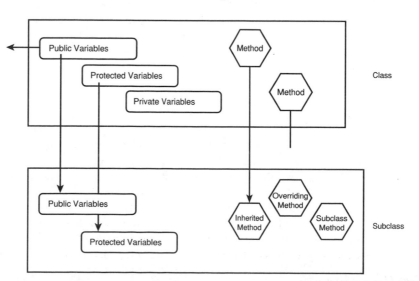

Part
III

Class

Ch
13

Subclass

# Packages in Java

The Java Class Hierarchy is the collection of all the classes that are provided as a standard part of Java. These classes are organized in a class hierarchy, as previously described, with a series of very general classes—such as the ubiquitous class known as Object—at the top of this hierarchy. This might lead you to guess that the class java.applet.Applet, which is the superclass of all applets, is a subclass of java.applet, which, in turn, is a subclass of an all-encompassing java class. This is an excellent guess but it is incorrect.

Java actually has two kinds of organization for its classes. It has a strict class hierarchy, which describes all the children of each class. It also has a more horizontal organizational structure known as the Java *package* system. Packages are used to group together similar, but not necessarily directly related, classes into a set of groups. These groups are the Java packages. Packages can be distinguished notationally from classes because they all begin with a lowercase letter, while classes always start with an uppercase letter. Thus, Applet is a class in the java.applet package, which is a part of the java package. As a class, Applet is derived as follows:

```
Object -> Component -> Container -> Panel -> Applet
```

An applet, therefore, is actually a specialized form of the graphic class Panel, which is derived from two other graphics classes, Container and Component, and ultimately from Object. This is an excellent example of the matrix organization of classes and packages. Applet is a member of the java.applet package; Panel, Container, and Component are members of the java.awt (Advanced Windowing Toolkit) package; and Object is the member of the java.lang package.

The top of the Java package hierarchy is the java package. There are other top level hierarchies, such as the sun hierarchy, which are platform and/or operating system dependent. The java hierarchy, however, is always guaranteed to be present. It contains the following main packages:

- lang
- net
- awt
- applet
- util
- io

**The *java.lang* Package**   The java.lang package is one of the most important and fundamental of the java packages. It defines the basic object types that correspond to elements of the language. It also includes several very interesting pieces of machinery that are used throughout Java programming, including the critical concept of a *thread*, which will be reviewed shortly.

The data type classes contained within `java.lang` include `Boolean`, `Character`, and `String`, as well as the numerical types `Integer`, `Long`, `Float`, and `Double`. These latter four classes are actually subclasses of a generic `Number` class. As one might expect, each of the numerical types defines conversion methods. You already have seen one of these, namely the `parseInt()` method of the `Integer` class, which is used to convert strings to integers.

▶ **See** "An Accounting Applet in Java," **p. 351**, for an example using the `Acex` applet.

The `java.lang` package also contains a class known as `Math`, which is very similar to the JavaScript object of the same name. `Math` provides an expanded set of mathematical operations. The same can be said for the `String` class, which is a full-fledged class (object) in Java. Java also provides a second string class, known as `StringBuffer`, within the `java.lang` package. This is used for extensible strings. Whenever you concatenate strings by using the plus sign (+) operator, you are actually using a `StringBuffer`. More precisely, whenever the Java compiler sees an expression that involves merging two strings, it rewrites that expression to use a `StringBuffer` behind the scenes.

Finally, the `java.lang` package contains two critical classes with enormous utility: `System` and `Thread`. The `System` class provides system-level functionality with a platform-independent interface. The way in which it is actually implemented, of course, heavily depends on the actual platform. You already have seen an example of the `System` class in the print statement, `System.out.println("message")`, which sends the string `"message"` with a subsequent carriage return to the *standard output*. Where this output actually goes is, of course, platform-dependent. `Threads` are the subject of the next section and are used in the "Image Viewer Applet" section at the end of this chapter.

**Using Java Threads**   It often is very useful to do several things at once. Not only does this accomplish more, but it also completes tasks earlier. Of course, in this aspect, most humans are like most computers. It really is not possible to do more than one meaningful thing at a time, such as reading two books at once, but it is often highly desirable (particularly for one's image) to make it appear this way. This is the advantage of modern multitasking. Each user process gets its own set of tiny slices of a single CPU and the illusion of simultaneous processing is maintained. Most modern operating systems enable you to appear to be performing several tasks, such as editing while printing.

There are often cases in which it is highly desirable to be able to perform many tasks within a single program. This is particularly true in graphics programs. In attempting to display multiple images, it is advantageous to be working on image 5 while image 4 is being displayed, for example. Java provides such capability as part of its `java.lang` package through the medium of the `Thread` class.

A Java thread is very similar to an ordinary thread in a garment. It has a definite starting point, a definite endpoint, and can weave through the garment in tandem with other threads. A complete description of Java threads is well beyond the scope of this chapter. However, we can examine the general structure of a threaded Java applet. This structure is used in the image display applet to realize precisely the goal described: interweaving graphic operations and other operations. The template for a multithreaded Java applet is shown in Listing 13.2.

Part
III

Ch
13

---

**Listing 13.2   The Structure of a Runnable Java Applet**

```
public class MTApplet extends java.applet.Applet implements Runnable {
    Thread mythread = null; // the thread we will create

    public void init() {     // init method, as before
        ...                  // initialization stuff goes here
    }

    public void start() {   // start method, creates thread
        if ( mythread == null ) {
            mythread = new Thread();
            mythread.start();
        }
    }

    public void stop() {     // stop method, stops thread
        if ( mythread != null ) {
            mythread.stop();
            mythread = null;
        }
    }

    public void paint( Graphics g ) {     // local paint method
        ...                               // custom drawing goes here
    }

    public void run() {     // the work method of the thread
        ...                 // the main body of the thread
    }
}
```

---

This template has several familiar features as well as some new wrinkles. First notice that the class declaration for this MTApplet class not only extends java.applet.Applet, as it must, it also "implements Runnable." Runnable is a new type of Java element: a Java *interface*. An interface, like a superclass, expresses a set of methods. A class, such as MTApplet, which implements this interface, must also implement these methods. In particular, it must implement a run() method. The purpose of the run() method will become clear in a moment.

The MTApplet class has the very familiar init() method, which is used to do whatever initialization is required. This usually involves parsing user parameters that are accessed via the getParameter() method. If images are to be manipulated, the init() method is also a good place to begin loading those images. The paint() method is also much as before: it is used to perform our applet-specific drawing operations. These operations now are done in parallel, however, using threads.

The start() and stop() methods shown in Listing 13.2 are not templates or place holders: they are shown in their entirety. The start() method examines the instance variable mythread to see if it is null (its initial value). If it is null, then the start() method creates a new Thread instance by invoking the new operator and by setting mythread to be that instance. The effect of creating a new thread is that there is now one extra task that can be run. However, this new thread is not running yet. The final statement in the start method launches this new thread by saying mythread.start(). This calls the start() method of the new thread. The new thread now runs as an independent entity within the applet.

The stop() method is the mirror image of the start() method. It also examines the mythread instance variable. If it is not null, then that thread is halted by calling its stop() method. Cleanup is performed then by setting the mythread variable back to null. The interplay between start() and stop() is such that, at most, one new thread will be created. If start() finds that mythread is not null, it will do nothing. Also, stop() ensures that the new thread will never be stopped twice. None of this yet explains how the new thread accomplishes anything, however.

The answer to this mystery is provided by the new run() method. When a class implements the Runnable interface and a new thread is created and set running by that class, then its run() method will be entered. In fact, every applet is already a thread, known as the main thread. Unless a new thread is created by instantiating the Thread class, the main thread is the only thread, so there is effectively no parallelism.

Once the second thread is activated and the run() method entered, the new thread can do one set of operations while the main thread is doing something else. This is the key idea behind parallelism in Java. If the run() method performs some graphical operations and ends up triggering paint(), the actual drawing is performed in the main thread, while the computations leading up to it are performed in the second thread.

**CAUTION**

The actual implementation of Java threads is platform-dependent at this time. This is because threads require some cooperation from the underlying operating system, and different operating systems cooperate in different ways. A thread-based applet that works perfectly under Solaris may fail on Windows NT, and vice versa. Applets using threads should be thoroughly tested on all major platform types (UNIX, Windows, Macintosh).

**The *java.net* Package**    The java.net package contains the basic classes and methods that are used for network communications. This package contains classes representing network connections (sockets), network addresses and, most significantly, URLs. This might sound like an extremely rich source for interesting Java programming ideas, but the Java security model limits quite severely what you can do with this package. It is worthwhile to review these limitations because they significantly affect what is possible and what is not.

Every Java applet is activated within the context of a Web page via that page's APPLET tag. This Web page, in turn, was obtained from some URL and therefore is associated with a particular Web server. We will refer to the Web page that activated the applet as that applet's document and the server from which that page was obtained as the applet's server.

The first restriction on network access within Java is that it is prohibited from opening a network connection to any host other than the applet's server. This means that it is not even possible to make a network connection to the user's own host! The second restriction is that a Java applet can access only those documents within the directory hierarchy rooted at the applet's document BASE. These two restrictions combined might seem quite grim because the set of documents accessible within Java is rendered very small.

Fortunately, there are no restrictions on documents that Java can ask its browser to open. This concept is one of the subtleties of Java. Java does not actually implement graphics, network connections, or anything else that impacts the external environment. It has a series of methods where it can ask its browser to do these things for it. When you create a button or open an URL in Java, it actually is the browser that is doing these things for you.

Having said all this, there is one very important class in the java.net package that you can (and will) use quite effectively: the URL class. As the name implies, this class is used to construct an abstract representation of an URL. This class has several different constructors, as follows:

URL(String)

URL(URL, String)

URL(String, String, String)

URL(String, String, int, String)

The first form takes a String, such as the literal http://www.microsoft.com, and attempts to construct an URL instance from it. The second form is used to concatenate a String representing a relative path name onto an existing URL. This form can be used to descend from the applet's document BASE to an HTML file within its tree.

The third and fourth forms are used to build an URL from its component parts. The third form takes a protocol name, such as http, a hostname, such as www.microsoft.com, and a filename, such as index.html, and produces an URL from that combination. The fourth form also enables you to explicitly set the port number for those rare cases in which the protocol is not being accessed on its default port. (http is occasionally received on port 1080 or 8080 rather than its default 80, for example.)

When we review our two major Java applets later in this chapter, you will see the first two forms of the URL class constructor and, also, how one politely asks one's browser to open a "foreign" URL. The upcoming discussion on the java.applet package also shows how to obtain the URL that corresponds to the applet's document BASE.

**The Advanced Windowing Toolkit**   We have already observed that Java cannot interact directly with HTML elements, unlike JavaScript. There are no HTML FORM components within the Java Class Hierarchy. This means that Java programmers must construct their own buttons, text entry fields, and the like, if they want such items to be part of their applets. The Advanced Windowing Toolkit (AWT) is Java's set of capabilities for doing this. It is contained within the package java.awt.

The classes in the AWT can be subdivided into three categories: display items (such as `Button`), layouts (such as `FlowLayout`), and overall graphics items (such as `Color` and `Font`). The first category is the largest and includes an extensive set of elements, including:

- `Button`—a standard button
- `Checkbox`—a button with an on/off indicator
- `CheckboxGroup`—a set of radio buttons
- `Choice`—a pop-up menu of choices
- `Dialog`—a pop-up dialog box
- `Frame`—an entirely new window
- `Image`—a GIF or JPEG image
- `Label`—a static text item
- `List`—a list box of items
- `Menu`—a menu of items
- `Panel`—an organizational item that can contain other items
- `Point`—a single pixel
- `Polygon`—a region bounded by line segments
- `Rectangle`—a rectangular region
- `Scrollbar`—a scroll bar, usually associated with a `List` or `TextArea`
- `TextArea`—an editable text item that can have more than one line and that can be scrolled
- `TextField`—a single-line editable text item with fixed size

As you can see from this enumeration, many familiar HTML elements are also present in the AWT. As in HTML, it is quite simple to glue together a set of graphical items in a page, but it is somewhat more difficult to make the presentation attractive and crisp. HTML has a number of markup styles and directives that can be used to control the visual format of various elements, including tables and forms.

The means to control where elements are placed, how they are aligned with one another, and how they are sized and spaced, is always an issue in graphics programming. This applies to all windowing systems. Java is no exception. The Java AWT has chosen an approach with several different, quite distinct, layout styles. Within each style, the display elements that you create, such as `Button`s and `TextArea`s, are placed according to a well-defined system. However, it can still take time to get things looking just the way you want and, if all else fails, you can still programmatically position objects at specific coordinates.

Part
III

Ch
13

 **T I P**  The default Java layout is `FlowLayout` with `CENTER` justification. Use this until you become more comfortable with the AWT.

At present, there are five Java layout styles. Each has its own peculiarities and you will almost certainly find yourself using a combination of styles once you acquire some skill with the AWT. The Java layout classes are:

- ◼ BorderLayout

- ◼ CardLayout

- ◼ FlowLayout

- ◼ GridLayout

- ◼ GridBagLayout

The BorderLayout approach is based on the idea of placing elements at one of the four cardinal points—North, South, East or West—or in the Center. It is often ideal for arranging items in case you want two or three arranged in a vertical (North, Center, South) or horizontal (West, Center, East) stacking order. BorderLayout is also used with Panels for hierarchical organization of items. If you want a top row of Buttons and perhaps a Label below, you create two Panels, place them at the North and South locations in a BorderLayout, and then add the Buttons to the northern Panel and a Label to the southern Panel. Listing 13.3 shows a code fragment that does this.

**Listing 13.3   An Example of Hierarchical Layout in Java**

```
BorderLayout bl;
Button but[];
Panel nopa, sopa;
Label la;

bl = new BorderLayout();    // 5; create a new BorderLayout instance
setLayout(bl);                   // 6; make it the default layout
nopa = new Panel();              // 7; create two new panels
sopa = new Panel();
add("North", nopa);              // 9; put nopa at the North edge
add("South", sopa);              // 10; add sopa at the South edge
but = new Button[4];             // 11; allocate space for 4 buttons
but[0] = new Button("Back");     // 12; create the buttons with various labels
but[1] = new Button("Forward");
but[2] = new Button("Home");
but[3] = new Button("Done");
for(int i = 0; i < 4; i++) {     // 16; add the buttons to North panel
    nopa.add(but[i]);            // 17; it will default to a FlowLayout
la = new Label("Southern Label"); // 18; create new label
sopa.add(la);                    // 19; add to south Panel
}
```

This example begins by allocating a new instance of the BorderLayout class (line 5) and then calling the setLayout() method to make this the current layout. Remember that a Java applet is actually a subclass of a Panel, so that the bare call to setLayout() on line 6 applies to the

`Panel` containing the entire applet. The next two statements create `Panel` instances. Note that instances of graphical items can be created all day long, but they are not displayed until they are added to the applet.

The North and South `Panel`s are added in lines 9 and 10 by using the `add()` method. The `add()` method is overridden in all the layout classes, which means that it has its own distinct syntax for each one. In the case of a `BorderLayout`, the first argument to `add()` must be one of the five permissible directions. We use North and South to split the applet vertically. The next five lines create four `Button`s with some text to name them. Lines 16 and 17 then add those buttons to the North panel. This is accomplished by explicitly invoking the `add()` method of `nopa`, the North panel instance. If we had mistakenly just used `add(but[i])` on line 17, this would have attempted to add these buttons to the entire applet's panel. Lines 18 and 19 create and add a `Label` to the south `Panel` in a similar way.

> **N O T E**  At the moment, button labels must be text. It currently is not possible to put an image inside a button by using the `Button` class. A subclass of the `Button` class would have to be written to do this.

The `FlowLayout` class implements an approach in which elements are added incrementally across one or more rows. Elements can be justified within a given row by using LEFT, CENTER (the default), or RIGHT justification. If an element does not fit on a given row, the layout wraps around to the beginning of the next row. `FlowLayout` is often used for rows of buttons or other components of similar size and shape. As mentioned previously, `FlowLayout` is the default layout for any newly created graphical container (such as a `Frame` or `Panel`).

The other three layout types are more specialized. `CardLayout` is used to create slide show-like presentations. Elements of a `CardLayout` are presented sequentially rather than being displayed simultaneously on the screen. `GridLayout` lives up to its name. It enables you to position elements based on their row and column location. It is used by first specifying the number of rows and columns to be allocated and then by placing individual elements in their desired (row, column) location. `GridBagLayout` is a much more powerful version of `GridLayout`. Regrettably, it is also complex because it is necessary to first construct a description of the layout by using the subsidiary class `GridBagConstraints` and then to actually build the layout on top of that.

Part

III

Ch

13

The final set of classes in the immense `java.awt` package are the classes that correspond to general graphical constructs rather than things that are actually drawn. We have already seen two examples of these classes in our tiny applets from Chapter 12, "A Java Tutorial": the `Color` and `Graphics` classes. The `Color` class is usually used by invoking its static instance variables that name the primary colors (such as `Color.Red`), although it also can be used to construct arbitrary color values directly from red, green, and blue levels. The `Graphics` class captures the entire graphical state of an applet. Recall that the method signature for the applet `paint()` method is `public void paint( Graphics g )`.

Within paint(), you can call a set of methods (too numerous to mention) to draw strings, rectangles, and other common, primitive graphics operations. Some of the other important classes in this general graphics category are the following:

- Event
- Font
- MediaTracker

The Event class is extremely important because it enables you to respond to user events such as a button being pushed inside the applet. The Applet class has another method, known as action(), that is called whenever user interaction takes place. Its method signature is public Boolean action( Event ev, Object arg ). It is called whenever the Object arg (a Button, for example) is pushed and generates the Event ev. If you override the default action() method, you can control what happens when events occur, just as in JavaScript.

---

**CAUTION**

Java Events and JavaScript events are not directly related. At present, Java cannot directly respond to events outside its applet. It also is not possible to install a JavaScript event handler for Events inside a Java applet.

---

The Font class is used to manipulate the text appearance of any item that contains text. It can be used to load a particular font by name (such as TimesRoman or Helvetica), to set the font style (such as PLAIN, BOLD, or ITALIC), and also to set the font size. The oddly named MediaTracker class is Java's answer to the patient projectionist. It is almost always used to track the progress of images being progressively loaded over the network. You will see examples of all three of these AWT classes below.

**The *java.applet* Package**   The java.applet package is quite small and has just one interesting class, Applet, with a small number of interesting methods. You have already seen the getParameter() method, which accepts a String argument giving the NAME of a PARAM, and returns the VALUE of the PARAM (or null if there is no matching name). The other three Applet methods that you will use most frequently are the following:

URL getDocumentBase();

URL getCodeBase();

AppletContext getAppletContext();

You probably can guess that the first of these methods returns an URL instance representing the value of the BASE attribute of the applet's document. It is the top of the document directory tree that the applet can access on the server host. The second of these methods is similar: it returns the URL representing the value of the CODEBASE attribute given in the APPLET tag, if any. This is used when all the Java class binaries are kept in a different server directory than the HTML files. That directory would be named in the CODEBASE attribute.

**TIP** The URLs returned by `getDocumentBase()` and `getCodeBase()` are always valid for use in Java applets, as long as they are not `null`.

▶ **See** "The *Applet* Tag," **p. 345,** for a description of the HTML elements used in declaring an applet.

The `getAppletContext` method is used to talk directly to the browser. The applet context really refers to the browser environment in which the applet is running. Once you have obtained the applet context, you then can use it to ask the browser to display an URL, for example. This is not a task that you can perform directly in Java because of security restrictions. You will see an example of this in the section titled "A Pop-Up Document Viewer Applet," later in this chapter.

**The *java.util* and *java.io* Packages**  These packages are the last two on our tour of the Java Class Hierarchy. The `java.util` package provides various utility classes, while the `java.io` package handles input and output to files and streams. The `java.util` package contains the `Date` object for manipulating date items, as in JavaScript. It also contains a series of classes that can be used to manipulate structured collections of things, including the `Vector`, `HashTable`, `Dictionary`, and `Stack` classes.

One the most useful utility classes is `StringTokenizer`. This class is used to solve the age-old problem of decomposing a string, such as the following:

`"this,is,a,comma,separated,list"`

into its individual components:

`"this" "is" "a" "comma" "separated" "list"`

The traditional way of solving this problem is to search for the separator character, which is the comma character (,) in this case, and keep track of the individual substrings that occurred between the separators. You would find the first comma and separate the initial string into `"this"` and `"is,a,comma,separated,list"` and then repeat the procedure until each of the individual elements was extracted. The `StringTokenizer` class completely automates this tedious, but extremely common, parsing task. Anyone who has ever written string manipulation code that attempts to interpret a string of a series of separate items (tokens) will appreciate the `StringTokenizer` class.

There is not much to be said about the `java.io` class for applet developers. One of Java's security restrictions prohibits local file access of any kind inside an applet. While we can certainly ask the browser to open a document by using the `file:` protocol, the applet cannot do so itself. This restriction may be weakened in some future version of Java, but at the moment, Java cannot touch the local file system.

# A Pop-Up Document Viewer Applet

This section analyzes and presents a pop-up document viewer applet in Java. This applet enables the user to specify the communication protocol to be used via a pop-up menu and permits a full document name to be entered into a text field. Once the user commits to a particular document name by pressing a button, the applet requests that the browser open that document in a new window. This applet is designed as a simple demonstration of some of the capabilities of the java.applet and java.awt packages. It also illustrates Java's variety of event handling. The code is shown in Listing 13.4.

**Listing 13.4   Viewing a Document in a New Browser Window Using Java**

```
/**
   A Java Applet to launch a document in a new window
   Comments for "javadoc" follow.
   @author Mark C. Reynolds
   @version 1.0
*/
import java.awt.*;                   // 1; get AWT components
import java.net.*;                   // 2; get URL and friends
import java.applet.*;               // 3; get Applet class methods

public class SD extends java.applet.Applet {
     String whatproto = "http";       // 5; initial protocol to use
     String prevproto = whatproto;    // 6; previous protocol used
     Choice ch;                       // 7; A pop-up menu choice
     TextField tf;                   // 8; User entered document name
     AppletContext ac;               // 9; Ask the browser...

     public void init() {            // 10; Init method
          FlowLayout fl;
          Button bu;
          Font fo;
// create a new left-justified flowlayout with 10 pixels of spacing
//on each side of each item
          fl = new FlowLayout(FlowLayout.LEFT, 10, 10); // 14
          setLayout(fl);     // 15; make it the current layout
          fo = new Font("TimesRoman", Font.PLAIN, 18); // 16;
          setFont(fo);       // 17; make it the current font
          ch = new Choice();       // 18; create a Choice instance
          ch.setFont(fo);          // 19; make this the current font
          ch.addItem(whatproto);   // 20; add "http" as a choice
          ch.addItem("gopher");    // 21; add literal "gopher" as a choice
          ch.addItem("ftp");
          ch.addItem("file");
          add(ch);           // 24; add pop-up menu to flowlayout
          bu = new Button("Open");       // 25; create "Open" button
          add(bu);           // 26; add button to flowlayout
// create a textfield of length 70, and put the string "http://" in it
          tf = new TextField(whatproto + "://", 70);     // 27
          tf.setEditable(true);  // 28; enable user to modify field
          add(tf);           // 29; add text field to flowlayout
          ac = getAppletContext();     // 30; discover our context
     }                       // 31; end of init method

     public void start() {    // 32; start method does nothing
     }
```

```
        public void stop() {         // 34; stop method does nothing too
        }

// change the text entry when user changes protocol
        private void modifytext() {           // 36;
            int len = prevproto.length();   // 37; len of prev proto
            String cur = tf.getText();         // 38; get the current text
            String left = cur.substring(len);  // 39; get doc name
// new name = new proto + old document name
            tf.setText(whatproto + left);      // 40;
        }           // 41; end of modifytext() private method

        private void launchdoc() {  // 42; ask browser to open a doc
            String doc = tf.getText();       // 43; get document name
            URL u = null;                     // 44; document's URL
// test to insure that there is a doc name, more than just proto://
            if ( doc.length() <= ( whatproto.length() + 3 ) ) return;      // 45
            try {  // 46; execute something that might abort
                u = new URL(doc);    // 47; convert doc name to URL
            } catch (MalformedURLException ue) {     // 48;
// if it failed then print a message indicating why
                System.err.println("Invalid URL: " + ue.getMessage()); // 49;
                return;                // 50; and give up
            }                          // 51; end of try clause
// ask for the document to be opened in a new window named "New Window"
            ac.showDocument(u, "New Window");        // 52
        }                          // 53; end of launchdoc

// event handler
        public boolean action(Event ev, Object arg) {       // 54;
            if ( ev.target instanceof Choice ) { // 55; Choice event
                prevproto = whatproto;           // 56; save prev proto
                whatproto = arg.toString(); // 57; get the choice
                modifytext();    // 58; change the text displayed
                return(true);    // 59; indicate event handled
            }                    // 60; end of Choice event
            if ( ev.target instanceof Button ) {      // 61; Button event
// if the "Open" button was selected then...
                if ( arg.toString().equals("Open") ) {      // 62;
                    launchdoc();     // 63; try to launch the doc
                    return(true);    // 64; event handled
                }                    // 65; end of if statement
            }                        // 66; end of Button event
            return(false);           // 67; did not handle event
        }                            // 68; end of action method
}                                    // 69; end of SD class
```

## Initializing the SD Applet

The init() method for the SD (Show Document) applet begins on line 10. Its job is to construct all the graphical elements that are displayed and, in the process, to initialize various instance variables that are used in the event handling methods, modifytext() and launchdoc(). It starts out by creating a FlowLayout instance on line 14. This instance is left-justified so that new elements are added starting at the left edge of each row. We also specify at least 10 pixels between each element in a row (the second argument to the constructor), and between rows (the third argument). Line 15 makes this layout the current layout. Because an applet is actually a Panel, this now applies to the entire applet.

Line 16 accesses a plain Times Roman font with 18-point type. If your system does not have this particular font, you may need to adjust this statement to choose another font name (such as Helvetica or Geneva) and perhaps another font size (such as 24-point). You can also specify the empty string " " as the first parameter to the Font constructor; this will select a default font. Line 17 makes this font the current font for the applet's panel. Next, three items are put into the flow layout, beginning at line 18: a pop-up menu, a button, and a single line text field.

The pop-up menu is created on line 18. Because pop-ups have their own fonts, which may be separate from the Panel in which they reside, you must set the font of the pop-up (line 19). This pop-up presents the user with a choice of four communication protocols that will be used. These are added to the pop-up in lines 20 through 23. Note that the default item, which represents the default protocol, is the one added first. This will be the initial value of the instance variable whatproto, which is the String "http." Finally, line 24 adds this pop-up to the layout.

Line 25 creates a Button whose label is Open. This is the button that the user presses to attempt to load a new document. It is added to the layout in line 26. The third item in our layout is an editable text field, which is created in line 27. The initial String that will be displayed is "http://", obtained by concatenating the default protocol "http" with the literal delimiter "://."

Line 28 makes this text field read/write, and line 29 adds it to the layout. Because this text field is quite long, it will be added in a new row below the pop-up menu and the Open button. Finally, line 30 initializes the instance variable ac to the applet's context. This is used in the launchdoc() method. Figure 13.2 shows the initial appearance of the SD applet after the init() method has been executed.

**FIG. 13.2**
The ShowDocument Applet uses AWT elements, which are very similar to HTML forms components.

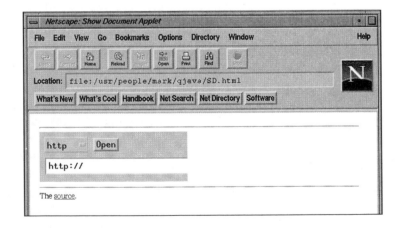

# Event Handling in the SD Applet

You will notice immediately that the start() and stop() methods of the SD applet do absolutely nothing. All of the activity in this applet is triggered in response to user interaction. As a result, all of our code is within the action() method and none in the start() or stop() methods. There is also no run() method in this applet because we are not implementing any threads (the next applet we consider uses threads).

There are many different ways of performing event handling in Java. For example, Java applets that desire to handle only mouse down events can override a specialized method known as mouseDown(). If you were only interested in button clicks on the Open button, you could use this approach. Because we are actually interested in handling events on the pop-up menu and button clicks on Open, the SD applet uses the more general approach.

If an applet overrides the action() method, this indicates that it wants to handle more than one event type. The code for the action() method begins on line 54. Note that this method accepts two arguments: an Event instance, indicating the type of event, and an Object instance, indicating where the event occurred. The target element of an Event indicates which graphical element was associated with the event

On line 55, the Java keyword instanceof is used to ask if the event was associated with a Choice item (a pop-up menu). If the result is true, then the code in lines 56 through 59 is executed. This code saves the previous choice value (line 56), stores the new choice value by extracting the String version of the Object selected (line 57), and then invokes the modifytext() private method to fix up the document name being displayed. It then returns true in line 59 to indicate that this event was successfully processed.

> **CAUTION**
>
> All applet event handling methods must return true to indicate that the event has been handled and false to say that it has not. Failure to do so may cause the applet (and the browser) to become horribly confused.

To understand what is going on, consider a concrete example. Suppose that the user had typed the document name "http://ftp.javasoft.com" in the text field and then suddenly realized that this was not going to work because it would require the ftp protocol rather than the http protocol. The user then invokes the pop-up choice menu and selects FTP.

This selection triggers the action() method of the SD applet. The test on line 55 will pass; prevproto becomes the string "http" and whatproto the string "ftp." The modifytext() method on line 36 is now executed. It gets the length of the prevproto string (which will be 4) and fetches the current document string on line 38 which will be the string "http://ftp.javasoft.com". It then peels off the substring that contains everything except the protocol name in line 39.

The local variable left will be the string "://ftp.javasoft.com." Finally, it glues the new protocol (stored in whatproto) onto the front of this substring and pushes that string out to the text field in line 40. The text now reads "ftp://ftp.javasoft.com." The reader is encouraged

Part
III

Ch
13

to perform this experiment and verify that the protocol part of the text field changes in lockstep with the value of the choice selected from the pop-up menu.

# Opening a New Document with the SD Applet

The action() method is also equipped to handle Button events. If the test on line 61 succeeds, this indicates that some button has been pressed, and the code on line 62 will be executed. Line 62 is a bit of defensive programming in which you test to make sure that it was the Open button that was pressed.

In our example, this test is superfluous because we have only one button. This line compactly converts the arg argument to a String and then uses its equals() method to test against the literal "Open". This test must pass in our case, so line 63 will be executed and the launchdoc() method invoked. When that method returns, the action() method returns true to indicate that the button press was handled (line 64). If this event was neither a pop-up selection nor a button press, then the action() method returns false on line 67.

The launchdoc() method is used to actually ask the browser to open a document URL. It first gets the text of the document name in line 43. It then checks to make sure that the string is long enough on line 45. If the string is just a bare protocol, such as "file://", this test fails and the method returns at that line. The extra 3 in the test accounts for the three characters ://.

You now have a string that represents an URL stored in the local variable doc, for example "http://www.microsoft.com." This needs to be converted to an URL instance because that is what you need for the subsequent request to the browser. This is executed in the try block beginning on line 46. A try block is required whenever a method invocation might generate a Java *exception*. Without being too specific, we can say that an exception results when you attempt to do something and it fails in a potentially unpleasant way. The URL constructor on line 47 is just such a statement.

How did we know this? Is it necessary to remember all the functions that can generate exceptions? Fortunately, the answer is *no*. If you had tried to write u = new URL(doc); without enclosing it in a try block, the Java compiler would thoughtfully tell you that URL constructors can generate exceptions and that you should try to catch the MalformedURLException. We have complied with this request and have enclosed the ominous statement in a try block, which always takes the following form:

```
try {
    ominous statement(s)
    } catch (SomeException e) {
        do something if an exception occurs
    }
```

In our case, if doc does not correspond to a valid URL, for any reason, the applet receives the MalformedURLException and the code on lines 49 and 50 (within the catch clause) is executed.

This code prints out a message indicating the reason for the failure on line 49 and then returns. Note that all exceptions have a `getMessage()` method that we have used to tell the user why the URL was malformed. An URL might be malformed because it was entered incorrectly, if it referred to a nonexistent server, or if it mentioned a document that the server did not want the user to see, among other reasons.

If the URL was well formed, then the `catch` clause will not be executed and the code will arrive at line 52. This is the critical statement that actually communicates with the browser. We use the `showDocument()` method of the `AppletContext ac` to ask it to open the URL `u` in a new window whose name is `"New Window."` This method call can still fail, of course, even if the URL `u` is well constructed. The reader should experiment with this applet by typing in various valid and invalid URLs, hitting the Open button, and observing the results.

## TROUBLESHOOTING

**I modified the code for SD.java to add a Clear button that clears out the contents of the TextField tf by using setText("").This works fine, but once Clear has been pressed, the popup Choice menu function no longer works. I get garbled output. Why?**

The `modifytext()` method is the workhorse that handles the event associated with changing the choice. When you clear the text field, you are wiping out the protocol part ("http" for example) of the document name. The applet does not know this, however, because it is assuming that you will only change the protocol by using the Choice item. Said another way, once you have cleared the text field, the protocol part of the document name is `null`, but the value of the instance variable, `whatproto`, is still set to the last protocol used.

If you are going to enable the user to change the protocol directly, then `modifytext()` has to become smarter. Use the following algorithm:

1. Read in the document string using `tf.getText()`.

2. Find the first colon character using the `String methodcharAt()`.

3. Set the local variable, `len`, to the length of the substring up to that colon.

4. Continue as written in Listing 13.4.

# An Image Viewer Applet

The real power of Java is its capability to rapidly display multiple images, giving the appearance of true animation on a Web page. You now have enough knowledge about Java threads and the AWT that you can present a simple image viewer applet in Java. This applet provides the first concrete example of something that is difficult to accomplish in JavaScript. This applet can also be used as a template for writing more-sophisticated applets that use Java threads. The code for the image viewer is shown in Listing 13.5.

### Listing 13.5   Displaying Multiple Images Is Easy Using Java Threads

```java
import java.applet.*;
import java.awt.*;
import java.net.*;

public class Simimg extends Applet implements Runnable {
    Image imgs[];                    // 6; the images themselves
    int imgidx = 0;                  // 7; image currently being displayed
    int nimg = 0;                    // 8; total number of images
    Thread mythread  = null;         // 9; animation thread

    public void init() {             // 10; get params and images
        MediaTracker mt;             // 11; track image loading
        String tmp;                  // 12; tmp string
        String imgloc;               // 13; location of images
        URL db;                      // 14; Applet's document BASE

        imgloc = getParameter("imgloc"); // 15; locate image dir
        if ( imgloc == null ) return;    // 16; no img dir—give up
        tmp = getParameter("nimg");      // 17; get # of images
        if ( tmp == null ) return;       // 18; no images—give up
        nimg = Integer.parseInt(tmp);    // 19; convert to int
        if ( nimg <= 0 ) return;   // 20; invalid # images—give up
        imgs = new Image[nimg];    // 21; alloc array for images
// create a mediatracker for the images
        mt = new MediaTracker(this);     // 22;
        db = getDocumentBase();          // 23; find Applet's doc BASE
// this loop starts loading all the images
        for(int i = 0, j = 1; i < nimg; i++, j++) {        // 24;
            imgs[i] = getImage(db, imgloc + j + ".gif");   // 25;
// tell the MediaTracker instance to track this image as ID 0
            mt.addImage(imgs[i], 0);                 // 26;
        }                          // 27; end of image loading loop
        try { mt.waitForID(0);     // 28; wait for all images
} catch (InterruptedException e) {
            nimg = 0;              // 30; if it failed set # images to 0
        }                          // 31; end of catch clause of try block
    }                              // 32; end of init method

    public void run() {            // 33; thread's run method
        Thread me;                 // 34; current thread

        me = Thread.currentThread();             // 35; get cur thread
        me.setPriority(Thread.NORM_PRIORITY-1); // 36; decrease pri
        while ( imgidx < nimg ) {      // 37; loop over images
            repaint();                 // 38; draw current image
            try {
                Thread.sleep(100);   // 40; wait a little while
                } catch (InterruptedException e) {}
            imgidx++;                  // 42; update index to next image
        }                              // 43; end of while loop
    }                              // 44; end of run method

    public void start() {
```

```
        if ( mythread == null ) {
            mythread = new Thread(this);
            mythread.start();
            }
        }

    public void stop() {
        if ( mythread != null ) {
            mythread.stop();
            mythread = null;
        }
    }

    public void paint( Graphics g ) {  // 57; draw current image
        if ( ( imgs != null ) && ( 0 <= imgidx ) && ( imgidx < nimg ) &&
            imgs[imgidx] != null ) { // 59; sanity check all values
            g.drawImage(imgs[imgidx], 0, 0, this); // 60; draw it!
        }
    }
```

## Initializing the Simple Image Viewer

The init() method for the Simimg applet performs two functions: it gets user parameters and it loads the images. This applet requires two PARAM tags to be specified, indicating where the images are to be found and how many there are. On line 15, the imgloc parameter is accessed; if it is not present, the init() method returns immediately (line 16). Lines 17 through 20 get the nimg parameter, convert it to an integer, and make sure that it is a positive number. If this parameter is not present or is not a valid positive number, the init() method returns.

Line 21 allocates an array just large enough to hold the indicated number of images. Line 22 initializes a MediaTracker instance. This instance will be used shortly to ensure that all images are loaded before the init() method completes. Line 23 uses the getDocumentBase() method from the java.applet package to discover the applet's document BASE, saving that value in the local URL variable db.

Statement 24 sets up a for loop to load all the images into the image array imgs. Note that two iteration variables, i and j, are used. This is because the imgs array is indexed from zero, but we are assuming that the names of the images will be something like IMG1.gif, IMG2.gif, and so forth. The i iteration variable marches through the array, while the j variable is used to build the names of the successive images.

The getImage() method is used on line 25 to launch the image-loading process. It takes two arguments: an URL specifying a server directory and a String giving the name of the file within that directory that is to be loaded. We are using the applet's document BASE as the first argument and we are constructing the successive image names by using the value of the imgloc parameter (with a numeric suffix) as the second argument. This particular version assumes that all the images are GIFs.

Part
III

Ch
13

**N O T E**  At present, the `getImage()` method only understands the GIF and JPEG image formats. Other formats may be added in the future. ▧

The `getImage()` method is slightly deceptive in that it does not guarantee that the image is actually received when the method returns. All it does is begin to load the image. This is the purpose of statement 26. We add the image being loaded to the `MediaTracker` instance `mt`, which indicates that we are going to subsequently watch the loading process, presumably to ensure that it is done.

The `addImage()` method takes two arguments: an `Image` instance and an integer ID. The ID is used to group images into pools. We could, for example, track the first half of the images as `ID 0` and the second half as `ID 1`. In this way, we could display the completely loaded `ID 0` images while the `ID 1` images were still being loaded.

This applet takes a brute force approach. All images are declared to have `ID 0`. On line 28, we actually wait for all the `ID 0` images, which are, in fact, all the images, to be fully loaded. Because this method can generate an `InterruptedException`, it must be executed within a `try` block, as we have seen in the `SD` applet. If this exception occurs, then we set the number of images `nimg` to `0`, ensuring that none will be displayed.

The `Simimg` applet, unlike the `SD` applet, requires `PARAM` tags to properly function. A sample HTML file that uses this applet is shown in Listing 13.6. Note that this particular HTML file indicates that we will load 16 images, that they will be located in the subdirectory "images" of the document's base directory, and that they will have the prefix "T." This means that the applet will attempt to load 16 images named images\T1.gif, images\T2.gif,…images\T16.gif. It is also worth noting that this HTML implicitly assumes that all the images will fit in a drawing area that is 300×150.

**Listing 13.6  HTML for the *Simimg* Applet**

```
<HTML>
<HEAD>
<TITLE>A Simple Image Player</TITLE>
</HEAD>
<BODY>
<HR>
<APPLET CODE="Simimg.class" WIDTH=300 HEIGHT=150>
<PARAM NAME="imgloc" VALUE="images\T">
<PARAM NAME="nimg" VALUE="16">
</APPLET>
<HR>
The <A HREF="Simimg.java">source</A>.
</BODY>
</HTML>
```

## Running the Simple Image Applet

The formal structure of this applet is exactly the same as previously described in the discussion of threads. The start() and stop() methods are each responsible for creating the "animation" thread and for stopping it, respectively. The actual work is done by the run() method and indirectly by the paint() method.

The run method first discovers the identity of its own thread by invoking the static method currentThread() of the Thread class on line 35. It then lowers its own priority to be just slightly less than the default priority for threads (line 36). This makes sense if you think of threads in terms of a standard multitasking operating system. Higher priority tasks get more of the real CPU and generally execute more frequently. The same model applies to Java threads. By declaring itself less important, it is implicitly declaring that the drawing activity is more important.

Line 37 is the main image loop. As long as the instance variable imgidx is less than the total number of images, nimg, the loop will continue. Each pass through the loop issues a call to repaint(), which results in the paint() method being executed (line 38). Each pass through the loop also puts the animation thread to sleep for 100 microseconds (line 40). This is another way to give the drawing activity even more time and to ensure that it is actually executed.

One of the side effects of using the static sleep() method of the Thread class is to ensure that other threads that are waiting to run get a chance to do so. This method also can generate an exception, which we dutifully ignore. Finally, at the end of the loop, we update imgidx to process the next image.

The paint() method, which begins on line 57, is a model of defensive programming. It checks to make sure that the imgs array is not null, that imgidx is neither too small nor too large, and that the actual image in the imgs array is not null. If all these tests pass, then it uses the drawImage() method of the Graphics instance, g, to actually draw the image (line 60). Figure 13.3 shows the result after 16 images, which depict a ladybug crawling across the screen. The reader is encouraged to experiment with this applet using his own images.

Part

III

Ch

13

**FIG. 13.3**

Java simplifies the tasks of image manipulation and animation.

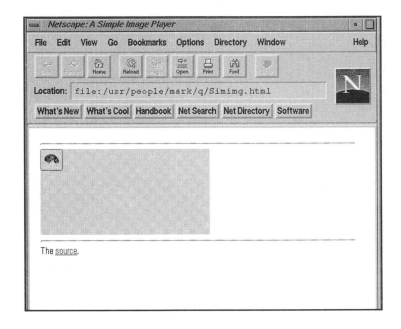

# CHAPTER 14

# LiveConnect and JavaScript

Individually, Java, JavaScript, and Navigator plug-ins are powerful tools that enable developers to field network-centric solutions. Each of these tools has its own strengths and weaknesses. Netscape's LiveConnect technology enables you to put these tools together in a single, integrated application.

With LiveConnect, Netscape gives sophisticated end-users a way to control complex components (plug-ins and Java applets) from a relatively simple language—JavaScript, bringing component architecture to the Web. ◼

**Find out why "small, sharp tools" that can be assembled into applications are more powerful than monolithic code**

In the "UNIX-style" versus "Microsoft-style" design war, history favors the little guy.

**Learn how to pass parameters to a plug-in**

Many applications don't even require JavaScript; you can configure a plug-in from the <EMBED> tag.

**Discover why LiveConnect is much more than a multimedia control**

LiveConnect is a key Netscape technology that promises to make plug-ins cost-effective (especially on intranets).

**Find out how Java classes talk to JavaScript**

Java is the central figure in LiveConnect, enabling client-side JavaScript to communicate with plug-ins.

**See how Java classes talk to plug-ins**

By completing the other side of the circuit, your Web pages can fully integrate Java, JavaScript, and plug-ins.

# Communicating Through LiveConnect

Although only experienced programmers are writing plug-ins and Java applets, almost anyone can learn to write JavaScript or HTML. If you're a C or C++ programmer, you can give the user a certain amount of control over your plug-in by passing parameters through the <EMBED> tag. (You can do the same thing with Java applets, using parameters to the <APPLET> tag.) If the HTML author writes

```
<EMBED SRC="http://www.somemachine.com/myFile.tst" HEIGHT=100 WIDTH=100
AUTOSTART=True LOOP=False AUTOSCALE=Often>
```

then a plug-in that handles the MIME media type that is associated with the ".tst" data stream can read the parameters HEIGHT, WIDTH, AUTOSTART, LOOP, and AUTOSCALE.

What it *does* with these parameters is, of course, determined by the programmer.

## What Is LiveConnect?

LiveConnect, introduced as part of Navigator 3.0, integrates applets that are written in the platform-independent language Java (from Sun Microsystems) with Netscape's JavaScript and with plug-ins. Figure 14.1 illustrates the communications paths between Java, JavaScript, and the plug-in.

**FIG. 14.1**
LiveConnect is
Netscape's approach
to integrating all of the
client-based program-
ming techniques.

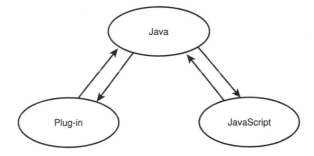

Note that LiveConnect doesn't allow a plug-in to communicate directly with a script written in JavaScript. All communications go through Java. This design isn't a problem, however, as you will read in a moment.

## A First Taste of LiveConnect

Suppose you have a plug-in that handles Windows AVI movies. Such a plug-in might be named npAVI. To add a movie to one of your pages, you might write

```
<EMBED SRC=myavi.avi NAME="myEmbed" WIDTH=320 HEIGHT=200>
```

When a user loads the page, Netscape finds the embedded avi file and looks for a plug-in to handle that type of movie. It loads npAVI and the movie begins playing.

If you'd like more control, you might want to communicate with the plug-in from JavaScript:

```
<FORM>
<INPUT TYPE="Button" onClick="document.myEmbed.Start();" value="Start">
<INPUT TYPE="Button" onClick="document.myEmbed.Stop(); value="Stop">
</FORM>
```

When the user clicks the Start button, JavaScript calls the Start() method of a Java class that is associated with the plug-in. The Java class passes the "Start" message through to the plug-in, and the movie starts playing. (The Stop button works the same way.)

Not only does LiveConnect enable you to talk to plug-ins and Java applets from JavaScript, but you can also access JavaScript objects from Java and plug-ins. A Java programmer can write an init function like that shown in Listing 14.1.

---

**Listing 14.1   Initialize the Window and Read Out JavaScript Objects**

```
public void init() {
  win = JSObject.getWindow(this);
  JSObject doc = (JSObject) win.getMember("document");
  JSObject myForm = (JSObject) doc.getMember("aForm");
  JSObject check = (JSObject) myForm.getMember("aCheckbox");
  Boolean isChecked = (Boolean) check.getMember("checked");
  }
```

---

Once the applet has a handle to the JavaScript window, the programmer can use such constructs as getMember to descend through the hierarchy of the document and its components.

The Java programmer can also call JavaScript methods. Once the Java applet has a handle to the JavaScript window, for example, the programmer can write:

```
public boolean mouseUp(Event e, int x, int y) {
  win.eval("alert(\"Hello world!\");");
  return true;
}
```

Java detects the mouseUp event in the applet's window and calls JavaScript's built-in method, alert().

> **N O T E**   In order for a plug-in or applet to take control of the JavaScript on your page, you must give permission by including the keyword MAYSCRIPT in the <EMBED> or <APPLET> tag. ■

In order to understand LiveConnect, you need to be familiar with its three components—Java applets, plug-ins, and JavaScript. You already know a great deal about JavaScript. The next section introduces plug-in technology. The following section introduces Java and applets. This chapter concludes with a detailed look at one of the most successful plug-ins, Shockwave, and how it integrates into a LiveConnect page.

Part
III

Ch
14

# What Are Plug-Ins?

Netscape Navigator is a well-designed, highly functional product. Netscape's innovations have catapulted the company to its position as leader of the Web browser vendors. Navigator provides native support for a variety of graphics formats as well as the Hypertext Markup Language (HTML), the language of Web pages.

Netscape, however, recognizes that the needs of the Web community change faster and grow wider than it can support in Navigator. Starting with version 1 of the product, Netscape provides ways to extend Navigator with helper applications, which support data formats beyond built-in graphics and HTML.

Starting in Netscape Navigator version 2, Navigator supports plug-ins, another way to extend the range of data types that can be presented on or with a Web page.

## Helper Applications

When a Netscape Navigator user attempts to open a document that Navigator does not recognize, the dialog box shown in Figure 14.2 appears. This dialog box allows the user to select an external viewer application through the "Pick App..." button, or to save the file.

**FIG. 14.2**

A Navigator user attempts to open an unrecognized file type.

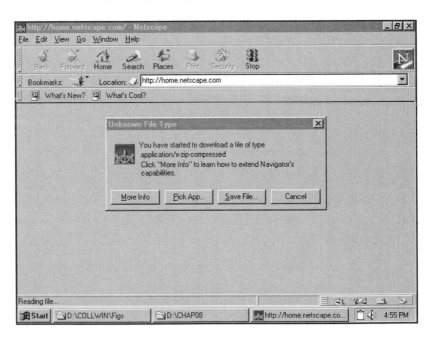

External viewers, also known as helper applications, allow the Web user to see a variety of data types that are not built into Netscape Navigator or other popular browsers. Figure 14.3, for example, shows a graphic stored in Computer Graphics Metafile (CGM) format—a format popular with the Computer-Aided Design (CAD) community. This image is viewed from Navigator by using FIGleaf, a plug-in from Carberry Technology.

**FIG. 14.3**
CGM graphics can be viewed through helper applications or plug-ins.

The downside of helper applications is that they are, indeed, applications. To view a file with a helper application, the user's machine must start an entirely new program, which means the following:

- They have to wait while the new program loads.
- They may run out of memory and not be able to launch the new program.
- If the helper application launches, they see the document in its own window, out of context from the Web document.
- No interaction exists between the Web document and the external file—for example, if the external file is a movie similar to that shown in Figure 14.4, no provision is available to allow the user to use buttons on the Web page to control the movie viewer.

## MIME Types

To understand helper applications and plug-ins, you must first understand *MIME* types. *Multimedia Internet Mail Extensions*, or MIME, was developed to enable users to exchange files by e-mail. Although the Web doesn't use the full MIME standard, it is convenient to use media types (formerly known as MIME types) to tell a Web browser how the file is formatted.

MIME is described in detail in Request for Comments (RFC) 1590, which updates the registration process originally described in RFC 1521. Although MIME was originally intended for use in e-mail systems (and RFC 1521 was written with this application in mind), today's user encounters MIME in a variety of multimedia settings.

Part
III

Ch
14

**FIG. 14.4**
This Macintosh QuickTime movie viewer has its own set of controls—the user cannot run it from the Web page.

**N O T E** You can obtain RFCs from any IETF mirror site. For example, **ftp://ds.internic.net/rfc/** serves the East Coast of the U.S. (though it is accessible from anywhere). ■

 For more information on MIME, check out the Frequently Asked Questions list at **ftp://ftp.uu.net/ usenet/news.answers/mail/mime-faq** or **http://www.cis.ohio-state.edu/text/faq/usenet/mail/ mime-faq/top.html**.

MIME is designed to have a limited number of top-level types, such as "application," "text," and "video," which can be extended by subtypes. Table 14.1 shows some typical MIME-compliant media types.

**Table 14.1   MIME Types Consist of a Type and a Subtype**

| Type | Subtype | Meaning |
|------|---------|---------|
| application | msword | Format for Microsoft Word documents |
| application | rtf | The "Rich Text Format" for word processors |
| application | octet-stream | A "catchall" type for a collection of bytes |
| application | zip | The compressed-file format for PKZIP and its kin |
| application | pdf | Adobe's Portable Document Format |
| audio | aiff | An audio interchange format developed by Apple Computer |
| audio | midi | A music format based on instruments |

| Type | Subtype | Meaning |
|------|---------|---------|
| audio | wav | The RIFF WAVE sound format developed by Microsoft and IBM |
| image | cgm | Computer Graphics Metafile image format |
| image | gif | Graphics Interchange Format image format |
| image | jpeg | File interchange format of the Joint Photographic Experts Group |
| text | plain | ASCII text |
| text | html | The Hypertext Markup Language |
| video | mpeg | Video format for the Motion Picture Experts Group |
| video | quicktime | Format developed by Apple Computer |

When a Web browser requests a document from a server, the server sends several header lines before it sends the document. One header is `Content-type`. This header line contains the MIME type and subtype, separated by a slash. Therefore, most Web pages are preceded by the following line:

```
Content-type: text/html
```

## How Web Servers Select a Media Type

Most Web servers have a file that associates file extensions with MIME types. On NCSA, Apache, and similar servers, the file is named mime.types. A typical line in mime.types says the following:

```
text/html html
```

This line tells the server that if the file has an extension of `.html`, the server should send `text/html` in the `Content-type` header.

Suppose that you wanted to serve Microsoft Word documents in their proprietary format directly from your Web server. If your MS Word documents use the file extension .doc and they are the only documents with that extension, you can add the following to mime.types:

```
application/msword    doc
```

Equivalently, you could put the following line into the configuration file srm.conf:

```
AddType    application/msword    doc
```

 **TIP** After changing a configuration file such as mime.types or srm.conf, you need to either restart your server or explicitly tell the server to reread the configuration files. In UNIX, you can tell the server to reread the configuration files by sending the following SIGHUP signal:

```
kill -SIGHUP processID
```

Here, *processID* is the process number of the parent server *daemon*.

Part
III

Ch
14

**N O T E** Under UNIX, many processes are detached from any terminal and run in the background
waiting for user requests. These processes are known as *daemons*. A typical UNIX machine
being used as a Web server may have several instances of the `httpd` daemon (the Web server
software) running, as well as an `ftp` dameon, a `telnet` daemon, and various service daemons such
as `timed` and `whois`. By convention, many daemon names end in the character 'd.' ▓

## How Web Browsers Handle Media Types

Start Netscape Navigator and go to Edit, Preferences, General Preferences. From this screen,
choose the Helpers tab. The result should resemble the screen shown in Figure 14.5.

**FIG. 14.5**
Navigator enables the
user to associate
applications with media
types.

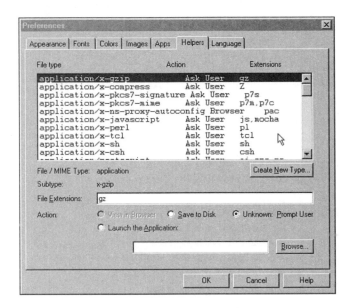

**N O T E** If Navigator recognizes the selected media type, it uses the common name (such as
CompuServe Image Format for image/gif). Some formats, such as GIF and JPEG, are
handled internally by Navigator. Others are handled by helper applications or plug-ins. ▓

Select a media type that is handled by a helper application and your selection will be displayed
in the lower half of the screen (refer to Figure 14.5). Note that you can specify the MIME-
compliant media type and subtype as well as a file extension.

**N O T E** Recall that plug-ins, by definition, are platform-specific. The example in this chapter shows
a Windows 95 plug-in, InterCAP InLine. InterCAP InLine was developed by InterCAP
Graphics Systems, Inc. (**inline@intercap.com**) for Windows NT and Windows 95 platforms. ▓

To add a new media type to the list that Navigator recognizes, return to the Helpers tab and
click the Create New Type button. Fill in the fields and click OK.

**N O T E**    The Macintosh operating system does not use file extensions to associate documents with applications. Instead, each file has two four-character fields called "Creator" and "Type." Most applications can handle more than one file type. Microsoft Word recognizes 18 file types.

Mac users can use the New... dialog box in the Helpers tab to specify which file type to associate with the media type. For example, "MSWD" is the "Creator" of a native MS Word document. "W6BN" is the type for Word 6.0.  ■

## Extending the Functionality of Netscape with Plug-Ins

In Navigator 2.0, Netscape introduced inline plug-ins as an alternative to helper applications. Plug-ins are platform-specific pieces of code that display their contents inside the Navigator window, in much the same way as the HTML <IMG> tag displays an image "inline" rather than in a separate window. This technology affords the following features:

- Plug-ins are small code resources, not full applications. They are run in the Navigator process. Consequently, they cost less to develop, take up less disk space, and load more quickly than full applications.

- Because plug-ins share address space with the Netscape application, they can run in the Navigator window. The HTML coder can embed references to the data directly in the HTML file, and the plug-in will open inline in the Navigator window. The coder can still get a full window if he or she chooses. There is also a provision to run plug-ins in the background when no graphical interaction is required, such as for an audio application.

- The plug-in is activated as soon as the data begins to flow from the server. The programmer has the option of waiting for the data to be stored as a file, but the recommended programming technique is to present the data as it arrives.

In mid-1996, Netscape released Navigator 3.0, which supports additional plug-in capabilities. In particular, it includes a technology Netscape calls LiveConnect, which integrates plug-ins with client-side JavaScript and Java.

The appeal of LiveConnect is that it gives non-programmers the ability to control Java and plug-in resources from JavaScript. JavaScript is an approachable language, and many programs have been written in JavaScript by people who do not consider themselves professional programmers.

Java is a powerful object-oriented language. Java programs can be compiled into *applets* and stored on the server. When the browser requests a page that references these applets, the applets are downloaded and run on the browser. For more information about Java, see Chapter 12, "A Java Tutorial," and Chapter 13, "Advanced Applets."

Although plug-ins are written in the native code of the client platform (OS/2, Windows, Macintosh, or a specific version of UNIX), Java is platform-independent. A Java applet can run on any platform that supports the Netscape Navigator browser.

With LiveConnect, a JavaScript programmer can include Java applets, as well as contents that require a plug-in on a Web page, and can issue calls to both entities to control them or to send them information. Plug-ins and applets can also call JavaScript functions to determine how they

Part
III

Ch
14

should proceed. This level of integration means that applets and plug-ins, which are usually written by skilled programmers, become a code resource for use by page designers, extending the reach of page designers who do not necessarily have the ability to write sophisticated programs.

> **N O T E** If you *are* a programmer, you may want to consider developing your own plug-in. You can learn how to write plug-ins in *Netscape Plug-Ins Developer's Kit* (Que, 1996). Chapter 18 of that book tells you how to integrate your plug-ins using LiveConnect. ■

> **N O T E** One example of an advanced plug-in is the Tool Command Language/Tool Kit (Tcl/Tk) plug-in, available from Sun Microsystems at **http://www.sun.com/960710/feature1/ index.html**. If your users have this plug-in, you can add scripts in the popular Tcl language directly to your Web page. For more information about the Tcl/Tk language, see **http://www.cis.ohio-state.edu/ hypertext/faq/usenet/tcl-faq/top.html**.
>
> To get started writing Tcl, visit Sun's site at **http://www.sunlabs.com/research/tcl/**. Sun has adopted Tcl as its prototyping language—Dr. John Ousterhout, developer of Tcl and a Sun Distinguished Engineer, says, "Tcl/Tk lets software developers get the job done ten times faster than with toolkits based on C or C++." ■

# JavaScript and Java Applets

Recall that LiveConnect doesn't give a JavaScript programmer direct access to the plug-in, or vice versa. If you're comfortable with C++ and object technology, you can write a plug-in, and then write a proxy class in Java that sits between your plug-in and JavaScript, giving a JavaScript programmer access to your plug-in.

You can download the latest version of the JDK, along with the Netscape modifications, as part of the Netscape Plug-ins SDK, at **http:// home.netscape.com/eng/mozilla/3.0/handbook/plugins/index.html**. The Netscape-specific packages are at **http:// home.netscape.com/eng/mozilla/3.0/handbook/plugins/wr3.htm**.

You can also use commercial packages, such as Symantec's Visual Café or Natural Intelligence's Roaster, but you'll need the classes from Netscape's version of the Kit. You'll also need Netscape's special version of the javah utility (also part of the Kit).

## Using LiveConnect to Talk to JavaScript

The first step in connecting a script in JavaScript to a plug-in is to connect JavaScript to Java. The plug-in programmer will supply a Java class that does its work by calling the plug-in. From the point of view of JavaScript, this Java class serves as a proxy for the plug-in.

**Calling JavaScript from Java**    In order for a Java class to talk to JavaScript, the Java programmer must import the Netscape javascript package in the Java class, as follows:

```
import netscape.javascript.*
```

The `netscape.javascript` package, described in a subsequent section of this chapter, includes two important classes—`JSObject`, which represents the JavaScript object, and `JSException`, which is raised to pass JavaScript errors back to your Java class.

For a Java class to call JavaScript, the HTML author must explicitly set the `MAYSCRIPT` attribute in the `APPLET` tag. For example:

```
<APPLET NAME="hello" CODE="hello.class" WIDTH=100 HEIGHT=100 MAYSCRIPT>
```

Note that in this example, a name was assigned to the applet. You will use the name when you begin talking to the applet from JavaScript.

---

**CAUTION**

If a Java applet attempts to run a page's JavaScript and the HTML author hasn't set `MAYSCRIPT`, Navigator raises an exception. You, the Java programmer, should catch this exception and put up an appropriate message to the user.

One good way to put up an error message is to use the *Java console* that is defined by Netscape. From inside Java, write the following:

```
System.out.println("Error: Applet unable to access JavaScript.
  Set the applet's MAYSCRIPT attribute and try again.");
```

---

To access JavaScript, your Java class must get a handle to the Navigator window, as shown in Figure 14.6. Your Java class's `init()` member is a good place to do this:

```
JSObject win;
public void init()
{
  win = JSObject.getWindow(this);
}
```

If the HTML page has a form named `theForm`, which, in turn, has a check box named `theCheckbox`, you can access the status of this check box by following the membership hierarchy from the form to the check box, as shown in Listing 14.2.

---

**Listing 14.2    Use Java to Read the JavaScript Check Box**

```
JSObject win;
public void init()
{
  win = JSObject.getWindow(this);
  JSObject doc = (JSObject) win.getMember("document");
  JSObject theForm = (JSObject) doc.getMember("theForm");
  JSObject check = (JSObject) myForm.getMember("theCheckBox");
  Boolean isChecked = (Boolean) check.getMember("checked");
}
```

Part
III

Ch

14

**FIG. 14.6**

Java gets a pointer to the JavaScript document in order to access its members.

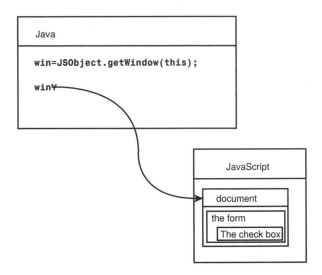

Just as `getMember()` gives you access to the components of the JavaScript form, `call()` and `eval()` give you access to the JavaScript methods. You can write the code shown in Listing 14.3.

**Listing 14.3   You Have Access to JavaScript Methods from Java**

```
public void init()
{
  win = JSObject.getWindow(this);
}
public boolean mouseUp(Event e, int x, int y)
{
  win.eval("alert(\"Hello, world!\");");
  return true;
}
```

Or, equivalently, you can write the code in Listing 14.4.

**Listing 14.4   Get to JavaScript Methods Through *call()* as well as *eval()***

```
public void init()
{
  win = JSObject.getWindow(this);
}
public boolean mouseUp(Event e, int x, int y)
{
  win.call("alert(\"Hello, world!\");");
  return true;
}
```

**Calling Java Methods from JavaScript**   You can communicate in the opposite direction, from JavaScript *to* the applet, by making sure that the applet has a name. Figure 14.7 illustrates this mechanism.

**FIG. 14.7**
The HTML author assigns the applet a name so that JavaScript can talk to it.

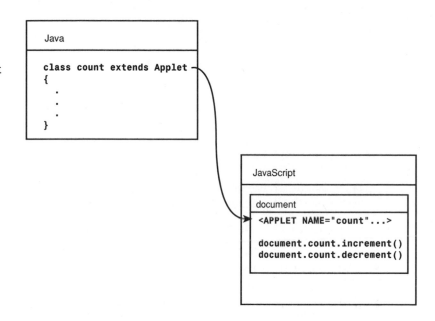

Suppose that you have a Java class like count, shown in Listing 14.5.

---

**Listing 14.5    A Simple Java Class that Accepts Two Commands**

```
import java.applet.*;
import java.awt.*;
public class count extends Applet
{
  int i;
  public void init()
  {
    i = 0;
  }
  public void paint (Graphics g)
  {
    g.drawString("The count is" + i, 10, 50);
  }
  public void increment()
  {
    i++;
    repaint();
  }
  public void decrement()
  {
```

Part
III

Ch

14

*continues*

**Listing 14.5    Continued**

```
    i—;
    repaint();
  }
}
```

You can install count on your Web page, as is shown in Listing 14.6.

**Listing 14.6    A Web Page with a Controllable Applet**

```
<HTML>
<HEAD>
<TITLE>Test count/TITLE>
</HEAD>
<BODY>
<H1>Test the Count Applet</H1>
<APPLET NAME="count" CODE="count.class" WIDTH=100, HEIGHT=100></APPLET>
<FORM>
<INPUT TYPE="Button" VALUE="Increment" NAME="IncrementButton"
➥onClick="document.count.increment()">
<INPUT TYPE="Button" VALUE="Decrement" NAME="DecrementButton"
➥onClick="document.count.decrement()">
</FORM>
</BODY>
</HTML>
```

Now that you know how Java and JavaScript can talk, you just have to get the plug-in to talk to Java.

## Talking to the Plug-In

When you add plug-ins to an HTML page, JavaScript puts them into an array named embeds. For example, if the following is the first <EMBED> tag on your page, JavaScript shows the associated plug-in in document.embeds[0]:

```
<EMBED SRC="http://www.somemachine.com/myFile.tst HEIGHT=100 WIDTH=100>
```

From JavaScript, you can access document.embeds.length to find out how many plug-ins are on the page.

> **N O T E**   Because full-page plug-ins are, by definition, on a page with no JavaScript (and no HTML), it only makes sense to talk about controlling embedded plug-ins, not full-page plug-ins. ▨

**T I P**   To increase readability, give your plug-ins names instead of referring to them as elements of the embeds array.

To make a plug-in visible from inside Java, your Java class must use `netscape.plugin.Plugin`. Netscape provides a file `java_40` with Netscape 4.0. This file contains three Java packages— `java`, `sun`, and `netscape`—with six major components:

- `java`
- `sun`
- `netscape.applet`
- `netscape.net`
- `netscape.javascript`
- `netscape.plugin`

The `java` and `sun` packages are replacements for packages of the same name in the Sun 1.0.2 Java Development Kit (JDK). They include security enhancements that are necessary for LiveConnect. Netscape and Sun are working together to ensure that these new packages are included in a future release of the Sun JDK.

`netscape.applet` is Netscape's replacement for `sun.applet`. Similarly, `netscape.net` replaces `sun.net`.

`netscape.javascript` implements `JSObject` and `JSException`, which are described previously in this chapter.

`netscape.plugin` implements the `Plugin` interface. As a Java programmer, you use methods of the `Plugin` interface to communicate with the plug-in.

**N O T E** To use the Netscape-supplied packages with the JDK compiler, add the path of the `java_40` and `classes.zip` to the compiler's `classpath`. You can either specify a `CLASSPATH` environment variable or use the `-classpath` command line option when you run `javac`. ▪

---

 **T I P** As a plug-in programmer, you have handy a C++ development environment such as Microsoft Visual C++. Don't waste time running `javac` from the command line. Put your plug-in's Java proxy class in the makefile and automatically call `javac` each time your plug-in is rebuilt. If you use Visual C++, just add the `javac` command line (with the `-classpath` option) to the Custom Build settings.

While setting up the makefile, add the call to `javah` described in the following section. It will save you time later.

---

**Calling Java Methods from the Plug-In**   The plug-in talks to Java through Netscape's Java Runtime Interface. Figure 14.8 illustrates the JRI.

Netscape has defined the Java Runtime Interface to allow native code (such as a plug-in) to call Java methods. The full specification of the Java Runtime Interface is available online (**http:// home.netscape.com/eng/jri/**). Netscape also supplies a new version of javah, named the JRI (Java Runtime Interface) version, which writes a C/C++ header file from a Java class.

To control the count class, previously described from your plug-in, start by typing (or including in the makefile) the following:

```
javah -jri -classpath pathTojava_40Andclasses.zip count
```

**FIG. 14.8**

The plug-in connects to the Java Runtime Interface, which handles communications with Java.

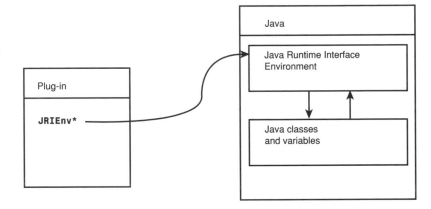

The result of running javah is a header file for class count. Recall that count has one public data member, are produced by i. In-line accessory functions are produced by javah.

```
jint i(JRIEnv* env);
```

and

```
void i(JRI* env, jint);
```

18 fig 07

to get and set this data member.

Note that javah has transformed the Java int into a variable of type jint. Table 14.2 shows the JRI definitions of the Java primitive types. Netscape's version of javah transforms Java variables into C/C++ variables with a new Java-specific type.

**Table 14.2   JRI Definitions of Java Primitive Types**

| Java Type | C/C++ Type | Size |
| --- | --- | --- |
| boolean | jbool | 1 byte |
| byte | jbyte | 1 byte |
| char | jchar | 2 bytes |
| short | jshort | 2 bytes |
| int | jint | 4 bytes |
| long | jlong | 8 bytes |
| float | jfloat | 4 bytes |
| double | jdouble | 8 bytes |

These sizes are defined through a series of `#ifdefs` in the file jri_md.h, which is included in the header file jri.h. Make sure that your compiler sets up the proper preprocessor symbols for your target machine, so your code gets the right size types.

> **CAUTION**
>
> Make sure that you use the JRI types described in Table 14.2 when talking to Java methods. If you use the compiler's types (in other words, `int`), you run the risk of a size mismatch when you move to a new compiler or a new platform.

> **CAUTION**
>
> `javah` doesn't do a very good job of protecting the privacy of data members in Java classes. You will be able to access private members from inside your plug-in. Avoid this temptation and use accessory methods and other public methods exclusively.
>
> By restricting yourself to public methods, your plug-in is less likely to need maintenance when the implementation of the Java class changes.

To call the `increment()` method of the Java class `count`, just write the following:

`count->increment(env);`

Here, env is the result of the function `NPN_GetJavaEnv()`, which has the following specification:

`JavaEnv* NPN_GetJavaEnv(void);`

Typically, you call `NPN_GetJavaEnv()` once, in `NPP_Initialize()`.

 Netscape starts the Java Runtime Interpreter when your plug-in first calls `NPN_GetJavaEnv()`. This first call can impose a delay on your plug-in. If you're sure that your plug-in needs to call Java, call `NPN_GetJavaEnv()` in `NPP_Initialize()` and get it out of the way. The user expects to wait a few seconds when he or she accesses the plug-in content, anyway.

 The pointer to the Java environment is thread-specific. If you call it in `NPP_Initialize()`, you can use it in any instance, but if you spawn a new thread, you need to call `NPN_GetJavaEnv()` for this thread and reserve the new `JavaEnv` pointer for use in this thread only.

Recall that most object-oriented languages, including both C++ and Java, support overloaded methods. That is, two or more methods can have the same name as long as they take different parameter types. (Sets of parameters are called *signatures*.) In C++, the compiler performs *name mangling* to make sure that the internal names are unique. Netscape's javah appends an index to all but the first occurrence of a name. If you have three functions named myFunc, javah produces myFunc, myFunc_1, and myFunc_2. To find out which name to call for which signature, just check the header file output by javah. Without the use of an index on all but one of the

Part
III

Ch

14

names, the function name myFunc would be ambiguous. For this reason, the index is sometimes known as a "disambiguating index."

**TIP**   If you have overloaded methods, declare first the one you plan to use most frequently from your plug-in. In this way, the declared version of the method will not have an index.

Similarly, if you have a Java-implemented version of a method and a native (such as C or C++) version of the same method, put the declaration of the native method first. In this way, you don't have to worry about index names when you write the native implementation.

**TIP**   Because javah uses the underscore followed by a number to disambiguate overloaded methods, it performs name-mangling on Java methods that contain an underscore in their name. Save yourself a headache—don't use underscores in Java method names.

**Calling the Plug-In from Java Methods**   You can define *native methods* in Java that are implemented in C or C++. These methods give your Java applet access to low-level library routines in the operating system and also can be more efficient than Java alone. Figure 14.9 illustrates a Java class calling its native method.

**FIG. 14.9**
Java invokes a native method, allowing access to the operating system.

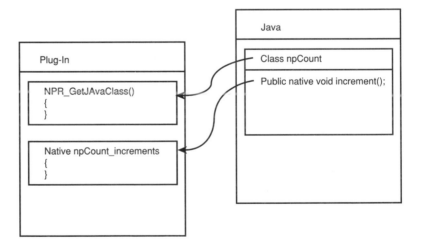

Just as calls to Java by the plug-in are made through the C or C++ header files produced by javah, Java methods call the plug-in by calling a Java peer of the plug-in. This peer is of type netscape.plugin.Plugin.

If you instantiate a Java object of type Plugin, your Java method will be able to refer to the plug-in, but will not be able to call any plug-in-specific methods. If you derive a new Java class from Plugin, you can define native methods in the derived class that corresponds to these plug-in methods you want to expose to Java.

Suppose that you want to write a plug-in that does the same work as count, the Java class shown previously. The new plug-in will be named npCount. For convenience, call the Java peer class npCount as well. Besides the increment() and decrement() methods defined for count, npCount has a new method, post(), which calls NPN_PostURL() and sends the current count back to a CGI script or LiveWire application on the Web site. The file shown in Listing 14.7 implements npCount.

### Listing 14.7  A Java Peer Class for the *npCount* Plug-In

```
import netscape.plugin.Plugin;
class npCount extends Plugin
{
  public native void increment();
  public native void decrement();
  public native boolean post();
}
```

Compile npCount.java with javac and run the JRI version of javah on it, as follows:

```
javah -jri -classpath pathTonpcount npCount
javah -jri -stubs -classpath pathTonpcount npCount
```

The second call to javah builds C stubs for the native methods. These stubs include a special initializer for each Java class. The initializer sets up the interface between Java and your plug-in. Be sure to call the initializer before you use the class! (If you have other Java classes with native methods outside of your plug-in, call their initializers, too.)

For npCount, the initializer is specified by the following line:

```
extern java_lang_Class* init_npCount(JRIEnv* env);
```

You can add initialization code to this init_ method. You can add balancing code to the Java peer's destroy() method. This method is called just before NPP_Destroy() is called on the instance. You also can check (from Java) to see if the native instance is still active by calling isActive(), which returns a boolean.

For Navigator to set up your Java peer class, it calls your plug-in's implementation of NPP_GetJavaClass(), which is specified as follows:

```
jref NPP_GetJavaClass(void);
```

For npCount, a reasonable implementation of NPP_GetJavaClass() is:

```
jref NPP_GetJavaClass()
{
  return init_npCount(NPN_GetJavaEnv());
}
```

If your plug-in uses other Java classes that have native methods, call their initializers before you return to register their native methods with the JRI.

Make sure that you add the stub file (here, npCount.c) into your project so that it will be compiled and linked into the plug-in.

**TIP** You should always include an implementation of `NPP_GetJavaClass()` in your plug-in, even if you don't plan to use it to connect to Java. Just write a stub implementation that returns NULL.

Follow the `javah` naming conventions (rather than C++ name mangling) when implementing the native methods. Therefore, you might write the code shown in Listing 14.8.

### Listing 14.8   A Native Implementation of *npCount*

```
jbool native_npCount_post(
  JRIEnv* env,
  npCount* self,
  JRIMethodThunk* methodThunk,
  other parameters…);
```

You can use the `self` parameter to access any other class members.

The *other parameters* in the last line are the parameters that you declared for this method in your Java class. The `env` parameter is supplied by the runtime in case you need to make calls back to Java.

From the `native` method, you can access the plug-in instance by writing the following:

```
NPP npp = (NPP)self->getPeer(env);
```

From the plug-in, you can access the Java peer by calling `NPN_GetJavaPeer()`. The prototype of that function is:

```
jref NPN_GetJavaPeer(NPP instance);
```

If your plug-in is embedded on a page with JavaScript, the HTML author can activate the plug-in by calling it through the `embeds` interface. The first time JavaScript needs the Java `peer` object, Navigator makes an internal call to `NPN_GetJavaPeer()`, which instantiates the Java `peer` object. As part of `NPN_GetJavaPeer()`, Navigator calls the `init` method.

JavaScript then actually communicates to the Java `peer` object, which does its work through the native methods.

## Putting It All Together

Figure 14.10 illustrates the flow of control from JavaScript through `npCount` and back again.

When the plug-in is loaded, it reads the current count from the Net—through `NPP_Write()`—and writes it to the window—through `NPP_SetWindow()`. When Navigator calls `NPP_GetJavaClass()`, `npCount` returns its `peer` object, which is made available to JavaScript through `embeds` (or by an explicit name in the `<EMBED>` tag). When the user clicks a button, Navigator calls the method on the Java `peer` object pointed to by `embeds[0]` (or the named plug-in). If the method is `add` or `decrease`, the `peer` object talks to JavaScript to read the contents of the `MoveBy` field. All the remaining work of the Java class is done back in the plug-in.

The plug-in runs the native method and calls `InvalidateRect()` to trigger an update of its window.

**FIG. 14.10**
The `npCount` plug-in communicates both to and from JavaScript.

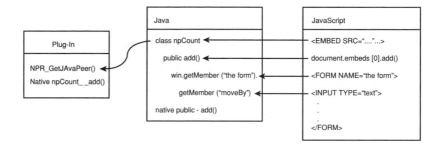

# Controlling Shockwave

Shockwave, from Macromedia, is an advanced plug-in that displays multimedia. Shockwave is downloadable for free and is available for all popular platforms. A high-end version, called Shockwave Deluxe, supports zoomable vector-based graphics.

**N O T E** Visit **http://www.macromedia.com/shockwave/download/** at the Macromedia site to download a version of Shockwave appropriate for your computer. You can learn more about Shockwave by following the links available here. ▪

## Adding Shockwave Content to Your Page

To add Shockwave content to your Web site, you'll need to use some tools from Macromedia, such as:

- Authorware
- Macromedia Director
- FreeHand
- SoundEdit 16

Once you have assembled your content, place it on the Web server. Be sure the server is configured to supply the proper MIME media type for your content. Macromedia supplies a configuration guide online at **http://www.macromedia.com/shockwave/config.html**. For example, if your content was produced using Macromedia Directory, specify a MIME type of `appliction/x-director`. For Authorware, use:

- `application/x-authorware-map` for the aam file;
- `application/x-authorware-seg` for the aas file; and
- `application/x-authorware-bin` for the aab file.

FreeHand documents should be set to use media type `image/x-freehand`.

***<EMBED>* Tag Basics**    To add Shockwave content to a Web page for Netscape Navigator, use the `<EMBED>` tag:

```
<EMBED SRC="pathToShockwaveContent/file.ext" WIDTH=width HEIGHT=height
➥PALETTE=ground BGCOLOR=color
➥PLUGINSPAGE="http://www.macromedia.com/shockwave/">
```

This tag instructs the browser to fetch the contents of the file at `pathToShockwaveContent/ file.ext`. When the contents begin to come down, the server sends the media type (e.g., `application/x-director`). The browser checks to see if it has a plug-in that handles this type.

 To see which plug-ins the browser has loaded, enter **about:plugins** in the location window.

If the user has the Shockwave plug-in installed, the browser reserves a section of the window based on the `WIDTH` and `HEIGHT` attributes of the `<EMBED>` tag. The background color is set in accordance with the `BGCOLOR` attribute. If `PALETTE` is set to `foreground`, Navigator loads the palette from the Shockwave content (for example, a Macromedia Director movie).

 If you specify `PALETTE=foreground`, the Shockwave contents will appear in their proper colors, but other images (including other Shockwave content) on the page may not appear correctly. `PALETTE=background` is the default for Navigator, so if you don't specify `PALETTE=foreground`, your Shockwave content will be displayed using the system palette.

If you scan your characters into Director, remember that each character will have a different palette. Specify a common palette for any Director movies you intend to use on the Web. (Use the Transform Bitmap item from the Modify menu.) Try to design your pages so that a single palette can span all of the images on the page, not just the Shockwave content. Better still, make sure all the images look good when rendered using the system palette, and allow the `<EMBED>` tag to default to `PALETTE=background`.

You can use Equilibrium Technology's DeBabelizer utility, which runs on the Macintosh, to integrate the palettes of all of the images on a page. If you're building pages with many complex graphics, DeBabelizer is essential.

 By keeping your color depth at eight bits or below, your Shockwave movies will be smaller. If it's more important to you that the colors be right than that the download time be low, consider setting the color depth to 16 bits or higher. Graphics with color depths of 16, 24, or 32 bits don't use color palettes—each color is fully specified.

Finally, the Shockwave plug-in is launched and control is passed to Shockwave.

If the Shockwave plug-in is not installed, the browser will offer to take the user to the `PLUGINSPAGE` you specified. The URL shown, **http://www.macromedia.com/shockwave/**, will take them directly to Macromedia's Shockwave center.

**TIP** For a quick way to steer users without Shockwave away from your Shocked pages, place a small Shockwave movie on the home page of your site. In that movie, include the line

```
gotoNetPage()
```

If the user has Shockwave, this code will redirect them to a new, shocked page. If they do not have Shockwave, you can give them a message about how to get the plug-in, or just keep them in a series of pages which do not require Shockwave.

Another way to catch browsers that don't understand JavaScript is to place the reference to the Shockwave movie *inside* a script. For example,

```
<SCRIPT LANGUAGE="JavaScript">
<!--
document.write( '<EMBED WIDTH=175 HEIGHT=135 SRC="mymovie.dcr">');
// -->
</SCRIPT>
```

will be visible only to browsers like Navigator and Microsoft Internet Explorer. If the browser understands JavaScript, chances are good that it will be able to use the Shockwave plug-in. (There's a Shockwave ActiveX control for MSIE, which MSIE will download automatically when the user visits the shocked page.)

 **TIP** When you use the <EMBED> tag, also include <NOEMBED>. If the user does not have a browser that supports the <EMBED> tag, the browser will display any HTML shown between <NOEMBED> and </NOEMBED>. For example, you could replace a Shockwave movie with a single image:

```
<NOEMBED><IMG SRC="pathToImage/imageName.jpeg"></NOEMBED>
```

### Adding Additional Parameters

Macromedia tools like Director support their own scripting language, called Lingo. You can add additional parameters to the <EMBED> tag and read them from Lingo.

Suppose you wrote

```
<EMBED SRC=... sw1=1 sw2="Yes">
```

In Lingo, you can write

```
on startMovie
  put externalParamCount()
    into field "Number of External Parameters"
end
```

The field Number of External Parameters would get the value 2.

You can read the parameters by name or by number. By name, write

```
on startMovie
  put externalParameterValue("sw1") into myVariable
  put myVariable into field "Display Variables"
end
```

Shockwave compares the string (in this case, sw1) with each of the parameters. Shockwave ignores case, so SW1 matches sw1. If Shockwave cannot find a match, or if the match has no associated value, externalParamValue() returns void.

By number, write

```
on startMovie
  put externalParamValue(1)
    into field "Display the First Parameter"
  put externalParameterValue(1) into myVariable
  put myVariable into field "Display Variables"
end
```

> **CAUTION**
>
> Shockwave movies can easily grow to several hundred kilobytes—a size that can require several minutes to download when using a dial-up connection. Use Macromedia's "Download-o-Matic" at **http://www. macromedia.com/shockwave/director5/moviedocs/download.html** to estimate how long your Shockwave content will take to download.
>
> Visit **http://www.macromedia.com/shockwave/director5/movielab.html** to get some ideas about how much you can do with just a small movie.

**N O T E**   Visit the links at **http://www.macromedia.com/shockwave/director5/index.html** of the Macromedia site to get even more ideas about how to tune Macromedia Director movies for use on the Web in Shockwave. ▦

# Controlling Shockwave with LiveConnect

Shockwave includes a MENU=FALSE attribute that you can add to the EMBED tag. This attribute disables the pop-up menu so the user can't accidentally take control of your movie.

You can call methods in the Shockwave Flash Player from JavaScript. Methods include:

- Play()—Start playing the animation.
- StopPlay()—Stop playing the animation.
- IsPlaying()—Returns true if the movie is currently playing.
- GotoFrame (int frameNum)—Go to a specific frame of the movie.
- TotalFrames()—Returns the total number of frames in the movie.
- Rewind()—Go to the first frame.
- SetZoomRect(int left, int top, int right, int bottom)—Zoom in on a rectangular area of the movie. Note that the units of the coordinates are in twips (1,440 units per inch).
- Zoom(int percent)—Zoom the view by a relative scale factor.
- Pan(int x, int y, int mode)—Pan a zoomed-in movie. The mode can be: 0 = pixels, 1 =% of window.

- PercentLoaded()—Returns the percent of the .spl file that has streamed into the browser so far (ranges 0-100).

If you want a button on your page that stops the movie, you might write:

```
<FORM>
<INPUT TYPE="Button" onClick="document.theMovie.StopPlay()" value="Stop">
</FORM>
```

You could add other controls to provide access to the remaining methods, depending upon the objectives of your page.

If you specify MAYSCRIPT in the <EMBED> tag, you can call JavaScript objects and methods from inside your .spl file. You can also take advantage of a Shockwave capability called FSCommand. From inside Flash Animator, you may associate an FSCommand with a button or frame. You give the command a name and pass it a set of arguments. In your JavaScript, you write something like Listing 14.8. In this case, the name of the Shockwave movie is mapcontrols.

**Listing 14.8    Handle *FSCommands* from the Flash Player**

```
<SCRIPT LANGUAGE="JavaScript">
<!--
// Handle special cases where we need different code
//  for Internet Explorer vs. Netscape navigator
var InternetExplorer = navigator.appName.indexOf("Microsoft") != -1;
// Handle all the the FSCommand messages in a Flash movie function
mapcontrols_DoFSCommand(command, args)
{

  // IE and Navgiator have slightly different document object models
  // IE treats objects as members of "window" while in Navigator,
  // embedded objects are members of "window.document"
  var map = InternetExplorer ? parent.fw_map.map :
    parent.fw_map.document.map;
  if ( command=="home" )
  {
    map.Rewind();
    map.Zoom(0);
  } else if ( command=="zoom" )
  {
    // Zoom in or out by a percentage specified in args
    map.Zoom(parseInt(args)); }
  }
}
//-->
</SCRIPT>
```

**N O T E**   Details of this and other techniques are available in Macromedia's Tech Note 4120, on the Web at **http://www.macromedia.com/support/technotes/flash/tn4120.html**.

Part
III

Ch
14

# JScript and Internet Explorer

**M**icrosoft's Internet Explorer Web browser represents Microsoft's attempt to get a portion of the Netscape-compatible browser market. Part of that attempt includes the introduction of the language JScript. In Microsoft's own words (at **http://www.microsoft.com/intdev/ script/scriptng-f.htm**), "Microsoft's implementation of JScript is 100% compatible with the JavaScript implementation in Netscape Navigator 2.0." Unfortunately, Microsoft's clone is not perfect. This chapter describes some of the differences between JScript and JavaScript. ■

**How JScript compares with JavaScript 1.0**

While JScript is a close match to JavaScript, the compatibility isn't perfect.

**How JScript compares with JavaScript 1.1**

JScript is Microsoft's attempt to match JavaScript 1.0. While Microsoft was cloning JavaScript, Netscape was developing JavaScript 1.1.

**How JScript compares with Java**

Some Microsoft literature leads you to believe that JScript is a Microsoft implementation of Java. This chapter describes how JavaScript and JScript are related to that Sun language.

**How to integrate JScript with ActiveX objects**

Microsoft is the champion of ActiveX—it's not surprising that JScript makes special provisions for the `<OBJECT>` tag.

**How implementation differences between JScript and JavaScript lead to some inconsistent behavior**

As a JavaScript programmer, be careful of the differences in the object hierarchies between JavaScript and JScript.

**N O T E** Links to online and downloadable versions of the JScript language standard and JScript tutorials can be found at **http://www.microsoft.com/jscript/us/techinfo/jsdocs.htm**. If you want to make sure your JavaScript is readable by MSIE users as well as Navigator users, or if you are focusing on the MSIE audience, be sure to bookmark this page. ▒

**N O T E** The site located at **http://www.microsoft.com/iesupport/default-news.htm** lists "peer-to-peer" newsgroups available to help Internet Explorer users support one another. For example, to talk to other users about scripting (in either JScript or VBScript), visit **news://msnews.microsoft.com/microsoft.public.internetexplorer.scripting**. ▒

# JScript and JavaScript Compared

Microsoft operates several sites that address its JScript language. One such site, **http://www.microsoft.com/intdev/script/scriptng-f.htm**, includes a December 20, 1996, article based on presentations given at the Site Builder Conference that was held October 28-30, 1996, in San José, California. This article describes scripting in the Microsoft Internet environment. In particular, the article compares Visual Basic Script (also known as VBScript) and JScript (Microsoft's implementation of JavaScript).

That article makes the following three claims about JScript:

- ▒ JScript is 100 percent compatible with the JavaScript implementation in Netscape Navigator 2.0.
- ▒ JScript is an open implementation of the Java language and can be extended.
- ▒ JScript enables developers to link and automate ActiveX controls and Java applets into a Web page.

## JScript and JavaScript 1.0—How Well Did Microsoft Clone?

JavaScript was introduced by Netscape in Navigator 2.0. That version of JavaScript is commonly called JavaScript 1.0. If Microsoft had implemented a perfect clone of JavaScript 1.0, then we, as Web site developers, would have a simple choice: We could use JavaScript 1.1 and live with the fact that those visitors who use Internet Explorer would not get the full benefit of our site, or we could limit ourselves to JavaScript 1.0, with the confidence that most users would be able to benefit from this "lowest common denominator" of JavaScript.

Unfortunately, Microsoft's clone is not perfect. This section describes some of the differences between JScript and JavaScript 1.0.

 **TIP** In addition to the incompatibilities described in this section, many programmers are confused by the fact that MSIE is more "forgiving" than Navigator. For example, JavaScript is a case-sensitive language, but MSIE does not enforce this restriction. A script that works correctly under MSIE may fail when it runs under Navigator.

The solution is to build all scripts with Navigator, then check them with MSIE. Navigator will catch errors like "Top" instead of "top" or "WINDOW" instead of "window," but MSIE will permit these erroneously-capitalized words.

**Some Features Disabled Offline**    Internet Explorer parses JScript in one way if the source of the code is an http: URL and a slightly different way if the source is a file: URL. These differences mean that some features will not work when you test them from your local hard drive, but will work okay once the page is online.

For example, several users have reported that MSIE will not write a cookie to your hard drive if the Web page is on your local drive. While this restriction makes a certain amount of sense, it also makes testing and debugging more complex because you cannot do complete testing from your hard drive.

Another example of this defect is in the <FORM> submission process. If you write code such as

```
<FORM ... onSubmit="return SendOrder()">
```

and run it from the server, control passes to the SendOrder() function when the user submits the form. If SendOrder() returns true, the contents of the form are submitted to the Action URL.

However, if the same page is loaded from the local hard drive, the form contents are *not* submitted. This behavior is almost certainly not intentional on the part of Microsoft but, instead, results from inadequate testing. The consequence, however, is that untold labor has been lost by JScript programmers attempting to debug their code from their local hard drive.

 **T I P**    If you've written what you think is valid JScript and it still doesn't work from the hard drive, try copying the file to a Web server and accessing it over the Internet. You may be surprised to find that the code suddenly begins working.

**No Support for the *Window* Object's *status* Property on Some Platforms**    JavaScript allows you to specify a message to appear in the window's status bar. For example, if you write

```
<A HREF="some URL" onMouseOver="window.status='Your message.';
➥return true">link</A>
```

then, when the user drags the cursor over the link, the status bar will read "Your message." Listing 15.1 shows an example of code that works in Netscape Navigator 4.0 on Windows 95 but not in Internet Explorer 3.0 on the Macintosh.

**Listing 15.1    IE 3.0 for the Mac Does Not Set the *window.status* Property**

```
<HTML>
<HEAD>
<TITLE>Status Bar Tester</TITLE>
</HEAD>
<BODY BGCOLOR="white">
```

*continues*

---

**Listing 15.1 Continued**

```
<H1>Status Bar Tester</H1>
This way to the <A HREF="http://www.whitehouse.gov"
➥onMouseOver="window.status='Your message.'; return true"> White House</A>.
</BODY>
</HTML>
```

---

**No Support for the *URL* Property of the *Document* Object**  From time to time, you will find it useful to let your program know "where it is." You can always give your document the current URL by referring to location.href. JavaScript 1.0 and later also has an URL property on the document object—you can get the current URL by asking for document.URL. Consider the difference between Netscape Navigator 4.0 (in Figure 15.1) and IE 3.0 (in Figure 15.2) when viewing the code in Listing 15.2.

**FIG. 15.1**

In Netscape Navigator, document.url works correctly.

---

**Listing 15.2 Internet Explorer Does Not Handle the *document.url* Property Properly**

```
<HTML>
<HEAD>
<TITLE>Document URL Tester</TITLE>
</HEAD>
<BODY BGCOLOR="white">
<H1>Document URL Tester</H1>
<P>The current URL is:<BR>
```

```
<SCRIPT LANGUAGE="JavaScript">
<!--
document.write(document.URL);
document.write("</P><P>and the location href is<BR>" + location.href);
// -->
</SCRIPT>
.</P>
</BODY>
</HTML>
```

**FIG. 15.2**

In Internet Explorer, `document.url` not only fails, but it also interrupts the rest of the `<SCRIPT>`.

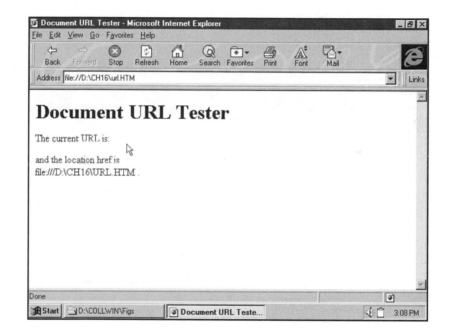

 **TIP** `location.href` seems to work better in MSIE than `document.url`. Since both properties return identical results, use `location.href` to get better cross-platform results.

**Limited Support for Cookies**  *Cookies* are a browser-based method of adding *state* to the Hypertext Transfer Protocol (HTTP)—the protocol of the Web. If you want to store some information about the user, you can put that information into a cookie and send it to the browser. If the browser supports cookies, and if the end user gives permission, the information is stored on the end user's local hard drive. Each domain (for example, **yahoo.com**, **dse.com**, or **mcp.com**) can write its own cookies so that information stored by one Web site will not be returned to another Web site.

All browsers that support cookies (the name is entirely whimsical) warn programmers that they have limited space for storage. If a cookie gets too old, or if the cookie file gets too full, any given cookie may be deleted. JavaScript 1.0 permits up to 20 cookies per domain, while JScript permits only one. Consequently, a large site that wants to set more than one cookie in

MSIE needs to look for its one cookie, read it if it exists, add information to it, and return it to the browser.

To do the same thing with Navigator, the server program just writes the cookie. Unless the server is particularly prolific (wanting to write more than 20 cookies for a given domain), this method will work reliably.

▶ **See** "Persistent Data and Cookies," **p. 628**, for a more detailed description of Cookies.

**N O T E**  Cookies were originally specified by Netscape, although the standard is widely distributed, and many browsers now support cookies. You can read the specification online at **http://www.netscape.com/newsref/std/cookie_spec.html**. ▪

Listing 15.3 shows a program that sends the text of the cookie to and from the browser.

**Listing 15.3    MSIE 3.0 Supports Only One Cookie per Domain**

```
<HTML>
<HEAD>
<TITLE>Cookie Tester</TITLE>
<SCRIPT LANGUAGE="JavaScript">
<!--
function getCookie(theForm)
{
  return document.cookie;
}

function setCookie()
{
  var theString = prompt("Enter a new cookie value:","Any text will do.");
  document.cookie = theString;
  document.theForm.cookieText.value = getCookie();
}
// -->
</SCRIPT>
</HEAD>
<BODY BGCOLOR="white">
<H1>Cookie Tester</H1>
<FORM NAME="theForm">
<P>The current cookie is:<BR>
<SCRIPT LANGUAGE="JavaScript">
<!--
document.write("<INPUT TYPE=Text NAME=cookieText VALUE=" + getCookie() + ">");
setCookie();
// -->
</SCRIPT>
</P>
<INPUT TYPE="Button" NAME=cookieButton VALUE="Set Cookie" onClick="setCookie()">
</FORM>
</BODY>
</HTML>
```

If you load this page into Netscape Navigator, you can specify up to 20 cookies per domain, but if you load the page into Internet Explorer, the first script (which calls getCookie() and writes it to the page) fails.

**Different Indexing Schemes for the History List**    Both Navigator and Internet Explorer support a history object, which contains a list of locations visited. You can see this list by choosing Window, History in Navigator. You can also see the ten most recent items under the Go menu.

Internet Explorer users access the history list by using the Go menu. Choosing Go, Open History opens a window showing the complete history list.

Netscape's JavaScript documentation says that the parameter of the go method of the history object describes a move *relative to* the current document. Thus, history.go(-1) directs the browser to move one position back on the history list. If your browser has the history window shown in Figure 15.3, history.go(1) takes you to the Status Bar Tester.

**FIG. 15.3**

Navigator uses a relative indexing scheme—history.go(1) takes you to the Status Bar Tester.

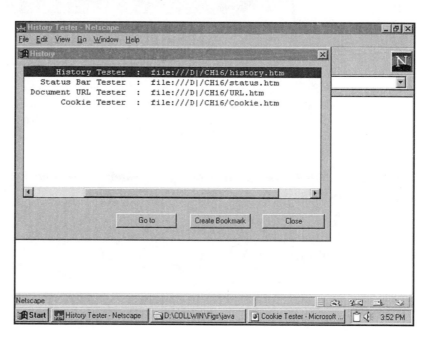

Microsoft's JScript documentation for the same method says that the parameter takes you to "the *n*th item in the history, where history.go 1 jumps to the first item in the history." Figure 15.4 shows the same history list, but from Microsoft Internet Explorer. Given the same history, you need two different commands to reach the same object.

**FIG. 15.4**

MSIE uses an absolute indexing scheme— `history.go` 3 takes you to the Status Bar Tester.

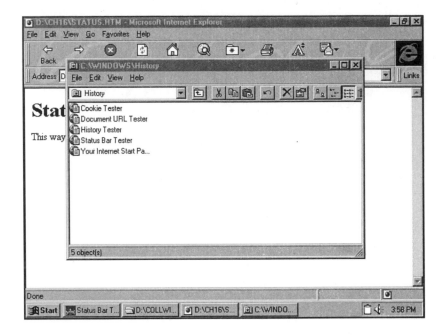

Listing 15.4 shows a script that offers to navigate the user around the history list. This script is tuned for Navigator. To go back, the script calls `history.go()` with a negative parameter. This script is valid JavaScript but will not work in JScript (due to the negative numbers).

---

**Listing 15.4 JScript Does Not Use the Relative Numbering System for the *history* Object**

```
<!DOCTYPE HTML PUBLIC "-//W3C//DTD HTML 3.2//EN">
<HTML>
<HEAD>
   <TITLE>History Tester</TITLE>
   <META NAME="GENERATOR" CONTENT="User-Agent: Mozilla/3.01Gold
➥(Macintosh; I; PPC)">
</HEAD>
<BODY BGCOLOR="white">
<H1>History Tester</H1>
<P>Go back
<FORM NAME="theForm">
<SELECT NAME="howFar" onChange="history.go(0 - this.selectedIndex);">
<OPTION SELECTED>0
<SCRIPT LANGUAGE="JavaScript">
<!--
for (var i=1; i<=history.length; i++)
{
  document.write("<OPTION> "+ i);
}
// -->
</SCRIPT>
</SELECT>
```

```
</FORM>
</P>
</BODY>
<SCRIPT LANGUAGE="JavaScript">
<!--
history.go(-1)
// -->
</SCRIPT>
</HTML>
```

**Different Interpretation of the *document.referrer* Property**  Both JavaScript and JScript support a `referrer` property for the `document` object, and both Netscape and Microsoft say that this property contains the name of the page from which the user arrived at the current page. Suppose the user is visiting the page described in Listing 15.5.

**Listing 15.5** **This Page Is the Start of the Referrer Test**

```
<!DOCTYPE HTML PUBLIC "-//W3C//DTD HTML 3.2//EN">
<HTML>
<HEAD>
    <TITLE>Referrer Tester</TITLE>
</HEAD>
<BODY BGCOLOR="white">
<H1>Referrer Tester</H1>
<P>
Go to the <A HREF="refer2.htm">next page</A>.
</P>
</BODY>
</HTML>
```

When the user selects the link to `refer2.htm`, the page described in Listing 15.6 is loaded into the browser.

**Listing 15.6** **This Page Tests the Browser's Understanding of *document.referrer***

```
<!DOCTYPE HTML PUBLIC "-//W3C//DTD HTML 3.2//EN">
<HTML>
<HEAD>
    <TITLE>Referrer Tester</TITLE>
</HEAD>
<BODY BGCOLOR="white">

<H1>Referrer Tester</H1>
<P>
<SCRIPT LANGUAGE="JavaScript">
document.write("The referrer is " + document.referrer + ".");
</SCRIPT>
</P>
</BODY>
</HTML>
```

According to the documentation supplied by both Netscape and Microsoft, we would expect to see the second page display `"The referrer is ...refer1.htm."` In Netscape Navigator, we see exactly this, but with MSIE 3.1, `document.referrer` returns the URL of the current page.

**No Support for .js Files**    JavaScript allows you to specify that functions are defined in a text file, downloaded, and cached separately from the HTML files. Listing 15.7 shows a tiny example of such a library file.

---

**Listing 15.7    A Single-Function Library File**

```
function doSomething()
{
  alert("Here I am, doing something.");
}
```

---

Now suppose you write an HTML page to load and call the function `doSomething()`. Listing 15.8 shows such a page.

---

**Listing 15.8    Testing the .js Library**

```
<!DOCTYPE HTML PUBLIC "-//W3C//DTD HTML 3.2//EN">
<HTML>
<HEAD>
   <TITLE>.js Tester</TITLE>
<SCRIPT SRC="library.js" LANGUAGE="JavaScript"></SCRIPT>
</HEAD>
<BODY BGCOLOR="white">
<H1>.js Tester</H1>
<P>
<SCRIPT LANGUAGE="JavaScript">
doSomething();
</SCRIPT>
</P>
</BODY>
</HTML>
```

---

If the browser understands the SRC attribute and loads the .js file correctly, it will display the alert upon loading. Navigator demonstrates this behavior. Internet Explorer does not load the file and fails to call the function.

**No Support for Stopping a Link**    JavaScript allows you to stop the browser from following a selected link by returning `false` to the `link` object. Listing 15.9 shows a link to the Yahoo! search engine, which executes only if the user enters "Yes" to the `confirm` dialog.

---

**Listing 15.9    Stop the Link If the User Says "Cancel"**

```
<!DOCTYPE HTML PUBLIC "-//W3C//DTD HTML 3.2//EN">
<HTML>
<HEAD>
```

```
    <TITLE>Stop Tester</TITLE>
</HEAD>
<BODY BGCOLOR="white">
<H1>Stop Tester</H1>
<P>
Visit <A HREF="http://www.yahoo.com/" onClick="return
➥confirm('Are you sure?');"> Yahoo!</A>.
</P>
</BODY>
</HTML>
```

If you run this script from Netscape Navigator, when you select the link, the browser displays a `confirm` dialog. If you choose "Yes," the `confirm` returns `true` and the browser attempts to load **http://www.yahoo.com/**. If you choose "No," `confirm` returns `false` and the browser does not attempt to follow the link.

In Internet Explorer, the same sequence of events does not produce a `confirm` dialog at all. In fact, MSIE appears to ignore the `onClick` handler completely. Like it or not, you're on your way to the Yahoo! site.

**Intermittent Defects with Relative URLs**   If you develop a site with multiple pages, you may sometimes want to copy all of the pages to a new site and use them as the basis for new development. In such cases, you typically use relative URLs so that all of the hyperlinks between the pages in the site still work after the move. For example, `<IMG SRC="../images/button.gif">` works whether the document base is `http://www.site1.com/bar/` or `http://www.site2.net/baz/`.

Unfortunately, some users have reported that JScript occasionally loses track of the root of a relative URL, leading to a series of `"File not found"` errors. The fix, of course, is to fully specify each URL.

## JScript and JavaScript 1.1—How Compatible Are They?

Of course, the previous section does not document the many areas in which JScript and JavaScript 1.0 *are* compatible. Microsoft is to be commended on getting things mostly right, but their claim to be "100% compatible" does not bear out under testing.

While Microsoft was cloning JavaScript 1.0, Netscape was moving on. Navigator 3.0 implements a newer version of the language—JavaScript 1.1. The result is that certain JavaScript 1.1 objects and features are not (yet) available in JScript. (You can be sure that Microsoft is running hard to catch up.) This section demonstrates some examples of the differences between the current versions of JavaScript and JScript.

**N O T E**   Microsoft posts known defects and other issues regarding Internet Explorer on its Web site at **http://www.microsoft.com/iesupport/content/issues/**. If you have a problem with MSIE, this site is a good place to check. ▪

**N O T E**   Netscape provides a nice summary of the features and capabilities that were added to
JavaScript as it moved from JavaScript 1.0 to JavaScript 1.1 at its site,
**http://home.netscape.com/comprod/products/navigator/version_3.0/building_blocks/**
**jscript/how.html**. These new features are not yet part of Microsoft's JScript language. A similar list of
new features is available at **http://home.netscape.com/eng/mozilla/3.0/handbook/javascript/**
**index.html**. Soon, Netscape will integrate JavaScript 1.1 features into the JavaScript Developers Guide,
available online in the developer's documentation library at **http://developer.netscape.com/library/**
**documentation/index.html**. ■

**No Support for the *image* Object**   Starting in Netscape 3.0, Netscape introduced the `image`
object. You can load a set of images by writing

```
document.images[i].src = "http://someURL/someImage;
```

This line will set the source attribute (`src`) of the *i*th image in the array `images` to the specified
image file.

While the preceding code works correctly in Netscape Navigator, MSIE complains that
`"'images' is not an object."`

**No Support for the *FileUpload* Object**   JavaScript's `FileUpload` object enables you to send
files to the server. Listing 15.10 shows how to use this object. Netscape Navigator renders it as
a text field with a Browse button, as shown in Figure 15.5. Internet Explorer does not recognize this tag.

---

**Listing 15.10   The *FileUpload* Object Is Supported by Navigator but Not MSIE**

```
<!DOCTYPE HTML PUBLIC "-//W3C//DTD HTML 3.2//EN">
<HTML>
<HEAD>
   <TITLE>Upload Tester</TITLE>
<BODY BGCOLOR="white">
<H1>Upload Tester</H1>
<P>
<FORM METHOD="POST"ACTION="http://www.dse.com/books/javascript/upload.cgi">
<INPUT TYPE="File">
<INPUT TYPE="Submit">
</FORM>
</P>
</BODY>
</HTML>
```

---

**No Support for the *onMouseout* Event**   JavaScript 1.1 added an `onMouseout` event. With this
event, you can detect the moment when the user moves the cursor out of a MAP AREA. JScript
does not yet have this event.

**FIG. 15.05**
MSIE does not support
the FileUpload
object, shown here in
Navigator 4.0.

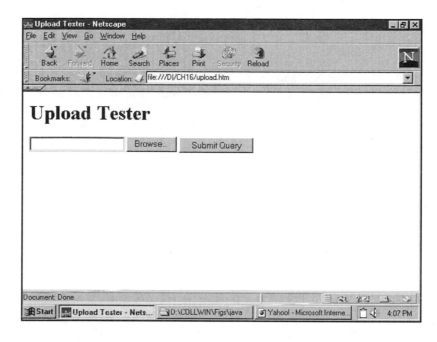

**No Support for the *onError()* Handler**   JavaScript 1.1 supports an error recovery mechanism based on the onError() handler. You can set onError for an image or a window. When an error occurs, your onError handler takes control. This mechanism is not available in JScript.

**No Support for *reload()***   In JavaScript 1.1, you can force the reload of a page by calling the reload() method. That method is not available in JScript.

**No Support for *reset()***   HTML forms typically have a Submit object and a Reset object. In JavaScript 1.1, you can simulate a click on the form's Reset object by calling reset(). That method is not available in JScript.

**No Support for *split()***   JavaScript 1.1 added the string method split(). This method, reminiscent of the Perl operator of the same name, allows you to write code like that shown in Listing 15.11.

**Listing 15.11   Test the JavaScript 1.1 *split()* Operator**

```
<!DOCTYPE HTML PUBLIC "-//W3C//DTD HTML 3.2//EN">
<HTML>
<HEAD>
    <TITLE>Split Tester</TITLE>
<SCRIPT LANGUAGE="JavaScript">
function passwdArray(theArray)
{
  this.length = 7;
  this[1] = "username";
  this[2] = "password";
```

*continues*

**Listing 15.11  Continued**

```
    this[3] = "userID";
    this[4] = "groupID";
    this[5] = "geos";
    this[6] = "home";
    this[7] = "shell";
    this["username"] = theArray[0];
    this["password"] = theArray[1];
    this["userID"] = theArray[2];
    this["groupID"] = theArray[3];
    this["geos"] = theArray[4];
    this["home"] = theArray[5];
    this["shell"] = theArray[6];
    return this;
}
</SCRIPT>
</HEAD>
<BODY BGCOLOR="white">
<H1>Split Tester</H1>
<P>
<SCRIPT LANGUAGE="JavaScript">
var passwdElements = "";
var theString = "kepilino:!:201:1::/home/kepilino:/usr/bin/ksh";
passwdElements = new passwdArray(theString.split(":"));
document.writeln("The username is " + passwdElements["username"] + "<BR>");
document.writeln("The user's shell is " + passwdElements["shell"] + "<BR>");
</SCRIPT>
</P>
</BODY>
</HTML>
```

This code takes a line, such as you might find in a UNIX /etc/passwd file, and splits it out by using the colon character as a separator. The `split()` method returns an array, which is passed into the constructor `passwdArray()` and stuffed into an associative array so that statements like `passwdElements["shell"]` return meaningful answers. JScript does not support `split()`.

▶ **See** "Substring Operations," **p. 130**, to learn more about `split()`.

**No Support for the *AREA* Object**   In Navigator 3.0, Netscape introduced the `<AREA>` tag, which is primarily used to support image maps. For example, you can write code like that shown in Listing 15.12. In this listing, a client-side image map named "lakeMap" is defined with one area: the bottom portion of the image, which contains the representation of the lake itself. If you click the specified `<AREA>`, the browser invokes `javascript:void(0)`, which does nothing. While your mouse is over the area, the status line displays `You are on the lake.` When your mouse leaves the image, an alert appears notifying you that you have left the lake.

### Listing 15.12 Navigator 3.0 or Later Enables You to Define an *AREA* Using HTML

```
<!DOCTYPE HTML PUBLIC "-//W3C//DTD HTML 3.2//EN">
<HTML>
<HEAD>
   <TITLE>Area Tester</TITLE>
<BODY BGCOLOR="white">
<H1>Area Tester</H1>
<P>
<MAP NAME="lakeMap">
   <AREA NAME="lake" COORDS="0, 350,640,480" HREF="javascript:void(0)"
      onMouseOver="self.status='You are on the lake.';return true"
      onMouseOut="alert('You have left the lake.');return true">
</MAP>
<IMG SRC="lake.gif" ALIGN="top" HEIGHT="480" WIDTH="640" USEMAP="#lakeMap">
</P>
</BODY>
</HTML>
```

MSIE understands the <AREA> tag at the HTML level, but Microsoft has not yet integrated <AREA> into JScript.

**N O T E** Visit **http://the-pages.com/netuner/** for a nice example of the <AREA> tag under MSIE. ▨

**No Support for the *Function* Object** In JavaScript 1.1, you can write functions on-the-fly. For example, you can write code like that shown in Listing 15.13, which builds onFocus and onBlur handlers for a frame.

**N O T E** While the names of the event handlers (onFocus and onBlur) are in mixed case, the properties that hold the handlers are all lowercase (onfocus and onblur). ▨

### Listing 15.13 You Can Set the *onFocus* and *onBlur* Handlers of a *<FRAME>* Only by Using JavaScript

```
<HTML>
<HEAD>
<TITLE>Hierarchy Tester</TITLE>
<SCRIPT LANGUAGE="JavaScript">
function setUp()
{
  frames[0].onfocus = new Function("document.bgColor = 'antiquewhite'");
  frames[0].onblur = new Function("document.bgColor = 'lightgrey'");
  frames[0].focus();
}
</SCRIPT>
```

*continues*

**Listing 15.13   Continued**

```
</HEAD>
<FRAMESET ROWS="40%,*" onLoad="setUp()">
  <FRAME SRC="hier-f.htm" >
  <FRAME SRC="blank.htm">
</FRAMESET>
</HTML>
```

**N O T E**   According to some of Netscape's documentation, putting an onFocus or an onBlur event handler in a <FRAMESET> tag has no effect when the page is loaded into any of the versions of Navigator for Windows. This problem has been corrected in Navigator 4.0. ■

**No Support for the LiveConnect Features**   Navigator provides an array, mimeTypes, which lists the MIME media types supported by either Navigator or by the current set of installed plug-ins. MSIE does not support plug-ins (though Microsoft's intent is that ActiveX controls offer similar functionality) so there is no MSIE counterpart to mimeTypes.

Similarly, MSIE has no plugin object (which is a read-only array called embeds that contains the plug-in instances used in the document), nor does it have the plugins array (which is an array of plug-ins currently installed in the browser).

These arrays and objects are integral parts of the LiveConnect mechanism that Navigator provides to integrate JavaScript with Java and plug-ins.

▶ **See** "What Are Plug-Ins?," **p. 386,** for more information about LiveConnect and plug-ins.

**No Support for the *Applet* Object**   Netscape's LiveConnect technology provides for integration not only with plug-ins, but also with Java applets. While MSIE does support Java, the internal mechanism is quite different than that used in Navigator. Consequently, there is no applet object.

In Navigator, the JavaScript programmer can use the applet object, which is a read-only array of the applets in the document, to communicate with a specific applet.

**Limited Support for the *Option* Object**   When you add a <SELECT> element to a form, JavaScript builds an array of the options associated with that <SELECT>. The components of this array are known as option objects. At runtime, you can change the text of the option by setting the text property. Listing 15.14 shows how to change option text on-the-fly. This script will work in Navigator, but not in MSIE.

**Listing 15.14   Navigator Enables You to Change *option* Text On-the-Fly**

```
<!DOCTYPE HTML PUBLIC "-//W3C//DTD HTML 3.2//EN">
<HTML>
<HEAD>
   <TITLE>Option Tester</TITLE>
<SCRIPT LANGUAGE="JavaScript">
```

```
function Greek()
{
  document.aForm.theAlphabet.options[0].text = "alpha";
  document.aForm.theAlphabet.options[1].text = "beta";
  document.aForm.theAlphabet.options[2].text = "gamma";
}
function Hebrew()
{
  document.aForm.theAlphabet.options[0].text = "aleph";
  document.aForm.theAlphabet.options[1].text = "beth";
  document.aForm.theAlphabet.options[2].text = "gimel";
}
function report(aList)
{
  var theChoice = aList.selectedIndex;
  alert("Your choice was " + aList.options[theChoice].text + ".");
}
</SCRIPT>
<BODY BGCOLOR="white">
<H1>Option Tester</H1>
<P>
<FORM NAME="aForm">
<SELECT NAME="theAlphabet" onChange="report(this)">
<OPTION>Aleph
<OPTION>Beth
<OPTION>Gimel
</SELECT><BR>
<INPUT TYPE="Button" onClick="Greek()" VALUE="Greek">
<INPUT TYPE="Button" onClick="Hebrew()" VALUE="Hebrew">
</FORM>
</P>
</BODY>
</HTML>
```

**Non-Standard Support for the *opener* Property of the *window* Object**    Both Netscape and Microsoft document an opener property for the window object. The code in Listing 15.15 tests how well the browser understands this property.

**Listing 15.15   Does Your Browser Understand *window.opener*?**

```
<!DOCTYPE HTML PUBLIC "-//W3C//DTD HTML 3.2//EN">
<HTML>
<HEAD>
   <TITLE>Opener Tester</TITLE>
</HEAD>
<BODY BGCOLOR="white">
<H1>Opener Tester</H1>
<P>
<SCRIPT LANGUAGE="JavaScript">
self.name = "topLevel";
document.writeln("My name is " + self.name + ".<BR>");
if (opener != null)
  document.writeln("This window opened by " + opener.name);
```

*continues*

**Listing 15.15   Continued**

```
else
  document.write("This window is the top window.");
myNewWindow = open('', "newWindow");
myNewWindow.document.writeln("<BODY BGCOLOR='white'><H1>Second Window</H1>");
if (myNewWindow.opener != null)
  myNewWindow.document.writeln("This window opened by " +
➥myNewWindow.opener.name + ".");
else
  myNewWindow.document.writeln("This window is the top window.");
myNewWindow.document.writeln("</BODY>")
myNewWindow.document.close();
</SCRIPT>
</P>
</BODY>
</HTML>
```

Figure 15.6 shows the result of loading the code in Listing 15.15 in Netscape Navigator. MSIE does not support opener.

Some users report that repeatedly opening new windows in Internet Explorer seems to eventually crash the browser.

If your application allows the user to open secondary windows, test your application thoroughly under MSIE, under various platforms, and under heavy load conditions. If you find that you are able to crash the browser, report the problem to Microsoft. Then, redesign your application or add a warning to the user if useragent tells you the user is running one of the versions of MSIE that you were able to crash.

# How Is JScript Related to Java?

Some of Microsoft's documentation would lead a reader to think that JScript is closely related to Java. For example, at **http://www.microsoft.com/intdev/script/scriptng-f.htm** they say, JScript "…is an open implementation of the Java language and can be extended." In fact, JavaScript and JScript bear only a distant relationship with Java. The language we know as JavaScript was developed by Netscape under the name LiveScript, while Java was developed by Sun Microsystems. The differences between the two languages are summarized in Table 15.1.

▶ **See** "JavaScript and Java," **p. 20**

**Table 15.1   The Differences Between JavaScript/JScript and Java Are Substantial**

| JavaScript/JScript | Java |
| --- | --- |
| Interpreted | Compiled |
| Object-based | Object-oriented |

| JavaScript/JScript | Java |
| --- | --- |
| Code integrated into HTML | Code in applets, loaded by HTML |
| Weakly typed | Strongly typed |
| Dynamic binding | Static binding |

**FIG. 15.6**
Netscape Navigator understands window.opener and writes the name of the parent window in the child.

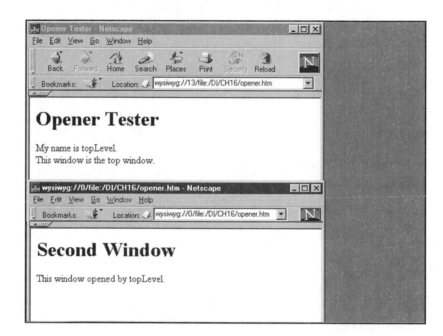

## How Is JScript Related to ActiveX Technology?

While JScript and JavaScript are only distantly related to Java, there are special provisions in JScript to support Microsoft's ActiveX technology. ActiveX encompasses several different technologies:

- ActiveX documents enable you to incorporate new media types into a Web document by using Microsoft's Object Linking and Embedding (OLE) technology to open an application and render the content. Viewers are available for some Microsoft Office applications, such as MS Word, Excel, and PowerPoint. See **http://www.microsoft.com/ie/most/howto/docs.htm** for more information about ActiveX documents and **http://www.microsoft.com/msoffice/** to download viewers.
- ActiveX controls enable you to add specific functionality to a Web page.
- ActiveX scripting enables you to add both client- and server-based interpreted programming to your page.

ActiveX scripting is available in Internet Explorer through either JScript or Visual Basic for Scripting (generally known as VBScript).

▶ **See** "Embedded Objects: ActiveX," **p. 434**, for more information about ActiveX controls.

▶ **See** "The VBScript Language," **p. 442**, for more information about VBScript.

An ActiveX control is a reusable piece of code that may be included in your Web page by using the <OBJECT> tag. Many Web page designers who have looked at applets, Navigator plug-ins, and ActiveX controls find ActiveX controls to be the most complex to use. For example, to use the Label control, you could use the code in Listing 15.16.

**Listing 15.16   Embedding an ActiveX Control**

```
<OBJECT
   classid="clsid:99B42120-6EC7-11CF-A6C7-00AA00A47DD2"
   id=label1
   width=75
   height=100
   vspace=0
   align=Left
>
<param name="Angle" value="0">
<param name="Alignment" value="100">
<param name="BackStyle" value="0">
<param name="Caption" value="Hello!">
<param name="FontName" value="Times New Roman">
<param name="FontSize" value="24">
</OBJECT>
```

Clearly, the potential for an error in the classid is high. You might also make a mistake in one of the parameter's names or values. For example, when you are typing an object's parameters while using an editor, there is nothing to remind you that BackStyle 0 means "transparent."

On the other hand, once a user has downloaded an ActiveX control and stored it to the hard drive, he or she need never download it again until a new version of the control is released. Furthermore, ActiveX controls can often take advantage of existing code in the Microsoft operating system or browser, so their size may be less than comparable plug-ins or applets.

 If you find yourself using many ActiveX controls, consider using the ActiveX Control Pad. This Microsoft utility enables you to embed ActiveX controls and "wire them up" by using JScript, while making it less likely that you will forget a parameter.

**N O T E**   An article on scripting in the Internet Explorer environment is located at **http:// www.microsoft.com/intdev/script/scriptng-f.htm**. See the section of that page titled "Make authoring scripts easy with ActiveX Control Pad" for a step-by-step procedure for embedding ActiveX objects by using the Control Panel. ▪

# Limitations of Internet Explorer 3.0

While Microsoft has attempted to make JScript fully compatible with JavaScript, their method of implementing some JavaScript features is quite different. Under certain conditions, these differences can lead to differences in behavior between the two browsers.

**N O T E**  As of the version 3.0 release of MSIE, Microsoft has not defined any objects for JScript that are not also part of JavaScript. However, Microsoft has defined its own scripting model and could add new objects in the future. ■

There are three potential solutions to the limitations of MSIE 3.0:

- **Code for Navigator only**  If you're programming for an intranet or other environment in which you can control the browser, this option may be feasible. On the Internet, however, this option cuts out the large (and growing) segment of the market that uses Internet Explorer.

- **Code to the "lowest common denominator"**  This chapter documents various inconsistencies between JavaScript and JScript. If you write for Navigator and then test your code in MSIE, and if you carefully avoid the JavaScript constructs that are not supported (or are supported differently) in JScript, you may be able to write pages that work well in either browser. Remember to test your pages thoroughly in both browsers and on various platforms. Keep reading the news groups and Web pages dedicated to tracking the differences to keep up with JScript fixes and newly discovered inconsistencies.

- **Write code that works well in any browser**  You can tune your pages so that different code is served depending upon the user's browser. For example, both MSIE and Navigator will load code labeled <SCRIPT LANGUAGE="JavaScript">, but only Navigator 3.0 or later will load code marked <SCRIPT LANGUAGE="JavaScript1.1">. You can also use properties of the navigator object, such as appName and appVersion, to steer the browser to browser-specific code. This approach requires more work on the part of the programmer and still demands thorough testing, but can lead to highly reliable pages regardless of which browser the end user chooses.

## Differences in the Object Hierarchy

Figure 15.7 illustrates the hierarchy of objects in Netscape Navigator. Figure 15.8 shows the same hierarchy in MSIE. These figures demonstrate that code like window.navigator will work in MSIE, but will fail in Navigator. This, by itself, is not a serious problem because most JavaScript programmers would not be tempted to preface a top-level object with a reference to the window.

Suppose, however, that a JavaScript programmer writes the code shown in Listing 15.17 for use in a frameset such as the one shown in Listing 15.18.

**FIG. 15.7**
In Navigator, many of
the objects are
document-level objects
and are only indirectly
part of the window.

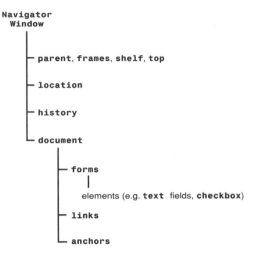

```
Navigator
 Window

  ─ parent, frames, shelf, top

  ─ location

  ─ history

  ─ document

        ─ forms
          │
            elements (e.g. text  fields, checkbox)
        ─ links

        ─ anchors
```

**FIG. 15.8**
In Internet Explorer,
many of the objects are
components of the
window object.

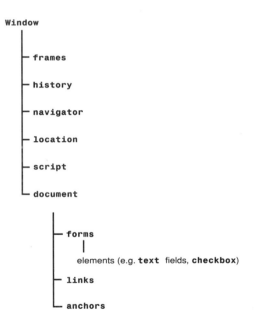

```
Window

  ─ frames

  ─ history

  ─ navigator

  ─ location

  ─ script

  ─ document

        ─ forms
          │
            elements (e.g. text  fields, checkbox)
        ─ links

        ─ anchors
```

**Listing 15.17  Netscape Navigator Cannot Find the *history* Object If This
Page Is Part of a *<FRAMESET>***

```
<HTML>
<HEAD>
<TITLE>Hierarchy Tester Frame</TITLE>
<SCRIPT LANGUAGE="JavaScript">
function goBack()
{
```

```
    alert("Document is " + document.title + ";\nParent document is " +
➥parent.document.title + ".");
    alert("My history list has " + history.length +
➥" element.\nMy parent's history list has " +
➥parent.history.length + " elements.");
    history.back();
}
</SCRIPT>
</HEAD>
<BODY BGCOLOR="white">
<H1>Hierarchy Tester</H1>
<FORM>
<INPUT TYPE="Button" VALUE="Go Back" onClick="goBack()">
</FORM>
</BODY>
</HTML>
```

### Listing 15.18   This *Frameset* Is Enough to Confuse the *goBack()* Function of Listing 15.17

```
<HTML>
<HEAD>
<TITLE>Hierarchy Tester</TITLE>
</HEAD>
<FRAMESET ROWS="40%,*" >
  <FRAME SRC="hier-f.htm">
  <FRAME SRC="blank.htm">
</FRAMESET>
</HTML>
```

If you load these pages into Internet Explorer, the browser adds the window reference to the front of history. Since the history object is, indeed, part of the window in MSIE, the attempt to move back down the history list succeeds.

In Navigator, however, the browser attempts to find window.history. As the alerts show, the window of the frame is associated with the document whose title is "Hierarchy Tester Frame"—this window has only the current document on its history list. The parent window, which is associated with the document titled "Hierarchy Tester," is the window with a longer history list. This difference is shown in Figure 15.9.

When Navigator attempts to run history.back() against a single-element list, it does not change documents, nor does it raise an error. Indeed, as far as the Navigator hierarchy is concerned, the code is correct, though it may not lead to the programmer's expected behavior.

If you need to access the history list from a document that may become part of a frameset, be sure to refer to parent.history to get to the history list that is part of the top-level document.

**FIG. 15.9**
The current window in a
<FRAMESET> has only
the current document
on its history list.

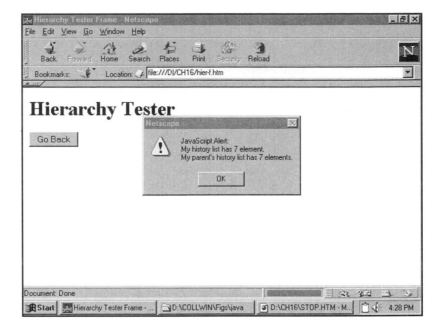

## Differences in How Java Is Implemented

Java applets are directly supported by Netscape Navigator, and Navigator allows the end user
to turn that support on or off. (Use the Options menu, choose Network Preferences, and then
click the Languages tab to find the Enable Java check box.) You can read the setting of this
check box from JavaScript by getting the value of navigator.javaEnabled.

JScript's navigator object does not include the javaEnabled property. Some developers have
speculated that Microsoft may find it difficult to offer such a property because MSIE does not
support Java natively. (Java in Internet Explorer is supported through ActiveX.) ●

# CHAPTER 16

# ActiveX Controls and VBScript

**N**ot long ago, you had some tough decisions to make if you wanted to build a dynamic Web page. You could use Java—but you probably needed to write your own applet. You could use JavaScript or JScript—but there are many things you *can't* do in those languages. You could write a platform-specific Netscape plug-in—but the plug-in audience was limited to Navigator users, and actually writing the code is a lot of work. Or, you could use an ActiveX control—there were plenty of these available, so you probably wouldn't have had to write one from scratch, but ActiveX controls were only usable in Microsoft Internet Explorer (MSIE).

On October 14, 1996, these tradeoffs changed. On that date, Netscape announced its support of ActiveX controls. Of course, MSIE already supports ActiveX controls. Now, you can build a page with an ActiveX control to add advanced functionality with confidence that users will be able to use the page with Netscape, as well as MSIE. ■

### Learn how ActiveX controls may be embedded as live content in pages

Since many ActiveX controls are already available, you can make your page dynamic with very little work.

### Discover the heritage of ActiveX controls

Even if you haven't previously worked with ActiveX, chances are you're familiar with its predecessors: COM, OLE, OCX, and DCOM.

### See how to script ActiveX controls with JScript

Allow the user—or your JScript program—to communicate with the ActiveX control at runtime.

### Find out how VBScript compares with JavaScript/JScript

While Microsoft supports JScript as its version of JavaScript, they believe VBScript and Visual Basic generally offer significant benefits.

### Control the Marquee control

Learn how to communicate with a specific ActiveX control by using either JScript or VBScript.

The tale of how Microsoft reinvented itself to focus on the Internet is now legendary. In fact, in order to position itself to take advantage of the fast-moving Internet market, Microsoft started with several existing technologies. ActiveX controls (one part of the ActiveX technology family) bear a close resemblance to OCX controls, which in turn are based on OLE 2 (Object Linking and Embedding). One big advantage of ActiveX controls is that programmers have been working with this technology for years—the Internet is thick with ActiveX controls, written for many different purposes. If you're not a professional programmer, you may find writing a Netscape plug-in or a Java applet to be a daunting task, but you certainly can use JavaScript to hook up an existing ActiveX control.

**NOTE** Many of the ActiveX controls you find on the Internet aren't digitally signed. By default, Internet Explorer 3.0 won't install unsigned controls—it doesn't even give you the chance to override it. Thus, Internet Explorer will ignore many of the controls that the Web page authors are using. Check your security configuration to make sure you have a choice: choose View, Options from the main menu; click the Security tab; click the Safety Level button; and make sure that you select Medium. (The default is High.) Then, Internet Explorer 3.0 will ask you before installing an unsigned control. If you choose not to install the control, the Web page may not work as the author intends. On the other hand, if you do install the control, you expose yourself to troubles that occur while running controls from unknown sources, such as bugs that can cause the browser to crash or, worse, controls that damage your system. ■

VBScript is a slimmed-down version of Visual Basic. Special precautions have been taken in VBScript to ensure that viruses and Trojan Horses cannot be downloaded to a user's machine.

# Embedded Objects: ActiveX

You can use ActiveX controls (which were formerly known as OLE controls or OCXs) to insert dynamic functionality into your Web page. For example, you can add a Timer control to your Web page that periodically updates the page's content, or you can use a Pop-up Window control to display tooltip-style help when the user holds the mouse pointer over a link. Considering that there are over a thousand ActiveX controls available for you to use, the possibilities are just about endless.

Simply dropping ActiveX controls onto your Web page isn't enough if you want to build dynamic and exciting Web pages. You have to make all those controls work together. That's where scripting comes in. You associate scripts with the events and values of the controls you put on a Web page so that you can make them interact. You can update the contents of a TextBox control when the user clicks a button, for example, or you can open a Web page in a frame when the user chooses an item from a Pop-up Menu control.

 **TIP** If your version of Netscape Navigator doesn't support ActiveX controls, you need to get the ActiveX plug-in from NCompass Labs. Visit **http://www.ncompass.com/** for more information.

# What Are ActiveX Controls?

Part of the promise of object-oriented programming is that much of what you do as a programmer isn't original. If one programmer has written a good component, other programmers may be able to reuse it. One of the best examples of the success of this approach has been OLE controls. OLE controls, also known as .OCXs, have been among the most popular code resources on the Net.

Microsoft has combined and enhanced its OLE 2 and OCX technologies and renamed the consolidated standard *ActiveX*. ActiveX refines the OLE specification for OLE controls, which makes them smaller and more efficient. New OLE interfaces are also defined, enhancing control over data and property management. By using the new ActiveX Control class, you can write .OCX controls that are lightweight and Internet-aware.

Part
III

Ch
16

**N O T E**   Microsoft has recently turned over ActiveX to a steering committee that will oversee the development of ActiveX standards. You can get more information at **http://www.activex.org/**. ■

In 1991, Microsoft introduced "Object Linking and Embedding" or OLE. OLE 1 was intended to start Microsoft down the road toward *compound documents*—documents that include objects from other documents and that can interact with those embedded or linked objects.

OLE 1 was not a success. It was slow and difficult to use. Most developers decided that OLE's learning curve was too steep to justify the benefits it offered.

In response to these problems, Microsoft reinvented OLE. OLE 2 is a whole new product, with new capabilities and a faster implementation. The learning curve is still about as steep as with OLE 1, but with end users demanding more functionality, OLE 2 is being accepted more widely than OLE 1. Because OLE 2 is now the standard, we call it simply *OLE* in this chapter.

**N O T E**   If you want to write your own ActiveX controls by using Microsoft's ActiveX SDK, you'll need to be well-grounded in OLE. For a technical introduction to OLE 2 and COM, see *Inside OLE 2* (Microsoft Press, 1994). ■

**N O T E**   For an in-depth look at ActiveX controls, see *Special Edition Using ActiveX* (Que, 1996). ■

If you're a programmer, you can write your own ActiveX controls by using tools from Microsoft. The latest version of Visual Basic includes provisions for writing ActiveX controls. You also can use the OLE Control development facilities in Visual C++, the ActiveX SDK, or the ActiveX Template Library (ATL).

Microsoft has announced its commitment to make ActiveX run on all major platforms and is working with Metrowerks (a leading tool vendor for Macintosh) and Bristol and Mainsoft (leading UNIX developers) to port ActiveX to these platforms.

**N O T E**   For current information about ActiveX technology in general, and ActiveX controls in particular, visit **http://www.microsoft.com/activex/activex-contents1.htm**.

**Building ActiveX Controls with Visual Basic**   Beginning with version 5.0, you can develop ActiveX controls right from Visual Basic. The new "Control Creation Edition" of the Visual Basic product is free and is downloadable from the Microsoft site. Using Visual Basic 5.0, you can write a simple ActiveX control in about 10 minutes—a dramatic savings compared to the other methods described in this section.

**N O T E**   **http://www.microsoft.com/vbasic/controls/** is loaded with the latest details on the Visual Basic Control Creation Edition. Visit here for the latest list of features, as well as a step-by-step procedure for building ActiveX controls with Visual Basic.

The Visual Basic Control Creation Edition follows the familiar "visual" programming paradigm. First you "draw" the interface, then you set some properties and write some event-driven code.

Visual Basic 5.0's ActiveX Control Interface Wizard enables you to easily define the properties, methods, and events for a user-developed ActiveX control. The Property Page Wizard automatically generates custom property pages for a user-defined control. By using custom property pages, you can build custom interfaces for the setting of properties.

If you're serious about writing your own ActiveX controls, you should take a serious look at the Visual Basic Control Creation Edition.

**Building ActiveX Controls with Visual C++**   A Visual C++ programmer can use Microsoft Foundation Classes (MFC) and the Visual C++ OLE control development facilities to build an ActiveX control.

Visual C++ AppWizard supports an OLE ControlWizard that builds a basic control in just two steps, as shown in Figure 16.1. Make sure that you link the control with MFC dynamically to avoid the download time associated with MFC.

**Building ActiveX Controls Based on the ActiveX SDK**   You can find the ActiveX SDK online. In this kit, Microsoft includes a sample named `BaseCtl`, which includes `FrameWrk`, `ToDoSvr`, and `WebImage` examples. You can use these examples as a basis for writing your own ActiveX control.

**N O T E**   Both Windows and Macintosh versions of the ActiveX SDK are at **http://www.microsoft.com/intdev/sdk**.

---

**CAUTION**

The Microsoft ActiveX SDK is over 13M *compressed*. Even if you're prepared to handle the learning curve, make sure you're prepared to handle the download time and the disk space.

---

**FIG. 16.1**
Use the Visual C++ OLE
ControlWizard to
quickly set up an OLE
control.

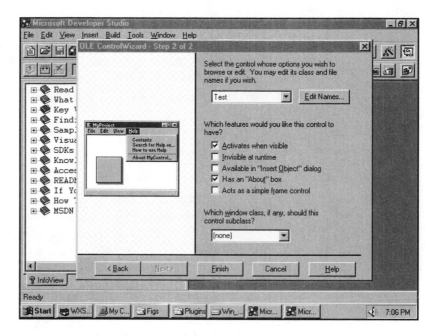

**Building ActiveX Controls with the ActiveX Template Library**   If you'd like to write some simple ActiveX controls without taking on the full details of COM and the ActiveX control architecture, check out the ActiveX Template Library, or ATL. The ATL comes with two examples— Beeper and Labrador.

These templates do some of the OLE work, but you still need to be familiar with COM and the ActiveX control architecture. Remember, too, that the ATL is designed only to build small ActiveX or OLE controls. What it does, it does well; but if you find yourself spending a lot of time adding interfaces and functions, chances are you could do better by using the ActiveX SDK.

**N O T E**   The ATL is available online at **http://www.microsoft.com/visualc/prodinfo/ default.htm** ▨

**N O T E**   The Windows 95/Windows NT 4.0 version of the ATL only takes up 590K compressed—and that's with all the documentation and sample code. The Windows NT 3.51 version is zipped and is even smaller. If you're looking for a kinder, gentler introduction to ActiveX, you may want to start with the ATL. ▨

Finally, note that Version 1.1 and later of the ATL use some of the newest features in Visual C++, such as the MIDL compiler (which replaces MkTypLib). If you have Visual C++ 4.0 or earlier, you need to upgrade to the latest version.

# Getting Microsoft's ActiveX Controls

Microsoft provides a collection of ActiveX Controls with Internet Explorer 3.0. You don't have to do anything other than install Internet Explorer 3.0 to get them. Microsoft provides other controls through its ActiveX Gallery Web site at **http://www.microsoft.com/activex/gallery**. Table 16.1 describes each control and how you get it. The sections that follow show you examples of some of these controls.

**Table 16.1   Microsoft's ActiveX Controls**

| Name | Description |
| --- | --- |
| *Provided by the Minimum, Typical, and Complete Installs of Internet Explorer 3.0* | |
| Web Browser | Displays HTML files, ActiveX Controls, and ActiveX documents |
| Timer | Executes a script at specific intervals |
| Marquee | Scrolls an HTML file horizontally or vertically |
| *Provided by the Complete Install of Internet Explorer 3.0* | |
| ActiveMovie | Displays streaming and nonstreaming video and audio |
| HTML Layout | Displays 2-D HTML regions created with the ActiveX Control Pad |
| Forms 2.0 Label | Displays a text label |
| Forms 2.0 Textbox | Prompts the user for text |
| Forms 2.0 Combo Box | Displays a drop-down list of options |
| Forms 2.0 List Box | Displays a scrollable list of options |
| Forms 2.0 CheckBox | Displays a check box option |
| Forms 2.0 Option Button | Displays an option button |
| Forms 2.0 Toggle Button | Displays a button that the user can toggle on and off |
| Forms 2.0 Command Button | Displays a basic button |
| Forms 2.0 Tabstrip | Displays multiple pages of controls that the user selects by clicking a tab |
| Forms 2.0 ScrollBar | Displays vertical and horizontal scroll bars |

| Name | Description |
|---|---|
| Forms 2.0 Spin Button | Displays a spin button that can be pushed up or down |
| Image | Displays a progressive image from a JPG, GIF, or BMP file |
| Hotspot | Adds a transparent hot spot to a layout |

*Provided at http://www.microsoft.com/activex/gallery*

| | |
|---|---|
| Animated Button | Displays an AVI file on a button |
| Chart | Draws various types of charts |
| Gradient | Shares an area with a range of colors |
| Label | Displays a text label with a given angle, color, and font |
| Menu | Displays a button that pops up a standard menu which fires an event when the user chooses an item |
| Popup Menu | Displays a pop-up menu that fires an event when the user chooses an item |
| Popup Window | Displays an HTML file in a pop-up window |
| Preloader | Downloads the file at the given URL into the user's cache |
| Stock Ticker | Displays data from a text file at regular intervals |
| View Tracker | Fires events when the control enters or leaves the browser's viewing area |

Part

III

Ch

16

## Label Control

The ActiveX Gallery shows an example of the use of the ActiveX Label control, shown in Figure 16.2. Using this control, you can display text within a Web page by using any installed font, with any style, color, and at any arbitrary angle you choose. In this example, the two regions change—either color, text, or orientation—whenever you click them.

## Preloader Control

The ActiveX Preloader control makes your Web site seem faster than all the rest. You use it to speed up the apparent throughput of a Web session by allowing Internet Explorer 3.0 to cache graphics, video, and audio for a subsequent Web page while the user is looking at the current page. Normally, you'd use the Preloader control to quietly preload images or other HTML elements while the user is reading the current Web page. Then, when you want to go on to the next page in the Web site, or when you want to view an image file, hear a sound, or watch a video clip, Internet Explorer has already downloaded it to the cache and the user can view it without any further delay. You can see an example of the Preloader control at Microsoft's ActiveX Gallery.

**FIG. 16.2**

The Label control gives you the ability to place text on the Web page without resorting to graphics.

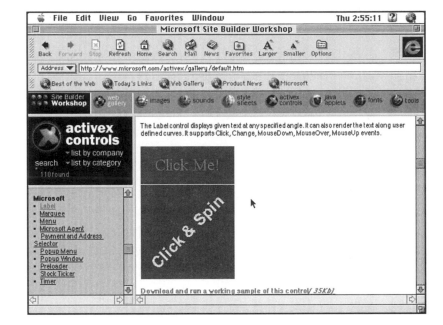

## Timer Control

The Timer control lets you periodically run a script that you can use to change the content of a Web page or perform some other task. Figure 16.3 shows a Web page that uses a timer to change the size and color of the two labels (each implemented with the Label control) over time. Both labels change at different intervals because this Web page uses two different Timer controls.

## Menu Control

You use the Menu control to put a button on your Web that, when clicked, displays a menu. When the user chooses a menu item, the control fires an event that you can handle with a script. Figure 16.4 shows you the example from Microsoft's ActiveX Gallery. It contains two Menu controls; each one displays a different submenu.

**FIG. 16.3**
You use the Timer control to execute a script at preset intervals, such as every second or every 10 seconds.

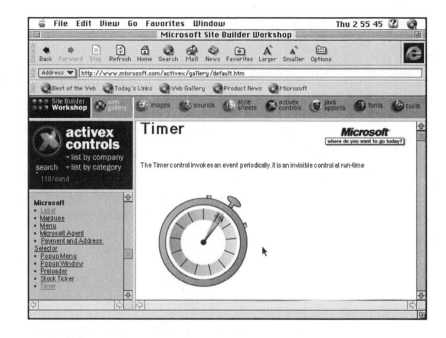

**FIG. 16.4**
You can use the Menu control to add menu-driven navigation to your Web site, like Microsoft's Site Builder Workshop.

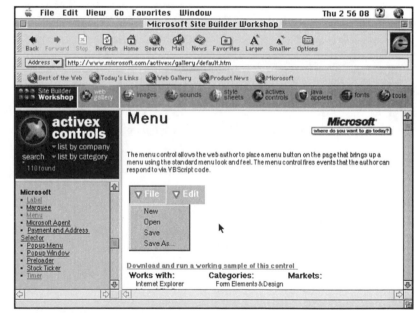

# The VBScript Language

Now that you have learned JavaScript (from the other chapters of this book), you can use that language as a starting point in learning VBScript. If you already know Visual Basic, you're even farther ahead. Many of the statements and operators in JavaScript have a counterpart in VBScript, and the object models of Navigator and Microsoft Internet Explorer are similar.

▶ **See** "Limitations of Internet Explorer 3.0," **p. 429**, for a discussion of the differences between the object models of Navigator and MSIE.

Microsoft started with a powerful set of tools that, in the past, was applied to building complete applications. This tool set is now available for use in enhancing HTML pages.

Each of the sections in this chapter talks about a different aspect of VBScript. To get started with VBScript, download the ActiveX SDK appropriate for your platform from **http://www.microsoft.com/intdev/sdk/**.

**N O T E**  For the latest information on VBScript, bookmark **http://www.microsoft.com/vbscript/vbsmain.htm** on the Microsoft site and visit it regularly. ∎

For more information on VBScript, be sure to see *Special Edition Using VBScript* (Que, 1996).

 **T I P**  Unlike JavaScript, VBScript is not case-sensitive. Nevertheless, you should adopt a coding convention that includes standards on capitalization. That way, you can use case-sensitive tools to manage your code. You'll also find it easier to port the code to a case-sensitive language (such as JavaScript) should you ever need to do so.

Microsoft provides a set of VBScript coding conventions that you may want to adopt at **http://www.microsoft.com/vbscript/us/vbstutor/vbscodingconventions.htm**.

Table 16.2 gives you an overview of the syntax of the language.

### Table 16.2  Visual Basic Script Syntax

| Element | Syntax |
|---|---|
| Arrays | Declaration (e.g., `Dim`, `Static`) |
| | `LBound`, `Ubound` |
| | `ReDim`, `Erase` |
| Assignment | `=` |
| | `Let` |
| | `Set` |
| Comments | `REM` |
| | Single Quote (`'`) |

| Element | Syntax | | |
|---------|--------|--|--|
| Control Flow | `Do...Loop`<br>`For...Next, For Each...Next`<br>`While...Wend`<br>`If...Then...Else` | | |
| Error trapping | `On Error`<br>`Err` Object | | |
| Literals | `Empty`<br>`Nothing`<br>`Null` | | |
| | `True, False` | | |
| | User-defined literals (e.g., `123.456`, `"baz"`) | | |
| Nonconforming identifiers | o. *MyLongMethodName* | | |
| Operators | Arithmetic: | `+, -, *, /, \, ^, Mod`<br>`Negation (-)` | |
| | String concatenation: | `(&)` | |
| | Comparison: | `=, <, >, <>, <=, >=, Is` | |
| | Logical: | `Not, And, Or, Xor, Eqv, Imp` | |
| Options | `Option Explicit` | | |
| Procedures | Declaring Procedures: | `Function`<br>`Sub` | |
| | Calling Procedures: | `Call` | |
| | Exiting Procedures: | `Exit Function`<br>`Exit Sub` | |
| | Parameters for procedures: | `ByVal, ByRef` | |
| Variables | Procedure-level: | `Dim, Static` | |
| | Module-level: | `Private, Dim` | |

**N O T E** You can follow links to download a full set of VBScript documentation or read the documentation online at **http://www.microsoft.com/vbscript/us/techinfo/vbsdocs.htm**. If you're not already a Visual Basic programmer, be sure to get this information before writing serious VBScript-based pages.

You will also find a nice VBScript tutorial at **http://www.microsoft.com/vbscript/us/vbstutor/vbstutor.htm**. ■

**Part**
**III**

**Ch**
**16**

# Variables

VBScript enables you to build and use many kinds of variables, which are generally similar to variables in JavaScript and other programming languages.

To declare a variable in VBScript, use the keyword DIM. DIM is analogous to JavaScript's var declaration:

```
<SCRIPT LANGUAGE="VBS">
<!--
DIM myVariable
-->
</SCRIPT>
```

VBScript variables follow the usual naming conventions: they must begin with an alphanumeric character, are limited to 255 characters, and must be unique within the scope in which they are declared.

> **N O T E**   In both JavaScript and VBScript, the memory associated with most variables is released as soon as the variable goes out of scope. In VBScript you can declare a variable to be static, telling VBScript that you want the variable to persist after it goes out of scope, and be reused if it's needed again. For example, you could write:
>
> ```
> <SCRIPT LANGUAGE="VBS">
> <!--
> function clockTime(aNumber)
>   static accumulator
>   accumulator = accumulator + number
>   clocktime = accumulator
> end function
> -->
> </SCRIPT>
> ```
>
> In this case, you would be able to execute the function clockTime over and over and be able to rely on the fact that the variable accumulator continued to persist between calls. In this way, accumulator would be able to consistently increase based on the variable aNumber that you pass to it each time. ▪

**Data Types**   VBScript uses only one data type: *variant*. If you use a parameter or other variable as a number, VBScript will attempt to cast the variable as a number. If you use the variable as a character string, VBScript will treat the variable as a string.

As you've seen in your JavaScript programming, making assumptions about the contents of a variable can lead to defects in your code. A good practice is to verify that the parameters into any function conform to your expectations before you pass them to any operators. VBScript supports such verification with the On Error statement, and with *subtypes*.

Table 16.3 lists the subtypes that VBScript understands.

### Table 16.3  Subtypes of the Data Type Variant

| Subtype | Description |
| --- | --- |
| Empty | Variable is not initialized. Value is treated as zero for numeric variables or an empty string (" ") for string variables |
| Null | Variable intentionally contains no valid data |
| Boolean | Either True or False |
| Byte | Integer in the range 0..255 |
| Integer | Integer in the range –32,768..32,767 |
| Long | Integer in the range –2,147,483,648..2,147,483,647 |
| Single | Floating-point number in the range –3.402823E38..–1.401298E–45 for negative numbers, and 1.401298E–45..3.402823E38 for positive numbers |
| Double | Floating-point number in the range –1.79769313486232E308..–4.94065645841247E–324 for negative numbers, and 4.94065645841247E–324.. 1.79769313486232E308 for positive numbers |
| Date (Time) | A number that represents a date between January 1, 100, and December 31, 9999 |
| String | A variable-length string that can be up to about two billion characters in length |
| Object | An ActiveX object |
| Error | An error number |
| Currency | From –922,337,203,685,477.5808 to 922,337,203,685,447.5807 |

**Arrays**   Recall that in JavaScript you build an array by calling a constructor and initializing the array. In VBScript, you simply use the DIM keyword and specify an upper limit to the size of the array. For example,

```
DIM baz(30)
```

reserves space for 31 variants, starting with baz(0) and ending with baz(30). You can assign a variable to any of these entries with the assignment operator =

```
baz(10) = 100
baz(11) = 99
```

In VBScript, you can build arrays with up to 60 dimensions. For example, if you want to build a three-dimensional array with 100 elements in the first dimension, 50 in the second, and 10 in the third, you would write:

```
DIM theArray(99, 49, 9)
```

**N O T E**  Remember that when you build an array in VBScript, you are not setting the size of the dimension, but the name of the largest element in that dimension. Thus, `theArray(99)` declares that `theArray` has 100 elements. 

In JavaScript, you can extend an array by initializing elements beyond the original length. In VBScript, you must explicitly declare an array to be dynamic by declaring it without an upper bound:

```
DIM myResizableArray()
```

Before using the array, call `ReDim` to specify the size of the array. Whenever you want to change the size of the array, call `ReDim` again.

**CAUTION**

If you use `ReDim` to decrease the size of an array, you will lose the data in the upper elements of the array.

## VBScript Constants

Although JavaScript has a few constants in its `Math` object and elsewhere, "VBScript has many more uses for constants." Table 16.4 lists a few common constants, and their JavaScript counterparts. Visit **http://www.microsoft.com/vbscript/us/vbslang/vsconString.htm** to see a full set of string constants. You can also declare your own constants by using the `Const` statement.

**Table 16.4  Commonly Used Constants**

| VBScript Constant | Description | JavaScript Equivalent |
|---|---|---|
| vbCr | Carriage return | \r |
| vbCrLf | Carriage return and line feed | \r\n |
| vbFalse | Boolean value represented by 0 | false |
| vbLf | Line feed | \n |
| vbTrue | Boolean value represented by 1 | true |

# VBScript Operators

VBScript operators resemble operators in other languages and follow the order of precedence common to JavaScript, Java, C++, and Perl. Table 16.5 shows the arithmetic, comparison, and logical operators in order of precedence.

**Table 16.5  VBScript Operators**

| Arithmetic Operators | | Logical Operators | | Comparison Operators | |
|---|---|---|---|---|---|
| **Description** | **Symbol** | **Description** | **Symbol** | **Description** | **Symbol** |
| Exponentiation | ^ | Equality | = | Negation | Not |
| Negation | – | Inequality | <> | Conjunction | And |
| Multiplication | * | Less Than | < | Disjunction | Or |
| Division | / | Greater Than | > | Exclusion | Xor |
| Integer Division | \ | Less Than or equal to | <= | Equivalence | Eqv |
| Modulo | Mod | Greater Than or equal to | >= | Implication | Imp |
| Addition | + | Equivalence | Is | | |
| Subtraction | - | | | | |
| String concatenation | & | | | | |

# Control Flow in VBScript

Control flow in VBScript is handled with statements that are similar to JavaScript, Java, and other modern programming languages. Unlike many languages, however, that group statements by using brackets or Begin...End statements, VBScript relies on explicit End statements to conclude each statement. Here's a side-by-side comparison of the same function in JavaScript and VBScript:

**JavaScript**

```
function respondToUser(aValue)
{
  if (aValue == false)
  {
    musicPlay.jazz = true;
    videoPlay.batman = slow;
  }
}
```

**VBScript**

```
Sub respondToUser(aValue)
if aValue = 0 Then
musicPlay.jazz = True
videoPlay.batman = Slow
Else
musicPlay.jazz = False
videoPlay.batman = Fast
```

*continues*

*continued*

| **JavaScript** | **VBScript** |
|---|---|

```
JavaScript
  else
  {
    musicPlay.jazz = false;
    videoPlay.batman = fast;
  }
}
```

```
VBScript
End If
End Sub
```

Most languages have a construct that allows you to loop until some condition is satisfied. In VBScript, this construct is `Do...While`. You can also use `Do...Until` (which continues until the specified condition becomes true). To break out of the loop early, use `Exit Do`.

VBScript enables you to build collections of objects (in arrays) and then manipulate those objects by using the `For Each...Next` construct, as shown here:

```
Sub
For Each state in myCountry
  If state.Governor = "Democrate" Then
    state.Color = "Green"
  End If
Next
End Sub
```

## VBScript Procedures

In C, C++, and JavaScript, any procedure may potentially return a value. Those procedures that do not return an explicit value are often said to return `void`.

In Pascal and VBScript, the language provides separate constructs for procedures that return values and those that don't. To return a value in VBScript, declare the procedure by using the keyword `function`. To declare a procedure that has no return value, use the keyword `sub`.

Thus, you might write

```
Sub convertTime()
  time = InputBox("Please enter the time in seconds.", 1)
  MsgBox "The time is " & Seconds(time) & " o'clock"
End Sub
```

or

```
Function Seconds(theTime)
  Seconds=theTime / 120
End Function
```

## Language Summary

Microsoft's online language reference is an invaluable aid during programming. If you use VBScript regularly, bookmark **http://www.microsoft.com/vbscript/us/vbslang/vbstoc.htm** or download the file.

| TIP |

If you prefer to use the online reference, use **View Source** to print out the source of **http://www.microsoft.com/vbscript/us/vbslang/vbstoc.htm**. That way, by reading the <OPTION> tags in each <SELECT>, you have a convenient reference sheet to the URL for each major VBScript topic. For example,

```
<OPTION VALUE="/vbscript/us/vbslang/vsstmCall.htm">Call Statement
```

tells you that you can get a full description of the Call statement by pointing your browser to **http://www.microsoft.com/vbscript/us/vbslang/vsstmCall.htm**.

Like many languages, much of the power of VBScript comes from its library of functions. Table 16.6 shows the extensive list of keywords associated with the functions, listed in alphabetical order from left to right. See *Special Edition Using VBScript* (Que, 1996) for details on these functions.

### Table 16.6   Built-In Functions in VBScript

| | | |
|---|---|---|
| Abs | Array | Asc |
| Atn | CBool | Cbyte |
| CCur | CDate | CDbl |
| Chr | Cint | CLng |
| Cos | CreateObject | CSng |
| Cstr | Date | DateAdd |
| DateDiff | DatePart | DateSerial |
| DateValue | Day | Exp |
| Filter | Fix | FormatCurrency |
| FormatDateTime | FormatNumber | FormatPercent |
| GetObject | Hex | Hour |
| InputBox | InStr | InStrRev |
| Int | IsArray | IsDate |
| IsEmpty | IsNull | IsNumeric |
| IsObject | Join | LBound |
| LCase | Left | Len |
| LoadPicture | Log | LTrim, RTrim, and Trim |
| Mid | Minute | Month |
| MonthName | MsgBox | Now |
| Oct | Replace | Right |
| Rnd | Round | ScriptEngine |
| ScriptEngineBuildVersion | ScriptEngineMajorVersion | ScriptEngineMinorVersion |
| Second | Sgn | Sgr |
| StrComp | String | Sin |
| Space | Split | StrReverse |
| Tan | Time | TextStream |
| TimeSerial | TimeValue | TypeName |
| UBound | UCase | VarType |
| Weekday | WeekdayName | Year |

VBScript statement keywords are shown in Table 16.7, listed alphabetically from left to right.

### Table 16.7 VBScript Statement Keywords

| | | |
|---|---|---|
| Call | Const | Dim |
| Do...Loop | Erase | Exit |
| For...Next | For Each...Next | Function |
| If...Then...Else | On Error | Option Explicit |
| Private | Public | Randomize |
| ReDim | Rem | Select Case |
| Set | Sub | While...Wend |

Built-in objects include `Dictionary`, `Err`, `FileSystem`, and `TextStream`.

## Should You Be Using VBScript?

Given the capabilities of VBScript, should you be using this language instead of JavaScript? If you are writing pages that may be loaded by Netscape Navigator, the answer is "No." Netscape has stated that it has no plans to support VBScript—Netscape's scripting language is JavaScript. Since JavaScript is a close match to Microsoft's VBScript, which runs in Microsoft Internet Explorer, a Web page written with JavaScript is likely to run correctly in Navigator and MSIE.

If you have a "captive audience" and know that your users are all running MSIE, then VBScript is a viable choice. If you already know Visual Basic, or at least some form of the original BASIC, you may feel more comfortable with the syntax of VBScript. Unlike JavaScript, VBScript is a subset of a robust language that has been around for quite some time. Microsoft will take advantage of that stability to seek a wider acceptance for VBScript than for JavaScript.

# Scripting ActiveX Controls

Recall from "Embedded Objects: ActiveX," earlier in this chapter, that ActiveX controls are embedded in an HTML page by using the <OBJECT> tag. ActiveX controls are true objects— they have properties associated with each instance. As a VBScript (or JScript) programmer, you can get and set the values of those properties. This capability is similar to Netscape's LiveConnect technology.

▶ **See** "What Are Plug-Ins?," **p. 386**, for more information on using LiveConnect to communicate with plug-ins.

## A Quick Example

Microsoft has several ActiveX controls available, including one called `Label`. Listing 16.1 shows an example of `Label` in use. You add the control to a page by using the <OBJECT> tag, and specify parameters by using the <PARAM> tags.

If you've used Visual Basic to work with OCX controls, you'll recognize the contents of the <PARAM> tags—they come directly from Visual Basic's property sheets. If you want to be sure that you set all the parameters correctly, use the ActiveX control pad to insert the control into your page.

ActiveX objects behave like the elements on a form. That is, you interact with each ActiveX object's properties, methods, and events in exactly the same way in which you interact with a form's elements. You handle an object's events when the object needs attention, you call an object's methods, and you get and set the object's properties.

Part

III

Ch

16

**N O T E** While most of the attributes of the <OBJECT> tag are self-explanatory, the CLASSID attribute is not. The CLASSID attribute uniquely identifies the control you're using. CLASSID is used to refer to the ActiveX control to be placed within the object's borders. Microsoft uses the clsid: URL scheme to specify the ActiveX class identifier.

One way to obtain the CLASSID for an ActiveX control is to look at the control's documentation. You can look up Microsoft's ActiveX controls at Microsoft's ActiveX Gallery. To save time, just use the ActiveX Control Pad to insert an ActiveX control into your Web page. That way you don't have to worry about the CLASSID at all.

If the CLASSID attribute is missing, ActiveX data streams will include a class identifier that can be used by the ActiveX loader to find the appropriate control. The CODEBASE attribute can be used to provide an URL from which the control can be obtained. ▧

The CODEBASE for Label is **http://activex.microsoft.com/controls/iexplorer/ ielabel.ocx#Version=4,70,0,1161**. Its content type is application/x-oleobject; if you open a page with the ActiveX control by using MSIE or Navigator 4.0, the browser will download the control. If you open the same page with an earlier version of Navigator, the browser will recognize the control as embedded data and will offer to take you to **http:// www.ncompasslabs.com/scriptactive/index.html**. At this site, you can download an evaluation copy of the plug-in, which allows you to view ActiveX controls from NCompass Labs.

**N O T E** Visit **http://www.w3.org/pub/WWW/Addressing/clsid-scheme/** for more information on the clsid: URL. ▧

### Listing 16.1  Microsoft's *Label* OLE Control

```
<HTML>
<HEAD>
<TITLE>ActiveX Control Demo</TITLE>
<SCRIPT LANGUAGE="VBScript">
<!--
Sub cmdChangeCaption_onClick
      theLabel.Caption = Document.LabelChange.newCaption.Value
```

*continues*

**Listing 16.1  Continued**

```
end sub
-->
</SCRIPT>
</HEAD>
<BODY BGColor="white">
<H1>ActiveX Control Demo</H1>
<OBJECT
     ID=theLabel
     CLASSID="clsid:99B42120-6EC7-11CF-A6C7-00AA00A47DD2"
     WIDTH=150
     HEIGHT=150
     VSPACE=0
     ALIGN=left
>
     <PARAM NAME="Angle" VALUE="0">
     <PARAM NAME="Alignment" VALUE="4" >
     <PARAM NAME="BackStyle" VALUE="1" >
     <PARAM NAME="BackColor" VALUE="#0000FF" >
     <PARAM NAME="Caption" VALUE="Default">
     <PARAM NAME="FontName" VALUE="Arial">
     <PARAM NAME="FontSize" VALUE="20">
     <PARAM NAME="ForeColor" VALUE="#F0F000" >
     <PARAM NAME="FontBold" VALUE="1" >
</OBJECT>
<FORM NAME=LabelChange>
<INPUT TYPE=Text Name=newCaption Size=10 Value="Default">
<INPUT TYPE=Button Name=cmdChangeCaption Value="Change Caption">
</BODY>
</HTML>
```

 **T I P** Browsers that understand the <OBJECT> tag ignore anything between the <OBJECT> tag and the </OBJECT> tag, except <PARAM> tags. Add some HTML in there for users whose browsers don't support ActiveX. You might tell them what they're missing, give them a link to download a better browser, or substitute a static image.

**N O T E** Note the "shortcut" way to associate controls with event handlers. The Visual Basic procedure cmdChangeCaption_onClick handles the onClick event of the button named cmdChangeCaption. ▪

## Changing the Control's Properties

In the example shown in Listing 16.1, clicking the form's button tells Internet Explorer to call cmdChangeCaption_onClick. That procedure, in turn, reads in the value of the text field and assigns that text string to the Caption property of the ActiveX control.

## Handling an Event

Recall from Chapter 3, "Events and JavaScript," that you can use several different methods of handling events for forms and elements. There's only one way to handle an ActiveX control's events: using the FOR and EVENT attributes of the SCRIPT tag.

The FOR and EVENT attributes let you associate a script with any named object in the HTML file and any event for that object. Take a look at this code:

```
<SCRIPT LANGUAGE="JavaScript" FOR="btnButton" EVENT="Click()">
<!--
 window.alert( "Oh! You clicked on me." )
-->
</SCRIPT>
<OBJECT ID="btnButton" WIDTH=96 HEIGHT=32
        CLASSID="CLSID:D7053240-CE69-11CD-A777-00DD01143C57">
        <PARAM NAME="Caption" VALUE="Click Me">
        <PARAM NAME="Size" VALUE="2540;847">
</OBJECT>
```

This code defines an ActiveX button (with an ID of btnButton) that executes the script when the user clicks it. Take a look at the <SCRIPT> tag. It contains the FOR and EVENT attributes, which define the object and event associated with that script. FOR="btnButton" EVENT="Click()" says that when an object named btnButton fires the Click event, this script is executed.

Some events pass arguments to the event handlers. You can pass arguments when you're handling the event using the FOR/EVENT syntax by writing code like:

```
<SCRIPT LANGUAGE="JavaScript" FOR="btnButton"
➡EVENT="MouseMove(shift, button, x, y)">
```

The enclosed script can then use any of the parameters passed to it by the MouseMove event.

 **TIP** Once you've specified a language in your HTML file, you don't need to do it again. Your browser defaults to the most recently used language in the HTML file. You can put `<SCRIPT LANGUAGE="JavaScript"></SCRIPT>` at the very beginning of your HTML file one time and forget about it. The rest of the scripts in your file will use JavaScript.

ActiveX controls support a wide variety of other events. The only way to know for sure which events a control supports is to consult the control's documentation or the ActiveX Control Pad's documentation. For your convenience, however, the following list describes the most prevalent and useful events:

- BeforeUpdate occurs before data in a control changes.
- Change occurs when the value property in a control changes.
- Click occurs when the user either clicks the control with the left mouse button or selects a single value from a list of possible values.

■ DblClick occurs when the user clicks twice with the left mouse button rapidly.

■ DropButtonClick occurs when a drop-down list appears or disappears.

■ KeyDown occurs when a user presses a key.

■ KeyUp occurs when a user releases a key.

■ KeyPress occurs when the user presses an ANSI key.

■ MouseDown occurs when the user holds down a mouse button.

■ MouseUp occurs when the user releases a mouse button.

■ MouseMove occurs when the user moves the mouse pointer over a control.

■ Scroll occurs when the user changes a scroll bar.

# The Marquee Control

If you visit Microsoft's ActiveX gallery (**http://www.microsoft.com/activex/gallery/**), you'll find a link to Microsoft's own Marquee control (**http://microsoft.saltmine.com/isapi/ activexisv/prmgallery/gallery-activex-info.idc?ID=157**). You'll also get this control if you install Microsoft Internet Explorer. This control can scroll the contents of an HTML page either vertically or horizontally across the screen. The HTML coder who installs the control can specify the amount of scrolling and the delay.

Here's the code that embeds this control into your HTML page:

```
<OBJECT
    ID="Marquee1"
  CLASSID="CLSID:1A4DA620-6217-11CF-BE62-0080C72EDD2D"
    TYPE="application/x-oleobject"
    WIDTH=100%
    HEIGHT=100
>
    <PARAM NAME="szURL" VALUE="http://www.microsoft.com/activex/gallery/
    ➥gallery.htm">
    <PARAM NAME="ScrollPixelsX" VALUE="0">
    <PARAM NAME="ScrollPixelsY" VALUE="-5">
    <PARAM NAME="ScrollDelay" VALUE="100">
    <PARAM NAME="Whitespace" VALUE="0">
</OBJECT>
```

In the example given on the Microsoft site, the delay is controlled by the end user, using one of three buttons and a few lines of VBScript:

```
...
<INPUT TYPE="Button" NAME="btnFaster" VALUE="Fast">
<INPUT TYPE="Button" NAME="btnNormal" VALUE="Normal">
<INPUT TYPE="Button" NAME="btnSlower" VALUE="Slow">
...
<SCRIPT Language="VBScript">
Sub btnFaster_Onclick
    Marquee1.ScrollDelay = 0
End Sub
```

```
Sub btnNormal_Onclick
    Marquee1.ScrollDelay = 100
End Sub

Sub btnSlower_Onclick
    Marquee1.ScrollDelay = 300
End Sub
</SCRIPT>
```

Figure 16.5 shows the finished result, available online at **http://microsoft.saltmine.com/activexisv/msctls/ie/marquee.htm**:

**Part**
**III**

**Ch**
**16**

**FIG. 16.5**

The end user can control the speed of the scrolling marquee by clicking one of three HTML buttons.

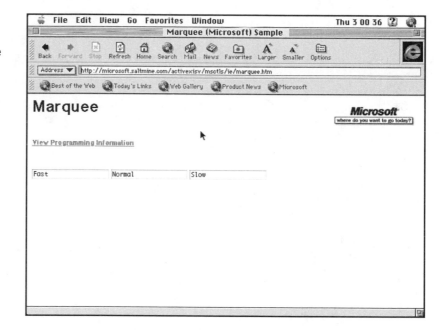

# JavaScript Special Effects

# CHAPTER 17

# Development Tools for JavaScript

**Locate JavaScript and VBScript source code you can use**

Find JavaScript source code you can use on your Web page and VBScript source code you can convert to JavaScript.

**Learn about Internet tools**

Many tools on the Internet now support JavaScript, with more on the way. Find out about the hottest tools here.

**Download the best shareware tools**

The Internet is swarming with shareware tools you can use to build classy Web pages—HTML editors, Java tools, and more.

In Chapter 12, "A Java Tutorial," you learned about some of the tools you can use to develop Java applets. And in Chapter 16, "ActiveX Controls and VBScript," you learned about the ActiveX SDK. This chapter expands on those chapters by introducing you to the tools you need to develop great Web pages with HTML, ActiveX, JavaScript, and Java.

Some of these tools are absolutely free; others are shareware programs that you can try free for a specified period of time. You pay for shareware programs only if you decide to keep and use them after the specified trial period. Other tools described in this chapter are commercial products that you can get through commercial channels such as your corner computer superstore.

# JavaScript Examples

The Internet is loaded with JavaScript (Microsoft calls it JScript) examples. In many cases, you can use these examples without worrying too much about copyright infringement. However, if you have any doubt about a program's copyright protection, get the original author's permission before you use his or her script in your Web page. If nothing else, you can rely on the scripts that you find on the Internet for inspiration when writing your own scripts. The following are some suggestions for finding scripts that you might be able to use:

- Open **http://www.yahoo.com/Computers_and_Internet/Programming_Languages/ JavaScript/Applets** in your Web browser. This is a list of JavaScript applets. Most of them have scripts from which you can learn and, in some cases, scripts you can reuse in your own Web page.

- Open your favorite Web search tool. Use the keyword **javascript** with either **demo**, **example**, or **sample**. You'll see a list of JavaScript examples from all over the Internet.

- Microsoft's JScript site at **http://www.microsoft.com/jscript/us/samples/ jssamp.HTM** contains a number of JScript examples, including a mortgage calculator, Webzee (a Yahtzee knockoff), and Hangman.

- Gamelan is an awesome Web site that contains hundreds of examples. As of this writing, it contains 372 JavaScript examples. Open **http://www.gamelan.com** in your Web browser and click the JavaScript link (in the middle of the Web page). You'll see several categories of JavaScript examples. In particular, click the Example link.

- Andrew Wooldridge, one of the authors of this text, maintains a list of JavaScript resources called the **JavaScript Index**, located at **http://www.c2.org/~andreww/ javascript/**.

# Microsoft Technologies

Many useful ActiveX and JavaScript development tools come from Microsoft. This section describes some of those tools, including the following:

The ActiveX Control Pad

Microsoft FrontPage

Microsoft Visual J++

Microsoft Visual Source Safe

Microsoft Visual C++

## ActiveX Control Pad

The ActiveX Control Pad is a must-have utility if you're using ActiveX controls and JavaScript. It's an authoring tool that enables you to automatically add ActiveX controls to your Web page—no hand-coding OBJECT tags or PARAM tags, just point and click, that's all. Figure 17.1 contains an example of the ActiveX Control Pad at work.

**FIG. 17.1**

The ActiveX Control Pad makes creating ActiveX Web pages much, much easier.

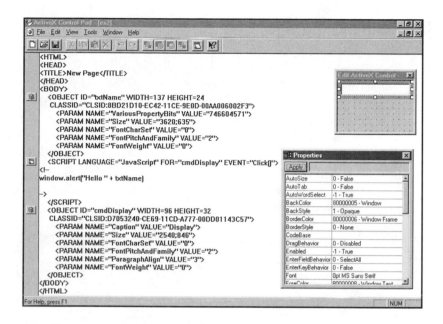

The ActiveX Control Pad also helps you to easily create JavaScript language scripts. In the Script Wizard, you associate an object's events with an object's properties and methods. Figure 17.2 shows an example of associating a button's `Click` event with the `Window` object's `alert` method.

**FIG. 17.2**

Choose the properties and methods from the right pane that you want to associate with the events in the left pane.

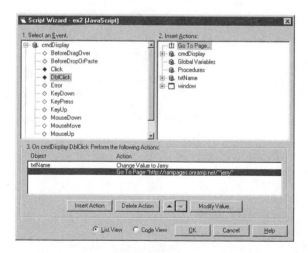

You'll learn everything you want to know about the ActiveX Control Pad in Chapter 16, "ActiveX Controls and VBScript." You'll learn how to download a free copy, how to use it to insert controls into your Web pages, how to create scripts using the Script Wizard, and how to use the HTML Layout control to create two-dimensional regions in your Web page.

## Microsoft FrontPage

Microsoft FrontPage is a popular HTML editor. Its popularity is due primarily to the fact that you don't have to know *any* HTML to use it to create great Web sites. However, it's much more than just a great HTML editor—you can use FrontPage to manage your entire Web site. FrontPage contains the following two components:

- ■ **FrontPage Explorer** enables you to create Web sites from scratch. It provides wizards and templates so that you can start with no site at all and build a foundational site in only a few minutes. FrontPage Explorer gives you a structural view of your site, too.

- ■ **FrontPage Editor** provides a what-you-see-is-what-you-get (WYSIWYG) editing environment for you to create individual pages or to edit the pages you have already created. Figure 17.3 shows you what the FrontPage Editor looks like.

**FIG. 17.3**

With FrontPage's server extensions, you can automatically stage and post your HTML files onto your Web server.

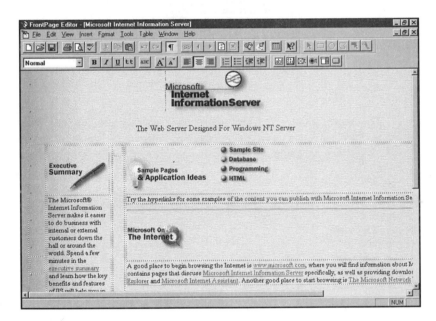

You can purchase Microsoft FrontPage at any computer retailer. More information about FrontPage is available at Microsoft's Web site: **http://www.microsoft.com/frontpage**.

**N O T E**  A good alternative to Microsoft FrontPage is Adobe PageMill. It's a similar product that makes creating Web pages easy for those who are not programmers. For example, it works just like a word processor, so you'll be familiar immediately with many of its features. You create links by dragging an icon that represents an URL and dropping it on an anchor. You even use a WYSIWYG editor to create tables. You can find more information about Adobe PageMill at **http://www.adobe.com/prodindex/pagemill/main.html**. ■

# Microsoft Visual J++

Microsoft has thrown its hat into the Java ring with Visual J++. This is Microsoft's first-rate development environment for Java Developers. Visual J++ is a comprehensive development tool that you can use to build software components for the Internet. The following are some of the highlights of Microsoft J++:

- It compiles over 10,000 lines of code per second.

- It includes an incredible debugger that you can use to disassemble bytecode, set breakpoints in your code, step through your code, watch variables, and more.

- You can work with classes, methods, and variables through the use of a class viewer (ClassView).

- You can build event-driven Java applets by using Visual J++ Wizards, which automatically generate basic code for you.

- You can use the Visual J++ resource editor to create menus, forms, toolbars, and images.

You can purchase Visual J++ at most computer stores. You can also learn more about Microsoft Visual J++ at its Web site by opening **http://www.microsoft.com/visualj** in your Web browser.

Part IV

Ch

17

# Microsoft Visual SourceSafe

If you've built a Web site of any magnitude, you probably have dozens or even hundreds of HTML files—not to mention hundreds of graphics files. What's worse, you probably have more than one person working on those files, too. You need something to help manage all those files, keep all the different versions straight, and manage conflicts between the different developers, artists, and the like. Take a look at Figure 17.4 to get an idea of Visual SourceSafe's interface.

Visual SourceSafe is precisely the right tool for managing your files and your project. It's a project-oriented version control system that manages your source files and the activities of the developers who work on them. When you want to work on a file, you check it out. This locks the file so that no one else can change it. Then, when you're finished with the file, you check it back in—unlocking the file. Visual SourceSafe keeps track of all the different versions so that you can keep a history of what's changed in the file. You can even roll back to a different version of the file if you make a mistake.

**N O T E**   Visual SourceSafe makes sharing files between multiple Web sites easy. You have one copy of a file that you share between multiple sites. Then, when you make a change to the file, that change is automatically reflected in all of the sites that share the file. ■

You can get more information about Visual SourceSafe from Microsoft's Web site by opening **http://www.microsoft.com/ssafe** in your Web browser.

**FIG. 17.4**
Visual SourceSafe's user interface looks very similar to Windows Explorer.

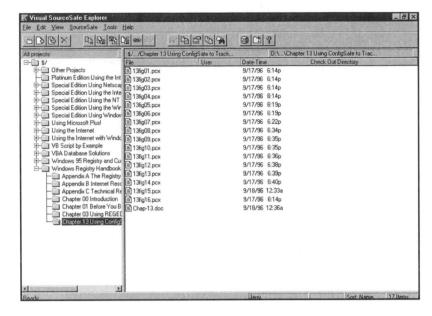

## Microsoft Visual C++

Currently, the only tool you can use to develop ActiveX controls is Microsoft's Visual C++, shown in Figure 17.5. You also need the ActiveX SDK, which you learned about in Chapter 16, "ActiveX Controls and VBScript."

**FIG. 17.5**
Microsoft Visual C++ contains a great editor, debugger, classes browser, resource editor, and more.

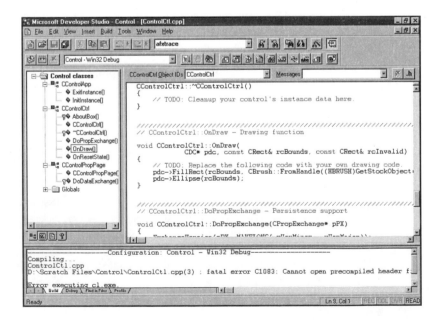

There are two ways to build ActiveX controls using Visual C++:

- You can build ActiveX controls that use the Microsoft Foundation Classes (MFC). This isn't a good idea, however, because the MFC code is large and takes longer to download over slower phone connections.

- You can build ActiveX controls by using the ActiveX Template Library. However, this requires a reasonably complete understanding of the Component Object Model (COM). These controls download much faster, though, because they don't carry the baggage of MFC.

You've learned about some of the shareware HTML editors found on the Internet. This section describes some of the shareware Java tools you can download and try out.

## CafeBabe

URL: **http://members.aol.com/opensolinc/opensolution.html**

CafeBabe is a freeware Java tool that you can use to view the revisions, super class name, and methods in a class file.

## ED

URL: **http://www.getsoft.com**

This is an evaluation copy of ED, which is an integrated development environment for Java. Soft As It Gets (the company) has also put out a new Java IDE.

## Jamba

URL: **http://www.aimtech.com/prodjahome.html**

This is an evaluation copy of Jamba, which is a Java tool you can use to create Java applets, without knowing much about Java programming.

## Java Developer's Kit

URL: **http://java.sun.com/JDK-1.0/index.html**

The Java Developer's Kit (JDK) from Sun Microsystems is the standard for Java. It is freeware and is compatible with most of the shareware Java environments that currently exist.

## JPAD

URL: **http://www.csn.net/express**

JavaPad is an editor you can use withSun's Java Development Kit (**http://java.sun.com/JDK-1.0**). You can edit, compile, debug, and run Java applets within JavaPad. Tracking down errors is easy with JavaPad, too.

# Shareware HTML Editors

The Web is just crawling with shareware HTML editors. Some of them are high-class, commercial-quality products. Others are kind of junky, but have features that make them worthwhile. This section describes some of the most popular HTML editors.

**N O T E**   I've listed only the most notable HTML editors in this section. You'll find a comprehensive list of editors at Tucows by opening **http://www.tucows.com** in your Web browser. ▨

## 1-4-All

URL: **http://ourworld.compuserve.com/homepages/minibbjd**

1-4-All is a shareware HTML editor that comes with a wizard for creating frames, a table editor, and some predefined JavaScripts.

## Almost Reality

URL: **http://www.lm.com/~pdixon/index.html**

Almost Reality is a freeware HTML editor for Windows 95.

## DerekWare HTML Author

URL: **http://shell.masterpiece.com/derek/derekware/**

DerekWare is a freeware HTML editor that supports all of the Internet Explorer HTML extensions. It has wizards for images, marquees, links, and forms. You can also add your own tags.

## Dummy

URL: **http://www.sausage.com/dummy.htm**

Dummy is a shareware utility published by Sausage Software (see HotDog Professional) that works more like a wizard. It provides step-by-step help for creating your home page from a predetermined style.

## FlexED for Windows 95

URL: **http://www.infoflex.com.au/flexed.htm**

FlexED for Windows 95 is a highly rated shareware HTML editor. You can edit the HTML directly by using dialog boxes to set the attributes for each tag. It also provides a lot of wizards that can automatically format your Web page for you, based on how you answer the questions provided. You can use this HTML editor even if you don't know any HTML.

# HotDog Professional

URL: **http://www.sausage.com**

HotDog Professional is one of the single-best shareware HTML editors available on the Internet. It has an easy-to-use user interface and it provides wizards to simplify your job. It also has advanced features such as a built-in animation editor. It contains JavaScript language scripts that you can use to add special effects to your Web page.

# HomeSite

URL: **http://www.dexnet.com/**

HomeSite is a basic shareware HTML editor that outputs HTML 3.0 code. It has some nice features in it, such as multifile search-and-replace and a Windows Explorer-like view of your HTML files.

# HTML Edit

URL: **http://www.iac.net/~afi/htmledit/htmledit.html**

HTML Edit is an easy-to-use freeware HTML editor. It's a good choice for beginners.

# HTML Express

URL: **http://www.pe.net/~coolkev/htmlexpress.html**

HTML Express is a shareware wizard-type program that creates HTML pages in a snap. If you don't want to mess with a bunch of HTML tags, you should give this one a try.

# HTMLPad

URL: **http://www.intermania.com/~imania**

HTMLPad is a simple shareware HTML editor. It looks a lot like Notepad but is geared toward editing HTML files.

# INP

URL: **http://inp.harbinger.net/products/index.htm**

INP is a great tool to create a corporate Web page quickly. You answer a questionnaire, which is industry-specific, and INP generates an eight-page Web site based on your answers. It comes with a bunch of predefined graphics that you can use on your Web site, including backgrounds and icons. ●

# CHAPTER 18

# Using Frames

One of the tremendous advantages of hypertext is its ability to link together many pieces of information in a nonlinear fashion. Rather than having to read a book one page at a time, you can leap from one link to the next as you explore different topics and their interconnections. However, sometimes this easy access to information can have unfortunate and cumbersome side effects.

One such side effect occurs when you find yourself moving back and forth between a small set of pages, over and over again. This happens because of a problem with *presentation*: the information you want is scattered over more than one page. If you are reading a tutorial, for example, you may find that you are revisiting the Table of Contents page with dreary repetitiveness. You can avoid this by having multiple browser windows open at the same time, but this often takes up too much of your display.

This chapter focuses on the emerging HTML *frames* technology, which addresses this issue of presentation. Both Microsoft's Internet Explorer version 3.0 and the Netscape Navigator 3.0 browser enable you to split a single browser window into multiple, independent sub-windows, each containing its own URL. These sub-windows are known as frames. We will explore frames technology and its close relationship to JavaScript in some detail.

## Build framesets and communicate between them

While framesets are easy to build, it is more challenging to have them talk to one another. Document loading and frameset addressing are covered in detail.

## Manage a JavaScript function library

Frames are an excellent place to store often-used JavaScript functions. Persistent functions can reside on one frame while other frames present dynamic data.

## Create nested framesets

Framesets can be nested in a single document or in more than one document, meaning that one frame can contain other sub-frames.

Please note that several listings are provided in this chapter for referenced example files. These listings are also included on this book's companion Web site. Unlike the other chapters in this book, file names are provided in the listing headings in this chapter to identify the individual frame files referenced. However, there are also files referenced in this chapter for which there are not corresponding listings in the text. Instead, these files' listings appear only on the Web site for this book. ■

# Frames and JavaScript

Frames are one of the most important new features to be added to HTML for some time. Frames allow multiple sub-windows—or panes—in a single Web page. This gives you the opportunity to display several URLs at the same time on the same Web page. It also enables you to keep part of the screen constant while other parts are updated. This is ideal for many Web applications that span multiple pages but also have a constant portion, such as a table of contents. Before you learn about the implications of frames on JavaScript, a very brief tutorial on frames will be presented.

## Specifying Frames in HTML

Frames in HTML are organized into sets that are known, appropriately enough, as *framesets*. To define a set of frames, one must first allocate screen real estate to this frameset and then place each of the individual frames within it. We will examine the syntax for the HTML FRAMESET and FRAME tags to understand how frames and framesets are organized.

One of the most important and most confusing aspects of frames is the parent/child relationships of frames, framesets, and the windows that contain them. The first frameset placed in a window has that window as its parent. A frameset can also host another frameset, in which case the initial frameset is the parent. Note that a top-level frameset itself is typically not named, but a frameset's child frames can be named. Frames can be referred to by name or as an index of the frames array.

You can divide your window real estate with a statement of the form <FRAMESET COLS=40%,*>. This frameset statement divides the window horizontally into two frames. It tells the browser to give 40% of the window width to the left frame, frames[0], and anything remaining to the right frame, frames[1]. You can explicitly give percentages or pixel widths for all frames, but it is more useful to use the asterisk for at least one parameter. Use this wild card character (*) for the widest frame or for the frame that is least likely to be resized. This helps ensure that the entire frameset is displayed on a single screen. You can also divide the window vertically with a statement like <FRAMESET ROWS=20%,*,10%>. This statement gives 20% of the available window height to the top frame, frames[0], 10% to the bottom frame, frames[2], and anything left to the middle frame, frames[1].

> **CAUTION**
> You cannot divide a window both horizontally and vertically with one frameset. To do that, you must use nested framesets.

The subsequent <FRAME...> statements define the name, source (URL), and attributes of each frame in the frameset. For example,

```
<FRAME SRC='menu.htm' NAME='menuframe'
MARGINWIDTH=2 MARGINHEIGHT=2 SCROLLING="YES">
```

defines a frame into which the Menu.htm file will be loaded. This frame is named menuframe.

Unless you are designing a *ledge* (a frame that never changes) and you know it will always appear in the frame, make the frame scrollable. You can enter an explicit SCROLLING attribute, which should equal the value YES or NO (the frame defaults to SCROLLING=YES). Scrolling is much kinder to your users. You might have a very high-resolution display, but a lot of computers, particularly laptops, do not. The MARGINWIDTH=*xx* and MARGINHEIGHT=*xx* attributes also allow you some latitude in how you present your document within a frame.

**N O T E**  Although Internet Explorer 3.0 and Netscape Navigator 3.0 both understand frames, many other browsers don't yet have that capability. Ideally, you should provide a version of your document that does not use frames for such browsers. At a minimum, you should warn the users about the presence of frames in your document by using a <NOFRAMES>...</NOFRAMES> clause. Anything contained within the clause will be ignored by frames-capable browsers. ■

Make sure that you have an initial URL to load into the frame, even if that URL is just a placeholder. Otherwise, you might find that the browser has loaded an index to the current directory. If you want to use a frame in the frameset to load other documents from a link, you must specify the target frame such as the following:

```
<A HREF='netcom.com/home' TARGET='menuframe'>Microsoft</A>
```

Frames are a sophisticated way to build Web pages; You can keep your menu in one frame and display your content in another. However, it is easy to go overboard and have too many frames. If you present too much information in several different small frames, the user will probably be scrolling quite often. Since the whole purpose of frames is to present information in a pleasing manner, it is important not to try the user's patience. Frames can be a powerful tool, but they should be used judiciously.

## Building a Frameset

Framesets are easy to build, although their hierarchy can become complex if they are nested. Listing 18.1 shows a simple frameset document. For it to display correctly, there must be HTML documents with the names given by the SRC attribute in each FRAME definition. When this code is loaded into the browser, the page shown in Figure 18.1 appears.

**Listing 18.1   C18-2.htm—A Simple Frameset**

```
<HTML>
<HEAD>
<TITLE>Simple Frame</TITLE>
```

*continues*

Part **IV**

Ch **18**

**Listing 18.1   Continued**

```
<SCRIPT></SCRIPT>
</HEAD>
<FRAMESET cols=40%,*>
<FRAME SRC="menu_2.htm" NAME="menuFrm" SCROLLING=YES
MARGINWIDTH=3 MARGINHEIGHT=3>
<FRAME SRC="display.htm" NAME="displayFrm" SCROLLING=YES
MARGINWIDTH=3 MARGINHEIGHT=3>
<NOFRAMES>
You must have a frames-capable browser to
<A HREF="noframes.htm">view this document</A> correctly.
</NOFRAMES>
</FRAMESET>
</HTML>
```

**FIG. 18.1**

Framesets contain multiple frames and reference multiple URLs.

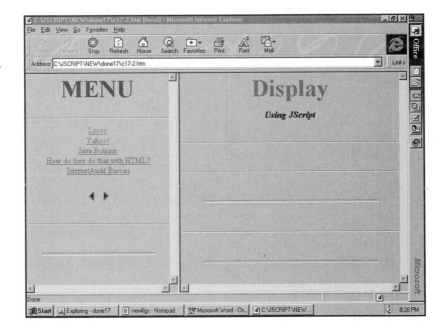

**N O T E**   When building a frameset, always remember the following rules:

1. The <FRAMESET>...</FRAMESET> block replaces the <BODY>...</BODY> block. It is incorrect to have both.

2. Always use a <NOFRAMES>...</NOFRAMES> clause for browsers that do not support frames. Include the <BODY> tag inside this clause so that those browsers will recognize the page; it will be ignored by the frames-capable browser.

3. Make all your frames scrollable, except in exceptional circumstances.

4. Make sure the HTML documents referenced by the SRC attributes are "live" before the frameset appears (meaning that there is an actual file for the SRC to retrieve when the page loads). ■

One of the most difficult concepts about framesets and frames is how they are referenced. For the simple frameset previously shown, you can make a simple roadmap of the object references. When you want to reference the child frames from the frameset, you can use the following references:

Menu_2.htm = `frames[0]` or `menuFrm`

Display.htm = `frames[1]` or `displayFrm`

When one of the frames references its parent frameset, the following object reference is used:

Either frame = `parent`

The contents of each frame are referenced as properties of the frame. For example, the frameset can access the document object of Menu_2.htm as `frames[0].document` or `menuFrm.document`. The latter usage is usually preferable because it is self-documenting.

# Frames Within Frames

Frames can be nested in two ways. We will illustrate both types of nesting by putting another frameset inside the `displayFrm` frame object defined in Listing 18.1. To understand the first method, call the original frameset, Frameset A. The frameset declaration shown in Listing 18.2 nests a second frameset, referred to as Frameset B, within Frameset A (see Figure 18.2). It does this by replacing `frames[1]` (the `displayFrm` frame) with another frameset. The auxiliary files Menu_3.htm, Pics.htm, and Text.htm are also required.

**Listing 18.2  Example of Nested Frames in Which a Frame Is Replaced with Another Frameset**

```
<HTML>
<HEAD>
<SCRIPT>
</SCRIPT>
</HEAD>
<FRAMESET COLS = 30%,*>
<FRAME SRC = 'menu_3.htm' NAME='menuFrame' MARGINWIDTH=3
MARGINHEIGHT=3>
<FRAMESET ROWS=66%,*>
<FRAME SRC='pics.htm' NAME='picFrame' SCROLLING=yes
MARGINWIDTH=3
MARGINHEIGHT=3>
<FRAME SRC='text.htm' NAME= 'textFrame' SCROLLING=yes
MARGINWIDTH=3 MARGINHEIGHT=3>
```

*continues*

Part
IV
Ch
18

**Listing 18.2   Continued**

```
</FRAMESET>
<NOFRAMES>
You must have a frames-capable browser to view this document correctly.
<A HREF=text.htm>Here is the main page</a>.
</NOFRAMES>
</FRAMESET>
</HTML>
```

**FIG. 18.2**

Replacing frames with framesets.

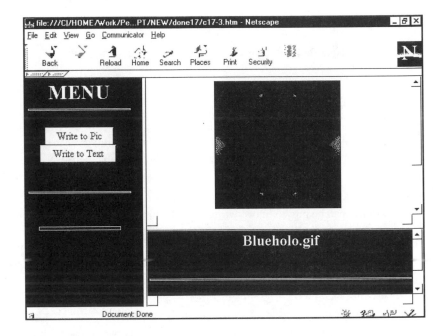

Referencing in this type of nested frameset is no different from the type of object references described for a simple frameset. When a frameset references a child frame, the following object references are used:

Menu_3.htm = `frames[0]` or `menuFrame`

Pics.htm = `frames[1]` or `picFrame`

Text.htm = `frames[2]` or `textFrame`

When any of the component frames refers to the frameset that contains it, the following reference is used:

Any frame = `parent`

The second method uses URLs to achieve nested framesets. We will set Frameset B's `displfrm` to an URL that contains a framed document. This URL comes from the file Displfrm.htm and creates the frames `picFrame` and `textFrame`. In this case, the object references are somewhat more complex. When the parent refers to its child frames, it uses the following:

Menu_4.htm = `frames[0]` or `menuFrm`

Displfrm.htm = `frames[1]` or `displayFrm`

Pics.htm = `frames[1].frames[0]` or `displayFrm.picFrame`

Text.htm = `frames[1].frames[1]` or `displayFrm.textFrame`

When the child frames refer to their frameset parent, the following object references are used:

Menu_4.htm = `parent`

Displfrm.htm = `parent`

Pics.htm = `parent.parent`

Text.htm = `parent.parent`

> **CAUTION**
>
> Specifying an empty URL in a frame declaration can cause the index file in the server's current directory to be loaded Into the frame. Anyone can then open any of the documents listed in that index file. This can be considerably detrimental if you do not want to allow users to view all of the files within that directory.

**Part**

**IV**

**Ch**

**18**

# Examples of Interframe Communication

At this point, you know how to refer to parent framesets in frames and you also know the correct object references for child frames of a frameset. The next topic explores interframe communication. The files C18-2.htm (Listing 18.1), Menu_2.htm (Listing 18.3), and Display.htm (Listing 18.4) are used in this example. Make sure you place all these files in the same directory, and then load C18-2.htm into your browser. The file Menu_2.htm that is loaded into the left frame provides a simple and useful example of interframe communication. Figure 18.3 shows an example of using nested framesets.

**Listing 18.3    Menu_2.htm—Using URLs to Create Nested Framesets**

```
<HTML>
<HEAD>
<TITLE>MENU.HTM</TITLE>
<SCRIPT>
function goback()
{
awin = self.parent.displayFrm
awin.history.back()
}
function gonext()
{
awin = self.parent.displayFrm
```

*continues*

**Listing 18.3    Continued**

```
awin.history.forward()
}
</SCRIPT>
</HEAD>
<BODY BGCOLOR='darkslateblue' TEXT='linen' LINK='corel'
VLINK='darkcorel' ALINK='yellow' >
<CENTER><FONT SIZE=7 COLOR="yellow"><B>MENU<B></FONT><CENTER>
<H3><HR></H3>
<A HREF="http://lycos-tmp1.psc.edu/lycos-form.html"
TARGET ="displayFrm">Lycos</A><BR>
<A HREF="http://www.yahoo.com/new"
TARGET ="displayFrm">Yahoo!</A><BR>
<A HREF="http://weber.u.washington.edu/~jgurney/java/"
TARGET ="displayFrm">Java Botique</A><BR>
<A HREF="http://www.nashville.net/~carl/htmlguide/index.html"
TARGET ="displayFrm">How do they do that with HTML?</A><BR>
<A HREF="http://www.internet-audit.com/"
TARGET ="displayFrm">InternetAudit Bureau</A><BR>
<H3><BR></H3>
<CENTER>
<A HREF=javascript:goback()>
<IMG WIDTH=24 HEIGHT= 21 VSPACE=2 HSPACE= 2 BORDER=0
SRC="Images/arw2_l.gif">
</A>
<A HREF="javascript:gonext()">
<IMG WIDTH=24 HEIGHT= 21 VSPACE=2 HSPACE= 2  BORDER=0
SRC="Images/arw2_r.gif">
</A>
</CENTER>
<BR>
<H3><BR><HR><BR></H3>
<H3><BR><HR SIZE=5 WIDTH=80%><BR></H3>
</BODY>
</HTML>
```

**Listing 18.4    Display.htm—Content for Display Frame**

```
<HTML>
<HEAD>
<TITLE>Display</TITLE>
<SCRIPT></SCRIPT>
</HEAD>
<BODY BACKGROUND= TEXT= LINK= VLINK= ALINK= >
<CENTER><FONT SIZE=7 COLOR="red"><B>Display<B></FONT><CENTER>
<CENTER><H3><i>Using JScript</i></H3></CENTER>
<H3><BR><HR><BR></H3>
<H3><BR><HR><BR></H3>
<H3><BR><HR SIZE=5 WIDTH=80%><BR></H3>
<H3><BR><HR><BR></H3>
<H3><BR><HR SIZE=5 WIDTH=80%><BR></H3>
</BODY>
</HTML>
```

**FIG. 18.3**

An example of nested framesets

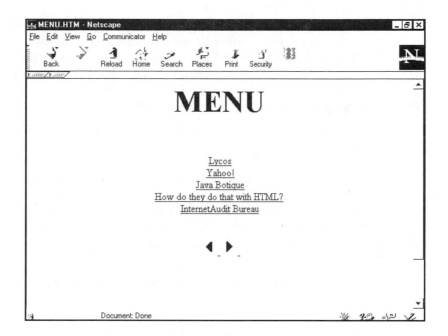

The Menu_2.htm file contains some links to well-known sites. A TARGET that points to the displayFrm frame is given for each link. If you click a link, the URL loads into the displayFrm frame instead of into the menuFrm frame. Note that you cannot refer to the "parent" object when you use a TARGET. To experiment with the page, click several links. After you have done this a few times, try to go backwards by using Netscape Navigator's Back button. Notice that if you are using Netscape Navigator 2.0, the whole frameset disappears; it is replaced by the document you were looking at before you loaded the C18-2.htm frameset, whereas in Navigator 3.0, you move back just one step in the frame you were in. Internet Explorer's navigational behavior is the same as Netscape 3.0.

**T I P** Earlier versions of Netscape Navigator 2.0's and Internet Explorer's Forward and Back buttons work on the entire document—not on individual frames, although in Internet Explorer you can go back in frames by using the backspace key.

This limitation in earlier browsers can certainly make life difficult, especially if you follow several links in the displayFrm and now want to get back to an intermediate one. Fortunately, there is a way to do this, but you must specifically provide for it. Notice the two small image buttons below the links. If you click the left arrow, the displayFrm frame reverts to the previously visited URL. Similarly, the right arrow takes you forward in the frame.

Another interesting aspect of frames is revealed if you attempt to use the View Source option of Internet Explorer or Netscape Navigator. Only the code for the frameset appears; the code for the frames contained in it does not appear. This is one approach to provide some simple protection for your source code. However, it keeps only novice users from seeing your code;

experienced users can defeat this by loading the URLs referenced in the individual frames into a single browser window and then by using View Source on that window. Newer versions of Navigator and Internet Explorer now give you the option of viewing the document source (the whole window) or the frame source (the HTML contained within the frame that has focus).

# Writing a New Document into a Frame

The examples in the files C18-2.htm and C18-3.htm do simple rewrites of documents into adjacent and foreign frames. We will now expand on that by taking the Note object example from Chapter 10, "Dynamic HTML and Netscape Objects," and writing it to a frame, rather than to a new window. The file C18-4.htm defines the frameset that loads the subsidiary documents Setnote.htm and Note.htm into its frames. The file Setnote.htm contains a button that calls a writeNote() routine to write the new HTML into the frames[1] frame. The file Note.htm is just a stub so that you don't have to write an empty URL. Listing 18.5 shows the code for the writeNote() function. Figure 18.4 shows what happens when the note is written into the frame.

**Listing 18.5   Setnote.htm—The Code for the *writeNote()* Function**

```
function writenote(topic)
{
topic = 'This is a little note about rewriting adjacent frames."
topic += " You do it the same way as you would to rewrite"
topic += " or originally write a window."
aWin = self.parent.displayFrm
ndoc= aWin.document
astr ='<HTML><HEAD><BR><TITLE>' + topic + '</TITLE>'
astr +='</HEAD>'
astr +='<SCRIPT>'
astr +='function closeNote(aName){'
astr +='self.close()'
astr +='}'
astr +='function saveNote(aName){'
astr +='}'
astr +='<\/SCRIPT>'
astr +='<BODY>'
astr +='<FORM>'
astr +='<TABLE ALIGN=LEFT BORDER><TR ALIGN=CENTER><TD>'
astr +='\<INPUT TYPE=button NAME=saveBtn VALUE="Save"
ONCLICK="saveNote()" \>'
astr +='</TD>'
astr +='<TD ROWSPAN=4>' + topic
astr +='</TD>'
astr +='</TR><TR ALIGN=CENTER><TD>'
astr +='\<INPUT TYPE=button NAME=closeBtn VALUE="Close"
ONCLICK="closeNote()" \>'
astr +='</TD></TR>'
astr +='<TR><TD><BR></TD></TR>'
astr +='<TR><TD><BR></TD></TR>'
astr +='</TABLE>'
astr +='</FORM>'
astr +='<BR CLEAR=ALL><H3><BR></H3>'
```

```
astr +='Note:  Save button is not active yet'
astr +='</BODY></HTML>'
ndoc.write(astr)
ndoc.close()
}
```

**FIG. 18.4**
Documents can be dynamically written into frames.

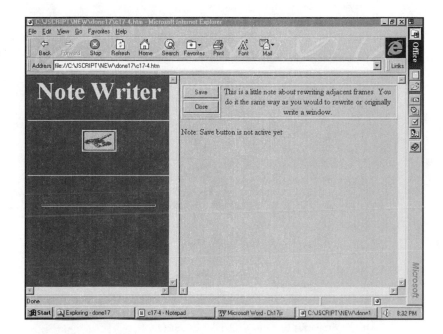

## Building a JavaScript Function Library in a Frameholder

You have already learned that a frameset document cannot contain any HTML other than frame definitions. It can, however, contain a script. In this script, you can keep window-global variables and functions. We will define a minimal string manipulator in a frameset. With this tool, you can do the following:

- Change a string to capital letters.
- Change a string to lowercase.
- Change all instances of a character.

The first two operations merely require calls to string functions. The latter can be accomplished by a routine that we have already written. You store these functions in the frameset of the file C18-5.htm (Listing 18.6). This frameset requires the files Funcs.htm (Listing 18.7) and Editor.htm (Listing 18.8) to be in the same directory.

### Listing 18.6   C18-5.htm—Storing Functions in a Frameset

```
<HTML>
<HEAD>
<TITLE><Simple Frame</TITLE>
<SCRIPT></SCRIPT>
</HEAD>
<FRAMESET cols=40%,*>
     <FRAME SRC="funcs.htm" NAME="menuFrm" SCROLLING=YES
      MARGINWIDTH=3 MARGINHEIGHT=3>
     <FRAME SRC="editor.htm" NAME="editFrm" SCROLLING=YES
      MARGINWIDTH=3 MARGINHEIGHT=3>
     <NOFRAMES>
       You must have a frames-capable browser to
       <A HREF="noframes.htm">view this document</A> correctly.
     </NOFRAMES>
</FRAMESET>
</HTML>
```

### Listing 18.7   Funcs.htm—The Text Converter Functions

```
<HTML>
<HEAD>
<TITLE>Text Converter</TITLE>
<SCRIPT>

function testit()
{
      var valu = document.choices.testtext.value
      var nvalu = valu.toUpperCase()
      document.choices.testtext.value = nvalu
}

function ucase()
{
      var adoc = parent.editFrm.document.edit.myedit
      var nval = adoc.value.toUpperCase()
      adoc.value = nval
}

function lcase()
{
      var adoc = parent.editFrm.document.edit.myedit
      var nval = adoc.value.toLowerCase()
      adoc.value = nval
}

function xreplace()
{
      var adoc = parent.editFrm.document.edit.myedit
      var valu = adoc.value
      var oldx = document.choices.oldtext.value
```

```
            var newx = document.choices.newtext.value
            var c
            var outv = ""

            for(var i=0;i<valu.length;i++)
                    {
                            c = valu.charAt(i)
                            if ( c == oldx )
                                    outv += newx
                            else
                                    outv += c
                    }
            adoc.value = outv
}

</SCRIPT>
</HEAD>
<BODY BGCOLOR='darkslateblue' TEXT='linen' LINK='lightblue' VLINK='darkcorel'
ALINK='yellow' >
<CENTER><FONT SIZE=6 COLOR="lightblue"><B>Text Converter<B></FONT><CENTER>
<HR>
<CENTER>
<FORM NAME="choices">
<TABLE WIDTH=90% CELLPADDING=3 CELLSPACING=2 BORDER=4>
<TR ALIGN=CENTER VALIGN=MIDDLE>
<TD>
<INPUT TYPE="RADIO" NAME="change" VALUE='upper' onClick='ucase()'>Upper Case<BR>
<INPUT TYPE="RADIO" NAME="change" VALUE='lower' onClick='lcase()'>Lower Case<BR>
<HR>
<INPUT TYPE="RADIO" NAME="change" VALUE='replace' onClick='xreplace()'>Replace
➥Char<BR>
Replace<INPUT TYPE="TEXT" NAME="oldtext" SIZE="10" MAXLENGTH="1"><BR>
With<INPUT TYPE="TEXT" NAME="newtext" SIZE="10" MAXLENGTH="80">
</TD></TR>
<TR><TD>
<CENTER>
<FONT SIZE=5>TEST</FONT>
<B><TEXTAREA  NAME="testtext" ROWS=6 COLS=15 WRAP=soft>
Use this text and button to test new function calls on objects in this frame
rather than the editor frame. The test function is currently set to uppercase
</TEXTAREA></B><BR>
<INPUT TYPE="BUTTON" NAME="test" VALUE='Test'
onClick='testit(this.form.testtext.value)'>
<CENTER>
</TD></TR>
</TABLE>
</FORM>
</CENTER>
<H3><BR><HR><BR></H3>
<H3><BR><HR SIZE=5 WIDTH=80%><BR></H3>
</BODY>
<SCRIPT>
</SCRIPT>
</HTML>
```

**Listing 18.8    Editor.htm—The Editor Window**

```
<HTML>
<HEAD>
<TITLE>Text</TITLE>
<SCRIPT></SCRIPT>
</HEAD>
<BODY BGCOLOR='linen' TEXT='darkslateblue' LINK='orange' VLINK='indianred'
➥ALINK='red' >
<CENTER><FONT SIZE=7 COLOR="darkblue"><B>Editor</B></FONT></CENTER>
<HR>
<CENTER><H5>Write the text you want to edit here. You can use the functions on
➥the left to change it.</H5></CENTER>
<HR>
<FORM NAME="edit">
<TEXTAREA NAME='myedit' ROWS="20" COLS="40" WRAP></TEXTAREA>
</FORM>
<H3><BR><HR SIZE=5 WIDTH=80%><BR></H3>
</BODY>
</HTML>
```

The frame named menuFrm contains buttons to call your frameset functions. These functions must be able to refer to objects in their own frame as well as the adjacent frame editFrm. In addition, you must be able to call these functions from the parent frame. The true value of a frameset function library is its reusability. It is easy to copy the HTML file that defines the library and create a new document by changing a small amount of code—the code that builds the frameset itself. In this way, you can reuse your code.

Another way to reuse code is to have all the functions in a small or hidden frame. When you want to use those functions, you simply load that frame. If you take this approach, you don't have to change the frameset code. In both cases, however, it is more difficult to address an adjacent frame than it is to address a parent or child.

The menuFrm frame loads the document defined in Listing 18.7—Funcs.htm. This file defines the buttons that access the frameset functions. Some of the object references are quite long, so this file makes liberal use of aliasing to shorten them. The file Funcs.htm is loaded into the frames[0] object, while a simple editor window is placed in frames[1]. This editor is implemented as a textarea. When this frameset is loaded, the browser displays something like what is shown in Figure 18.5.

The file Funcs.htm also has a test window and a button, so you can try out the functions it provides. These functions act on objects in its document. The code is such that the button always calls a routine named testit. The testit function has calls to the three routines in the function library. You can easily adapt this code for your own purposes by replacing the testit function.

**FIG. 18.5**
A frameset library can
be used to implement a
string processor.

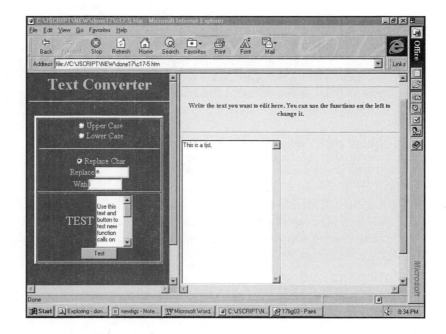

The most complex part of using functions stored in the frameset is determining the appropriate name of the frameset window. This depends on the window from which the function call is made. The example previously shown offers a very simple solution: just use `self.parent.myfunc()`. The `self` portion of this expression can be omitted, but you might want to keep it to discourage ambiguity.

# Other Frame Techniques

Netscape improved its implementation of frames with 3.0 to include frames that have no borders (which give the page a more continuous feel). Also, there are ways to use frames that the user doesn't see to hide code or store information.

## Borderless Frames

Although Internet Explorer first implemented borderless frames, Netscape has added this capability in Navigator 3.0. To take advantage of this, you need to use two attributes of the FRAME tag: FRAMEBORDER and BORDER. FRAMEBORDER specifies whether frames will appear with borders by indicating either "yes" or "no." The BORDER attribute specifies with a number the width of the borders, if you have them. For no borders, set this to 0. Although you might confuse these two attributes, it is necessary to include both for Netscape to hide the borders on frames. Perhaps in the future, the FRAMEBORDER attribute will disappear and BORDER=0 will be sufficient to direct the browser to hide the borders.

Part
IV

Ch

18

## "Hidden" Frames

Another technique used to build frame-based pages is to place all the code you don't want changed or replaced into a "hidden" frame. This frame is not really hidden and often appears as two borders with a tiny space on the browser page. To specify a "hidden" frame, simply add another frame to your frameset, but make sure that all the other frames take up all the available space on the page. For example:

```
<FRAMESET ROWS="50%,50%,*">
<FRAME SRC="one.html" NAME=first>
<FRAME SRC="two.html" NAME=second>
<FRAME SRC="hidden.html" NAME=hidden>
</FRAMESET>
```

With this HTML, the first two frames each take up 50% of the page. Therefore, the last frame will be made as small as the browser can make it. Experiment with this technique to see how much easier it is to place persistent code into this hidden frame, while dynamically replacing the other frames. ●

# CHAPTER 19

# Controlling Web Page Appearance

**A**s you already know, HTML is not desktop publishing. It provides structure and style to your Web page, but no control of the page width, size, or typography. This is what enables the Web to work on so many different platforms. Now, with JavaScript and recent extensions to the HTML specification, you have more control over page appearance. In fact, your whole site can almost be considered one application.

This chapter focuses on the appearance of text on your user's Web browser. The first section covers building JavaScript applications with a control panel. Next, text properties, font colors, and font methods are discussed. The chapter ends with a detailed example of a message editor, which uses all of the font methods of JavaScript. ∎

**JavaScript applications**

Designing an application can involve building multiple, related pages with JavaScript. You can do this using frames and multiple windows.

**Storing data**

Though you cannot save data to the user's hard drive in the traditional way, there are ways to save information into cookies via the browser.

**Color properties**

Colors can be specified by name, without using hexadecimal numbers. You can specify colors by a commonly used table of names as well.

**Designing a frame application**

Learn about child-parent relations when referring to objects between frames.

**JavaScript for text editing**

Learn how to develop a message editor application. Although text-editing methods are minimal, you can still create a practical application.

**Hyperlinks as controls**

Use color, text, and hyperlinks as control buttons.

# Page Building with JavaScript

Before applying specific JavaScript properties, methods, and techniques, you must be aware of layout. This includes how the browser processes a page and its related documents, as well as some design principles about good layout. You can build multiple pages with JavaScript to design your application.

## Even the First Page Can Come Alive

When a user requests a page from your site for the first time, the user has not yet given you any feedback, so you simply serve the page. When the page reaches the browser, however, the following two facts become available and can make the page come alive:

■ JavaScript-enhanced browsers recognizes code that other browsers ignore. You may add a special welcome to your opening document that only JavaScript users can view. The code in Listing 19.1 makes a menu of links available only to JavaScript users.

■ JavaScript-enhanced browsers know the time of day and the date. By using this information, you can change the appearance of the page. Although this has limited application, it is still worth considering. For example, you can display holiday greetings. Listing 19.1 also contains code for a greeting based on the hour of the day. As an example, look at Katipodesign at **http://www.katipodesign.com/**, shown in Figure 19.1.

### Listing 19.1   JavaScript-Only Greeting and Menu

```
<HTML><HEAD><TITLE>greeting.htm by Ray Daly</TITLE></HEAD>
<BODY><H1>WTFIN:  Where to Find It Now</H1>
<SCRIPT LANGUAGE="JavaScript">
<!-- hidden from other browsers
today=new Date()     //..get date and time
x=today.getHours()   //..pull out the hours
document.write ('<H2>Welcome JavaScript Surfers</H2>')
if (x<12) {
   document.write('<H3>Good Morning!</H3>')
} else {
   document.write('<H3>Hello on this beautiful day!</H3>')
}
//...you could substitute graphics instead of text greetings.
document.write('<P>Hidden away for your use only are several applications:</P>')
// Add your own application link(s) here
document.write('<OL><LI><A HREF="mypage.htm">Message Editor</A></LI>')
document.write('<LI>More applications here.</LI></OL>')
//  all done with JavaScript-->
</SCRIPT>
<!-- Add you own forward link here -->
<A HREF="mypage2page.htm">Continue to <I>Find it Now</I>.</A>
</BODY></HTML>
```

**FIG. 19.1**
Katipodesign shows how graphic design can be enhanced with JavaScript, but you have to visit it at different times of the day to see it all.

One of the first things you learn about JavaScript is that you cannot really change much about a page that is already displayed. Change a property, and most likely it doesn't change the appearance. The text and layout of form elements are fixed.

You can, however, change the background color. For most pages, this may seem trivial, and it probably is. But you can be creative with this feature. This is covered in more detail later in the section titled, "Practical Uses of Text Properties."

## First Page as a Control Panel

Although the user can't control the currently displayed page, data from this page can change the appearance and content of related documents. In many ways, you can consider the first page to be a *control panel* that enables users to make choices that affect all related documents.

As an example, you can create a frameset in which one frame is the control panel. In this frame, the user can click a choice of font and background colors. The rest of the documents in the other frames then appear with this selection.

With frames, you have the frame document and related documents. You may not want the user to be able to load the related documents without the frameset. In these related documents, you can use the onLoad event handler to verify that the document was loaded with the frameset. Just check to see if window.frames.length is greater than zero. If it is, then your page has been loaded inside a frameset.

The first page can also control content. For example, a sports site might start by asking which sports interest you. The rest of the site can omit links and information on teams and games that don't match your interest.

## JavaScript-Enhanced Pages as an Application

These control panels could be more sophisticated to the point of becoming a full-fledged application. You might develop a whole series of questions, something like a registration page, and all subsequent documents could be modified by the registration data from the control panel. These control panels are coming up more and more often on sites (see Figure 19.2).

**FIG. 19.2**

Dave's Tekno Dive, **http://www.dream.com** gets better with each visit. If you register, he saves your background preference for 30 days. The control panel changes the way you browse his site.

It is possible to build very advanced JavaScript applications using this technique. The dependence on data from the first page is like a parent-child relationship. (This is very different from today's Web sites, in which most pages can stand on their own.) Although the server can send what appears to be static pages, the JavaScript in these pages makes them come alive in the browser.

**N O T E** As you will see in this chapter, you can create documents that are only a part of an application. Often, these pages make little or no sense on their own. Yet all pages look the same to a search engine. To discourage people from directly accessing these secondary documents, consider hiding these pages from the search engines.

This is usually done with a Robots.txt file. When a search engine indexes a site, it use a program called a robot or a spider. When the engine visits a site, the first file it reads is Robots.txt. By using the information in this file, the search engine's robot omits specified areas from its search on the site. Take a moment to read "A Standard for Robot Exclusion," which is available at

**http://info.webcrawler.com/mak/projects/robots/norobots.html** ▪

# Storing Control Panel Information

As you develop JavaScript applications, you will have multiple related documents. Sharing information amongst these documents is part of the process of building these applications. But now that you have collected all of this information, you may want to start storing it.

**Cookies Store Information in the Browser**    One means of storing information amongst pages is to use *cookies* (client-side persistent information). The browser, not the server, maintains this information. When using cookies, each time the browser makes a certain request to a server, the request includes this stored information. The server may or may not use this information.

Let's look at a simple example. Say you want to store a customer's name, such as "Smith." The information is stored by the browser, and when the browser requests another related page, this information is sent to the server by the browser.

Cookie data uses the format *NAME=VALUE*. For this example it would be `customer=Smith`. If you have multiple pairs of data, just separate them with semicolons—for example:

```
customer=Smith ; phone=8005551212.
```

To store information in a cookie with JavaScript, you can use the `cookie` property of the document object. To store a value, use a statement such as the following:

```
document.cookie = "customer=Smith"
```

In the default mode, the cookie information is maintained until a session ends. Also, the information is sent only when requesting pages from the same server. More details are available in Netscape's Preliminary Specification (http://home.netscape.com/newsref/std/cookie_spec.html).

You also retrieve information from the cookie by using the `cookie` property. Then, by using string methods, you can extract the information. For our customer Smith example, use the following code:

```
var pair=document.cookie
lastname = pair.substring(pair.indexOf("=")+1,pair.length)
///...lastname should now equal Smith
```

You can store cookie information in two ways. First, as you gather important information, you might want to store it immediately in the cookie. The other method is to create an exit function. This function is called by an `unLoad` event and saves the information into the cookie.

While the cookie specification is considered preliminary, the standard is supported, to varying degrees, by a wide number of browsers, including Internet Explorer 3.0 and Netscape Navigator 3.0. So, while you should use it with some degree of caution, cookies will certainly become more common.

**URLs for Storage**    Though this is infrequently used, you can store information in the URL for your page. Using the search property of a location object, you can add text to the end of your URL. While extremely long URLs can cause server problems, storing small amounts of data should work flawlessly. Search data is the information after a question mark in an URL. In the following example, `?info=htmljive` is the search portion of the URL:

```
http://www.yoursite.com?info=htmljive
```

After a user enters registration information, you can take him or her to a post-registration page. Your code can add registration information to the URL by using the `search` property (see Listing 19.2). Recommend to the user that he or she make that page a bookmark. This saves the user's registration information as part of the bookmark's list.

When the customer returns to your site by using the bookmark's list, you can read the search property of the URL. Now you have the registration information, and your user can be immediately directed into your site.

**Listing 19.2   Store Information in an URL**

```
<HTML><HEAD><TITLE>search.htm by Ray Daly </TITLE></HEAD>
<BODY>
<P>Save this page as a bookmark to avoid the
registration page on your next visit...</P>
<SCRIPT LANGUAGE="JavaScript">
if (location.search==""){
   //...need this if control to avoid an endless loop
   window.location.search="?infohere"
  //..add information to URL
   document.write(window.location.href)
}
</SCRIPT></BODY></HTML>
```

Most often, you will see search information stored in a format of associative pairs. In this format, you have *field=value*. Multiple pairs are separated by the ampersand and spaces are not permitted. Go to almost any search engine and do a simple search. The page that is returned to you will have search text in its URL. For example,

```
http://www.altavista.digital.com/cgi-bin/query?pg=q&what=web&q=htmljive
```

Though the format of associative pairs is common, there appears to be no requirement to use them. I've found that you can put almost any text or numeric data you want into this portion of the URL.

**Parent Knows All**    While cookies and bookmarks with search information allow user information to be stored between visits, you can also maintain information during the current visit by using the control panel concept. JavaScript works with both frames and multiple windows. As long as a window from your application stays open, the browser can store data. For example, a user can work within your application and then hyperlink to another site. You can design all of your external links to open new browser windows. This way, your original window is not unloaded and your data is retained.

## Good Design

Whether a Web page looks good is a matter of taste: what you like, others might avoid. This factor should be part of your design. Enable users to change the appearance of the page, even to a style that you personally would not normally choose. For example, many people set their word processor to use vibrant colors, such as bright green and rich purple. This is a style others might use only occasionally, if at all.

Although everyone has individual tastes, the following are various principles that can produce good-looking pages (see Figure 19.3):

- Keep it simple: focus the document on a topic.
- Leave white space: don't fill your page with text or images (especially large ones).
- Employ only the styles you need: don't use every option.
- Shorter lines of text are easier to read.

**FIG. 19.3**

Almost everyone agrees that Yahoo!'s design is elegant and to-the-point. The graphic is all that is necessary and it is functional. The text is easy to read in multiple columns with spacing between the lines.

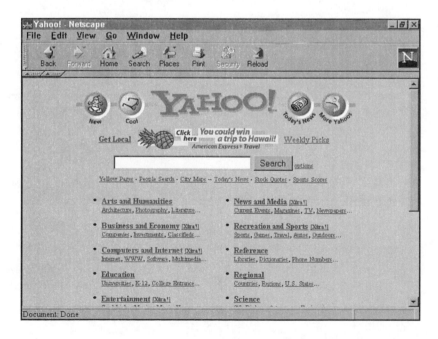

# Text Properties and Color Values

Background color and tiles have changed the Web forever. Many sites now use the background to further convey the style of the site. This puts a burden on the designer to be a color coordinator.

If you change the background color, you must also be able to modify the colors used to display text. Having the background color match the text color makes the text invisible. Although you might want to use this as an effect, most of the time you will want a pleasant contrast between these two colors.

## Text Properties

There are five text properties available from the browser. These all reflect the values of the TEXT attribute of the BODY tag. The first two are the color for the background and for the text of the document. These properties are called bgColor and fgColor.

The three other text properties reflect the three different colors applied to hyperlink text. Usually, your hyperlinks should stand out from the rest of the text. Although early browsers displayed these links by underlining the text, now most browsers distinguish these links by color. They also provide feedback to the user by changing this color momentarily when the user clicks the link. After a link is visited, the color is also changed. These properties are called linkColor, alinkColor, and vlinkColor, respectively.

The syntax for these properties is as follows:

```
document.fgColor [= [RGB Triplet ¦ Color Name]]
document.bgColor [= [RGB Triplet ¦ Color Name]]
document.alinkColor [= [RGB Triplet ¦ Color Name]]
document.linkColor [= [RGB Triplet ¦ Color Name]]
document.vlinkColor [= [RGB Triplet ¦ Color Name]]
```

While *RGB Triplet* is a string of hexadecimal values representing a combination of the colors red, green, and blue; *Color Name* is a string representing a specific color's name as defined in the color table.

## Color Values

You specify the color for TEXT properties just as you would any other color element. The general syntax is

```
document.textproperty = "colorvalue"
```

where *colorvalue* is either a hexadecimal value or a literal name representing a color.

**Hexadecimal Values for Color**    Prior to JavaScript, all color values were specified by using the RGB hexadecimal values. This is a six-digit number. It is often called a triplet because it is divided into three sets of two digits each: The first two digits specify the amount of red, the second two specify the amount of green, and the last two specify the amount of blue.

Because the numbers are hexadecimal, the values range from 00 to FF. (255 is the decimal equivalent of FF hexadecimal.) For example, black is FFFFFF and white is 000000. Aqua, which is an equal mix of green and blue, is represented by 00FFFF. You might want this color as your background and type:

```
document.bgColor = "00FFFF"
```

**Using Color Names**    JavaScript provides another option, besides hexadecimal numbers, for specifying color values: you can use names. Instead of coding:

```
document.fgColor = "0000FF"
```

you can use the word "blue" as in the following:

```
document.fgColor = "blue"
```

You have a choice of over 150 predefined colors. Of course, you have standard colors such as blue, violet, cyan, and maroon. But now, such colors as dodger blue, tomato, Navajo white, Indian red, peach puff, and Alice blue are available directly from JavaScript.

▶ **See** "Color Values," **p. 803**, for a list of color names.

**N O T E**    You probably remember the primary colors: red, yellow, and blue. Why are the colors red, green, and blue used for computers? Why green instead of yellow?

Red, yellow, and blue paints are commonly used on paper to learn about primary colors. In that case, white light reflects off the mixture of paints to produce the desired color. No paint produces white, and equal amounts of each color absorb all of the reflected light, producing black. The important point is the reflected light because that is the color you see.

Red, blue, and green (RGB) are the primary colors when the light itself provides the color (additive). It doesn't matter whether you mix red, green, and blue lights on a darkened theatrical stage or from inside a monitor or television. No light produces black; an equal amount of all lights produces white.

So RGB is used, given that the colors are additive, and many other graphic-related software programs have used RGB in the past. ▉

**Color Tools**    As you work with color, you will find that having a few tools will make things easier. For example, what is the hexadecimal number for light purple? What color text looks good on a coral background?

A chart that shows the hexadecimal representation of a desired color is a great tool to own. There are numerous charts available. The *RGB Hex Triplet Color Chart* at **http:// www.phoenix.net/~jacobson/rgb.html** is an excellent example. Whenever you need to see what a color really looks like, you can just load the page and see it displayed on the monitor.

A program that actually lets you experiment with color properties and background tiles is hIdaho Design's ColorCenter (**http://www.hidaho.com/colorcenter/**) by Bill Dortch (see Figure 19.4). You select colors and actually see the results on your screen. Not only is it a great way to find pleasant color schemes, but it is also a brilliant JavaScript application.

Part
**IV**

Ch

**19**

**FIG. 19.4**

hIdaho Design's Color-Center is even more brilliant on your monitor. You can work in hexadecimal, decimal, or percentage. The logo is an animated GIF file.

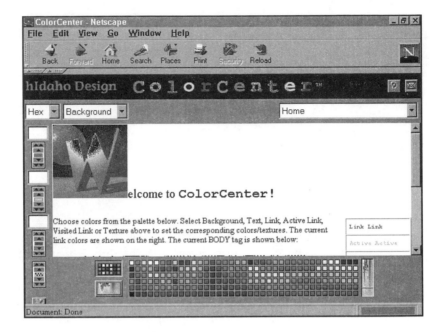

## Practical Uses of Text Properties

By knowing the text properties of the current document, you can use these values to set the text properties for any new documents. Make the new documents the same as the current one, or create a new color by manipulating the current property values.

Another use for text properties is to provide feedback that the user's action was recognized. You can either replace the existing background or possibly flash the background. You can also use text properties with a countdown sequence, like ticks of a clock.

For example, upon a user's action, such as clicking a hyperlink, you can make the background color change to the standard text color (Listing 19.3). This makes the text "disappear" and notifies the user that his or her action was accepted.

---

**Listing 19.3 Changing Background Color**

```
<HTML>
<HEAD>
<TITLE>color16.htm by Ray Daly</TITLE>
</HEAD>
<BODY bgColor="red" fgColor="black" >
<P>Simple example of changing background color.</P>
<P><FONT COLOR="green">Why did the chicken cross the road?</P>
<P><FONT COLOR="document.bgColor">To get to the other side.</P>
<!--...make color same as background to make invisible -->
<FORM>
<INPUT TYPE="button" VALUE="Red"  onclick='document.bgColor="red" '>
```

```
<INPUT TYPE="button" VALUE="Green" onclick='document.bgColor="green" '>
<BR>
</FORM>
<P>
<A HREF="http://www.yahooligans.com/"
onClick='document.bgColor="black" '>Yahooligans</A>
</BODY></HTML>
```

## Overriding *fgColor*

Normally, the color specified with `fgColor` is the color of all the text on the page, except hyperlinks. You can override this color by using the `fontcolor` element. For example, you can place one paragraph of text between `<FONT COLOR="chocolate">` and `</FONT>`. The text of this paragraph then appears in the color chocolate instead of the color specified by `fgColor`.

JavaScript provides a method for placing `FONTCOLOR` tags around a string. This is the topic of the next section.

# Fonts and Font Methods

You certainly have used physical styles such as `bold`, `fixed`, and `italics` for your HTML pages. JavaScript has methods for these three styles as well as `blink`, `strikeout`, `subscript`, and `superscript`. It also has methods for `big`, `small`, `fontsize`, and `fontcolor`. This chapter groups these methods under the name of *font methods*.

## Description of Font Methods

The result of a font method is that it places the appropriate tags at the beginning and end of the string. For example, for the physical style of `bold`, if `testString="example"`, then the result of `testString.bold()` is `<B>example</B>`. In other words, the result of a font method is a new string with HTML code embedded in it.

In Listing 19.4, you will see three figures that demonstrate all the JavaScript font methods. This listing shows the use of each font method on the same string. Listing 19.5 shows the equivalent HTML code. Figure 19.5 is a screen shot showing the display of each style.

## Using Font Methods

The font methods are useful in three primary ways, as follows:

- Your page can directly create a new document in a new window or a frame.
- Your page can collect a sequence of inputs and build the new document only when the user signals completion.
- Your user can create an HTML document that is submitted to the server. The server can then save this page and make it available to other users. Your user might not ever see the new document.

**Using Font Methods Directly**   You create new documents by using the `document.write` or `document.writeln` methods. As part of the string used in a `document.write` method, you can use the font methods instead of hard-coding in the style tags.

▶ **See** "Browser Objects," **p. 120**, for details on the `document.write` method.

Using `document.write (promptstring.bold())` can make it easier to debug than by using `document.write ("<B>" + promptstring + "</B>")`. Using `document.write` also enables the browser to handle implementation of HTML tags because the specifications may change in the future. In the following example, you see the JavaScript code using `document.write` (see Listing 19.4), the equivalent HTML code (see Listing 19.5), and the display of that HTML code in Figure 19.5, which shows the use of each of the different font methods. Figure 19.5 shows how either one of these documents appears on a browser. Because the HTML code does not actually specify a font, the results will vary depending on your browser preferences.

**Listing 19.4   All Font Methods in Use**

```
<HTML><HEAD><TITLE>fontmeth.htm by Ray Daly</TITLE>
<SCRIPT LANGUAGE="JavaScript">
var testString = "JavaScript Font Methods "
document.write ('<P>')
document.write (testString.bold()+"<BR>")
document.write (testString.fixed()+"<BR>")
document.write (testString.italics()+"<BR>")
document.write (testString.blink()+"<BR>")
document.write (testString.strike()+"<BR>")
document.write (testString.sub()+"<BR>")
document.write (testString.sup()+"<BR>")
document.write (testString.big()+"<BR>")
document.write (testString.small()+"<BR>")
document.write (testString.fontsize(1)+"<BR>")
document.write (testString.fontsize(2)+"<BR>")
document.write (testString.fontsize(3)+"<BR>")
document.write (testString.fontsize(4)+"<BR>")
document.write (testString.fontsize(5)+"<BR>")
document.write (testString.fontsize(6)+"<BR>")
document.write (testString.fontsize(7)+"<BR>")
document.write (testString.fontcolor("FA8072")+"<BR>")
document.write (testString.fontcolor("salmon")+"<BR>")
document.write ('</P>')
</SCRIPT></HEAD><BODY<</BODY></HTML>
```

**TIP**   You can combine font methods to act on one string. For example, to produce a bold, size 4 font in the salmon color, use the following code:

```
testString.bold.fontsize(4).fontcolor("salmon")
```

### Listing 19.5  Equivalent HTML Code for Font Methods

```
<HTML><HEAD><TITLE>fontactu.htm by Ray Daly</TITLE></HEAD><BODY>
<B>JavaScript Font Methods </B><BR>
<TT>JavaScript Font Methods </TT><BR>
<I>JavaScript Font Methods </I><BR>
<BLINK>JavaScript Font Methods </BLINK><BR>
<STRIKE>JavaScript Font Methods </STRIKE><BR>
<SUB>JavaScript Font Methods </SUB><BR>
<SUP>JavaScript Font Methods </SUP><BR>
<BIG>JavaScript Font Methods </BIG><BR>
<SMALL>JavaScript Font Methods </SMALL><BR>
<FONT SIZE="1">JavaScript Font Methods </FONT><BR>
<FONT SIZE="2">JavaScript Font Methods </FONT><BR>
<FONT SIZE="3">JavaScript Font Methods </FONT><BR>
<FONT SIZE="4">JavaScript Font Methods </FONT><BR>
<FONT SIZE="5">JavaScript Font Methods </FONT><BR>
<FONT SIZE="6">JavaScript Font Methods </FONT><BR>
<FONT SIZE="7">JavaScript Font Methods </FONT><BR>
<FONT COLOR="FA8072">JavaScript Font Methods </FONT><BR>
<FONT COLOR="salmon">JavaScript Font Methods </FONT><BR>
</P></BODY></HTML>
```

**FIG. 19.5**

This is how the browser displays the HTML code for font methods (see Listings 19.4 and 19.5). The code is different, but the results are the same.

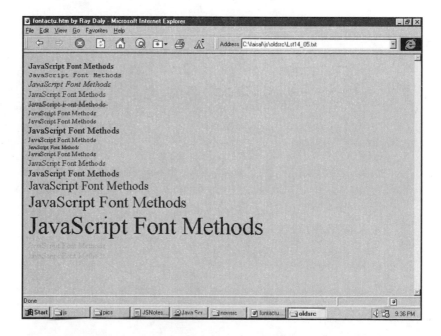

Part
**IV**

Ch

**19**

**Using Font Methods Indirectly**   There may be many cases in which you want to build a document as user inputs are gathered, instead of building it immediately. This enables users to select components to be used for their documents. By putting the components together in different sequences, users create different HTML pages. By using an indirect technique, they can preview the page prior to finalizing it.

A very practical example is an HTML editor (see Figure 19.6). The user builds the page by using various form inputs, such as buttons. These activate functions that insert HTML tags using the font methods. As the user builds the page by making various choices, the raw HTML code appears in a text area of a form. The text area functions like a text editor in which the user can make changes prior to finalizing the document.

**FIG. 19.6**

HTMLjive is an HTML editor written in JavaScript. You build a document in the text area with the option to preview it.

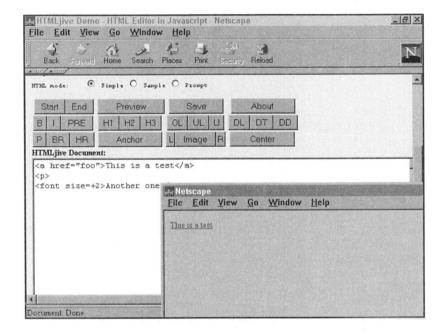

In other cases, you may not want the user to be capable of directly editing the HTML code. Instead of building the HTML page in a text area, you can use a hidden form element. Just use the value of that hidden element to store the code until it is ready to be directed to a new document (see Figure 19.7). The code for this example is in Listing 19.6.

**Listing 19.6   Storing New Document in Hidden Value**

```
<HTML><HEAD><TITLE>hidden.htm by Ray Daly</TITLE>
<SCRIPT LANGUAGE="JavaScript">
<!-- hide code from other browsers
function preview (form) {
    msg=open ("", "DisplayWindow","toolbar=yes,scrollbars=yes")
      msg.document.write(form.storage.value)
}
// end hiding -->
</SCRIPT>
</HEAD><BODY>
<P>Demo of building a hidden HTML document.  Click several times
on the Holiday buttons before asking for a preview.</B>
<FORM>
```

```
<INPUT TYPE="hidden" NAME="storage"
VALUE="<HTML><HEAD><TITLE>Greetings</TITLE></HEAD><BODY>">
<!--...this hidden element is where the HTML document is created -->
<INPUT TYPE="button" VALUE="Happy Fourth"
onClick='this.form.storage.value += "<H1>Happy Fourth</H1>" '>
<INPUT TYPE="button" VALUE="Happy Halloween"
onClick='this.form.storage.value += "<H1>Happy Halloween</H1>" '>
<INPUT TYPE="button" VALUE="Show New Document" onClick="preview(this.form)">
</BODY></HTML>
```

**FIG. 19.7**

In this example, code is stored in the hidden form element, but you don't see it until you click the Show New Document button.

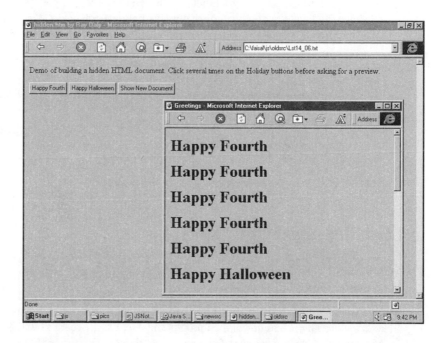

Part **IV**

Ch **19**

**HTML Strings as a Submission**   There is also the case in which the new HTML code is never directly displayed by the browser. Instead, using the various user inputs, the HTML code is stored either in a text box or in a hidden value. When complete, the resulting code is submitted to the server, which processes it.

A practical example is a Web-based message board. Users can compose messages by using a JavaScript-enhanced message editor. Because the messages become part of a Web page, they contain various physical styles, such as bold and italic. Buttons can be part of the form, so users do not necessarily need to know the HTML code to add italic or bold to their messages. When a message is complete, it can be sent to the server and appended to an existing page.

Another example is a salesperson's weekly report. A salesperson can complete a Web form about his or her activity. This might include invoice numbers, dollar amounts, and comments. When the report is complete, the JavaScript code adds HTML code to the various inputs. The final document is submitted to the server, where it is simply appended to the sales manager's page for his or her review on Monday morning.

# The Design of a JavaScript Message Editor

For a detailed and practical example, we will build a message editor. This JavaScript-enhanced page provides controls so that the user can easily add HTML style tags to messages. This final text is then submitted to a server, where the message is added to a guest book, a message board, or any other site that accepts HTML-enhanced messages.

Designing JavaScript applications often works best if you lay out the interface first. This is a way to decide not only the layout, but also the events for which you need to write code. Once you have the layout, write the code that works behind each event. This is a common technique for event-driven programs and it is the approach taken for our message editor.

> **CAUTION**
>
> The initial release of JavaScript had limited methods available for text editing. First, the string methods were limited. For example, there is no search-and-replace method.
>
> The other limitation relates to the fact that text editing takes place in a text area. The `textarea` object has no properties related to the cursor position. Therefore, text functions can append new text only to the end of the text and not at the cursor.
>
> Despite these limitations, interesting applications can be created.

## How the Message Editor Works

This application basically works like any other page with a text box in a form. The users complete their information and they can then edit it. When it is finalized, the text is submitted to a server where it is processed.

JavaScript enhances this process. We will design a control panel in which the user can select a text style. The program will then prompt the user to type the text that is to be highlighted with a style. After the user has finished typing, the text and the HTML code are appended to the message in the text area.

The other main feature of the message editor is the preview window. Users will be able to preview their HTML documents prior to submitting them to the server. This will be activated by a button on the control panel. Because all of this activity takes place in the browser (on the client side), the load on the server is reduced. It also provides a much quicker response time than waiting for the server to return a previewed document.

## Layout Decision

You must decide whether to create this application in one document or in multiple documents. There are trade-offs with either choice.

You can make one long document with all of the HTML and JavaScript code. The user may then need to scroll around the page to use it. This choice can also be easier to code. The real benefit is that the user can save and recall the application in a single file on his or her hard drive.

The other option is to create one frame for the control panel and another for the text window. Users will not be able to easily save the application on their hard drives because it is now in several files, but the real benefit is ease of use because the user will not have to scroll around as much.

For our example, we will use a page with frames. There will also be a dialog box and two other windows.

# Framing the Message Editor

For the message editor, there are two main frames. The top frame displays the control panel. It is as wide as the browser allows and it has a fixed height large enough to contain all of the controls.

The top panel is subdivided into a left and right section. The left simply displays the last font color used. This is a fixed width. The right contains all of the controls and extends to the edge of the screen.

The second frame will contain the text box. This is where the message is edited. Like the other frame, the width is the same as the screen. Its height is variable, taking up the remainder of the vertical space.

Listing 19.7 is the code for creating the frames. To test the frames, three test documents are created (see Listings 19.8, 19.9, and 19.10). These documents will be modified as we develop the application. Our test result is shown in Figure 19.8.

**Listing 19.7   Frameset Document for Message Editor**

```
<HTML><HEAD><TITLE>Message Editor by Ray Daly</TITLE>
<FRAMESET ROWS = " 110, * ">
    <FRAMESET COLS="20,*">
    <!-- this is the upper frame, divided into two more frames -->
            <FRAME NAME="messcolr" SRC="messcolr.htm">
    <FRAME NAME="messcont" SRC = "messcont.htm">
    </FRAMESET>
    <FRAME NAME="messarea" SRC="messarea.htm">
    <!-- this is the lower frame -->
</FRAMESET>
</HTML>
```

Using frames with Netscape Navigator and Internet Explorer requires multiple documents. The primary document is a new type of HTML document because it has no <BODY>. Instead, the document uses the FRAMESET element. The contents of the FRAMESET tag are FRAME tags. The primary attribute of the FRAME is the source document, which appears in the frame. So for a page with two frames, you would have two FRAME elements, each specifying a source document. The subsidiary files for the FRAMESET shown in Listing 19.7 are found in Listings 19.8, 19.9, and 19.10.

One other optional element of a FRAMESET is another FRAMESET. You use this in the case where you want to subdivide a frame into different frames. This is how we create the message editor example.

---

**Listing 19.8   Test Document for Upper Frame**

```
<HTML><HEAD><TITLE>Message Editor by Ray Daly</TITLE>
<BODY bgcolor ="white">
<H1>messcont.htm</H1>
</BODY></HTML>
```

---

**Listing 19.9   Test Document for Lower Frame**

```
<HTML><HEAD><TITLE>Message Editor by Ray Daly</TITLE>
<BODY bgcolor ="white">
<H1>messarea.htm</H1>
</BODY></HTML>
```

---

**Listing 19.10   Test Document for Color Frame**

```
<HTML><HEAD><TITLE>Message Editor by Ray Daly</TITLE>
<BODY bgcolor ="black">
</BODY></HTML>
```

---

**FIG. 19.8**

It's always a good idea to test your frames to see if they are the size you expect.

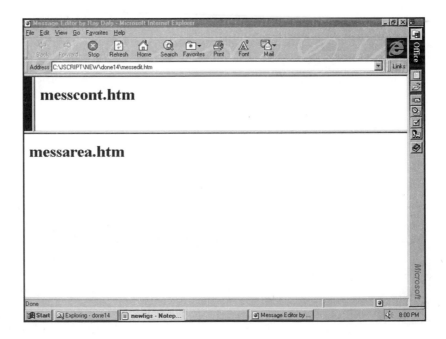

> **CAUTION**
>
> Netscape Navigator and Internet Explorer will cache frame information if possible. If you modify the frame dimensions and just reload, this does not always change the frame sizing. To be certain, you may have to load a different page and then reload your page.

## Framesets Nest, Frames Objects Don't

The message editor contains a set of nested framesets. The primary, or top, frameset contains another frameset. This is done to subdivide a frame into two other frames. You might think of these frames and framesets as a tree structure. Using the file names from our example, a tree might break down to resemble the following:

```
Frameset: Messedit.htm        Parent
    Frame: Messtext.htm       Child
    Frameset:                 Child
        Frame: Messcont.htm   Grandchild
        Frame: Messcolr.htm   Grandchild
```

Because the top file is considered the parent by JavaScript, you would consider Messtext and the Frameset to be children. So the other two frames would be considered grandchildren, right? Surprisingly, the answer is no!

When JavaScript creates the objects from the framesets, all of the frames get "flattened." In other words, each frame, regardless of how deeply it is nested, is considered a child and is placed into the same frame array. All frames are placed into the array in the same sequence that they appear in the HTML file. All nesting is ignored, for example:

```
frames[0].document.name is messcolr
frames[1].document.name is messcont
frames[2].document.name is messarea
```

This makes it easier to properly refer to a property in another frame. You don't need to know the relative relationship between frames because they are each a child to the parent.

If we add a text area (called `messaret`) in a form (called `heavy`) in a frame (named `messarea`) from a function in the other frame (called `messcont`), then we could reference the contents of this text area by using the following:

```
parent.messarea.document.heavy.messaret.value
```

Please note the word `document` in this code. Since a frame has several properties, you must specify that you are referring to the `document` property.

## HTML Code for a Layout

In deciding on a layout, we will provide just enough code to see what the application will look like. For the text area, no further coding is needed other than layout. For the control panel, we will display the various buttons and other controls with practically no JavaScript coding.

**HTML Code for the Text Area**   This frame will consist primarily of a form. You can also select a background color for the form elements to sit on. There will also be one line of instruction at the top of the text area. As defined by the preceding frame coding, this document is called Messarea.htm.

Let's start with the standard tags and define the background color as aqua:

```
<HTML><HEAD><TITLE>Message Editor by Ray Daly</TITLE></HEAD>
<BODY bgcolor="aqua">
```

Next is the start of the form and the single line of instruction:

```
<FORM NAME="heavy"><P><B>Type your message in this box:</B><BR>
```

This form contains only three elements. The first element of the form is the text area: this one is defined with a column width of 70 and a height of 16 lines. You can make these whatever dimensions you choose.

 **T I P**   You can choose a text area that is longer than the frame. Then the user will have to scroll the frame to get to the Submit and Reset buttons. In this case, you might consider putting one set of buttons at the top of the text area and another at the bottom. This is a design choice.

The coding of the text area follows the standard format. There is also an attribute of `wrap=virtual`:

```
<TEXTAREA NAME="messtext" ROWS="10" COLS="70" WRAP="virtual">
</TEXTAREA>
```

**N O T E**   The TEXTAREA element has a tag called WRAP. There are three different options for this tag, as follows:

> `off`   This is the default setting. There is no wrapping; lines are sent exactly as typed.
>
> `virtual`   With this option, the display is word-wrapped, but the actual text is not. In other words, you see a long line wrapped, but the browser sends it as one long line to the server.
>
> `physical`   With this option, the display is word-wrapped and the text is sent with all wrap points.

The syntax is

```
<TEXTAREA WRAP="wrapvalue">
```

The final two elements are the buttons for submitting the document and an optional Reset button. The default wording is not used. Because this program is like a word processor or text editor, those types of terms are used:

```
<INPUT TYPE="submit" VALUE="Submit Message">
<INPUT TYPE="reset" VALUE="Reset:  Erase all text">
```

To finish this document, we only need to close the tags for both the FORM and HTML:

```
</FORM> </HTML>
```

The code for this entire document is shown in Listing 19.11. Figure 19.9 shows how this document looks inside our frame.

### Listing 19.11   Text Area in Lower Frame

```
<HTML><HEAD><TITLE>Message Editor by Ray Daly</TITLE></HEAD>
<BODY bgcolor ="aqua">
<FORM NAME="heavy"><P><B>Type your message in this box:</B><BR>
<TEXTAREA NAME="messaret" ROWS="10" COLS="70" WRAP="virtual">
</TEXTAREA>
<INPUT TYPE="submit" VALUE = "Submit Message" >
<INPUT TYPE="reset" VALUE = "Reset:  Erase all text">
</BODY></HTML>
```

**FIG. 19.9**

Notice the large message area waiting for a user to type something. The WRAP attribute is set to virtual to force word-wrapping.

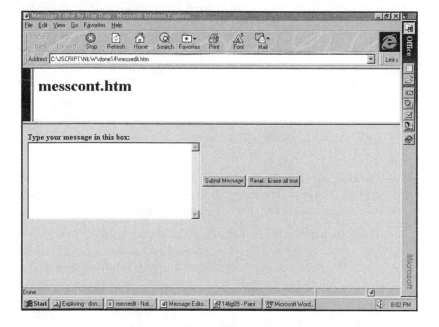

You can add another button to this frame, as users might appreciate having a Preview button right next to the Submit button. This button allows users to preview their messages prior to submitting them. The Preview button is detailed in the section "The Preview," later in this chapter.

At this point, three of the four documents that make up the message editor are complete. The main code is in the control panel, which we will now develop.

**The Controls in the Control Panel**   The control panel has three rows of controls. These controls prompt the user for text to be appended to the text in the text area with the appropriate HTML codes.

The first row contains eight buttons, all of which are approximately the same size. These buttons are named for their corresponding physical text styles: Bold, Italic, Fixed, Strike, Blink, Sup (Superscript), and Sub (Subscript). (The buttons will display these words.) There is an eighth button on this row called About.

The second row contains nine controls. The first two buttons are the same size as those in the first row. These are for the Big and Small styles. Then there are much smaller buttons for font sizes 1 to 7. The last button on this row is for Help.

The third row is a set of seven hyperlinks. The text for these are eight standard colors, except white. Each text appears in its corresponding font color. The last control on the row is a Preview button.

**Putting the Controls into a Table**   These controls should appear properly spaced to make it easier for the user to find the button he or she wants. Aligning the buttons also makes it easier on the eyes.

To accomplish the desired layout of these controls, each is centered within a cell of a table. The <TABLE> is used only for layout purposes, it has no borders, and it is effectively invisible to the user.

Given three rows of controls, the table also has three rows. With both the top and bottom rows having eight controls, we know the minimum number of columns is also eight. Because the middle row has several smaller buttons and a total count of ten, we are going to double the number of columns to sixteen.

The standard size buttons—those from the top and bottom rows—will be placed in cells that span two columns. The seven smaller buttons for font sizes, in the second row, are each placed within single cells. The coding for this table is in Listing 19.12.

There are comments inserted into the cells where coding goes for each control. Also, the entire table is between FORM tags because each button is a form element. The standard elements that define an HTML document are also there, including a background color of light gray.

### Listing 19.12   Tabled Layout of Controls

```
<HTML><HEAD><TITLE>Message Editor by Ray Daly</TITLE>
</HEAD><BODY bgcolor ="white">
<TABLE WIDTH="100%" HEIGHT="100%" BORDER="0">
   <TR><TD COLSPAN=2><!--bold here-->bold</TD>
<TD COLSPAN=2><!--italics here-->italics</TD>
      <TD COLSPAN=2><!--blink here-->blink</TD>
      <TD COLSPAN=2><!--strike here-->strike</TD>
      <TD COLSPAN=2><!--fixed here-->fixed</TD>
      <TD COLSPAN=2><!--sub here-->sub</TD>
      <TD COLSPAN=2><!--sup here-->sup</TD>
      <TD COLSPAN=2><!--about here-->about</TD>
   </TR><TR><TD COLSPAN=2><!--big here-->big</TD>
      <TD COLSPAN=2><!--small here-->small</TD>
      <TD><!--fontsize 1 here-->1</TD>
```

```
<TD><!--fontsize 2 here-->2</TD>
<TD><!--fontsize 3 here-->3</TD>
<TD><!--fontsize 4 here-->4</TD>
<TD><!--fontsize 5 here-->5</TD>
<TD><!--fontsize 6 here-->6</TD>
<TD><!--fontsize 7 here-->7</TD>
<TD><BR></TD><TD COLSPAN=2><BR></TD>
<TD COLSPAN=2><!--help here-->help</TD>
</TR><TR><TD COLSPAN=2><!--black fontcolor-->black</TD>
<TD COLSPAN=2><!--red fontcolor-->red</TD>
<TD COLSPAN=2><!--green fontcolor-->green</TD>
<TD COLSPAN=2><!--blue fontcolor-->blue</TD>
<TD COLSPAN=2><!--cyan fontcolor-->cyan</TD>
<TD COLSPAN=2><!--magenta fontcolor-->magenta</TD>
<TD COLSPAN=2><!--yellow fontcolor-->yellow</TD>
<TD COLSPAN=2><!--preview button-->Preview</TD>
</TR></TABLE>
</BODY></HTML>
```

**Putting Buttons into the Table**   The coding for each of the buttons follows the same format. The HTML code creates a button displaying the name of the style (for instance, Bold). Each contains an onClick event, which calls a function specifically to implement that feature. However, this code will not be written until the next phase of developing this program. The following is the code for the Bold button:

```
<INPUT name="bold" type="button" value="  Bold  "onClick="stylemethod('bold')">
```

This same coding is created for Italic, Fixed, Blink, Strike, Sub, Sup, Big, Small, 1, 2, 3, 4, 5, 6, and 7. Insert this coding into the correct cells of the table. The coding for all of these buttons is shown in Listing 19.13.

Part
IV

Ch
19

### Listing 19.13   Button Inputs Defined

```
<INPUT name="bold" type="button" value="  Bold  " onClick="stylemethod('bold')">
<INPUT NAME="italics" TYPE="button" VALUE="Italics"
➥onClick="stylemethod('italics')">
<INPUT NAME="blink" TYPE="button" VALUE="  Blink  "
➥onClick="stylemethod('blink')">
<INPUT NAME="strike" TYPE="button" VALUE=" Strike "
➥onClick="stylemethod('strike')">
<INPUT NAME="fixed" TYPE="button" VALUE=" Fixed "
➥onClick="stylemethod('fixed')">
<INPUT NAME="sub" TYPE="button" VALUE="  Sub  " onClick="stylemethod('sub')">
<INPUT NAME="sup" TYPE="button" VALUE="  Sup  " onClick="stylemethod('sup')">
<INPUT NAME="big" TYPE="button" VALUE="  Big  " onClick="stylemethod('big')">
<INPUT NAME="small" TYPE="button" VALUE="Small" onClick="stylemethod('small')">
<INPUT NAME="1" TYPE="button" VALUE="  1 " onClick="stylemethod('Size 1')">
<INPUT NAME="2" TYPE="button" VALUE="  2 " onClick="stylemethod('Size 2')">
<INPUT NAME="3" TYPE="button" VALUE="  3 " onClick="stylemethod('Size 3')">
<INPUT NAME="4" TYPE="button" VALUE="  4 " onClick="stylemethod('Size 4')">
<INPUT NAME="5" TYPE="button" VALUE="  5 " onClick="stylemethod('Size 5')">
<INPUT NAME="6" TYPE="button" VALUE="  6 " onClick="stylemethod('Size 6')">
<INPUT NAME="7" TYPE="button" VALUE="  7 " onClick="stylemethod('Size 7')">
```

About, Help, and Preview have their own specialized functions, so they do not call the same `stylemethod`. The code for these buttons is

```
<INPUT NAME="about" TYPE="button" VALUE="  About  " onClick="aboutalert()"><
<INPUT NAME="help" TYPE="button" VALUE="   Help  " onClick="helppage()">
<INPUT NAME="preview" TYPE="button" VALUE="Preview" onClick="apreview(this.form)">
```

 **TIP** When you create a button, JavaScript makes the button just large enough to hold the text stored in the `VALUE` property. You can widen a button by adding extra spaces to the text of the `VALUE` property.

With a little experimenting, you can make most buttons appear to be the same width. However, browsers on other platforms and with other preferences may display different widths.

**Hyperlinks as Controls**   The third row of the control panel has seven hyperlinks that are used as controls. These are used instead of buttons to enable the user actually to see the different colors. This is essentially a simple color selector.

**N O T E**   A color selector can be done in a variety of ways. You can have a `SELECT` list showing the string literals for all 150 colors. You can create a text box for users to input hexadecimal values, or you can create a Select drop-down list that has the names of the colors.

An exciting way to make the color selector is to create a client-side image map of a color bar. The user can select a color and execute the appropriate JavaScript code by clicking anywhere on the color bar. ◼

Originally, the coding for these hyperlinks used the `OnClick` event. The problem with that approach is that it is necessary to specify an `HREF` for either an anchor or an URL. If you only want to implement a JavaScript function without jumping to an anchor or loading an URL, set the `HREF` to a nonexistent anchor. This works; however, a future version of JavaScript might produce an error message. The following is an example of the code originally used:

```
<A HREF=#bold  onClick="stylemethod('red')"> <FONT color="red">Red </FONT></A>
```

It turns out that this is a perfect case for using the new `javascript:` protocol. Instead of specifying an anchor, an URL, or even a `mailto:`, you can specify JavaScript code. In our case, we want to specify a function for the color represented by the hyperlink. So now the code looks like the following:

```
<A HREF="javascript: stylecolor('red')"> <FONT color="red">Red </FONT></A>
```

 **TIP** *Easter eggs* is a term in video games for undocumented, hidden features. By using `fontcolor` methods, you can make a hyperlink an invisible Easter egg. Just make the `fontcolor` the same as the normal text color. The only clue would be in the status bar.

 **TIP** The `javascript:` protocol allows you to make hyperlinks behave like buttons. So if you don't like being limited to the predefined buttons, use a hyperlink, the `javascript:` protocol, and your own image as an icon.

Create this same coding for black, green, blue, yellow, cyan, and magenta. Obviously, if you don't like these colors, just pick another set. Insert this code into the correct cells of the table. The complete code for the tables with all of the hyperlinks and buttons is shown in Listing 19.14.

### Listing 19.14 Tabled Layout of Buttons

```
<HTML><HEAD><TITLE>Message Editor by Ray Daly</TITLE>
</HEAD><BODY bgcolor ="lightgrey">
<TABLE WIDTH="100%" HEIGHT="100%" BORDER="0">
 <FORM><TR><TD COLSPAN=2>
   <INPUT NAME="bold" TYPE="button" VALUE=" Bold "
onClick="stylemethod('bold')"></TD>
   <TD COLSPAN=2>
   <INPUT NAME="italics" TYPE="button" VALUE="Italics"
onClick="stylemethod('italics')"></TD>
   <TD COLSPAN=2>
   <INPUT NAME="blink" TYPE="button" VALUE="  Blink  "
onClick="stylemethod('blink')"></TD>
   <TD COLSPAN=2>
   <INPUT NAME="strike" TYPE="button" VALUE=" Strike "
onClick="stylemethod('strike')"></TD>
   <TD COLSPAN=2>
   <INPUT NAME="fixed" TYPE="button" VALUE=" Fixed "
onClick="stylemethod('fixed')"></TD>
   <TD COLSPAN=2>
   <INPUT NAME="sub" TYPE="button" VALUE="  Sub  "
onClick="stylemethod('sub')"></TD>
   <TD COLSPAN=2>
   <INPUT NAME="sup" TYPE="button" VALUE="  Sup  "
onClick="stylemethod('sup')"></TD>
   <TD COLSPAN=2>
   <INPUT NAME="about" TYPE="button" VALUE="  About  "
onClick="aboutalert()"></TD>
 </TR><TR><TD COLSPAN=2>
   <INPUT NAME="big" TYPE="button" VALUE="  Big  "
onClick="stylemethod('big')"></TD>
   <TD COLSPAN=2>
   <INPUT NAME="small" TYPE="button" VALUE="Small"
onClick="stylemethod('small')"></TD>
   <TD><INPUT NAME="1" TYPE="button" VALUE="  1 "
onClick="stylemethod('Size 1')"></TD>
   <TD><INPUT NAME="2" TYPE="button" VALUE="  2 "
onClick="stylemethod('Size 2')"></TD>
   <TD><INPUT NAME="3" TYPE="button" VALUE="  3 "
onClick="stylemethod('Size 3')"></TD>
   <TD><INPUT NAME="4" TYPE="button" VALUE="  4 "
onClick="stylemethod('Size 4')"></TD>
   <TD><INPUT NAME="5" TYPE="button" VALUE="  5 "
onClick="stylemethod('Size 5')"></TD>
   <TD><INPUT NAME="6" TYPE="button" VALUE="  6 "
onClick="stylemethod('Size 6')"></TD>
   <TD><INPUT NAME="7" TYPE="button" VALUE="  7 "
```

Part
IV

Ch
19

*continues*

**Listing 19.14 Continued**

```
onClick="stylemethod('Size 7')"></TD>
    <TD><BR></TD>
    <TD COLSPAN=2><BR></TD>
    <TD COLSPAN=2>
    <INPUT NAME="help" TYPE="button" VALUE="   Help   "
onClick="helppage()"></TD>
</TR><TR><TD COLSPAN=2 ALIGN="center">
<A HREF="javascript: stylecolor('black')">
            <FONT COLOR="black"><B>Black</B></FONT></A></TD>
        <TD COLSPAN=2 ALIGN="center">
        <A HREF="javascript: stylecolor('red')">
            <FONT COLOR="red"><B>Red</FONT></B></A></TD>
        <TD COLSPAN=2 ALIGN="center">
        <A HREF="javascript: stylecolor('green')">
            <FONT COLOR="green"><B>Green</B></FONT></A></TD>
        <TD COLSPAN=2 ALIGN="center">
        <A HREF="javascript: stylecolor('blue')">
            <FONT COLOR="blue"><B>Blue</B></FONT></A></TD>
        <TD COLSPAN=2 ALIGN="center">
        <A HREF="javascript: stylecolor('cyan')">
            <FONT COLOR="cyan">Cyan</FONT></B></A></TD>
        <TD COLSPAN=2 ALIGN="center">
        <A HREF="javascript: stylecolor('magenta')">
            <FONT COLOR="magenta"><B>Magenta</B></FONT></A></TD>
        <TD COLSPAN=2 ALIGN="center">
        <A HREF="javascript: stylecolor('yellow')">
            <FONT COLOR="yellow"><B>Yellow</B></FONT></A></TD>
        <TD COLSPAN=2>
        <INPUT NAME="preview" TYPE="button" VALUE="Preview"
          onClick="apreview(this.form)">></TD>
    </TR></FORM></TABLE>
</BODY></HTML>
```

**Double-Check the Layout**    You now have enough code to check your layout. Start your browser and load the code you have so far. You should see a layout like that shown in Figure 19.10.

Normally, at this point in your program development, you would spend some time polishing the layout. You might rearrange the controls, change a description, or decide on a different color background. You may or may not want to do this now, depending on how you like the choices made so far. If you like what you see, let's proceed and make this thing do some work.

**FIG. 19.10**
The layout of the message editor is only a façade at this point, but it is just as well to get the layout done and then put code behind it.

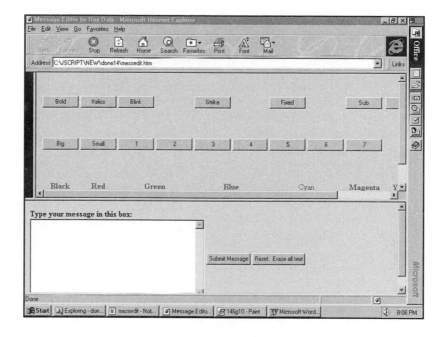

# Program Structure or Coding the Events

Although the message editor has 26 different controls on the control panel, most perform nearly identical functions. Most controls prompt for a text string, apply a font method to the string, and then append it to the text in the text area. The Help and About buttons simply display text. And finally, we have the best feature of all: the Preview button.

## Font Methods

For all of the font-style buttons, there is one function. Each button calls this function and passes a single value: the name of the style. The function uses this value in both the prompt box text and to decide which method to apply to the text. Although it creates a rather long function, it does keep down the number of functions.

**The Function *stylemethod()*** The first thing `stylemethod()` does is to display a dialog box in which the user can enter the text. This is the text that is highlighted in the given style. You note that the prompt message reminds the user of the style selected. This goes after `</TITLE>` and before `</HEAD>` and is shown in Listing 19.15.

Part
**IV**

Ch
**19**

### Listing 19.15   Start Adding Functions

```
<SCRIPT LANGUAGE = "JavaScript">
<!-- hide code from other browsers
function stylemethod (style) {
    x = prompt ("Enter your text for the style:" + style, "")
     if ((x!=null) && (x!="")) {
           //<!-- many if statements will go here -->
     }
}
// no more hidding -->
</SCRIPT>
```

The next several lines of code are a series of `if` statements. We must now apply the proper font method to the text string returned from the prompt dialog box. This is the section of code for the condition in which the style was bold:

```
if (style=="bold") {
    x = x.bold()
}
```

Additional `if` statements must be created for each of the additional 15 font methods using buttons. This code is shown in Listing 19.16.

Each of the `if` statements in Listing 19.16 produces a string with the appropriate HTML tags surrounding the string to be highlighted. This string is now simply appended to the existing text in the text area.

### Listing 19.16   *If* Statements of the *style* Function

```
        if (style == "bold") {
           x = x.bold()
        }
        if (style == "italics") {
           x = x.italics()
        }
        if (style == "blink") {
           x = x.blink()
        }
        if (style == "strike") {
           x = x.strike()
        }
        if (style == "fixed") {
           x = x.fixed()
        }
        if (style == "sub") {
           x = x.sub()
        }
        if (style == "sup") {
           x = x.sup()
        }
        if (style == "big") {
           x = x.big()
```

```
}
if (style == "small") {
    x = x.small()
}
if (style == "Size 1") {
    x = x.fontsize(1)
}
if (style == "Size 2") {
    x = x.fontsize(2)
}
if (style == "Size 3") {
    x = x.fontsize(3)
}
if (style == "Size 4") {
    x = x.fontsize(4)
}
if (style == "Size 5") {
    x = x.fontsize(5)
}
if (style == "Size 6") {
    x = x.fontsize(6)
}
 if (style == "Size 7") {
    x = x.fontsize(7)
}
```

**The Function *stylecolor()*** Though the method of applying color to strings is the same as other font methods, we are going to add a feature when using the fontcolor method. So, we need a function just for colors, which we call stylecolor(). When you select a color control, you change the color in the small frame in the upper-left corner. This provides the user with feedback and visually reminds the user which color he or she has selected. The code for this function is shown in Listing 19.17. Note that the final statement of this function first extracts the value field of the MESSARET text area of the heavy form of the document window of the MESSAREA frame and then appends the new value of the x parameter to it.

Part
IV

Ch
19

**Listing 19.17   The Function *stylecolor()***

```
function stylecolor(style) {
  parent.messcolr.document.bgColor = style
  x = prompt ("Enter your text for the style: "+ style, "")
     if ((x!=null)&&(x!="")) {
          x = x.fontcolor(style)
parent.messarea.document.heavy.messaret.value =
                    parent.messarea.document.heavy.messaret.value + x + ' '

     }
```

## The About and Help Features

So far, we have treated the About and Help buttons as part of the style function. This was great for testing the application, but we now want to make these buttons work.

The About button simply tells the user such information as where the program originated, the name of the author, and the version number. The coding is straightforward:

```
function aboutalert () {
    alert ("Message Editor by Ray Daly from Using JavaScript")
}
```

The Help function opens a new window with a help message, as seen in Figure 19.11. This comes from the code given in Listing 19.18. The code to open this window is as follows:

```
function helppage () {
    helpwin=open ("messhelp.htm", "HelpWindow","toolbar=no,scrollbars=yes")
}
```

**FIG. 19.11**

The Help screen for Message Editor is static. A more elaborate Help screen could contain the same controls as the control panel and provide help for each control.

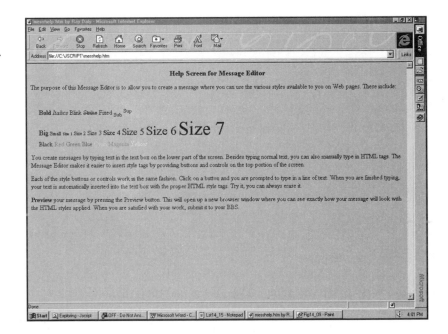

**Listing 19.18  Implementation of the Help Screen**

```
<HTML><HEAD><TITLE>messhelp.htm by Ray Daly </TITLE></HEAD><BODY>
<CENTER><H3>Help Screen for Message Editor</H3></CENTER>
<P>The purpose of this Message Editor is to
allow you to create a message where you
can use the various styles available to you on
 Web pages.   These include:</P>
<DL><DD>
<B>Bold</B> <I>Italics</I> <BLINK>Blink</BLINK> <STRIKE>Strike</STRIKE> Fixed
<SUB>Sub</SUB> <SUP>Sup</SUP> <BR>
<BIG>Big</BIG> <SMALL>Small</SMALL> <FONT SIZE="1">Size 1</FONT>
<FONT SIZE="2">Size 2</FONT>
<FONT SIZE="3">Size 3</FONT>
<FONT SIZE="4">Size 4</FONT>
```

```
<FONT SIZE="5">Size 5</FONT>
<FONT SIZE="6">Size 6</FONT>
<FONT SIZE="7">Size 7</FONT> <BR>
<FONT COLOR="black">Black</FONT>
<FONT COLOR="red">Red</FONT>
<FONT COLOR="green">Green</FONT>
<FONT COLOR="blue">Blue</FONT>
<FONT COLOR="cyan">Cyan</FONT> <
FONT COLOR="magenta">Magenta</FONT>
<FONT COLOR="yellow">Yellow</FONT>
</DD></DL>
<P>You create messages by typing text in
the text box on the lower part of the screen.
Besides typing normal text, you can
also manually type in HTML tags.
The Message Editor
makes it easier to insert style tags
by providing buttons and controls on the top
portion of the screen.</P>
<P>Each of the style buttons or controls
works in the same fashion.  Click on a button
and you are prompted to type in a line of text.
When you are finished typing, your text
is automatically inserted into the text box
with the proper HTML style tags.  Try it;
you can always erase it.</B>
<P><B>Preview</B> your message by clicking
the Preview button.  This will open up a new
browser window where you can see
exactly how your message will look with the HTML styles
applied.  When you are satisfied with
your work, submit it to your BBS.</P>
</BODY></HTML>
```

## The Preview

You have waited to the very end of this chapter for the best feature of this program. You may be disappointed at how short this code is. The purpose of this code is to take the HTML document created in the text area and display it on its own page. The code is shown in Listing 19.19. Figures 19.12 and 19.13 show the message center with the text entered, as well as that same text in the Preview window.

**Listing 19.19** *apreview* Function

```
function apreview (form) {
      msg = open ("","DisplayWindow","toolbar=yes")
      starttags ="<HTML><HEAD><TITLE>Preview</TITLE></HEAD><BODY><P><PRE>"
      endtags = "</PRE></P></BODY></HTML>"
      y = starttags + parent.messarea.document.heavy.messaret.value + endtags
      msg.document.write (y)
}
```

Part
IV

Ch
19

**CAUTION**

The function for preview is called `apreview`, not `preview`. This is because the button itself is already using the name preview. Unlike some other languages, function and object names can conflict.

**FIG. 19.12**

The message in the text box can be typed in or entered by clicking the control buttons. You can see how your message appears in a browser in Figure 19.13.

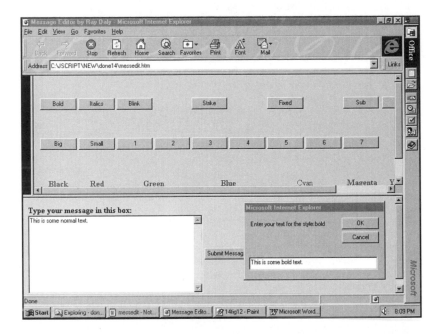

**FIG. 19.13**

This is the Preview window, which shows how your message appears in a browser. Once you approve, you submit your message.

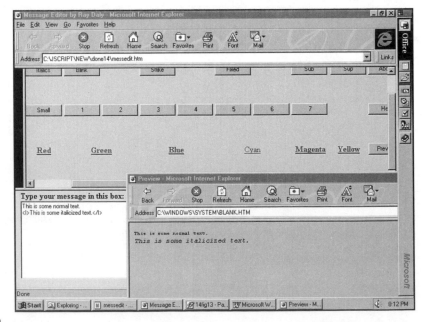

The limitation built into this design is that only one style can be applied at a time. For example, the controls do not allow bold, italic, green, or big. Of course, you can manually enter the codes in the text area to create these physical styles. This limitation does force your users to keep their effects simple. Such simplicity can produce better design. One useful addition that you could make would be to include a control that adds paragraph tags. As it stands, the message editor allows only a single paragraph message. ●

# CHAPTER 20

# Visual Effects

The flat, static Web page may not yet be a thing of the past. But, as the number of pages on the Web spirals into the tens of millions, new creative approaches are required both to catch viewers' attention and to hold their interest. Web page designers may now choose from a growing array of tools to lend visual impact to their creations.

In this chapter, you'll see how JavaScript can be used to create several useful visual effects, including alternating color schemes, fades, scrolling marquees, and dynamic graphics. Unlike effects created using other tools, JavaScript effects load quickly as part of your document and can start even before a page is completely loaded.

## Create a color alternator

The `Alternator` object alternates between two color schemes, producing a flashing effect.

## Build an event scheduler

The `Event` and `EventQueue` objects are used to manage timer-based events. They provide the basis for many of the effects described in this chapter.

## Write a color fader

The `Fader` object produces a smooth fade from one color scheme to another.

## Make a scrolling marquee

The `Marquee` object is used to create a scrolling marquee. Marquees can include multiple fonts, font sizes, colors, and can scroll left or right.

## Make a highlighted link menu

Using the new built-in `Image` object, a list of options are highlighted via the Image replacement method when the mouse passes over them.

## Generate XBM images

The `xbmImage` object is used to generate graphic images in real time.

# Creating Dynamic Framesets

Before getting started, let's take a look at the frameset environment we'll use to create visual effects.

Because Netscape Navigator and Internet Explorer 3.0 do not provide a way to update a document directly once it has been written to the screen, most of the effects we create here require that we write a new document to the screen for each step in an animation, marquee, or other effect—the exception being the Image replacement through use of the built-in Image object. Rather than load each successive document from the server (which would be much too slow), we'll generate our documents on-the-fly and then slap them into frames. Listing 20.1 shows the skeleton frameset that will be developed in the examples that follow.

**Listing 20.1   Skeleton Frameset**

```
<html>
<head>
<title>Visual Effects</title>
<script language="JavaScript">
<!-- begin script
var emptyFrame = '<html></html>';
function headFrame () {
  return '<html><body bgcolor="#FFFFFF" text="#000000">' +
    '<h1 align="center">Visual Effects</h1>' +
    '</body></html>';
}
function initialize () {
  self.head.location = "javascript:parent.headFrame()";
}
// end script -->
</script>
<frameset rows="52,*" onLoad="initialize()">
  <frame name="head" src="javascript:parent.emptyFrame"
    marginwidth=1 marginheight=1 scrolling="no" noresize>
  <frame name="body" src="javascript:parent.emptyFrame">
</frameset>
<noframes>
<h2 align="center">JavaScript or
JavaScript-enabled browser required</h2>
</noframes>
</html>
```

Some of the syntax and techniques used here are a bit different from what you've seen so far. But it's all perfectly legal. Let's take a minute to dissect this skeleton script.

## The *javascript*: Protocol

You've often seen http: or ftp: at the beginning of an URL. This is the *protocol:* It tells the browser which protocol handler to use to retrieve the object referred to after the colon. The `javascript:` protocol is really no different; it simply instructs the browser to let JavaScript retrieve the object. But, rather than initiate communication with another server, the JavaScript handler returns the value of the variable or function cited after the colon. The value returned should be HTML or some other MIME type the browser is able to display.

When using a `javascript:` URL, keep in mind that the reference after the colon is specified from the perspective of the receiving frame; in our example, from the point of view of the head frame—the `headFrame()` function is in the parent frame.

## Empty Frames

Sometimes it's desirable to leave a frame blank initially and load the contents later. For instance, the value of the frame may depend on user input or the result of a lengthy calculation or process. You could load an empty document from the server, but that wastes a server access. It's faster and easier to use the `javascript:` protocol to load the empty document internally.

The `<HTML></HTML>` pair used in our `emptyFrame` variable isn't strictly necessary under Netscape or Internet Explorer—an empty string works just as well. But other JavaScript-enabled browsers may not be as forgiving.

You may be wondering why we need to use an empty frame at all in this example, at least for the head frame, as we could load it directly. In fact, it sometimes happens that frames loaded by using the `javascript:` protocol align incorrectly if they are loaded directly from a `FRAME` tag. So instead, we must load an empty document in the `FRAME` tag and then load the intended document from the `onLoad` handler for the frameset.

You might also be tempted to simply leave off the `SRC=` attribute. However, frames that do not have an initial location specified cannot be updated with a new location.

**N O T E**  You may have seen frameset documents that use `about:blank` to specify an empty frame. This is a Netscape-specific construction and should be avoided. Internet Explorer does not support the `about:` construction. ■

## Content Variables versus Functions

In our skeleton frameset, `emptyFrame` is a variable containing HTML, while `headFrame()` is a function that returns HTML. Either method can be used. In general, use variables if the content will not change. Use functions to return dynamic content.

# A Simple Color Alternator

One of the easiest visual effects to create is a color alternator, which switches between two color schemes in a frame. This effect is best used in small frames containing large, bold headlines. In general, it should not be used with smaller, more detailed text, as it will make such text difficult to read while the effect is in progress. It would also be wise to use this effect in

Part
**IV**

Ch
**20**

moderation—a brief burst of alternating colors can be very effective when your page first loads, when making a transition to a new topic, or to underscore a point. However, continuous flashing quickly becomes annoying to the viewer. (Remember the fate of the BLINK tag!)

Let's start with a simple, direct example. Building on our skeleton frameset in Listing 20.2, the headFrame() function is modified to return one of two BODY tags, depending on the state of a variable called headColor.

### Listing 20.2   The Modified *headFrame()* Function

```
var headColor = "white";
function headFrame () {
  return '<html>' +
    ((headColor == "white") ?
      '<body bgcolor="#FFFFFF" text="#000000">' :
      '<body bgcolor="#000000" text="#FFFFFF">') +
    '<h1 align="center">Visual Effects</h1>' +
    '</body></html>';
}
```

In Listing 20.3, we create a function called setHead() that uses JavaScript's setTimeout() function to create a timer loop. The head frame will be updated six times, alternating colors each time.

### Listing 20.3   The *setHead()* Function Alternates Colors

```
var headLoops = 6;
function setHead () {
  if (headColor == "white")
    headColor = "black";
  else
    headColor = "white";
  if (--headLoops > 0)
    setTimeout ('setHead()', 100);
  self.head.location = "javascript:parent.headFrame()";
}
```

Finally, we'll call setHead() in our initialize() function:

```
function initialize() {
  setHead();
}
```

When the example page is loaded, the head frame alternates rapidly between white-on-black and black-on-white. The entire effect lasts less than one second. The output is shown in Figure 20.1 and Figure 20.2.

**N O T E**   The absolute update rate that can be achieved with timer events will vary from platform to platform. On some systems, it might be as few as three per second. ▪

**FIG. 20.1**

The heading frame alternates between white-on-black (shown here) and black-on-white (shown in Figure 20.2).

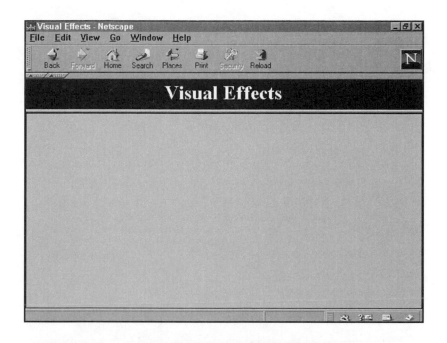

**FIG. 20.2**

Here is an example of black-on-white.

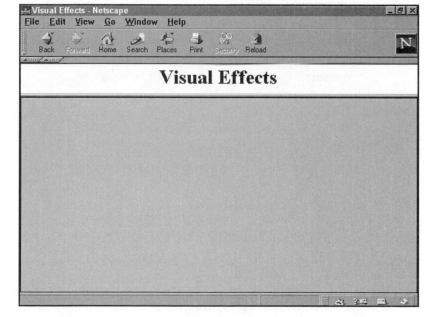

Listing 20.4 shows the complete code for this example.

**Listing 20.4   The Simple Color Alternator**

```
<html>
<head>
<title>Visual Effects</title>
<script language="JavaScript">
<!-- begin script
var emptyFrame = '<html></html>';
var headColor = "white";
function headFrame () {
  return '<html>' +
    ((headColor == "white") ?
      '<body bgcolor="#FFFFFF" text="#000000">' :
      '<body bgcolor="#000000" text="#FFFFFF">') +
    '<h1 align="center">Visual Effects</h1>' +
    '</body></html>';
}
var headLoops = 6;
function setHead () {
  if (headColor == "white")
    headColor = "black";
  else
    headColor = "white";
  if (--headLoops > 0)
    setTimeout ('setHead()', 125);
  self.head.location = "javascript:parent.headFrame()";
}
function initialize () {
  setHead();
}
// end script -->
</script>
<frameset rows="52,*" onLoad="initialize()">
  <frame name="head" src="javascript:parent.emptyFrame"
     marginwidth=1 marginheight=1 scrolling="no" noresize>
  <frame name="body" src="javascript:parent.emptyFrame">
</frameset>
<noframes>
<h2 align="center">JavaScript or
JavaScript-enabled browser required</h2>
</noframes>
</html>
```

# A Better Color Alternator

The first color alternator works fine if you plan to use the effect only once with one set of colors in a single frame. But, if you plan to use this effect more extensively, you'll end up duplicating a lot of code. In this section, we'll develop a generalized version of the color alternator that offers greater flexibility and that can easily be reused.

An object-oriented, component-based approach will be used in this example. Initially this might appear to be overkill but, as you will see, the components created here provide the foundation for more complex effects.

▶ **See** "JavaScript Objects," **p. 87**, for more information about objects.

## Color Objects

Let's start by defining a Color object and some related functions. Colors in HTML (and JavaScript) are represented by hexadecimal triplets of the form RRGGBB, in which each two-digit hexadecimal code represents the red, green, or blue component of a color. Values range between 00 and FF hex, corresponding to zero to 255 decimal. The Color object constructor, shown in Listing 20.5, accepts a hexadecimal string, but stores the individual components as numbers, which are easier to manipulate.

### Listing 20.5  The *Color* Object Constructor

```
var hexchars = '0123456789ABCDEF';
function fromHex (str) {
  var high = str.charAt(0);
  var low = str.charAt(1);
  return (16 * hexchars.indexOf(high)) +
    hexchars.indexOf(low);
}
function toHex (num) {
  return hexchars.charAt(num >> 4) + hexchars.charAt(num & 0xF);
}
function Color (str) {
  this.red = fromHex(str.substring(0,2));
  this.green = fromHex(str.substring(2,4));
  this.blue = fromHex(str.substring(4,6));
  this.toString = ColorString;
  return this;
}
function ColorString () {
  return toHex(this.red) + toHex(this.green) + toHex(this.blue);
}
```

As you might expect, the fromHex() and toHex() functions convert between numeric and hexadecimal values. Note that these functions will only work with values in the range 00 to FF hex (zero to 255 decimal). By the way, it should be possible to write the fromHex() function more compactly as

```
function fromHex (str) {
return (16 * hexchars.indexOf(str.charAt(0))) +
    hexchars.indexOf(str.charAt(1));
}
```

The ColorString() function is defined as the Color object's toString() method. This function converts the color back to an RGB triplet and is automatically invoked any time a Color object is used in a context that requires a string.

**TIP** Any JavaScript object can be given a `toString()` method, which is automatically called whenever an object needs to be converted to a string value.

In the following, the `Color` constructor is used to define a few colors:

```
var black = new Color ("000000");
var white = new Color ("FFFFFF");
var blue = new Color ("0000FF");
var magenta = new Color ("FF00FF");
var yellow = new Color ("FFFF00");
```

Now that the colors are in a convenient form, let's define an object to contain all the colors in use by a document at a given moment. We'll call this the `BodyColor` object. Its constructor is shown in Listing 20.6.

### Listing 20.6  The *BodyColor* Object Constructor

```
function BodyColor (bgColor,fgColor,linkColor,vlinkColor,alinkColor) {
   this.bgColor = bgColor;
   this.fgColor = fgColor;
   this.linkColor = linkColor;
   this.vlinkColor = vlinkColor;
   this.alinkColor = alinkColor;
   this.toString = BodyColorString;
   return this;
}
function BodyColorString () {
   return '<body' +
      ((this.bgColor == null) ? '' : ' bgcolor="#' + this.bgColor + '"') +
      ((this.fgColor == null) ? '' : ' text="#' + this.fgColor + '"') +
      ((this.linkColor == null) ? '' : ' link="#' + this.linkColor + '"') +
      ((this.vlinkColor == null) ? '' : ' vlink="#' + this.vlinkColor + '"') +
      ((this.alinkColor == null) ? '' : ' alink="#' + this.alinkColor + '"') +
      '>';
}
```

The `BodyColor()` constructor accepts up to five `Color` objects as parameters, one for each HTML body color attribute. The colors are specified in the order of generally accepted importance; trailing colors can be omitted if they will not be used. So, for instance, if a document does not contain any links, the last three parameters can safely be left off.

Like the `Color` constructor, the `BodyColor` constructor includes a `toString()` method named the `BodyColorString()` function. In this case, a complete BODY tag is returned, including any color attributes specified.

Note that the individual `Color` objects are used directly in the construction of the BODY tag string. Because the objects are used in a context requiring a string, the `Color` object's `toString()` method will automatically be called to translate these into hexadecimal triplet strings!

The following are a few definitions for `BodyColor` objects. Because no links will be used in this example, the three link parameters are omitted:

```
var blackOnWhite = new BodyColor (white, black);
var whiteOnBlack = new BodyColor (black, white);
var blueOnWhite = new BodyColor (white, blue);
var magentaOnYellow = new BodyColor (yellow, magenta);
var yellowOnBlue = new BodyColor (blue, yellow);
```

In this case, previously defined colors are used. Because these colors will likely be reused, it was worthwhile to assign them to named variables. But, suppose you wanted to use a color only once in a specific `BodyColor` object. It seems—and is—inefficient to define a variable just to hold an object that is going to be used immediately:

```
var weirdOne = new Color ("123ABC");
var oddBody = new BodyColor (weirdOne, yellow);
```

Instead, we can invoke the `Color` constructor directly from the `BodyColor` constructor parameter list without ever assigning a name to the color:

```
var oddBody = new BodyColor (new Color ("123ABC"), yellow);
```

 **TIP**
When creating an object that is referred to by name only once, you can invoke its constructor in the parameter list of the function or method that will use it instead of assigning it to a named variable.

## The *Alternator* Object

Our next step is to create an object that generates HTML that alternates between two `BodyColor` specifications. This will be called the `Alternator` object. Its constructor is shown in Listing 20.7.

**Listing 20.7   The *Alternator* Object Constructor**

```
function Alternator (bodyA, bodyB, text) {
  this.bodyA = bodyA;
  this.bodyB = bodyB;
  this.currentBody = "A";
  this.text = text;
  this.toString = AlternatorString;
  return this;
}
function AlternatorString () {
  var str = "<html>";
  with (this) {
    if (currentBody == "A") {
      str += bodyA;
      currentBody = "B";
    }
    else {
```

Part
**IV**

Ch
**20**

*continues*

> **Listing 20.7   Continued**
>
> ```
>        str += bodyB;
>        currentBody = "A";
>     }
>     str += text + '</body></html>';
>   }
>   return str;
> }
> ```

The `Alternator()` constructor accepts two `BodyColor` objects plus a string containing that which is to appear between `<BODY>` and `</BODY>`. In theory, the text string can be arbitrarily long, but 4K seems to be the maximum usable length on most platforms. In our examples, this string will be much shorter.

The `currentBody` variable indicates which `BodyColor` object is used to generate the `BODY` tag. This variable is switched by the `toString()` method, `AlternatorString()`, each time it is invoked. Let's now create an `Alternator` object by using the same text that appeared in the head frame of our simple alternator example:

```
var flashyText = new Alternator (blackOnWhite, whiteOnBlack,
  '<h1 align="center">Visual Effects</h1>');
```

Each time `flashyText` is referenced, it will alternate between black-on-white and white-on-black output. For example, suppose we loaded `flashyText` into three frames consecutively:

```
self.frameA.location = "javascript:parent.flashyText";
self.frameB.location = "javascript:parent.flashyText";
self.frameC.location = "javascript:parent.flashyText";
```

## Events and the Event Queue

All that's left is to write a `flashyText` object to the screen at regular intervals. To do this, you need to create an object called an `Event`, which—in this context—is an action that is scheduled to take place at a particular time. You can define the `Event` object so that a separate event is required for each write to the screen, but this would require a lot of extra coding. Instead, build a looping mechanism into the `Event` object because most of the effects created in this chapter involve multiple writes to the screen. Listing 20.8 shows the `Event` constructor.

> **Listing 20.8   The *Event* Object Constructor**
>
> ```
> function Event (start, loops, delay, action) {
>   this.start = start * 1000;
>   this.next = this.start;
>   this.loops = loops;
>   this.loopsRemaining = loops;
>   this.delay = delay * 1000;
>   this.action = action;
>   return this;
> }
> ```

The Event constructor takes the start time for the event (relative to the time the program is launched or the time the EventQueue is started), the number of times (loops) to execute the event, the delay between each execution, and the action to be performed for the event.

The start time and delay are specified in seconds but are converted to milliseconds for internal use. The action can be any valid JavaScript statement enclosed in quotes. (This is similar to the way you specify an action for JavaScript's setTimeout() function.) The following is the Event constructor for the flashyText object:

```
var flashEvent = new Event (0, 10, 0.1,
  'self.head.location="javascript:parent.flashyText"');
```

We will start the event at time zero, that is, as soon as the EventQueue is started. We'll loop ten times with each loop one-tenth of a second apart. The action for the event is to load the flashyText object into the head frame.

We've defined an Event, but it's still just sitting there. This is where the EventQueue object comes in. The EventQueue contains a list of Event objects to be acted upon. It handles the scheduling and looping of events and executes the associated actions. Listing 20.9 shows the EventQueue constructor and related functions. This is a fairly complex bit of code; we won't go through it line-by-line, but we'll cover the key parameters and methods.

### Listing 20.9 The *EventQueue* Object Constructor

```
function EventQueue (name, delay, loopAfter, loops, stopAfter) {
  this.active = true;
  this.name = name;
  this.delay = delay * 1000;
  this.loopAfter = loopAfter * 1000;
  this.loops = loops;
  this.loopsRemaining = loops;
  this.stopAfter = stopAfter * 1000;
  this.event = new Object;
  this.start = new Date ();
  this.loopStart = new Date();
  this.eventID = 0;
  this.addEvent = AddEvent;
  this.processEvents = ProcessEvents;
  this.startQueue = StartQueue;
  this.stopQueue = StopQueue;
  return this;
}
function AddEvent (event) {
  this.event[this.eventID++] = event;
}
function StartQueue () {
  with (this) {
    active = true;
    start = new Date();
    loopStart = new Date();
```

Part
IV

Ch
20

*continues*

**Listing 20.9  Continued**

```
      loopsRemaining = loops;
      setTimeout (name + ".processEvents()", this.delay);
   }
}
function StopQueue () {
  this.active = false;
}
function ProcessEvents () {
  with (this) {
    if (!active) return;
    var now = new Date();
    if (now.getTime() - start.getTime() >= stopAfter) {
      active = false;
      return;
    }
    var elapsed = now.getTime() - loopStart.getTime();
    if (elapsed >= loopAfter) {
      if (--loopsRemaining <= 0) {
        active = false;
        return;
      }
      loopStart = new Date();
      elapsed = now.getTime() - loopStart.getTime();
      for (var i in event)
        if (event[i] != null) {
          event[i].next = event[i].start;
          event[i].loopsRemaining = event[i].loops;
        }
    }
    for (var i in event)
      if (event[i] != null)
        if (event[i].next <= elapsed)
          if (event[i].loopsRemaining-- > 0) {
            event[i].next = elapsed + event[i].delay;
            eval (event[i].action);
          }
    setTimeout (this.name + ".processEvents()", this.delay);
  }
}
```

The first parameter to the EventQueue constructor is the queue name. This *must* be the same as the variable name to which the EventQueue object is assigned. (This is a bit of a kludge, but is required for the event processor to make setTimeout() calls to itself.)

Next, the delay parameter specifies how often the events in the queue are checked. This is important because it determines the maximum rate of actions for all events in the queue. If you specify a queue delay of 0.10 seconds, but an event delay of 0.05 seconds, the event will only be executed every 0.10 seconds. Therefore, the delay should be set to the smallest value required by your events. Values smaller than 0.05 seconds are not recommended.

The `loopAfter` parameter specifies the number of seconds after which the entire `EventQueue` starts over. This enables entire complex sequences of events to be repeated. The `loops` parameter specifies the number of times the entire `EventQueue` repeats. Set this to zero if you do not want the queue to repeat.

The `stopAfter` parameter indicates the number of seconds after which the queue stops processing events, regardless of the number of loops remaining. Set this to an arbitrarily chosen high number, such as `99999`, if you do not want the queue to stop after any particular length of time. Once the `EventQueue` has been defined, you can then use the `addEvent()` method to add events to the queue. Let's create an event queue and add our `flashEvent` object to it, as follows:

```
var evq = new EventQueue ("evq", 0.1, 30, 10, 99999);
evq.addEvent (flashEvent);
```

Our event queue (`EventQueue`) will check for events every 0.1 seconds. It will start over every 30 seconds, repeating 10 times. If for some reason it is still active after 99,999 seconds, it will stop processing.

The final step is to start the queue. This is done in the `initialize()` function, which is the `onLoad` handler for our frameset.

```
function initialize () {
  evq.startQueue();
}
```

That's it! We're in business! After creating numerous functions and scores of lines of code, we now have exactly what we started with in our first, "simple" example. But wait—there's more.

## Scheduling Multiple Events

As noted at the beginning of this section, this somewhat complex approach to generating the `Alternator` effect isn't really necessary if you are going to use a single effect only once in your program. But, the advantages quickly multiply when you create complex effects or sequences of events. Each new event requires just a few lines of code, as Listing 20.10 demonstrates.

Part
**IV**

Ch
**20**

---

**Listing 20.10    Adding *New Alternator* Events**

```
var dance1 = new Alternator (yellowOnBlue, magentaOnYellow,
  '<h1 align="center">Dancing...</h1>');
var inthe1 = new Alternator (magentaOnYellow, yellowOnBlue,
  '<h1 align="center">...in the...</h1>');
var streets1 = new Alternator (whiteOnBlack, yellowOnBlue,
  '<h1 align="center">...streets!</h1>');
var d1e = new Event (0, 10, .1,
  'self.f1.location="javascript:parent.dance1"');
var i1e = new Event (3, 10, .1,
  'self.f1.location="javascript:parent.inthe1"');
var s1e = new Event (6, 10, .1,
  'self.f1.location="javascript:parent.streets1"');
```

*continues*

**Listing 20.10   Continued**

```
evq.addEvent(d1e);
evq.addEvent(i1e);
evq.addEvent(s1e);
```

Listing 20.11 shows the complete code for the improved alternator with an expanded example, the output of which is shown in Figure 20.3. In the sections that follow, you'll see how you can easily build on our event model to create even more interesting effects.

**FIG. 20.3**

Alternating text events are scheduled in four frames.

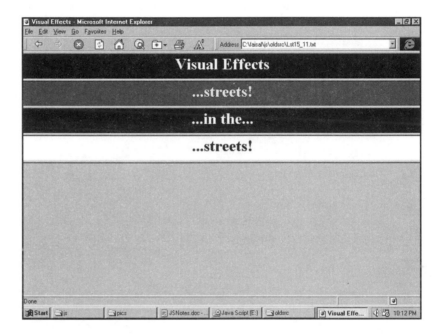

**Listing 20.11   Complete Code for the Improved Alternator**

```
<html>
<head>
<title>Visual Effects</title>
<script language="JavaScript">
<!-- begin script
var emptyFrame = '<html></html>';
var hexchars = '0123456789ABCDEF';
function fromHex (str) {
  var high = str.charAt(0);
  var low = str.charAt(1);
  return (16 * hexchars.indexOf(high)) +
    hexchars.indexOf(low);
}
function toHex (num) {
  return hexchars.charAt(num >> 4) + hexchars.charAt(num & 0xF);
```

```
}
function Color (str) {
  this.red = fromHex(str.substring(0,2));
  this.green = fromHex(str.substring(2,4));
  this.blue = fromHex(str.substring(4,6));
  this.toString = ColorString;
  return this;
}
function ColorString () {
  return toHex(this.red) + toHex(this.green) + toHex(this.blue);
}
function BodyColor (bgColor,fgColor,linkColor,vlinkColor,alinkColor) {
  this.bgColor = bgColor;
  this.fgColor = fgColor;
  this.linkColor = linkColor;
  this.vlinkColor = vlinkColor;
  this.alinkColor = alinkColor;
  this.toString = BodyColorString;
  return this;
}
function BodyColorString () {
  return '<body' +
    ((this.bgColor == null) ? '' : ' bgcolor="#' + this.bgColor + '"') +
    ((this.fgColor == null) ? '' : ' text="#' + this.fgColor + '"') +
    ((this.linkColor == null) ? '' : ' link="#' + this.linkColor + '"') +
    ((this.vlinkColor == null) ? '' : ' vlink="#' + this.vlinkColor + '"') +
    ((this.alinkColor == null) ? '' : ' alink="#' + this.alinkColor + '"') +
    '>';
}
function Alternator (bodyA, bodyB, text) {
  this.bodyA = bodyA;
  this.bodyB = bodyB;
  this.currentBody = "A";
  this.text = text;
  this.toString = AlternatorString;
  return this;
}
function AlternatorString () {
  var str = "<html>";
  with (this) {
    if (currentBody == "A") {
      str += bodyA;
      currentBody = "B";
    }
    else {
      str += bodyB;
      currentBody = "A";
    }
    str += text + '</body></html>';
  }
  return str;
}
function Event (start, loops, delay, action) {
  this.start = start * 1000;
  this.next = this.start;
```

*continues*

**Listing 20.11    Continued**

```
    this.loops = loops;
    this.loopsRemaining = loops;
    this.delay = delay * 1000;
    this.action = action;
    return this;
  }
  function EventQueue (name, delay, loopAfter, loops, stopAfter) {
    this.active = true;
    this.name = name;
    this.delay = delay * 1000;
    this.loopAfter = loopAfter * 1000;
    this.loops = loops;
    this.loopsRemaining = loops;
    this.stopAfter = stopAfter * 1000;
    this.event = new Object;
    this.start = new Date ();
    this.loopStart = new Date();
    this.eventID = 0;
    this.addEvent = AddEvent;
    this.processEvents = ProcessEvents;
    this.startQueue = StartQueue;
    this.stopQueue = StopQueue;
    return this;
  }
  function AddEvent (event) {
    this.event[this.eventID++] = event;
  }
  function StartQueue () {
    with (this) {
      active = true;
      start = new Date();
      loopStart = new Date();
      loopsRemaining = loops;
      setTimeout (name + ".processEvents()", this.delay);
    }
  }
  function StopQueue () {
    this.active = false;
  }
  function ProcessEvents () {
    with (this) {
      if (!active) return;
      var now = new Date();
      if (now.getTime() - start.getTime() >= stopAfter) {
        active = false;
        return;
      }
      var elapsed = now.getTime() - loopStart.getTime();
      if (elapsed >= loopAfter) {
        if (--loopsRemaining <= 0) {
          active = false;
          return;
        }
```

```
      loopStart = new Date();
      elapsed = now.getTime() - loopStart.getTime();
      for (var i in event)
        if (event[i] != null) {
          event[i].next = event[i].start;
          event[i].loopsRemaining = event[i].loops;
        }
    }
  for (var i in event)
    if (event[i] != null)
      if (event[i].next <= elapsed)
        if (event[i].loopsRemaining-- > 0) {
          event[i].next = elapsed + event[i].delay;
          eval (event[i].action);
        }
    setTimeout (this.name + ".processEvents()", this.delay);
  }
}
var black = new Color ("000000");
var white = new Color ("FFFFFF");
var blue = new Color ("0000FF");
var magenta = new Color ("FF00FF");
var yellow = new Color ("FFFF00");

var blackOnWhite = new BodyColor (white, black);
var whiteOnBlack = new BodyColor (black, white);
var blueOnWhite = new BodyColor (white, blue);
var yellowOnBlue = new BodyColor (blue, yellow);
var magentaOnYellow = new BodyColor (yellow, magenta);

var flashyText = new Alternator (blackOnWhite, whiteOnBlack,
  '<h1 align="center">Visual Effects</h1>');
var dance1 = new Alternator (yellowOnBlue, magentaOnYellow,
  '<h1 align="center">Dancing...</h1>');
var dance2 = new Alternator (whiteOnBlack, yellowOnBlue,
  '<h1 align="center">Dancing...</h1>');
var dance3 = new Alternator (new BodyColor(black,yellow), magentaOnYellow,
  '<h1 align="center">Dancing...</h1>');
var inthe1 = new Alternator (magentaOnYellow, yellowOnBlue,
  '<h1 align="center">...in the...</h1>');
var inthe2 = new Alternator (blackOnWhite, whiteOnBlack,
  '<h1 align="center">...in the...</h1>');
var inthe3 = new Alternator (yellowOnBlue, blueOnWhite,
  '<h1 align="center">...in the...</h1>');
var streets1 = new Alternator (whiteOnBlack, yellowOnBlue,
  '<h1 align="center">...streets!</h1>');
var streets2 = new Alternator (blueOnWhite, magentaOnYellow,
  '<h1 align="center">...streets!</h1>');
var streets3 = new Alternator (yellowOnBlue, blackOnWhite,
  '<h1 align="center">...streets!</h1>');

var flashEvent = new Event (0, 10, 0.1,
  'self.head.location="javascript:parent.flashyText"');
var d1e = new Event (0, 10, .1,
  'self.f1.location="javascript:parent.dance1"');
```

Part

**IV**

Ch

**20**

*continues*

**Listing 20.11    Continued**

```
var d2e = new Event (5, 10, .1,
  'self.f2.location="javascript:parent.dance2"');
var d3e = new Event (10, 10, .1,
  'self.f3.location="javascript:parent.dance3"');
var i1e = new Event (3, 10, .1,
  'self.f1.location="javascript:parent.inthe1"');
var i2e = new Event (8, 10, .1,
  'self.f2.location="javascript:parent.inthe2"');
var i3e = new Event (13, 10, .1,
  'self.f3.location="javascript:parent.inthe3"');
var s1e = new Event (6, 10, .1,
  'self.f1.location="javascript:parent.streets1"');
var s2e = new Event (11, 10, .1,
  'self.f2.location="javascript:parent.streets2"');
var s3e = new Event (16, 10, .1,
  'self.f3.location="javascript:parent.streets3"');

var evq = new EventQueue ("evq", 0.1, 20, 10, 60);
evq.addEvent (flashEvent);
evq.addEvent(d1e);
evq.addEvent(i1e);
evq.addEvent(s1e);
evq.addEvent(d2e);
evq.addEvent(i2e);
evq.addEvent(s2e);
evq.addEvent(d3e);
evq.addEvent(i3e);
evq.addEvent(s3e);

function initialize () {
  evq.startQueue();
}
// end script -->
</script>
<frameset rows="52,52,52,52,*" onLoad="initialize()">
  <frame name="head" src="javascript:parent.emptyFrame"
    marginwidth=1 marginheight=1 scrolling="no" noresize>
  <frame name="f1" src="javascript:parent.emptyFrame"
    marginwidth=1 marginheight=1 scrolling="no" noresize>
  <frame name="f2" src="javascript:parent.emptyFrame"
    marginwidth=1 marginheight=1 scrolling="no" noresize>
  <frame name="f3" src="javascript:parent.emptyFrame"
    marginwidth=1 marginheight=1 scrolling="no" noresize>
  <frame name="body" src="javascript:parent.emptyFrame">
</frameset>
<noframes>
<h2 align="center">JavaScript or
  JavaScript-enabled browser required</h2>
</noframes>
</html>
```

# A Color *Fader*

Like the `Alternator` effect, the `Fader` effect involves the transition from one color scheme to another. But, instead of jumping abruptly between colors, the `Fader` displays a series of intermediate shades, creating the illusion of a smooth transition. Although the `Alternator` effect is noisy and jarring, the `Fader` effect is calm, serene, even solemn. In particular, a slow fade up from (or down to) black can lend a somber, serious tone to the message being conveyed. Or the `Fader` can be used to create wild, psychedelic effects—whichever best suits your purpose.

By now, it should come as no surprise that we'll start by creating a new object type. However, before we create the `Fader` object itself, we need to create a special object that calculates an intermediate color value between two `Color` objects. I'll call this the `IntColor` object. Its constructor is shown in Listing 20.12.

**Listing 20.12    The *IntColor* Object Constructor**

```
function IntColor (start, end, step, steps) {
  this.red =
    Math.round(start.red+(((end.red-start.red)/(steps-1))*step));
  this.green =
    Math.round(start.green+(((end.green-start.green)/(steps-1))*step));
  this.blue =
    Math.round(start.blue+(((end.blue-start.blue)/(steps-1))*step));
  this.toString = ColorString;
  return this;
}
```

The `IntColor()` constructor takes two `Color` objects—`start` and `end`—plus the number of steps between the start and end colors, and the current step. The resultant object is identical to a `Color` object and can be used as such. It may be convenient to think of `IntColor()` as just another constructor for a `Color` object.

Now that we have a way to calculate intermediate colors, we can create our `Fader` object. Listing 20.13 shows its constructor.

**Listing 20.13    The *Fader* Object Constructor**

```
function Fader (bodyA, bodyB, steps, text) {
  this.bodyA = bodyA;
  this.bodyB = bodyB;
  this.step = 0;
  this.steps = steps;
  this.text = text;
  this.toString = FaderString;
  return this;
}
function FaderString () {
  var intBody = new BodyColor();
```

Part
IV

Ch
20

*continues*

**Listing 20.13 Continued**

```
with (this) {
  if (bodyA.bgColor != null && bodyB.bgColor != null)
    intBody.bgColor =
      new IntColor (bodyA.bgColor, bodyB.bgColor, step, steps);
  if (bodyA.fgColor != null && bodyB.fgColor != null)
    intBody.fgColor =
      new IntColor (bodyA.fgColor, bodyB.fgColor, step, steps);
  if (bodyA.linkColor != null && bodyB.linkColor != null)
    intBody.linkColor =
      new IntColor (bodyA.linkColor, bodyB.linkColor, step, steps);
  if (bodyA.vlinkColor != null && bodyB.vlinkColor != null)
    intBody.vlinkColor =
      new IntColor (bodyA.vlinkColor, bodyB.vlinkColor, step, steps);
  if (bodyA.alinkColor != null && bodyB.alinkColor != null)
    intBody.alinkColor =
      new IntColor (bodyA.alinkColor, bodyB.alinkColor, step, steps);
  step++;
  if (step >= steps)
    step = 0;
}
return '<html>' + intBody + this.text + '</body></html>';
}
```

The Fader object is similar in construction to the Alternator object. The Fader() constructor takes a beginning BodyColor object (bodyA), an ending BodyColor object (bodyB), and a text string containing the HTML and text to be displayed. In addition, the Fader() constructor takes the number of steps to be used in the transition from the beginning colors to the ending colors.

The toString() method, FaderString(), is a bit more complex than its Alternator counterpart. It creates a temporary BodyColor object and populates it with IntColor objects for each color attribute that is present in both the beginning and ending BodyColor objects. FaderString() then increments the current step. When all steps have been completed, it resets the current step to zero, so the object can be reused. It returns the specified text along with an embedded BODY tag generated from the temporary BodyColor object.

You may have recognized that a Fader object with steps set to 2 performs exactly the same function as an Alternator object, but the code is a little longer and involves more processing.

 **TIP**

If you are using both Alternator and Fader objects, you can use a Fader object with two steps in place of an Alternator object and omit the alternator code to save space.

A Fader object is defined much the same way as an Alternator object, as shown in Listing 20.14.

---

**Listing 20.14  Using the *Fader* Object**

```
var fadingText = new Fader (yellowOnBlue, magentaOnYellow, 10,
  '<h1 align="center">Visual Effects</h1>');
var evq = new EventQueue ("evq", 0.1, 20, 10, 60);
evq.addEvent (new Event (0, 10, 0.1,
  'self.head.location="javascript:parent.fadingText"'));
```

---

Notice that, instead of creating a named variable for our `Fader` event, we defined it in the parameter list for the `addEvent()` method. If you have a lot of events, making up names for them can be a chore—not to mention a source of confusion.

When creating events for `Fader` objects, it's important to remember that the number of loops specified for the event should normally be the same as the number of steps in the fade. If you specify a smaller number of loops, you'll get an incomplete fade; specify a larger number and the fade will start over with the initial color.

# A Scrolling Marquee

By now, you've probably seen dozens of pages with a scrolling text ticker down at the bottom in the status area. Besides being hard to read, these tend to block out the usual status messages associated with cursor actions. The Java applet and ActiveX marquees and tickers are much better, but they can take a while to load or won't run on all platforms. However, you can enjoy the best of both worlds by creating a JavaScript marquee that's both readable and quick to load.

Ideally, our marquee should be able to display text in a variety of fonts, sizes, and colors, in any combination. So, before we define the `Marquee` object itself, let's create some text-handling objects that will help us do just that. The `Text` and `Block` object constructors are shown in Listing 20.15.

---

**Listing 20.15  The *Text* and *Block* Object Constructors**

```
function Text (text, size, format, color) {
  this.text = text;
  this.length = text.length;
  this.size = size;
  this.format = format;
  this.color = color;
  this.toString = TextString;
  this.substring = TextString;
  return this;
}
function TextString (start, end) {
  with (this) {
    if (TextString.arguments.length < 2 || start >= length) start = 0;
    if (TextString.arguments.length < 2 || end > length) end = length;
```

*continues*

**Listing 20.15   Continued**

```
      var str = text.substring(start,end);
      if (format != null) {
        if (format.indexOf("b") >= 0) str = str.bold();
        if (format.indexOf("i") >= 0) str = str.italics();
        if (format.indexOf("f") >= 0) str = str.fixed();
      }
      if (size != null) str = str.fontsize(size);
      if (color != null) {
        var colorstr = color.toString();
        str = str.fontcolor(colorstr);
      }
    }
    return str;
}
function Block () {
    var argv = Block.arguments;
    var argc = argv.length;
    var length = 0;
    for (var i = 0; i < argc; i++) {
      length += argv[i].length;
      this[i] = argv[i];
    }
    this.length = length;
    this.entries = argc;
    this.toString = BlockString;
    this.substring = BlockString;
    return this;
}
function BlockString (start, end) {
    with (this) {
      if (BlockString.arguments.length < 2 || start >= length) start = 0;
      if (BlockString.arguments.length < 2 || end > length) end = length;
    }
    var str = "";
    var segstart = 0;
    var segend = 0;
    for (var i = 0; i < this.entries; i++) {
      segend = segstart + this[i].length;
      if (segend > start)
        str += this[i].substring(Math.max(start,segstart)-segstart,
          Math.min(end,segend)-segstart);
      segstart += this[i].length;
      if (segstart >= end)
        break;
    }
    return str;
}
```

The Text object is used to contain a string, along with font, size, and color information. If you look closely, you'll see that the Text object has some interesting properties, both figuratively and literally.

The Text object is designed to mimic JavaScript strings, but with some important differences. The Text object has a length property, for instance, and a substring() method. But while the length property returns the length of the text itself, the substring() method returns the requested substring *plus* the HTML tags required to render the substring in the desired font, size, and color.

Why is this important? Because the Marquee object must display segments of text to produce its scrolling effect. Therefore, to maintain proper formatting, the Marquee object needs to be able to retrieve substrings as small as a single character with all their HTML attributes intact.

The Text() constructor takes a text string and, optionally, a font size, a Color object, and a format string. The format string can contain the lowercase letters b, i, or f, or any combination of the three, which stand for bold, italic, and fixed, respectively. The Color object specifies the foreground color to be used when displaying the text.

**N O T E** The font size must be passed as a string (for example, "7") rather than a number when specified as a parameter to the Text() constructor.

The Block object is used to combine two or more Text objects, JavaScript strings, or even other Block objects, in any combination. Like the Text object, the Block object mimics JavaScript string behavior. A call to its substring() method might return portions of several of its constituent objects, with all their HTML formatting intact.

The Block() constructor accepts any number of Text, String, or Block objects. These are considered to be logically concatenated in the order specified in the argument list. Listing 20.16 shows an example of using Text and Block objects.

**Listing 20.16   Using *Text* and *Block* Objects**

```
var t1 = new Text ("When shall ", "5", "", blue);
var t2 = new Text ("we three ", "6", "fb", red);
var t3 = new Text ("meet again, ", "5", "bfi", yellow);
var t4 = new Text ("or in rain? ", "6", "ib", red);
var b1 = new Block (t3, "In thunder, lightning, ", t4);
var b2 = new Block (t1, t2, b1);
```

A call to b2.substring(5,25) would then return the following:

```
<FONT COLOR="#0000FF"><FONT SIZE="5">shall </FONT></FONT>
<FONT COLOR="#FF0000"><FONT SIZE="6"><TT><B>we three </B></TT></FONT></FONT>
<FONT COLOR="#FFFF00"><FONT SIZE="5"><I><B>meet </B></I></FONT></FONT>
```

Part
IV

Ch
20

Using `Text` and `Block` objects, you can create marquees in a wide variety of styles. Now let's take a look at the `Marquee` object itself. Listing 20.17 shows its constructor.

**Listing 20.17   The *Marquee* Object Constructor**

```
function Marquee (body, text, maxlength, step) {
  this.body = body;
  this.text = text;
  this.length = text.length;
  this.maxlength = maxlength;
  this.step = step;
  this.offset = 0;
  this.toString = MarqueeString;
  return this;
}
function MarqueeString () {
  with (this) {
    var endstr = offset + maxlength;
    var remstr = 0;
    if (endstr > text.length) {
      remstr = endstr - text.length;
      endstr = text.length;
    }
    var str = nbsp(text.substring(offset,endstr) +
      ((remstr == 0) ? "" : text.substring(0,remstr)));
    offset += step;
    if (offset >= text.length)
      offset = 0;
    else if (offset < 0)
      offset = text.length - 1;
  }
  return '<html>' + this.body + '<table border=0 width=100% height=100%><tr>' +
    '<td align="center" valign="center">' + str + '</td></tr></table></body></
html>';
}
function nbsp (strin) {
  var strout = "";
  var intag = false;
  var len = strin.length;
  for(var i=0, j=0; i < len; i++) {
    var ch = strin.charAt(i);
    if (ch == "<")
      intag = true;
    else if (ch == ">")
      intag = false;
    else if (ch == " " && !intag) {
      strout += strin.substring(j,i) + " ";
      j = i + 1;
    }
  }
  return strout + strin.substring(j,len);
}
```

The body parameter to the Marquee() constructor accepts a BodyColor object. This object determines the overall color scheme for the marquee.

The text parameter can be a Block object, a Text object, or a JavaScript String object. The text produced by this object will be scrolled across the screen to create the marquee effect. Any colors embedded in this object will override the foreground color specified in the body parameter for the corresponding section of text.

The maxlength parameter is the maximum length of the text returned by the Marquee object, not counting HTML formatting tags. You will need to experiment with this a bit to get the right width. A good starting point is to use the width of the marquee frame divided by ten. So, for a 400-pixel-wide window, start with 40 and then adjust as necessary. It's okay to specify a length slightly larger than the frame width, but if you specify a much longer length, it will slow down processing and increase memory usage.

The step parameter specifies the number of characters the marquee will scroll each time it is invoked. You will generally want to set this to 1 or 2 or, to scroll backwards, -1 or -2. Combined with the delay time defined for the Marquee event, the step parameter determines how fast the Marquee scrolls across the screen.

The toString() method, MarqueeString(), uses a table to center the text vertically and horizontally within the frame. (Depending on how you use the Alternator and Fader objects, you may want to modify their toString() methods to do this as well.) Note that if you use a combination of large and small fonts in your marquee, the text may "wobble" vertically during the transition from one size to another.

The nbsp() function is used to replace all space characters with non-breaking spaces ( ). This enables you to include consecutive spaces (normally ignored by HTML) in your text. It also prevents the scrolling text from breaking into two or more lines when the font is small enough or the marquee window large enough that this would otherwise occur. In Listing 20.18, we create a marquee, using the opening lines from Shakespeare's Macbeth for our text.

### Listing 20.18   Using the *Marquee* Object

```
var mbScene = new Block (
  new Text ("When shall we three meet again, ", "5", "b", red),
  new Text ("In thunder, lightning, or in rain? ", "6", "bf", blue),
  new Text ("When the hurlyburly\'s done, ", "5", "ib", yellow),
  new Text ("When the battle\'s lost and won. ", "6", "bfi", magenta),
  new Text ("That will be ere the set of sun. ", "6", "fb", red),
  "..............."
  );

var mbMarquee = new Marquee (whiteOnBlack, mbScene, 50, 2);
var evq = new EventQueue ("evq", 0.1, 120, 5, 600);
evq.addEvent (new Event (0, mbMarquee.length * 3, 0.125,
  'self.f1.location = "javascript:parent.mbMarquee"'));
```

There are several points to note in this example. First, rather than define a separate named variable for each `Text` object, they are created in the parameter list for the `Block` constructor. Again, this is usually preferable to cluttering your program with a lot of variables that are only referenced once.

Next, notice that the apostrophes in the text are *escaped* by using the \ character. It's easy to forget to do this when you're working with real-world text in JavaScript applications. The line of dots at the end of the `Block` acts as a separator between the end of the text and the beginning when the marquee wraps around. In this particular case, it would have been better to use a `Text` object with a larger font size because the rest of the text in the block uses larger fonts. But the point to keep in mind is that you *can* use plain strings in `Block` objects if you want.

Finally, when creating the `Event` for the marquee, the number of loops is specified as a multiple of the length of the `Marquee` object. This is much easier than counting all the characters in the `Block` object manually. Its output is shown in Figure 20.4.

**FIG. 20.4**
A scrolling marquee can include multiple font styles, colors, and sizes.

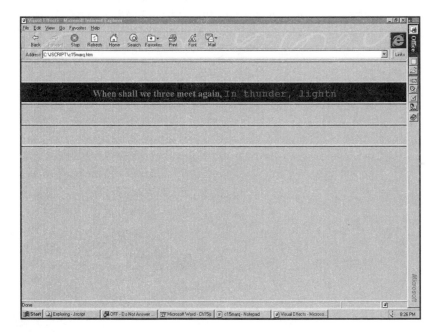

# The *Static* Object

In some cases, you may just want to put some text in a frame at a particular time. This isn't really an effect, per se, but it is convenient to have an object similar to the rest of your objects for this purpose. The `Static` object fills this need. Its constructor is shown in Listing 20.19.

**Listing 20.19   The *Static* Object Constructor**

```
function Static (body, text) {
  this.body = body;
  this.text = text;
  this.toString = StaticString;
  return this;
}
function StaticString () {
  return '<html><body>' + this.body + this.text + '</body></html>';
}
```

The `Static()` constructor takes a `BodyColor` object and a text string, which may contain HTML. You can also use a `Text` object or a `Block` object for the text parameter. The following is an example of using the `Static` object:

```
var beHere = new Static (blackOnWhite, '<h1 align="center">Be Here Now</h1>');
var evq = new EventQueue ("evq", 0.1, 120, 5, 600);
evq.addEvent (new Event (12, 1, 10,
  'self.f1.location = "javascript:parent.beHere"'));
```

# Animating Images

Using JavaScript to animate images is not the best way because Netscape Navigator and Internet Explorer 3.0 support GIF89a multi-part images, which contain built-in timing and looping instructions. These load faster and run more smoothly than animation created by using JavaScript. A number of inexpensive shareware utilities are available for creating GIF animation, the best-known of which is probably *GIF Construction Set* by Alchemy Mindworks.

The latest version (3.0) of Netscape Navigator has added some very exciting features to JavaScript. You can now preload and animate images directly on the page by using the built-in `Image` object. Before 3.0, if you wanted to create animations via JavaScript, you had to use some kind of dynamic frames, which limited the usefulness and adaptability of the animation. Now you can replace images on-the-fly—create icons that change when the mouse interacts with them and animate images directly on the page, even after it has completely loaded.

If you have used the `LOWSRC` attribute of the `IMG` tag, you have seen that Netscape has been able to replace images directly on the screen for some time. The `Image` object has many properties and has three event handlers. The example we will build involves creating a graphical list of links that are sensitive to your mouse location. As you pass your mouse over each link, the icon to the left of it changes to indicate that you are currently focused on that link. This script is very simple, yet it can give your pages a very dynamic feel. Listing 20.20 contains the complete script.

Part

**IV**

Ch

**20**

**Listing 20.20    The *Link* Focus List**

```html
<html>
<head>
<title>Link Focus List</title>
<script language="javascript">
firstImage = new Image()
secondImage = new Image()
focusImage = new Image()

firstImage.src = "one.gif"
secondImage.src="two.gif"
focusImage.src = "three.jpg"

// this preloads the images into cache
</script>
</head>
<body>
<h1>Link Focus List</h1>
<font size=4>Move your mouse over each selection</font>
<P>
<a href="javascript:alert('first image link')"
onMouseOver="document.images[0].src=focusImage.src"
onMouseOut ="document.images[0].src=firstImage.src"
onError = "alert('error loading image 0')"
><img src="one.gif" border=0 height=20 width=100></a> <br>
<a href="javascript:alert('second image link')"
onMouseOver="document.images[1].src=focusImage.src"
onMouseOut ="document.images[1].src=secondImage.src"
onError = "alert('error loading image 1')"
><img src="two.gif" border=0 height=20 width=100></a> <br>
</body>
</html>
```

We simply created three `Image` objects, assigned an URL to their `SRC` attribute, and used `onMouseOver` and `onMouseOut` to control the image replacement.

TIP    To preload images into the cache, create Image objects in the <HEAD></HEAD> and set each `Image.src` attribute to the desired image URL.

It is good practice, if you are going to dynamically change images on a page, to preload them into the browser's cache before you attempt to display them on the page. If you do not preload them, you will see the browser's empty image icon until the image is loaded. This often will appear strange to the page user and can have other unexpected effects.

Whenever you want to replace one image with another on a page, via whatever event is triggered, just reset that image's `src` attribute to the new URL. If the image is not already loaded, it will cause the browser to retrieve the image.

Notice also in the preceding script the onError handler. If for some reason the image fails to completely load into that location, this event is triggered. This is handy in that you might try loading another image in its place to ensure that there are no "broken image" icons on the screen.

# Generating Images

Loading images from a server has its limitations. Apart from the amount of time this can take—especially over a slow connection—you generally have a fixed set of images with which to work (unless you generate images on the server by using a CGI program). There are times when it is useful to create images on-the-fly, perhaps in response to user input or to create a dynamic animation.

JavaScript offers two solutions. The first is to use single-pixel GIF files to construct images. Because Netscape Navigator and Microsoft Internet Explorer automatically scale images to the specified width and height, you can create rectangles of various dimensions from a 1×1 GIF image of a particular color by specifying the height and width in the IMG tag. This technique is especially useful for creating dynamic bar charts; but, beyond that, its applications are very limited. I won't cover this technique here, but encourage you to experiment with it on your own.

To start you off, though, here is a small example of setting an image's width via JavaScript:

```
<SCRIPT LANGUAGE="JavaScript">
var imageWidth=30
document.write("<IMG SRC='greenpixel.gif' HEIGHT=5 WIDTH="+imageWidth+">")
</SCRIPT>
```

The second solution is to generate XBM-format images. You may not have heard of these before, but you've probably seen them. They're often used as icons in server directory listings. You are most likely to see one when downloading a file via FTP.

The greatest drawback to XBM images is that they're monochromatic (black-and-white) though Navigator and IE render them as black-and-gray. But this is also something of an advantage to us because they can be represented internally as a string of bits, one per pixel, on or off (which allows bits of information to be represented as images—such as graphs). This also makes manipulating XBM images fairly straightforward and not too costly in terms of processor cycles—an important consideration when working with an interpreted language such as JavaScript. Also of importance is that the XBM file's native format is plain (ASCII) text, which can be represented by using text strings in JavaScript.

## The XBM Format

An XBM image consists of a header, which specifies its width and height in pixels, and a string of hexadecimal byte codes. As shown in Listing 20.21, it looks much like something you'd find in a C-language source file.

---

**Listing 20.21   An XBM Image File Header**

```
#define xbm_width 32
#define xbm_height 32
static char xbm_bits[] = {
  0xFF,0x02,0x88,0x25,0x3C,0xB4,0x11,0xDB,
  ...
};
```

---

The names `xbm_width`, `xbm_height`, and `xbm_bits` are not part of the specification. We chose these because they are descriptive, but the names could be any valid C-style identifiers—it's the format that's important.

Each byte code is a bitmap that corresponds to eight pixels in a row of pixels. The first byte code represents the upper-leftmost eight pixels in an image. Bits are processed from left to right until the specified width is reached. The next set of bits then defines the next row of pixels, and so on, until the entire image is drawn.

# Representing an XBM Image

We'll represent the XBM bits internally as JavaScript numbers. Because JavaScript uses 32-bit integers, it makes sense to store 32 XBM bits in each JavaScript number. However, it turns out that the high-order sign bit can't be set on some platforms, so we'll use 16-bit numbers instead. This wastes some space, but the math is much easier if we stick with powers of 2.

Our XBM images will be made up of two types of objects: the `xbmRow` object, which contains an array of 16-bit numbers, and the `xbmImage` object, which contains an array of `xbmRow` objects. These objects both contain additional information that is used in manipulating the image and in translating it to ASCII text for display. Listing 20.22 shows their constructors.

---

**Listing 20.22   The *xbmRow* and *xbmImage* Object Constructors**

```
function xbmRow (parent, columns, initialValue) {
  this.redraw = true;
  this.text = null;
  this.parent = parent;
  this.col = new Object();
  for (var i = 0; i < columns; i++)
    this.col[i] = initialValue;
  this.toString = xbmRowString;
  return this;
}
function xbmImage (width, height, initialValue) {
  this.width = (width+15)>>4;
  this.pixelWidth = this.width<<4;
  this.height = height;
  this.head = "#define xbm_width " + (this.pixelWidth) +
    "\n#define xbm_height " + this.height +
    "\nstatic char xbm_bits[] = {\n";
  this.initialValue = ((initialValue == null) ? 0 : initialValue);
```

```
    this.negative = false;
    this.row = new Object();
    for (var i = 0; i < height; i++)
        this.row[i] = new xbmRow(this, this.width, this.initialValue);
    this.drawPoint = xbmDrawPoint;
    this.drawLine = xbmDrawLine;
    this.drawRect = xbmDrawRect;
    this.drawFilledRect = xbmDrawFilledRect;
    this.drawCircle = xbmDrawCircle;
    this.drawFilledCircle = xbmDrawFilledCircle;
    this.reverse = xbmReverse;
    this.clear = xbmClear;
    this.partition = xbmPartitionString;
    this.toString = xbmString;
    return this;
}
```

The xbmImage() constructor takes the width and height of the image, in pixels, as parameters. An optional initial value can also be specified—if supplied; this will create a pattern of vertical lines in the image. Otherwise, a zero is assumed, which results in a blank image.

The xbmImage() constructor calls the xbmRow() constructor to create each row in the image. xbmRow() should be considered an internal function. You don't need to call it directly. Both xbmImage and xbmRow have toString() methods: xbmImageString() and xbmRowString(), respectively. These create the ASCII representation of the XBM image when it's time to display it. A third method, xbmPartitionString(), optimizes the string-building process, which would otherwise consume an excessive amount of memory. These are shown in Listing 20.23.

### Listing 20.23  The *xbmImage toString()* Methods

```
function xbmRowString () {
    if (this.redraw) {
        this.redraw = false;
        this.text = "";
        for (var i = 0; i < this.parent.width; i++) {
            var pixels = this.col[i];
            if (this.parent.negative)
                pixels ^= 0xFFFF;
            var buf = "0x" + hexchars.charAt((pixels>>4)&0xF) +
                hexchars.charAt(pixels&0xF) + ",0x" +
                hexchars.charAt((pixels>>12)&0xF) +
                hexchars.charAt((pixels>>8)&0xF) + ",";
            this.text += buf;
        }
    }
    return this.text;
}
function xbmPartitionString (left,right) {
    if (left == right) {
        var str = this.row[left].toString();
```

Part

IV

Ch

20

*continues*

**Listing 20.23    Continued**

```
    if (left == 0)
      str = this.head + str;
    else if (left == this.height - 1)
      str += "};\n";
    return str;
  }
  var mid = (left+right)>>1;
  return this.partition(left,mid) + this.partition(mid+1,right);
}
function xbmString () {
  return this.partition(0,this.height - 1);
}
```

# XBM Drawing Methods

The foundation of our XBM drawing capability is the drawPoint() method, xbmDrawPoint(), shown in Listing 20.24. As with all of the XBM drawing methods, the drawPoint() method doesn't actually draw anything on the screen. Instead, it updates the internal state of the xbmImage object to indicate that the specified point needs to be drawn.

**Listing 20.24    The *xbmDrawPoint()* Function**

```
function xbmDrawPoint (x,y) {
  if (x < 0 || x >= this.pixelWidth ||
      y < 0 || y >= this.height)
    return;
  this.row[y].col[x>>4] |= 1<<(x&0xF);
  this.row[y].redraw = true;
}
```

The drawPoint() method takes the *x* and *y* coordinates of the point to be drawn. These are specified relative to the upper left corner of the image, which is point (0,0).

The *y* coordinate is used as an index into the array of xbmRow objects. The high-order bits of the *x* coordinate are used to compute an index into the array of JavaScript numbers that represent the row. The low-order bits are then used to calculate the bit offset for the desired pixel coordinate, which is turned on.

Let's create an xbmImage object and draw a point:

```
var picture = new xbmImage (64,64);
picture.drawPoint(10,15);
```

Drawing points can be useful for creating fine detail within an image, but it would take a lot of drawPoint() calls to create a useful image. Fortunately, we have some more-powerful drawing methods at our disposal (Listing 20.25).

## Listing 20.25   The *xbmDrawLine()* Function

```
function xbmDrawLine (x1,y1,x2,y2) {
  var x,y,e,temp;
  var dx = Math.abs(x1-x2);
  var dy = Math.abs(y1-y2);
  if ((dx >= dy && x1 > x2) || (dy > dx && y1 > y2)) {
    temp = x2;
    x2 = x1;
    x1 = temp;
    temp = y2;
    y2 = y1;
    y1 = temp;
  }
  if (dx >= dy) {
    e = (y2-y1)/((dx == 0) ? 1 : dx);
    for (x = x1, y = y1; x <= x2; x++, y += e)
      this.drawPoint(x,Math.round(y));
  }
  else {
    e = (x2-x1)/dy;
    for (y = y1, x = x1; y <= y2; y++, x += e)
      this.drawPoint(Math.round(x),y);
  }
}
```

The drawLine() method, xbmDrawLine(), shown in Listing 20.25, draws a line between two points by making a series of calls to drawPoint(). It takes two pairs of coordinates, (x1,y1) and (x2,y2), as parameters. The algorithm is reasonably efficient, at least in the context of an interpreted language. The drawLine() method forms the basis of our rectangle-drawing algorithms, shown in Listing 20.26.

## Listing 20.26   Rectangle Drawing Functions

```
function xbmDrawRect (x1,y1,x2,y2) {
  this.drawLine (x1,y1,x2,y1);
  this.drawLine (x1,y1,x1,y2);
  this.drawLine (x1,y2,x2,y2);
  this.drawLine (x2,y1,x2,y2);
}
function xbmDrawFilledRect (x1,y1,x2,y2) {
  var x,temp;
  if (x1 > x2) {
    temp = x2;
    x2 = x1;
    x1 = temp;
    temp = y2;
    y2 = y1;
    y1 = temp;
  }
  for (x = x1; x <= x2; x++)
    this.drawLine(x,y1,x,y2);
}
```

Part
IV

Ch
20

The drawRect() method, xbmDrawRect(), draws a hollow rectangle, given two opposing corner coordinate pairs, (x1,y1) and (xy,y2). The drawFilledRect() method, xbmDrawFilledRect(), draws a filled rectangle (as you probably guessed).

Let's draw some lines and rectangles. Note this only modifies the contents of an xbmImage object named picture—it does not actually draw anything. The technique for actual drawing is described later.

```
var picture = new xbmImage (64,64);
picture.drawLine (0,0,63,63);
picture.drawRect (32,0,63,32);
picture.drawFilledRect (0,32,32,63);
```

Our last two drawing methods, shown in Listing 20.27, draw hollow and filled circles.

### Listing 20.27 Circle Drawing Functions

```
function xbmDrawCircle (x,y,radius) {
  for (var a=0, b=1; a < b; a++) {
    b = Math.round(Math.sqrt(Math.pow(radius,2)-Math.pow(a,2)));
    this.drawPoint(x+a,y+b);
    this.drawPoint(x+a,y-b);
    this.drawPoint(x-a,y+b);
    this.drawPoint(x-a,y-b);
    this.drawPoint(x+b,y+a);
    this.drawPoint(x+b,y-a);
    this.drawPoint(x-b,y+a);
    this.drawPoint(x-b,y-a);
  }
}
function xbmDrawFilledCircle (x,y,radius) {
  for (var a=0, b=1; a < b; a++) {
    b = Math.round(Math.sqrt(Math.pow(radius,2)-Math.pow(a,2)));
    this.drawLine(x+a,y+b,x+a,y-b);
    this.drawLine(x-a,y+b,x-a,y-b);
    this.drawLine(x+b,y+a,x+b,y-a);
    this.drawLine(x-b,y+a,x-b,y-a);
  }
}
```

The drawCircle() method, xbmDrawCircle(), and the drawFilledCircle() method, xbmDrawFilledCircle(), take the coordinates of the center point of the circle plus the radius. These methods take advantage of the fact that it's necessary only to compute the points for a single octant (one-eighth) of a circle. They compute these points relative to an origin of (0,0) and then translate them to the eight octants relative to the x and y coordinates.

Because the drawPoint() method automatically "clips" any points that don't lie within the image area, we can draw circles that only partially intersect our image, by using the following code:

```
var picture = new xbmImage (64,64);
picture.drawCircle (32,32,20); // completely within image
```

## Displaying Generated Images

A generated xbmImage object can be displayed in much the same way that an ordinary image would be displayed, except that it has a javascript: URL. Listing 20.28 shows an example of using the Static object to supply the surrounding HTML.

---

**Listing 20.28  Displaying an *xbmImage* Object**

```
picture = new xbmImage (64,64);
picture.drawLine (0,0,63,63);
picture.drawLine (0,63,63,0);
var pictureFrame = new Static (whiteOnBlack,
  '<img src="javascript:parent.picture" width=64 height=64>');
self.frameA.location = "javascript:parent.pictureFrame";
```

---

Note, however, that once an xbmImage has been displayed, any subsequent changes to it will not be displayed when you redraw the frame. Internet Explorer assumes that images of a given name don't change, so it uses its cached copy after the first draw. The workaround is to assign the xbmImage object to an object with a different name and then redraw it. ●

# CHAPTER 21

# Creative User Interaction

**J**avaScript offers tremendous flexibility in interacting with the user. You can create entire documents on-the-fly. You can dynamically customize both the content of a document and its appearance according to user criteria and other factors. User input also benefits from this flexibility: Prompts can be dynamically generated and freeform input can even be processed. In this chapter, you develop techniques for performing all these tasks.

This chapter builds on several of the objects you created in Chapter 20, "Visual Effects," and some of the techniques you developed there, so you might want to review that chapter before you begin, or refer to it as you go along. ■

### Create dynamic output

Page content and layout are generated on-the-fly based on user input and other factors.

### Generate random numbers

The RandomNumberGenerator object is used to create random phrases and to display them using random fonts and color schemes.

### Sort an array

A Quicksort array-sorting algorithm is used to sort words for the phrase generator and to rank scores in a database-lookup application.

### Parse freeform user input

Keywords are extracted from a query string and are used for database lookup.

### Create an indexed database

A multiple-key indexing and retrieval mechanism is used to build a bookstore catalog with author, title, and subject indexes.

# Creating Dynamic Output

JavaScript provides two methods for updating the screen with dynamic content: You can use the document.write() function, or you can write the entire contents of a frame to the screen by using the javascript: protocol as an HREF in a link. As in Chapter 20, you use the latter approach here because it is better suited to the examples in this chapter.

The skeleton frameset shown in Listing 21.1 is essentially the same as that used in Chapter 20.

## Listing 21.1  The Skeleton Frameset

```html
<html>
<head>
<title>Creative User Interaction</title>
<script language="JavaScript">
<!-- begin script
var emptyFrame = '<html></html>';
function headFrame () {
  return '<html><body bgcolor="#FFFFFF" text="#000000">' +
    '<h1 align="center">Creative User Interaction</h1>' +
    '</body></html>';
}
function initialize () {
  self.head.location = "javascript:parent.headFrame()";
}
// end script -->
</script>
<frameset rows="52,*" onLoad="initialize()">
  <frame name="head" src="javascript:parent.emptyFrame"
      marginwidth=1 marginheight=1 scrolling="no" noresize>
  <frame name="body" src="javascript:parent.emptyFrame">
</frameset>
<noframes>
<h2 align="center">JavaScript  or
JavaScript enabled browser required</h2>
</noframes>
</html>
```

In this listing, you start by initializing the frames to point to the emptyFrame variable in the FRAME SRC= tag and then set the true location from the initialize() function, which is the onLoad handler for the frameset. As noted in the preceding chapter, this gets around an alignment bug that appears when loading a frame directly by using the javascript: protocol as an HREF in an anchor or link.

You can specify either a variable or a function name to the right of the colon in a javascript: URL. Normally you use a variable to return an unchanging, or static, value; whereas, you use a function to return dynamic content. If a variable name refers to an object, however, and that object has a toString() method defined, the function associated with the toString() method is called when the object is referenced in a `javascript:` URL, in which case, dynamic content may be returned. You see an example of this behavior later, in the section titled "A Random Phrase Generator."

You have defined `headFrame()` as a function, although it currently returns a static value. You can jazz it up with a bit of dynamic content, as shown in Listing 21.2.

**Listing 21.2   Returning Dynamic Content**

```
function headFrame () {
  var now = new Date();
  var body;
  if (now.getHours() >= 6 && now.getHours() < 18)
    body = '<body bgcolor="#FFFFFF" text="#000000">';
  else
    body = '<body bgcolor="#000000" text="#FFFFFF">';
  return '<html>' + body +
    '<h1 align="center">Creative User Interaction</h1>' +
    '</body></html>';
}
```

Now, when `headFrame()` is loaded between 6:00 A.M. and 6:00 P.M., it comes up in daylight mode, with a white background. From 6:00 P.M. until 6:00 A.M., the function displays its nocturnal mode. You can also give the user an appropriate greeting, as shown in Listing 21.3 (you might want to adjust the frame size to accommodate the new line). One result of this listing is shown in Figure 21.1.

**Listing 21.3   Returning a Timely Greeting**

```
function headFrame () {
  var now = new Date();
  var hour = now.getHours();
  var body;
  var greeting;
  if (hour >= 6 && hour < 18)
    body = '<body bgcolor="#FFFFFF" text="#000000">';
  else
    body = '<body bgcolor="#000000" text="#FFFFFF">';
  if (hour < 6)
    greeting = "Up late, or up early?";
  else if (hour < 12)
    greeting = "Good morning!";
  else if (hour < 18)
    greeting = "Good afternoon!";
  else
    greeting = "Good evening!";
  return '<html>' + body +
    '<h1 align="center">Creative User Interaction</h1>' +
    '<h3 align="center">' + greeting + '</h3>' +
    '</body></html>';
}
```

**FIG. 21.1**

The current time is used to generate an appropriate greeting.

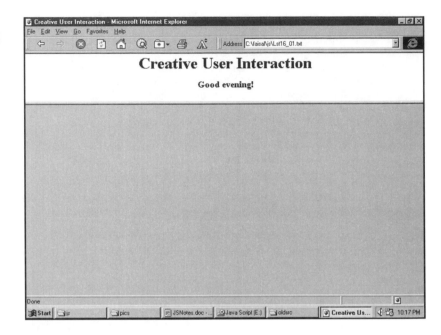

# Generating Random Numbers

In the preceding example, you used the time of day to determine which colors and messages to use in generating a dynamic header frame. You can take this example even further; for instance, you might define a different message for every hour of the day, or even for every minute of the hour. You can use this technique to give your pages many different looks.

For many applications in which a degree of apparent randomness is desirable, using the Date object alone yields acceptable results. However, when you need a series of random numbers, one after another, the Date object isn't of much help. In this situation, the chances are that the calculations you're performing or the effects you're creating will be finished before the Date object advances to a new value. This is where a *Random Number Generator* (RNG) comes into play.

In truth, no such thing as a software-generated random number really exists. Software is hopelessly logical—given a particular set of input values, a function performs a predefined set of steps in a predictable order, yielding predictable results. (Even a buggy function yields predictable, albeit undesirable, results.)

Even the best algorithms, such as the one presented in the next paragraph, don't generate truly random numbers. Instead, they generate very long sequences of numbers that simulate random behavior. However, eventually the sequences repeat. The numbers generated are, therefore, properly known as *pseudo-random* numbers.

The RNG shown in Listing 21.4 is an implementation of the Park-Miller algorithm. (See "Random Number Generators: Good Ones Are Hard to Find," by Stephen K. Park and Keith W. Miller, Communications of the ACM, 31(10):1192—1201, 1988.) The JavaScript version was written by David N. Smith of IBM's T.J. Watson Research Center. Mr. Smith notes that his version has not been subjected to the rigorous testing required of a mission-critical RNG.

**Listing 21.4   The *RandomNumberGenerator* Object**

```
function NextRandomNumber()  {
  var hi   = this.seed / this.Q;
  var lo   = this.seed % this.Q;
  var test = this.A * lo - this.R * hi;
  if (test > 0)
    this.seed = test;
  else
    this.seed = test + this.M;
  return (this.seed * this.oneOverM);
}
function RandomNumberGenerator() {
  var d = new Date();
  this.seed = 2345678901 +
    (d.getSeconds() * 0xFFFFFF) +
    (d.getMinutes() * 0xFFFF);
  this.A = 48271;
  this.M = 2147483647;
  this.Q = this.M / this.A;
  this.R = this.M % this.A;
  this.oneOverM = 1.0 / this.M;
  this.next = NextRandomNumber;
  return this;
}
```

In the preceding listing, the `RandomNumberGenerator()` constructor uses the system time, in minutes and seconds, to "seed" itself—that is, to create the initial values from which it will generate a sequence of numbers. If you are familiar with random number generators, you may use some other value for the seed. Otherwise, you should probably not change it.

This RNG is implemented as an object. To use it, you create an instance of the object and then invoke its `next()` method to return a number. Each call to the `next()` method returns a new random number, as in the following:

```
var rand = new RandomNumberGenerator();

// Display five random numbers
for (var i = 0; i < 8; i++)
  document.write ("The number is: " + rand.next() + "<br>");
```

Part

IV

Ch

21

Like many random number generators, this RNG returns a fraction between 0 and 1; for example, .2755983265971, or something similar. To convert this number to an integer between 0 and *n,* you must multiply *n* times the random number and then round the result. Here's an example that returns a random number between 0 and 255:

```
function random255 () {
  return Math.round(255 * rand.next());
}
```

This example works fine if you need only random integers between 0 and 255. But you can rewrite it to return a number between 0 and any integer, as follows:

```
function random (n) {
  return Math.round(n * rand.next());
}
```

By now you might be wondering, "Why all the fuss about random numbers? What use are they, anyway?" Well, they have many serious and important uses in simulations, in software testing and verification, and so on. They also happen to be great for creating games and other fun things, as you see in the next section.

**N O T E**  You might have noticed that JavaScript's Math object includes a built-in random()
method. The version presented here should work as well as, if not better than, the built-in
implementations, and will work uniformly on all platforms.

# A Random Phrase Generator

According to one popular theory, if you put enough monkeys in a room full of typewriters, eventually, by hit and miss, they will bang out the complete works of Shakespeare. Although we suspect it would take several generations of monkeys just to tap out a decent sonnet, try a similar but less ambitious experiment by using the random number generator in place of monkeys.

The goal is to generate some simple phrases by randomly combining words from lists of verbs, articles, adjectives, and nouns. In this exercise, you can cheat a bit by imposing a structure on the phrases. Your formula is as follows:

> verb + article (or possessive pronoun) + adjective + noun.

For example,

> Have a nice day.

## Random Words

Start creating the random phrase generator by defining an object to contain a list of words, as shown in Listing 21.5.

### Listing 21.5 The *Word* Object Constructor

```
function Word () {
  var argv = Word.arguments;
  var argc = argv.length;
  this.list = new Object();
  for (var i = 0; i < argc; i++)
    this.list[i] = argv[i];
  this.count = argc;
  this.toString = WordString;
  return this;
}
function WordString () {
  var i = Math.round((this.count - 1) * rand.next());
  return this.list[i];
}
```

The Word() constructor is designed to accept a variable number of parameters or arguments. Every JavaScript function has a built-in property called arguments. The arguments property is an array containing all the arguments passed to the function, indexed beginning at 0. The arguments property also has a length property, which is the number of arguments passed to the function. You assign them to variables argv and argc, primarily because variables by those names play a similar role in C programs.

The Word() constructor takes the words passed in the argument list and puts them in an internal array called list. To keep the numbering scheme simple, you can make list a separate object rather than making each word a property of the Word object itself.

The toString() method WordString() does the monkey's job of returning random words. As you learned in Chapter 20, "Visual Effects," JavaScript automatically calls an object's toString() method any time the object is used in a context requiring a string. WordString() uses the random number object rand to generate an integer between 0 and the number of words in the list, minus one. (If you have a list containing five words, the generated integer is 0–4.) This integer is then used as the index into the list array.

To start, use the Word() constructor to create a list of nouns:

```
var noun = new Word ("dog", "cat", "shoe", "doorknob", "umbrella");
```

Now, each time you refer to the noun object in a context requiring a string (thus, invisibly calling its toString() method), you get a random selection from the list. For instance, consider this code snippet:

```
for (var i = 0; i < 5; i++)
  document.write ("Have a " + noun + "<br>");
```

It returns a list of offerings that might look something like the following:

```
Have a shoe
Have a umbrella
Have a umbrella
Have a dog
Have a doorknob
```

Sample output is shown in Figure 21.2.

**FIG. 21.2**
The RNG object is used
to construct simple
random sentences.

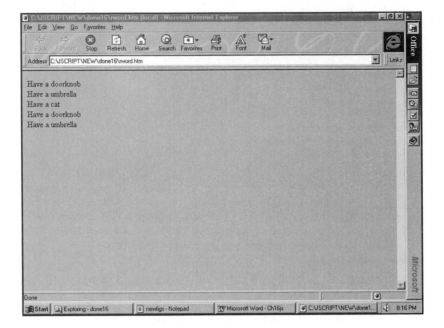

As you can see, just because you reference the noun object five times does not mean that each of the five words will be listed. Randomness means that you might get just one of the words repeated five times. Or you might get all five perfectly alphabetized. Over time, these instances will roughly average out, but you have no way of knowing what you'll get in any given sample.

Now go ahead and define the rest of the word types and then take a crack at some random phrases, as follows:

```
var verb = new Word ("have", "get", "eat", "pet", "feed");
var article = new Word ("a", "the", "my", "your");
var adjective = new Word ("nice", "pretty", "smelly", "hairy", "yellow");

for (var i = 0; i < 5; i++)
  document.write (verb + " " + article + " " +
    adjective + " " + noun + "<br>");
```

To add variety to the phrases, you can include a couple of possessive pronouns in the article object, as shown in the preceding code. Here's one possible set of generated phrases:

```
get your nice shoe
pet a smelly umbrella
pet your hairy shoe
feed my yellow dog
eat the hairy doorknob
```

How many different phrases can you generate? Right now, you can calculate the number of phrases as the number of verbs (5) times the number of articles (4) times the number of adjectives (5) times the number of nouns (5), or a total of 500 phrases. But you're about to increase that number more than tenfold.

# The Phrasemaker

Having a function that returns a complete phrase would be convenient. Your random phrase generator can be enhanced by adding the ability to return a complete phrase, the ability to vary the structure of phrases, the ability to specially handle plural nouns, and by adding adjectives or nouns that begin with vowels. Listing 21.6 gets you started.

### Listing 21.6  The *phrase()* Function

```
function isVowel (ch) {
  if (ch == 'a' || ch == 'e' || ch == 'i' ||
      ch == 'o' || ch == 'u')
    return true;
  return false;
}
function phrase (adjs) {
  var plural = (rand.next() >= .5); // Sets plural to true or false
  var vb = verb.toString();
  var first = vb.charAt(0);
  var vb = first.toUpperCase() + vb.substring(1,vb.length);
  var art = article.toString();
  var adj = new Object();
  for (var i = 0; i < adjs; i++)
    adj[i] = adjective.toString();
  var nn = (plural) ? pluralNoun.toString() : singularNoun.toString();
  if (plural && art == "a")
    art = "some";
  if (art == "a") {
    if (adjs > 0)
      first = adj[0].charAt(0);
    else
      first = nn.charAt(0);
    if (isVowel(first))
      art = "an";
  }
  var ph = vb + " " + art + " ";
  for (i = 0; i < adjs; i++)
    ph += adj[i] + " ";
  ph += nn;
  return ph;
}
var singularNoun = new Word ("dog", "cat", "shoe", "doorknob", "umbrella");
var pluralNoun = new Word ("dogs", "cats", "shoes", "doorknobs", "umbrellas");
```

In this listing, the `phrase()` function takes the number of adjectives to be included in the phrase as a parameter and returns a complete phrase with the first letter capitalized. The function uses the random number generator to decide whether the noun will be singular or plural. The article `"a"` is also given special handling: If the noun is plural, `"a"` is changed to `"some"`, and if `"a"` precedes a word beginning with a vowel, `"a"` is changed to `"an."`

Notice that you call the `toString()` methods for the `Word` objects directly here. Because of the special handling you're doing, you aren't using the objects in a string context, so `toString()` isn't called automatically by JavaScript.

In this listing, you also define new `Word` objects for singular and plural nouns. Although plural nouns can be created from the singular nouns used here by appending `"s"` to the end of each, many irregular nouns cannot be transformed easily. Note that the `singularNoun` and `pluralNoun` objects can contain completely different words and even different numbers of words.

Here's an example of using the `phrase()` function:

```
document.write (phrase(0) + "<br>");
document.write (phrase(1) + "<br>");
document.write (phrase(2) + "<br>");
```

The phrases generated might look something like this:

```
Buy an umbrella
Eat your smelly cats
Have the nice yellow doorknob
```

## Colors, Fonts, and All

Up to this point, you've been testing the phrase generator by using simple `document.write()` calls. Now put it in a frameset with all the trimmings. Because you're experimenting with random numbers, you can also use them in the display process to generate random color schemes and fonts for the phrases.

Briefly review a few of the objects you created in Chapter 21 for placing text on the screen. These objects simplify the process of creating random colors and fonts for the phrase generator. Listing 21.7 shows the `Color` object.

### Listing 21.7  The *Color* Object Constructor

```
var hexchars = '0123456789ABCDEF';
function fromHex (str) {
  var high = str.charAt(0);
  var low = str.charAt(1);
  return (16 * hexchars.indexOf(high)) +
    hexchars.indexOf(low);
}
function toHex (num) {
  return hexchars.charAt(num >> 4) + hexchars.charAt(num & 0xF);
```

```
}
function Color (str) {
  this.red = fromHex(str.substring(0,2));
  this.green = fromHex(str.substring(2,4));
  this.blue = fromHex(str.substring(4,6));
  this.toString = ColorString;
  return this;
}
function ColorString () {
  return toHex(this.red) + toHex(this.green) + toHex(this.blue);
}
```

The Color object holds a color. It stores the red, green, and blue components as numbers (0–255). The Color() constructor accepts a hexadecimal triplet of the form RRGGBB, whereas the toString() method ColorString() converts the internal values back to this format.

Listing 21.8 shows the BodyColor object.

### Listing 21.8   The *BodyColor* Object Constructor

```
function BodyColor (bgColor,fgColor,linkColor,vlinkColor,alinkColor) {
  this.bgColor = bgColor;
  this.fgColor = fgColor;
  this.linkColor = linkColor;
  this.vlinkColor = vlinkColor;
  this.alinkColor = alinkColor;
  this.toString = BodyColorString;
  return this;
}
function BodyColorString () {
  return '<body' +
    ((this.bgColor == null) ? '' : ' bgcolor="#' + this.bgColor + '"') +
    ((this.fgColor == null) ? '' : ' text="#' + this.fgColor + '"') +
    ((this.linkColor == null) ? '' : ' link="#' + this.linkColor + '"') +
    ((this.vlinkColor == null) ? '' : ' vlink="#' + this.vlinkColor + '"') +
    ((this.alinkColor == null) ? '' : ' alink="#' + this.alinkColor + '"') +
    '>';
}
```

The BodyColor object contains one or more Color objects that correspond to the HTML color attributes that can be specified in a body tag. Its toString() method returns a formatted Body tag, including any specified colors. Listing 21.9 shows the Text constructor.

Part

IV

Ch

21

### Listing 21.9   The *Text* Object Constructor

```
function Text (text, size, format, color) {
  this.text = text;
  this.length = text.length;
  this.size = size;
  this.format = format;
  this.color = color;
  this.toString = TextString;
  this.substring = TextString;
  return this;
}
function TextString (start, end) {
  with (this) {
    if (TextString.arguments.length < 2 ¦¦ start >= length) start = 0;
    if (TextString.arguments.length < 2 ¦¦ end > length) end = length;
    var str = text.substring(start,end);
    if (format != null) {
      if (format.indexOf("b") >= 0) str = str.bold();
      if (format.indexOf("i") >= 0) str = str.italics();
      if (format.indexOf("f") >= 0) str = str.fixed();
    }
    if (size != null) str = str.fontsize(size);
    if (color != null) {
      var colorstr = color.toString();
      str = str.fontcolor(colorstr);
    }
  }
  return str;
}
```

The Text object contains a text string, along with optional font size, font color, and format information. The format string can contain any combination of the letters "b", "i", and "f", corresponding to bold, italic, or fixed (<tt>) formatting. Text objects mimic some JavaScript string behaviors—they have a length property and a substring() method. Listing 21.10 shows the Static object.

### Listing 21.10   The *Static* Object Constructor

```
function Static (body, text) {
  this.body = body;
  this.text = text;
  this.toString = StaticString;
  return this;
}
function StaticString () {
  return '<html>' + this.body + this.text + '</body></html>';
}
```

The Static object holds a BodyColor object and any text, including HTML, that is to appear between the BODY and /BODY tags. Its toString() method returns a complete HTML page ready for display.

Now you can also create a new helper function, center(), to center the text on the page, as follows:

```
function center (text) {
  return '<table width=100% height=100% border=0 ' +
    'cellpadding=0 cellspacing=0>' +
    '<tr><td align="center" valign="center">' +
    text + '</td></tr></table>';
}
```

The center() function accepts a text parameter, which can be either a JavaScript string or any object that has a toString() method. The function returns the text embedded in a one-cell table with width and height set to 100 percent and horizontal and vertical centering specified. This way, the text is centered within the frame.

To generate random colors for the display, create two new objects called DarkColor and LightColor, as shown in Listing 21.11.

**Listing 21.11   The *DarkColor* and *LightColor* Object Constructors**

```
function DarkColor () {
  this.red = Math.round (127 * rand.next());
  this.green = Math.round (127 * rand.next());
  this.blue = Math.round (127 * rand.next());
  this.toString = ColorString;
  return this;
}
function LightColor () {
  this.red = Math.round (127 * rand.next()) + 128;
  this.green = Math.round (127 * rand.next()) + 128;
  this.blue = Math.round (127 * rand.next()) + 128;
  this.toString = ColorString;
  return this;
}
```

As you know, color component values can range from 0 to 255. The DarkColor() constructor generates a random color with component values between 0 and 127. The LightColor() constructor generates a random color with component values between 128 and 255. When used together to create foreground and background colors, DarkColor and LightColor almost always produce a readable combination, though it may not always be an attractive combination.

The DarkColor and LightColor objects have an internal structure that is identical to that of the Color object, so they can be used anyplace a Color object can be used. Therefore, it is convenient to think of DarkColor and LightColor as simply being different constructors for a Color object.

Now you can modify the phrase() function to return a complete HTML page, including random foreground and background colors, font size, and format. The modified function is shown in Listing 21.12. Note that in another application, placing the phrase-generation and page-generation code in separate functions might make sense; but for this example, a single function will do.

Part
IV

Ch
21

## Listing 21.12   The Modified *phrase()* Function Returns a Complete Page

```
function phrase (adjs) {
  var size = "" + (Math.round(rand.next() * 3) + 4);
  var format = " ";
  if (rand.next() >= .5)
    format += "b";
  if (rand.next() >= .5)
    format += "i";
  if (rand.next() >= .5)
    format += "f";
  var body;
  if (rand.next() >= .5)
    body = new BodyColor (new DarkColor(), new LightColor());
  else
    body = new BodyColor (new LightColor(), new DarkColor());
  var plural = (rand.next() >= .5);
  var vb = verb.toString();
  var first = vb.charAt(0);
  var vb = first.toUpperCase() + vb.substring(1,vb.length);
  var art = article.toString();
  var adj = new Object();
  for (var i = 0; i < adjs; i++)
    adj[i] = adjective.toString();
  var nn = (plural) ? pluralNoun.toString() : singularNoun.toString();
  if (plural && art == "a")
    art = "some";
  if (art == "a") {
    if (adjs > 0)
      first = adj[0].charAt(0);
    else
      first = nn.charAt(0);
    if (isVowel(first))
      art = "an";
  }
  var ph = vb + " " + art + " ";
  for (i = 0; i < adjs; i++)
    ph += adj[i] + " ";
  ph += nn;
  var screen = new Static (body,center(new Text(ph,size,format)));
  return screen.toString();
}
```

First you generate a random font size from 4 to 7. Smaller fonts can be difficult to read, especially when shown in a fixed-width (<tt>) font or italics. Besides, the generated phrase is the only text in its frame, so you might as well make it big.

Next you choose format specifiers. Note that you start with a string containing a single space. This is a workaround for the fact that the indexOf() method call in the Text object may generate an alert if it is called for an empty string. (It should simply return -1, indicating the substring was not found.)

For each format specifier, generate a random number to determine whether it will be included. Testing for greater than or equal to .5 means you have a 50-50 chance that any specifier will be included.

Then decide whether to use a dark-on-light or light-on-dark color scheme—again, by generating a random number and comparing it to .5. Note that you specify only the foreground and background colors in the BodyColor() constructor because you aren't using any links.

At the end of the phrase() function, you create a Static object, using the generated BodyColor object, and a centered Text object that includes the generated font size and format specifiers, in addition to the generated phrase. You call the Static object's toString() method directly to return the completely formatted HTML page.

All that is left now is to provide a button so the user can request a new phrase and a selection list, enabling the user to specify the number of adjectives to use in the phrase. You put these controls in a separate control frame (named head), as shown in Listing 21.13.

### Listing 21.13  The Control Frame

```
function printPhrase () {
  var adj = self.head.document.cont.adj.selectedIndex;
  if (adj == 3)
    adj = Math.round (rand.next()*2);
  self.body.location = "javascript:parent.phrase(" + adj + ")";
}
var controlFrame =
  '<html><body bgcolor="#808080" text="#FFFFFF">' +
  '<form name="cont">' +
  '<table width=100% height=100% border=0 cellpadding=0 cellspacing=0>' +
  '<tr align="center">' +
  '<td colspan=2><b>Number of Adjectives</b> <select name="adj">' +
  '<option>None' +
  '<option>1' +
  '<option>2' +
  '<option selected>Random' +
  '</select></td>' +
  '<td colspan=2><input type="button" value="Generate Phrase!" ' +
  'onclick="parent.printPhrase()"></td>' +
  '</tr>' +
  '</table>' +
  '</form>' +
  '</body></html>';
```

When the user presses the Generate Phrase! button, the printPhrase() function is called. This function determines how many adjectives to use by examining the selectedIndex property of the selection list adj. If the user has selected the fourth option, Random, a random value between 0 and 2 is calculated. Then the frame where you show the phrase, body, is updated by using a javascript: URL that calls the phrase() function.

Figure 21.3 shows an example of the output.

**FIG. 21.3**

The random phrase generator at work.

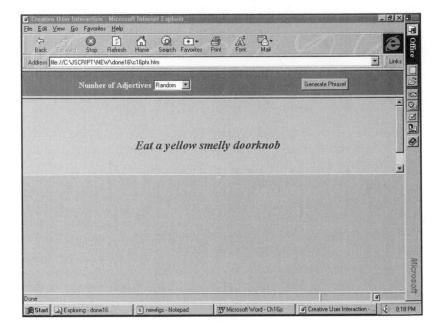

## Adding and Sorting Words

The phrase generator can produce some pretty amusing results just as it is, but sooner or later, users will want to get into the act and add some words of their own. They also will want to see which words are already defined. In this section, you extend the Word object so that it can accept additional words and produce a sorted (alphabetized) list of its contents. You also add some additional controls to the control (head) frame so that the users can view and add words.

Start by taking a look at the sorting function. Many sorting algorithms are available. The simplest to comprehend and write is the *bubble sort*. The bubble sort algorithm makes $n-1$ passes through a list of $n$ items, comparing and, if necessary, exchanging adjacent pairs. After the last pass, the list is sorted.

Unfortunately, the bubble sort is also about the slowest sorting algorithm available. If you're sorting only a handful of items it doesn't make much difference which algorithm you use. But, if you are sorting dozens or hundreds of items, or more, that difference becomes very significant. It can mean the difference between waiting a fraction of a second or a couple minutes for your sort to complete.

Fortunately, much faster algorithms are available and, although they're not as easy to comprehend, you can implement them by using only a little more code than a bubble sort. One of the best is the *Quicksort* algorithm. This chapter won't get into the details of its operation, except to say that it takes a divide-and-conquer approach to its comparisons and exchanges.

The JavaScript Quicksort algorithm, shown in Listing 21.14, was written by Achille Hui of Stanford University.

## Listing 21.14   A JavaScript Quicksort Implementation

```
function _pm_array_qsort(vec,lo,up,cmp_fun){
  var i, j, t;
  while(up > lo){
    i = lo;
    j = up;
    t = vec[lo];
    while(i < j){
      while(cmp_fun(vec[j],t) > 0)
        j -= 1;
      vec[i] = vec[j];
      while((i < j) && (cmp_fun(vec[i],t) <= 0))
        i++;
      vec[j] = vec[i];
    }
    vec[i] = t;
    if(i - lo < up - i){
      _pm_array_qsort(vec,lo,i-1,cmp_fun); lo = i+1;
    } else {
      _pm_array_qsort(vec,i+1,up,cmp_fun); up = i-1;
    }
  }
}
function _pm_array_defcmp(a,b){
  return (a == b) ? 0 : (a > b) ? 1 : -1;
}
function pm_array_qsort(vec,lo,hi,cmp_fun){
  if(vec == null){
    return;
  } else if(cmp_fun == null){
    _pm_array_qsort(vec,lo,hi,_pm_array_defcmp);
  } else {
    _pm_array_qsort(vec,lo,hi,cmp_fun);
  }
}
```

To use this Quicksort, call the pm_array_qsort() function and pass it an array object (vec), the starting item number in the array (lo), the ending item number (hi), and optionally, a comparison function (cmp_fun).

The lo and hi parameters you use depend on how your array object is constructed. If you use the first entry (entry[0]) to contain the array length, for instance, then you should pass 1 as the lo parameter and the number of entries in the array as the hi parameter. If you use a zero-based array, you should pass 0 as the lo parameter, and the number of entries minus one as the hi parameter.

Your Quicksort function includes a default comparison function, which is used to compare two items. The default comparison function can be used if your array consists of strings or numeric items. If you are sorting an array of objects, however, you need to supply a comparison function. The comparison function compares two items, a and b. If they are equal, it returns 0. If a is greater than b, then the function returns 1. If a is less than b, it returns –1.

Part

IV

Ch

21

Now you can beef up your Word object, as shown in Listing 21.15. The improved Word object will let you add new words, sort the words in the object, produce a list of sorted words, and find a particular word.

**Listing 21.15   An Improved *Word* Object Constructor**

```
function Word () {
  var argv = Word.arguments;
  var argc = argv.length;
  this.list = new Object();
  for (var i = 0; i < argc; i++)
    this.list[i] = argv[i];
  this.count = argc;
  pm_array_qsort (this.list,0,this.count-1);
  this.add = AddWord;
  this.find = FindWord;
  this.print = PrintWords;
  this.toString = WordString;
  return this;
}
function AddWord (str) {
  this.list[this.count++] = str;
  pm_array_qsort(this.list,0,this.count-1);
}
function FindWord (str) {
  for (var i = 0; i < this.count; i++)
    if (this.list[i] == str)
      return i;
  return -1;
}
function PrintWords () {
  var str = "";
  for (var i = 0; i < this.count; i++)
    str += this.list[i] + '<br>';
  return str;
}
```

The Word() constructor calls the pm_array_qsort function to sort the original list of words that was supplied when the object was constructed. You can keep them unsorted, instead, and sort them only when output is required. In this case, the design decision is arbitrary, but sometimes it is desirable to maintain an array in sorted form at all times.

The add() method AddWord() adds a new word to the end of the array and then sorts the array back into alphabetical sequence. The find() method FindWord() searches the array to see whether a word is present. You use this method in conjunction with the add() method to prevent the user from adding duplicate words. The print() method PrintWords() returns the sorted list of words, separated by HTML <BR> tags.

In Listing 21.16, you add some functions that prompt the user for a new word. You also add functions to list all the words for each type.

**Listing 21.16  Functions to Prompt the User and List Words**

```
function addVerb () {
  var str = prompt ("Enter a verb (eat, kiss, bite, etc.):","");
  if (str == null || str == "")
    return;
  if (verb.find(str) != -1) {
    alert ("\nThat verb is already listed!");
    return;
  }
  verb.add(str);
  listVerbs();
}
function addAdjective () {
  var str = prompt ("Enter an adjective (pretty, smelly, nice, etc.):","");
  if (str == null || str == "")
    return;
  if (adjective.find(str) != -1) {
    alert ("\nThat adjective is already listed!");
    return;
  }
  adjective.add(str);
  listAdjectives();
}
function addSingular () {
  var str = prompt ("Enter a singular noun (dog, cat, knife, etc.):","");
  if (str == null || str == "")
    return;
  if (singularNoun.find(str) != -1) {
    alert ("\nThat noun is already listed!");
    return;
  }
  singularNoun.add(str);
  listSingular();
}
function addPlural () {
  var str = prompt ("Enter a plural noun (dogs, cats, knives, etc.):", "");
  if (str == null || str == "")
    return;
  if (pluralNoun.find(str) != -1) {
    alert ("\nThat noun is already listed!");
    return;
  }
  pluralNoun.add(str);
  listPlural();
}
function listVerbs () {
  self.body.location =
    "javascript:parent.showList('Verbs',parent.verb.print())";
}
function listAdjectives () {
  self.body.location =
    "javascript:parent.showList('Adjectives',parent.adjective.print())";
```

Part

IV

Ch

21

*continues*

**Listing 21.16   Continued**

```
}
function listSingular () {
  self.body.location =
    "javascript:parent.showList('Singular Nouns',parent.singularNoun.print())";
}
function listPlural () {
  self.body.location =
    "javascript:parent.showList('Plural Nouns',parent.pluralNoun.print())";
}
function showList (title,str) {
  return '<html><body bgcolor="#FFFFFF" text="#0000FF"><h1 align="center">' +
    title + '</h1><div align="center"><font size=5>' + str +
    '</font></div></body></html>';
}
```

The addVerb(), addAdjective(), addSingular(), and addPlural() functions prompt the user for a word. If the word is already present in the list, an error message is displayed. Otherwise, the word is added and the updated list is displayed.

The listVerbs(), listAdjectives(), listSingular(), and listPlural() functions display the word lists by updating the body frame location using a javascript: URL. This URL includes a call to the showList() function, which returns a formatted HTML page listing the words for the given word type.

Finally, you update the control frame to include a set of buttons for adding and listing words, as shown in Listing 21.17.

**Listing 21.17   The Updated Control Frame**

```
var controlFrame =
  '<html><body bgcolor="#808080" text="#FFFFFF">' +
  '<form name="cont">' +
  '<table width=100% height=100% border=0 cellpadding=0 cellspacing=0>' +
  '<tr align="center">' +
  '<td colspan=2><b>Number of Adjectives</b> <select name="adj">' +
  '<option>None' +
  '<option>1' +
  '<option>2' +
  '<option selected>Random' +
  '</select></td>' +
  '<td colspan=2><input type="button" value="Generate Phrase!" ' +
  'onclick="parent.printPhrase()"></td>' +
  '</tr>' +
  '<tr align="center">' +
  '<td><input type="button" value="Add Verb" ' +
  'onclick="parent.addVerb()"></td>' +
  '<td><input type="button" value="Add Adjective" ' +
  'onclick="parent.addAdjective()"></td>' +
  '<td><input type="button" value="Add Singular Noun" ' +
  'onclick="parent.addSingular()"></td>' +
```

```
  '<td><input type="button" value="Add Plural Noun" ' +
  'onclick="parent.addPlural()"></td>' +
'</tr>' +
 '<tr align="center">' +
 '<td><input type="button" value="List Verbs" ' +
 'onclick="parent.listVerbs()"></td>' +
 '<td><input type="button" value="List Adjectives" ' +
 'onclick="parent.listAdjectives()"></td>' +
 '<td><input type="button" value="List Singular Nouns" ' +
 'onclick="parent.listSingular()"></td>' +
 '<td><input type="button" value="List Plural Nouns" ' +
 'onclick="parent.listPlural()"></td>' +
'</tr>' +
 '</table>' +
 '</form>' +
 '</body></html>';
```

An example result after adding the adjective "spongy" is shown in Figure 21.4.

**FIG. 21.4**

The improved phrase generator includes controls to add and view words.

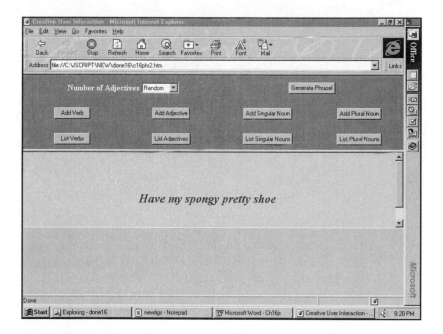

# An Online Bookstore

In this section, you develop an online bookstore application. You create a small database of books and provide a way for the user to look up books by subject, author, or title. Along the way, you learn how to parse freeform user input and how to look up items in an indexed database.

Of course, in real life, you can't expect to keep the entire inventory of a bookstore in a single JavaScript document. But the techniques you develop here can be applied to many smaller databases or to results returned by a CGI program on the server.

# Parsing Freeform User Input

Usually, when you process input entered in a text field, the value is treated as a whole. If you are expecting a numeric value, you might check to ensure that the value is, indeed, numeric. You might also check to see that it falls within a certain range or ranges. If you expect an alphanumeric value, you might check it against a list of expected values.

Suppose you want to allow the user to enter a series of values in a single field but process the values individually? A good example is a database lookup or search function where the user can enter a set of keywords. In that case, you need to *parse* the input field; that is, break it into a list of individual words or terms.

The process of parsing is fairly straightforward. The first step is to define the *whitespace* characters that can separate the terms in your input field. Whitespace is usually defined as blank (or space) characters, and tabs. It may also include carriage returns and linefeeds, as well as certain other non-displaying characters.

The isWhitespace() function, shown in Listing 21.18, determines whether the input character is whitespace.

### Listing 21.18   The *isWhitespace()* Function

```
function isWhitespace (ch) {
  if (ch == ' ' || ch == '\n' || ch == '\r' || ch == '\t' || ch == '\f' ||
      ch == '\v' || ch == '\b')
    return true;
  return false;
}
```

You also may want to test for certain *delimiter* characters. Common delimiters include commas, forward or backward slashes, periods, and so on. Delimiters can be a meaningful part of the input, or they can be nonessential characters that can be discarded.

The isDelimiter() function, shown in Listing 21.19, tests for delimiters.

### Listing 21.19   The *isDelimiter()* Function

```
function isDelimiter (ch) {
  if (ch == ',' || ch == '?' || ch == '-' || ch == '.' ||
      ch == '\\' || ch == '/')
    return true;
  return false;
}
```

After you decide which whitespace and delimiter characters can separate your terms, you need a place to put the individual terms you extract from the input field. A simple array can do the trick. In this case, you can define a KeywordList object to hold them, shown in Listing 21.20. This object will come in handy in the bookstore example.

**Listing 21.20   The *KeywordList* Object Constructor**

```
function KeywordList () {
  this.count = 0;
  this.word = new Object ();
  this.add = AddKeyword;
  return this;
}
function AddKeyword (word) {
  for (var i = 0; i < this.count; i++)
    if (this.word[i] == word)
      return;
  this.word[this.count++] = word;
}
```

In the bookstore example, you want to allow only unique keywords. Therefore, the add() method AddKeyword() prevents duplicate keywords from being added. However, this method is not appropriate in many applications. If you don't want to suppress duplicates in your application, then omit the first three lines in the body of the AddKeyword() function.

Now you are ready to write the parser, which is shown in Listing 21.21.

**Listing 21.21   The *parseKeywords( )* Function**

```
function parseKeywords (str) {
  var list = new KeywordList ();
  var inword = false;
  var word = "";
  var len = str.length;
  for (var i = 0; i < len; i++) {
    var ch = str.charAt(i);
    if (isWhitespace(ch) || isDelimiter(ch)) {
      if (inword) {
        list.add(word);
        word = "";
        inword = false;
      }
    }
    else {
      word += ch;
      inword = true;
    }
    if (i + 1 == len && inword)
      list.add(word);
  }
  return list;
}
```

Part
**IV**

Ch

**21**

The parseKeywords() function accepts a string, which can be the contents of an input field. It returns a KeywordList object containing a list of the extracted terms.

The parseKeywords() function examines each character in the input string to decide if it is a whitespace or delimiter character. If it is neither, the character is added to the current word. If it is either one, the current word, if any, is added to the list and preparation is made for a new word. You also add the current word to the list when you reach the last character of the input string.

The parseKeywords() function discards delimiter characters because they are not important to the bookstore application. However, delimiters can have special meaning to your application, in which case you might want to add them to the keyword list.

## Building an Index

For the example, you want users of your online bookstore to be able to look up books by title, author, or subject. To do so, you must build some indexes for the book database. You use JavaScript's *associative array* feature to create the indexes.

Associative arrays enable you to associate a value with an array entry. You can then use that value to retrieve the desired entry. For example, suppose that you create a simple array named animal and associate a name with each entry, as follows:

```
var animal = new Object();
animal["dog"] = "Woof!";
animal["cat"] = "Meow!";
animal["pig"] = "Oink!";
```

To retrieve an item, you use the value associated with it, as follows:

```
document.write("A dog says " + animal["dog"] + "<br>");
```

To take advantage of this capability, you index each word in the book titles, subjects, and author names by creating an entry in an associative array.

The only hitch is that you can have only one entry per value. What if, as is very likely, more than one of the books uses that value in its title, subject, or author? The solution, as it turns out, is fairly simple. Instead of associating an individual Book object with each entry in the array, you create a special object that contains a list of the items that match a given value and associate that object with the value.

Listing 21.22 shows the Index object, along with its methods and the internal list object.

### Listing 21.22   The *Index* and *IndexItemList* Object Constructors

```
function IndexItemList () {
  this.count = 0;
  this.item = new Object();
  this.add = AddIndexItem;
```

```
      return this;
    }
    function AddIndexItem (object) {
      this.item[this.count++] = object;
    }
    function Index () {
      this.count = 0;
      this.item = new Object();
      this.add = AddToIndex;
      return this;
    }
    function AddToIndex (object, keywords) {
      for (var i = 0; i < keywords.count; i++) {
        var kw = keywords.word[i];
        var ilist = this.item[kw];
        if (ilist == null) {
          ilist = new IndexItemList();
          this.item[kw] = ilist;
        }
        ilist.add(object);
      }
    }
```

The IndexItemList object is used internally to store a list of objects that contain a particular keyword value. In the bookstore example, it will contain references to one or more Book objects (which you define shortly) that share a given keyword. The IndexItemList object has a single method, AddIndexItem(). You don't need to access the IndexItemList object directly.

The Index object contains the associative array item. The item array contains a list of IndexItemList objects. Each entry in the array is associated with a value, in this case a keyword. The Index object includes a method to add items to the array. You will soon write another method to look up entries.

The Index object's add() method, AddToIndex(), accepts an object to be indexed and a list of keywords in the form of a KeywordList object. For each keyword in the KeywordList, AddToIndex() first checks to see whether an IndexItemList object is associated with the keyword. Note that it uses the keyword value itself as an index into the array. If no IndexItemList object exists for the keyword, a new object is created and added to the array, again using the keyword as the index. Finally, the object to be indexed is added to the IndexItemList for that keyword value. This process is repeated for each keyword, so a given object can have several index entries.

# Defining *Book* and *Catalog* Objects

Now you're ready to create the Book object. In Listing 21.23, you also create a Catalog object that contains a list of all books, as well as subject, title, and author indexes.

Part
IV

Ch
21

**Listing 21.23   The *Book* and *Catalog* Object Constructors**

```
function Book (author, title, subject, code, price) {
  this.author = author;
  this.title = title;
  this.subject = subject;
  this.code = code;
  this.price = price;
  return this;
}
function Catalog () {
  this.count = 0;
  this.book = new Object;
  this.author = new Index();
  this.title = new Index();
  this.subject = new Index();
  this.add = AddToCatalog;
  return this;
}
function AddToCatalog (book) {
  this.book[this.count++] = book;
  this.author.add(book,parseKeywords(book.author));
  this.title.add(book,parseKeywords(book.title));
  this.subject.add(book,parseKeywords(book.subject));
}
```

The `Book()` constructor simply creates an object that contains each of the relevant pieces of information about the book. The `Catalog()` constructor creates a simple array called `book`, which contains a single entry for each book. It also creates three `Index` objects: `author`, `title`, and `subject`.

The `Catalog` object's `add()` method, `AddToCatalog()`, does the really interesting work. First, it adds the `book` object to the `book` array. Next, it updates the author, title, and subject indexes. For each of the indexes, it calls the `parseKeywords` function to create a list of keywords from the value of the field. The `Index` object's `add()` method then creates an index entry for each of these values.

In Listing 21.24, you create a catalog and add some books to it.

**Listing 21.24   Creating a Catalog and Adding Books**

```
var cat = new Catalog();
cat.add (new Book ("Kingsolver, Barbara", "Animal Dreams",
  "fiction animals dreams environment Native-American love",
  "ISBN 0-06-092114-5", 13.00));
cat.add (new Book ("Calasso, Roberto", "The Marriage of Cadmus and Harmony",
  "fiction Greek myth mythology Zeus Athens",
  "ISBN 0-679-73348-5", 13.00));
cat.add (new Book ("Le Carre, John", "The Night Manager",
  "fiction suspense spy arms drugs",
```

```
    "ISBN 0-345-38576-4", 6.99));
cat.add (new Book ("Rice, Anne", "Interview with the Vampire",
    "fiction vampire New Orleans gothic horror",
    "ISBN 0-345-33766-2", 4.95));
cat.add (new Book ("Garcia Marquez, Gabriel", "One Hundred Years of Solitude",
    "fiction South America magic dreams war love",
    "ISBN 0-06-091965-5", 13.00));
cat.add (new Book ("Barkakati, Naba", "Object-Oriented Programming in C++",
    "nonfiction computer language programming object C",
    "ISBN 0-672-22800-9", 29.95));
cat.add (new Book ("Petzold, Charles", "Programming Windows",
    "nonfiction computer programming C windows",
    "ISBN 1-55615-264-7", 29.95));
```

Well, so far so good. You have a catalog loaded with books that are all cross-referenced by author, subject, and title. But how do you use this information?

You now need a search mechanism. You want the search to return multiple matches for a given set of keywords. Ideally, the results should also be ranked by how well they match the keywords supplied. To accomplish this task, you first create an object to hold a list of search results, as shown in Listing 21.25.

### Listing 21.25  The *Result* and *ResultList* Object Constructors

```
function Result (object, score) {
  this.object = object;
  this.score = score;
  return this;
}
function ResultList () {
  this.count = 0;
  this.item = new Object();
  this.add = AddResult;
  this.sort = SortResults;
  return this;
}
function AddResult (object) {
  for (var i = 0; i < this.count; i++)
    if (this.item[i].object == object) {
      this.item[i].score++;
      return;
    }
  this.item[this.count++] = new Result (object,1);
}
function SortResults () {
  pm_array_qsort (this.item,0,this.count - 1,CompareResults);
}
function CompareResults (a,b) {
  return (a.score == b.score) ? 0 : (a.score <  b.score) ? 1 : -1;
}
```

Part
IV

Ch
21

The Result object holds an individual object—in this case, a Book object. It also contains a score field. This field indicates the number of "hits" the query gets for this particular object; that is, how many of the keywords specified in the query match this object.

The ResultList object contains a list of Result objects. It contains one Result for each object (book) that matches one or more of the specified keywords. The add() method, AddResult, searches the ResultList for a matching object. If it finds one, it increments the score by one. Otherwise, it creates a new Result entry for the object and sets the score to one.

The sort() method, SortResults(), sorts the Result objects in the ResultList in descending order according to score. That is, the objects with the highest score go to the top of the list. Because you are sorting objects rather than simple strings or numbers, you must supply a comparison function, CompareResults, to the pm_array_qsort() function.

Now you can add the search function. In Listing 21.26, you update the Index object to make SearchIndex() the find() method.

### Listing 21.26   Adding a *find()* Method to the *Index* Object

```
function Index () {
  this.count = 0;
  this.item = new Object();
  this.add = AddToIndex;
  this.find = SearchIndex;
  return this;
}
function SearchIndex (keywords) {
  var rlist = new ResultList();
  for (var i = 0; i < keywords.count; i++) {
    var kw = keywords.word[i];
    var ilist = this.item[kw];
    if (ilist != null)
      for (var j = 0; j < ilist.count; j++)
        rlist.add(ilist.item[j]);
  }
  rlist.sort();
  return rlist;
}
```

The find() method, SearchIndex(), takes a KeywordList object containing a list of words for which to search. It first uses the keyword value to do an associative array lookup to retrieve the IndexItemList object, if any, for the given keyword. Then it calls the ResultList object's add() method to add each matching object to the result list, or increment the score for that object if it was already added to the list. This process is repeated for each search term specified. Finally, the ResultList is sorted by score and returned to the caller.

## The Bookstore

You've got all the tricky pieces worked out, so you now can build an interface and open your bookstore. You can make a control frame with a selection list for author, title, or subject, and a text field for keyword entry. A Search button starts the search. In Listing 21.27, some functions are written to process this information and to display the results.

**Listing 21.27  Creating the Bookstore Interface**

```
var controlFrame =
  '<html><body bgcolor="#808080" text="#FFFFFF">' +
  '<form name="cont">' +
  '<table border=0 width=100% height=100% cellpadding=0 cellspacing=0>' +
  '<tr align="center" valign="center">' +
  '<td><b>Search by: </b><select name="stype">' +
  '<option selected>Title' +
  '<option>Author' +
  '<option>Subject' +
  '</select></td>' +
  '<td><b>Keywords: </b><input size=30 name="keywords"></td>' +
  '<td><input type="button" value="Search" onclick="parent.doSearch()"></td>' +
  '</tr></table>' +
  '</form>' +
  '</body></html>';

var results = null;

function doSearch () {
  var index = self.head.document.cont.stype.selectedIndex;
  var keywords = parseKeywords (self.head.document.cont.keywords.value);
  if (index == 0)
    results = cat.title.find (keywords);
  else if (index == 1)
    results = cat.author.find (keywords);
  else
    results = cat.subject.find (keywords);
  self.body.location = "javascript:parent.showList()";
}

function showBook (item) {
  var book = results.item[item].object;
  var detail = book.author + '<br>' + book.title + '<br>' +
    book.subject + '<br>' + book.code + '<br>$' + book.price + '<br>' +
    '<h3><a href="javascript:parent.showList()">Return to list</h3>';
  return '<html><body bgcolor="#FFFFFF" text="#000000" link="#0000FF" ' +
    'alink="#FF0000"><div align="center"><table border=0><tr><td>' +
    detail + '</td></tr></table></body></html>';
}
```

Part
IV

Ch

21

*continues*

**Listing 21.27  Continued**

```
function showList () {
  var list = "";
  for (var i = 0; i < results.count; i++)
    list += '<a href="javascript:parent.showBook(' + i + ')">' +
      '(' + results.item[i].score + ')  ' +
      results.item[i].object.author + ':  ' +
      results.item[i].object.title + '</a><br>';
  if (list.length == 0)
    list = '<h2 align="center">Sorry, no matches found</h2>';
  return '<html><body bgcolor="#FFFFFF" text="#000000" link="#0000FF" ' +
    'alink="#FF0000"><div align="center"><table border=0><tr><td>' +
    list + '</td></tr></table></body></html>';
}
```

Clicking the Search button calls the doSearch() function. This function examines the selection list and performs the appropriate search. The results list is placed in a global variable called results. The doSearch() function then loads the show frame with a javascript: URL that calls showList().

The showList() function, in turn, reads the results list and creates a one-line entry for each book, consisting of the score (number of matching terms), along with the book's author and title. Each entry is enclosed in an HREF that calls the showBook() function to display details about the book.

The showBook() function displays each of the fields in the Book object. It also includes an HREF back to the showList() function so that the user can return to the result list of the current search. That's it! Your bookstore is open for business. Figure 21.5 shows the resulting list of titles based on a subject search of the keyword love, and Figure 21.6 shows the complete author, title, and subject information for one book.

## Improved Indexing and Searching

The indexing and searching algorithms do a good job of finding matching entries, but they suffer from a couple of drawbacks.

First, the user must enter keywords exactly as they were specified when the Book object was created. One obvious improvement is to store all keywords in lowercase and convert search words to lowercase before beginning the search.

But what if the user enters the plural or past tense version of a word? What if the user includes (or fails to include) apostrophes, quotation marks, or other punctuation symbols? The search engine will break down and will fail to return any matching items.

You can address this problem to some extent by *normalizing* all keywords before adding them to the index or performing a lookup. Normalizing a word means reducing it to something akin to a root word. This process is not easy; volumes have been written and fortunes spent on developing effective indexing and searching algorithms. But you can use a few simple techniques to improve your search results dramatically.

**FIG. 21.5**
Each book matching
the search term is
listed.

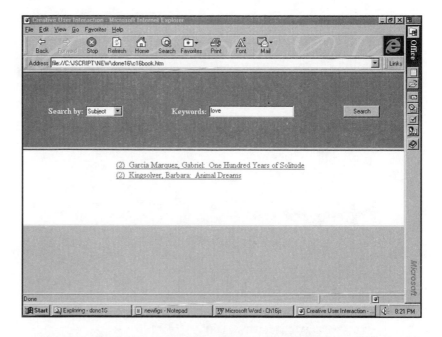

**FIG. 21.6**
Selecting a book shows
a detailed listing.

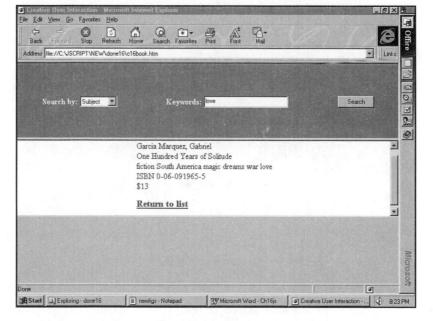

First, create a function to normalize a word, as shown in Listing 21.28.

**Listing 21.28   The *normalizeWord()* Function**

```
function normalizeWord (keyword) {
  var esc = escape (keyword.toLowerCase());
  var kw = "";
  for (var i=0; i < esc.length; i++) {
    var ch = esc.charAt(i);
    if (ch == '%')
      i += 2;
    else
      kw += ch;
  }
  var len = kw.length;
  if (kw.charAt(len-1) == "s" && kw.charAt(len-2) != "s") {
    kw = kw.substring(0,len-1);
    len--;
  }
  if (kw.substring(len-2,len) == "ly") {
    kw = kw.substring(0,len-2);
    len -= 2;
  }
  if (kw.substring(len-2,len) == "ed") {
    kw = kw.substring(0,len-1);
    len--;
  }
  if (kw.substring(len-2,len) == "er") {
    kw = kw.substring(0,len-1);
    len--;
  }
  if (kw.substring(len-2,len) == "ie") {
    kw = kw.substring(0,len-2) + "y";
    len--;
  }
  if (kw.substring(len-3,len) == "ing" && len > 5) {
    kw = kw.substring(0,len-3);
    len -= 3;
    if (isVowel(kw.charAt(len-2)) && !isVowel(kw.charAt(len-3))) {
      kw += "e";
      len++;
    }
  }
  if (kw.charAt(len-1) == "e")
    if (!isVowel(kw.charAt(len-3))) {
      kw = kw.substring(0,len-1);
      len--;
    }
  if (len > 1 && (kw.charAt(len-1) == kw.charAt(len-2))) {
    kw = kw.substring(0,len-1);
    len--;
  }
  return kw;
}
```

The `normalizeWord()` function starts by converting the keyword to lowercase. Next, it strips out any punctuation marks or other unusual characters. To strip the characters, it calls JavaScript's `escape()` function, which converts all unusual characters to a percent sign (%), followed by two ASCII characters. These characters are then removed.

The `normalizeWord()` function then makes a series of transformations based on the word ending. Note that the order of these transformations is important. We won't go into detail on each transformation. The goal is to reach a root version of the word. It isn't necessarily the true English root, but as long as you perform the same transformations on both the indexed words and the search words, you should improve chances of getting a match.

**N O T E**  The transformations applied by the `normalizeWord()` function are useful only for English words. The call to `escape()` strips out accented letters, for instance, and the word-ending transformations are meaningful only for English words. However, creating a similar function for other languages should be possible. ■

The second of the two problems with this indexing scheme is that it indexes and searches for many words that are extraneous, such as "the," "and," "a," and so on. Most indexing and searching programs use a list of *stop words* to exclude extraneous words. These lists are often quite extensive, but you can write a simple function to deal with the worst offenders. Listing 21.29 shows a simple `isStopword()` function.

### Listing 21.29   The *isStopword()* Function

```
function isStopword (word) {
  var wd = word.toLowerCase();
  if (wd == "a" || wd == "an" || wd == "and" ||
      wd == "or" || wd == "the")
    return true;
  return false;
}
```

Finally, you can modify the `parseKeywords()` function to call `normalizeWord()` and `isStopword()`, as shown in Listing 21.30.

### Listing 21.30   The Improved *parseKeywords()* Function

```
function parseKeywords (str) {
  var list = new KeywordList ();
  var inword = false;
  var word = "";
  var len = str.length;
  for (var i = 0; i < len; i++) {
    var ch = str.charAt(i);
    if (isWhitespace(ch) || isDelimiter(ch)) {
      if (inword) {
```

Part
IV

Ch
21

*continues*

**Listing 21.30  Continued**

```
          if (!isStopword(word))
            list.add(normalizeWord(word));
          word = "";
          inword = false;
        }
      }
      else {
        word += ch;
        inword = true;
      }
      if (i + 1 == len && inword)
        if (!isStopword(word))
          list.add(normalizeWord(word));
    }
    return list;
  }
```

You can try this more sophisticated code by doing a subject search for "the love". The results that you will obtain will be identical to those shown in Figure 21.5, since the stop word "the" has been removed. A number of additional improvements could be made, including better handling of symbols, as well as Boolean AND and OR operations, to name a few. ●

# CHAPTER 22

# JavaScript on the Server

Starting with Netscape Navigator 2.0, Web users have been able to run JavaScript programs on their desktop machines. Sometimes, however, client-side JavaScript is not enough. The Web developer may want to provide services for users of all browsers—not just Navigator. Or the application may need to access a database or server file or reach out over the Net. Any of these needs may induce a Web developer to look to server-side JavaScript (also known as LiveWire JavaScript).

Server-side JavaScript is a feature of LiveWire. Using LiveWire, the developer can write a *server-side script* (a JavaScript program that runs on the server) and have it compiled before starting the application. Then, when the visitor connects to the application pages, the compiled versions of the scripts run and send HTML to the client. ■

**Learn how an HTTP request works**

Understanding how LiveWire interacts with the server can help you avoid making design defects in your application.

**Find out how to call server-side JavaScript from inside *<SERVER>* tags**

<SERVER> tags let you write large scripts right in the HTML page.

**See how to call server-side JavaScript from inside a tag**

The special backquote notation is convenient but is often misunderstood and misused.

**Find out how to lock server-side objects**

If you're using LiveWire Pro, you might need to lock your server-side objects to prevent database corruption.

**Learn about built-in functions**

Use them to build some example applications; then use those applications as the foundation for your own code.

**N O T E** Netscape offers two versions of its application development tool: LiveWire and LiveWire
Pro. Both versions include a database connectivity library, which allows you to access
relational databases (including an ODBC interface, which can get you into most Windows-based
database managers). LiveWire Pro includes a developer's version of Informix, a popular relational
database manager. Check the release notes for your platform at **http://home.netscape.com/eng/
LiveWire/relnotes/**. Depending upon your platform, you may be able to access data in Informix,
Sybase, or Oracle databases or through ODBC. ■

▶ **See** Chapter 5, "Working with Multiple Tables," of *Visual FoxPro Expert Solutions* (Que, 1996)
and Chapter 8, "A SQL Primer," of *Special Edition Using Netscape LiveWire* (Que, 1996) to learn
more about SQL, the Structured Query Language, and its use with relational database managers.

# The Dynamics of the HTTP Request

Anyone who has spent more than a few minutes on the Web has wondered about the ubiquitous http that appears at the beginning of each URL. The *Hypertext Transfer Protocol* (HTTP) is
the protocol of the Web. By making it a part of each URL, the designers left room for other
protocols to be added in the future.

The standard (non-LiveWire) HTTP is a five-step process:

1. The client establishes a TCP connection with the server.
2. The client sends a request to a well-known port on the server (by default, port 80).
3. The server looks up the requested entity on the server (which may include running a
   CGI script).
4. The server sends back a header with status codes, followed by the requested entity.
5. After sending the requested entity, client and server disconnect.

You can experiment with this protocol by using Telnet to substitute for the browser. Establish a
Telnet session to port 80 of your favorite server. Type the following request line:

> **GET pathToEntity HTTP/1.0**

Now press the Enter key twice.

**N O T E** The latest version of HTTP is 1.1, which has some important new features. For the purposes
of this chapter, however, both HTTP 1.0 and HTTP 1.1 work about the same way. ■

For example, if you want the welcome page from the DSE Web server, you can establish a
Telnet session (on a UNIX machine) by typing

> **telnet www.dse.com 80**

Once connected, you can request the default document with

> **GET / HTTP/1.0**

▶ **See** "The Dynamics of the HTTP Request," **p. 590**, which describes HTTP in more detail.

The server responds with several lines of header, followed by the requested file. After that, the TCP connection is torn down. The remainder of this section describes how this process proceeds when the server is a Netscape server that is running LiveWire.

## Receiving the Request

When the Webmaster installs an application using the LiveWire Application Manager, he or she specifies the URL at which the application is served. The Application Manager writes a line into the livewire.conf file similar to the following line (for the sample application named `world`):

```
world uri=/world object=D:/Netscape/Server/LiveWire/Samples/world/
➥hello.web home=hello.html client-mode=client-cookie maxDBConnects=0
```

The first two fields of this line say that the application named `world` should be served when a client requests **http://name-of-our-server/world**.

Once the server has the request, it passes the request through its usual security checks before checking to see whether the URL may be a pointer to a LiveWire application.

## Checking with LiveWire

When a client requests an URL from a Netscape Web server, the server checks the contents of the livewire.conf file to see whether the URL is on the list of LiveWire applications. If it is, control is turned over to LiveWire.

> **CAUTION**
>
> If you have a directory in your document root directory and you install a LiveWire application with the same name as the directory, the application takes precedence and the directory becomes unreachable.

## Starting LiveWire

To see what LiveWire does when it takes control, launch the Application Manager (or, equivalently, connect to your Netscape server at **http://www.yourserver.com/appmgr/**). Select the sample application named `world` from the menu in the left pane. Your screen should look like Figure 22.1.

Now choose `Debug` in the left pane. (It's below the row of links that says `Start`, `Stop`, and `Restart`. You may have to scroll down to see `Debug`.) The left pane holds the debug information—the right pane shows the application's initial page. The debugger says in the left pane that the application is now `Waiting for first request...`, but the debugger does not yet show the application's activity.

**FIG. 22.1**

Launch the Application Manager and select the world application.

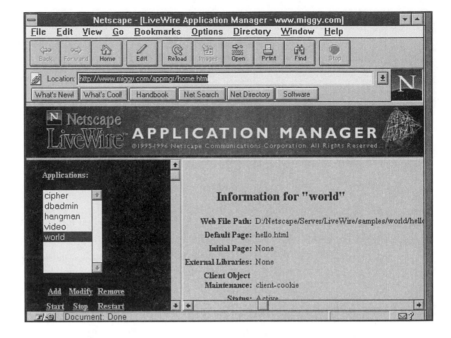

The Netscape Web server, like all of Netscape's new servers, has a layer called the *Java Virtual Machine* (see Figure 22.2), which can understand compiled Java and JavaScript. On Web servers, that layer supports the LiveWire Object Framework—four prebuilt objects that offer an interface with the server, the application (called the project in server-side JavaScript), the client, and the request.

**FIG. 22.2**

Each Netscape server— not just the Web servers—includes Java and JavaScript support.

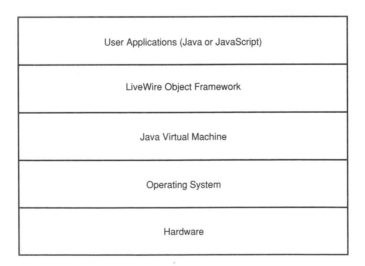

## Runtime Interpreter

The LiveWire compiler converts server-side JavaScript into a file of bytecodes that are read by the server's Java Virtual Machine (JVM) at runtime. To understand the JVM, recall that conventional processors accept binary instructions in a *machine language*, which is specific to each processor family. That is, the machine language for an Intel 80x86 processor in a PC is different from the machine language for an IBM/Motorola PowerPC processor in a Macintosh. The JVM is a software implementation of a "virtual processor." Java and JavaScript are platform-independent because compilers can generate Java machine language that runs on the JVM. Netscape has built a version of the JVM for each major platform.

**N O T E** In addition to writing JavaScript that can be compiled for the JVM, Sun provides documentation that allows developers to take further advantage of the JVM built into each server. You can extend the JVM, port it to new processors, or write your own compiler to output bytecodes for the JVM. Anything you write that is targeted for the JVM is highly portable because the JVM is available on so many machines and can easily be ported to new processors and architectures. Sun's documentation on the JVM is available at **http://java.sun.com:80/doc/language_vm_specification.html**. ■

## Running the Application

The application has already instantiated the four default objects: `server`, `project`, `client`, and `request`. Enter your name in the field provided and press Enter to see LiveWire in action. LiveWire fills in your response as a property of its `request` object. The resulting screen should look like Figure 22.3.

**FIG. 22.3**
The debugger frame on the left shows the internal processing of LiveWire.

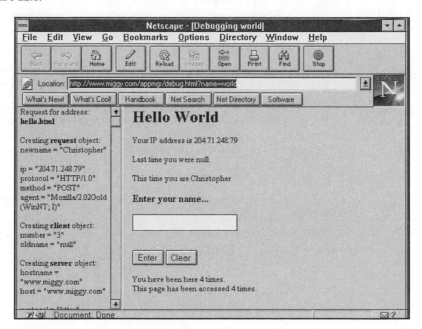

Scroll through the debugging frame. Here are some of the things you see LiveWire doing:

- LiveWire recognized the request for the LiveWire application hello and called for the application's initial page, hello.html.

- LiveWire instantiated a new `request` object. The `request` object has properties such as the IP address and the protocol (HTTP/1.0), which the `request` object gets from the browser's header during the HTTP exchange. The `request` object also puts up the `METHOD` (`POST`) and the agent, which the `request` object gets from the HTTP exchange. The `request` object also has one property for every `text`, `radioButton`, and `checkbox` element on the form, so the debug pane shows `newname` = "your name".

- Next, LiveWire instantiated the `client` object. A look at home.html reveals that the programmer has set up `number` and `oldname` properties in the client. These properties are duly reported out. If this is the first time this user has visited this site, a new `client` object is built (based on the application's defined state maintenance mechanism). If the client state is already defined, the `client` object is reloaded from that mechanism.

- LiveWire now accesses the existing `server` object, which has default properties of `hostname`, `host`, `protocol`, and `port`. This information comes from the server's configuration file, magnus.conf.

- Now that the stage is set, LiveWire begins to execute the bytecodes in hello.web that are associated with this page. Follow along in hello.html, but remember that LiveWire is executing the compiled version. The debug pane says, `Serving page....`

- Note that three write statements are in hello.html: one for `request.ip`, one for `client.oldname`, and one for `request.newname`. None of these writes is reported in the debug pane. Next you see `client.oldname` = `request.newname`, and the debug pane duly reports the property assignment, `client.oldname` = `"Christopher"` (or whatever name you entered most recently).

- Next in the source file is a bit of logic to determine whether the `client.number` and `project.number` have been set up yet. Note that only the outcome of this logic—the assignment statements—is reported in the debug pane.

- Finally, all of the `<SERVER>` work has been performed and LiveWire is about to conclude the transaction. It reports out the final state of each of the three objects: `client`, `project`, and `server`. (The `request` object is discarded after it is used.) Then LiveWire sends the finished page to the client.

**N O T E**  Although only a part of the HTML file is server-side JavaScript, all of the file is converted into JavaScript bytecodes. All of the HTML file is generated dynamically, not just the portion built from JavaScript. If you examine the compiler's output (called a .web file), you'll see a mixture of bytecodes and HTML.

**CAUTION**

The debug facility (also known as the trace facility in some of Netscape's literature) is intended for use in a development environment. Do not use this tool on your production machine. If more than one user attempts to trace the same application at the same time, the Web server can crash.

## LiveWire and the .web File

If you use the View, Document Source menu choice to examine the page of a LiveWire application, the source can appear rather confusing. None of the server-side JavaScript comes down to the client—only its output does. For example, the source of the hangman application shows the same page—hangman.html—being repeatedly loaded. Each time it is loaded, it changes slightly, based on the user's answers.

When the page is served, LiveWire runs the bytecodes from the application's Web page on the server. Only the output is sent to the client.

 LiveWire reads the Web file only when the application is started. If you change the HTML file, the application is not updated. If you recompile, the application is not updated. You must use the Application Manager to restart the application in order to force LiveWire to reread the Web file. For convenience, bookmark some of the common Application Manager commands such as **http://our-server/appmgr/debug.html?name=your-application** during development.

## Attaching the Built-In Objects

Before it runs the Web page, LiveWire loads the user's environment with the built-in objects such as request, client, and server.

Notice from the debug pane, examined earlier, that these objects are preloaded with information that is based on the HTTP request and the server configuration files.

## The LiveWire Interpreter

After the JavaScript context is loaded with the prebuilt objects and the bytecodes from the application's Web file, the <SERVER> code is run by the JavaScript Runtime Interpreter. The application may read or write files, access the database, or make calls around the Internet. Anything that is passed through write() is sent back to the client browser. Note that the output may include client-side JavaScript—the browser does not begin to interpret the JavaScript in the document until the server-side JavaScript has finished running.

# HTML with JavaScript

This section shows how to write server-side JavaScript into a page. Note that, unlike client-side JavaScript, server-side JavaScript must be compiled and the application must be installed before it can be used.

**TIP** If you see server-side JavaScript in your page when you access the application, make sure you have installed the pages as a LiveWire application with the Application Manager. If you have, examine your server-side code carefully—chances are good that a <SERVER> tag is missing or has a typo.

If the LiveWire compiler finds an error, it reports it and exits without generating a .web file. The LiveWire compiler doesn't catch all errors, however, so you'll need to check your code carefully to remove all defects.

## *<SERVER>*-Delimited Example

For most large chunks of server-side JavaScript, you want to wrap the code in <SERVER>... </SERVER> tags. This section shows how to set up JavaScript code that uses this notation.

**The Syntax**    The proper syntax for server-side JavaScript with the <SERVER> tags is

```
<SERVER>
Java statements, including one or more write statements
</SERVER>
```

**JavaScript Statements**    Listing 22.1 shows a simple example of server-side JavaScript.

**Listing 22.1    Simple Example of Server-Side JavaScript**

```
<HTML>
<HEAD>
<TITLE>Simple Example</TITLE>
</HEAD>
<BODY>
<H1>Hello, World!</H1>
<P>
Your IP address is
<SERVER>
write(request.ip)
</SERVER>
</BODY>
</HTML>
```

Up until the first <SERVER> tag, this file appears to be a typical HTML static file. Inside the <SERVER> tag pair, however, you see something new—a call to a write method. In this case, the write writes the ip property of the built-in request object.

JavaScript is dynamically typed. The runtime environment easily converts between numbers and text, so the IP address is written in its conventional dotted-decimal form.

**N O T E**  Without a call to `write()` somewhere in the JavaScript, nothing gets written back to the client. Only rarely will you write server-side JavaScript for its side effects alone. If your server-side JavaScript does not include at least one `write()`, think it through carefully to be sure you haven't missed something.

**T I P**  Some of the state maintenance mechanisms (for example, client-cookies) have to send information back to the client in the headers. It is good practice, therefore, to set all `client` properties before doing any calls to `write`.

## The *request* Object

If you've done any CGI programming, you are quite familiar with the difference between GET and POST methods. Those methods are less visible in server-side JavaScript because all of the form's fields become properties of the `request` object. Thus, you can write code like that shown in Listings 22.2 and 22.3.

**Listing 22.2  A *Request* Object Demo**

```
<HTML>
<HEAD>
<TITLE>A Request Object Demo</TITLE>
</HEAD>
<BODY>
<FORM NAME="theForm" ACTION="Request2.html" METHOD="GET">
Enter text:
<INPUT TYPE="Text" NAME="Text">
<BR>
Enter a number:
<INPUT TYPE="Text" NAME="Number">
<INPUT TYPE="Submit" NAME="Submit" VALUE="Enter">
</FORM>
</BODY>
</HTML>
```

**Listing 22.3  Processing the Form**

```
<HTML>
<HEAD>
<TITLE>A Request Object Demo</TITLE>
</HEAD>
<BODY>
<SERVER>
write("<P>The form's text field contained " + request.text + "</P>");
write ("<P>The form's number field contained " + request.number + "</P>");
</SERVER>
<A HREF="home.html">Home</A>
</BODY>
</HTML>
```

Of course, more interesting applications may send the form elements to the site owner by e-mail or write them to a file or the database, or even use them to look something up in a file or database. The end result, however, is nearly always a write() of something back to the client.

# Locking

The built-in objects, like project, contain a lock() method that operates in much the same way as transactions do in a SQL database. After a lock is set, no other application can change the locked object until the lock is released. This section shows how to set locks and explains why they are needed.

**Why Lock?**   Suppose you want a simple counter that keeps track of how many times someone visits your site. Hundreds of versions of this program exist in CGI scripts—Listing 22.4 shows one in server-side JavaScript.

## Listing 22.4   An Access Counter in Server-Side JavaScript

```
<HTML>
<HEAD>
<TITLE>An Access Counter</TITLE>
</HEAD>
<BODY>
<H1>Welcome!</H1>
<SERVER>
project.lock();
if (project.lastCount == NULL)
{
  project.lastCount == 1;
  write ("<P>You are the first person to use this application.</P>");
}
else
{
  if (!client.logged)
    project.lastCount = 1 + parseInt(project.lastCount, 10);
write("<P>This application has been accessed " + project.lastCount + " times.
➥</P>");
}
project.unlock();
client.logged = true;
</SERVER>
<A HREF="home.html">Home</A>
</BODY>
</HTML>
```

Once again, the interesting part begins with the first <SERVER> tag. The script locks the project to prevent anyone else from changing the values of the project properties while it is using them. If this is the first time that anyone has accessed this project, the script initializes project.lastCount. If the script finds project.lastCount already initialized, it checks to see whether the current client has been to this application before. If the current client has not, the script increments the project.lastCount value. In either case, the script reports out the value of lastCount.

Finally, the script unlocks the `project` and (perhaps redundantly) sets a `client` variable to log the fact that this particular client has been to this application.

**T I P** The `parseInt` construct in Listing 22.4 is used so often that it has become a JavaScript idiom. `parseInt` is a built-in function in server-side JavaScript. It takes the string in the first parameter and interprets it as a number in the base that is given by the second parameter. If the string contains certain key characters, then the base is overridden. For example, `parseInt("0x10", 10)` is 16 because `0x` denotes a hexadecimal interpretation.

> **CAUTION**
>
> If `parseInt` cannot interpret its first parameter as a number, `parseInt` will return a zero on Windows platforms and `NaN` (for Not a Number) on other platforms. This function is one of the few times that JavaScript behaves differently depending on the platform. This behavior has been changed in JavaScript 1.1, but only JavaScript 1.0 (not 1.1) is used in LiveWire 1.0.

**Locking at the *project* Level**    At any given time, dozens, or even hundreds, of people may be accessing a given page. When the `project` is locked, no one else can read or change any `project` property. Consider what might happen in the previous example if two users accessed a `project` property at about the same time without using locking:

1. User 1 reads `project.lastCount` and finds that it is 10.
2. User 2 reads `project.lastCount` and finds that it is 10.
3. User 1 increments `project.lastCount` and sets it to 11.
4. User 2 increments `project.lastCount` and sets it to 11.

If `project.lastCount` is used, for example, as an ID for a shopping cart, two users are now putting items into the same cart. This design is risky—with enough users over a long enough time, this design will cause an error sooner or later.

With locking, the following sequence occurs:

1. User 1 locks the `project` and reads `project.lastCount`, finding that it is 10.
2. User 2 attempts to read `project.lastCount` and finds that the `project` is locked.
3. User 1 increments `project.lastCount` and sets it to 11.
4. User 1 releases the lock on `project`.
5. User 2 now locks the `project` and reads and increments `project.lastCount`, setting it from 11 to 12.

**T I P** LiveWire implicitly locks the `project` whenever you read or set a `project` property. You only need to lock the `project` explicitly when, having read a `project` property, you intend to set something in the `project` based on what you read.

> **CAUTION**
>
> While you have `project` locked, no one else can read or set any `project` property. Keep `project` locked for as short a period as possible.

**An Example from a Shopping Cart System**   Many shopping cart scripts want to assign a sequential number to each shopper so that the script can keep track of the shopping baskets and orders. Listing 22.5 shows a simple way to do that by using `project` locking.

**Listing 22.5   A Script to Assign an ID to a Shopper**

```
<HTML>
<HEAD>
<TITLE>A Shopping Cart ID Generator</TITLE>
</HEAD>
<BODY>
<H1>Welcome!</H1>
<SERVER>
project.lock();
if (project.lastID == NULL)
{
  project.lastID == 1;
}
else
{
  if (client.ID == NULL)
  {
    project.lastID = 1 + parseInt(project.lastID, 10);
    client.ID = project.lastID;
  }
}
project.unlock();
write("<P>Now proecessing order number " + client.ID + ".</P>");
</SERVER>
<A HREF="home.html">Home</A>
</BODY>
</HTML>
```

**N O T E**   When you install a LiveWire application, Application Manager allows you to specify both a default page and an initial page. Suppose you install an application named myApp, with a default page of home.html and an initial page of start.html. When a user first asks for **http://your-server/myApp**, LiveWire serves start.html. That page is typically used for initialization (for example, establishing a connection with the database). The initial page will usually finish by redirecting the user to the default page. On every subsequent request for **http://your-server/myApp** by that client, LiveWire will return home.html.

Because the `project` can be initialized in a starter page, you may prefer the simplified version of this script, shown in Listing 22.6.

**Listing 22.6  A Simplified Version of the Shopper's ID**

```
<HTML>
<HEAD>
<TITLE>A Shopping Cart ID Generator</TITLE>
</HEAD>
<BODY>
<H1>Welcome!</H1>
<SERVER>
project.lock();
if (client.ID == NULL)
{
    project.lastID = 1 + parseInt(project.lastID, 10);
    client.ID = project.lastID;
}
project.unlock();
write("<P>Now proecessing order number " + client.ID + ".</P>");
</SERVER>
<A HREF="home.html">Home</A>
</BODY>
</HTML>
```

Note that, for this version of the script to work, the developer must initialize the
`project.lastID`. The application's starter page is a reasonable place to do this step so
that each page does not have to check to see whether the application is initialized.

## Calling JavaScript from Inside a Tag

For short pieces of JavaScript, the `<SERVER>...</SERVER>` construct can be cumbersome. It is
often preferable to just "drop" a bit of server-side JavaScript into an otherwise conventional
HTML tag.

**The Syntax**   Of course, conventional HTML tags have the form

```
<TAG ATTRIBUTE=VALUE...>
```

By surrounding either an attribute or a value (or both) in backquotes, the developer can force a
call to server-side JavaScript. The next section shows some examples.

**Some Examples**   The following line puts up the appropriate image during a game of
Hangman:

```
<IMG SRC='"Graphics/hang"+client.numberOfMisses+".gif">
```

Here's a line that works with the preceding shopping cart script:

```
<A HREF='"addToOrder.html?ID="+cursor.productID'>
```

Here's another line from a shopping cart application:

```
<A HREF='"product.html?category=" + categoryString'>
```

## Using a .js File

Experienced programmers will have noted earlier in the book that no way was given of building up a library of functions (such as is commonly done in other languages). Because all of the pages are stored on the server but executed on the client, no easy way existed in the original version of JavaScript to send a library of functions to the client for use by all pages.

In the latest version of JavaScript you can write

```
<SCRIPT SRC="http://yourserver/someDirectory/filename.js"></SCRIPT>
```

This technique allows you to build a library of JavaScript functions on the server which are downloaded and run on the client. You cannot include any HTML in a .js file, but you can use this feature to share common functions among several pages. Once the file is in the client's cache, you can avoid the time required to download JavaScript for each page.

> **CAUTION**
>
> If you write a <SCRIPT> tag with the SRC attribute, don't forget to include the closing tag, </SCRIPT>. It's easy to forget, but without it, Navigator will ignore all the HTML in your file!

With server-side JavaScript, it makes sense to define a file of common functions and compile them only once. The LiveWire compiler recognizes files with a .js extension as containing function declarations only. The developer can put all of the application's common routines in .js files and compile them into the Web file. Then the only code in the .html files is the local logic and function calls.

# Built-In Functions

Like Java and client-side JavaScript, server-side JavaScript is an object-oriented language. Although most functions are really methods on one object or another, a few functions, like parseInt, are true functions built right into the JavaScript language. This section lists the most common of these functions in server-side JavaScript.

Your copy of LiveWire comes with plenty of documentation. For the latest information on server-side JavaScript, check out **LiveWire/doc/index.html** in your server's root directory. For information on both client-side and server-side JavaScript, follow the server-specific link on the **LiveWire/doc/index.html** page to the JavaScript Guide. The actual locations differ depending on whether you use Netscape's Enterprise or FastTrack Web server, but the documentation is the same.

Be sure to get the LiveWire release notes appropriate to your platform at **http:// home.netscape.com/eng/LiveWire/relnotes/**. LiveWire is most mature on Windows NT. Some of the newer releases have additions to the documentation and have known problems.

You'll also need to set up environment variables specific to your platform. For even more help getting LiveWire set up, use the resources at **http://help.netscape.com/**. If you find a LiveWire bug, report it using the form at **http://cgi.netscape.com/cgi-bin/ livewire_bug.cgi**.

# write

You have seen the write function throughout this chapter. You use it to generate HTML that is sent back to the client.

# writeURL

If an application generates URLs dynamically, it should use writeURL instead of trying to build the URL with a write function. writeURL encapsulates any URL encoding that is being used to maintain the client's state.

 Even if you are using a non-URL method of maintaining state (such as client-cookies), it is a good idea to use writeURL to generate any dynamically generated URLs. This way, you can change your mind later and switch the state-saving mechanism in the Application Manager without having to change the source code.

# flush

In general, operating systems do not write data as soon as a write or print statement is executed. Instead, data is buffered into fairly large "chunks." When the buffer is full, the data in the buffer is written all at once. This approach is much more efficient than stopping to do small writes of a few bytes each. LiveWire flushes after every 64K of generated content.

Usually this mechanism is transparent to the user, but sometimes the buffering gets in the way. You can use flush() to send the data immediately and allow the user to see your response. For example, unless the flush() is included, the following code gives the user the impression that nothing is happening:

```
while (!In.eof())
{
  theLine = In.readln();
  if (!In.eof())
    write(LPad(LineCount + ": ", 5), theLine, "\n");
  LineCount++;
  flush();
}
```

# redirect

The redirect function works like a call to print("Location: *some new page*\n\n"); in a CGI script—as soon as it is executed, LiveWire transfers the client to the indicated URL. None of the statements following the redirect are executed.

**TIP** If you have any standard "wrap-up" code at the end of your page (such as `database.disconnect()` or `project.unlock()`), be sure to run this final code before issuing the `redirect()`.

## debug

The `debug` function writes its parameter to the trace facility. Use it like you'd use a `write()`, to make sure you know what's happening at each step in your script.

## registerCFunction

The `registerCFunction` is part of the mechanism for calling C from JavaScript. If you need to do something that can't easily be done from JavaScript (such as make direct calls to operating system functions), use this external call mechanism to link C code into your .web file.

# Predefined Objects

The LiveWire application developer has several ways to add dynamic content to the site: plug-ins, Java, client-side JavaScript, server-side JavaScript, and CGI. Of these mechanisms, all except server-side JavaScript and CGI run on the user's machine. As a result, Netscape's designers started their extension to JavaScript by examining how CGI programmers spent their time.

Thousands of CGI applications are on the Web—many of them are very simple programs, some of them are great, complex affairs. An examination of CGI code and a discussion with CGI programmers reveals three facts:

- Nearly all CGI programs have many lines of code that are responsible for pulling the user's data out of a query string or input stream and putting it into variables for the program to use.

- Many CGI programs spend a lot of time keeping track of user state. Because HTTP is a stateless protocol, programs that need to know who the user is, such as shopping cart scripts, have to use a variety of schemes to get each client's request to identify itself.

- Many CGI programmers wish they could access databases on the server. Although such access is possible, the techniques have been something of a "mysterious art" for many CGI programmers.

To meet these and other needs on the server, Netscape defined the four objects that are available automatically to every server-side JavaScript program:

- The `server` object, which contains information about the Netscape server
- The `project` object, which contains information that is shared among all users of a particular application
- The `client` object, which contains information associated with a particular user
- The `request` object, which contains information about this particular client request

Collectively, these four objects are known as the *LiveWire Object Framework*. The LiveWire Object Framework is illustrated in Figure 22.4.

**FIG. 22.4**
The LiveWire Object Framework consists of four predefined objects, shown here in order from the longest-lived to the shortest-lived.

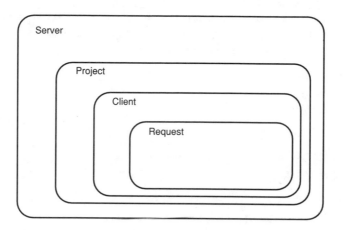

# The *server* Object

The server object comes into existence when the server is started and is destroyed when the server is stopped. Each application can read and, to a limited extent, write server data. Every application on a server shares the same server object, but if more than one Web server is running on the same computer (listening to different TCP ports), each has its own server object.

**Properties**    The server object supports four properties, as shown in Table 22.1.

**Table 22.1    Properties of the *server* Object**

| Property | Description | Example |
|---|---|---|
| hostname | The full server hostname, including the port number | www.dse.com:80 |
| host | The server name, subdomain, and domain name | www.dse.com |
| protocol | The communications protocol of the server | http: |
| port | The port on which the server is listening | 80 |

**T I P** In addition to the properties of the `server` object, you can get the values of the Netscape server environment variables through the LiveWire external function interface.

Netscape provides sample code to access environment variables in the **LiveWire/samples/lwcall/ lwccall.c** file, part of the documentation supplied with LiveWire in your server's root directory. The variables you can get using external functions include the following:

- SERVER_URL
- REMOTE_USER
- AUTH_TYPE
- SERVER_PROTOCOL
- REQUEST_METHOD
- QUERY_STRING
- USER_AGENT

Before you write code to extract these variables from the Netscape server, check the properties of the other built-in objects. USER_AGENT, for example, is available as the `agent` property of the `request` object. LiveWire decodes the QUERY_STRING and provides each field as a property of the `request` object.

**Methods**    Any application may call the `lock()` method of the server. Doing so makes it possible to read and update server properties without interference from any other application. While the server is locked, no one else can read or set any server property, nor can anyone else lock the server. Call the `unlock()` method to release the lock on the server.

> **CAUTION**
>
> While the server is locked, other applications that try to access to the server's properties are blocked. Do not keep the server locked any longer than necessary.

## The *project* Object

The `project` object is associated with the application. The developer uses the LiveWire Application Manager to install, start, stop, and remove applications. When the application is started, LiveWire makes a new `project` object. Everyone accessing that application uses the same `project` object. On a well-run server, the application and, consequently, the `project` object have a lifetime of many weeks.

The application may add properties to the `project` object as the application runs. Suppose the application wants to count the number of times it is accessed by a unique client. Recall from the section "HTML with JavaScript" that an application developer can put the following server-side JavaScript on the default page:

```
<SERVER>
project.lock();
if (project.count == NULL)
```

```
    project.count = 1;
else
    project.count = 1 + parseInt (project.count, 10);
project.unlock();
</SERVER>
```

This bit of code locks the `project` (so you can read and increment `project.count` without fear of someone else changing it before you are done with it). If you are the first client to access this `project` since it started, the count is set to one. Otherwise, the count is incremented.

 **TIP** Recall, too, that `parseInt()` is a built-in, top-level function that transforms strings into integers. You should always use string functions when reading or writing properties of objects in the LiveWire Object Framework. These objects store their properties internally as strings. By acknowledging that fact and dealing with the conversion explicitly, you are less likely to get subtle defects in your code.

Like the `server` object, the `project` object supports `lock()` and `unlock()` methods. Also like the `server` object, locking the `project` blocks other users from the application, so the `project` should be unlocked as quickly as possible.

## The *client* Object

The HTTP is called a stateless protocol. This statement means that if a Web server gets two requests in a row, it has no way of knowing whether those requests came from a single user or from two different users. Several mechanisms can be built into a CGI script by which the server can tell one user from another, but these mechanisms require advanced programming skills and can be tricky to set up.

When a user first requests access to a LiveWire application, LiveWire instantiates a new client object and makes it available to the application. Any information that is associated with that user can be stored in the client object. Upon completion of the request, LiveWire stores the client information. If the same user makes another request before the client object expires, the application restores the client object with the stored information.

The mechanisms LiveWire uses to store client information are fairly complex, but the application programmer doesn't have to be concerned with those mechanisms. The programmer specifies a mechanism in the Application Manager and lets LiveWire do the work.

 **TIP** Some of the state preservation mechanisms, like client-cookies, rely on LiveWire to send information back to the client. This information must be sent with the HTTP headers before any content is sent.

The LiveWire buffers can store 64K of data. After you have issued calls to send that much data, the buffers are sent and your opportunity to put data into the header is lost. Therefore, you should set any client properties before you do many calls to `write`, making sure that the header can be sent before the content is returned to the client.

Do not rely upon the installer to use one mechanism over another. Strive to make your code independent of the state preservation mechanism so that Webmasters can set the state preservation mechanism to whatever is appropriate for their site.

**Properties**   There are no predefined properties for the `client` object. Instead, the `client` object is the place for the application to store any information about this particular user that the application needs. A shopping cart script may store information about the items the visitor has selected. A multipart form may store information about the choices the visitor has already made. A multipage survey may store information about the visitor's choices so that coefficients of correlation can be calculated between questions on one page and another.

**Methods**   One of the problems with state-preserving systems is that no one knows when the visitor is gone. Suppose a visitor arrives at a shopping site like the one shown in Figure 22.5. Because this visitor arrives with no `client` object (he or she is not known to the site), the application's initial page issues a shopper ID which it stores in the `client` object. The application then redirects the visitor to a welcome page and returns control back to the visitor.

**FIG. 22.5**

A shopping cart script must have some way to keep track of which request goes with which order file.

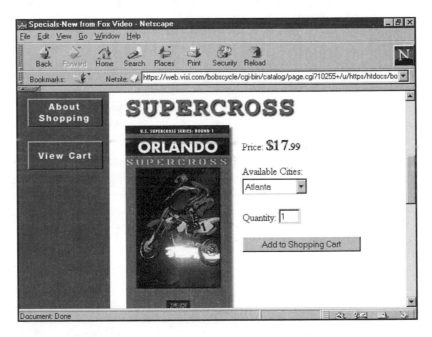

A few minutes later, the visitor requests a catalog page. Because the visitor is now known to the site, the application does not issue a new ID but serves the requested page directly. The visitor makes a series of requests, each one asking that an item be added to the shopper's order. Each request contains information about the item, such as size, color, and style. The requests arrive two to three minutes apart as the shopper navigates the site.

Then—nothing. Minutes pass, and nothing is heard from the shopper. The application is keeping a record of the shopper's order so far. How long should that record be retained? Five minutes? Ten? An hour? A day? At what point can you confidently say that the visitor is gone, or—if not gone for good—at least gone so long that the visitor would not expect to return and find the order waiting for them?

The answer, of course, depends on the application. LiveWire enables the application to call the client method expiration() that takes a single parameter: seconds. Using this method, the application can set the timeout period. The default is ten minutes.

Of course, sometimes the application designer has just the opposite problem. The shopper has completed the order (the visitor has completed the last page of the form or the survey) and it's time to destroy the client object and bid farewell to the client. Call client.destroy() and the deed is done.

# The *request* Object

The LiveWire Object Framework includes four prebuilt objects: the server, the project, the client, and the request. The request object has more built-in properties and methods than the other three combined. This section describes the capabilities of the request object.

If you've written CGI scripts to process form data, you known that HTTP supports two methods that enable data to go from the client to the server. The first, called GET, appends the data to the URL—it is available as the environment variable QUERY_STRING to the CGI script. If the form uses POST, the data is sent to the TCP port following the request headers. The data is pulled out by the server and delivered to the CGI script on its STDIN.

Either way, the CGI programmer must write code to take the fields out of the query string or STDIN, separate the field names from their values, and decode any characters from hexadecimal back to ASCII. With LiveWire, that coding and decoding is a thing of the past. (This feature alone may be enough to justify some programmers buying the product!) As shown in this section, when the request object is delivered to the application, it comes with all of the form elements attached to it as properties.

The request object is the shortest-lived of the four LiveWire Object Framework objects. It is brought into existence when the client sends a request and destroyed after the response is sent. A new request is generated whenever the following happens:

- A user requests a new URL with the browser
- A user clicks a link to a new page or requests a document, like a frame parent, that references another page
- A client-side JavaScript program sets the document.location property
- A client-side JavaScript program invokes the history.go() method
- Server-side JavaScript calls redirect()

**Built-In Properties**    The four built-in properties of the request object are shown in Table 22.2.

**Table 22.2   The Built-In Properties of the *request* Object**

| Property | Description | Example |
| --- | --- | --- |
| agent | Name and version of the client software | Mozilla/2.02Gold (WinNT; I) |
| ip | The IP address of the client | 207.2.80.1 |
| method | The HTTP method associated with the request | GET, POST, or HEAD |
| protocol | The HTTP protocol level supported by the browser | HTTP/1.0 |

Netscape browsers understand extensions that are not part of standard HTML (not the least of which is client-side JavaScript). The agent property can be used to serve one version of a page to Netscape browsers (identified by the distinctive name, Mozilla), and a different version to browsers that do not understand Netscape's extensions.

T I P    Before you spend much time building browser-specific versions of your pages, take note of how close standard HTML (HTML 3.2) is coming to Netscape's interpretation of the language. Information about the official HTML specification is available at **http://www.w3.org/pub/WWW/MarkUp/Wilbur/**.

In general, the World Wide Web Consortium (W3C) is adopting many of Netscape's recommended enhancements. Netscape, in turn, is getting out ahead of W3C and experimenting with new capabilities (including JavaScript) that are likely to become part of the official standard in the future.

You can get the latest summary of the capabilities of the most popular browsers through the BrowserCaps site at **http://www.pragmaticainc.com/bc/Generated/browser-Mozilla-3-01b1-Win95.html**. This URL reports the test results for Netscape Navigator 3.01b1 for Windows 95. Similar pages are available for all popular combinations of platform and browser.

**Properties from Form Elements**    In addition to the four predefined properties, every element of every form on a page becomes a property of the request object. Consider the tax calculator in Listings 22.7 and 22.8.

**Listing 22.7   The First Half of a Real Estate Tax Calculator**

```
<HTML>
<HEAD>
<TITLE>Tax Calculator</TITLE>
</HEAD>
<BODY>
```

```
<FORM NAME="taxcalc" METHOD=GET ACTION="taxcalc2.html">
What is the assessed value of the property?
<INPUT TYPE=text NAME=assessed>
<BR>
In which city is the property located?
<SELECT NAME=city>
<OPTION Chesapeake>Chesapeake
<OPTION Norfolk>Norfolk
<OPTION Portsmouth>Portsmouth
<OPTION VirginiaBeach>Virginia Beach
</SELECT>
<INPUT TYPE=submit NAME=submit VALUE=Enter>
<INPUT TYPE=reset NAME=reset VALUE=Clear>
</FORM>
<A HREF="home.htm">Home</A>
</BODY>
</HTML>
```

## Listing 22.8   The Second Half of a Real Estate Tax Calculator

```
<HTML>
<HEAD>
<TITLE>Calculated Tax</TITLE>
</HEAD>
<BODY>
<P>
<SERVER>
write("The tax rate for " + request.city + " is " +
taxrate(request.city) + ". At that rate your
monthly taxes will be $" +
computeTax(request.city, request.assessed) + ".");
</SERVER>
<A HREF="home.htm">Home</A>
</BODY>
</HTML>
```

In this case, the programmer can get access to the form elements just by asking for them by name from the `request` object.

**N O T E**   The code in Listings 22.7 and 22.8 could have been run as client-side JavaScript. By implementing it as server-side JavaScript, however, the application developer can offer the application to non-Netscape browsers without having to maintain two versions of the page.

Note that, unlike client-side JavaScript, Listing 22.8 does not have to include all of the functions in the HTML file. Server-side JavaScript functions can be declared in a separate JavaScript file (with a .js extension) and compiled into the application. ■

**Properties from URLs**   The `request` object also picks up values passed in the URL. The general syntax is

```
URL?name=value[&name=value...]
```

For example, when the link

```
<A HREF="remove.html?ID=112">Remove Item 112</A>
```

is selected, it requests that the server load the page named remove.html and passes the value 112 in a variable named ID. Inside remove.html, the programmer can refer to `request.ID` and get back the value 112.

An advanced technique is to call some server-side JavaScript to build a part of a page from a database and then call server-side JavaScript to handle the request. For example,

```
<SERVER>
cursor = new database.cursor(SELECT name, id FROM publishers);
while (cursor.next())
  write ("<A HREF=&quot;remove.html?id=" + cursor.id + "&quot;>" + cursor.name +
"</A><BR>\n");
cursor.close();
</SERVER>
```

uses the database extension (part of LiveWire) to read a list of publishers from the database.

The resulting HTML that is sent to the client may resemble the following code:

```
<A HREF="remove.html?id=201">Addison-Wesley</A><BR>
<A HREF="remove.html?id=471">Wiley and Sons</A><BR>
<A HREF="remove.html?id=55615">Microsoft Press</A><BR>
<A HREF="remove.html?id=937175">O'Reilly & Associates</A><BR>
```

When a user selects one of these links, the browser requests the remove.html page. The browser passes the ID that is to be removed to the server-side JavaScript on that page. Remove.html deletes the entry from the database.

# The *file* Object

Although the `file` object is not part of the LiveWire Object Framework, it is one of the most useful objects a programmer can instantiate. A file can be used to store data when the full power of a relational database is not needed. You can also write an application that writes HTML files so that an application can build its own pages.

Listing 22.9 shows an example of how to use a `file` object.

---

**Listing 22.9   Read and Write Files on the Server Host**

```
// file names are platform dependent; this example favors UNIX
var theFile = new File("/tmp/aFile.dat")

// check to see if the file exists and is readable
var fileIsOpen = theFile.open("r")
```

```
if (fileIsOpen)
{
  write("File name is "+theFile+"<BR>")
  while (!theFile.eof())
  {

    //keep reading the file and writing out lines
    line = theFile.readln()

    // as long as there is data to be read
    if (!theFile.eof())
      write(line+"<BR>")
  }
  if (theFile.error() != 0)
    write("Error reading file " + theFile + ".<BR>")
  theFile.close()
}
```

> **CAUTION**
>
> Most Web servers are run as an unprivileged user. For example, UNIX servers often run as user nobody. Nevertheless, be careful about where your applications write. Your application can write (and overwrite!) anywhere on the server machine that the unprivileged user can write to.

Note that the `file` constructor makes a new `file` object, not a new file on the hard drive. The path specified with the constructor is relative to the application directory. Specify the path in the manner that is consistent with the platform. (Thus, Windows NT users should use backslashes to separate levels of directories, and UNIX users should use forward slashes.)

Note, too, that the name of the `file` object is synonymous with the name of the file. In the example, `write(theFile)` causes /tmp/aFile.dat to be written to the output stream.

## Static Methods

Recall from Chapter 7, "The *Date* and *Array* Objects," that static methods apply to the class and not to any particular instance of the class. Class `file` supports two static methods: `byteToString()` and `stringToByte()`. To call a static method, call it on the class, not an instance. Thus,

`File.byteToString(number)`

converts the number to a one-character string, but

`myFile.byteToString(number)`

causes a compile-time error.

In general, files can contain ASCII text or binary data. These methods make it easy to convert from one format to the other.

***byteToString***    `byteToString()` outputs a one-character string. If the argument is not a number, the output is the empty string.

***stringToByte***    `stringToByte()` takes a string as its parameter and returns the numeric code of the first character.

# State Management Methods

Class `file` supports five methods that can be used to change the state of the file itself: `open()`, `close()`, `flush()`, `setPosition()`, and `clearError()`.

***open***    The `file` constructor makes a new `file` object that is associated with the specified path. Before you read or write the file, you must call `open`, specifying the mode. Valid modes are given in Table 22.3.

**Table 22.3   The Modes of *open***

| Mode | Description | Fails If... |
|------|-------------|-------------|
| r | Opens the file for reading | File does not exist or is not readable |
| w | Opens the file for writing | Cannot write to the specified directory |
| a | Opens the file for appending | Cannot write to the file (if it exists) or the directory |
| r+ | Opens the file for reading and writing | File does not exist or is not readable |
| w+ | Opens the file for reading and writing | Cannot write to the file (if it exists) or the directory |
| a+ | Opens the file for reading and writing, starting at the end of the file | Cannot write to the file (if it exists) or the directory |

**N O T E**   Windows makes a distinction between text files and binary files. (UNIX does not.) If the application may run on a Windows server, append a "b" to the mode to denote binary mode. The default is text mode.

**N O T E**   In addition to the reasons for failure given in Table 22.3, `open()` also fails if the file is already open.

***close***    When you are done with the file, call its `close()` method. `close()` fails if the file is not open.

***flush***    `flush()` is used with the `write` methods. JavaScript's `write` methods are buffered. To force a `write`, call `flush()`.

**setPosition**    The `file` object maintains an internal pointer to the current read/write position. If you open a file in append mode, this pointer is at the end of the file. Otherwise, when the file first opens, the pointer is at the beginning. Use `setPosition()` to move the pointer around the file. The syntax is

```
fileObject.setPosition(position [, reference])
```

where `position` is an integer offset from the reference and `reference` can be

- `0` to denote the beginning of the file
- `1` to denote the current position
- `2` to denote the end of the file
- `Other` (or unspecified) to denote the beginning of the file

Thus, at the end of the following code, the position is five characters from the beginning of the file if all of the function calls succeed.

```
var theFile = new File("/tmp/theFile.txt")
theFile.open("r+")
theFile.setPosition(3)
theFile.write("xy")
```

The `file` position is at the beginning when the file is opened. `setPosition()` advances the position three characters from the beginning, and the `write()` function advances the position two more characters.

***clearError***    `clearError()` resets the error number and the `eof()` method, both of which are described later in this section.

# Info Methods

Six methods on `file` report information about the file without changing anything about it: `getPosition()`, `getLength()`, `exists()`, `eof()`, `error()`, and `toString()`.

***getPosition***    `getPosition()` is the companion function to `setPosition()`. `getPosition()` returns the read/write position, with `0` being the first character in the file. If there is an error, `getPosition()` returns `-1`.

***getLength***    `getLength()` returns the number of bytes in the file. If the file is a text file on a Windows system, the answer represents the number of characters in the file.

***exists***    To check to see whether the file named by the `file` object actually exists, call its `exists()` method.

***eof***    `eof` returns `true` if the read/write position is at the end of the file. Thus, an application can open a file for read (positioning the pointer at the beginning of the file) and issue a series of reads until `eof()` is true.

eof() returns true after the first read operation that attempts to read past the end of the file. Thus, the last read() before eof() that becomes true cannot be relied on to hold the expected result. The common idiom is to write

```
while (!theFile.eof())
  {
    line = theFile.readln()
    if (!theFile.eof())
        write(line)
  }
```

so that eof() is called twice—once after the read to determine whether the data is meaningful to write it and again at the top of the loop to be sure it is safe to read again.

**error**   If error() returns a -1, the file is not open. If error() returns 0, the file is open and has no error. Error codes (positive non-zero values) are operating system-dependent. By using error(), you can now interpret the last few lines in the demo code that appeared at the beginning of this section:

```
if (theFile.error() != 0)
    write("Error reading file " + theFile + ".<BR>")
```

If, after the series of calls to readln(), error() is set to a non-zero value, either the file failed to open or an error occurred during one of the reads. Either way, the application complains about the problem and closes the file.

## *read* Methods

The file class enables the programmer to issue a read of a predefined number of bytes or of a single byte. For text files, however, it is often convenient to read until the end of the line.

**read**   The read() method is most commonly used when the data is binary. When reading files of fixed-length records, the read() method may also be used. This method takes one parameter—a count—and reads that number of bytes from the file. The read() method returns a string. If the read attempts to read past the end of the file, the valid characters are returned and eof() becomes true.

**readln**   readln() is appropriate for text files—it reads to the end of the line.

 The end of the line in a text file depends on the computer on which the server is running. UNIX machines signify the end of the line with a *linefeed*, also known as a *newline*, and denoted with \n. Windows machines use a carriage return followed by a newline (\r\n). These line separator characters are not included in the returned string.

**readByte**   readByte() reads a single byte from the file and returns its numeric value. This is most appropriate for use with binary files.

## *write* Methods

Like the read methods, file can handle writes at several levels of granularity: the byte, the character string, or the line.

 **T I P** JavaScript write methods are internally buffered. To force the write, call flush() on the file object.

***write*** write() takes a single parameter, a string, and writes it to the file.

***writeln*** writeln() works like write but includes the line separator characters appropriate for the operating system (\n for UNIX, \r\n for Windows).

***writeByte*** writeByte() outputs a single numeric parameter that is useful when writing to binary files or devices. For example, to write an ASCII null character, use writeByte(0).

## Locking Files

When multiple users attempt to write to the same file, the potential always exists for one user's activity to interfere with another's activity—and a strong likelihood exists that the file will become corrupted. In server-side JavaScript, this problem is easily solved by using the lock() and unlock() methods of the project object. Before accessing the file (for either read or write), call project.lock(). Be sure to call project.unlock() when the file operation is done.

If a file is shared between applications, use server.lock() and server.unlock() instead of the calls to the project object.

 **T I P** Do not rely on the read/write pointer being where you left it after the last unlock. After you unlock, another user of your application can get a lock and move the pointer. After they unlock and you get the lock back, you should reposition the pointer if its location is important to you.

---

### More on Server-Side JavaScript and Netscape LiveWire

For a more complete discussion of server-side JavaScript and Netscape LiveWire, see *Special Edition Using Netscape LiveWire* (Que, 1996).

Chapter 8, "A SQL Primer," of that book describes SQL, the Structured Query Language, and its use with relational database managers.

Chapter 14, "Building LiveWire Applications," gives more details on compiling server-side JavaScript.

Details of the registerCFunction mechanism and the external function interface that allows you to call C from server-side JavaScript are given in Chapter 15, "Calling C and C++ Code."

For more information on LiveWire debugging and the Trace facility, see Chapter 16, "Testing and Debugging Server-Side JavaScript."

---

# CHAPTER 23

# Using Cookies in Advanced Applications

**O**ne of the limitations of the Hypertext Transfer Protocol (HTTP), the protocol of the Web, is that it is stateless. That is, if a Web server gets a request for page A, then page B, and then page C, it has no way of determining whether those requests came from one, two, or even three different users. In truth, most sites don't care. But some services, such as multipart forms and shopping carts, absolutely must be able to tell one user from another.

While several mechanisms have been developed by Webmasters and Web programmers to add state to their Web pages, Netscape has built such a technology into Navigator. Microsoft and other browser vendors have incorporated this technology into their products as well.

The mechanism for adding state and persistent data to a Web page goes by the whimsical name, *cookie*. When you use cookies to build state and persistence into your Web pages, you are using a mechanism that is available to nearly all Web users. By using LiveWire to read and write cookies, without extra programming, you avoid having to construct the tedious CGI code required to build or dissect cookies on-the-fly. ∎

---

**Learn why Web page designers want to add state and persistent data to their Web pages**

Once you learn how to store information on the client's machine, you will want to utilize this capability everywhere.

**Learn how Webmasters added state to pages before cookies were available**

You can append "command-line parameters" to an URL and read them at the server.

**Find out how cookies work in modern browsers such as Navigator and Internet Explorer**

You can save information about users and their activity and read it back again.

**Learn how to specify how long a cookie will remain on the client's machine**

For many purposes, you may never even need to store a cookie on the hard drive.

**Find out how your JavaScript can read and set the contents of the cookie**

Once you see how cookies are read and written, you can decide whether cookies are likely to be "poached" by another site.

# Using the Command Line

While the Hypertext Transfer Protocol does not support state, it does enable you to append extra information after the URL. Forms use this mechanism (when their method is GET) to send data back to the server, though the mechanism is not limited to use by forms. For example, you could write a server program using the Common Gateway Interface (CGI) that reads the following URL:

**http://www.myserver.com/processData.cgi?myName=John+P.+Smith&myOrderID=001270&productToAdd=1178&size=small&color=navy**

When the server sees that URL, it invokes the specified CGI script. When the CGI script starts running, the server puts everything after the question mark into the environment variable QUERY_STRING. It's up to the CGI program to

1. Split the pairs of *variable=value* at each ampersand (&)

2. Decode any spaces, which are encoded to plus signs

3. Decode any characters encoded with the percent sign (e.g., a forward slash has an ASCII code of $2_F16$, so %2F is a forward slash)

4. Read the *value* into a local variable that matches the name *variable*.

In the example used here, the CGI script might end up with:

- a variable named myName set to the string "John P. Smith";

- a variable named myOrder set to the integer 001270;

- a variable named productToAdd set to the integer 1178;

- a variable named size set to the string "small"; and

- a variable named color, set to the string "navy".

If you're writing a CGI script, you may want to use the Perl language, which has lots of built-in tools to unpack strings like QUERY_STRING. If you're using LiveWire, name-value pairs on the command line are transformed to properties of the request object, so you don't have to do anything to read them or decode them.

JavaScript uses the same encoding mechanism to put the current URL into location.search. If you want to take apart strings such as this on the client, and you have JavaScript 1.1, you can use the string operator split(). Otherwise, you need to do a bit more coding.

▶ **See** "HTML with JavaScript," **p. 596**, for more information about server-side JavaScript.

Listing 23.1 is a function, parameterArray, that dissects a command line such as the one used in this example. It puts its output into an associative array and returns the array. You'll find an example of this function in action in Listing 23.2.

## Listing 23.1   With JavaScript 1.0, You Need to Split the Command Line Yourself

```
function parameterArray(inputString)
{
  var theLength = inputString.length;
  inputString = inputString.substring(0, theLength);
//document.write("Input String is " + inputString + "<BR>");
//document.write("theLength is " + theLength + "<BR>");
  var theStringSoFar = '';
  var aCounter = 1;
  for (var i=0; i<=theLength; i++)
  {
    var theCurrentCharacter = '';
    theCurrentCharacter = inputString.substring(i, i+1);
//document.write(theCurrentCharacter);
    if (theCurrentCharacter == '+') theCurrentCharacter = ' ';
    if (theCurrentCharacter == '%')
    {
      var aHexString = inputString.substring(i, i+3);
      theCurrentCharacter = unescape(aHexString);
      i +=2;
//document.write("(" + theCurrentCharacter + ")");
    }
    if (theCurrentCharacter == '=')
    {
      this[aCounter] = theStringSoFar;
      theStringSoFar = '';
//document.write(" is ");
      continue;
    }
    if (theCurrentCharacter == '&')
    {
      this[this[aCounter]] = theStringSoFar;
//document.write("<BR>");
      aCounter++;
      theStringSoFar = '';
      theCurrentCharacter = '';
      continue;
    }
    theStringSoFar += theCurrentCharacter;
  }
  // output the final value
  this[this[aCounter]] = theStringSoFar;
//document.write(".");
//document.close();
  this.length = aCounter;
}
```

Associative arrays are one-dimensional arrays of pairs. The left member specifies a name—the right member is a value associated with that name.

**Listing 23.2   *parameterArray()* in Action**

```
<HTML>
<HEAD>
<TITLE>Split Tester</TITLE>
<SCRIPT LANGUAGE="JavaScript">
<!--
function parameterArray(inputString)
{
  var theLength = inputString.length;
  inputString = inputString.substring(0, theLength);
//document.write("Input String is " + inputString + "<BR>");
//document.write("theLength is " + theLength + "<BR>");
  var theStringSoFar = '';
  var aCounter = 1;
  for (var i=0; i<=theLength; i++)
  {
    var theCurrentCharacter = '';
    theCurrentCharacter = inputString.substring(i, i+1);
//document.write(theCurrentCharacter);
    if (theCurrentCharacter == '+') theCurrentCharacter = ' ';
    if (theCurrentCharacter == '%')
    {
      var aHexString = inputString.substring(i, i+3);
      theCurrentCharacter = unescape(aHexString);
      i +=2;
//document.write("(" + theCurrentCharacter + ")");
    }
    if (theCurrentCharacter == '=')
    {
      this[aCounter] = theStringSoFar;
      theStringSoFar = '';
//document.write(" is ");
      continue;
    }
    if (theCurrentCharacter == '&')
    {
      this[this[aCounter]] = theStringSoFar;
//document.write("<BR>");
      aCounter++;
      theStringSoFar = '';
      theCurrentCharacter = '';
      continue;
    }
    theStringSoFar += theCurrentCharacter;
  }
  // output the final value
  this[this[aCounter]] = theStringSoFar;
//document.write(".");
//document.close();
  this.length = aCounter;
}

function showResults(theArray)
{
  for (var i=1; i<=theArray.length; i++)
```

```
      alert("" + theArray[i] + "=" + theArray[theArray[i]]);
}

// -->
</SCRIPT>
</HEAD>
<BODY BGCOLOR="white">
<FORM NAME="theForm">
<P>
Enter a string:
<INPUT Type="text" NAME="theTextField" Value="default">
<INPUT Type="button" NAME="Parse" Value="Parse" onClick="myArray=new
parameterArray(document.theForm.theTextField.value)">
<INPUT TYPE="button" Value="Show Results" onClick="showResults(myArray)">
</FORM>
</BODY>
</HTML>
```

▶ **See** "JavaScript's Associative Arrays," **p. 289**, for more information about associative arrays.

## Using Command-Line Encoding with *location.search*

From a JavaScript script, the "command line" information in the current URL (starting with the question mark) is stored in `location.search`. Listing 23.3 shows JavaScript that reads and decodes `location.search`.

---

**Listing 23.3    A Dynamic Page in JavaScript 1.1**

```
<HTML>
<HEAD>
<TITLE>Command Line Tester</TITLE>
<SCRIPT LANGUAGE="JavaScript1.1">
<!--
function parameterArray(inputString)
{
  // strip off the question mark;
  //subString's 2nd parameter defaults to end of string
  inputString = inputString.substring(1);
  aLocalArray = inputString.split('&');
  this.length = aLocalArray.length;
  for (var i=0; i<aLocalArray.length; i++)
  {
    // If the browser follows the encoding of JavaScript's 'escape'
    // and 'unescape' functions, replace these two while loops with
    // aLocalArray[i] = unescape(aLocalArray[i]);
    while (aLocalArray[i].indexOf("+") != -1)
    {
      var theLocation = aLocalArray[i].indexOf("+");
      aLocalArray[i] = aLocalArray[i].substring(0, theLocation) + " " +
      aLocalArray[i].substring(theLocation+1);
    }
    while (aLocalArray[i].indexOf("%") != -1)
    {
```

*continues*

**Listing 23.3    Continued**

```
        var theLocation = aLocalArray[i].indexOf("%");
        aLocalArray[i] = aLocalArray[i].substring(0, theLocation) +
          unescape(aLocalArray[i].substring(theLocation, theLocation+3)) +
          aLocalArray[i].substring(theLocation+3);
      }
      this[i] = aLocalArray[i].substring(0,aLocalArray[i].indexOf("="));
      this[this[i]] = aLocalArray[i].substring(aLocalArray[i].indexOf("=")+1);
    // alert("Slot " + i + " is " + this[i] + "\nand contains " +
➥this[this[i]] + ".");
  }
  return this;
}
// -->
</SCRIPT>
</HEAD>
<BODY>
<SCRIPT LANGUAGE="JavaScript1.1">
<!--
var aString = location.search;
var anotherString = new String;
if (aString != null && aString != '')
{
   gParameters = new parameterArray(aString);
   anotherString = "<BODY BGCOLOR='linen' ";
   anotherString += "TEXT='" + gParameters["textColor"] + "' ";
   anotherString += "LINK='" + gParameters["linkColor"] + "' ";
   anotherString += "VLINK='" + gParameters["vlinkColor"] + "' ";
   anotherString += "ALINK='red'";
   anotherString += "BACKGROUND = 'images/" +
➥gParameters['image'] + "' ";
   anotherString += "><HR><BR>";
   document.writeln(anotherString);
}
else
document.writeln("<BODY>");

document.writeln("<H1>Command Line Tester</H1>");
document.writeln("<P>This page is an example of a
➥dynamically revised page. ");
document.writeln("Some of the information on this page comes from " +
  "the 'command line.'");

if (aString != null && aString != '')
{
   anotherString = "<CENTER><FONT SIZE=7 COLOR='"+
```

```
      gParameters["linkColor"] + "'><EM>";
    anotherString += gParameters["name"] + "</EM></FONT></CENTER>"
    document.write(anotherString);
  }
  else
  {
    anotherString = "<P>This page understands the following parameters:";
    anotherString += "<DL>";
    anotherString +="<DT>textColor<DD>Use hash or word notation to
➥set the text color.";
    anotherString +="<DT>linkColor<DD>Set the color of the unvisited link.";
    anotherString +="<DT>vlinkColor<DD>Set the color of the visited link.";
    anotherString +="<DT>image<DD>Specify a background image from the " +
      "<TT>image</TT> directory.";
    anotherString +="<DT>name<DD>Your name.";
    anotherString +="</DL></P>";
    document.writeln(anotherString);
    anotherString = "<P>Pass these parameters in the URL. For
➥example:<BR>";
    anotherString += "Follow the <A HREF=" + location.href +
        "?textColor=darkblue&linkColor=indianred&vlinkColor=blue&"+
        "image=dots3.gif&name=John+P.+Smith>";
    anotherString += " link</A> to <BR>";
    anotherString += location.href +
      "?textColor=darkblue&linkColor=indianred&vlinkColor=blue&"+
      "image=dots3.gif&name=John+P.+Smith";
    document.writeln(anotherString);
  }
  document.write("<HR></BODY>");
  document.close();
  // -->
</SCRIPT>
</BODY>
</HTML>
```

Note that some of the code in Listing 23.3 relies upon JavaScript 1.1 features, so the <SCRIPT> language is specified as JavaScript1.1. If the user calls the page without passing anything on the command line, the page displays instructions for its use. If the user calls the page as,

**http://*someServer.domain*/cmdLine.com? textColor=darkblue&linkColor=indianred&vlinkColor=blue&image=dots3.gif&name=John+P.+Smith**

the browser displays a page similar to the one shown in Figure 23.1.

**FIG. 23.1**

You can build a page dynamically by specifying the page's parameters on the URL "command line."

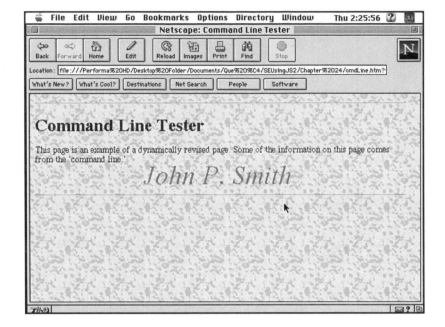

# Cookie Format Specification

While you can certainly use languages like Perl or server-side JavaScript to take apart information on the server, or use client-side JavaScript to pass state information from page to page on the client, these mechanisms are tedious. Netscape supplies an easier method, called *cookies*. Microsoft and other browser vendors have adopted the cookies mechanism, so you can now use cookies with confidence that nearly all browsers handle cookies correctly.

**N O T E**  The complete cookie specification is available online from the Netscape site, located at **http://home.netscape.com/newsref/std/cookie_spec.html**. ▨

To start using a cookie, the server must ask the user's browser to set up the cookie. The server sends a header like:

```
Set-Cookie: NAME=VALUE; expires=DATE; path=PATH; domain=DOMAIN_NAME; secure
```

Let's go through these fields one at a time.

## NAME

The server sets the name to something meaningful for this script. In a shopping cart script, the name might be `OrderID` and the field might read `OrderID=12345`. In a multipart form, the name might be `PRODUCT` and the field might read `PRODUCT=BaffleBlaster`. `NAME` is the only required field in `Set-Cookie`.

## *expires*

Once the server asks the browser to set up a cookie, that cookie remains on the user's machine until the cookie expires. If the server does not set the `expires` field, the cookie is retained only until the user exits the browser. If the user sets `expires` to some date and time in the future, the client writes the cookie to the hard drive (typically when the browser exits).

 If you need to delete a cookie, just set the `expires` field to some time in the past. The client will respond by making the cookie unavailable.

If you direct the client to store the cookie, then, when the user visits your site again, you can read the cookie and recall information you stored about the user on previous visits. You can also download pages with JavaScript and read and process cookie information in your scripts.

For some applications, a cookie might be useful for an indefinite period. For others, the cookie has a definite lifetime. If you are using cookies to build a multipart survey form, the cookie is not useful after the survey ends.

 The format of the expiration date must be followed exactly. Here's an example of that format:

Mon, 03-Jun-96 00:00:00 GMT

GMT, or Greenwich Mean Time, is the only time zone allowed. If you want your cookie to expire at a particular time, you must convert to GMT.

In JavaScript, you can make a new `Date` object, then convert to the proper format by calling the `Date` method `toGMTString()`.

▶ **See** "Using the *Date* Methods," **p. 165**, for more information on the JavaScript `Date` object.

Once the expiration date has been reached, the cookie is no longer stored or given out.

> **CAUTION**
>
> Unexpired cookies are deleted from the client's hard drive if certain internal limits are hit. For example, Netscape has a limit of 300 cookies, with no more than 20 cookies per path and domain. The maximum size of one cookie is 4K.
>
> Microsoft's JScript supports only a single cookie per domain. If several pages on your server set up cookies, be sure to test your site with several versions of Microsoft Internet Explorer (MSIE) to be sure MSIE users do not lose some of your cookies.

## *domain*

Each cookie has only one domain for which it is valid. When a CGI script asks a browser to set up or send its cookie, the browser compares the URL of the server with the domain attributes of its cookies. The browser looks for a *tail match*. That is, if the cookie domain is `xyz.com`, the domain will match `www.xyz.com` or `pluto.xyz.com` or `mercury.xyz.com`. If the domain is one of the seven special top-level domains, the browser expects there to be at least two periods in the matching domain. If the domain is not one of the special seven, there must be at least three periods. The seven special domains are com, edu, net, org, gov, mil, and int. Thus www.xyz.com matches xyz.com, but atl.ga.us does not match ga.us.

If no domain is specified, the browser uses the name of the server as the default domain name.

> **CAUTION**
> Order is important in Set-Cookie. Do not put the domain before the NAME or the browser will become confused and may not assign the correct value to either the NAME or the domain.

## path

If the server domain tail-matches a cookie's domain attribute, the browser performs a path match. The purpose of path-matching is to allow multiple cookies per server. For example, a user visiting **www.xyz.com** might take a survey at **http://www.xyz.com/survey/** and get a cookie named XYZSurvey12. That user might also report a tech support problem at **http://www.xyz.com/techSupport/** and get a cookie called XYZTechSupport. Each of these cookies should set the path so that the appropriate cookie is retrieved later.

Paths match from the top down. A cookie with path /techSupport matches a request from **http://www.xyz.com/techSupport/wordProcessingProducts/**. By default, the path attribute is set to the path of the URL that responded with the Set-Cookie request.

## secure

A cookie is marked secure by putting the word secure at the end of the request. A secure cookie will be sent only to a server offering HTTPS (HTTP over SSL). Netscape's Enterprise and FastTrack Web servers offer HTTPS.

By default, cookies are sent in the clear over nonsecure channels.

**N O T E**   To learn more about setting up a secure server, see Chapter 16, "Establishing RSA Encryption on the FastTrack Server," in *Running a Perfect Netscape Site* (Que, 1996). ▨

# Persistent Data and Cookies

Once you know you are talking to a browser that understands cookies, you can use them in three different ways:

- You can read and write cookies from the server by using a CGI script
- You can read and write persistent data by using server-side JavaScript and LiveWire
- You can manipulate the cookie from your client-side JavaScript

# Getting and Setting Cookies from a CGI Script

Suppose you want to write a server CGI script that reads and writes cookies. You might use Perl and write a script something like the one in Listing 23.4. This script gets and sets a cookie for the fictitious myDomain.net domain. The path is simply root ('/') and the *NAME=VALUE* pair is the number of times this user has visited this site. Since this value should remain on the client's machine for many months, the expiration date is set well into the future (November 9, 1999).

### Listing 23.4   How to Get and Set Cookies

```perl
#!/usr/local/bin/perl
$expirationDate = 'Wed, 09-Nov-99 00:00:00 GMT';
$thePath = '/';
$theDomain = 'myDomain.net';
$header = "Content-type: text/html\nSet-Cookie:";
&RespondToCookie;

sub RespondToCookie
{
  if ($ENV{'HTTP_COOKIE'} =~ /Count/)
  {
    $theCount = &GetTheCount($ENV{'HTTP_COOKIE'});
    &WrapUp;
  }
  else
  {
    $theCookieData = "Count=1\; expires=$expDate\; path=$thePath;
➥Domain=$theDomain\n\n";
    $theText = "$header $theCookieData";
    print $theText;
    print "<HTML><HEAD><TITLE>Welcome</TITLE></HEAD>\n";
    print "<BODY><H1>Welcome</H1>\n";
    print "<P>This visit is your first!</P>\n";
    print "</BODY></HTML>\n";
  }
}

sub GetTheCount
{
  @theCookies = split(/; /,@_[0]);
  foreach (@theCookies)
  {
    ($key, $val) = split(/=/,$_);
    $cookie($key) = $val;
  }
  return $cookie{'count'};
}

sub WrapUp
{
  $theCount++;
```

*continues*

**Listing 23.4    Continued**

```
  $theCookieData = "count=$theCount\; expires=$expDate\; path=$thePath\;
➥Domain=$theDomain\n\n";
  $theText = "$header $theCookieData";
  print $theText;
  print "<HTML><HEAD><TITLE>Thanks again!</TITLE></HEAD>\n";
  print "<BODY><H1>Nice to see you again!</H1>\n";
  print "<P>You have visited this page $theCount times.<P>\n";
  print "</BODY></HTML>\n";
}
```

**N O T E**    If you'd like to learn more about building state into Web pages through CGI scripts, see Chapter 20, "Preserving Data," in *Webmaster Expert Solutions* (Que, 1996). ▪

# Getting and Setting Cookies in LiveWire

If you write CGI scripts that read and write cookies, you need to include code similar to Listing 23.4, shown in the previous section, on every page that needs the cookie's information. For simple purposes, such as keeping a count of the number of visits to your site's home page, that Perl script is adequate. For more complex purposes, such as a shopping cart script, the Perl becomes difficult and the busy programmer looks for another solution.

One such solution is Netscape LiveWire. LiveWire includes many components—only a few of them have anything to do with cookies. Nevertheless, LiveWire so unclutters the process of maintaining user state that, if your site requires user state at all, you should consider LiveWire.

▶ **See** "HTML with JavaScript," **p. 596**, for details about LiveWire and server-side JavaScript.

**N O T E**    For even more information on server-side JavaScript, and LiveWire in general, read *Special Edition Using LiveWire* (Que, 1996). That book dedicates ten chapters to various aspects of JavaScript, including LiveWire's Database Connectivity Library, which allows your server-side JavaScript program to access a relational database. ▪

Fundamentally, state information can be retained in one of only two places: the client or the server. This section describes the mechanisms available to the LiveWire application developer.

The LiveWire Application Manager enables you, as the programmer, to choose from five techniques for state preservation. These choices appear in the right pane of the Application Manager, in the field titled Client Object Maintenance, shown in Figure 23.2.

The client-based choices are:

- client-cookie
- client-url

**FIG. 23.2**
Application Manager affords the developer five techniques for preserving client state.

The server-based choices are:

- server-ip
- server-cookie
- server-url

The remainder of this section describes how these options work and identifies when they are appropriate choices. First, this section describes the non-cookie methods, since they still have a place. Then this section concludes by discussing the two cookie-based solutions.

**Client URL**   The Client URL mechanism takes advantage of the "command line" mechanism described earlier in this chapter, in the section titled "Using the Command Line." Suppose you are running one of LiveWire's built-in demonstration programs—hello.html. If you set Client Object Maintenance to Client URL, you'll see the URL change. The demo program keeps track of the name you enter. If you just entered "Sue" as your name, your URL might be **http://*your.server.domain*/world/hello.html?NETSCAPE_LIVEWIRE.oldname=Sue**.

LiveWire and server-side JavaScript take care of decoding the command line. In your JavaScript program, all you need to do to get the variable oldname is read client.oldname.

The principal advantage of the Client URL method is that it works with all browsers. Most Web sites get an overwhelming majority of their visits from Netscape Navigator or MSIE, but if you have a significant number of visits from browsers that don't understand cookies, Client URL may be worth consideration.

The principal disadvantage of this approach is that, as the number of parameters grows, the URL can become quite long. Some applications have five, ten, or more parameters attached to their client object. Using the client to remember these parameters can take up a fair amount of bandwidth.

> **CAUTION**
>
> Remember from Listing 23.4 that all of the encoding for the URL must be in place before the content is sent back to the client machine. After the page is returned to the client, no more opportunity exists to add or change properties in the LiveWire client object.
>
> If you use any LiveWire methods, try to finish the setup of the client object before you begin to write to the client. Output to the client is written to a 64K buffer. After you've written 64K (or if your server-side JavaScript application calls flush()), the buffer is sent and your opportunity to set any client properties is lost.

> **CAUTION**
>
> Another drawback of both client and server URLs is that the client must stay in the application to preserve the information in the URL. If a user is in the middle of an application and then goes out to another site, their URL information can be lost.

**Server URL**   If you change the Client Object Maintenance option in LiveWire to server-url and rerun the hello.html application, you'll see that the URL has changed to something like **http://***your.server.domain***/world hello.html?NETSCAPE_LIVEWIRE_ID =002822754597**. The URL no longer holds the contents of the client object. Instead, it holds an ID number that points to a bit of shared memory on the server. The client maintains the pointer just like it maintained the data itself when you used client-url. When the user submits the form, LiveWire strips off the ID and uses it to look up the client properties, which it then loads into the client object.

The Server URL mechanism for preserving state offers the same advantage as the Client URL—it works with any browser, not just those which understand cookies. It also consumes less bandwidth because only the ID number is passed back and forth to the server.

**Server IP**   Another approach that works with all browsers—though not with all service providers—is the Server IP mechanism.

If you switch LiveWire's Client Object Maintenance option to server-ip, you won't see anything unusual appearing in the URL. Instead, the server keeps track of which user is which by examining the client's Internet Protocol (IP) address. This approach works well as long as each client has a unique, fixed IP address. On the Internet, though, that assumption often breaks down.

Intranets—internal networks typically found in larger organizations—often have most of their machines permanently online. A large company may have a single Class B license, giving them over 65,000 unique addresses. For most intranets, server-ip can offer all of the advantages of the URL-based methods, yet consumes no extra bandwidth at all.

Of course, many intranets are large enough for applications to be accessed through in-house proxy servers. This design can break the server-ip method as well because each request comes to the application from the IP address of the proxy server.

Furthermore, there is a growing trend to put some applications on the *extranet*—an intranet that makes some sites available to select Internet users, such as customers or suppliers.

In short, feel free to use Server IP if you can, but be aware of the restrictions.

**Client Cookies** In order to see LiveWire's cookie-based mechanisms in action, you need to be able to read the cookie on the server. Persistent cookies (those that survive the shutdown of the browser) are stored in a disk file on the client machine. For example, Netscape Navigator stores cookies on a Windows computer in a file called cookies.txt. On a UNIX machine, Navigator uses the file name cookies. On the Mac, the file is called MagicCookie. These files are simple ASCII text—you can examine them with a text editor. Don't change them, though, or you may confuse the applications that wrote them.

Most LiveWire applications' cookies don't make it into the cookies file, however, because they are set to expire when the user quits the browser. The easiest way to see a LiveWire application's cookie is to pretend to be the browser.

**N O T E**  As an application programmer, you can set the `client` to expire a given number of seconds after the last request. The default is 600 seconds, or 10 minutes. ■

If an application calls the `client.expiration()` method and uses one of the cookie-based `client` state maintenance mechanisms, the browser saves the cookie to the hard drive (though often not until the user quits the browser).

If you'd like to see a LiveWire cookie, set the Client Object Maintenance option for the world application to client-cookie. Then use Telnet to call your server.

By default, Web servers listen to port 80. If the URL for the world application is **http://your.server.domain/world/**, connect to port 80. If the URL looks like **http://your.server.domain:somePort/world/**, connect to the indicated port.

After you are connected, send

```
HEAD /world/hello.html http/1.0
```

Press the Enter key *twice* after typing that line—once to end the line, and once to tell the server that you've sent all the header lines (in this case, none). Note that the HEAD method is used because you don't want to see all the lines of the page—just the header.

Your server responds with something like this:

```
HTTP/1.0 200 OK
Server: Netscape-FastTrack/2.0a
Date: Sat, 28 Dec 1996 10:52:32 GMT
Set-cookie: NETSCAPE_LIVEWIRE.number=0; path=/world
Set-cookie: NETSCAPE_LIVEWIRE.oldname=null; path=/world
Content-type: text/html
```

You'll recognize the Set-cookie: header lines from the discussion in "Cookie Format Specification," earlier in this chapter. The Set-cookie: lines tell the browser to remember this information and send it back with subsequent requests.

> **CAUTION**
>
> Like the URL mechanisms, Set-cookie: header lines must be sent to the client before the page contents. Try to set up the client object's properties before sending content. You must set up the client's properties before the buffer flushes at 64K or you'll miss your chance to put the properties in the cookie.

**Server Cookies**   Like client URLs, client cookies can start consuming a fair amount of bandwidth. More importantly, large numbers of client properties can overflow the browser cookie table. Recall that Netscape has a limit of 300 cookies, with no more than 20 cookies per path and domain. Microsoft Internet Explorer's limits are even tighter. The maximum size of one cookie is 4K. If your application requires more client properties, consider switching to *short cookies*, called server-cookie in LiveWire Application Manager.

Using the short cookie technique, the cookie contains an ID number that identifies where on the server the data may be found. For example, a shopping cart script may use a cookie on the user's machine to store the fact that this shopper is working on order number 142. When the shopper connects to the server, the server looks up its record of order 142 to find out what items are on the order.

If you change the Client Object Maintenance for the world application to server-cookie and rerun the Telnet experiment described in the last section, you'll find that the header only has one Set-cookie: line. That line now looks something like:

```
Set-cookie: NETSCAPE_LIVEWIRE_ID=002823513984; path=/world;
➥expires Sun, 29 Dec 1996 19:13:44 GMT
```

All of the other header lines look like they did before.

Note first that the short cookie is an ID number—it works the same way the ID did in the server URL. Note, too, the expiration date. A user can get this cookie, exit the browser, and then restart the browser and still join their old client object (as long as the server and the LiveWire application have not been shut down in the meantime).

On intranets, where many of the browsers are cookie-aware, server-cookies have a lot of advantages. Because they write only one cookie (with the ID) to the browser, the network overhead is negligible, and the browser's cookie table is unlikely to overflow.

On the Internet, a Webmaster still has to deal with the possibility of getting visits from browsers that don't know about cookies. These visits are becoming increasingly infrequent. Nevertheless, if this issue is important at your site, you may be best served by setting Client Object Maintenance to a mechanism like server-url, which is browser-independent.

 **TIP** If you use LiveWire, you can set a default state-preservation mechanism. After you've chosen the mechanism that will work for most of your applications, go back to Application Manager, choose the `Config` link, and select your chosen mechanism as the default.

Part
IV
Ch
23

## Reading and Writing Cookies in Client-Side JavaScript

In general, servers are more powerful machines than desktop clients. Often, you can take advantage of this fact by distributing processing between the two machines and piggybacking information for the client onto the client's state preservation mechanism.

Here's an example of how that works: Suppose you are using client cookies as your state preservation mechanism (either through LiveWire or through a CGI script). The client-side JavaScript object `document.cookie` contains the cookies which match the domain and path of your Web page. If you're setting up cookies through LiveWire, the cookies all have names which begin with `NETSCAPE_LIVEWIRE`. The client-side JavaScript function `getCookie()` gives the client access to its cookies. (If you're not using LiveWire, you should modify or delete the `NETSCAPE_LIVEWIRE.` string in these functions.) Listing 23.5 shows `getCookie()`.

**Listing 23.5   Use This Function to Read Cookies from the Client**

```
function getCookie(Name)
{
  var search = "NETSCAPE_LIVEWIRE." + Name + "=";
  var RetStr = "";
  var offset = 0;
  var end    = 0;
  if (document.cookie.length > 0)
  {
    offset = document.cookie.indexOf(search);
    if (offset != -1)
    {
      offset += search.length;
      end = document.cookie.indexOf(";", offset);
      if (end == -1)
        end = document.cookie.length;
      RetStr = unescape(document.cookie.substring(offset, end));
    }
  }
  return (RetStr);
}
```

Likewise, the tiny setCookie() function sets up a LiveWire cookie from the client. Be sure to change or remove the reference to NETSCAPE_LIVEWIRE. if you build your own cookies in a CGI script. Listing 23.6 shows setCookie().

**Listing 23.6   This Function Writes the Cookie from Client-Side JavaScript**

```
function setCookie(Name, Value, Expire)
{
  document.cookie = "NETSCAPE_LIVEWIRE." + Name + "=" +
    escape(Value) +
    (Expire == null ? "" : ("; expires = " +
        Expire.toGMTString()));
}
```

Listing 23.7 shows these two functions in action. The functions getCookie() and setCookie() are omitted here for clarity.

**Listing 23.7   Use a Cookie from the Client Script**

```
<HTML>
<HEAD>
<TITLE>Cookie Tester</TITLE>
<SCRIPT LANGUAGE="JavaScript">
<!--
function getCookie(...)
{
...
}
function setCookie(...)
{
...
}
// -->
</SCRIPT>
</HEAD>
<BODY BGCOLOR="white">
<H1>Cookie Tester</H1>
<SCRIPT LANGUAGE="JavaScript">
<!--
var killDate = new Date();
killDate.setDate(killDate.getDate = 7);
var value = getCookie("answer")
if (value == "")
  setCookie("answer", "42", killDate);
else
  document.write("The answer is " + value + ".");
// -->
</SCRIPT>
</BODY>
</HTML>
```

# CHAPTER 24

# Debugging JavaScript Applications

In an ideal world, our code would work right the first time, would never need maintenance, and the customer would always be delighted with the product.

It's not an ideal world. Oh, boy, is it ever not an ideal world.

Whether our defect rate is one defect per hundred lines of code, or one defect per thousand, we'd all like perfect code. This chapter contains hints, tips, and lessons learned from hard development, tailored to the server-side JavaScript environment. ▨

## What testing is good for

You can't rely on it, but you don't dare skip it.

## How to prepare for testing

You can reduce test time and increase product quality by getting ready for testing before you write a single line of code.

## How to prepare to debug your code

Put debug hooks into the design, not just the code.

## How to use JavaScript's debugger

Speed up the debug process by knowing what to expect from the debugger.

## Where to look for error messages

Many software tools generate misleading error messages. Learn how to interpret them properly to save time during test and deployment.

# Testing 101

Everyone in the software industry agrees that our defect rates are too high. Software products—many of them mission-critical systems—fail far too often, sometimes making headlines in ways that most of us would like to forget.

This section provides a high-level look at why applications fail, and a few tips on how to reduce the defect rate.

## Five Reasons Why Software Fails

Among the top causes of software defects and project failures are the following:

- **Inadequate analysis** The developer and the customer never agreed on what the product must do. This problem is notorious in large projects, where the customer's needs may change dramatically during the life of the product.

- **Inadequate design** The developer, feeling the press of the schedule, begins to code before many of the design issues are thought out.

- **Unrealistic budget and schedule expectations** All too many projects are bid with "price-to-win" budgets and development schedules. Too late, management discovers that the resources are stretched too thin, and they solve the problem by cutting analysis, design, and test time—anything that doesn't look like coding.

- **Unrealistic quality expectations** Although everyone wants zero defects, no one has figured out how to get there. The measures of quality in software projects are expressed in defects per thousands of lines of code—or sometimes, in defects per hundreds of lines of code. Good analysis, design, and coding practices can bring those defect rates down. Good testing can confirm that the process was done right.

- **Failure to build a test plan** If the test plan is built before the code is written, directly from the design document, it becomes almost easy to pass the test. It's like taking an exam when you've had access to the key. Write the test plan early and pass the test every time.

## What Testing Can't Do

At its worst, software testing pokes and prods the product a bit, uncovers some obvious defects, and finally runs out of time before the schedule and the budget say the product has to ship.

At its best, software testing can confirm that the defect rate is very, very low by exercising the function of the software under a variety of loads and input conditions.

No amount of testing, no matter how thorough, can ever prove the product is defect-free. And no amount of testing, no matter how many defects it discovers, ever adds value to a product.

If testing doesn't add value, what does it add? One answer is confidence. The best software engineering organizations develop processes that, when followed, result in code with a low defect rate. The organizations use these tests as one way of confirming that the processes worked.

Another thing testing adds is cost. Other ways—often less expensive ways—can build confidence in the software. Table 24.1 shows the defect-detection rates of ten different Software Quality Assurance (SQA) activities.

**Table 24.1  The Best Way to Detect Defects Is by Using a Combination of Methods**

| Removal Step | Lowest Rate | Modal Rate | Highest Rate |
| --- | --- | --- | --- |
| Personal checking of design documents | 15% | 35% | 70% |
| Informal group design reviews | 20% | 40% | 60% |
| Formal design inspections | 35% | 55% | 75% |
| Formal code inspections | 30% | 60% | 70% |
| Modeling or prototyping | 35% | 65% | 80% |
| Personal desk-checking of code | 20% | 40% | 60% |
| Unit testing (single routines) | 10% | 25% | 50% |
| Function testing (related routines) | 20% | 35% | 55% |
| Integration testing (complete systems) | 25% | 45% | 60% |
| Field testing (live data) | 35% | 50% | 65% |
| Cumulative effect of complete series | 93% | 99% | 99% |

Part
**IV**

Ch
**24**

As you can see in this table, the best modal defect-detection rate for any kind of *test* (field testing) is only 50 percent, and the best single *technique* (modeling or prototyping) has a modal defect- detection rate of only 65 percent. The effect of using all of these techniques is the detection of 99 percent of all defects.

Watts Humphrey of the Software Engineering Institute at Carnegie-Mellon University found that, in a 1989 study (reported in his book *Managing the Software Process*, published by Addison-Wesley), organizations get more efficient at finding defects through inspections as they gain experience.

A 1987 study at the Software Engineering Laboratory (Basili and Selby, "Comparing the Effectiveness of Software Testing Strategies," *IEEE Transactions on Software Engineering*, SE-13, no. 12 (December): 1278-96) found that code reading detected about 80 percent more faults per hour than testing. The evidence suggests that as an organization gains experience in non-test mechanisms for finding defects, the cost of defect detection begins to favor combinations of techniques, with much of the effort spent in inspections and other forms of review.

 **T I P**  Don't rely on general data. Do your own study of an organizational or even a personal level. Keep track of how much time you spend on various kinds of defect-detecting activities. Keep a time sheet and measure the labor at 15-minute increments. Then, keep a log of how many defects you find in each activity.

While you're at it, try to identify where in the software development process the defect was inserted—analysis, design, implementation, or even debug and maintenance.

## Designing for Test

One reason testing is difficult is the complexity of software. The classic measure of complexity in software is Tom McCabe's *Complexity Metric*. McCabe's metric says to compute complexity through a simple three-step process designed to count the number of paths through the code.

1. Start with 1 to capture the straight-line path through the code.

2. Add 1 for each of the keywords if, while, repeat, for, and, and or.

3. Add 1 for each case in a case statement. If the case statement doesn't have a default case, add 1 more.

Now consider the following function, written in pseudocode. This function can be implemented in C, C++, JavaScript, or any of a number of languages, but the issues discussed in this section should come up during design, when the modules are still in pseudocode or similar design-level notation.

```
function bubbleSort(array of integers theInts)
{
do
{
Boolean switched = false;
for (int i=0; i<the number of elements in theInts - 1; i++)
if (theInts[i] > theInts[i+1])
{
int temp = theInts[i+1];
theInts[i+1] = theInts[i];
theInts[i] = temp;
switched = true;
}
} while (true == switched);

// pass theInts back by reference
return;
}
```

Start with 1 for the straight-line path. Add 1 for the for, 1 for the if, and 1 for the while. This implementation of BubbleSort has four decision points; to properly test this function, the designer may have to look at $2^4$ or 16 test cases.

The number of test cases rises quickly as the system's average complexity metric climbs. Suppose the system has 25 decision points—a very modest number. If all of that logic is in a single routine, there are potentially $2^{25}$ test cases. That's a whopping 33,554,432 steps in the testing procedure. If the same system is rearranged into 5 independent modules, with 5 decision points each, the number of test cases drops to $5 \times 2^5$, or 160.

As a rule of thumb, strive to keep the complexity of each module between 1 and 5. As it climbs above 5, look for ways to simplify the design. If the complexity is above 10, break some of the logic into another function that can be called from the first. That's not a hard and fast rule, but you should very carefully think through any design that has a McCabe's metric higher than 10, and be prepared to defend your decision to not simplify it.

*Functional testing* is used by outsiders to verify that the requirements are met. *White-box* (also known as "glass-box" testing) is done in the context of the source code and takes advantage of special knowledge the programmer might have, such as where the decision points are. Complexity analyses, such as the McCabe computation shown here, help you do functional testing in a white-box context.

**TIP** During analysis, prepare a test plan from the requirements documents. Format the requirements documents with number requirements of the form, "The system shall do this" and "The system shall do that."

Then carry the numbering over to the test plan—each numbered requirement results in one or more procedures in the test plan. Select the test procedures based on the decision points identified during the computation of McCabe's metric.

For example, one requirement may say, "The system shall generate a list of scores, sorted from lowest to highest." The test plan may say, "Verify that the scores are correctly sorted." The procedure may call for the following:

- A test case in which the array is already sorted
- A test case in which the array is empty
- A test case in which the array has exactly one element
- A test case in which the array has exactly two elements and they are out of order
- All the meaningful combinations of these cases, such as a two-element array with the elements already sorted, and so forth

# Unit Testing

Unit testing is the white-box testing of a single routine, usually by the programmer who developed the routine. The work of building a successful routine (or unit) begins long before formal testing; the early steps of unit testing begin during analysis and design. Here's a recommended process for conducting unit tests:

1. During analysis, develop test cases to cover each requirement. Expand the requirements to include security issues, installation procedures, and disk, memory, and performance goals.

2. As soon as the units are identified, allocate test cases (or portions of them) to each unit. As the unit is designed, add and refine test cases to cover all of the decision points. Look for opportunities to simplify the unit, either by redesigning the code or by moving complexity into separate routines.

3. Use basis testing (described later in this chapter) to select test cases for the first round of unit testing.

4. Add data-flow tests (also described later) after the initial tests are working.

5. Add other test cases not already run to ensure that all requirements are met.

6. As changes are made to correct defects, rerun all test cases—a process known as *regression testing*.

**T I P**

Design the module and the test cases so that the module can read test data from an ASCII file and write results the same way. If the module cannot be set up to read and write ASCII, build a test harness that does use ASCII and that converts commands into the module's required format.

Save each test case in an ASCII command file. After the module is working, save the output in a file of known correct results—called *golden output*. Then write a command script that reruns all the commands during regression testing by feeding the test cases to the module, one at a time, and comparing the output files with the golden output to ensure that there are no changes.

With this setup, you can run a complete regression test just by typing **regress** from the command line and waiting for the results.

When you initially estimate the size and cost of an application, consider the time required to build test harnesses as well. Sometimes you may want to change a design to be able to reuse existing test-support code or to eliminate a requirement for such support code.

**Basis Testing**  Basis testing is a method of using McCabe's complexity metric to identify a minimal set of test cases. Using McCabe's metric, identify each decision point in the code. At each decision point, the execution can go one of two ways. Design test cases to cover each of the two paths—but combine them into as small a number of test cases as possible. In the BubbleSort example, you may have four test cases, as follows:

- One in which the for statement immediately exits because the number of elements in the array is zero or one
- One in which the for statement runs through one loop (two elements in the array) and finds that the elements are already sorted
- One in which a two-element array is out of order and must be iterated twice
- One in which the loop counter can increment—so there are at least three elements in the array—and the array is completely reversed

Basis testing certainly does not prove your code is correct; no testing can do that. But once you pass basis testing, your confidence that the code is essentially correct goes up.

**Data-Flow Testing** By some estimates, half of all modern routines consist of data declarations and initializations. In *data-flow analysis*, each piece of data is considered to have two attributes: a state and where it is in its life cycle.

Here are the states:

- *Defined* The variable has been initialized but not yet used.
- *Used* The variable has been read or written into.
- *Killed* The variable has gone out of scope or in some other way is no longer meaning-ful. An object pointed to by a pointer may have been deleted, or a record may be in a database that has been closed.

---

 **TIP** In languages like C, C++, and Java, you have to declare the type of each variable. JavaScript is dynamically typed; you don't need to think as much about types. In fact, the JavaScript variable-declaration keyword var is optional.

Use var anyway. That way, you can spot at a glance the places where a variable is declared for the first time. The compiler won't care, but it can make it easier to spot problems and can serve as the basis for writing your own testing tools.

Part IV
Ch 24

---

Here are the steps in the data life cycle:

- *Entered* A routine that uses the variable has started, but the variable hasn't been used yet.
- *Exited* The control flow has passed out of the routine that uses the variable.

Figure 24.1 shows nine combinations of states for data. The usual life cycle is that the data is defined, used (one or more times), and then perhaps killed. A problem may be indicated, for example, if a variable skips steps in that life cycle or runs through a single step more than once (except for used).

**FIG. 24.1**

Data-flow analysis identifies variables as having one of nine possible life cycles.

 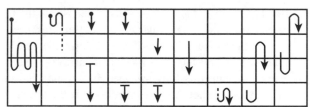

To conduct data-flow testing, add test cases to those identified during basis testing. The new test cases should, as a minimum, test every place in the unit where data is defined.

Preferably, your test cases will cover every defined-used combination. Review the test cases identified during basis testing. If there are paths through the code in which a variable is de-fined in one place and used in another, make sure you have test cases to cover all the possible combinations. For example, in the `BubbleSort`, if two elements need to be switched, the variable `temp` is both declared and used. If no elements need to be swapped, `temp` is never declared at all.

> **TIP**
> Studies have found that the closer a variable's declaration is to its point of use, the less likely the programmer is to make a mistake in using it. Both C++ and JavaScript enable you to declare variables anywhere. If your experience is in C, try to lose the habit of declaring all variables at the top. Dropping that habit decreases the number of data-flow test cases you have to add, and it decreases the likelihood of making an error.

**Equivalence Partitioning**   Analyze the routine to find out how much of the function's input is equivalent to each test case. For example, in the `BubbleSort` function, sorting the five-element array [1,2,3,4,5] doesn't appear to test anything that wasn't already tested with the four-element array [1,2,3,4]. Save yourself some time by recognizing that two test cases are equivalent and by running only one of them.

**Redesigning Trouble Spots**   As you continue with tests, you often discover that one piece of the code has far more defects than the others. Pick a limit as to how many defects you'll tolerate. For example, say you average 10 defects per 1,000 lines of code, with a variance of about 10 lines. You may decide that 20 defects per 1,000 may be a good starting point—or 2 defects allowed in a 100-line module.

Adjust the "kill" threshold up or down as you gain experience with your own defect rate. When a piece of code is responsible for too many defects, don't try to fix it. Scrap it, and redesign it. Because 10 to 20 percent of the code is responsible for up to 80 percent of the defects, you'll usually save time and money redoing it right rather than trying to tinker with it. Scrapping a few troublesome routines may reduce your test time by 80 percent.

**Boundary Analysis**   Most programmers are familiar with the off-by-one error. Should that condition be less-than, or less-than or equal-to? Should the comparison be with x or $x - 1$?

Don't guess. Build in test cases that demonstrate the boundaries are handled correctly. For a given boundary, you may be able to run three test cases—the boundary minus 1, the boundary plus 1, and the boundary itself. Clearly, two elements is an interesting boundary in the `BubbleSorter` because the two-element array is the smallest test case where the numbers are compared and, potentially, swapped. If your machine supports up to 32,767 positive integers, what happens when 32,768 elements are in the array?

Look at complex combinations of boundaries. Suppose your code has two numbers that are multiplied. What happens when they are both large at the same time?

**Load Testing**   Look for ways to give the program valid data, but give it too much; if the maximum integer is 32,757, load in 32,767 of them—each one, 32,767!

If performance is a factor (as it typically is in Web applications), have dozens, or even hundreds, of people access your application simultaneously. Instrument the code—add code to report what is happening internally—to find out where it is bottlenecking. Is everyone waiting for the `project` to unlock? Does someone lock the server and forget about it?

**Stress Testing**   Finally, give the routine invalid data to check out the user interface. What happens to the `BubbleSorter` if one of the integers in the array is the letter j? What should happen?

With integer input, think about negative input or integers that exceed MAXINT for the architecture. Enter negative values. Put in too many values. Put in no data. If your routine expects another routine to preprocess the data for it, test your routine without the preprocessor. Does your routine recognize the problem and reject the data? (That situation will occur someday during maintenance.)

Also, test data that is marginally valid. Run with integers that are set to MAXINT. Test nominal cases, and test at the edges of the valid range.

> **TIP**  If the routine must work with old data from a legacy system or prior version, be sure to test for backwards compatibility.
>
> When you choose data, choose data that will be easy to spot if something goes wrong. For example, the sorted array input for the bubble sort can be 111, 222, 333, and so on. If the bubble sort fails, the out-of-sequence numbers should be readily obvious.

**Test for the "I Did It Again" Error**   For most of us, bad habits are difficult to break. Develop (or reuse) an error taxonomy that suits your language, environment, and kinds of programs. Every time you make an error, classify it and add it to the count.

After you have a feel for the kinds of mistakes you make (or the kind that are common in your organization), add test cases to look for those errors. If you know that you often mess up `switch` statements, pay particular attention to the test results of the cases. Consider adding some tests that exercise that code better.

Eventually, you'll learn not to make those kinds of mistakes. Keep your statistics updated. When the problem gets better, rerun your evaluation and start focusing on the new kind of mistakes you make.

> **TIP**  The very best software engineers keep a multi-section project notebook. Three-ring binders with tabs work well. In these binders, the engineers keep their time logs, design notes, test plans, and test results for their units. Periodically, they read through their old notebooks, looking for trends and insights. They use this information to improve their personal processes and reduce their defect rate.

# Designing for Debug

As testing proceeds, you and other testers will identify defects in your code. Expect these because you know that no one has a zero-defect rate; you know your code has defects. If the defects don't come out during inspections, walk-throughs, or testing, don't presume that your code is clean; it just means you haven't found the defects yet.

This section shows how to organize to repair defects quickly, especially in server-side JavaScript.

**Organizing the Process**   Make sure that everyone who touches the product—from testers and programmers to end users—has an opportunity to report defects. Provide them with a form to fill out that gives you the information you will need to reproduce and isolate the problem. Figure 24.2 shows a trouble report you might provide an end user.

**FIG. 24.2**

Every application should have a Customer Trouble Report (CTR).

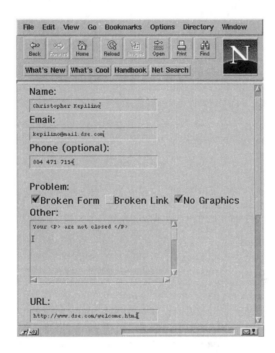

As Defect Reports and CTRs come in, follow this seven-step procedure to resolve the errors:

1. Log in the CTRs and Defect Reports. If the product is fielded, use the date of the CTR to give the customer regular feedback on how the fix is coming along.

2. Rank the reports by severity.

3. Assign the reports to engineers who try to reproduce the failure. Once they have a reproducible failure, they should proceed to fault-isolate it.

4. Most faults can be isolated to a single module. Send isolated modules to the engineer responsible for that unit.

5. After the defect is reported as fixed, run a regression test on the module. Modify the regression test, adding a test case that would have caught the defect.

6. Depending on the severity, decide when you will release the maintenance fix. You may release one for a fatal error or accumulate several cosmetic and minor defects into a later release.

7. Fully regression test the product before each release.

**Using *make* and the *cpp*** C development environments nearly always include a program called the *C Preprocessor* (cpp). This program accepts directives like

```
#define MOBILE
#ifdef MOBILE
// use this code for the mobile version
  .
  .
  .
#else
// use this code for the fixed version
  .
  .
  .
#endif
```

Despite its name, nothing about cpp ties it to the C language. You can put a cpp directive in your .html and .js files and pass them through the C Preprocessor. That way, you can include chunks of code that dump all of the interesting variables in a routine or that call special debug versions of functions.

To further automate this process, use the make utility, which also comes with most C and C++ development environments. make enables you to specify a series of targets and declare which files those targets depend on. When you make target, make looks at each component of the target to figure out which files it needs to update. It updates each file by running programs specified in rules you give it.

Give each version of your files a unique file extension, and then you can set up a Makefile (the command file for make) that knows enough to build your whole application. You can call JavaScript files with cpp directives .jsc. When you type make, the utility knows enough to run cpp on those files, naming the output .js. Now, by switching on a -dDEBUG switch, you can build a debug version of your application. If you have many files that make up the application, you can turn DEBUG on in just those modules where you suspect trouble.

Statements that provide some useful debugging information are covered later in this chapter in the section, "JavaScript Debugging Features."

**Psychology of Debugging** Some people approach testing and debugging with a defensive attitude: "Prove there's a problem in my code." There is something to be said for surprise; with a regimen of design and code reviews, walk-throughs, inspections, and code reading, defects that make it into testing should be so rare that a raised eyebrow and a bit of skepticism are justified.

But the defect-free application hasn't been built yet. If you know that you typically have about 10 defects per 1,000 lines of code when you begin testing, and you have a 1,000-line application (a modest size by today's standards), you can expect about 10 defects. If testing only finds 3, something is probably wrong. Somewhere around 7 defects are waiting to be found. If they're found before deployment, you'll have to rush to fix them to stay on schedule. But if they are still in the code when it ships, you can count on them being found: one at a time, painfully, by an increasingly irate customer or user.

With a bit of attitude adjustment, you begin to welcome defect reports; it's easier to fix the problem during testing than after the application is in use.

**N O T E**   The term bug is dropping out of favor among the better software engineers. Bugs connote some cute little creature that needs to be hunted down, examined, and then exterminated. The term has been in use so long that it doesn't carry the shock value of the word defect. ■

**A Debugging Toolkit**   With most defects, half the battle is duplication, the other half is fault isolation. Web applications live in a changing environment. A defect that was reported this morning may not be reproducible this afternoon. Work with testers and users to ensure that defect reports come in with a complete set of data, which is needed to reproduce the problem. Try to get defect reports turned in quickly, and try to have one of the maintenance programmers get right to work on them. Reproduce the problem before the changing Web environment makes the problem irreproducible.

If you can't reproduce the problem, leave the trouble report open and accumulate similar defect reports until a pattern becomes apparent. Form hypotheses, and then examine the code or devise tests to confirm or deny the hypotheses.

After a defect is reproducible, trace the failure page-by-page and function-by-function through the application. In the interest of time, you may want to print the current values of all variables in a routine or page in the middle of the application. Continue to cut the suspect code in half until you spot the problem. Figure 24.3 illustrates this technique.

**FIG. 24.3**
Track a reproducible failure through the application by successively splitting in half the section with the defect.

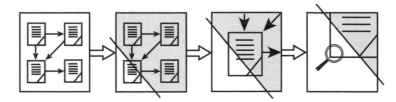

 **T I P**   If you're not getting anywhere with a defect, try consulting someone else for help. The other person need not be a programmer; he or she may not even understand a word you say. Often, just the act of describing the problem to a person who has little understanding of the technology gives you insight that leads to a solution.

Of course, if no one else is around, you can try describing the problem to yourself. Be careful about performing this exercise aloud, though. Your coworkers may begin to worry about you.

**TIP** Here's another thing to try if you're stuck: Go back and reread your test notebook on this module. See whether you tested these cases before. Look at what kinds of problems you and others have had with this code. Check to see whether it's an "I did it again" error.

If all else fails, rewrite the offending section of code. Implement things a little differently. You'll either fix the problem with the new code, or you'll get insight as to why the old code failed—and possibly be able to go back and fix the old code faster than you can bring up the new.

# Debugging Server-Side JavaScript

JavaScript was designed for simple scripting, not for programs with thousands of lines of code. However, JavaScript is growing up fast with its increasingly sophisticated server-side programs, server-side integration with relational databases, and client-side integration into Java and plug-ins through LiveConnect.

## The Trace Utility

Go to Application Manager and select the application "world" in the left pane. Now click the debug link near the bottom of the left pane. Enter a few characters and press Enter to get the trace rolling. The resulting window is shown in Figure 24.4.

**N O T E** Notice from the URL that you can put an application in the trace utility without going through Application Manager's home page. Just point your browser to **http:// your.server.com/appmgr/debug.html?name=world.** n ▪

**FIG. 24.4**
Although the link says "Debug," this window is the trace utility.

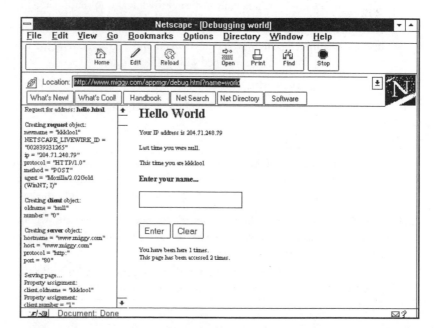

Scroll through the information in the left pane. You will want to be familiar with the application or have the source code in front of you to determine whether the application's behavior is reasonable.

## The *debug* Function

Server-side JavaScript includes a top-level function called debug(). Pass a variable or other expression as the parameter to debug(), and run the application in the trace facility. You then see the output of the debug() call as a "Debug message" in the left pane.

 **TIP**  If you need more room to see the application and its trace, go to the Config link in Application Manager, and set "Debug Output" to "Other Window."

## Calling *write()*

Often, all of the variables appear to have the correct answer, but the output in the browser window is not correct. Look for critical values and use write() to send them to the browser. Couple this technique with View | Document Source and the make/cpp technique described earlier in this chapter, and you have a powerful mechanism for turning on debug statements that send their output to the browser rather than the trace facility.

## *lwcomp -d -c*

Another tool to use is the LiveWire compiler's debug switch. The -d switch on the compiler causes the compiler to output the same code that it is converting to bytecodes. Because the output can be long, you'll usually just want to look at one routine at a time.

To avoid rebuilding the Web file while you are examining the output, don't use the -o switch. Instead, use the -c switch, which tells the compiler to just check the file. Check just one file at a time to keep from being swamped with output. Thus,

```
lwcomp -d -c hello.html
```

returns the compiler's interpretation of the code in hello.html.

## Searching the Logs

Software at all levels of the system are writing messages to logs that may help you isolate a problem. For that matter, consider opening a file yourself and keeping your own error log. This section describes four logs that may give you some insight during debugging.

**The Server Error Log**   The Netscape server keeps several logs. The most useful of these for debugging is the error log. The *Web server error log* contains a record of all output sent by the application to the program's "standard output" file handle. This log also records the client requests that generate a server error—any request answered with a status code outside the 200-series.

Bear in mind that the status codes were defined when the Web was defined by static HTML. Some of the messages may require a bit of interpretation to understand them in the context of an application.

**The System Error Log**   Most operating systems maintain a *system error log*. On a Windows NT system, examine entries in the Event Viewer, in the Administrative Tools Program Group. Figure 24.5 shows the Event Viewer window.

Most versions of UNIX have built-in tools to display and filter the error log, similar to the Windows NT Event Viewer. Figure 24.6 shows the AIX System Management Interface Tool (SMIT) running the errpt command.

**FIG. 24.5**

The Windows NT Event Viewer can show a System Log, an Application Log, and a Security Log.

| Event Viewer - Application Log on \\MIGGY | | | | | | |
|---|---|---|---|---|---|---|
| Log   View   Options   Help | | | | | | |
| Date | Time | Source | Category | Event | User | Computer |
| 7/2/96 | 11:13:56 AM | DNS | None | 3 | N/A | MIGGY |
| 7/2/96 | 10:52:45 AM | nsctrs | None | 2000 | N/A | MIGGY |
| 7/2/96 | 10:42:37 AM | DNS | None | 3 | N/A | MIGGY |
| 7/2/96 | 10:41:51 AM | DNS | None | 3 | N/A | MIGGY |
| 7/2/96 | 10:41:51 AM | DNS | None | 3 | N/A | MIGGY |
| 7/2/96 | 10:41:51 AM | DNS | None | 3 | N/A | MIGGY |
| 7/2/96 | 10:41:51 AM | DNS | None | 3 | N/A | MIGGY |
| 7/2/96 | 10:41:50 AM | DNS | None | 3 | N/A | MIGGY |
| 7/2/96 | 10:41:50 AM | DNS | None | 3 | N/A | MIGGY |
| 7/2/96 | 10:36:57 AM | DNS | None | 3 | N/A | MIGGY |
| 7/2/96 | 10:16:04 AM | DNS | None | 3 | N/A | MIGGY |
| 7/2/96 | 9:57:38 AM | DNS | None | 3 | N/A | MIGGY |
| 7/1/96 | 2:12:26 PM | DNS | None | 3 | N/A | MIGGY |
| 7/1/96 | 2:11:41 PM | DNS | None | 3 | N/A | MIGGY |
| 7/1/96 | 2:10:16 PM | DNS | None | 3 | N/A | MIGGY |
| 7/1/96 | 1:40:00 PM | DNS | None | 3 | N/A | MIGGY |
| 7/1/96 | 1:39:59 PM | DNS | None | 3 | N/A | MIGGY |
| 7/1/96 | 1:39:59 PM | DNS | None | 3 | N/A | MIGGY |
| 7/1/96 | 1:39:59 PM | DNS | None | 3 | N/A | MIGGY |
| 7/1/96 | 1:39:59 PM | DNS | None | 3 | N/A | MIGGY |
| 7/1/96 | 1:39:53 PM | Autochk | None | 1024 | N/A | MIGGY |
| 7/1/96 | 3:45:30 AM | DNS | None | 3 | N/A | MIGGY |
| 6/30/96 | 6:16:39 PM | DNS | None | 3 | N/A | MIGGY |
| 6/30/96 | 6:16:39 PM | DNS | None | 3 | N/A | MIGGY |
| 6/30/96 | 6:16:39 PM | DNS | None | 3 | N/A | MIGGY |

**The Database Error Log**   If your application uses a relational database, be sure to visit the RDBMS's *error log*. Even if the application is showing no defects, you should review this log regularly; some kinds of problems are logged long before they cause operational impact to the user.

**The Server Access Log**   For some kinds of problems, the *server access log* can give additional insight. This log shows each request. If necessary, you can use this log, the information about HTTP, and the technique of using telnet to mimic the browser to get a copy of exactly what the browser gets, including headers.

**FIG. 24.6**

AIX, IBM's UNIX, shows the error log through the SMIT utility.

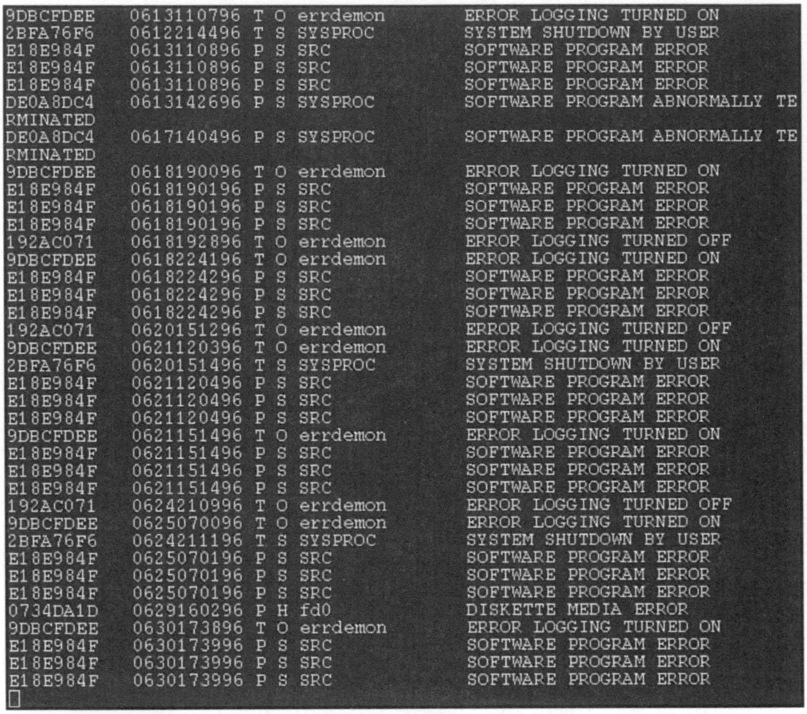

```
9DBCFDEE    0613110796  T  O  errdemon    ERROR LOGGING TURNED ON
2BFA76F6    0612214496  T  S  SYSPROC     SYSTEM SHUTDOWN BY USER
E18E984F    0613110896  P  S  SRC         SOFTWARE PROGRAM ERROR
E18E984F    0613110896  P  S  SRC         SOFTWARE PROGRAM ERROR
E18E984F    0613110896  P  S  SRC         SOFTWARE PROGRAM ERROR
DE0A8DC4    0613142696  P  S  SYSPROC     SOFTWARE PROGRAM ABNORMALLY TE
RMINATED
DE0A8DC4    0617140496  P  S  SYSPROC     SOFTWARE PROGRAM ABNORMALLY TE
RMINATED
9DBCFDEE    0618190096  T  O  errdemon    ERROR LOGGING TURNED ON
E18E984F    0618190196  P  S  SRC         SOFTWARE PROGRAM ERROR
E18E984F    0618190196  P  S  SRC         SOFTWARE PROGRAM ERROR
E18E984F    0618190196  P  S  SRC         SOFTWARE PROGRAM ERROR
192AC071    0618192896  T  O  errdemon    ERROR LOGGING TURNED OFF
9DBCFDEE    0618224196  T  O  errdemon    ERROR LOGGING TURNED ON
E18E984F    0618224296  P  S  SRC         SOFTWARE PROGRAM ERROR
E18E984F    0618224296  P  S  SRC         SOFTWARE PROGRAM ERROR
E18E984F    0618224296  P  S  SRC         SOFTWARE PROGRAM ERROR
192AC071    0620151296  T  O  errdemon    ERROR LOGGING TURNED OFF
9DBCFDEE    0621120396  T  O  errdemon    ERROR LOGGING TURNED ON
2BFA76F6    0620151496  T  S  SYSPROC     SYSTEM SHUTDOWN BY USER
E18E984F    0621120496  P  S  SRC         SOFTWARE PROGRAM ERROR
E18E984F    0621120496  P  S  SRC         SOFTWARE PROGRAM ERROR
E18E984F    0621120496  P  S  SRC         SOFTWARE PROGRAM ERROR
9DBCFDEE    0621151496  T  O  errdemon    ERROR LOGGING TURNED ON
E18E984F    0621151496  P  S  SRC         SOFTWARE PROGRAM ERROR
E18E984F    0621151496  P  S  SRC         SOFTWARE PROGRAM ERROR
E18E984F    0621151496  P  S  SRC         SOFTWARE PROGRAM ERROR
192AC071    0624210996  T  O  errdemon    ERROR LOGGING TURNED OFF
9DBCFDEE    0625070096  T  O  errdemon    ERROR LOGGING TURNED ON
2BFA76F6    0624211196  T  S  SYSPROC     SYSTEM SHUTDOWN BY USER
E18E984F    0625070196  P  S  SRC         SOFTWARE PROGRAM ERROR
E18E984F    0625070196  P  S  SRC         SOFTWARE PROGRAM ERROR
E18E984F    0625070196  P  S  SRC         SOFTWARE PROGRAM ERROR
0734DA1D    0629160296  P  H  fd0         DISKETTE MEDIA ERROR
9DBCFDEE    0630173896  T  O  errdemon    ERROR LOGGING TURNED ON
E18E984F    0630173996  P  S  SRC         SOFTWARE PROGRAM ERROR
E18E984F    0630173996  P  S  SRC         SOFTWARE PROGRAM ERROR
E18E984F    0630173996  P  S  SRC         SOFTWARE PROGRAM ERROR
```

# Debugging Client-Side JavaScript

You now know for which browser you are writing and you have pored over the manual so much that you are getting eyestrain. Now what? Here are some techniques that I have used in writing JavaScript code that you might find useful.

## Using *alert()*

The alert() method is one of the big guns in your arsenal against JavaScript bugs. Most variables can be converted automatically to strings in JavaScript , so they can be exposed and displayed by an alert message on the screen while a script is running. Using alert() also enables you to "step" through your scripts because the script usually will pause in what it is doing to wait for you to click OK. If a function is giving you errors, check the values of all of the variables just before and just after a function is called. To do this, place an alert() just above the function call, and place one on the first line inside the function definition. Here is an example:

```
function buggyDivide(top, bottom) {
alert("top=" + top + ", bottom=" + bottom)
return top/bottom
}
oneVar=1
twoVar=99
alert("oneVar=" +oneVar + ", twoVar" + twoVar)
buggyDivide(twoVar,oneVar-1)
```

In this example, you will find out immediately why the function gives you an error—you are trying to divide by zero, something that perhaps is not immediately obvious by looking at the oneVar assignment or at the call to buggyDivide. (Although, for this example, it is fairly obvious.)

## Using *document.write()*

If you find constantly clicking the OK button for every step in your code to be annoying, you can alternatively use document.write(). You can take advantage of the same ability to convert most variables into strings to display on-screen. When you are creating a dynamically generated HTML page, you can place additional document.write() statements to see just which variable is changing when, or even if, a given function returned the value you expected.

Also, you can use document.write() to "label" different aspects of your script. When you create some dynamically generated pages, you can write such things as "This is the first call to foo()" or "here is where I test for null." Once your code is bug-free, you can easily delete these lines.

## Start Small

JavaScript is highly object-oriented. Functions that you create for one script can be cut and pasted into new scripts, usually with little difficulty. Because of this, it is a very good practice when you are creating a complicated script to break it into smaller pieces—each performing some specific sub-task. You then write the code for each sub-task, debug that smaller part, and then assemble each component together into a workable whole.

For instance, if your script will be checking a form for valid input entries, you might write functions that just check one input field apiece. Then, successively add other functions one at a time until your script is complete. Adding only one function at a time is a good practice because if you get an error after you have added it, you know immediately which function is the culprit. Whereas, if you added two or more functions, you have no way of knowing if it was the first or second one that you added, or even if some interaction between them caused the error. This may seem tedious, but it is a sure-fire way to avoid many errors.

## Get Small (Using Comments)

You are assigned to debugging someone else's script. Their code is so garbled that you can't make heads or tails of the script logic. Or, perhaps you were on a coding roll and you wrote a large amount of code before you stopped to test it, and now you get many overlapping errors.

What do you do? A good practice is to systematically eliminate functions, variables, and so on, until the script runs without errors—even if it does nothing else! JavaScript enables you to create comments using `//` or `/* */`. If your script is giving you problems, try commenting out the newest feature you added. If it runs without errors after checking, then you know that the bug relates to the section of code you commented out—although it might not necessarily reside there since the new code might actually be exposing some bug elsewhere in your script.

## Other Tips

Here are some other tips that might help you avoid common errors in your scripts:

- JavaScript arrays begin counting at 0. If you assume they start at 1, you might be throwing off your code in subtle ways.
- Lines in JavaScript cannot be over 254 characters long due to a bug in the HTML parser. To avoid this, concatenate two smaller lines with a "+" as in `"this is a short string"` `+ "this is another short string"`.
- Don't mix static HTML with JavaScript-generated HTML. If you must use generated HTML, then generate the whole page in JavaScript.

## Debugging Tools

Until just a few months ago, it would have been impossible to find any software products that have debugging capabilities. But, as time has passed, software tools are now catching up to authors' demands.

**Microsoft Debugger**   Microsoft Script Debugger for Internet Explorer is an add-on that enables you to take greater control over your HTML. Your pages can be previewed dynamically as your code changes; you can switch between JScript (Microsoft's version of JavaScript), VBScript, and Java. It also has a built-in interpreter for JScript objects, breakpoints (which can stop a script at a given interval), and stepping—which allows you to slowly move through a script to see where some error occurs.

Microsoft Script Debugger can help you clean up your code. You can find the Microsoft Script Debugger at **http://www.microsoft.com/workshop/prog/scriptie/**.

**Acadia Infuse**   Acadia Infuse is more than just a JavaScript debugger, it is a full-fledged JavaScript authoring environment. You have complete access to all of the objects, methods, properties, and so forth, via a handy, hierarchical tree-style view, with the ability to drag and drop objects, methods, and more, into your scripts.

Also, you can view your script as a tree of nested objects and quickly jump to any part of your script. Not only can Infuse be used to write scripts, but it also enables you to quickly store and retrieve pieces of code that you can reuse across scripts.

Infuse also contains a large number of pre-built scripts that enable you to quickly begin programming. You can find Acadia Infuse at **http://www.acadians.com/Infuse/**.

**Other Debuggers**    Table 24.2 provides a short list of other JavaScript development software—most of which contains some form of debugger.

### Table 24. 2    Other JavaScript Development Software

| | |
|---|---|
| SiteXtras | A site management tool; located at **http://www.hyperact.com/** |
| Borland Intrabuilder | A robust and visual Web site builder that supports JavaScript. Located at **http://intrabuilder. borland.com/intrabuildernet/** |
| NetObjects Fusion | Another outstanding visual Web site builder. Contains a built-in JavaScript interpreter. Located at **http://www.netobjects.com/** |

# Debugging Resources

Once you have exhausted all of your resources by trying to track down your JavaScript problems, the next step is to get outside help. On the Internet, there are literally thousands of people who share your interest in JavaScript programming, and who are sharing their own information with others. The resources listed in Table 24.3 are just a few of the many places to which you can go to look for help. For more resources, see Chapter 17, "Development Tools for JavaScript."

### Table 24.3    Internet-Based Debugging Resources

| | |
|---|---|
| JavaScript Debugger | **http://www.media.com/ users/public/jsdb.html** |
| JavaScript Properties Browser | **http://www.usyd.edu.au/~doug/ javascript/prop_set.html** |
| Netscape's Documentation | **http://home.netscape.com/eng/ mozilla/3.0/handbook/javascript/index.html** |
| Netscape's Discussion Group | **snews://secnews.netscape.com/ netscape.devs-javascript** |
| UseNet JavaScript Newsgroup | **news:comp.lang.javascript** |

# Learning from the Pros

# CHAPTER 25

# Learning from the Pros: Site Outlines

**O**ne of the ways JavaScript has made navigating Web sites easier is through the use of multiple frames, typically implemented with a static list of links or a toolbar.

However, with JavaScript's capability to manipulate the contents of a window—including clearing and rewriting it—what would happen if the list of links was a dynamic object that could be expanded or collapsed? That's the idea Stefan Raab began to develop when he started to put together an indexing system for the Cue Systems' Web site that would enable easy navigation and a visual key to its structure. ■

### The purpose of a navigation outline

Stefan Raab of Cue Systems considered several options to help users navigate his company's site. He settled on the outline format since it was a natural way to represent the structure of the site.

### Problems implementing the plan

JavaScript wasn't the first choice for the outline. Raab worked through several ideas, including CGI scripting and forms-based alternatives. Finally, he discovered that JavaScript offered the right combination of speed and flexibility.

### Outlines beyond navigation

Raab's simple outline is a unique application of JavaScript that extends its use beyond its typical use in forms. Since Raab first implemented the idea, his outline has found its way into online books, corporate directories, and hardware structures.

# Stefan Raab of Cue Systems, LLC

Using JavaScript as part of a corporate Web site was practically an accident for Stefan Raab, Communications Development Manager for Cue Systems, which is located on the World Wide Web at **http://www.cuesys.com** (see Figure 25.1).

**FIG. 25.1**

Implementation of a navigation outline with JavaScript required only a few days of coding and testing by Raab after learning the basics of scripting.

The menu includes a button for eliminating the frames.

Each heading includes a graphical button for expanding or collapsing that portion of the outline.

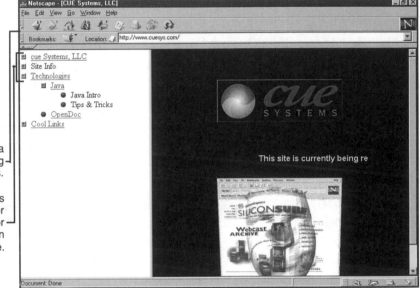

The company's mission is to develop integration between Java and OpenDoc for universal document handling, regardless of the hardware platform. According to Raab, "We call it, 'Reinventing the wheel for the information age.'"

When it comes to learning new tools such as JavaScript, reinventing the wheel means sharing ideas and solutions with other programmers and developers by letting the flow of information on the Web help drive program development through shared source code.

"It really frustrates me when someone just lifts a section of code and doesn't try to do anything else with it," Raab said. He contends that it defeats the purpose of making common items available, and it slows down the process that takes simple ideas and transforms them into powerful applications.

"I love just to watch stuff evolve," Raab said, adding that one of his favorite moments is when people modify his outline and make it work for applications he never thought of. "People take it and do something new, and that's the exciting part about this."

Most of Raab's time is spent on everything except Web site management, including documentation, system support, and patent registration. "This was strictly a spare-time enterprise," Raab stated; "As I found a few minutes, I started to put the pieces together."

With an original plan revolving around learning CGI and Perl, Raab had planned on spending up to a month getting familiar with the programming before tackling the Web outline project.

# The Collapsing and Expanding Outline

"The outline is more than a menu," Raab explains. "It's a natural way to organize information," which applies to everything from books and magazines to shopping lists and lists of home-improvement projects.

When developing Cue Systems' public Web site, Raab wanted to use an outline model to relay navigational information to the user. His plan was for an application to automatically track the pages and links and assemble the outline based on that information. Each time a user accessed his site, the server would search for folders and documents, then use the information to build an outline, which in turn would be used as a hot-linked table of contents.

The initial plan involved CGI scripting to accomplish site searching and page creation to update the outline. In addition to assembling and testing CGI scripts, this option also meant increased traffic and loading on the server.

Using CGI also meant increased difficulties on both sides of the development process. First Raab had to learn Perl, and then develop the necessary script to search a site and build pages. A functioning script also meant a decrease in server performance, as the script spent time looking for Web documents and writing the outline.

As the plan for CGI began to fade, Raab still didn't want to abandon the idea. "The outline is the most powerful way to organize information," he said. "It's something people do automatically whether they know it or not."

Part

V

Ch

25

# Getting Up to Speed

"Getting this implemented was not a real priority," Raab said. The first thoughts of putting up a site for public consumption was in October 1995, but there was no serious development toward completion. Cue Systems maintains an intranet for its own use, but a site on the World Wide Web was not a pressing concern.

Raab saw the possibilities in JavaScript for putting together a site outline without CGI. After trial-and-error experimentation and working with a JavaScript newsgroup, Raab picked up the fundamentals of implementing JavaScript in HTML.

For additional research, Raab and his colleagues went browsing for other pages that used outlines as a navigational tool. "We looked at other sites, but they just didn't use the function of an outline." Raab said other sites had an outline's appearance, but not the usability. In most cases they were too simple, with links to the top page of a general location, or they were too unwieldy, with a list of links to an entire site.

Once Raab knew how his site shouldn't work, he put together an idea of how it could work and began assembling HTML and JavaScript code. With three days of work, a mock-up of the outline was completed.

# The First Attempt: Forms

The first implementation of a dynamic outline used JavaScript's form manipulation features. This led to some unexpected behavior created by the way forms and form elements are implemented in JavaScript. Each level of the outline was represented by a form element, which worked well at first. The problems surfaced when adding or subtracting form check-box elements as particular items were removed when the outline was collapsed.

Form elements are implemented in JavaScript as arrays and not true objects. As a form element was removed from the array, the other elements moved up in the array to occupy the vacant position. However, in addition to occupying the space by its neighbor, the check-box element also assumed the value its neighbor left behind.

▶ **See** "HTML Objects in JavaScript," **p. 189**

So, if a form element was changed from `false` (for expanded) to `true` (for collapsed), the major topics below the changed element assumed the check box values of the newly collapsed items' subtopics, resulting in bizarre behavior. Selecting or deselecting an outline item resulted in an almost random state of outline items below the affected form element.

## *onClicks* and *Anchors*

The next attempt at the outline implementation was an outline that used the `onClick` method in conjunction with `anchors`. This option utilized a set of pages representing the different states of the outline, with hashes to ensure the right portion was displayed when selected.

▶ **See** "Events and Actions," **p. 60**

The problem was the use of hashes. To reference the top of a form, the URL included a hash with no anchor, which again resulted in unpredictable behavior and frequent crashes caused by the referral to a "nonexistent" hash.

# Those Persistent Objects

By continued experimentation with JavaScript, Raab learned about a quirk that held the key to the final solution: If a value is assigned to an object and the page is reloaded, the object will retain the value of its properties.

▶ **See** "Dynamic Documents," **p. 264**

The implications were immediately clear. The form of the outline could be stored as objects with properties relating to the current state. When the user changed the state, the page was reloaded and redrawn based on the new object information.

This was accomplished with another "hidden" feature of the language. JavaScript became a valid document type for URLs. By selecting an item in the outline, a JavaScript command is invoked with an event handler using the URL format.

The key to implementing the outline lies in the persistent state of objects during page reloading and the capability to embed JavaScript commands in URLs. This results in an URL reflected in the status bar that displays the two functions that update the outline display.

# Losing Automatic Outline Building

By choosing an HTML JavaScript solution over CGI scripting, Raab had to give up the option of an outline that automatically updated itself. That meant more up-front work implementing the idea because he now had to organize his site with pencil and paper to see how it would be implemented in JavaScript code.

"The worst part was building the outlines by hand," he said. Organizing the site on paper also led to organizing the site on the server. "It really took planning."

Like a lot of Web sites, most of Raab's pages were lumped together in a common content directory. By breaking out the pages into directories that reflected site organization, the site outline began to materialize. As the outline took shape, so did the site, and he was ready to implement the information into his script.

Raab insists it was a valuable exercise in the development of a coherent and usable site. Taking the time to "build a good plan straight from the beginning" has saved more time later when it has been necessary to update the site. It also leads to the one drawback of his implementation: when a page or a link changes on his site, it must be recorded in the outline HTML document. "Every time I add, change, or remove a link, I have to change the code," stated Raab.

Although this can be an inconvenience, the majority of the links for the Cue Systems site only occur within the outline. If a link is changed, it's usually in the outline document where the outline data can also be changed. If the link is also contained on another page, Raab's organization and outline speeds its identification and change.

Part
**V**

Ch

**25**

# Simple Idea—Broad Application

After Raab finished the code, he posted the results on a newsgroup with a "here's my simple outline" note. He didn't think he had accomplished much until the mail started to overflow in his electronic mailbox.

"I was just overwhelmed. People were writing things like, 'This is the best use of JavaScript I've ever seen.' It was just message after message. I still get four or five messages a week like that as more people find it."

Some other implementations of the outline that Raab has heard about from other developers include a table of contents for an online book and an outline of graphics files. Other possibilities he's considered, but hasn't yet seen, include personnel and corporate directories for both Internet and intranet sites, departments for electronic stores, and illustration of hardware-connection structures.

Listing 25.1 is the source code for Stefan Raab's dynamic outline menu. Each menu level is implemented with its own object, which can contain other objects for outline subtopics. To work with the quirks of JavaScript's `write` method, the object properties are initialized and the initial display is created by using Raab's `draw()` function. After a user changes the outline, the page is cleared and re-created by using a `redraw()` function.

**Listing 25.1   Cue Systems' Expanding and Collapsing Navigation Outline**

```
<!-- So, you think the outline is pretty cool huh? Yeah me too! -->
<!-- Well feel free to take it and use it to your heart's content -->
<!-- I just ask two things of you:                               -->
<!-- 1. Please send me the URL of the page that uses it! I want -->
<!--    to see what other people are doing with it! :)           -->
<!-- 2. Please keep this Comment attached. Feel free to add to   -->
<!--    it as you see fit!                                        -->
<!-- This is version 2.0                                          -->
<!-- Stefan Raab, cue Systems — stefan@cuesys.com          -->

<HTML><HEAD>
<TITLE>CUE Systems, LLC</TITLE>
</HEAD>

<SCRIPT LANGUAGE="JavaScript">

<!-- Beginning of JavaScript -

chk = 'if (top.root == null) {top.location = "http://www.cuesys.com"} else
{'function element(objName, name, location, modified)
{
  this.objName = objName
  this.open = false
  this.name = name
  this.location = location
  this.modified = modified //new Date(modified)
  this.kid = null
  this.nextPeer = null
  this.addKid = addKid
  this.addPeer = addPeer
  this.draw = draw
}

function addPeer(item)
{
  if (this.nextPeer != null)
  {
    this.nextPeer.addPeer(item)
  }
  else
  {
    this.nextPeer = item
  }
}

function addKid(item)
{
  if (this.kid != null)
  {
    this.kid.addPeer(item)
  }
  else
  {
    this.kid = item
```

```
    }
}

function open(item) {
    if (root ==null) {
       outline
    }
    item.open = true
}

function close (item) {
    if (root ==null) {
       outline
    }
    item.open = false
}


function draw()
{
  if (this.kid == null) {
     print("\n<DT><IMG SRC='http://www.cuesys.com/icons/bul.gif' " +
       "HEIGHT = 10 WIDTH = 20>")
     if (this.location != null) {
       print("<A HREF =" + this.location +" TARGET='doc'>" + this.name + "</A>")
          }
       else {
         print(this.name)
          }
     if (this.nextPeer != null) {
       this.nextPeer.draw()
        }
       else {
         print("</DL>")
         return
          }
     }
     else {
       if (this.open) {
         print("\n<DT><A HREF='javascript:" + chk + ";top.close(top." +
             this.objName+ ");top.redraw()}'>")
         print("<IMG SRC='http://www.cuesys.com/icons/minus.gif' " +
             "HEIGHT = 10 WIDTH = 20 BORDER = 0></A>")
         if (this.location != null) {
           print("<A HREF =" + this.location +" TARGET='doc'>" + this.name +
           ➡"</A> <DL>")
            }
           else {
             print(this.name+"<DL>")
            }
         this.kid.draw()
         if (this.nextPeer != null) {
           this.nextPeer.draw()
          }
         else {
```

*continues*

**Listing 25.1 Continued**

```
                print("</DL>")
                }
        }
      else {
        print("\n<DT><A HREF='javascript:" + chk + ";top.open(top."+
            this.objName + ");top.redraw()}'>")
        print("<IMG SRC='http://www.cuesys.com/icons/plus.gif' " +
            "HEIGHT = 10 WIDTH = 20 BORDER = 0></A>")
        if (this.location != null) {
          print("<A HREF =" + this.location +" TARGET='doc'>" + this.name +
          ➥"</A>")
          }
          else {
            print(this.name)
            }
        if (this.nextPeer != null) {
          this.nextPeer.draw()
        }
        else {
          print("</DL>")
          }
      }
    }
}

function print(text)
{
if (navigator.appVersion.lastIndexOf('Win') == -1 &&
➥navigator.appVersion.lastIndexOf('2.0') == -1) {
  top.out.document.write(text)
  }
  else {
    top.out.print(text)
  }
}

function redraw()
{
if (navigator.appVersion.lastIndexOf('Win') == -1 &&
➥navigator.appVersion.lastIndexOf('2.0') == -1) {
  top.out.document.open()
  top.out.document.clear()
  dr()
  top.out.document.close()
  }
  else {
    top.out.location = "winhack.html"
    }
}

function outline()
{
root = new element("root","cue Systems, LLC", "/home.html", "Sep 4 00:16")
```

```
root.addKid(new element(null, "About cue Systems",  "/cue/index.html",
➥"Sep 4 00:16"))
root.addKid(new element(null, "Contacting cue Systems",  "/cue/contact.html",
➥"Sep 4 00:16"))
root.addKid(new element(null, "Copyright and Disclaimer",  null,  "Sep 4
00:16"))
root.addPeer(site = new element("site", "Site Info", null, "Sep 9 15:21"))
site.addKid(new element(null, "General Information", "/site_info.html",
➥"Sep 9 15:21"))
site.addKid(new element(null, "Statistics", "/ps.html", "Sep 9 15:21"))
root.addPeer(tech = new element("tech", "Technologies", "/tech/index.html",
➥"Sep 4 00:17"))
tech.addKid(java =new element("java", "Java",  "/objects/java",  "Sep 4 00:16"))
java.addKid(new element(null, "Java Intro",  null,  "Sep 4 00:16"))
java.addKid(new element(null, "Tips & Tricks",  null,  "Sep 4 00:16"))
java.addPeer(new element(null, "OpenDoc",  "/objects/od",  "Sep 4 00:16"))
root.addPeer(links = new element("links", "Cool Links", "/links", "Sep 4,
00:14"))
links.addKid(new element(null, "Graphics", "/links/index.html#graphics",
➥"Sep 4 00:14"))
links.addKid(new element(null, "Mac", "/links/index.html#mac", "Sep 4 00:14"))
links.addKid(new element(null, "Random", "/links/index.html#random", "Sep 4
➥00:14"))
links.addKid(new element(null, "Unix", "/links/index.html#unix", "Sep 4 00:14"))

tech.open = true
java.open = true
}

function dr()
{
  print("<DL>")
  root.draw()
}

// - End of JavaScript - -->

</SCRIPT>
<FRAMESET COLS="33%,*">
<FRAME NAME="out" SRC="blank.html" MARGINWIDTH="2" MARGINHEIGHT="2">
<FRAME NAME="doc" SRC="home.html" MARGINWIDTH="2" MARGINHEIGHT="2">
</FRAMESET>

<NOFRAME>
<CENTER>
<p><p>
<IMG SRC="icons/newlogo.gif" ALIGN=bottom WIDTH=253 HEIGHT=84><BR>
<BR><P><P><P><BR>
<A HREF="lists/jod">
<H1>The Java-OpenDoc Connection.</H1></a>

<HR><A HREF="cue/"><IMG SRC="icons/cue.gif" BORDER="0" WIDTH="100" HEIGHT="50"
➥ALIGN=bottom NATURALSIZEFLAG= "3" ></A>
<A HREF="people/"><IMG SRC="icons/people.gif" BORDER="0" WIDTH="100" HEIGHT="50"
➥ALIGN=bottom NATURALSIZEFLAG= "3"></A>
```

Part
V

Ch
25

*continues*

**Listing 25.1    Continued**

```
<A HREF="objects/"><IMG SRC="icons/objects.gif" BORDER="0" WIDTH="100"
➥HEIGHT="50"
ALIGN=bottom NATURALSIZEFLAG= "3"></A>
<A HREF="links/"><IMG SRC="icons/links.gif" BORDER="0" WIDTH="100" HEIGHT="50"
➥ALIGN=bottom NATURALSIZEFLAG= "3"></A>
<A HREF="freebies/"><IMG SRC="icons/freebies.gif" BORDER="0" WIDTH="100"
➥HEIGHT="50"
ALIGN=bottom NATURALSIZEFLAG="3"></A><BR>
<HR>
<H4>Please Address all comments, questions and concerns to
<A HREF="mailto:Webmaster@cuesys.com">Webmaster@cuesys.com</A>.<BR>
<A HREF="ps.html">Site statistics</A> are available.</H4>
<H6>Copyright 1995 CUE Systems, LLC. All Rights Reserved<BR>
<A HREF="http://www.freebsd.org/">
<IMG SRC="powerlogo.gif" WIDTH="171" HEIGHT="64" ALIGN=bottom
NATURALSIZEFLAG="3"
➥ALT="Powered by FreeBSD"></A></H6>
</NOFRAME>
</HTML>
```

"What you see (on our site) is a façade," Raab said, "a simple tool to aid navigation." But its simplicity is its power. Like Java, JavaScript is making what were once complicated programming applications easier to understand and implement in less space.

Raab doesn't view the current version of the script as a static product. He has more refinements and revisions planned, including making the code more modular and even smaller. And there's always the question of what someone else is going to try to do with it. ●

# CHAPTER 26

# Learning from the Pros: Adding Frames and Controlling Navigation

**P**robably the most widely used new feature provided by JavaScript is the capability to use multiple frames to organize Web site content, especially when used in conjunction with navigation bars and toolbars. For many Web authors, this means converting existing pages and sites into a frame-based format. But this can be tricky. Although frames are a powerful new tool, if misplaced and misused, they can be a hindrance to the user because they can eat up screen space and slow down the browser.

Another key capability offered with JavaScript is control over browser behavior. New windows and new browsers are opened and closed by using simple commands that also control the availability of the browser's tools.

Properly used, these two capabilities enable a Web developer to create a portal into the site and to provide the tools the developer wants the user to have to navigate inside. Content presentation and access are controlled in one simple step (see Figure 26.1). ■

### Use multiple frames to organize your Web site's content

Among JavaScript's new features is the capability to create multiple frames to maximize the organization and presentation of your Web site content. Learning how to master this feature requires patience and practice.

### Control Web site access and the presentation of content

JavaScript enables you to control the manner in which your browser windows appear and function. Simple commands open and close new windows and browsers, and provide access to browser tools. You can also use JavaScript to help potential users who don't have proper software to view your Web site.

### Convert your old Web site into the new JavaScript format

You don't need to start from scratch; convert your old Web site into the new JavaScript format. Consider options such as providing a link to a mirror site for non-JavaScript users, containing the same general content but without JavaScript.

**FIG. 26.1**

The Start Demo button on CyberExplorer's Web site opens a new browser without the traditional Netscape menu bar items. This enables the Web author to control entrance, exit, and navigation within the site.

A button serves as the doorway to CyberExplorer's Web site. Access to the right software is provided for users who need to upgrade before entering.

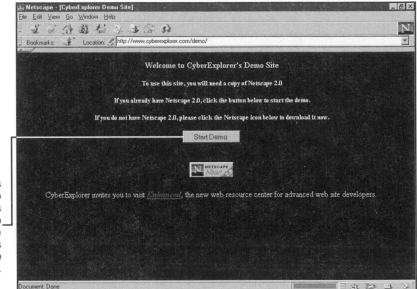

# Matthew Fusfield of CyberExplorer

As an Internet consultant, Matthew Fusfield spends a lot of time keeping up with hardware and software advances that can be integrated into clients' Web sites. Because Web technology is changing on virtually a day-to-day basis, it has been a constant process, but one he has enjoyed watching.

"It's good to have new things to do," he said, noting that if nothing new were developed, the capabilities would get old and stale. Emerging technologies enable him to continue providing new services and capabilities to his clients. Future projects include a Web-based bulletin board system that utilizes new Web technologies, including JavaScript.

**N O T E**   CyberExplorer's home page, **http://www.cyberexplorer.com/demo/**, operates by opening a new browser to control the user's navigation options. Fusfield welcomes comments and suggestions about his site from visitors, and can be reached at **matfusf@cyberexplorer.com**. ▪

# The One-Way-Out Web Site

With JavaScript, it is possible to control the appearance and functionality of browser windows. Fusfield capitalized on this with his Web site. Users are greeted by a button that is used to enter the site. This page also serves to help screen users who may not have the proper software to view the pages within.

When the Start Demo button is clicked, a new browser is loaded with a custom set of navigation buttons (see Figure 26.2).

**FIG. 26.2**

All pages of CyberExplorer's JavaScript demo include a navigation frame and a tool/ navigation bar. An Exit button returns the user to the original browser window.

The custom tool/ navigation bar

A standard navigation frame

A custom status bar message

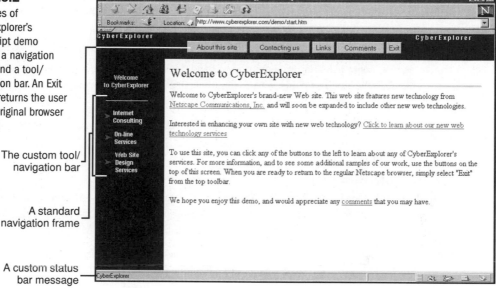

As a reminder that users are not in an average Web site, a confirmation alert is used to let them know they're leaving CyberExplorer pages (see Figure 26.3). This is the preferred way to leave the site, although a user can always use the close button on the top right corner of the screen.

**FIG. 26.3**

After pressing the Exit button, a confirmation box appears, confirming that you want to exit CyberExplorer.

Part
**V**

Ch
**26**

# New Web Site Formats = Old-Fashioned Organization

Converting an old Web site into its new JavaScript format is a straightforward process that involves refining the existing content, organizing it for frame presentation, and then creating new pages with JavaScript code with the new content pasted in—a process Fusfield uses for most of his projects.

"Generally, if it's a clean site with clean HTML, it takes a few hours over a few days," he said. "But planning is the important part."

After deciding how the site should work and what it should include, Fusfield sketches his ideas on paper, including flow charts and screen layouts. After refining the idea on paper, he gets the HTML documents currently in use.

Any changes to the content or artwork are made in the old files. Then in separate files, Fusfield creates the JavaScript code that controls navigation and other browser behavior. When scripts in the new files are complete, the content is inserted from the old files.

"I put it on a password-protected server to see how it behaves," Fusfield said. This gives him a chance to use the site in its natural environment and decide what works and what doesn't. This is also a crucial step when working with a client because it enables the customer to review the site before it is generally available.

When the new site is running without a hitch, an important decision is left: what to do with the old files.

## To Mirror or Replace

Fusfield said the decision to delete the old files in lieu of the JavaScript-enabled versions depends on the end-user's alternatives. For a JavaScript-dependent site, such as CyberExplorer, it's "tough luck" for the user who's not using an up-to-date Netscape or Microsoft browser.

Another option is to provide access to a mirror site, which contains the same content but without JavaScript. This ensures that no users are left out and is especially important for general-interest sites.

# Creating Entrance to a Controlled Site

Creating a controlled environment, like Fusfield created for CyberExplorer, is quite simple, apart from the frames.

If the entrance page also provides access to a mirror site that doesn't require JavaScript, then a hot link can be embedded inside script comment markers, /* and */, to the alternative site. In this example, an all-or-nothing approach is used.

Listing 26.1 shows the HTML code used to create access to the CyberExplorer demo. Note the startdemo() function, which creates a new window without a tool bar or menu bar, but provides for scrolling and a status bar. This enables the author to provide a unique set of tools and navigation aids while in the site.

### Listing 26.1   Code for Creating the First Page of the CyberExplorer Demo

```
<HTML>
<HEAD>
<TITLE>CyberExplorer Demo Site</TITLE>

<SCRIPT LANGUAGE="JavaScript">

<!--
function startdemo(){
```

```
        cyber=window.open('start.htm', 'CyberExplorer',
➥'toolbar=no,location=no,directories=no,status=yes,
➥menubar=no,scrollbars=yes,resizable=yes,copyhistory=no')
}
//-->

</SCRIPT>

</HEAD>
<BODY BGCOLOR="#000000" TEXT="#ffffff">
<center>
<P>
<P>
<P>
<P>
<P>
<h4>Welcome to CyberExplorer's Demo Site</h4>
<h5>To use this site, you will need a copy of Netscape 2.0</h5>
<h5>If you already have Netscape 2.0, click the button below
➥to start the demo.</h5>
<h5>If you do not have Netscape 2.0,
please click the Netscape icon below to download it now.</h5>
<FORM>
<input type="button" value=" Start Demo  " onClick="startdemo()">
</FORM>
<BR>
<a href="http://cgi.netscape.com/comprod/mirror/index.html"
 onMouseOver="self.status='Download Netscape'; return true">
<img src="ns20.gif" border=0></A>

<P>
CyberExplorer invites you to visit <B><I><a href="/enhanced/"
➥onMouseOver="self.status='Visit Enhanced'; return true">
Enhanced</A></I></B>, the new web resource center for
advanced web site developers.

</center>

</BODY>
</HTML>
```

When the button is clicked, a new window is created using the window.open() method. This directs the browser to create a new window and load it with the contents from start.htm—the file that creates the frames and loads the toolbars for the rest of the site tour.

With the tool definitions in the window.open method, Fusfield's site has captured the user's browser. "The ability to control how a browser behaves is very powerful. Basically, you can't leave until you hit the Exit button."

# Using Frames

"Frames can be clunky at times," Fusfield says, "At times, I think of ways the actual syntax would have been easier."

Learning how to effectively include frames in a site takes practice and a healthy dose of trial and error. "It's a little more difficult than other HTML tags," Fusfield said. His starting point included documentation and examples available online, followed by a lot of experimentation.

Fusfield thinks the price is worth it, however. "They make sense in a lot of places," he said. "We're seeing the groundwork laid for complex interfaces," such as those available for America Online, Prodigy, and CompuServe. It's one of the good ideas that can actually make a page or Web site easier to view and navigate for the user, and serves as the basis for more sophisticated tools.

The problem is that frames require screen space. "With each frame, the screen (for content) is getting smaller." This is especially true when Web authors start creating frames for displaying advertising. "The spirit in which this capability was created was to help navigate...not advertise," he said. "Its best use is for navigation and toolbars." Although advertising is a valid use for frames, it shouldn't interfere with or overpower the frame used for content. "Put it where it's not obtrusive," Fusfield advises. ●

# CHAPTER 27

# Learning from the Pros: Online Ordering System

**O**ne of the underutilized areas of JavaScript is client-side integration with CGI and server-side databases. With JavaScript's capability to validate information and keep a running total of items and prices, it can serve as a powerful tool to reduce the dependence on CGI scripts in generating catalog pages and order forms for users, thereby reducing the load on the server and the user's time spent on waiting for client/server communication.

Although the Books Galore! site (see Figure 27.1) is simple in structure and application, the fundamentals used illustrate what can be done, even with a simple CGI operation on a text-based data set. ■

## Portability is key

As David Nagy-Farkas developed the Books Galore! site, he kept in mind that it should remain generic enough to apply to other situations, from bookstores to candy shops to technical support sites.

## Working with variables

One of the problems Nagy-Farkas had to work around was the loose variable typing used in JavaScript. He offers some advice on making this an easier process.

## Working with databases

Part of the portability of the Books Galore! concept is how it works with databases. A CGI script wraps the database information with the JavaScript code and returns it to the browser. This enables the pages to share the processing load between server and client, even as the user browses the selected items.

**FIG. 27.1**

The opening page of Books Galore! is a simple form that enables the user to choose which types of books to browse. The results of the form are used to parse a database and retrieve the product information.

**N O T E** The Books Galore! ordering demo is found at **http://weber.u.washington.edu/~davidnf/ java/bookstore.html**. As you try out the system, don't worry about the bill: It's only a demo, so no one is waiting on the other end of the line to take your money. ■

# David Nagy-Farkas of LiveWeb

David Nagy-Farkas is a computer engineering student at the University of Washington in Seattle. With exposure to a wide variety of computer languages over the course of his studies, including C, C++, and SmallTalk, it was only natural that he trained his sights on two new entries in the programming fray: Java and JavaScript.

"I heard about them when they were released, and started checking them out," he said. After consulting online documentation from Netscape and other sources, he started to spend some of his spare time looking at how other people were using them, and generating applets and scripts of his own. Nagy-Farkas now spends a portion of his time creating HTML, Java, JavaScript, and CGI scripts on a freelance basis.

"Initially, I was just looking at what could be done," Nagy-Farkas said. He looked at a lot of other Web sites to see what other developers were doing with JavaScript. "What I found really wasn't that practical. There were a lot of calculators and stuff like that," but nothing that really indicated some of the more powerful client-side functions that are useful when dealing with data and a server.

**N O T E** David Nagy-Farkas's home page for Live Web Designs is found at **http:// weber.u.washington.edu/~davidnf/**. ■

# Books Galore!

The product-ordering system began as a simple project to keep a running total of items as a user selected or deselected items. "It was really pretty simple," Nagy-Farkas said. "I just worked with 'on-event' handlers. Anytime any field was changed that could affect the price, I recalculated the total."

As he worked with JavaScript's capability to write HTML, the rest of the project fell into place through the use of arrays to keep track of items inserted into the page that is using the CGI script (see Figure 27.2). "All that I needed was a section of code to add the item to the array. The JavaScript functionality really made it pretty easy."

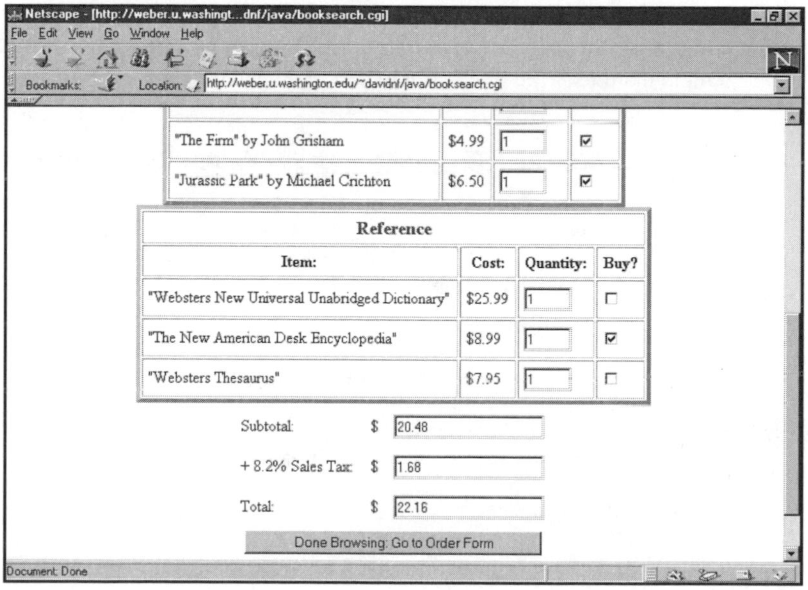

**FIG. 27.2**
This page is used to choose which books to order and how many. Note the form fields at the bottom of the screen that contain the running totals. These are updated as soon as one of the fields above it is changed or clicked.

Because the project was for his own curiosity, Nagy-Farkas took his time to learn how JavaScript worked as he assembled each piece. The total time—including weeding out bugs that would pop up as each Netscape beta progressed—was about two weeks. "Wrapping it up in a book order" lasted three days, including developing the CGI scripts in Perl.

# Portability by Design

The first version of the Running Total program wasn't very modular. When the idea evolved to turn it into an ordering system, Nagy-Farkas realized it would be a much simpler project if the JavaScript code were converted into a series of functions for each task.

As each section was converted into a JavaScript function, it was thoroughly tested. Nagy-Farkas learned his lessons about debugging JavaScript early. "Netscape's error messages aren't that helpful," he said, citing vague system responses when a piece of code fails, compounded by a line-numbering system that defies explanation.

"I only write a few lines at a time and then test them to make sure they work," he said. "When something goes wrong, it's a lot easier to track down where and what it is." The other result is robust code that the programmer knows works "every step of the way."

Listing 27.1 shows a sample section of code generated by the CGI script from the introductory page. The first section, including all of the JavaScript functions, is a standard header that never changes, regardless of which book categories are chosen by the user.

Information from the database is inserted into JavaScript templates containing HTML formatting, which is also written to the document and finally to the screen by utilizing `document.write` functions. The only items in the document that are considered "true" HTML content are the page title and directions. By creating a generic template for the products, it is a simple matter for the CGI script to parse the database and add the items to the page.

### Listing 27.1   An HTML Page with JavaScript Generated by a CGI Script

```html
<!--     Copyright 1996 David Nagy-Farkas. All Rights Reserved     -->
<!--     David Nagy-Farkas reserves all rights regarding this      -->
<!--      code and any derived works. You may not reproduce        -->
<!--     this code without the explicit permission of the author.  -->

<HTML>
<HEAD>
<BODY BACKGROUND="../chalk.jpg"></BODY>
<SCRIPT LANGUAGE="JavaScript">

<!-- hide the script's contents from feeble browsers

// Global Variables
var ForceSub = 0;
var subt = 0, addtax = 0, tot = 0; // subtotal, tax, and total
var tax = 0.082;                    // tax rate

/******************
** Add a decimal point to a number
*/
function AddDecimal(number) {
  var withdecimal = "";
  var num = "" + number;
  if (num.length == 0) {
    withdecimal += "0";
  } else if (num.length == 1) {
    withdecimal += "0.0" + num;
  } else if (num.length == 2) {
    withdecimal += "0." + num;
  } else {
  withdecimal += num.substring(0, num.length - 2);
  withdecimal += "."
  withdecimal += num.substring(num.length - 2, num.length);
  }
```

```
    return withdecimal;
}

/****************
** Creates a new array of length n
*/
function MakeArray(n) {
    for (var i = 0; i <= n; i++)
        this[i] = 0;
    this.length = n;
    return this;
}

/****************
** Creates a new Product object
*/
function Product(name, price) {
  this.name = name;
  this.quantity = 1;
  this.price = price;
  this.itemtot = 0;
}

/****************
** Outputs HTML for a product object
*/
function DisplayItem(item, number) {
  var result = "<TR><TD>";
  result += item.name + "</TD>";
  result += "<TD>$" + AddDecimal(item.price) + "</TD>";
  result += "<TD><INPUT TYPE='text' SIZE=5 VALUE=1 ";
  result += "name='" + item.name + "_quantity' ";
  result += "onFocus='reset(" + number + ")' onBlur='unreset(" + number + ")'>
➥</TD>";
  result += "<TD><INPUT TYPE='checkbox' VALUE='off' ";
  result += "name='" + item.name + "_buy' ";
  result += "onClick='toggle(" + number + ")'></TD>";
  result += "<INPUT TYPE='hidden' name='" + item.name + "_itemprice'
➥VALUE="+ AddDecimal(item.price) +"></TR>";
  document.write(result);
}

/****************
** Outputs HTML for the top of a table column
*/
function PrintHead(header) {
  var result = "<CENTER><TABLE BORDER=4 CELLPADDING=5 CELLSPACING=2>";
  result += "<TR><TH COLSPAN=4><FONT SIZE=4 COLOR='maroon'>" + header +
      "</FONT></TH></TR>"
  result += "<TR><TH>Item:</TH><TH>Cost:</TH><TH>Quantity:</TH>" +
      "<TH>Buy?</TH></TR>";
  document.write(result);
}

/****************
```

Part

V

Ch

27

*continues*

**Listing 27.1   Continued**

```
** Ends a table column
*/
function PrintTail() {
  document.write("</TABLE></CENTER>");
}

/****************
** Executed when the quantity of a product is selected
*/
function reset(index) {
  if (document.forms[0].elements[3*index+1].value == "on") {
    ForceSub = 1;
    compute(index);
    ForceSub = 0;
  }
  document.forms[0].elements[3*index].value = "";
}

/***************
** Executed when done changing the quantity of a product
*/
function unreset(index) {
  if (document.forms[0].elements[3*index].value == "")
    document.forms[0].elements[3*index].value = inv[index].quantity;
  else
    inv[index].quantity = eval(document.forms[0].elements[3*index].value);
  if (document.forms[0].elements[3*index+1].value == "on")
    compute(index);
}

/***************
** Toggles the value of a checkbox
*/
function toggle(index) {
  if (document.forms[0].elements[3*index+1].value == "off") {
    document.forms[0].elements[3*index+1].value = "on"; }
  else if (document.forms[0].elements[3*index+1].value == "on") {
    document.forms[0].elements[3*index+1].value = "off"; }
  compute(index);
}

/***************
** Perform updates of totals and tax
*/
function compute(index)
{
  if (document.forms[0].elements[3*index+1].value == "on" && !ForceSub) {
    inv[index].itemtot = eval(inv[index].itemtot) + (eval(inv[index].price) *
➥eval(inv[index].quantity));
    subt = (eval(subt) + (eval(inv[index].price) * eval(inv[index].quantity)));
  } else {
    inv[index].itemtot = eval(inv[index].itemtot) - (eval(inv[index].price) *
➥eval(inv[index].quantity));
    subt = (eval(subt) - (eval(inv[index].price) * eval(inv[index].quantity)));
```

```
    }
    addtax = Math.round(subt * tax);
    tot = (eval(subt) + eval(addtax));
    retotal();
}

/***************
**  Redisplay the totals
*/
function retotal() {
    document.forms[0].subtotal.value = AddDecimal(subt);
    document.forms[0].addedtax.value = AddDecimal(addtax);
    document.forms[0].total.value = AddDecimal(tot);
}

<!-- done hiding from old browsers -->

</SCRIPT>
</HEAD>

<CENTER><H1> Browse the Store! </H1></CENTER>
<HR>
<DL><DT><H3>Here are the available items you requested:</H3>
    <DD>Browse the selection of items and select the items you want by
checking the "buy" box next to your selection. You may also specify the
quantity of items you wish to purchase. At any time, you can check the
bottom of the page to see a running total of the items you have selected.
When you are finished, please <B>click on the "Finished" button</B> at the
bottom of the page. Don't worry... there is no obligation to buy at this
point... this is just a demo.
</DL>
<HR>

<SCRIPT>
<!-- Hide the script from unworthy browsers
inv = new MakeArray(9);
inv[0] = new Product('"The Joy of Cooking" - Hardcover', 2000);
inv[1] = new Product('"The Frugal Gourmet and our Immigrant Ancestors" by Jeff
➥Smith', 795);
inv[2] = new Product('"Interview with the Vampire" by Anne Rice', 599);
inv[3] = new Product('"Patriot Games" by Tom Clancy', 699);
inv[4] = new Product('"The Firm" by John Grisham', 499);
inv[5] = new Product('"Jurassic Park" by Michael Crichton', 650);
inv[6] = new Product('"Websters New Universal Unabridged Dictionary"', 2599);
inv[7] = new Product('"The New American Desk Encyclopedia"', 899);
inv[8] = new Product('"Websters Thesaurus"', 795);
document.write("<FORM METHOD='POST' ACTION='bookinvoice.cgi'>");
PrintHead('Cooking');
DisplayItem(inv[0], 0);
DisplayItem(inv[1], 1);
PrintTail();
PrintHead('Popular Fiction');
DisplayItem(inv[2], 2);
DisplayItem(inv[3], 3);
DisplayItem(inv[4], 4);
```

Part

V

Ch

27

*continues*

**Listing 27.1    Continued**

```
DisplayItem(inv[5],5);
PrintTail();
PrintHead('Reference');
DisplayItem(inv[6], 6);
DisplayItem(inv[7], 7);
DisplayItem(inv[8], 8);
PrintTail();
document.write("<CENTER><TABLE CELLPADDING=4 CELLSPACING=4><TR>");
document.write("  <TD>Subtotal: </TD>");
document.write("  <TD>$</TD>");
document.write("  <TD><INPUT NAME='subtotal' VALUE=0.00
➥onBlur='retotal()'></TD></TR><TR>");
document.write("  <TD>+ 8.2% Sales Tax: </TD>");
document.write("  <TD>$</TD>");
document.write("  <TD><INPUT NAME='addedtax' VALUE=0.00
➥onBlur='retotal()'></TD></TR><TR>");
document.write("  <TD>Total: </TD>");
document.write("  <TD>$</TD>");
document.write("  <TD><INPUT NAME='total'
➥VALUE=0.00 onBlur='retotal()'></TD></TR>");
document.write("  </TABLE><INPUT TYPE='submit' " +
      "VALUE='Done Browsing: Go to Order Form'></CENTER></FORM>");
// stop hiding -->
      </SCRIPT>

<HR>
<A HREF="http://weber.u.washington.edu/~davidnf/java/bookstore.html">
<B>Head back to the starting page</A></B>
</HTML>
```

# Working with Databases

If it were just a matter of hard-wiring the JavaScript code with the product items, this would be a simple—albeit limited—project. But it is designed to work with a database that can change in content and size from day to day. This is where CGI becomes a necessary companion to JavaScript.

"The page is pretty standardized," Nagy-Farkas said. "The user submits a choice for book categories, and the CGI script returns with a brand new page." With the JavaScript functions in place, it becomes a matter of getting the right information into the document.

"The toughest part is parsing the database, especially if it's a large one," he said. Books Galore! is designed to take the extraneous parsing load off the server. Current CGI online ordering systems require parsing the database after each selection and then generating a new total with a new page to display it. "If you have a big list of items, redrawing is a pain."

With Books Galore!, the database is parsed once to get the information for the initial ordering screen and is not referenced again until the final invoice (see Figure 27.3). Any changes to a customer's order on the order form is handled by JavaScript.

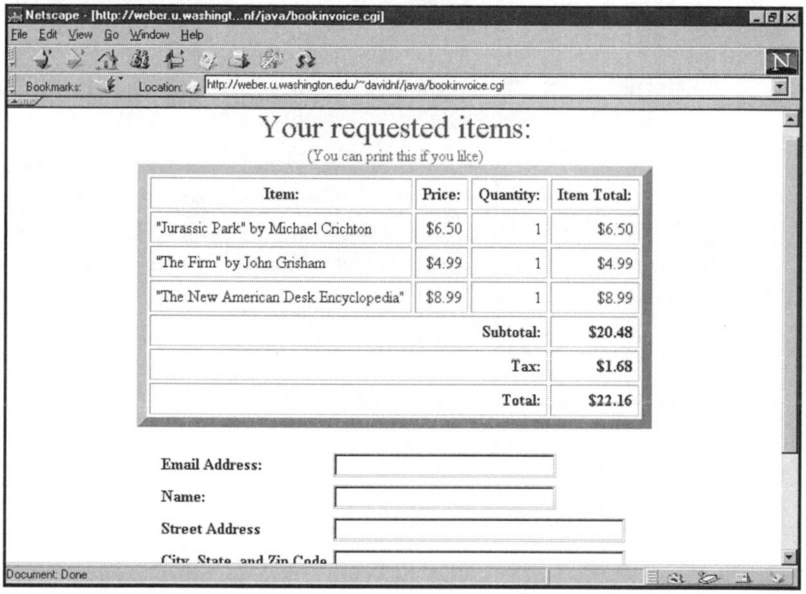

**FIG. 27.3**
After the user submits an order, another CGI script generates the final invoice with information from the order screen, including a form at the bottom for entering name, address, and payment information.

# Determining Variable Types

One of the key items that slowed down the development process was the lack of variable typing in JavaScript. Depending on its use, a variable can be a string or a number. To make matters worse, there aren't effective methods in place to determine what a variable thinks it is at any given moment.

"It's really a nightmare keeping track of how things are typed," Nagy-Farkas said. A variable acts according to how it's being used—which affords a lot of flexibility, but also causes a lot of confusion, in passing parameters. "It takes a little time to figure out whether that integer you just passed into a function thinks it's an integer or a string."

When this snag started to become a bigger issue in application development, he also started to realize that JavaScript is more than just an extension of HTML. "You really have to have a basic feel for programming to get this to do anything," he said. Putting workable JavaScript pages together isn't "a ten-minute project...If you have a grasp of object-oriented programming structure, it helps a lot."

Part
**V**

Ch
**27**

# Will It Work for a Candy Store?

When Nagy-Farkas posted the first running total calculation application, no one seemed to be too interested. After adding the CGI script and the book order wrapping, "Feedback has been very positive" in spite of the fact the basic functionality of the page hasn't changed much—it still keeps a running total based on the most current user input.

"A lot of people have been asking for a 'vanilla' version of the Books Galore! program," Nagy-Farkas said. "It's really pretty portable right now."

By building the page at an early stage in modular components, the JavaScript code is virtually independent of the database that supplies its information. The section of the project that will change from application to application is the CGI script, which must be modified for each database. With portable code and the right CGI script, Books Galore! could be used for any virtual storefront operation. ●

# PART VI

# Netscape Communicator Update

# CHAPTER 28

# Creating Netscape Layers

**I**n the desktop publishing world, layers are rectangular blocks of text and artwork that you can position anywhere on the page that you like. You can also overlap layers so that one is hidden behind another, or so that one bleeds through another. Publishers use layers to create some pretty awesome layouts. Take a look at some print advertisements or brochures, for example. Chances are, the publisher used layers.

While desktop publishers take layers for granted (even the simplest of desktop publishing programs enable you to create and overlap layers), HTML designers don't. They've never had the capability to overlap blocks of text and artwork because HTML is *streaming*. That is, each preceding HTML element is displayed before the next, in order. HTML has never provided for the positioning of an HTML element, much less for overlapping HTML elements—until now.

Netscape Navigator 4.0 introduces the <LAYER> tag. You use this tag to create layers, which you can position anywhere on the HTML document, overlapping the HTML document and other layers. You can use it to create advanced layouts in your HTML document, to create simple animation effects such as a curtain that unveils the contents of your document, or even to provide simple fly-over help for each link on the HTML document.

## Easily add layers to your HTML documents

The <LAYER> tag gives you real desktop publishing capabilities in a straightforward way.

## Overlap multiple layers

You have complete control over how overlapped layers appear in your HTML document.

## Control your layers with scripts

The real power of layers comes from controlling them with scripts. This chapter shows you how.

## Create groups by nesting layers

You can insert one layer within another. The nested layer always moves with the outside layer.

## Create fly-over help by using layers

The example at the end of this chapter shows you how to create fly-over help for each of your links.

The real excitement in using layers comes from your ability to control the position, visibility, and so forth, with a JavaScript script. For example, you can move a layer across the screen by using a script. By using a script, you can overlap ten layers and then peel them away to create an animation effect. This chapter contains several examples that use JavaScript to control one or more layers. ■

 **TIP**   You can put any valid HTML within a layer. You can even put plug-ins within a layer.

# Creating a Basic Layer

Listing 28.1 shows the most basic usage of the <LAYER> tag. You simply enclose the contents of the layer within <LAYER> and </LAYER>. No attributes are given. As shown in Figure 28.1, however, you can hardly tell the difference between this result and streaming HTML.

The sections that follow show you how to really use the <LAYER> tag. You can position a layer anywhere you like, change the size of a layer, or even change the background of the layer. A bit later in this chapter, you also will learn how to overlap layers and control layers with scripts.

**Listing 28.1   A Simple *<LAYER>* Tag**

```
<HTML>
<HEAD>
<TITLE>Layer 1</TITLE>
</HEAD>
<BODY>

<P>This example shows what a basic layer that contains an image looks like.
Note that the layer isn't positioned in any way whatsoever. Thus,
you can hardly tell it from in-line HTML.</P>

<LAYER>
<IMG SRC=init.gif>
</LAYER>

</BODY>
</HTML>
```

**CAUTION**

<LAYER> is not part of HTML 3.2 and is supported only by Navigator 4.0. Thus, if you're concerned about compatibility with Internet Explorer, you should avoid the <LAYER> tag or provide an alternate HTML document for those users.

**FIG. 28.1**
Without positioning the layer, you can't tell the difference between this result and streaming HTML.

**N O T E**  Internet Explorer does have support for layers using a different technology. You instead use the ActiveX HTML Layout Control. ▦

## Positioning a Layer

Positioning a layer on your HTML document is real power. You no longer have to struggle to get just the look you want with HTML. Now, you can create any look you like by creating individual blocks of HTML and positioning them individually, using the LEFT and TOP attributes of the <LAYER> tag, like this:

```
<LAYER TOP=100 LEFT=20>
```

LEFT and TOP are represented in pixels and are relative to the top-left corner of the containing area within the HTML document. That is, these attributes are relative to the area created if you remove the <LAYER> and </LAYER> tags. For example, to create a layer 10 pixels from the left edge of the browser window and 40 pixels from the top edge, use LEFT=10 and TOP=40. The browser draws the HTML document as though the entire <LAYER> container did not exist, and then the layer is overlapped with the Web page at the given offset.

Listing 28.2 shows an HTML document with a layer positioned at 0, 0. Notice in Figure 28.2 how the contents of the HTML document show through the layer.

Part

VI

Ch

28

**Listing 28.2    Positioning a Layer**

```
<HTML>
<HEAD>
<TITLE>Layer 2</TITLE>
</HEAD>
<BODY>

<P>This example shows what the same basic layer looks like.</P>

<P>This layer is positioned, however, so that it overlaps
the HTML document below it. Notice how this text displays
through the image's transparent background.</P>

<P>This layer is positioned, however, so that it overlaps
the HTML document below it. Notice how this text displays
through the image's transparent background.</P>

<P>This layer is positioned, however, so that it overlaps
the HTML document below it. Notice how this text displays
through the image's transparent background.</P>

<P>This layer is positioned, however, so that it overlaps
the HTML document below it. Notice how this text displays
through the image's transparent background.</P>

<LAYER TOP=0 LEFT=0>
<IMG SRC=init.gif>
</LAYER>

</BODY>
</HTML>
```

**N O T E**   Positioning a layer at 0,0 isn't the same as omitting the LEFT and TOP attributes from the <LAYER> tag. Positioning a layer at 0, 0 causes the layer to overlap the Web page at the top-left corner. Omitting the LEFT and TOP attributes causes the contents of the layer to appear inline. ▧

Listing 28.3 is a similar example that positions the layer in the middle of the Web page. As shown in Figure 28.3, the contents of the HTML document show through the contents of the layer.

**Listing 28.3    Positioning a Layer in the Middle of the Web Page**

```
<HTML>
<HEAD>
<TITLE>Layer 3</TITLE>
</HEAD>
<BODY>
```

```
<P>You can position the layer anywhere you like.</P>

<P>This layer is positioned, however, so that it overlaps
the HTML document below it. Notice how this text displays
through the image's transparent background.</P>

<P>This layer is positioned, however, so that it overlaps
the HTML document below it. Notice how this text displays
through the image's transparent background.</P>

<P>This layer is positioned, however, so that it overlaps
the HTML document below it. Notice how this text displays
through the image's transparent background.</P>

<P>This layer is positioned, however, so that it overlaps
the HTML document below it. Notice how this text displays
through the image's transparent background.</P>

<LAYER TOP=40 LEFT=100>
<IMG SRC=init.gif>
</LAYER>

</BODY>
</HTML>
```

**FIG. 28.2**

Using a layer positioned at 0, 0, you can write HTML that fits snugly against the left border of the browser window.

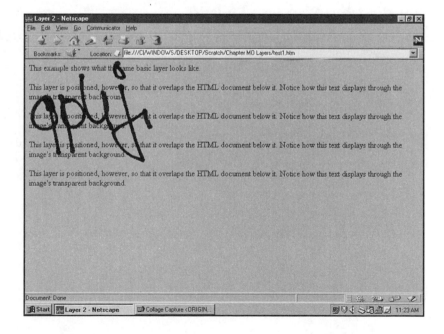

**FIG. 28.3**

If the layer doesn't entirely fit within the browser window, the browser clips the layer.

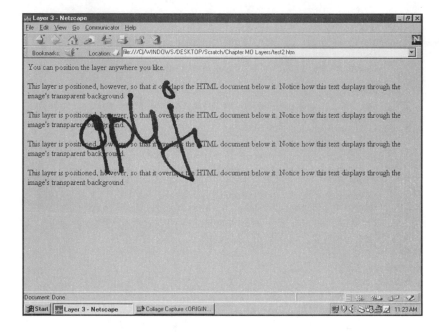

## Changing the Size of a Layer

You can't change the height of a layer because the height is determined by the size of the layer's content. You can control the width of a layer, however, and let the browser determine the appropriate height. You use the <LAYER> tag's WIDTH attribute to set the width of the layer in pixels:

```
<LAYER TOP=5 LEFT=5 WIDTH=300>
```

You don't use the WIDTH attribute to define the absolute width of the layer. Instead, this attribute is used to suggest a width for purposes of wrapping the text contained within the layer. If the text doesn't completely fill the layer, however, the layer will not actually be as wide as the specified value. If you're inserting an image (or another element that the browser can't wrap) inside of a layer and the image is wider than the suggested width, the actual width of the layer will be bigger than the suggested value.

Listing 28.4 shows an example of a layer positioned 100 pixels from the top that is 60 pixels wide. As shown in Figure 28.4, the text wraps within the layer, just like it would wrap within a table cell that's 60 pixels wide.

**Listing 28.4   Specifying the Width of a Layer**

```
<HTML>
<HEAD>
<TITLE>Layer 6</TITLE>
</HEAD>
<BODY>
```

```
<LAYER TOP=0>
This text is contained within the first layer. It starts in the
upper, left-hand corner of the browser window. Notice that the
width of this layer isn't controlled.
</LAYER>

<LAYER TOP=100 WIDTH=160>
This text is contained within the first layer. It starts in the
upper, left-hand corner of the browser window. Notice how the width
of this layer is controlled.
</LAYER>

</BODY>
</HTML>
```

**FIG. 28.4**

You can leave out either the TOP or LEFT attributes and the browser will position the layer as though the omitted attribute is 0.

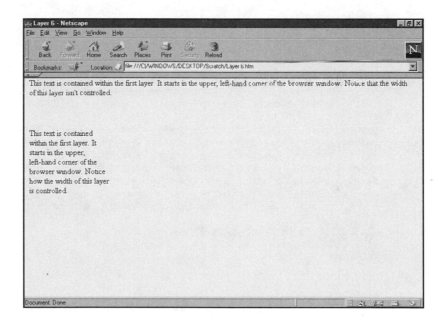

**TIP** You can use a layer to do many of the same formatting tricks you've learned to do with the <TABLE> tag.

## Using a Background Image or Color

By default, the empty space in a layer is transparent. That is, if a pixel in the layer doesn't contain any rendered text, or it contains a portion of an image that's transparent, anything underneath the layer shows through at that point. You can use this to create some incredible effects.

However, if a layer contains mostly text and it's overlapped, the content of the layer might be hard to read. Regardless, you might want the layer to occupy a well-defined space on the HTML document. You can use a background image or background color with a layer so that what's behind the layer doesn't show through.

Listing 28.5 shows a layer that defines a background color for a layer using the BGCOLOR attribute. You can set this attribute to any valid color name or color value (#FF0000, for example) just as you would with any other color attribute in HTML. As Figure 28.5 shows, the content behind the layer no longer shows through.

### Listing 28.5   Setting a Layer's Background Color

```
<HTML>
<HEAD>
<TITLE>Layer 4</TITLE>
</HEAD>
<BODY>

<P>Change the background color of a layer.
Notice that this text doesn't show through a layer
that uses the BGCOLOR attribute.</P>

qwerty. qwerty. qwerty. qwerty. qwerty. qwerty. qwerty. qwerty. qwerty.
qwerty. qwerty. qwerty. qwerty. qwerty. qwerty. qwerty. qwerty. qwerty.
qwerty. qwerty. qwerty. qwerty. qwerty. qwerty. qwerty. qwerty. qwerty.
qwerty. qwerty. qwerty. qwerty. qwerty. qwerty. qwerty. qwerty. qwerty.
qwerty. qwerty. qwerty. qwerty. qwerty. qwerty. qwerty. qwerty. qwerty.
qwerty. qwerty. qwerty. qwerty. qwerty. qwerty. qwerty. qwerty. qwerty.
qwerty. qwerty. qwerty. qwerty. qwerty. qwerty. qwerty. qwerty. qwerty.

<LAYER TOP=40 LEFT=100 BGCOLOR=GRAY>
<IMG SRC=init.gif>
</LAYER>

</BODY>
</HTML>
```

Listing 28.6 shows you a similar example that sets a background image for the layer using the BACKGROUND attribute. You set the BACKGROUND attribute to the URL (relative or absolute) of the image you want to tile in the background of the layer. Unlike normal tiled backgrounds in HTML, if a layer's background image has transparent areas, the content behind the layer shows through those areas. Figure 28.6 shows what this example looks like in the browser window.

**FIG. 28.5**

When you use a
background color, the
content behind the
layer doesn't peek
through.

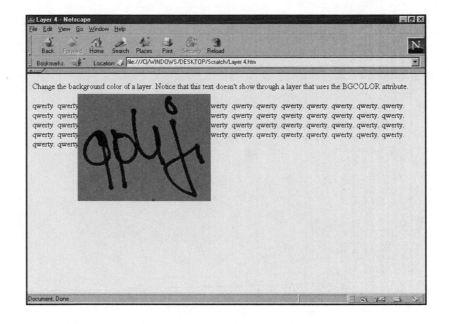

---

### Listing 28.6    Setting a Layer's Background Image

```
<HTML>
<HEAD>
<TITLE>Layer 5</TITLE>
</HEAD>
<BODY>

<P>Use a background image with a layer.
Notice that this text doesn't show through a layer
that uses the BACKGROUND attribute.</P>

qwerty. qwerty. qwerty. qwerty. qwerty. qwerty. qwerty. qwerty. qwerty.
qwerty. qwerty. qwerty. qwerty. qwerty. qwerty. qwerty. qwerty. qwerty.
qwerty. qwerty. qwerty. qwerty. qwerty. qwerty. qwerty. qwerty. qwerty.
qwerty. qwerty. qwerty. qwerty. qwerty. qwerty. qwerty. qwerty. qwerty.
qwerty. qwerty. qwerty. qwerty. qwerty. qwerty. qwerty. qwerty. qwerty.
qwerty. qwerty. qwerty. qwerty. qwerty. qwerty. qwerty. qwerty. qwerty.
qwerty. qwerty. qwerty. qwerty. qwerty. qwerty. qwerty. qwerty. qwerty.

<LAYER TOP=40 LEFT=100 BACKGROUND=bg.gif>
<IMG SRC=init.gif>
</LAYER>

</BODY>
</HTML>
```

**FIG. 28.6**
Use your favorite graphics editor to create a border and then insert it into the layer.

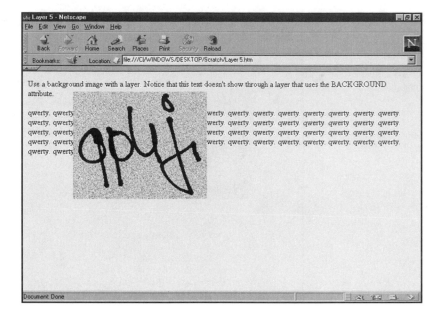

## Using Multiple Layers

Thus far, you've seen examples that use a single layer. However, you can add as many layers as you like in your HTML document, as shown in Listing 28.7 and Figure 28.7. Each layer can contain any valid HTML, including images, text, and plug-ins. Naturally, additional layers consume additional resources—browser memory and download time in particular.

**Listing 28.7   Using Multiple Layers**

```
<HTML>
<HEAD>
<TITLE>Layer 7</TITLE>
</HEAD>
<BODY>

<LAYER TOP=40 LEFT=60 BACKGROUND=bg.gif>
<B>This is the first layer.</B><BR>
<B>This is the first layer.</B><BR>
<B>This is the first layer.</B><BR>
<B>This is the first layer.</B><BR>
<B>This is the first layer.</B><BR>
<B>This is the first layer.</B><BR>
<B>This is the first layer.</B><BR>
<B>This is the first layer.</B><BR>
</LAYER>
```

```
<LAYER TOP=40 LEFT=220>
<IMG SRC=init.gif>
</LAYER>

</BODY>
</HTML>
```

**FIG. 28.7**

You can build your entire HTML document using layers and then arrange them as you like.

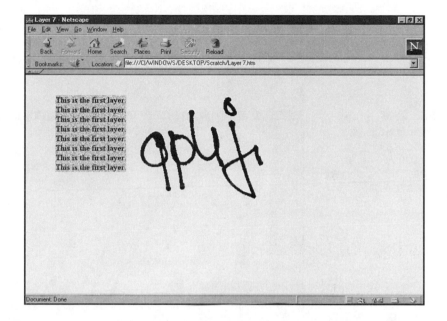

You can also cause layers to overlap by setting each layer's TOP and LEFT attributes so that one layer appears on top of another. Figure 28.8 shows two layers. The first layer contains a handful of text and has a background image. The second layer contains an image with a transparent background. The second layer is positioned so that it overlaps the first layer.

**Listing 28.8   Positioning Two Layers so that They Overlap**

```
<HTML>
<HEAD>
<TITLE>Layer 8</TITLE>
</HEAD>
<BODY>

<LAYER TOP=40 LEFT=60 BACKGROUND=bg.gif>
<B>This is the first layer. It's behind the second layer.</B><BR>
<B>This is the first layer. It's behind the second layer.</B><BR>
<B>This is the first layer. It's behind the second layer.</B><BR>
<B>This is the first layer. It's behind the second layer.</B><BR>
<B>This is the first layer. It's behind the second layer.</B><BR>
```

*continues*

Part
**VI**

Ch
**28**

**Listing 28.8 Continued**

```
<B>This is the first layer. It's behind the second layer.</B><BR>
<B>This is the first layer. It's behind the second layer.</B><BR>
<B>This is the first layer. It's behind the second layer.</B><BR>
</LAYER>

<LAYER TOP=80 LEFT=200>
<IMG SRC=init.gif>
</LAYER>

</BODY>
</HTML>
```

**FIG. 28.8**

Because the image in the second layer has transparent areas, the content behind this layer bleeds through.

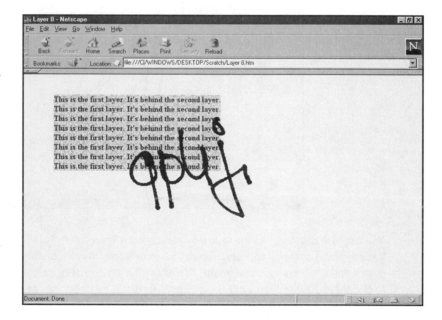

**N O T E** By default, the browser draws overlapped layers in the order it encounters them. That is, it draws the first layer, overlaps that with the second layer, and so on. ▪

## Changing a Layer's *Z-INDEX*

If you don't like the order in which the browser overlaps layers, you can easily change it. The most straightforward way to change the order in which layers overlap is by using the <LAYER> tag's Z-INDEX attribute, which defines the stacking order for layers:

```
<LAYER Z-INDEX=1>
```

You can set this attribute to any positive integer value. Layers are drawn in increasing stacking order. For example, a layer with a stacking order of 10 overlaps a layer with a stacking order of 5. On the other hand, a layer with a stacking order of 3 is overlapped by a layer with a stacking order of 5.

Listing 28.9 is an example of three layers, each of which uses the Z-INDEX attribute to define its stacking order. The first layer has a stacking order of 2, the second has a stacking order of 1, and the third has a stacking order of 3. Thus, the browser draws the second layer first, the first layer second, and the third layer last, as shown in Figure 28.9.

**Listing 28.9    Using Z-INDEX**

```
<HTML>
<HEAD>
<TITLE>Layer 9</TITLE>
</HEAD>
<BODY>

<LAYER TOP=40 LEFT=60 BACKGROUND=bg.gif Z-INDEX=2>
<B>This is the first layer. It's in the middle.</B><BR>
<B>This is the first layer. It's in the middle.</B><BR>
<B>This is the first layer. It's in the middle.</B><BR>
<B>This is the first layer. It's in the middle.</B><BR>
<B>This is the first layer. It's in the middle.</B><BR>
<B>This is the first layer. It's in the middle.</B><BR>
<B>This is the first layer. It's in the middle.</B><BR>
<B>This is the first layer. It's in the middle.</B><BR>
</LAYER>

<LAYER TOP=80 LEFT=200 BACKGROUND=bg2.gif Z-INDEX=1>
<B>This is the second layer. It's behind the first layer.</B><BR>
<B>This is the second layer. It's behind the first layer.</B><BR>
<B>This is the second layer. It's behind the first layer.</B><BR>
<B>This is the second layer. It's behind the first layer.</B><BR>
<B>This is the second layer. It's behind the first layer.</B><BR>
<B>This is the second layer. It's behind the first layer.</B><BR>
<B>This is the second layer. It's behind the first layer.</B><BR>
<B>This is the second layer. It's behind the first layer.</B><BR>
</LAYER>

<LAYER TOP=100 LEFT=80 Z-INDEX=3>
<IMG SRC=init.gif>
</LAYER>

</BODY>
</HTML>
```

**FIG. 28.9**

The Z-INDEX attribute essentially defines the order in which each layer is drawn.

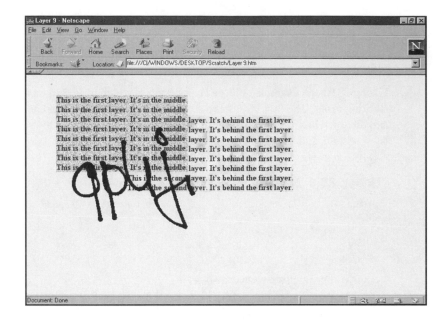

 **T I P** You can overlap several layers at the same position, define each layer's stacking order in sequence, and then peel away the layers one at a time (using a script) to create a simple animation.

## Overlapping Two Layers with *ABOVE* and *BELOW*

The Z-INDEX attribute specifies the order in which layers are drawn by ranking each layer. You can get much more specific than that, however, by defining exactly which layer you want to display above or below another layer. For example, if you have a layer containing an image, and you want to make sure that a specific layer containing text is displayed over it, you can tell the browser to specifically draw the text layer over the image layer.

Before you can do that, however, you have to give each layer a name. Use the NAME attribute, like this:

```
<LAYER NAME=MYLAYER>
```

Then, you use the <LAYER> tag's ABOVE or BELOW attributes to specify exactly which layer you want to draw above or below the current layer, referring to each layer by its name. For example, if you have an existing layer called MYLAYER, and you want to make sure that the browser draws it below a layer named Fridnee, you write a <LAYER> tag that looks like this:

```
<LAYER NAME=Fridnee BELOW=MYLAYER>
```

On the other hand, if you want to make sure that the browser draws MYLAYER on top of a layer named Xemag, you write a <LAYER> tag that looks like this:

```
<LAYER NAME=Xemag ABOVE=MYLAYER>
```

Listing 28.10 shows the example from Listing 28.9, rewritten to use the ABOVE and BELOW attributes. Instead of defining a Z-INDEX for each layer, it specifies that the layer called FIRST is above the layer called SECOND, and below the layer called THIRD (see Figure 28.10).

### Listing 28.10   Using *ABOVE* and *BELOW* to Specify Order

```
<HTML>
<HEAD>
<TITLE>Layer 10</TITLE>
</HEAD>
<BODY>

<LAYER NAME=FIRST TOP=40 LEFT=60 BACKGROUND=bg.gif>
<B>This is the first layer. It's in the middle.</B><BR>
<B>This is the first layer. It's in the middle.</B><BR>
<B>This is the first layer. It's in the middle.</B><BR>
<B>This is the first layer. It's in the middle.</B><BR>
<B>This is the first layer. It's in the middle.</B><BR>
<B>This is the first layer. It's in the middle.</B><BR>
<B>This is the first layer. It's in the middle.</B><BR>
<B>This is the first layer. It's in the middle.</B><BR>
</LAYER>

<LAYER NAME=SECOND TOP=80 LEFT=200 BACKGROUND=bg2.gif ABOVE=FIRST>
<B>This is the second layer. It's behind the first layer.</B><BR>
<B>This is the second layer. It's behind the first layer.</B><BR>
<B>This is the second layer. It's behind the first layer.</B><BR>
<B>This is the second layer. It's behind the first layer.</B><BR>
<B>This is the second layer. It's behind the first layer.</B><BR>
<B>This is the second layer. It's behind the first layer.</B><BR>
<B>This is the second layer. It's behind the first layer.</B><BR>
<B>This is the second layer. It's behind the first layer.</B><BR>
</LAYER>

<LAYER NAME=THIRD TOP=100 LEFT=80 BELOW=FIRST>
<IMG SRC=init.gif>
</LAYER>

</BODY>
</HTML>
```

Part
VI

Ch
28

**FIG. 28.10**
If you specify an order that doesn't make sense, the browser will often get very confused and display nonsense.

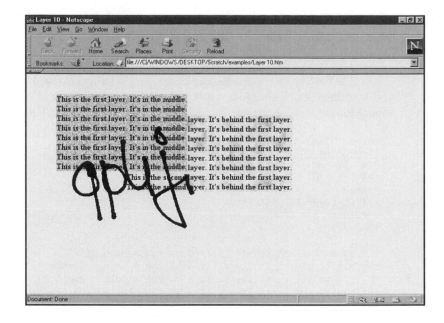

# Attaching Scripts to Layers

The ability to position a layer anywhere in an HTML document, and to overlap that layer with other layers, gives you a wealth of publishing capabilities. Additionally, you can create a variety of special effects by attaching a script to a layer, which can then be used to hide, show, or move the layer within the browser window.

You can reference a layer by using its name, like this:

```
Layers.LayerName
```

*LayerName* is the name of the layer as defined by the <LAYER> tag's NAME attribute. You can also reference a layer by using the layers array: document.layers. You can use an index with the layers array or you can reference a layer in the array by name.

▶ **See** "The *Date* and *Array* Objects," **p. 163**, if you're unsure of how to use arrays.

```
document.layers[2]
document.layers["MyLayer"]
```

Layers have a variety of properties and methods. Properties of a layer are written as *LayerName.PropertyName* and *LayerName.MethodName(Parameters)*. For example, to make a layer invisible, you set its visibility property to HIDE, like this:

```
layers.MyLayer.visibility = "hide";
```

▶ **See** "Objects, Properties, and Methods in JavaScript," **p. 88,** for more information about using objects with JavaScript.

Table 28.1 describes the properties of the Layer object. These properties roughly correspond to the attributes you've already learned about in this chapter.

**Table 28.1   The *Layer* Object's Properties**

| Property | Description |
| --- | --- |
| name | The name of the layer; you can't change this property |
| left | Specifies the left offset of the layer |
| top | Specifies the top offset of the layer |
| visibility | Set to "hide", "show", or "inherit"; note that these are strings, not keywords |
| clip | Defines the region of the layer that's displayed; clip has the sub-properties left, top, right, bottom, width, and height |
| siblingAbove | The name of the layer displayed immediately above the referenced layer |
| siblingBelow | The name of the layer displayed immediately below the referenced layer |
| parentLayer | The name of the layer that contains the referenced layer, if the layer is nested |
| layers | An array that contains all of the child layers that are nested within the referenced layer |

Table 28.2 describes the methods of the Layer object. Note that every method corresponds to a property so that you can control layers by setting their properties or calling their methods (or both).

**Table 28.2   The *Layer* Object's Methods**

| Method | Description |
| --- | --- |
| offset($dx,dy$) | Offsets the layer by the given deltas so that LEFT = LEFT + $dx$ and TOP = TOP + $dy$ |
| moveTo($x,y$) | Changes the layer's position so that LEFT = $x$ and TOP = $y$ |
| resize(*width, height*) | Changes the height and width of the layer's clipping rectangle |
| moveAbove(*layer*) | Stacks the referenced layer above the layer called *layer* |
| moveBelow(*layer*) | Stacks the referenced layer below the layer called *layer* |

Part
VI

Ch
28

# Using a Script to Hide or Show a Layer

You can use a script to hide and show layers in an HTML document. For example, you can create a layer that is displayed only when the user moves the mouse across an image. In that case, you set the layer's VISIBILITY attribute to "HIDE" so that it's not displayed initially. Then, in the image's OnMouseOver event, you set the layer's visibility property to "SHOW", like this:

```
Layers.MyLayer.visibility = "show";
```

Listing 28.11 shows you an example that does something similar. It contains three layers and three buttons. The script associated with each button toggles the visibility of each layer. Click a button associated with a visible layer and the script makes the layer invisible (see Figure 28.11).

Take a look at the function called ToggleFirst(). It toggles the state of the flag called ShowFirst, which indicates whether or not the layer called FIRST is visible. Then, it sets the layer's visibility property to "HIDE" if ShowFirst is false; otherwise, it sets the property to "INHERIT".

### Listing 28.11   Hiding and Showing Layers

```
<HTML>
<HEAD>
<TITLE>Layer 11</TITLE>

<SCRIPT LANGUAGE=JAVASCRIPT>

ShowFirst = true;
ShowSecond=false;
ShowThird=true;

function ToggleFirst()
{
  ShowFirst = !ShowFirst;
  document.layers["FIRST"].visibility = ShowFirst ? "INHERIT" : "HIDE";
}

function ToggleSecond()
{
  ShowSecond = !ShowSecond;
  document.layers["SECOND"].visibility = ShowSecond ? "INHERIT" : "HIDE";
}

function ToggleThird()
{
  ShowThird = !ShowThird;
  document.layers["THIRD"].visibility = ShowThird ? "INHERIT" : "HIDE";
}

</SCRIPT>
```

```
</HEAD>
<BODY>
<LAYER NAME=FIRST TOP=80 LEFT=60 BACKGROUND=bg.gif>
<B>This is the first layer. It's in the middle.</B><BR>
<B>This is the first layer. It's in the middle.</B><BR>
<B>This is the first layer. It's in the middle.</B><BR>
<B>This is the first layer. It's in the middle.</B><BR>
<B>This is the first layer. It's in the middle.</B><BR>
<B>This is the first layer. It's in the middle.</B><BR>
<B>This is the first layer. It's in the middle.</B><BR>
<B>This is the first layer. It's in the middle.</B><BR>
</LAYER>

<LAYER NAME=SECOND TOP=120 LEFT=200 BACKGROUND=bg2.gif Z-INDEX=1 BELOW=FIRST
VISIBILITY=HIDE>
<B>This is the second layer. It's behind the first layer.</B><BR>
<B>This is the second layer. It's behind the first layer.</B><BR>
<B>This is the second layer. It's behind the first layer.</B><BR>
<B>This is the second layer. It's behind the first layer.</B><BR>
<B>This is the second layer. It's behind the first layer.</B><BR>
<B>This is the second layer. It's behind the first layer.</B><BR>
<B>This is the second layer. It's behind the first layer.</B><BR>
<B>This is the second layer. It's behind the first layer.</B><BR>
</LAYER>

<LAYER NAME=THIRD TOP=140 LEFT=80 BELOW=FIRST>
<IMG SRC=init.gif>
</LAYER>

<LAYER TOP=0 LEFT=0>
<FORM NAME=TOGGLE>
  <TABLE ALIGN=CENTER>
    <TD>
      <INPUT NAME=FIRST TYPE=BUTTON VALUE="Toggle First Layer "
onclick="ToggleFirst();">
    </TD>
    <TD>
      <INPUT NAME=SECOND TYPE=BUTTON VALUE="Toggle Second Layer"
onclick="ToggleSecond();">
    </TD>
    <TD>
      <INPUT NAME=THIRD TYPE=BUTTON VALUE="Toggle Third Layer "
onclick="ToggleThird();">
    </TD>
  </TABLE>
</FORM>
</LAYER>

</BODY>
</HTML>
```

**FIG. 28.11**

As you click buttons to hide a layer, the browser peels that layer away, unveiling what's underneath it.

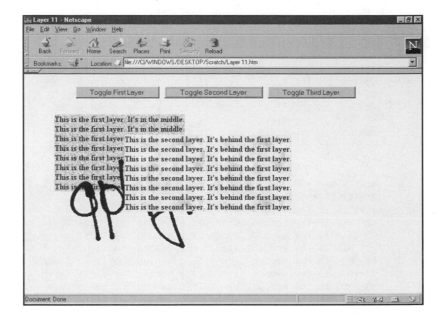

 **T I P**   In Windows 95, there are dialog boxes that contain a button with the text More>>. When you click that button, additional fields are presented. You can achieve the same effect in an HTML form by attaching a script to a form's button, which shows another form hidden within a layer.

## Moving a Layer with a Script

Besides showing and hiding a layer, you can also move it around on the Web page. You can use this to create some pretty fancy animation effects, such as a curtain that appears to open, unveiling the contents of the page. Moving a layer around is easy. You can either use the offset or moveTo methods; or you can set the value of the left and top properties, which is the approach taken in Listing 28.12; the result is shown in Figure 28.12.

This example contains two layers. It also contains four buttons labeled Up, Down, Left, and Right. Each button is associated with a function that moves the second layer in the appropriate direction. For example, the Up function subtracts 10 from the second layer's top property, which has the effect of moving the layer up 10 pixels. The Right function adds 10 to the second layer's left property, which has the effect of moving the layer right 10 pixels.

### Listing 28.12   Moving a Layer with a Script

```
<HTML>
<HEAD>
<TITLE>Layer 12</TITLE>
```

```
<SCRIPT LANGUAGE=JAVASCRIPT>

function Up()
{
  document.layers["SECOND"].top -= 10;
}

function Down()
{
  document.layers["SECOND"].top += 10;
}

function Left()
{
  document.layers["SECOND"].left -= 10;
}

function Right()
{
  document.layers["SECOND"].left += 10;
}

</SCRIPT>

</HEAD>
<BODY>

<LAYER NAME=FIRST TOP=200 LEFT=300 BACKGROUND=bg.gif>
<B>This is the first layer. It's always on top.</B><BR>
<B>This is the first layer. It's always on top.</B><BR>
<B>This is the first layer. It's always on top.</B><BR>
<B>This is the first layer. It's always on top.</B><BR>
<B>This is the first layer. It's always on top.</B><BR>
<B>This is the first layer. It's always on top.</B><BR>
<B>This is the first layer. It's always on top.</B><BR>
<B>This is the first layer. It's always on top.</B><BR>
<B>This is the first layer. It's always on top.</B><BR>
</LAYER>

<LAYER NAME=SECOND TOP=180 LEFT=0 ABOVE=FIRST>
<IMG SRC=init.gif>
</LAYER>

<LAYER TOP=0 LEFT=0>
<FORM NAME=BUTTONS>
  <TABLE>
    <TR>
      <TD></TD>
      <TD ALIGN=CENTER>
        <INPUT WIDTH=100% NAME=UP TYPE=BUTTON VALUE="Up" onclick="Up();">
      </TD>
      <TD></TD>
    </TR>
```

*continues*

**Listing 28.12   Continued**

```
    <TR>
      <TD ALIGN=CENTER>
        <INPUT NAME=LEFT TYPE=BUTTON VALUE="Left " onclick="Left();">
      </TD>
      <TD></TD>
      <TD ALIGN=CENTER>
        <INPUT WIDTH=100 NAME=RIGHT TYPE=BUTTON VALUE="Right"
        ➥onclick="Right();">
      </TD>
    </TR>

    <TR>
      <TD></TD>
      <TD ALIGN=CENTER>
        <INPUT WIDTH=100 NAME=DOWN TYPE=BUTTON VALUE="Down "
        ➥onclick="Down();">
      </TD>
      <TD></TD>
    </TR>

  </TABLE>
</FORM>
</LAYER>

</BODY>
</HTML>
```

**FIG. 28.12**

As you move the second layer relative to the first layer, it will disappear under it. This is because the second layer's ABOVE property is set to FIRST.

**TIP** Resizing the Web browser causes the layers to return to their original position.

# Nesting Layers

So far, you've only seen cases where a handful of layers were added to the HTML document. They were siblings insofar as one was not contained within another. You can insert one layer inside of another layer, however, to create a parent-child relationship. In that case, the child (inside) layer is relative to the parent (outside) layer. Thus, if you create a layer called PARENT and locate it at 10, 10, and then nest a layer inside of PARENT that is called CHILD, located at 5, 5, the child layer will actually be displayed at 15, 15 on the HTML document. If you move the parent layer to 20, 20, the child layer will move right along with it to 25, 25.

Listing 28.13 shows you an example of nested layers. The parent layer contains an image of a Christmas tree (sorry about the bad artwork). It contains a number of nested layers that represent bulbs. The coordinates of each nested layer are relative to the upper-left corner of the parent layer. If you move the Christmas tree to another location on the Web page, the bulbs will move right along with it.

**Listing 28.13    Nesting Layers**

```
<HTML>
<HEAD>
<TITLE>Layer 13</TITLE>
</HEAD>
<BODY>

<LAYER TOP=0 LEFT=0 CLIP=300,400>
<IMG SRC=xtree.gif>

<LAYER TOP=160 LEFT=60>
</LAYER>

<LAYER TOP=150 LEFT=60>
<IMG SRC=ball1.gif>
</LAYER>

<LAYER TOP=20 LEFT=100>
<IMG SRC=ball2.gif>
</LAYER>

<LAYER TOP=130 LEFT=120>
<IMG SRC=ball1.gif>
</LAYER>

<LAYER TOP=170 LEFT=140>
<IMG SRC=ball2.gif>
</LAYER>
```

*continues*

**Listing 28.13 Continued**

```
<LAYER TOP=200 LEFT=120>
<IMG SRC=ball2.gif>
</LAYER>

<LAYER TOP=80 LEFT=80>
<IMG SRC=ball3.gif>
</LAYER>

<LAYER TOP=90 LEFT=125>
<IMG SRC=ball3.gif>
</LAYER>

<LAYER TOP=200 LEFT=60>
<IMG SRC=ball3.gif>
</LAYER>

<LAYER TOP=200 LEFT=180>
<IMG SRC=ball3.gif>
</LAYER>

</LAYER>

</BODY>
</HTML>
```

**FIG. 28.13**

By capturing the mouse events for each bulb, you can allow the user to move the bulbs around on the Christmas tree.

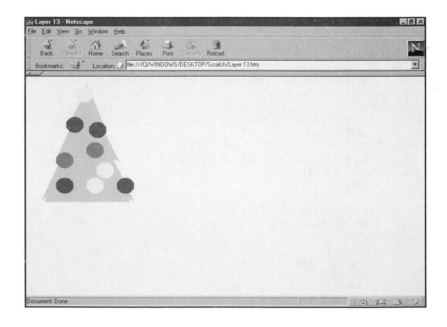

# Putting Layers to Practical Use: Fly-Over Tips

One of the practical uses for layers is to create fly-over help or tips for links and objects on the HTML document. For example, you can insert a number of art images on a page and then display more information about the image when the user moves the mouse across the image.

The example shown in Listing 28.14 gives the user additional information about each link on the HTML document. When the user moves the mouse over the second link shown in Figure 28.14, for example, the function associated with that link shows the appropriate layer, which contains additional information about the link.

**Listing 28.14  Providing Fly-Over Help for Links**

```
<HTML>
<HEAD>
<TITLE>Layer 14</TITLE>
</HEAD>
<BODY>

<SCRIPT LANGUAGE="JAVASCRIPT">

// Hide all of the layers (tips) in this HTML document

function ClearHelp()
{
  for( i=0; i < document.layers.length; i++)
    document.layers[i].visibility = "HIDE";
}

// Clear all the displayed layers; then, display the layer by the
// given name. Set a timer to automatically clear the layers after
// five seconds.

function OnLink( Name )
{
  ClearHelp()
  document.layers[Name].visibility="INHERIT";
  window.window.setTimeout( "ClearHelp()", 5000 );
}
</SCRIPT>

<A OnMouseOver='OnLink("LINK1")'
HREF="http://rampages.onramp.net/~jerry">Jerry's Home Page</A>
<LAYER NAME=LINK1 VISIBILITY=HIDE>
<TABLE BORDER=1 BGCOLOR=YELLOW>
  <TD>
    Click on this link to jump to Jerry's home page.
  </TD>
</TABLE>
</LAYER>
```

Part

**VI**

Ch

**28**

*continues*

**Listing 28.14  Continued**

```
<BR>

<A OnMouseOver='OnLink("LINK2")' HREF="http://www.netscape.com">Netscape's Home
➥Page</A>
<LAYER NAME=LINK2  VISIBILITY=HIDE>
<TABLE BORDER=1 BGCOLOR=YELLOW>
  <TD>
    Click on this link to jump to Netscape's home page.
  </TD>
</TABLE>
</LAYER>

<BR>

<A OnMouseOver='OnLink("LINK3")' HREF="http://www.yahoo.com">Yahoo!</A>
<LAYER NAME=LINK3  VISIBILITY=HIDE>
<TABLE BORDER=1 BGCOLOR=YELLOW>
  <TD>
    Click on this link to jump to Yahoo!
  </TD>
</TABLE>
</LAYER>
</BODY>
</HTML>
```

**FIG. 28.14**

Using a bordered table within a layer helps better set it off from the underlying HTML document.

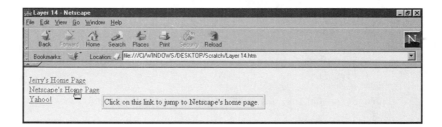

At the bottom half of the listing, you see three links. Each link uses the OnMouseOver attribute to associate a JavaScript function with that link. In this case, each link is associated with the function called OnLink. That function is passed the name of the layer to be shown. The first link calls OnLink like this:

```
OnLink("LINK1")
```

Just under each link, you see a layer. Each layer has a unique name and is hidden. Each layer also contains the help text associated with the preceding link.

At the top of the listing, you see two functions. Here's a description of each:

| | |
|---|---|
| OnLink(*Name*) | Hides all of the layers on the HTML document, then displays the layer called *Name*. Set a timer to call ClearHelp() in 5 seconds (5,000 milliseconds) so that the browser will hide the layer at that time. |
| ClearHelp() | Hide all of the layers in the HTML document. It uses the layers array to visit each layer and to set its visibility property to "HIDE". Note that you can get the size of the layers array by using the property document.layers.length. ● |

# CHAPTER 29

# Style Sheets

**S**tyle sheets are a W3C recommendation that defines a standard by which you can format Web pages through the use of desktop publishing concepts. Microsoft Internet Explorer 3.0 was the first browser to support style sheets, but Netscape is committed to supporting style sheets in the full release of Communicator. You can get more information about the W3C recommendation at its Web site: **http://www.w3.org/pub/WWW/TR/WD-css1.html**. Note that W3C uses the terminology "Cascading Style Sheets Level 1." This chapter, however, uses the simpler language, "style sheet."

Netscape has its own style sheet "thing" going on, too. It's called JavaScript Style Sheets, which you'll learn about in this chapter. JavaScript Style Sheets, at first, might seem a bit daunting, but in reality, it's nothing more than the ability to write style sheets by using JavaScript keywords and statements. In other words, Netscape exposes a few new style sheet-related objects that you can manipulate in a script.

Before you go any further, you need to understand what you can do with style sheets. Most word processors let you specify styles that describe how a block of text will be formatted. For example, you can specify a paragraph style that sets the line spacing to one, the font to Courier, and the left margin to one inch. Then, you can assign this style to any number of paragraphs in your document. You can use HTML style sheets to do essentially the same thing. ■

## Attach style sheets to your HTML file

This chapter shows you four different ways to associate a style sheet with your HTML document.

## Set a variety of properties within a style

Style sheets support a large variety of properties you can set within your style definitions.

## Save time and space by grouping properties

You can group the most common properties together to save time and make your HTML files more readable.

## Learn about more-advanced topics

In this chapter, you learn more-advanced style sheet topics such as classes and inheritance.

## Provide for browsers lacking style sheet support

If you follow a few simple rules, users that don't have browsers with style sheet support will be okay.

## Use JavaScript Style Sheets (JSSS) in your Web page

Netscape has introduced JavaScript Style Sheets to expand the intrinsic capabilities of cascading style sheets.

Here's a sample of the techniques you'll learn in this chapter:

- Change the spacing between text lines, individual words, and individual characters.
- Set the left, right, top, and bottom margins for an element (block of text within an HTML container).
- Set the indent for an element.
- Change the font size, style, and other font attributes of the text in an element.
- Create a border around an element and set the border's width and style.
- Set the background color or background image of an element (kind of like a watermark).

> **CAUTION**
>
> At the time of this writing, the W3C recommendation hasn't been approved as an official standard. Browser support for style sheets is very limited. Thus, the capabilities described in this chapter should be regarded as influx. In addition, many portions of the W3C recommendation are optional and thus need not be supported by all browsers claiming to support style sheets.

# Attaching a Style Sheet to Your HTML Document

The main benefit of using HTML style sheets is in being able to separate the format of your Web pages from the content. You specify how the text will look in a different location than the contents of the text itself. If you later decide that you want all your headings to be displayed in blue characters, you only have to change the style for those headings, instead of changing each heading within the HTML file.

So, how do you attach a style sheet to an HTML file? There are four methods:

**Linking**    You can link an HTML file to a style sheet contained in a separate file.

**Embedding**    You can embed the style sheet within the HTML file by using the <STYLE> container.

**Inline**    You can define styles on-the-fly within an HTML tag such as <P>.

**Import**    You can use the @import keyword to import a style sheet into your HTML file.

## Linking a Style Sheet

As noted earlier, you can create a style sheet in a separate file and then apply that style sheet to all of the pages on your Web site. I recommend this method to you only because it makes creating a consistent Web site much easier. In fact, you can create a corporate style sheet and have everyone in your organization use it with their Web sites (imagine an intranet with a common look).

You store a linked style sheet in a text file with the CSS file extension. It's a plain text file that you can create with your favorite text editor. The format of the text file is readable by humans and is easy to understand. Thus, you won't have any trouble creating your style sheets by hand.

To link to a style sheet stored in a separate file, store all of the style definitions in the CSS file and link your HTML files to it through use of the <LINK> tag, like this:

```
<LINK REL=STYLESHEET HREF="http://www.myserver.com/mysheet.css"
➡TYPE="text/css">
```

Assign the URL of the style sheet to the HREF attribute. Set TYPE to "text/css" so browsers that don't support style sheets can avoid the download.

 **TIP** Store your corporate style sheets in a common location on the Web server and then have everyone in the company who is creating Web pages reference that style sheet from their HTML files. Everyone can even use the same <LINK> tag. In this way, you can have a more consistent look across all of the Web pages on the server.

## Embedding a Style Sheet

You don't have to store your style sheet in a separate file. You can embed the style sheet inside each HTML file. Note that the styles within an embedded style sheet only affect the HTML within that file. Thus, you can't embed a style sheet in an HTML file and expect to use that across multiple HTML files without copying and pasting it into each file (thus, my earlier recommendation that you use linked style sheets).

The <STYLE> container is used to embed a style sheet in your HTML file. Put this container between the <HTML> and <BODY> tags of your file, like this:

```
<HTML>
<HEAD>
</HEAD>
<STYLE TYPE="text/css">
Style definitions go here
</STYLE>
<BODY>
</BODY>
</HTML>
```

The following example shows you what a real <STYLE> tag looks like. You can ignore the actual style definitions for now—they will be covered soon.

```
<STYLE TYPE="text/css">
H1 {color: BLUE}
</STYLE>
```

## Defining Styles Inline

Inline styles are simply styles that you define on-the-fly. You can use inline styles to quickly change the appearance of a single tag—on-the-run. You can also use inline styles to override a style for a particular tag. For example, if you've defined a style that sets the color of the H1 tag to blue, you can set the color of a specific element by setting its H1 tag to red.

Inline styles affect the individual tag for which it is defined; that is, you define a tag's style within the tag itself. You do this by using the STYLE attribute, which is supported by all the child tags of the BODY tag. To define an inline style, add the STYLE attribute to the tag whose style you want to change and set its value to the string representing the style definition, like this:

```
<H1 STYLE="color: blue">
```

**N O T E**  If an inline style conflicts with an embedded or linked style, the inline style wins. This enables you to change individual elements without modifying the overall style. ▪

You can use inline styles with the <DIV> tag to set the style for an entire block of HTML within your document. This works because of the concept of inheritance, which you'll learn about later in this chapter. For example, if you want to change the text color of an entire block of tags to blue, you can put those tags in the DIV container and define a style for the <DIV> tag that sets the text color to blue. It looks like this:

```
<DIV STYLE="color: blue">
<H1>This is a heading</H1>
<P>This is a paragraph. It will look blue in the user's browser</P>
</DIV>
```

You can also use inline style sheets with the <SPAN> tag to change the formatting for a few words, or even just a few letters. For example:

```
This is a <SPAN STYLE="color: blue">simple</SPAN> block of text.
```

**CAUTION**

Don't rely on inline styles too much. They'll quickly clutter your HTML file so that it's harder to read and much, much harder to maintain. This obviously diminishes the greatest advantage of style sheets: separating format from content. If you don't want to take full advantage of style sheets, however, but you still want to add a bit of special formatting to just a few elements, go ahead and use inline styles.

## Importing Style Sheets

Earlier in the chapter, you learned about linking to a style sheet. You can also use the @import keyword to import a style sheet into your HTML file. Remember that you're just importing the text file, thus, you have to insert it in the <STYLE> container. In this manner, importing a style sheet works just like embedding a style sheet into your HTML file. For example:

```
<STYLE TYPE="text/css">
@import url(http://www.myserver.com/style.css);
</STYLE>
```

**N O T E**  As of this writing, Internet Explorer 3.01 doesn't support the @import keyword. Therefore, you should link to your style sheet if you want to store it in a separate file. ▪

# Understanding What Style Sheets Look Like (Syntax)

As noted earlier, style sheets are stored in text files that you can easily read and understand. They're also very easy to create by hand. Note that, in the future, you'll be able to create and use styles sheets with the more popular HTML editors, such as Microsoft's FrontPage™.

Linked and embedded style sheets enable you to define styles for one or more individual tags. For example, you can create a style sheet that defines styles for the <H1>, <H2>, <P>, and <EM> tags. Each style definition is called a *rule*. A rule contains a selector (the HTML tag), followed by the declaration (the definition of the style). The rule's selector is what ties the style's definition to tags you use in the HTML file. Here's an example of a rule that defines a style for each occurrence of the <H1> tag:

```
H1 {color: blue}
 |  └────┬────┘
Rule  Declaration
```

The declaration is enclosed in curly braces ({}). Each item in the declaration has two parts: the property name and the value you're assigning to the property, separated by a colon (:). In the previous example, color is the property name and blue is the value you're assigning to it. HTML predefines dozens of property names (font-size, font-style, color, margin-right, and so on), which you'll learn about a bit later in this chapter. Each property also accepts a predefined type and range of values.

## Setting Multiple Properties

The examples you've seen so far only set a single property: color. You can also set multiple properties within a declaration. You do this by separating each assignment with a semicolon (;), like this:

```
H1 {color: blue; font-size: 12pt; text-line: center}
```

In this example, the browser will display each occurrence of the <H1> tag in the color blue, in a font size of 12 points, and centered in the browser window. For all other properties, the browser uses its default values. For example, it sets the font-style property to normal.

## Grouping Selectors

If you want to define a similar style for several tags, you can list them individually in your style sheet, like this:

```
P {font-size: 12pt}
UL {font-size: 12pt}
LI {font-size: 12pt}
```

This isn't the most efficient way to do this, however, considering that you can group the selectors together and define a rule for them as a group. The following example groups the selectors in the previous example on one line, and defines a rule that sets the font-size property to 12pt:

```
P, UL, LI {font-size: 12pt}
```

Note the comma between each selector in the list. Leaving this comma out means a totally different thing (see "Using Contextual Selectors," later in this chapter).

## Adding Comments to Your Style Sheet

If your style sheet gets a bit complicated or you need to explain why you've made a particular design decision, you can add a comment to the style sheet. Comments only serve to document your style sheet, they don't have any impact on how the browser displays the HTML document.

Enclose your comments between /* and */. The following example shows you what a one-line comment looks like:

```
BODY {margin-left: 1in}          /* Create space for sliders */
H1 {font-size: 16; margin-left: -1in}     /* Out one inch */
H2 {font-size: 14; margin-left: -1in}     /* Out one inch */
```

You can also use the /* and */ characters to create block comments. This is useful to explain an entire portion of your style sheet, like this:

```
/*--------------------------------------------------------------
   The margin-left property is set to one inch for the BODY tag.
   Since all of its enclosed tags will inherit this setting, the
   entire page will appear to be indented by one inch. The first-
   and second-level headings are indented to the left by one inch
   so that they slide out into the margin.
   ------------------------------------------------------------*/

BODY {margin-left: 1in}          /* Create space for sliders */
H1 {font-size: 16; margin-left: -1in}     /* Out one inch */
H2 {font-size: 14; margin-left: -1in}     /* Out one inch */
```

# Exploring the Properties of a Style

HTML style sheets define a wide variety of properties you can use to change how your HTML document looks in the browser. Most of the names contain multiple words, each separated by a dash (-). In property names that contain multiple words, the first word usually indicates a category. As well, most categories will also have a *shorthand* property name you can use to simplify your style sheet.

Table 29.1 provides an overview of the properties available in HTML style sheets. The property column contains the name of the property. Each name is explained in much more detail later in this chapter. The shorthand property column indicates whether or not that particular property can be set within a shorthand property. The inherited column indicates whether or not that particular property is inherited by its child tags.

## Table 29.1    Properties in HTML Style Sheets

| Property | Shorthand | Inherited? |
|---|---|---|
| background-attachment | background | No |
| background-color | background | No |
| background-image | background | No |
| background-position | background | No |
| background-repeat | background | No |
| border-bottom-width | border | No |
| border-color | border | No |
| border-left-width | border | No |
| border-right-width | border | No |
| border-style | border | No |
| border-top-width | border | No |
| clear | | No |
| color | | Yes |
| float | | No |
| font-family | font | Ycs |
| font-size | font | Yes |
| font-style | font | Yes |
| font-variant | | Yes |
| font-weight | font | Yes |
| height | | No |
| letter-spacing | | Yes |
| line-height | | Yes |
| list-style-image | list-style | Yes |
| list-style-position | list-style | Yes |
| list-style-type | list-style | Yes |
| margin-bottom | margin | No |
| margin-left | margin | No |
| margin-right | margin | No |
| margin-top | margin | No |

*continues*

**Table 29.1   Continued**

| Property | Shorthand | Inherited? |
|----------|-----------|-----------|
| padding-bottom | padding | No |
| padding-left | padding | No |
| padding-right | padding | No |
| padding-top | padding | No |
| text-align | | Yes |
| text-decoration | | No |
| text-indent | | Yes |
| text-transform | | Yes |
| vertical-align | | No |
| white-space | | Yes |
| width | | No |
| word-spacing | | Yes |

# Background Properties

HTML style sheets provide you with the capability to decorate the background of an element with color and images. Note that using the properties described in the following sections doesn't define the background for the Web page as a whole. Instead, these properties set the background of an element on the Web page. For example, if you define a background for the <UL> tag, as shown later, then the background only appears within each occurrence of that tag on the Web page.

UL {background-image: URL(http://www.myserver.com/images/watermark.gif)}

**N O T E**   Internet Explorer 3.01 doesn't fulfill the W3C recommendation with regard to the background properties. It has a single property called background to which you can assign a background color or the URL of a background image. ■

***background-attachment***   The background-attachment property determines whether the background image is fixed in the browser window or if it scrolls as the user scrolls the window. You can use this to create a watermark behind your Web page that stays put regardless of which portion of the Web page the user is viewing.

You can assign two possible values to background-attachment, as described in Table 29.2.

**Table 29.2** *background-attachment* **Values**

| Value | Description |
| --- | --- |
| fixed | The image is fixed within the browser window. |
| scroll | The image scrolls as the user scrolls the window. |

***background-color***   You can change the background color for an element by using the background-color property. You can assign one of the valid color names to background-color; an RGB value like #808080 (white) can also be used. For example, if you define a style for the <UL> tag that changes the background color to blue, then all of the unordered lists in your HTML file will be displayed with a blue background.

**TIP**   Changing the background color for certain types of tags is useful to highlight information on the Web page.

***background-image***   You can display a background image in an element by setting the value of the background-image property to the URL of an image. This has the effect of a watermark displayed behind that element on the Web page (the element's content is displayed over the background image).

You set the URL by using the URL(*address*) format, like this:

```
H1 {background-image: URL(http://www.myserver.com/images/heading.gif)}
```

Most of the style sheet properties accept some sort of length. You can use many different units to specify a length, too. HTML supports two types of units: relative and absolute. Table 29.3 describes the relative units.

**Table 29.3   Relative Units**

| Unit | Example | Description |
| --- | --- | --- |
| em | 0.5em | The height of the element's font. |
| ex | 0.75ex | The height of the letter X. |
| px | 15px | Pixels, relative to the output device. |

Whenever possible, you should use relative units so that your Web pages will scale better from one display to the next. You can also use the absolute units described in Table 29.4.

**Table 29.4    Absolute Units**

| Unit | Example | Description |
|------|---------|-------------|
| in | .5in | Inches |
| cm | 1cm | Centimeters |
| mm | 20mm | Millimeters |
| pt | 12pt | Points (1pt 1/72 inch) |
| pc | 1pc | Pica (1pc 12pt) |

Aside from relative and absolute lengths, you can also specify most lengths in terms of percentages. With HTML style sheets, percentages are almost always relative to the parent element. For example, if you're specifying a font size of 50 percent, what you're really saying is that you want the element's font size to be half as big as the font size of the parent.

**background-position**    You can change the position of the background image by using the background-position property. The position is always relative to the top-left corner of the element in which you're positioning the image. That is, if you're positioning an image for the <UL> tag, the image's position will be relative to the top-left corner of the unordered list.

The background-position property looks like

background-position: *x y*

where *x* is the horizontal position and *y* is the vertical position of the image. *x* and *y* can be a percentage that is relative to the size of the element, a fixed amount such as 1in, or one of the keywords that indicate a relative position as described in Table 29.5.

**Table 29.5    *background-position* Positions**

| Keyword | Description |
|---------|-------------|
| top | Aligns the image with the top of the containing element; only useful when substituted for *y*. |
| left | Aligns the image with the left side of the containing element; only useful when substituted for *x*. |
| right | Aligns the image with the right side of the containing element; only useful when substituted for *x*. |
| bottom | Aligns the image with the bottom of the containing element; only useful when substituted for *y*. |
| center | Centers the image within the containing element; when substituted for *x*, the image is centered horizontally; when substituted for *y*, the image is centered vertically. |

***background-repeat*** You can cause the user's browser to tile the background image so that it fills the entire area of the containing element. The background-repeat property can have four values, as described in Table 29.6.

**Table 29.6** *background-repeat* **Values**

| Value | Description |
|---|---|
| repeat | Repeats the image both vertically and horizontally |
| repeat-x | Repeats the image horizontally |
| repeat-y | Repeats the image vertically |
| no-repeat | Doesn't repeat the image |

# Box Properties

W3C's style sheet recommendation provides the capability to define borders, margins, and padding for elements on the Web page. You can wrap a border around a heading, for example, or change the margins of the <P> tag so that any occurrence of this tag is indented into the page. Here's an overview of the properties that you can use to change the boxes that are associated with an element:

**Border** Use the border properties to set the left, right, top, and bottom borders of an element. You can set the border's width, color, and style.

**Margin** Use the margin properties to set the left, right, top, and bottom margins of an element. With these properties, you only specify the size of the margin.

**Padding** Use the padding properties to specify how much space the browser displays between the border and the content of the element. With the padding properties, you only specify the size of the margin.

Figure 29.1 shows you how the border, margin, and padding properties work with the height and width properties to form the boxes around the element. The following list describes these in more detail:

- The height and width properties determine the overall size of the element's containing box.

- The margin properties determine the element's margins within its containing box.

- The border properties determine the position of the border within the element's margins.

- The padding properties determine the amount of space between the element's border and the contents of the element itself.

**FIG. 29.1**
There are actually four boxes around each element.

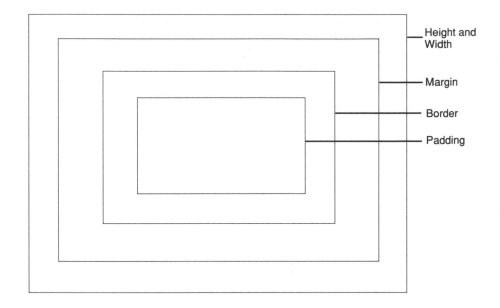

Height and Width

Margin

Border

Padding

***border-bottom-width***   Set the width of the bottom border by using the `border-bottom-width` property. This doesn't affect the other sides of the border. You can assign any of the values described in Table 29.7 to this property.

**Table 29.7** *border-bottom-width* **Values**

| Value | Description |
|---|---|
| thin | Displays the border by using a thin line. |
| medium | Displays the border by using a medium line. |
| thick | Displays the border by using a thick line. |
| length | You can define the exact width of the border by using points (pt), inches (in), centimeters (cm), or pixels (px). |

***border-color***   The `border-color` property sets the color of the element's border. You can use a named color, such as RED, or an RGB value, such as #FF0000.

***border-left-width***   You set the width of the left border by using the `border-left-width` property. This doesn't affect the other sides of the border. You can assign any of the values described in Table 29.7 to this property.

***border-right-width***   You set the width of the right border by using the `border-right-width` property. This doesn't affect the other sides of the border. You can assign any of the values described in Table 29.7 to this property.

***border-style*** The `border-style` property determines the style of the border that the browser displays. You can specify from one to four values for this property:

**One Value**    All four borders are set to the style.

**Two Values**    The top and bottom borders are set to the style in the first value; the left and right borders are set to the style in the second value.

**Three Values**    The top border is set to the style in the first value; the right and left borders are set to the style in the second value; and the bottom border is set to the style in the third value.

**Four Values**    The top border is set to the style in the first value; the right is set to the second value; the bottom is set to the third value; and the left is set to the fourth value.

Table 29.8 describes the values you can use for a border's style.

**Table 29.8    *border-style* Values**

| Value | Description |
| --- | --- |
| none | No border. |
| dotted | Dotted line drawn over the top of the element. |
| dashed | Dashed line drawn over the top of the element. |
| solid | Solid line. |
| double | Double line drawn over the top of the element; the width of the two lines, and the space between them, equals the `border-width` value. |
| groove | 3-D groove drawn in colors based upon `color`. |
| ridge | 3-D ridge drawn in colors based upon `color`. |
| inset | 3-D inset drawn in colors based upon `color`. |
| outset | 3-D outset drawn in colors based upon `color`. |

***border-top-width***    You set the width of the top border by using the `border-top-width` property. This doesn't affect the other sides of the border. You can assign any of the values described in Table 29.7 to this property.

**TROUBLESHOOTING**

**I've set the width of my border but it still doesn't display. Why?** Setting the width of the border isn't enough. You also have to set the border style by using the `border-style` property. This is because the default style for every border is none.

***clear***   The `clear` property determines whether the browser can display floating elements on the sides of an element. The property's value indicates the sides on which floating elements are not allowed. For example, `clear: left` means that the browser can't float elements on the left side of the element. Table 29.9 describes the values you can assign to this property.

**Table 29.9   *clear* Values**

| Value | Description |
| --- | --- |
| none | Floating elements are allowed on all sides. |
| left | Floating elements are not allowed on the left. |
| right | Floating elements are not allowed on the right. |
| both | Floating elements are not allowed on either side. |

***float***   The `float` property specifies that the element is floated to the left or right side, with the surrounding elements flowing around it. Table 29.10 describes the values you can assign to this property.

**Table 29.10   *float* Values**

| Value | Description |
| --- | --- |
| none | Displays the element where it is. |
| left | Move to the left and wrap text around it. |
| right | Move to the right and wrap text around it. |

***height***   Set the total height of the element with the `height` property. You can set this property for text blocks or images. For example, you can use the `height` and `width` properties to create a special warning on the Web page that has a fixed size. Height is more useful with images, however. You can set this property to any length, a percentage value, or `auto`, which lets the browser determine the best size for the element.

***margin-bottom***   Set the bottom margin by using the `margin-bottom` property. You can specify any valid length, a percentage value (relative to the `height` and `width`) of the element, or `auto`, which lets the browser determine the best margins to use for the element. You can also use a negative margin size to create special effects.

***margin-left***   Set the left margin by using the `margin-left` property. You can specify any valid length, a percentage value (relative to the `height` and `width`) of the element, or `auto`, which lets the browser determine the best margins to use for the element. You can also use a negative margin size.

***margin-right*** Set the right margin by using the `margin-right` property. You can specify any valid length, a percentage value (relative to the `height` and `width`) of the element, or `auto`, which lets the browser determine the best margins to use for the element. You can also use a negative margin size.

***margin-top*** Set the top margin by using the `margin-top` property. You can specify any valid length, a percentage value (relative to the `height` and `width`) of the element, or `auto`, which lets the browser determine the best margins to use for the element. You can also use a negative margin size.

***padding-bottom*** The `padding-bottom` property specifies the amount of space to display between the element's bottom border and the element's contents. You can set this property to a valid length or a percentage value (relative to the `height` and `width`) of the element.

***padding-left*** The `padding-left` property specifies the amount of space to display between the element's left border and the element's contents. You can set this property to a valid length or a percentage value (relative to the `height` and `width`) of the element.

***padding-right*** The `padding-right` property specifies the amount of space to display between the element's right border and the element's contents. You can set this property to a valid length or a percentage value (relative to the `height` and `width`) of the element.

***padding-top*** The `padding-top` property specifies the amount of space to display between the element's top border and the element's contents. You can set this property to a valid length or a percentage value (relative to the `height` and `width`) of the element.

***width*** Set the total width of the element with the `width` property. You can set this property for text blocks or images. You can set this property to any length, a percentage value, or `auto`, which lets the browser determine the best size for the element.

## List Properties

You use the list properties to specify how lists display in the browser window. You can change the position of the marker (`list-style-position`) and the style or image used for the marker (`list-style-type` and `list-style-image`). The sections that follow describe each property in more detail.

The list properties are inherited, so if you define a property for the `<UL>` tag, all of its enclosed `<LI>` tags inherit those properties. This is only meaningful for HTML list tags.

***list-style-image*** You use the `list-style-image` property to specify an image that the browser will display as the marker for a list item. The property's only value is the URL, using the `URL(address)` format, of the image to use as the marker, like this:

```
list-style-image: url(http://www.myserver.com/images/marker.gif)
```

To affect all of the list items within a list, set this property for the list container, such as `<UL>`, instead of the list item `<LI>`. You can override an individual list item, however, by setting this property in a single occurrence of the `<LI>` tag.

***list-style-position***   The `list-style-position` property determines the relative position of the marker. Table 29.11 describes the possible values you can assign to this property.

**Table 29.11**   *list-style-position* **Values**

| Value | Description |
|-------|-------------|
| Inside | The list item's text wraps to the next line underneath the marker. |
| Outside | The list item's text wraps to the next line underneath the start of the text on the previous line (hanging indent). |

***list-style-type***   Use the `list-style-type` property to specify the type of marker the browser will display. Use this instead of a marker image. Table 29.12 describes each of the possible values you can assign to this property.

**Table 29.12**   *list-style-type* **Values**

| Value | Description |
|-------|-------------|
| disc | Disc |
| circle | Circle |
| square | Square |
| decimal | Numbered (1, 2, 3, …) |
| lower-roman | Lowercase Roman numerals (i, ii, iii, …) |
| upper-roman | Uppercase Roman numerals (I, II, III, …) |
| lower-alpha | Lowercase alphabet (a, b, c, …) |
| upper-alpha | Uppercase alphabet (A, B, C, …) |
| none | No markers |

# Text Properties

The text properties give you complete control over how the browser displays an element's text. You can change its color, size, font, spacing, and so on. The sections that follow describe each text property you can set. Figure 29.2 shows a combination of these properties.

**FIG. 29.2**
HTML style sheets support most of the text formatting capabilities that many word processors do.

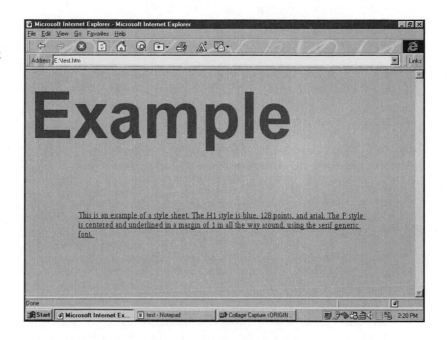

***color*** The `color` property determines the foreground color for the element. Thus, the browser displays the element's text using this color. You can set `color` to a named color or an RGB value. Named colors include the following:

| | | | |
|---|---|---|---|
| black | silver | gray | white |
| maroon | red | purple | fuchsia |
| green | lime | olive | yellow |
| navy | blue | teal | aqua |

***font-family*** `font-family` is a prioritized list of typefaces for the element. You can specify a single typeface or a list of alternatives, separated by commas; for example:

```
font-family: Courier, Times, Serif
```

You can use a font name that you expect to be on the user's computer, such as Courier or Helvetica, or you can use a generic font name. Table 29.13 shows the generic font names and provides an example of a font that looks similar.

### Table 29.13   Generic Fonts

| Name | Similar to: |
| --- | --- |
| serif | Times New Roman |
| sans-serif | Arial |
| cursive | Script |
| fantasy | Comic |
| monospace | Courier New |

In case the font you've requested is unavailable, you should always use a generic font name as the last item in the list. In the previous example, serif is the last font in the list. If the user doesn't have courier or times, the browser will use the generic font, instead.

If you're using a font name that has multiple words, enclose the font name in quotes, for example:

```
font-family: "Courier New", serif
```

**font-size**   font-size determines the size of the text in points (pt), inches (in), centimeters (cm), or pixels (px). You can also use a percentage, which is relative to the parent element's font size. You can also use one of the values shown in Table 29.14.

### Table 29.14   *font-size* Values

| Value | Description |
| --- | --- |
| xx-small | 50 percent smaller than the x-small font. |
| x-small | 50 percent smaller than the small font. |
| small | 50 percent smaller than the medium font. |
| medium | A medium-sized font, probably 10 points. |
| large | 50 percent larger than the medium font. |
| x-large | 50 percent larger than the large font. |
| xx-large | 50 percent larger than the x-large font. |
| larger | 50 percent larger than the parent element's font. |
| smaller | 50 percent smaller than the parent element's font. |

**N O T E**   The W3C recommendation that browsers use a scaling factor of 50 percent is only a recommendation. Browsers are free to use any scaling factor. Thus, the values in Table 29.14 are only guidelines. ■

***font-style***   You can change the style of the font by using the font-style property. Table 29.15 describes each of the possible values.

**Table 29.15   *font-style* Values**

| Value | Description |
| --- | --- |
| normal | Selects a normal face. |
| oblique | Selects an oblique face. |
| italic | Selects an italic face. |

***font-variant***   Use the font-variant property to display text in small-caps. Setting this property to normal causes the browser to display the text normally. Setting this property to small-caps causes the browser to display the text in small-caps.

***font-weight***   font-weight determines the thickness of the font. You can assign normal, bold, bolder, or lighter to this property. You can also assign one of the series of numbers from 100, 200, ... 900 to this property, with each successive number representing a weight that is thicker than the previous number. For example, font-weight: 700 sets a thicker font weight than does font-weight: 400.

 A font weight of 400 is roughly equivalent to that of a normal font.

***letter-spacing***   letter-spacing determines the spacing between each letter in a line of text. You can set this property to normal and let the browser worry about it, or you can set this property to any valid length, such as 1px.

***line-height***   Use the line-height property to set the leading for an element. An element's leading is the distance between the baselines of two text lines. You can use any valid length, a percentage (which is relative to the parent element's line-height property), or you can set this property to normal. Note that the spacing is added before each line, not after.

**CAUTION**

This setting doesn't work well on text lines that use multiple font sizes on the same line.

***text-align***   text-align defines how text is aligned in an element. You can set this property to any of the values shown in Table 29.16.

**Table 29.16**   *text-align* **Values**

| Value | Description |
|-------|-------------|
| left | Text is left justified. |
| right | Text is right justified. |
| center | Text is centered within the element. |
| justify | Text is left and right justified. |

***text-decoration***   Add special decorations, such as underlining, to an element by using the text-decoration property. Table 29.17 describes the values you can assign to this property. You can combine these values, too.

**Table 29.17**   *text-decoration* **Values**

| Value | Description |
|-------|-------------|
| none | No decorations |
| underline | Underlined text |
| overline | Text with a line over it |
| line-through | Strike through |
| blink | Blinking text |

 **TIP**   You can prevent the browser from underlining anchors by setting text-decoration to none for the <A> tag.

***text-indent***   The text-indent property is used to indent the first line of an element's text. You can set this property to any valid length. For example, here's how to indent the <P> tag's text to the right by one inch:

```
P {text-indent: 1in}
```

 **TIP**   You can create a hanging indent by setting a tag's style text-indent to a negative value and margin-left to a positive value.

***text-transform***   text-transform specifies that the text should be changed according to the values in Table 29.18.

### Table 29.18  *text-transform* Values

| Value | Description |
|---|---|
| capitalize | Capitalize first letter of each word. |
| uppercase | Uppercase all letters in the element. |
| lowercase | Lowercase all letters in the element. |
| none | No transformation. |

**vertical-align**   Use the vertical-align property to change the vertical position of the element's text within the element itself. You can use one of the keywords described in Table 29.19.

### Table 29.19  *vertical-align* Values

| Value | Description |
|---|---|
| baseline | Align the baseline of the element with the baseline of the parent. |
| middle | Align the middle of the element with the middle of the parent. |
| sub | Subscript the element. |
| super | Superscript the element. |
| text-top | Align the top of the element with the top of the parent element's text. |
| text-bottom | Align the bottom of the element with the bottom of the parent element's text. |
| top | Align the top of the element with the tallest element on the line. |
| bottom | Align the bottom of the element with the lowest element on the line. |

**white-space**   The white-space property defines how the browser handles white space within the element. You can leave things alone and let the browser collapse all of the white space, or you can specify that the browser treat white space as if you're within a <PRE> container. Table 29.20 shows the values you can assign to this property.

### Table 29.20  *white-space* Values

| Value | Description |
|---|---|
| normal | White space is collapsed. |
| pre | Handle white space like the <PRE> tag. |
| nowrap | Wrapping is only permitted with <BR>. |

***word-spacing***   word-spacing determines the spacing between each word in a line of text. You can set this property to normal and let the browser worry about it, or you can set this property to any valid length, such as 1px.

# Grouping Properties to Simplify Style Definitions

Many of the properties described in the previous section can be grouped together. Thus, instead of writing a rule that looks like this:

```
H1 {font-weight: bold; font-style: normal; font-size: 12pt; font-family: serif}
```

you can write a rule that looks like this:

```
H1 {font: bold normal 12pt serif}
```

HTML style sheets provide groups for the border, background, font, list, margin, and padding properties. You'll learn more about each of these in the following sections.

## Border Properties

You can group border properties in five different ways. You can specify the properties for a particular side of the element, using border-top, border-right, border-bottom, or border-left. You can also specify all sides of the border at one time by using border.

With any of these attributes, you specify the width, style, and color of the border; for example:

```
border-top: thin dotted black
```

## Background Properties

You can group the background properties by using background. Specify the background color, image, repeat, attachment, and position, like this:

```
background: white =URL(http://www.myserver.com/images/bg.gif)
➥repeat-x fixed top, left
```

## Font Properties

You can group the font properties by using font. You specify the weight, style, size, and family; for example:

```
font: bold normal 12pt times, serif
```

## List Properties

You can group the list properties by using list-style. You specify the marker type, marker image, and position, like this:

```
list-style: square =URL(http://www.myserver.com/images/marker.gif) inside
```

# Margin Properties

You can group the margin properties by using `margin`. You specify the top, right, bottom, and left margins, like this:

```
margin: .5in 1in .5in 1in
```

If you specify only one value, the browser uses that value for all sides. If you leave out one or two values, the browser takes the missing value from the opposite side. For example, if you leave off the last value (left), the browser sets the left margin to the value you specified for the right margin.

# Padding Properties

You can group the margin properties by using `padding`. You specify the top, right, bottom, and left padding values, like this:

```
padding: .25in .25in .25in .25in
```

If you specify only one value, the browser uses that value for all sides. If you leave out one or more values, the browser takes the missing value from the opposite side. For example, if you leave off the last value (`left`), the browser sets the left padding to the value you specified for the right margin.

# Using Inheritance

In HTML, tags inherit certain properties from their parents. For example, all of the tags within the `<BODY>` tag (`<P>` and `<UL>`) inherit certain properties from the `<BODY>` tag. Likewise, an `<LI>` tag inherits properties from the `<UL>` tag that contains it.

Consider the following bit of HTML:

```
<STYLE TYPE="text/css">
P {color: blue}
</STYLE>
<BODY>
<P>Hello. This is a paragraph of text. <EM>This text is emphasized</EM></P>
</BODY>
```

The style sheet for this example sets the color for the `<P>` tag to blue. There is no definition for the `<EM>` tag, however. You might expect that the text in the `<EM>` tag to suddenly change back to the default color: black. That's not the case. Since the `<EM>` is within the container tag `<P>` (it's a child, in other words), the `<EM>` tag inherits the color property from the `<P>` tag.

Table 29.1, earlier in this chapter, indicates which properties are inherited by child tags.

# Using Contextual Selectors

With HTML style sheets, you can get very specific about when a style is applied to a tag. For example, you may want to define two styles for the `<LI>` tag: one that's applied when it's a child of the `<UL>` tag and another when it's a child of the `<OL>` tag. You do this with contextual selectors.

Contextual selectors define the exact sequence of tags for which a style will be applied. In other words, you can specify that a style applies to a particular tag, such as <LI> only, if it's a child of the <OL> tag, like this:

```
OL LI {list-style-type: decimal}
```

You can also specify that a particular style applies to the <LI> tag only, if it's a child of the <UL> tag, like this:

```
UL LI {list-style-type: square}
```

Note the list of selectors is not comma-separated. Separating each selector with a comma would cause all of the tags in the list to be assigned the rule.

# Understanding the Cascade

W3C refers to style sheets as "cascading style sheets" because you can use multiple styles to control how your Web page looks; the browser follows a certain set of rules to determine the precedence and to resolve conflicts between styles (cascading order). For example, you can define a style sheet for your Web site and the reader can have their own style sheet. The cascading rules determine who wins if both style sheets define a style for a particular type of text.

So how does this work? Each rule is assigned a weight by the browser. When the browser is working with the occurrence of a particular tag, it finds all of the rules that apply to it. The browser then sorts those rules by their weight, applying the style with the greatest weight.

In general, there are just a few rules that you need to be aware of when dealing with competing style sheets:

- The author's style sheet overrides the user's style sheet; while the user's style sheet overrides the browser's default values.
- Inline styles sheets take precedence over embedded style sheets; while embedded style sheets take precedence over linked style sheets.

You can also override the precedence for a rule by using the important keyword. In the following example, the assignment of red to the property color, and the assignment of sans-serif to the property font-family, are marked as important. Thus, the browser will not override these styles. If two competing style sheets mark the same property as important, however, the rules in the previous list apply:

```
H1 {color: red ! important font-weight: bold font-family: sans-serif ! important}
```

# Working with Classes in Your Style Sheets

A class defines a variation of style, which you refer to in a specific occurrence of a tag by using the CLASS attribute. For example, you can define three variations of the H1 style, and then use each one in the appropriate context. You define a class much like you normally define a style, only you add an arbitrary class name to the end of the tag, separating them with a period; for example:

```
H1.blue {color: blue}
H1.red {color: red}
H1.black {color: black}
```

Then, when adding the <H1> tag to your HTML document, you set the CLASS attribute to indicate exactly which style you're using:

```
<H1 CLASS=red>Red Heading</H1>
```

**TIP** You can address all of the tags within a particular class by omitting the tag name from the selector, like this: red {color: red}. After defining this style, any tag that you associate with the red class will be displayed using the color red.

# Taking Care of Browsers that Don't Support Style Sheets

HTML style sheets are new. Internet Explorer and Netscape Communicator are the first browsers to support them. You still need to consider all those browsers that don't support style sheets, however.

Most browsers are designed to simply ignore the tags and attributes they don't understand. Thus, they'll ignore the <STYLE> tag, for example. They won't necessarily ignore what you put in the <STYLE> tag, though, and will display its contents as text on the Web page. To get around this problem, you can use an HTML comment within the <STYLE> tag to hide the style definitions, like this:

```
<STYLE TYPE"text/css">
<!--
H1 {color: red}
-->
</STYLE>
```

Browsers that don't support style sheets will display the HTML files with their default styles. They'll ignore the style definitions.

**TIP** Take a look at your HTML documents without the associated style sheets so that you can verify how your Web pages look in browsers that don't support style sheets.

# Using JavaScript Style Sheets (JSSS)

With the introduction of JSSS—or JavaScript Style Sheets— Netscape is helping to automate and simplify the process of adding style to your pages. Just as JavaScript can be used in place of complicated CGI programs, JSSS can be used to build style sheets. We have spent the first part of this chapter reviewing the HTML aspects of style sheets. This section will explore how JavaScript integrates with those style sheets.

## Including JSSS in HTML

Including JavaScript Style Sheets in your HTML file works about the same as you learned in "Attaching a Style Sheet to Your HTML Document," earlier in this chapter. There is one minor difference, however. Instead of setting the TYPE attribute to text/css, set it to text/javascript. This indicates to the browser that you are using a JavaScript Style Sheet as opposed to a cascading style sheet:

```
<HTML>
<HEAD>
<title>My Wow Page</title>
<LINK REL=STYLESHEET TYPE="text/javascript"
➥HREF="http://www.server.com/styles/wow" TITLE="Neato">
</HEAD>
```

## Understanding the New JSSS Functions and Objects

JavaScript Style Sheets introduce a number of new objects that make it possible to manipulate style sheets with lines of JavaScript code, instead of the simple rules you learned about earlier in this chapter. The sections that follow describe each of these functions and objects.

**The *tags* Object**   The most notable new object is the document.tags object. All of the tags on a page are reflected in this object, as well as all of the style attributes for those tags. For instance, to specify that you want all bold text to be red, you can use:

```
document.tags.b.color = "red";
```

Since tags always applies to the document object, you can omit the document portion of this statement:

```
tags.b.color  ="red";
```

**The *classes* Object**   Another object introduced in JSSS is classes. This object does not pertain to Java classes but, instead, to the new JSSS proposal that enables you to assign a class to a set of elements (tags) within an HTML document. Suppose you had created a class called cool and had assigned to that class a number of tags, illustrated as follows:

```
<html>
<head>
<title>My Cool Page</title>
</head>
<body bgcolor="green">
<h1 class=cool>Welcome to my cool page</h1>
<div align=left class=cool>
Too bad it's just an example page.
</div>
<P>
More text <b>here</b>.
</body>
</html>
```

You could add a style element to just the tags that you have set as cool or to any subset—such as just the <div> tags that have the class of cool. To set this style in the header, you could use classes.cool.div.color="blue".

If you wanted all the tags assigned to the class to be blue, you could use:

```
classes.cool.all="blue".
```

**The *ids* Object** JSSS adds another attribute to tags that is called `id`. This attribute comple-ments the `class` attribute because, instead of grouping tags together, it uniquely identifies each tag that contains the `id` attribute. Another way of looking at `class` versus `id` is this: German Shepherds, Dobermans, and Poodles are all in the `class` Dog. Your Poodle has the name, or `id`, of "Poopsie." Just as you would not name two dogs the same name, you must give each tag that uses the `id` attribute a unique name. For example:

```
<em id=br549>Emphasized Text</em>
```

To use the `ids` object, you might say: `ids.br549.paddingTop=auto`.

**The *contextual* Function** JSSS adds a new base-level function called `contextual`. This func-tion enables you to specify style attributes that are based on the position of other tags. This means that you can set default styles—say "all level one headers (`H1`) are green with 12pt font"—across your page, but override this for special cases. The contextual function enables you to add exceptions, such as "except the level one headers that are enclosed by `<DIV>` tags of class `'rad'` that are red." The two previous statements are translated into JSSS as follows:

```
<style type="text/javascript">
    with (tags)
    {
        h1.color="green";
        h1.fontSize="12pt";
    }
    contextual(classes.rad.div, tags.h1).color="red"
</style>
```

**The *tags.x.apply* Property** You will often find yourself setting numerous style functions to a tag because there are many attributes that can be modified to suit any particular style. Instead of manually setting each of these functions (like `tags.b.color="purple"`), you can define a function to the `apply` property of that tag. Essentially, the `apply` property is a style "construc-tor" in a way similar to building objects with a function that returns an object. For example:

```
function setStyle()
{
    if (textDecoration == "blink")
    {
        textDecoration = "none";
        color="blue";
    }
    else
    {
        textDecoration = "underline";
        color = "green";
    }
}
tags.h1.textDecoration="blink";
tags.all.apply = setStyle();
```

This code defines a function that sets attributes to all the tags. You then set one of the tags to have the textDecoration style of blink. The function will convert all blinking headers to normal and change their color to blue. All other tags will now present green underlined text.

## Setting Multiple Attributes in JSSS

Here is a shortcut for setting multiple attributes of a tag within JavaScript. You may remember seeing this with the Math object:

```
<STYLE>
<!--
    with (tags.DIV)
    {
        color="green"; align='=left';
        textTransform="uppercase";
    }
-->
</STYLE>
```

# Appendixes

# JavaScript Resources

**B**ecause JavaScript is designed for content presentation on the World Wide Web, it's only appropriate that the largest collection of resources for its implementation is found on the Internet. Because of JavaScript's specific platform base (currently supported by Netscape Navigator and Microsoft Internet Explorer), the number of "official" online resources that directly address JavaScript is relatively small. However, the "unofficial" resources (put up by experimenting individuals who want to share their discoveries of this new technology) are growing at a rapid rate. In addition, because Microsoft's JScript is very closely related to Netscape's JavaScript, many of the resources for JScript contain valuable information about JavaScript as well.

Also, because JavaScript works well as a "glue" to bind together ActiveX controls, Java applets, frames, and Netscape plug-ins, it's well worth the effort to keep up-to-date on the latest in these technologies. This appendix introduces you to the growing base of information available.

This list is by no means comprehensive—new sites appear on the Web daily—but it's a good place to start looking for information on JavaScript, JScript, ActiveX, Java, plug-ins, and other related technologies. ▪

## Learn about World Wide Web resources

Find JavaScript information sources and other resources on the Web.

## Explore UseNet newsgroups

UseNet has plenty of discussion groups for problem-solving.

## Discover e-mail mailing lists

Tap into topical lists for your mailbox.

## Visit search engines for further exploring

This appendix lists sites from which to start searching for more information.

## Find out about resources for the Macintosh

Macintosh users need not be left out anymore.

## Get an overview of the ActiveX SDK

The ActiveX SDK is one of the best tools available to develop and install the files you need to build ActiveX controls.

## See the author's recommendations on books

Many of the topics that come up during a discussion of JavaScript deserve a book of their own. This appendix ends with a list of other Que books that provide more in-depth treatment of these topics.

# The World Wide Web

Because JavaScript is *for* the Web, it's only appropriate that the best sources of information on its use are found *on* the Web. As with most other Internet-based sources, the bulk of Java and JavaScript sites are primarily Java-oriented with JavaScript covered as a subsection. Again, the following list is not all-inclusive; to stay current of new offerings on the Web, your best bet is to take advantage of the "Other Hot Links" pages that many of the sites have.

## Netscape

**http://home.netscape.com/**

Netscape's home site is a good place to check periodically, especially for updates and additions to the JavaScript language specification. The JavaScript Authoring Guide at **http://home.netscape.com/eng/mozilla/Gold/handbook/javascript/** provides a good overview of the language. Netscape has promised to fold JavaScript 1.1 information into this Guide. Until it does, be sure to check out **http://home.netscape.com/eng/mozilla/3.0/handbook/javascript/index.html** to learn about the latest features.

**http://developer.netscape.com/**

Netscape's developer's site contains links to a library of documentation on Java, JavaScript, and the other core technologies of the Netscape Open Network Environment (ONE), at **http://developer.netscape.com/library/documentation/index.html**. You can also download the complete specification as a PostScript file and print it off.

> **CAUTION**
>
> The complete JavaScript 1.1 specification, downloadable from **ftp://ftp.netscape.com/pub/review/jsspec.ps.gz**, may be *more* information than you want to know about JavaScript. It provides enough detail that you could use it as the basis for writing your own JavaScript interpreter. On the other hand, if you truly need the comprehensive specification, here it is!

## Microsoft Corporation

**http://www.microsoft.com/**

Microsoft developed the JScript implementation of JavaScript and is also the developer of the ActiveX technologies (including ActiveX documents, scripting, and controls). As a result, there is a wide variety of pages at the Microsoft site that will be of interest to JavaScript programmers, ActiveX developers, and Java enthusiasts. Obvious choices include **http://www.microsoft.com/jscript/** and **http://www.microsoft.com/activex/**. This site changes frequently, with more material being added all the time. It is well worth frequent visits.

## JavaScript Index

http://www.c2.org/~andreww/javascript/

JavaScript Index is a solid compendium of JavaScript implementations and experimentation, including a growing list of personal home pages that show off a variety of JavaScript tricks. A subset of the site is the JavaScript Library, a small but expanding collection of source code from around the Web community.

## Voodoo JavaScript Tutorial

http://rummelplatz.uni-mannheim.de/~skoch/js/script.htm

Voodoo JavaScript Tutorial is an ongoing tutorial that is presented in easy-to-digest sections covering the basics of JavaScript. It includes examples that are built into the page, along with descriptive text and code examples. It's a good place to get started.

## Danny Goodman's JavaScript Pages

http://www.dannyg.com/javascript/index.html

This is a collection of examples covering more-advanced concepts in JavaScript, including cookies. Danny Goodman, one of the de facto experts of JavaScript on the Web, provides some good examples from which to learn and adapt other applications.

## *The Complete Idiot's Guide to JavaScript* Home Site

http://www.epicmedia.com/ javascript/

This is the online companion to the book by the same name (also published by Que). Source code for the printed examples, links to other resources and sites, and regular tutorial sections on various parts of JavaScript are offered.

## Gamelan

http://www.gamelan.com/

Called "*the* online Java index," EarthWeb's Gamelan has an extensive collection of links to other sites, examples, tools, utilities, and other interesting resources. Although primarily targeting Java, the JavaScript section is quite sizable as well.

## Netscape World

http://www.netscapeworld.com/

This is another new online *eZine*, dedicated to Netscape products. If you're interested in seeing just how powerful JavaScript can be, this is an excellent example of JavaScript in action.

## TeamJava

http://www.teamjava.com/

TeamJava is a group consisting of Web gurus, consultants, Internet programmers, Webwriters, and other such denizens of the net. Their home page has links to other Java and JavaScript resources, as well as information on how to contact the consultants themselves.

## Symantec

http://www.symantec.com/

Symantec led the pack when it came to providing a development platform for Java applet creation. With *Café*, the commercially available Java development add-on to their popular C++ package, Symantec provided the Web community with the first GUI-based development environment for applet creation.

## Dimension X

http://www.dnx.com/

Dimension X is the home of *Liquid Reality*, a Java applet development platform that merges the capabilities of a 3-D modeling package with a Java application builder.

## The Java Developer

http://www.digitalfocus.com/faq/

Sponsored by Digital Focus, The Java Developer serves as the home site for The Java Developer FAQ and is one of the more interesting implementations of frames to present search-and-question submission buttons as you browse the site.

## Sun Microsystems

http://www.javasoft.com/

The place where it *all* started, Sun hosts the Java home site. Additionally, Sun maintains several mailing and notification lists to keep developers informed of the latest events.

# UseNet Newsgroups

Several UseNet newsgroups have sprung up to provide channels for developers who are looking for guidance with Java, JavaScript, and Web programming in general. They all have global distribution and should be available from your Internet provider.

## comp.lang.javascript

As the only newsgroup specifically dedicated to JavaScript development, this one gets somewhat lively at times.

## news.livesoftware.com

This site hosts two popular discussion groups: **news://news.livesoftware.com/livesoftware.javascript.developer** and **news://news.livesoftware.com/livesoftware.javascript.examples**.

## microsoft.public.internetexplorer.scripting

**http://www.microsoft.com/iesupport/default-news.htm** lists "peer-to-peer" newsgroups that are available to help Internet Explorer users support one another. For example, to talk to other users about scripting (in either JScript or VBScript), visit **news://msnews.microsoft.com/microsoft.public.internetexplorer.scripting**.

## comp.lang.java

Although this collection of groups is focused on the discussion of Java programming tricks and tips, integrating JavaScript into Web content is also discussed. This group has several interesting subgroups, including **.announce**, **.api**, and **.setup**.

## comp.infosystems.www.authoring

The traditional collection of newsgroups for WWW-oriented discussion has been **comp.infosystems.www**. As the Web has expanded, so have they, covering everything from browsers to announcements of newly opened Web sites.

Even though there is no group specifically for JavaScript in the comp.infosystems hierarchy, the following groups—which cover various facets of Web authoring—are of interest:

- **comp.infosystems.www.authoring.cgi**
- **comp.infosystems.www.authoring.html**
- **comp.infosystems.www.authoring.images**
- **comp.infosystems.www.authoring.misc**

# E-Mail Mailing Lists

For those who prefer receiving e-mail, there are mailing lists dedicated to Java and JavaScript that offer similar information to that found in UseNet newsgroups. Keep in mind, however, that mailing lists are a lot like a party line and can get rather chatty (the downside being that you have to wade through all the flotsam in your in-box to figure out what you can use). If you plan to use mailing lists heavily, you might want to use an e-mail program, such as Netscape Messenger (part of Netscape Communicator Standard Edition), that supports *threading*: the linking together of messages that share the same subject. This feature helps organize the flood of information.

**N O T E**  Although you post your questions and comments to the address of the list (for broadcast to the rest of the list's readers), subscribing to and unsubscribing from the list are done through *a separate e-mail address*, specifically the address of the *list server*.

The lists discussed later in this appendix mention both the list address and the list server address. Sending subscription requests to the list address (so everyone on the list knows you don't know what you're doing) is a guaranteed way to get branded a *newbie*.

If you want more information regarding how to communicate with the list server (or about other lists a particular server might have), you can send a message to the list server address with "help" in the message body. ▪

# avascript@obscure.org

Sponsored by the Obscure Organization (**http://www.obscure.org/**) and TeleGlobal Media, Inc. (**http://www.tgm.com/**), the JavaScript Index is the only mailing list (at the time of this writing) dedicated specifically to JavaScript. The discussion gets pretty varied and ranges from introductory questions to more-involved discussions on how best to handle animation, framing, reloads, and so on. To subscribe, send a message to **majordomo@obscure.org** with "**subscribe javascript**" in the message body. Alternatively, you can point your browser at **http://www.obscure.org/javascript/** for further information.

# listserv@listserv.msn.com

This list server sponsors a number of mailing lists devoted to Web-related topics. While there is no JavaScript list at the time of this writing, there are lists for ActiveX, Java, and other topics of interest to Webmasters.

# Search Engines

There are several search engines available to JavaScript, including AltaVista, Yahoo!, Lycos, and WebCrawler.

## AltaVista

**http://www.altavista.digital.com/**

A relative newcomer to the search engine world, AltaVista sports over 15 *million* entries, making it the largest search site currently in cyberspace. This site attempts to catalog not only sites and pages but also *words* within pages, making it very easy to generate thousands of matches for a particular search term. For example, searching "*JavaScript*" will find not only sites that deal with JavaScript, but also sites that *use* it within their pages because that word is always part of the <SCRIPT> tag. To make the best use of this site, try to be as specific as possible, or be prepared to refine and narrow your search parameters.

## Yahoo!

http://www.yahoo.com/Computers_and_Internet/Programming_Languages/
JavaScript/

Yahoo! is short for "You Always Have Other Options," and although this is most definitely true on the Internet, you'd be hard pressed to find others as broad.

## Lycos

http://www.lycos.com/

One of the granddaddies of the search world, Lycos has a massive database and a large collection of references to Java, JavaScript, and Web design in general.

## WebCrawler

http://www.webcrawler.com/

Supported by America Online, WebCrawler is a broad-spectrum search system that's *fast* (one of the fastest reply systems on the Internet).

# General Web Sites

There are several sites on the Web that serve as a central clearinghouse for Internet-related applications (many of which are being developed as low-cost shareware by individuals). Although these sites address a broader base than Java or JavaScript, they are expanding their coverage to include Java editors, extended HTML tools, and the like.

## The Consummate Winsock Software List

http://cws.iworld.com/

The Consummate Winsock Software (CWS) list is just as the name implies: a very complete collection of the best, the latest, the greatest, and the not so great. Combining a five-star rating system and a thorough collection of product reviews (including both pro and con analysis of all products), CWS is an excellent place to keep up with what's new and different.

## TUCOWS

http://www.tucows.com/

The Ultimate Collection of Winsock Software (hence the acronym), TUCOWS rivals CWS for its completeness and variety in content. There is naturally some duplication between the two sites (the most popular pieces of software on the Internet are found at both), but one complements the other quite nicely. (For the broadest picture of what's available, it's worth stopping by both.)

Similar to CWS, TUCOWS has a "cow" rating system, which highlights hot, "get it" titles.

## Shareware.COM

http://www.shareware.com/

What started as the Virtual Shareware Library (VSL), this site has been taken over by clnet central, an online/on-TV source for the latest-breaking information on Internet technology. Although it doesn't attempt to rate software, it does provide a "top downloads" list to indicate what "Netizens" have deemed the hot products of the moment.

Unlike CWS and TUCOWS, which link one product to one download link, Shareware.COM's download section presents a list of sites (rated by reliability) around the world from which you can retrieve a particular file.

# Macintosh

Both Java and JavaScript draw much of their success from the fact that they are platform-independent languages. While most Internet users run one version of Windows or another, a significant number use the Macintosh. Symantec (**http://www.symantec.com/product/index_devtools.html**), Metrowerks (**http://www.metrowerks.com/products/discover/mac/withjava.html**), and Natural Intelligence (**http://www.natural.com/**) are among the companies shipping Java development environments for the Mac. In addition, there are other Internet resources that are Mac-specific.

## Internet Explorer 3.0

The Macintosh version of Internet Explorer provides the same set of features as the Windows version, including support for JScript and Java. If you want to take advantage of IE, you need to stop by MSE for Mac's home site (**http://www.microsoft.com/ie/mac/**) and download a copy of Internet Explorer for the Macintosh.

## Symantec's Café and Visual Café

http://www.symantec.com/product/index_devtools.html

Symantec's *Café* and *Visual Café* development platform is available for Windows 95, Windows NT, and the Macintosh. Check out the Java Center for additional Java-related product information.

## Roaster

http://www.natural.com/

Roaster was the first Mac development environment to provide a GUI platform for the development of Java applets.

## CodeWarrior

**http://www.metrowerks.com/products/discover/mac/withjava.html**

CodeWarrior is the most popular C++ development platform for Macintosh and PowerPC developers today. Metrowerks has extended its development environment to also support Java.

# Various ActiveX Resources

In Chapter 16, "ActiveX Controls and VBScript," you learned how to use ActiveX controls in your Web pages. You learned how to insert them by using the OBJECT tag and how to set their properties by using the PARAM tag. You also learned how to associate scripts with controls by using the FOR and EVENT attributes of the SCRIPT tag. These are all authoring details.

This appendix shows you how to find more-technical information about ActiveX technology. It introduces you to the ActiveX SDK, for example, and points you to some of the best resources on the Internet for ActiveX information and resources.

# A Brief Tour of the ActiveX SDK

The ActiveX SDK contains the tools you need to build Internet applications. It contains the files you need to build ActiveX controls, for example, or to integrate Internet technology into your existing applications. For that matter, you can use the ActiveX SDK to build your own Internet tools, such as browsers and news readers. Here's a quick rundown of what you'll find in the SDK:

- The SDK contains specifications that describe various aspects of ActiveX, such as ActiveX controls.

- The SDK contains utilities that you use to certify your ActiveX controls so that people who download them know that the controls haven't been tampered with.

- The SDK is loaded with examples that you can use as a starting point or to learn more about building Internet applications with the SDK.

- The SDK contains all of the interface files (LIB, H, and so on) and redistributable files that you need to build Internet applications with Visual C++ and the WIN32 SDK.

You can get your own copy of the ActiveX SDK from Microsoft's Web site. In your favorite Web browser, open **http://www.microsoft.com/msdownload/activex.htm**, and follow the instructions you see on the Web page. To read about the SDK before you download it, visit **http://www.microsoft.com/intdev/sdk/**. For the Mac-specific version of the SDK, see **http://www.microsoft.com/intdev/sdk/mac/**.

**TIP** Microsoft updates the ActiveX SDK quite frequently. Thus, you should check Microsoft's Web site often for new versions of the SDK.

# ActiveX Resources on the Web

It's tough to keep current with Microsoft. By necessity, they keep a pace that makes most people's heads spin.

The best way to stay up-to-date is to visit the resources available on the Internet for ActiveX folks like you. You'll find a plethora of Web sites, newsgroups, and mailing lists that'll help you stay at the head of the pack.

## Web Sites

The Web is your number one resource for ActiveX documentation. You'll find Web pages about ActiveX controls and other ActiveX technologies. You'll also find information about Microsoft's technological strategy. Take a look at the sites in the following sections.

### The ActiveX Working Group    http://www.activex.org/

Microsoft has very recently turned over ActiveX to a steering committee that will oversee the development of the ActiveX standards. Microsoft's hope is that ActiveX will gain broader acceptance if the technology remains open and customer-driven. They also hope to evolve ActiveX across multiple platforms such as UNIX. This site is the place to check for information about ActiveX standardization efforts.

### Microsoft's Knowledge Base Online    http://www.microsoft.com/kb

Microsoft's Knowledge Base contains thousands of articles, each of which provides information about a specific problem. Each article describes the problem's symptoms, causes, resolution, and, sometimes, status. For example, you might learn that the reason your desktop redraws so painfully slow is because the video driver has a bug that you can repair by changing a setting in the Registry. Open **http://www.microsoft.com/kb** in your Web browser and you'll see Microsoft's Knowledge Base.

The types of articles that the Knowledge Base contains are quite impressive. The following are the categories that you will find as of this writing:

Application Notes Available

Confirmed Bugs

Display (video, monitor, resolution) Issues

Documentation Errors

Environment and Configuration Issues

Error Message Follow-Up Information

Files Available for Download

Fixed Bugs

General Programming Issues

Hardware

Interaction Between Microsoft Products

Interactions with Third-Party Products

Multimedia, Including Programming Issues

Networking, Including Programming Issues

OLE, Including Programming Issues

Product Features or Functionality

Printing, Including Programming Issues

Problems Not Classified as Bugs (Features?)

Sample Code

Sample Macros

Setup and Installation Issues

Step-by-Step Procedures for Tasks

Sound (Audio) Issues

Tools, Utilities, Wizards, etc.

Troubleshooting Information

User Interface, Including Programming Issues

**Microsoft Site Builder Workshop**    **http://www.microsoft.com/workshop/**

The Site Builder Workshop is a huge Web site that documents every facet of Microsoft's Internet technology, including ActiveX. You'll find the following six different types of information for Internet professionals:

■ Authoring/Editing is for professionals who create Web pages. You'll find information to help you build Web pages, such as an HTML reference.

■ Design/Creative is for graphically-oriented professionals. You'll find information about graphics and Web page layout.

■ Programming is for those responsible for building Internet applications or ActiveX controls. It contains update specifications, samples, and more.

■ Site Administration is all about administering large Web sites. You'll find information such as using Visual Source Safe to manage HTML files.

■ Planning/Production contains information about Internet business. You'll learn about production issues, marketing, and planning.

■ Web Gallery is a huge resource of multimedia that you can use in your Web pages. You can lift graphics, sounds, and controls from this site.

**TIP** For even more resources from Microsoft, consider joining the Site Builder Network. You can get information about membership online at **http://198.68.191.189/**.

### World Wide Web Consortium    http://www.w3.org/

The World Wide Web Consortium (W3C) is the organization that defines many of the standards that drive the Web. For example, W3C is responsible for defining HTML 3.2, which includes innovations such as style sheets, the OBJECT tag and, of course, the <SCRIPT> tag. The working documents on these two Web pages are of particular interest. They are as follows:

**http://www.w3.org/pub/WWW/TR/WD-object.html** is a working document for the multimedia object specification—the OBJECT tag.

**http://www.w3.org/pub/WWW/TR/WD-script.html** is a working document for the specification that describes HTML extensions to support executable scripts such as JavaScript, JScript, and VBScript.

## Newsgroups

UseNet newsgroups are a good place to get your questions answered by other professionals. You'll find a newsgroup for just about every topic imaginable. The following is a list of the most useful newsgroups for ActiveX programmers:

- Newsgroups on low-level communications under Windows

  **alt.winsock**

  **alt.winsock.programming**

- Newsgroups on various aspects of the World Wide Web

  **comp.infosystems.www.authoring.cgi**

  **comp.infosystems.www.authoring.html**

  **comp.infosystems.www.authoring.images**

  **comp.infosystems.www.authoring.misc**

  **comp.infosystems.www.browsers.ms-windows**

  **comp.infosystems.www.servers.ms-windows**

- Newsgroups on programming, especially C and C++

  **comp.lang.c**

  **comp.lang.c++**

- Newsgroups on Microsoft Windows networking and programming

  **comp.os.ms-windows.apps.winsock.mail**

  **comp.os.ms-windows.apps.winsock.misc**

  **comp.os.ms-windows.apps.winsock.news**

  **comp.os.ms-windows.networking.tcp-ip**

comp.os.ms-windows.networking.win95

comp.os.ms-windows.programmer.controls

comp.os.ms-windows.programmer.misc

comp.os.ms-windows.programmer.networks

comp.os.ms-windows.programmer.ole

comp.os.ms-windows.programmer.tools.mfc

comp.os.ms-windows.programmer.tools.misc

comp.os.ms-windows.programmer.tools.winsock

comp.os.ms-windows.programmer.win32

- Newsgroups on computer security

comp.security.announce

comp.security.misc

- Microsoft's own newsgroups on its Internet technology

microsoft.public.activex.controlpad

microsoft.public.inetserver.iis

microsoft.public.inetserver.misc

microsoft.public.internetexplorer

microsoft.public.vb.controls.internet

microsoft.public.vc.activextemplatelib

- A newsgroup on the science of cryptography

sci.crypt

## Getting Your Questions Answered

You can find millions of postings on UseNet every day. You have to believe that at least one person in the world has already answered the question that is currently on your mind, right? The problem is that you can't wade through all of the postings to find the answer. It's not practical.

DejaNews, at **http://www.dejanews.com/**, is a perfect resource for locating those answers. Open it in your Web browser, type a few keywords that are related to your questions, and click Find. DejaNews presents you with a list of all the postings it finds that contain those keywords. You may notice that many of the message headers begin with RE:. These are replies to original questions and are great places to start when you're looking for answers to your questions.

You can also use DejaNews to locate newsgroups that discuss a particular topic. The second text box on this Web page lets you specify a couple of keywords to which DejaNews responds with a list of newsgroups that frequently use those keywords. You can use DejaNews to locate the newsgroups that discuss the ActiveX Menu control, for example.

# Mailing Lists

Microsoft sponsors a number of mailing lists to facilitate communication about its technology. It has a number of notable ActiveX-related mailing lists, too. The following sections describe each list and show you how to subscribe to it.

**ActiveXControls**    The ActiveXControls mailing list includes discussion about the development of ActiveX controls. To subscribe, send an e-mail message to **listserv@listserv.msn.com** with **subscribe ActiveXControls *Your Name*** in the body of the message.

**ActiveXScript**    The ActiveXScript mailing list includes discussions about the development of ActiveX scripting engines and the usage of the ActiveX scripting languages. To subscribe, send an e-mail message to **listserv@listserv.msn.com** with **subscribe ActiveXScript *Your Name*** in the body of the message.

**Authenticode**    The Authenticode mailing list includes discussion about the Windows Trust Verification Services, which is a set of APIs that verifies the digital certificate of a software component. To subscribe, send an e-mail message to **listserv@listserv.msn.com** with **subscribe Authenticode *Your Name*** in the body of the message.

**CodeDownload**    The CodeDownload mailing list includes discussion about component downloading. To subscribe, send an e-mail message to **listserv@listserv.msn.com** with **subscribe CodeDownload *Your Name*** in the body of the message.

**Denali**    The Denali mailing list includes discussion about the ActiveX Server Framework, which is the component for developing Web server applications. To subscribe, send an e-mail message to **listserv@listserv.msn.com** with **subscribe Denali *Your Name*** in the body of the message.

**DocObjects**    The DocObjects mailing list includes discussion about the development of document objects. To subscribe, send an e-mail message to **listserv@listserv.msn.com** with **subscribe DocObjects *Your Name*** in the body of the message.

**IE-HTML**    The IE-HTML mailing list includes discussion about writing HTML for Internet Explorer and includes discussion of the OBJECT and SCRIPT tags. To subscribe, send an e-mail message to **listserv@listserv.msn.com** with **subscribe IE-HTML *Your Name*** in the body of the message.

**OLEHyperlinking**    The OLEHyperlinking mailing list includes discussion about the ActiveX hyperlinking services and interfaces. To subscribe, send an e-mail message to **listserv@listserv.msn.com** with **subscribe OLEHyperlinking *Your Name*** in the body of the message.

**URLMonikers**    The URLMonikers mailing list includes discussion about URL monikers and asynchronous monikers. To subscribe, send an e-mail message to **listserv@listserv.msn.com** with **subscribe URLMonikers *Your Name*** in the body of the message.

**VBScript**    The VBScript mailing list includes discussion about VBScript. To subscribe, send an e-mail message to **listserv@listserv.msn.com** with **subscribe VBScript *Your Name*** in the body of the message.

**WebPost**   The WebPost mailing list includes discussion about the WebPost API. To subscribe, send an e-mail message to **listserv@listserv.msn.com** with **subscribe WebPost *Your Name*** in the body of the message.

# Book Recommendations

In the course of describing JavaScript, this book has touched upon many topics related to Web site development. This section highlights additional Que books you may find useful as you work with JavaScript.

## General Web Site Development

*Webmaster Expert Solutions* (Que, 1996) is a comprehensive guide to HTML and CGI development. This book emphasizes hands-on development.

*Platinum Edition Using HTML 3.2, Java 1.1, and CGI* (Que, 1996) is similar in scope to *Webmaster,* but is intended more as a reference volume.

## Netscape Technology

*Developing with Netscape ONE* (Que, 1997) describes Netscape's Open Networking Environment (ONE), which ties together LiveConnect, Java, JavaScript, and numerous other Netscape technologies.

*Netscape Plug-Ins Developer's Kit* (Que, 1996) describes browser plug-in technology, with an emphasis on LiveConnect and JavaScript integration.

*Running a Perfect Netscape Site* (Que, 1996) describes the Netscape FastTrack server and the steps necessary to get it connected to the Internet.

## Java Applet Development

*Special Edition Using Java* (Que, 1996) gives an in-depth look at this programming language.

For an introductory book on Java, check out *Java by Example* (Que, 1996).

## ActiveX Development

*Special Edition Using ActiveX* (Que, 1996), *Special Edition Using JScript* (Que, 1996) and *Special Edition Using VBScript* (Que, 1996) will get you started if you're using Microsoft-specific technology. Remember that, starting with Navigator 4.0, Netscape now supports ActiveX controls.

*VBScript by Example* (Que, 1996) provides an introduction to this important technology.  ●

# JavaScript Glossary

This appendix is an expanded discussion of JavaScript's language elements. This enhanced glossary defines the common terms associated with JavaScript, and lists the objects, methods, properties, and event handlers that make JavaScript such a growing, powerful language.

Cross-references are included for individual terms, where appropriate, and are structured such that the term is listed first, followed by a colon, and then the category under which it can be found. These categories appear in all-uppercase letters and they include: TERMS, OBJECTS, PROPERTIES, METHODS, and EVENT HANDLERS. ■

# Terms

While the following items are not necessarily JavaScript objects or keywords, they can help in your understanding of JavaScript and how it works. These are the general terms that are used in most discussions about JavaScript and its implementation.

## Cookie

A special object containing state/status information about the client that can be accessed by the server. Included in that `state` object is a description of the range of URLs for which that state is valid. Future HTTP requests from the client that fall within a range of URLs described within the `state` object will include transmission of the current value of the `state` object from the client back to the server.

This simple form of data storage enables the server to provide "personalized" service to the client. Online merchants can store information about items currently in an "electronic shopping basket," services can post registration information and automate functions such as typing a user-ID, and user preferences can be saved on the client and retrieved by the server when the site is contacted. For limited-use information, such as shopping services, it is also possible to set a time limit on the life of the cookie information.

CGI scripts are typically used to set and retrieve cookie values. To generate the cookie requires sending an HTTP header in the following format:

```
Set-Cookie: NAME=Value; [EXPIRES=date;] [PATH=pathname;]
↪[DOMAIN=domainname;] [SECURE]
```

When a request is made for cookie information, the list of cookie information is searched for all URLs that match the current URL. Any matches are returned in this format:

```
cookie: NAME1=string1; NAME2=string2; ...
```

*Cookie* was an arbitrarily assigned name. For more information about the cookie and its function, see **http://home.netscape.com/newsref/std/cookie_spec.html**. Also see Chapter 23, "Using Cookies in Advanced Applications."

## Event Handler

Attributes of HTML tags that are embedded in documents. The attribute assigns a JavaScript command or function to execute when the event happens.

## Function

A user-defined or built-in set of statements that perform a task. It can also return a value when used with the `return` statement.

# Hierarchy

Browser objects exist in a set relation to one another that reflects the structure of an HTML page. This is referred to as *instance hierarchy* because it works only with specific instances of objects, rather than general classes.

The `window` object is the parent of all other browser objects. Underneath `window`, `location`, `history`, and `document`, all share precedence. `Document` includes forms, links, and anchors.

Each object is a descendant of the higher object. A form called `orderForm` is an object, but is also a property of `document`. As such, it is referred to as `document.orderForm`.

# Java

An object-oriented, platform-independent programming language developed by Sun Microsystems that is often used to add additional functionality to Web pages (although it is also used for creating full-scale applications). Programming in Java requires a Java compiler, such as the Java Development Kit, and the Java core classes.

# JavaScript

A scripting language developed by Netscape for HTML documents. Scripts are performed after specific triggered events (triggered by the user or otherwise—as in time-based events). Creating JavaScript Web documents requires a text editor and a compatible browser. JScript is Microsoft's implementation of JavaScript for its Internet Explorer browser.

# Literal

An absolute value not assigned to a variable. Examples include `1`, `3.1415927`, "Bob," `true`.

# Method

A function assigned to an object. For example, `bigString.toUpperCase()` returns an uppercase version of the string contained in `bigString`.

# Object

A construct with properties that are JavaScript variables or other objects. Functions associated with an object are known as the object's *methods*. You access the properties of an object with a simple notation:

```
objectName.propertyName
```

Both object and property names are case-sensitive.

# Operator

Performs a function on one or more operands or variables. Operators are divided into two classes: binary and unary. Binary operators need two operands, whereas unary operands can operate on a single operand.

For example, addition is a binary operand:

```
sum = 1 + 1
```

Unary operands are often used to update counters. The following example increases the variable by 1:

```
counter++
```

See Appendix C, "JavaScript Commands and Grammar," for a list of operators and their precedence.

# Property

Used to describe an object. A property is defined by assigning it a value. There are several properties in JavaScript that contain *constants:* values that never change. A property can be anything that adds further description to the object. Properties can also be other objects or methods.

# Script

One or more JavaScript commands enclosed with a `<script>` tag.

# Objects

JavaScript is an object-oriented language, so at its heart is a predefined set of objects that relates to the various components of an HTML page and their relation to one another. To view or manipulate the state of an object requires the use of properties and methods, which are also covered in this appendix. If an object is also used as a property of another object, that relationship is listed following the definition. Related properties, methods, and event handlers for each object are listed following the definition.

## *anchor*

An object (usually a text string) that can be the target of a hypertext link. This is a read-only object that is set in HTML with `<A>` tags. To determine how many anchors are included in a document, use the `length` property. Property of `document`.

```
document.anchors.length
```

See `link`: OBJECTS; see `anchor`: METHODS.

## *applet*

An object that contains references to all of the Java applets on a page, stored in an array. Property of `document`.

See `mimetypes`: OBJECTS.

## area

An object that is tied to the links object array. Refers to a clickable image-map area containing, among other things, links and coordinates of clickable areas. Referred via the links array, such as document.links[2]. Property of document.

See Image: OBJECTS.

## button

An object that is a form element, requiring that it be defined within a <form> tag, and that can be used to perform an action. Property of form.

See reset and submit: OBJECTS; see name and value:PROPERTIES; see click: METHODS; see onClick: EVENT HANDLERS.

## checkbox

A form element that the user clicks to set to *on* or *off* and that must be defined in a <form> tag. Using the checkbox object, you can see whether the box is checked and review the name and value. Property of form.

See radio: OBJECTS; see checked, defaultChecked, name, and value:PROPERTIES; see click: METHODS; see onClick: EVENT HANDLERS.

## Date

Replaces a normal date type. Although it does not have any properties, it is equipped with a wide range of methods. In its current release, Date does not work with dates prior to 1/1/70.

Methods for getting and setting time and date information are divided into four classes: set, get, to, and parse/UTC.

Except for the date, all numerical representation of date components begin with zero. This should not present a problem except with months, which are represented by zero (January) through 11 (December).

The standard date syntax is "Thu, 11 Jan 1996 06:20:00 GMT". U.S. time zone abbreviations are also understood; but for universal use, specify the time zone offset. For example, "Thu, 11 Jan 1996 06:20:00 GMT+0530" is a place five hours and 30 minutes west of the Greenwich meridian.

See getDate, getDay, getHours, getMinutes, getMonth, getSeconds, getTime, getTimezoneOffset, getYear, parse, setDate, setHours, setMinutes, setMonth, setSeconds, setTime, setYear, toGMTString, toLocaleString, and toString:METHODS.

App

B

## *document*

An object created by the browser when a page is loaded, containing information on the current document, such as title, background color, and forms. These properties are defined within <body> tags. It also provides methods for displaying HTML text to the user.

You can reference the anchors, forms, and links of a document by using the anchors, forms, and links arrays of the document object. These arrays contain an entry for each anchor, form, or link in a document. Property of window.

See frame: OBJECTS; see alinkColor, anchors, bgColor, cookie, fgColor, forms, lastModified, linkColor, links, location, referrer, title, and vlinkColor: PROPERTIES; see clear, close, open, write, and writeln METHODS; see onLoad and onUnload: EVENT HANDLERS.

## *elements*

An array of form elements in source order, including buttons, check boxes, radio buttons, text and textarea objects. The elements can be referred to by their index:

```
formName.elements[index]
```

Elements also can be referenced by the element name. For example, a password element called newPassword is the second form element on an HTML page. Its value is accessed in three ways:

```
formName.elements[1].value
formName.elements["newPassword"].value
formName.newPassword.value
```

Values cannot be set or changed by using the read-only elements array. Property of form.

See length: PROPERTIES.

## *embed*

An object containing information about data on a page obtained from an <EMBED></EMBED>. Usually this will be Java code to allow an interface to a plug-in. This is not widely used.

## *FileUpload*

A form element object that contains a read-only property called value that corresponds to the name of the file to upload. Property of elements.

See text: OBJECTS.

## *form*

A property of the document object. Each form in a document is a separate and distinct object that can be referenced by using the form object. The form object is an array created as forms are defined through HTML tags. If the first form in a document is named orderForm, then it could be referenced as document.orderForm or document.forms[0]. Property of document.

See hidden: OBJECTS; see action, elements, encoding, forms, method, name, and target: PROPERTIES; see submit: METHODS; see onSubmit: EVENT HANDLERS.

## frame

A window containing HTML sub-documents that are independently scrollable. Frames can point to different URLs and can be targeted by other frames—all in the same window. Each frame is a window object that is defined by using the <frameset> tag to define the layout that makes up the page. The page is defined from a parent HTML document. All sub-documents are children of the parent.

If a frame contains definitions for SRC and NAME attributes, then the frame can be identified from a sibling by using the parent object as parent.frameName or parent.frames[index]. Property of window.

See document and window: OBJECTS; see defaultStatus, frames, parent, self, status, top, and window: PROPERTIES ; see setTimeout and clearTimeout: METHODS.

## function

An object that specifies a JavaScript code string to be compiled as a function. Function objects are evaluated every time they are used—less efficient than declaring a function to be called within your code.

## hidden

A text object that is suppressed from appearing on an HTML form. Hidden objects can be used in addition to cookies to pass name/value pairs for client/server communication. Property of form.

See cookie, defaultValue, name, and value: PROPERTIES.

## history

This object contains URL link information for previously visited pages. Property of document.

See location: OBJECTS; see length: PROPERTIES; see back, forward, and go: METHODS.

## image

An image object contains information about an image embedded in an HTML document. An array images[] contains references to all of the images embedded on a page, and can refer to images using document.images[]. Internet Explorer 3.0 currently does not support the image object. Property of document.

See border, complete, height, hspace, lowsrc, name, prototype, src, vspace, and width:PROPERTIES.

## link

A location object. In addition to providing information about existing hypertext links, the link object can also be used to define new links. Property of document.

See anchor: OBJECTS; see hash, host, hostname, href, length, pathname, port, protocol, search, and target: PROPERTIES; see link: METHODS; see onClick and onMouseOver: EVENT HANDLERS.

## location

Contains complete URL information for the current document, while each property of location contains a different portion of the URL. Property of document.

See history: OBJECTS; see hash, host, hostname, href, location, pathname, port, protocol, search, and target: PROPERTIES.

## Math

Includes properties for mathematical constants and methods for functions. For example, to access the value of pi in an equation, use:

```
Math.PI
```

Standard trigonometric, logarithmic, and exponential functions are also included. All arguments in trigonometric functions use radians.

See E, LN10, LN2, PI, SQRT1_2, and SQRT2: PROPERTIES; see abs, acos, asin, atan, ceil, cos, exp, floor, log, max, min, pow, random, round, sin, sqrt, and tan: METHODS.

## mimetypes

When mimetypes is a property of navigator, it is an object containing information in an array of all of the MIME types supported by the client browser. When it is a property of the plugin object, it contains all of the MIME types supported by that specific plug-in —which is a subset of the navigator.mimetypes[] array. Property of navigator.

## navigator

Contains information on the current version of the browser used by the client.

See link and anchors: OBJECTS; see appName, appCodeName, appVersion, and userAgent: PROPERTIES.

## password

Created by HTML password text fields and is masked when entered by the user. It must be defined with an HTML <form> tag. Property of form.

See text: OBJECTS; see defaultValue, name, and value: PROPERTIES; see focus, blur, and select: METHODS.

## radio

Objects that are created within HTML <form> tags to represent radio buttons. A set of radio buttons enables the user to select one item from a list. When it is created, it takes the form of document.formName.radioName[index], where the index is a number representing each button beginning with zero. Property of form.

See checkbox and select:OBJECTS; see checked, defaultChecked, index, length, name, and value: PROPERTIES; see click: METHODS; see onClick: EVENT HANDLERS.

## reset

Correlates with an HTML Reset button, which resets all form objects to their default values. A reset object must be created within a <form> tag. Property of form.

See button and submit: OBJECTS; see name and value: PROPERTIES; see click: METHODS; see onClick: EVENT HANDLERS.

## select

A selection list or scrolling list on an HTML form. A selection list enables the user to choose one item from a list, while a scrolling list enables the choice of one or more items from a list. Property of form.

See radio: OBJECTS; see length, name, options, and selectedIndex: PROPERTIES; see blur and focus:METHODS; see onBlur, onChange, and onFocus: EVENT HANDLERS.

For the options property of select, see defaultSelected, index, selected, text, and value.

## string

A series of characters defined by double or single quotes. For example:

```
myDog = "Brittany Spaniel"
```

returns a string object called myDog with the value "Brittany Spaniel". Quotation marks are not a part of the string's value—they are used only to delimit the string. The object's value is manipulated by using methods that return a variation on the string, for example myDog.toUpperCase() returns "BRITTANY SPANIEL". It also includes methods that return HTML versions of the string, such as bold and italics.

See text and textarea: OBJECTS; see length: PROPERTIES; see anchor, big, blink, bold, charAt, fixed, fontcolor, fontsize, indexOf, italics, lastIndexOf, link, small, strike, sub, substring, sup, toLowerCase, and toUpperCase: METHODS.

## submit

Causes the form to be submitted to the program specified by the action property. It is created within an HTML <form> tag. It always loads a new page, which may be the same as the current page if an action isn't specified. Property of form.

See `button` and `reset`:OBJECTS; see `name` and `value`:PROPERTIES; see `click`: METHODS; see `onClick`: EVENT HANDLERS.

## text

A one-line input field on an HTML form that accepts characters or numbers. A `Text` object can be updated by assigning new contents to its value. Property of `form`.

See `password`, `string`, `textarea`: OBJECTS; see `defaultValue`, `name`, and `value`: PROPERTIES; see `focus`, `blur`, and `select`: METHODS; see `onBlur`, `onChange`, `onFocus`, and `onSelect`: EVENT HANDLERS.

## textarea

Similar to a `text` object, with the addition of multiple lines. A `textarea` object can also be updated by assigning new contents to its value. Property of `form`.

See `password`, `string`, and `text`: OBJECTS; see `defaultValue`, `name`, and `value`: PROPERTIES; see `focus`, `blur`, and `select`: METHODS; see `onBlur`, `onChange`, `onFocus`, and `onSelect`: EVENT HANDLERS.

## window

Created by the browser when a page containing properties that apply to the whole window is loaded. It is the top-level object for each `document`, `location`, and `history` object. Because its existence is assumed, you do not have to reference the name of the window when referring to its objects, properties, or methods. For example, the following two lines have the same result (printing a message to the status line):

```
status = "Go away from here."
window.status = "Go away from here."
```

A new window is created by using the `open` method:

```
aNewWindow = window.open("URL","Window_Name",["windowFeatures"])
```

The variable name is used to refer to the window's properties and methods. The window name is used in the target argument of a form or `anchor` tag.

See `document` and `frame`: OBJECTS; see `defaultStatus`, `frames`, `opener`, `parent`, `self`, `status`, `top`, and `window`: PROPERTIES; see `alert`, `close`, `confirm`, `open`, `prompt`, `setTimeout`, and `clearTimeout`: METHODS; see `onLoad` and `onUnload`: EVENT HANDLERS.

# Properties

Properties are used to view or set the values of objects. An object is simply a vague generality until a property is used to define the values that make it specific.

## action

The action property is a reflection of the action attribute in an HTML <form> tag, consisting of a destination URL for the submitted data. This value can be set or changed before or after the document has been loaded and formatted.

In this example, the action for a form called outlineForm is set to the URL contained in the variable outlineURL:

```
outlineForm.action=outlineURL
```

Property of form. See encoding, method, and target: PROPERTIES.

App
B

## alinkColor

The color of a link after the mouse button is depressed—but before it's released—and expressed as a hexadecimal RGB triplet or string literal. It cannot be changed after the HTML source is processed. Property of document. Both of these examples set the color to Alice blue.

```
document.alinkColor="aliceblue"
document.alinkColor="F0F8FF"
```

See bgColor, fgColor, linkColor, and vlinkColor: PROPERTIES.

## anchors

An array of all the defined anchors in the current document. If the length of an anchor array in a document is 5, then the anchors array is represented as document.anchors[0] through document.anchors[4]. Property of document.

See anchor: OBJECT; see length and links: PROPERTIES.

## appCodeName

Returns a read-only string with the code name of the browser:

```
document.write("The code name of your browser is " + navigator.appCodeName)
```

For Internet Explorer, this returns:

```
The code name of your browser is Microsoft Internet Explorer 3.0A
```

Property of navigator.

See appName, appVersion, and userAgent: PROPERTIES.

## appName

Returns a read-only string with the name of the browser. Property of navigator.

See appCodeName, appVersion, and userAgent: PROPERTIES.

## appVersion

Returns a string with the version information of the browser in the format `"releaseNumber (platform; country)"`. For a release of Internet Explorer 3.0:

```
document.write(navigator.appVersion)
```

returns

```
3.0 (Win95; U)
```

This specifies IE 3.0 running on Windows 95. The U country code specifies a U.S. release, while an I indicates an international release. Property of `navigator`.

See `appName`, `appCodeName`, and `userAgent`: PROPERTIES.

## bgColor

The document background color expressed as a hexadecimal RGB triplet or string literal. It can be reset at any time. Property of `document`. Both of these examples set the background to Alice blue.

```
document.bgColor = "aliceblue"
document.bgColor = "F0F8FF"
```

See `alinkColor`, `fgColor`, `linkColor`, and `vlinkColor`: PROPERTIES.

## checked

A Boolean value (`true` or `false`), indicating whether a check box or radio button is selected. The value is updated immediately when an item is checked. It's used in the following form:

```
formName.checkboxName.checked
formName.radioButtonName[index].checked
```

Property of `checkbox` and `radio`.

See `defaultChecked`: PROPERTIES.

## cookie

String value of a small piece of information stored by the browser in a client-side cookies folder or file. The value stored in the `cookie` is found by using substring, `charAt`, `IndexOf`, and `lastIndexOf`. Property of `document`.

For more information, see the discussion under TERMS.

See `hidden`: OBJECTS.

## defaultChecked

A Boolean value (`true` or `false`) indicating whether a check box or radio button is checked by default. Setting a value to `defaultChecked` can override the checked attribute of a form element. The following section of code will reset a group of radio buttons to its original state by finding and setting the default button:

```
for (var i in menuForm.choices) {
   if (menuForm.choices[i].defaultChecked) {
      menuForm.choice[i].defaultChecked = true
   }
}
```

Property of `checkbox` and `radio`.

See `form`: OBJECTS; see `checked`: PROPERTIES.

## defaultSelected

A Boolean value (`true` or `false`) representing the default state of an item in a form select element. Setting a value with this property can override the selected attribute of an `<option>` tag. The syntax is identical to `defaultChecked`. Property of `options`.

See `index`, `selected`, and `selectedIndex`: PROPERTIES.

## defaultStatus

The default message displayed in the status bar at the bottom of a browser window when nothing else is displayed. This is preempted by a priority or transient message, such as a `mouseOver` event with an `anchor`. For example:

```
window.defaultStatus = "Welcome to my home page"
```

displays the welcome message while the mouse is not over a link, or Internet Explorer is not performing an action about which it needs to notify the user. Property of `window`.

See `status`: PROPERTIES.

## defaultValue

The initial contents of `hidden`, `password`, `text`, `textarea`, and `string` form elements. For password elements, it is initially set to `null` for security reasons, regardless of any set value.

Property of `hidden`, `password`, `text`, `textarea`. See `value`: PROPERTIES.

## E

The base of natural logarithms, also known as Euler's constant. The value is approximately 2.718. Property of `Math`.

See `LN2`, `LN10`, `LOG2E`, `LOG10E`, `PI`, `SQRT1_2`, and `SQRT2`: PROPERTIES.

## elements

An array of objects containing form elements in HTML source order. The array index begins with zero and ends with the number of `form` elements –1. Property of `form`.

See `elements`: OBJECTS.

# encoding

Returns a string reflecting the MIME encoding type, which is set in the `enctype` attribute of an HTML `<form>` tag. Property of `form`.

See `action`, `method`, and `target`: PROPERTIES.

# fgColor

The color of foreground text represented as a hexadecimal RGB triplet or a string literal. This value cannot be changed after a document is processed. It can take two forms:

```
document.fgColor="aliceblue"
document.fgColor="F0F8FF"
```

Property of `document`.

See `alinkColor`, `bgColor`, `linkColor`, and `vlinkColor`: PROPERTIES; see `fontcolor`: METHODS.

# forms

An array of objects corresponding to named forms in HTML source order and containing an entry for each `form` object in a document. Property of `document`.

See `form`: OBJECTS; see `length`: PROPERTIES.

# frames

An array of objects corresponding to child-frame windows that are created by using the `<frameset>` tag. To obtain the number of child frames in a window, use the `length` property.

Property of `window`. See `frame`: OBJECTS; see `length`: PROPERTIES.

# hash

Returns a string with the portion of an URL beginning with a hash mark (#), which denotes an anchor name fragment. It can be used to set a `hash` property, although it is safest to set the entire URL as an `href` property. An error is returned if the `hash` isn't found in the current location. Property of `link` and `location`.

See `anchor`: OBJECTS; see `host`, `hostname`, `href`, `pathname`, `port`, `protocol`, and `search` properties: PROPERTIES.

# host

Returns a string formed by combining the `hostname` and `port` properties of an URL, and provides a method for changing it:

```
location.host = "www.montna.com:80"
```

Property of `link` and `location`.

See `hash`, `hostname`, `href`, `pathname`, `port`, `protocol`, and `search`: PROPERTIES.

## hostname

Returns or changes a string with the domain name or IP address of an URL. Property of link and location.

See hash, host, href, pathname, port, protocol, and search: PROPERTIES.

## href

Returns a string with the entire URL. All other location and link properties are substrings of href, which can be changed at any time. Property of link and location.

See hash, host, hostname, pathname, port, protocol, and search: PROPERTIES.

## index

Returns the index of an option in a select element with zero being the first item. Property of options.

See defaultSelected, selected, and selectedIndex: PROPERTIES.

## lastModified

A read-only string containing the date that the current document was last changed, based on the file attributes. The string is formatted in the standard form used by JavaScript (see Date object). A common usage is:

```
document.write("This page last modified on " + document.lastModified)
```

Property of document.

## length

An integer reflecting a length- or size-related property of an object.

| Object | Property Measured |
|---|---|
| history | Length of the history list |
| string | Integer length of the string; zero for a null string |
| radio | Number of radio buttons |
| anchors, forms, frames, links, options | Number of elements in the array |

Property of anchors, elements, forms, frame, frames, history, links, options, radio, string, and window.

App
B

## linkColor

The hyperlink color displayed in the document, expressed as a hexadecimal RGB triplet or as a string literal. It corresponds to the `link` attribute in the HTML `<body>` tag, and cannot be changed after the document is processed. Property of `document`.

See `alinkColor`, `bgColor`, `fgColor`, and `vlinkColor`: PROPERTIES.

## links

An array representing `link` objects defined in HTML using `<a href=URL>` tags with the first `link` identified as `document.links[0]`. See `link` object.

See `anchors` and `length`: PROPERTIES.

## LN2

A constant representing the natural logarithm of 2 (approximately 0.693). Property of `Math`.

See `E`, `LN10`, `LOG2E`, `LOG10E`, `PI`, `SQRT1_2`, and `SQRT2`: PROPERTIES.

## LN10

A constant representing the natural logarithm of 10 (approximately 2.302). Property of `Math`.

See `E`, `LN2`, `LOG2E`, `LOG10E`, `PI`, `SQRT1_2`, and `SQRT2`: PROPERTIES.

## location

Returns a string with the URL of the current document. This read-only property (`document.location`) is different from the `location` object's properties (`window.location.propertyName`), which can be changed. Property of `document`.

See `location`: OBJECTS.

## LOG2E

A constant representing the base 2 logarithm of `e` (approximately 1.442). Property of `Math`.

See `E`, `LN2`, `LN10`, `LOG10E`, `PI`, `SQRT1_2`, and `SQRT2`: PROPERTIES.

## LOG10E

A constant representing the base 10 logarithm of `e` (approximately .434). Property of `Math`.

See `E`, `LN2`, `LN10`, `LOG2E`, `PI`, `SQRT1_2`, `SQRT2`: PROPERTIES.

## method

Reflects the `method` attribute of an HTML `<form>` tag: either `<GET>` or `<POST>`. It can be set at any time. The first function returns the current value of the `form` object, while the second function sets the method to the contents of `newMethod`.

```
function getMethod(formObj) {
    return formObj.method
}
function setMethod(formObj,newMethod) {
    formObj.method = newMethod
}
```

Property of `form`.

See `action`, `encoding`, and `target`: PROPERTIES.

## name

Returns a string with the `name` attribute of the object. This is the internal name (set using the HTML NAME attribute) for `button`, `reset` and `submit` objects, not the on-screen label.

For example, after opening a new window with `indexOutline = window.open("http://www.wossamatta.com/outline.html","MenuPage")` and issuing the command `document.write(indexOutline.name)`, JavaScript returns `MenuPage`, which was specified as the `name` attribute.

Property of `button`, `checkbox`, `frame`, `password`, `radio`, `reset`, `select`, `submit`, `text`, `textarea`, and `window`.

See `value`:PROPERTIES.

## opener

Returns the `window` object from which the current window was opened. For example, if window A issues a `window.open()` call to create window B, then the value of `document.opener` in window B is "A." Property of `window`.

See `parent` and `top`:PROPERTIES.

## options

An array of `option` objects created by a `select` form element. The first option's index is zero, the second is 1, and so on.

See `select`: OBJECTS.

## parent

Refers to the calling document in the current frame created by a `<frameset>` tag. Using `parent` grants access to other frames created by the same `<FRAMESET>` tag. For example, two frames invoked are called "index" and "contents." The "index" frame can write to the "contents" frame by using the syntax:

```
parent.contents.document.write("Kilroy was here.")
```

Property of `frame` and `window`.

App

B

## pathname

Returns the path portion from an URL. Although the `pathname` can be changed at any time, it is always safer to change the entire URL at once by using the `href` property. Property of `link` and `location`.

See `hash`, `host`, `hostname`, `href`, `port`, `protocol`, and `search`:PROPERTIES.

## PI

Returns the value of pi (approximately 3.1415927). This is the ratio of the circumference of a circle to its diameter. Property of `Math`.

See `E`, `LN2`, `LN10`, `LOG2E`, `LOG10E`, `SQRT1_2`, and `SQRT2`:PROPERTIES.

## port

Returns the port number of an URL address, which is a substring of the `host` property in `href`. Property of `link` and `location`.

See `hash`, `host`, `hostname`, `href`, `pathname`, `protocol`, and `search`:PROPERTIES.

## protocol

Returns a string with the initial portion of the URL, up to and including the colon, which indicates the access method (`http`, `ftp`, `mailto`, etc.).

Property of `link` and `location`.

See `hash`, `host`, `hostname`, `href`, `pathname`, `port`, and `search`:PROPERTIES.

## referrer

Returns a read-only URL of the document that called the current document. In conjunction with a CGI script, it can be used to keep track of how users are linked to a page.

```
document.write("You came here from a page at " + document.referrer)
```

Property of `document`.

## search

Returns a string containing any query information appended to an URL. Property of `link` and `location`.

See `hash`, `host`, `hostname`, `href`, `pathname`, `port`, and `protocol`:PROPERTIES.

## selected

Returns a Boolean value (`true` or `false`) indicating the current state of an option in a `select` object. The selected property can be changed at any time and the display will immediately update to reflect the new value. The selected property is useful for `select` elements that are created using the multiple attribute. Using this property, you can view or change the value of any element in an options array without changing the value of any other element in the array. Property of options.

See defaultSelected, index, and selectedIndex: PROPERTIES.

## selectedIndex

Returns an integer specifying the index of a selected item. The selectedIndex property is useful for select elements that are created without using the multiple attribute. If selectedIndex is evaluated when the multiple option is selected, the property returns the index of the first option only. Setting the property clears any other options that are selected in the element. Property of select, options.

See defaultSelected, index, and selected: PROPERTIES.

## self

Refers to the current window or form and is useful for removing ambiguity when dealing with window and form properties with the same names. Property of frame and window.

See window: PROPERTIES.

## SQRT1_2

The square root of 1/2, also expressed as the inverse of the square root of 2 (approximately 0.707). Property of Math.

See E, LN2, LN10, LOG2E, LOG10E, PI, and SQRT2: PROPERTIES.

## SQRT2

The square root of 2 (approximately 1.414). Property of Math.

See E, LN2, LN10, LOG2E, LOG10E, PI, and SQRT1_2: PROPERTIES.

## status

Specifies a priority or transient message to display in the status bar at the bottom of the window, usually triggered by a mouseOver event from an anchor. To display when the mouse pointer is placed over a link, the usage is:

```
<A anchor definition onMouseOver="window.status='Your message.'; return
true">link</A>
```

Note the use of nested quotes and the required return true statement at the end of the event handler. Property of window.

See defaultStatus: PROPERTIES.

App
B

## target

A string specifying the name of a window to which responses are to be posted after a form is submitted. For a link, `target` returns a string specifying the name of the window that displays the content of a selected hypertext link:

```
homePage.target = "http://www.wossamatta.com/"
```

Property of `form`, `link`, and `location`. See `action`, `encoding`, and `method`: PROPERTIES.

## text

Returns the value of text following the `<option>` tag in a `select` object. It also can be used to change the value of the option, with an important limitation—while the value is changed, its appearance on-screen is not. Property of `options`.

## title

Returns the read-only value set within HTML `<title>` tags. If a document doesn't include a title, the value is `null`. Property of `document`.

## top

The topmost window, called an ancestor or Web browser window, that contains `frames` or nested `framesets`. Property of `window`.

## type

A property that specifies the type of form element. Can be obtained from *objectname*`.type` or `mimeTypes[`*index*`].type`.

## userAgent

Header sent as part of HTTP protocol from client to server to identify the type of client. Internet Explorer currently returns the string `"Mozilla/2.0 (compatible; MSIE 3.0A; Windows 95)"` on a Windows 95 platform. Property of `navigator`.

See `appName`, `appVersion`, and `appCodeName`: PROPERTIES.

## value

The value of an object depends on the type of object to which it is applied.

| Object | Value Attribute |
|---|---|
| button, reset, submit | Value attribute that appears on-screen, not the button name |
| checkbox | ON if item is selected, OFF if not |
| radio | String form of value |

| Object | Value Attribute |
|--------|-----------------|
| hidden, text, textarea | Contents of the field |
| select | Reflection of option value |
| password | Returns a valid default value, but an encrypted version if modified by the user |

Changing the value of a text or textarea object results in an immediate update to the screen. All other form objects are not graphically updated when changed.

Property of button, checkbox, hidden, options, password, radio, reset, submit, text, and textarea.

For password, text, and textarea, see defaultValue: PROPERTIES.

For button, reset, and submit, see name: PROPERTIES.

For options, see defaultSelected, selected, selectedIndex, and text: PROPERTIES.

For checkbox and radio, see checked and defaultChecked: PROPERTIES.

## vlinkColor

Returns or sets the color of visited links using hexadecimal RGB triplets or a string literal. The property cannot be set after the document has been formatted. To override the browser defaults, color settings are used with the onLoad event handler in the <BODY> tag:

```
<BODY onLoad="document.vlinkColor='aliceblue'">
```

Property of document.

See alinkColor, bgColor, fgColor, and linkColor: PROPERTIES.

## window

A synonym for the current window, used to remove ambiguity between a window and form object of the same name. While it also applies to the current frame, it is less ambiguous to use the self property. Property of frame and window.

See self: PROPERTIES.

# Methods

Methods are functions and procedures used to perform an operation on an object, variable, or constant. With the exception of built-in functions, methods must be used with an object:

```
object.method()
```

Even if the method does not require any arguments, the parentheses are still required.

The object that utilizes the method is listed after the definition as `"Method of object,"` followed by any cross-references to other methods. Stand-alone functions that are not used with objects are indicated with an asterisk (*).

## abs

Returns the absolute (unsigned) value of its argument.

```
document.write(Math.abs(-10));
document.write(Math.abs(12))
```

These examples return 10 and 12, respectively. Method of `Math`.

## acos

Returns the arc cosine (from zero to pi radians) of its argument. The argument should be a number between –1 and 1. If the value is outside the valid range, a zero is returned. Method of `Math`.

See `asin`, `atan`, `cos`, `sin`, and `tan`: METHODS.

## alert

Displays a JavaScript alert dialog box with an OK button and a user-defined message. Before the user can continue, they must press the OK button. Method of `window`.

See `confirm` and `prompt`: METHODS.

## anchor

Used with `write` or `writeln` methods, `anchor` creates and displays an HTML hypertext target. The syntax is:

```
textString.anchor(anchorName)
```

where `textString` is what the user sees, and `anchorName` is equivalent to the `name` attribute of an HTML `<anchor>` tag. Method of `string`.

See `link`: METHODS.

## asin

Returns the arc sine (between –pi/2 and pi/2 radians) of a number between –1 and 1. If the number is outside the range, a zero is returned. Method of `Math`.

See `acos`, `atan`, `cos`, `sin`, and `tan`: METHODS.

## atan

Returns the arc tangent (between –pi/2 and pi/2 radians) of a number between –1 and 1. If the number is outside the range, a zero is returned. Method of `Math`.

See `acos`, `asin`, `cos`, `sin`, and `tan`: METHODS.

## *back*

Recalls the previous URL from the history list. This method is the same as `history.go(-1)`. Method of `history`.

See `forward` and `go`:METHODS.

## *big*

Formats a string object as a big font by encasing it with HTML `<big>` tags. Both of the following examples result in the same output—displaying the message `"Welcome to my home page"` in a big font:

```
var welcomeMessage = "Welcome to my home page."
document.write(welcomeMessage.big())
```

```
<BIG> Welcome to my home page.</BIG>
```

Method of `string`.

See `fontsize` and `small`:METHODS.

## *blink*

Formats a `string` object as a blinking line by encasing it with HTML `<blink>` tags. Both of the following examples produce a flashing line that says `"Notice"`:

```
var attentionMessage = "Notice"
document.write(attentionMessage.blink())
```

```
<BLINK>Notice</BLINK>
```

Method of `string`.

See `bold`, `italics`, and `strike`:METHODS.

## *blur*

Removes focus from the specified `form` element or `window` object. For example, the following line removes focus from `feedback`:

```
feedback.blur()
```

assuming that `feedback` is defined as:

```
<input type="text" name="feedback">
```

Method of `password`, `select`, `text`, and `textarea`.

See `focus` and `select`:METHODS.

## *bold*

Formats a string object in bold text by encasing it with HTML `<B>` tags. Method of `string`.

See `blink`, `italics`, and `strike`:METHODS.

## ceil

Returns the smallest integer greater than, or equal to, its argument. For example:

```
Math.ceil(1.01)
```

returns a 2. Method of Math.

See floor: METHODS.

## charAt

Returns the character from a string at the specified index. The first character is at position zero and the last at length –1.

```
var userName = "Bobba Louie"
document.write(userName.charAt(4)
```

returns an "a". Method of string.

See indexOf and lastIndexOf: METHODS.

## clear

Clears the contents of a window, regardless of how the window was filled. Method of document. See close, open, write, and writeln: METHODS.

## clearTimeout*

Cancels a timeout set with the setTimeout method. A timeout is set using a unique timeout ID, which must be used to clear it:

```
clearTimeout(waitTime)
```

Method of frame and window.

See setTimeout: METHODS.

## click

Simulates a mouse click on the calling form element with the effect dependent on the type of element.

| Form Element | Action |
|---|---|
| Button, Reset, and submit | Same as clicking button |
| Radio | Selects radio button |
| Checkbox | Marks check box and sets value to ON |

Method of button, checkbox, radio, reset, and submit.

# close

For a document object, closes the current output stream and forces its display. It also stops the browser icon animation and displays Done in the status bar.

For a window object, closes the current window. As with all window commands, the window object is assumed. For example:

```
window.close()
close()
self.close()
```

all close the current window. Method of document and window.

See clear, open, write, and writeln: METHODS.

# confirm

Displays a JavaScript confirmation dialog box with a message and buttons for OK and Cancel. Confirm returns a true if the user selects OK and false for Cancel. The following example loads a new window if the user presses OK:

```
if (confirm("Are you sure you want to enter.") {
    tourWindow = window.open("http:\\www.haunted.com\","hauntedhouse")
}
```

Method of window.

See alert and prompt: METHODS.

# cos

Returns the cosine of the argument. The angle's size must be expressed in radians. Method of Math.

See acos, asin, atan, sin, and tan: METHODS.

# escape*

Returns ASCII code of its argument based on the ISO Latin–1 character set in the form %xx, where xx is the ASCII code. It is not associated with any other object, but is actually part of the JavaScript language.

See unescape: METHODS.

# eval*

This built-in function takes a string or numeric expression as its argument. If a string, it attempts to convert it to a numeric expression. Eval then evaluates the expression and returns the value:

```
var x = 10
var y = 20
document.write(eval("x + y"))
```

This method can also be used to perform JavaScript commands included as part of a string, as in this example:

```
var doThis = "if (x==10) { alert("Your maximum has been reached") }
function checkMax () {
    x++;
    eval(doThis)
}
```

This can be useful when converting a date from a form (always a string) into a numerical expression or number.

## exp

Returns e (Euler's constant) to the power of the argument. Method of `Math`.

See `log` and `pow`: METHODS.

## fixed

Formats the calling string into a fixed-pitch font by encasing it in HTML `<tt>` tags. Method of `string`.

## floor

Returns the integer less than, or equal to, its argument. For example:

```
Math.floor(2.99)
```

returns a 2. Method of `Math`.

See `ceil`: METHODS.

## focus

Navigates to a specific `form` element and gives it focus. From that point, a value can be entered by JavaScript commands or the user can complete the entry. Method of `password`, `select`, `text`, and `textarea`.

See `blur` and `select`: METHODS.

## fontcolor

Formats the string object to a specific color expressed as a hexadecimal RGB triplet or a string literal, similar to using `<font color=color>`. Method of `string`.

## fontsize

Formats the string object to a specific font size: one of the seven defined sizes using an integer through the `<fontsize=size>` tag. If a string is passed, then the size is changed relative to the value set in the `<basefont>` tag. Method of `string`.

See `big` and `small`: METHODS.

## forward

Loads the next document on the URL history list. This method is the same as `history.go(1)`. Method of `history`.

See `back` and `go`: METHODS.

## getDate

Returns the day of the month as an integer between 1 and 31. Method of `Date`.

See `setDate`: METHODS.

## getDay

Returns the day of the week as an integer from zero (Sunday) to six (Saturday). There is no corresponding `setDay` method because the day is automatically computed when the date value is assigned. Method of `Date`.

## getHours

Returns the hour of the day in 24-hour format, from zero (midnight) to 23 (11 PM). Method of `Date`.

See `setHours`: METHODS.

## getMinutes

Returns the minutes as an integer from zero to 59. Method of `Date`.

See `setMinutes`: METHODS.

## getMonth

Returns the month of the year as an integer between zero (January) and 11 (December). Method of `Date`.

See `setMonth`: METHODS.

## getSeconds

Returns the seconds as an integer from zero to 59. Method of `Date`.

See `setSeconds`: METHODS.

## getTime

Returns an integer representing the current value of the `date` object. The value is the number of milliseconds since midnight, January 1, 1970 (known as The Epoch). This value can be used to compare the length of time between two date values.

For functions involving computation of dates, it is useful to define variables by giving the minutes, hours, and days in milliseconds:

```
var dayMillisec = 1000 * 60 * 60 * 24 //1,000 milliseconds x 60 sec x 60 min x 24 hrs
var hourMillisec = 1000 * 60 * 60 //1,000 milliseconds x 60 sec x 60 min
var minuteMillisec = 1000 * 60 //1,000 milliseconds x 60 sec
```

Method of `Date`.

See `setTime`: METHODS.

## getTimezoneOffset

Returns the difference in minutes between the client machine and Greenwich Mean Time. This value is a constant except for Daylight Savings Time. Method of `Date`.

## getYear

Returns the year of the `Date` object minus 1900. For example, 1996 is returned as `96`. Method of `Date`.

See `setYear`: METHODS.

## go

Loads a document specified in the history list relative to the current position on the list. If the value given to `go` is out of range (before the beginning of the history list, or after its end), the nearest valid value is used. Method of `history`.

See `back` and `forward`:METHODS.

## indexOf

Returns the location of a specific character or string, starting the search from a specific location. The first character of the string is at location zero and the last is at location `length-1`. The syntax is:

```
stringName.indexOf([character¦string], [startingPoint])
```

The `startingPoint` is zero by default. Method of `string`.

See `charAt` and `lastIndexof`:METHODS.

## italics

Formats a string object into italics by encasing it in an HTML `<I>` tag. Method of `string`. See `blink`, `bold`, and `strike`:METHODS.

## javaEnabled

Indicates whether Java is enabled on the client browser. Method of `navigator`.

See `appName`, `appCodeName`, and `userAgent`:PROPERTIES.

## *join*

A method that joins array elements into a continuous string, with each element divided by an optional delimiter. Opposite of the `string` method `split`. Method of `array`.

See `split`:METHODS.

## *lastIndexOf*

Returns the index of a character or string in a string object by looking backwards from the end of the string or from a user-specified index. Method of `string`.

See `charAt` and `indexOf`:METHODS.

App

B

## *link*

Creates a hypertext link to another URL by defining the `<href>` attribute and the text representing the link. Method of `string`.

See `anchor`: METHODS.

## *log*

Returns the natural logarithm (base e) of a positive numeric expression. An out-of-range number always gives an error. Method of `Math`.

See `exp` and `pow`:METHODS.

## *max*

Returns the greater of its two arguments. For example:

```
Math.max(1,100)
```

returns `100`. Method of `Math`.

See `min`: METHODS.

## *min*

Returns the lesser of its two arguments. Method of `Math`.

See `max`: METHODS.

## *open*

For a document, opens a stream to collect the output of `write` or `writeln` methods. If a document already exists in the target window, then the `open` method clears it. The stream is ended by using the `document.close()` method.

For a window, it opens a new browser window in a similar fashion to choosing New Window from the File menu. Using the URL argument, it loads a document into the new window; otherwise, the new window is blank. When used as part of an event handler, the form must include the `window` object; otherwise, the `document.open` method is assumed. Window features are defined by a comma-separated list of options with `=1` or `=yes` to enable and `=0` or `=no` to disable. Window features include toolbar, location, directories, status, menu bar, scroll bars, resizable, copy history, width, and height. Method of `document` and `window`.

See `clear`, `close`, `write`, and `writeln`:METHODS.

## parse

Takes a date string, such as `"Jan 11, 1996"`, and returns the number of milliseconds since midnight, Jan. 1, 1970. This function can be used to set date values based on string values. When passed a string containing a date, it returns the time value.

Because `parse` is a static function of `Date`, it is always used as `Date.parse()` rather than as a method of a created `Date` object. Method of `Date`.

See `UTC`: METHODS.

## parseFloat*

Parses a string argument and returns a floating-point number if the first character is a plus sign, minus sign, decimal point, exponent, or a numeral. If it encounters a character other than one of the valid choices after that point, it returns the value up to that location and ignores all succeeding characters. If the first character is not a valid character, `parseFloat` returns zero.

## parseInt*

Parses a string argument and returns an integer based on a specified radix or base. A radix of 10 interprets the string as a decimal number, while eight implies an octal number, and 16 a hexadecimal number.

Floating-point values are converted to integers. The rules for evaluating the string are identical to `parseFloat`.

See `parseFloat`: METHODS.

## pow

Returns the base argument raised to the exponent. Method of `Math`.

See `exp` and `log`: METHODS.

## prompt

Displays a prompt dialog box that accepts user input. If an initial value is not specified for `inputDefault`, the dialog box displays a blank value. Method of `window`.

See `alert` and `confirm`: METHODS.

## random

Returns a pseudo-random floating-point number between zero and 1. Method of `Math`.

## reload

Reloads the current window. Will force a document retrieval (instead of a conditional retrieval from cache) if argument passed is true—such as `location.reload(true)`. Method of `location`.

See `replace` (next method).

App
B

## replace

Current window location is replaced by new location. The previous location entry in the browser's history is removed and replaced with the new location. Useful when many transient pages are created but do not need to be seen again. Method of `location`.

See `reload` (previous method).

## reset

This method simulates a mouse click on a form's Reset button. Method of `form`.

See `onReset`: EVENT HANDLERS; `reset`: OBJECTS.

## reverse

This method reverses the order of elements in an array. The first element is now the last; the last element is now the first. Method of `array`.

## round

Returns the value of a floating-point argument rounded to the next highest integer if the decimal portion is greater than, or equal to, .5, or the next lowest integer, if it is less than .5. Method of `Math`.

## scroll

This method will scroll a window to coordinates passed as arguments. The coordinates are integers representing pixels. Method of `window`.

## select

Selects the input area of a specified form element. Used in conjunction with the `focus` method, JavaScript can highlight a field and position the cursor for user input. Method of `password`, `text`, and `textarea`.

See `blur` and `focus`: METHODS.

## setDate

Sets the day of the month. Method of `Date`.

See `getDate`: METHODS.

## setHours

Sets the hour for the current time. Method of `Date`.

See `getHours`: METHODS.

## setMinutes

Sets the minutes for the current time. Method of `Date`.

See `getMinutes`: METHODS.

## setMonth

Sets the month with an integer from zero (January) to 11 (December). Method of `Date`.

See `getMonth`: METHODS.

## setSeconds

Sets the seconds for the current time. Method of `Date`.

See `getSeconds`: METHODS.

## setTime

Sets the value of a `Date` object. Method of `Date`.

See `getTime`: METHODS.

## setTimeout*

Evaluates an expression after a specified amount of time, expressed in milliseconds. This is not repeated indefinitely. For example, setting a timeout to three seconds will evaluate the expression once after three seconds—not every three seconds. To call `setTimeout` recursively, reset the timeout as part of the function invoked by the method. Calling the function `startclock` in the following example sets a loop in motion that clears the timeout, displays the current time, and sets the timeout to redisplay the time in one second.

```
var timerID = null;
var timerRunning = false;
function stopclock () {
  if(timerRunning) cleartimeout(timerID);
  timerRunning=false;
}
function startclock () {
```

```
      stopclock();
      showtime();
}
function showtime () {
  var now = new Date();
  ...
  document.clock.face.value =   timeValue;
  timerID = setTimeout("showtime()",1000);
  timerRunning = true;
}
```

Method of window.

See clearTimeout: METHODS.

## setYear

Sets the year in the current date by using an integer representing the year, minus 1900. Years before 1970 are not currently permitted. Method of Date.

See getYear: METHODS.

## sin

Returns the sine of an argument. The argument is an angle expressed in radians and the returned value is from -1 to 1. Method of Math.

See acos, asin, atan, cos, and tan: METHODS.

## small

Formats a string object into a small font using the HTML <small> tag. Method of string.

See big and fontsize: METHODS.

## sort

A method that sorts elements in an array based on either a built-in or user-specified sorting algorithm. Method of array.

## split

Splits a string object into an array of strings, based on a delimiter passed as an argument. Opposite of the array method join. Method of string.

See join: METHODS.

## sqrt

Returns the square root of a positive numeric expression. If the argument's value is outside the range, the returned value is zero.

## strike

Formats a string object as strikeout text using the HTML `<strike>` tag. Method of `string`.

See `blink`, `bold`, and `italics`: METHODS.

## sub

Formats a string object into subscript text using the HTML `<sub>` tag. Method of `string`.

See `sup`: METHODS.

## submit

Performs the same action as clicking a submit button. Method of `form`.

See `submit`: OBJECTS; see `onSubmit`: EVENT HANDLERS.

## substring

Returns a subset of a string object based on two indexes. If the indexes are equal, an empty string is returned. Regardless of order, the substring is built from the smallest index to the largest. Method of `string`.

## sup

Formats a string object into superscript text using the HTML `<sup>` tag. Method of `string`.

See `sub`: METHODS.

## tan

Returns the tangent of an argument. The argument is an angle expressed in radians. Method of `Math`.

See `acos`, `asin`, `atan`, `cos`, and `sin`: METHODS.

## toGMTString

Converts a date object to a string using Internet Greenwich Mean Time (GMT) conventions. For example, if `today` is a date object:

```
today.toGMTString()
```

then the string `"Mon, 18 Dec 1995 17:28:35 GMT"` is returned. Actual formatting may vary from platform to platform. The time and date are based on the client's machine. Method of `Date`.

See `toLocaleString`: METHODS.

## toLocaleString

Converts a date object to a string using the local conventions, such as *mm/dd/yy hh:mm:ss*. Method of `Date`.

See `toGMTString`: METHODS.

## toLowerCase

Converts all characters in a string to lowercase. Method of `string`.

See `toUpperCase`: METHODS.

## toString

Converts an object to a string. In addition to working on the built-in `Date` and `location` objects, it will also work with user-defined objects. Method of `Date`, `location`.

## toUpperCase

Converts all characters in a string to uppercase. Method of `string`.

See `toLowerCase`:METHODS.

## unEscape *

Returns a character based on its ASCII value, expressed as a string in the format %xx where xx is a hexadecimal number between 0x0 and 0xFF.

See `escape`: METHODS.

## UTC

Returns the number of milliseconds for a date in Universal Coordinated Time (UTC) since midnight, January 1, 1970. `UTC` is a static method and is always used as `Date.UTC()`, not with a created `Date` object. Method of `Date`.

See `parse`: METHODS.

## write

Writes one or more lines to a document window and can include HTML tags and JavaScript expressions, including numeric, string, and logical values. The `write` method does not add a new line (`<br>` or `\n`) character to the end of the output. If called from an event handler, the current document is cleared if a new window is not created for the output. Method of `document`.

See `close`, `clear`, `open`, and `writeln`: METHODS.

## writeln

Writes one or more lines to a document window, followed by a new line character; can include HTML tags and JavaScript expressions, including numeric, string, and logical values. If called from an event handler, the current document is cleared if a new window is not created for the output. Method of document.

See close, clear, open, and write:METHODS.

# Event Handlers

Event handlers are where JavaScript gets its power. By looking for specific user actions, JavaScript can confirm or act on input immediately, without waiting for server intervention.

## onAbort

If the loading of an image is aborted by the user before it is complete, this event handler will be triggered. Event handler of image.

See onError and onLoad: EVENT HANDLERS.

## onBlur

Blurs occur when a select, text, or textarea field in a form, or when a window, loses focus. Event handler of select, text, textarea, and window.

See onChange and onFocus:EVENT HANDLERS.

## onChange

A change event happens when a select, text, or textarea element on a form is modified before losing focus. Event handler of select, text, and textarea.

See onBlur and onFocus:EVENT HANDLERS.

## onClick

Occurs when an object, such as a button or check box, is clicked. Event handler of button, checkbox, radio, link, reset, and submit.

## onError

Occurs when there is an error loading an image or document. Setting this to null turns off error checking, and assigning an error checking function will redirect errors to that function. Event handler of image, window.

## onFocus

A form element receives focus by tabbing to, or clicking, the input area with the mouse. Selecting within a field results in a `select` event. Event handler of `select`, `text`, and `textarea`.

See `onBlur` and `onChange`: EVENT HANDLERS.

## onLoad

A load event is created when the browser finishes loading a window or a frame within a `<frameset>` tag. Event handler of `window`.

See `onUnload`: EVENT HANDLERS.

**App**
**B**

## onMouseMove

A Microsoft-specific extension of the `onMouseOver` event. This form of the event permits the event handler to receive the x and y coordinates of the mouse at the time the event occurred, as well as the current state of the mouse button(s) and the shift key. Currently, this event is only implemented for ActiveX controls.

See `onMouseOver`: EVENT HANDLERS.

## onMouseOut

A `mouseout` event is triggered when the mouse leaves an area defined in an image map or a link. Event handler of `area` and `link`.

## onMouseOver

Occurs when the mouse pointer is placed over a `link` object. To function with the `status` or `defaultStatus` properties, the event handler must return `true`. Event handler of `link`.

## onReset

Occurs when a `reset` event occurs—when a user clicks the Reset button in a form. Event handler of `form`.

## onSelect

A `select` event is triggered by selecting some or all of the text in a `text` or `textarea` field. Event handler of `text` and `textarea`.

## onSubmit

Triggered by the user submitting a form. The event handler must return `true` to allow the form to be submitted to the server. Conversely, it returns `false` to block the form's submission. Event handler of `form`.

See `submit`: OBJECTS and METHODS.

## *onUnload*

Occurs when exiting a document. For proper operation, place the onUnload handler in the <body> or <frameset> tags. Event handler of window.

See onLoad: EVENT HANDLERS. ●

# JavaScript Commands
# and Grammar

**F**inding information on programming in JavaScript can be
challenging. With Netscape's and Microsoft's sites, online
tutorials, and examples, information seems to be everywhere but at your fingertips. Here is the information
you're looking for, all in one place, including statements,
operators, and color values. ■

# JavaScript Statements

The statements used to control program flow in JavaScript are similar to Java and C. A statement may span several lines if needed, or several statements may be placed on the same line. The important key to remember is that a semicolon must be placed between multiple statements on a single line. Since JavaScript is not strict in its formatting, you must provide the line breaks and indentation to make sure the code is readable and easy to understand later.

**break**   Terminates the current `for` or `while` loop and passes control to the first statement after the loop.

**comment**   Notes from the script author that are ignored by the interpreter. Single line comments are preceded by `//`. Multiple line comments begin with `/*` and end with `*/`. Do not use HTML comment delimiters (`<!--` and `-->`) with JavaScript code.

**continue**   Passes control to the condition in a `while` loop and to the `update` expression in a `for` loop.

**for**   Creates a loop with three optional expressions enclosed in parentheses and separated by semicolons, followed by a set of statements to be executed during the loop:

```
for( initialExpression; condition; updateExpression) {
statements...
}
```

The `initial` expression is used to initialize the counter variable, which can be a new variable declared with `var`. The `condition` expression is evaluated on each pass through the loop. If the condition is `true`, the loop statements are executed. The `update` expression is used to increment the counter variable.

**for...in**   Iterates a variable over all the properties of an object:

```
for (var vtmp in object) {
statements...
}
```

For each property, it executes the statement block with `vtmp` set to the current property.

**function**   Declares a JavaScript function with a name and parameters. To return a value, the function must include a `return` statement. A function definition cannot be nested within another function.

```
function name ([parameter] [...,parameter]) {
statements...
}
```

**if...else**   A conditional statement that executes the first set of statements if the condition is `true`, and the statements following the `else` if `false`. `If...else` statements can be nested to any level.

```
if (condition) {
statements...
} [else {
```

```
 statements...
}]
```

***return***   Specifies a value to be returned by a function.

```
return expression;
```

***var***   Declares a variable and optionally initializes it to a value. The scope of a variable is the current function or—when declared outside a function—the current document.

```
var variableName [=value] [..., variableName [=value]]
```

***while***   Repeats a loop while a conditional expression is true.

```
while (condition) {
statements...
}
```

***with***   Establishes a default object for a set of statements. Any property references without an object are assumed to use the default object.

```
with (object) {
statements...
}
```

This statement is especially useful when applied to the Math object for a set of calculations. For example:

```
with (Math) {
var Value1 = cos(angle);
var Value2 = sin(angle);
}
```

replaces:

```
{
var Value1 = Math.cos(angle);
var Value2 = Math.sin(angle);
}
```

# Operator Precedence

Precedence refers to the order in which compound operations are computed. Operators on the same level have equal precedence. Calculations are computed from left to right on all binary operations, beginning with the operators at the top of the list and working down.

| call, member | . | [ ] | ( ) | | |
|---|---|---|---|---|---|
| negation/increment | ++ | - - | ! | ~ | - |
| multiply/divide | * | / | % | | |
| addition/subtraction | + | - | | | |
| shift | << | >> | >>> | | |
| relational | < | > | <= | >= | |
| equality | == | != | | | |

App
C

| bitwise AND | & |  |
|---|---|---|
| bitwise XOR | ^ |  |
| bitwise OR | ¦ |  |
| logical AND | && |  |
| logical OR | ¦¦ |  |
| conditional | ?: |  |
| assignment | = | *op=* |
| comma | , |  |

# JavaScript Objects

JavaScript is an object-oriented language and, as such, includes a set of built-in objects to represent the HTML document, especially form elements. Built-in objects can be accessed by both the client and the server.

**String**   Contains a string of characters.

**Math**   Provides numerical constants and mathematical functions.

**Date**   Stores a date in the number of milliseconds since 1/1/1970, 00:00:00, and returns a date string in the format `"Thu, 11 Jan 1996 06:20:00 GMT"`.

**Array**   Holds an array of elements.

**Document**   The foundation object created with an HTML `<BODY>` tag and used to write other information to the page.

**Form**   An object for gathering and echoing data, created by HTML `<FORM>` tags.

**Window**   The highest precedence object accessible by JavaScript relating to the currently open browser window. New windows and frames can also be constructed.

**Area**   Defines an area of an image as an image map. When the user clicks the area, the area's hypertext reference is loaded into its target window.

**Function**   Specifies a string of JavaScript code to be compiled as a function.

**Image**   Reflects images such as those included by using the HTML `<IMG>` tag.

**N O T E**   The `Image` object is included by Netscape, but is not supported by Microsoft Internet Explorer at this time. ▨

# Reserved Words

The following words cannot be used as user objects or variables in coding JavaScript. Not all are currently in use by JavaScript—they are reserved for future use.

| | | |
|---|---|---|
| abstract | boolean | break |
| byte | case | catch |
| char | class | const |
| continue | default | do |
| double | else | extends |
| false | final | finally |
| float | for | function |
| goto | if | implements |
| import | in | instanceof |
| int | interface | long |
| native | new | null |
| package | private | protected |
| public | return | short |
| static | super | switch |
| synchronized | this | throw |
| throws | transient | true |
| try | var | void |
| while | with | |

# Color Values

Colors can be referenced in a variety of properties in two ways: by using the string literal, or an RGB hexadecimal triplet formed by combining the three color values. For example, aliceblue is represented as F0F8FF.

| Color/String Literal | Red | Green | Blue |
|---|---|---|---|
| aliceblue | F0 | F8 | FF |
| antiquewhite | FA | EB | D7 |
| aqua | 00 | FF | FF |
| aquamarine | 7F | FF | D4 |
| azure | F0 | FF | FF |
| beige | F5 | F5 | DC |
| bisque | FF | E4 | C4 |

*continues*

*continued*

| Color/String Literal | Red | Green | Blue |
| --- | --- | --- | --- |
| black | 00 | 00 | 00 |
| blanchedalmond | FF | EB | CD |
| blue | 00 | 00 | FF |
| blueviolet | 8A | 2B | E2 |
| brown | A5 | 2A | 2A |
| burlywood | DE | B8 | 87 |
| cadetblue | 5F | 9E | A0 |
| chartreuse | 7F | FF | A0 |
| chocolate | D2 | 69 | 1E |
| coral | FF | 7F | 50 |
| cornflowerblue | 64 | 95 | ED |
| cornsilk | FF | F8 | DC |
| crimson | DC | 14 | 3C |
| cyan | 00 | FF | FF |
| darkblue | 00 | 00 | 8B |
| darkcyan | 00 | 8B | 8B |
| darkgoldenrod | B8 | 86 | 0B |
| darkgray | A9 | A9 | A9 |
| darkgreen | 00 | 64 | 00 |
| darkkhaki | BD | B7 | 6B |
| darkmagenta | 8B | 00 | 8B |
| darkolivegreen | 55 | 6B | 2F |
| darkorange | FF | 8C | 00 |
| darkorchid | 99 | 32 | CC |
| darkred | 8B | 00 | 00 |
| darksalmon | E9 | 96 | 7A |
| darkseagreen | 8F | BC | 8F |
| darkslateblue | 48 | 3D | 8B |
| darkslategray | 2F | 4F | 4F |
| darkturquoise | 00 | CE | D1 |
| darkviolet | 94 | 00 | D3 |
| deeppink | FF | 14 | 93 |
| deepskyblue | 00 | BF | FF |

| Color/String Literal | Red | Green | Blue |
| --- | --- | --- | --- |
| dimgray | 69 | 69 | 69 |
| dodgerblue | 1E | 90 | FF |
| firebrick | B2 | 22 | 22 |
| floralwhite | FF | FA | F0 |
| forestgreen | 22 | 8B | 22 |
| fuchsia | FF | 00 | FF |
| gainsboro | DC | DC | DC |
| ghostwhite | F8 | F8 | FF |
| gold | FF | D7 | 00 |
| goldenrod | DA | A5 | 20 |
| gray | 80 | 80 | 80 |
| green | 00 | 80 | 00 |
| greenyellow | AD | FF | 2F |
| honeydew | F0 | FF | F0 |
| hotpink | FF | 69 | B4 |
| indianred | CD | 5C | 5C |
| indigo | 4B | 00 | 82 |
| ivory | FF | FF | F0 |
| khaki | F0 | E6 | 8C |
| lavender | E6 | E6 | FA |
| lavenderblush | FF | F0 | F5 |
| lawngreen | 7C | FC | 00 |
| lemonchiffon | FF | FA | CD |
| lightblue | AD | D8 | E6 |
| lightcoral | F0 | 80 | 80 |
| lightcyan | E0 | FF | FF |
| lightgoldenrodyellow | FA | FA | D2 |
| lightgreen | 90 | EE | 90 |
| lightgray | D3 | D3 | D3 |
| lightpink | FF | B6 | C1 |
| lightsalmon | FF | A0 | 7A |
| lightseagreen | 20 | B2 | AA |
| lightskyblue | 87 | CE | FA |
| lightslategray | 77 | 88 | 99 |

*continues*

App
C

*continued*

| Color/String Literal | Red | Green | Blue |
| --- | --- | --- | --- |
| lightsteelblue | B0 | C4 | DE |
| lightyellow | FF | FF | E0 |
| lime | 00 | FF | 00 |
| limegreen | 32 | CD | 32 |
| linen | FA | F0 | E6 |
| magenta | FF | 00 | FF |
| maroon | 80 | 00 | 00 |
| mediumaquamarine | 66 | CD | AA |
| mediumblue | 00 | 00 | CD |
| mediumorchid | BA | 55 | D3 |
| mediumpurple | 93 | 70 | DB |
| mediumseagreen | 3C | B3 | 71 |
| mediumslateblue | 7B | 68 | EE |
| mediumspringgreen | 00 | FA | 9A |
| mediumturquoise | 48 | D1 | CC |
| mediumvioletred | C7 | 15 | 85 |
| midnightblue | 19 | 19 | 70 |
| mintcream | F5 | FF | FA |
| mistyrose | FF | E4 | E1 |
| moccasin | FF | E4 | B5 |
| navajowhite | FF | DE | AD |
| navy | 00 | 00 | 80 |
| oldlace | FD | F5 | E6 |
| olive | 80 | 80 | 00 |
| olivedrab | 6B | 8E | 23 |
| orange | FF | A5 | 00 |
| orangered | FF | 45 | 00 |
| orchid | DA | 70 | D6 |
| palegoldenrod | EE | E8 | AA |
| palegreen | 98 | FB | 98 |
| paleturquoise | AF | EE | EE |
| palevioletred | DB | 70 | 93 |
| papayawhip | FF | EF | D5 |

| Color/String Literal | Red | Green | Blue |
|---|---|---|---|
| peachpuff | FF | DA | B9 |
| peru | CD | 85 | 3F |
| pink | FF | C0 | CB |
| plum | DD | A0 | DD |
| powderblue | B0 | E0 | E6 |
| purple | 80 | 00 | 80 |
| red | FF | 00 | 00 |
| rosybrown | BC | 8F | 8F |
| royalblue | 41 | 69 | E1 |
| saddlebrown | 8B | 45 | 13 |
| salmon | FA | 80 | 72 |
| sandybrown | F4 | A4 | 60 |
| seagreen | 2E | 8B | 57 |
| seashell | FF | F5 | EE |
| sienna | A0 | 52 | 2D |
| silver | C0 | C0 | C0 |
| skyblue | 87 | CE | EB |
| slateblue | 6A | 5A | CD |
| slategray | 70 | 80 | 90 |
| snow | FF | FA | FA |
| springgreen | 00 | FF | 7F |
| steelblue | 46 | 82 | B4 |
| tan | D2 | B4 | 8C |
| teal | 00 | 80 | 80 |
| thistle | D8 | BF | D8 |
| tomato | FF | 63 | 47 |
| turquoise | 40 | E0 | D0 |
| violet | EE | 82 | EE |
| wheat | F5 | DE | B3 |
| white | FF | FF | FF |
| whitesmoke | F5 | F5 | F5 |
| yellow | FF | FF | 00 |
| yellowgreen | 9A | CD | 32 |

App
C

# Error Messages

**C**ompiled languages such as C++ and Java report many programming defects to the programmer when they are compiled, but interpreted languages such as JavaScript don't get "compiled" until they are run. This means that certain errors may not show up until the user finds them at runtime.

This appendix lists the major errors that the JavaScript interpreter can report. Use this list as you code, and check it frequently as you test and debug your JavaScript programs. ▪

# Top Six Errors that New Programmers Encounter

This section explains the errors most new (and many experienced) JavaScript programmers are likely to see.

◼ `x is not defined`

If you fail to initialize a logical variable, it assumes a value of `null`, but if you use an uninitialized variable in a string or arithmetic expression, or if you try to call an undefined function, you'll get this runtime error.

If you're trying to call a function and JavaScript claims the function is not defined, make sure the function is defined in the `<HEAD>` section of the document. If you call the function before the browser loads it, you'll get the `not defined` error.

◼ `x has no property named y`

With this error, the interpreter seems to be telling you that you have referenced the *y* property of the object named *x*. In fact, this message could just as easily mean that the object named *x* does not exist.

In the following code snippet, the form named `"theForm"` is used before the browser has a chance to load the form. You'll get the message `"document.theForm has no property named name."`

```
<P><SCRIPT LANGUAGE="JavaScript">
alert(document.theForm.name.value);
</SCRIPT>

<FORM NAME="theForm">
<INPUT TYPE="text" NAME="name" VALUE="Default">
<INPUT TYPE="submit" NAME="submit" VALUE="Send">
</FORM>
```

If you reverse the order so that the form is defined before its field is used, you won't get an error—although the value is `undefined`. But if you attempt to reference a nonexistent form, you'll go back to the error `"document.theForm2 has no property named name."`

```
<FORM NAME="theForm">
<INPUT TYPE="text" NAME="name" VALUE="Default">
<INPUT TYPE="submit" NAME="submit" VALUE="Send">
</FORM>

<P><SCRIPT LANGUAGE="JavaScript">
alert(document.theForm2.name.value);
</SCRIPT>
```

◼ `Function.x has no property indexed by i`

You've attempted to use an array associated with a function. The function is defined, but the interpreter cannot find the array. For example, functions have a built-in array named `arguments`. Inside a function, you can refer to the arguments as, say, `arguments[3]`. Outside the function definition, you'll get this error message, because `arguments` is not defined.

■ `Unterminated string literal`

Carefully examine the line and string named in the error message. You're missing a quote somewhere. If you don't see it, check the line above the referenced line.

■ `test for equality == mistyped as assignment (=)?`

`Assuming equality test`

The equality operator is `==`. If you're not careful, you may sometimes type only a single equals sign—completely changing the meaning of the statement. JavaScript knows about this common error, warns you about it, and goes on to behave as though you had typed `==` in the first place. Go back and clean up the code so that this warning goes away.

■ `function does not always return a value`

Carefully trace through all paths of control through the function. Look at `if` statements and other conditionals. There's at least one way to get out of the function without passing through a `return` statement.

---

**CAUTION**

Some Netscape documentation warns against explicitly setting the properties of the `location` object: `hash`, `host`, `hostname`, `pathname`, `port`, `protocol`, and `search`. Netscape says that if you set these properties to a value that is not available, the interpreter will generate an error. Instead, they recommend you make all changes to `href`.

While Netscape seems to have fixed this problem in recent versions of Navigator, there may be a few Version 2 users around for a while. It's a good idea to set all of `href` when changing to a new location, instead of setting just one component.

App
D

---

# Other Runtime Errors You May See

This section lists errors that may show up at runtime as your code attempts to execute an illegal operation.

■ `x can't be set by assignment`

You can't set read-only properties.

■ `x can't be deleted`

You can't delete permanent objects; the latest versions of Navigator don't even try. If you try to replace a permanent object such as `location` with a new object, the existing object just takes on the value of the new object. Since this behavior is probably not what you want, your program won't work correctly, but it won't give you an error message.

■ `illegal array length x`

Integer array lengths are legal. The most frequent cause of this error is that you've inadvertently called for an array of negative length.

# Internal Errors and the Like

You may occasionally run into an error that announces it is an "Internal error." That's a good time to contact Netscape technical support. More frequently, you may cross some internal limit and get one of these errors:

- too much with and for-in statement nesting

  The nesting limits are undocumented but are quite generous. If you see this error and you don't have an unusually large number of nesting levels, report it to Netscape as an internal error.

- stack overflow in *x*

  Often, the cause of this error is excessive recursion. Look for places where your function calls itself, either directly or indirectly. Trace through the stopping condition to ensure that there really is an end to the recursion.

# Syntax Errors and Their Kin

These errors often indicate a typing error. The names are self-explanatory. Double-check the code carefully against the standard. Sometimes, just a single missing or extra character can trigger one of these errors.

Remember, too, to take these messages with a grain of salt. Often a syntax error is telling you that *something* is wrong, but the interpreter's parser is not powerful enough to tell you exactly *what*. For example, the line

```
myArray = new array[10];
```

generates a complaint that the semicolon is missing before the next statement. The problem is that the parser gets to the end of the string array and is expecting another statement. When it sees a left bracket instead, it gives up and complains that it didn't see the semicolon it expected. The following are common syntax errors you may encounter:

- illegal formal argument name *x*
- illegal radix

  The latest version of Navigator flywheels through radix errors in parseInt(). This practice makes it more important than ever to test thoroughly. Your application will put up fewer JavaScript Error dialog boxes, but its behavior may not be correct.

- missing exponent

  JavaScript doesn't always raise the error you'd expect, even when the code is wrong. For example,

  ```
  Math.pow(2,3)
  ```

  returns 8, but

  ```
  Math.pow(2)
  ```

  returns undefined is not a number.

- integer literal too large
- nested comment
- unterminated comment
- illegal character
- malformed floating point literal
- missing function name
- missing formal parameter
- missing { before function body
- missing } after function body
- missing ( before condition
- missing ) after condition
- missing ( after for
- missing } in compound statement
- missing variable name
- missing operator in expression
- missing ] in index expression
- missing ) after argument list
- missing ) after parenthetical
- missing operand in expression
- syntax error
- missing name in expression
- missing ( before formal parameters
- missing ) after formal parameters
- missing ; after for-loop initializer
- missing ; after for-loop condition
- missing ) after for-loop control
- missing semicolon before statement
- missing ; in conditional expression
- missing ) after constructor argument list

# Errors Caused by Incorrect Program Design

If you get one of these errors and don't understand why, go back and reread the chapters on JavaScript syntax. Once you're comfortable in the language, these errors most often are found when you're maintaining code and have moved things around incorrectly. Some common errors are:

- break used outside a loop
- continue used outside a loop
- return used outside a function
- illegal variable initialization
- identifier is a reserved word
- function defined inside a function
- *x* is not a function
- *x* is not a number
- *x* is not an object
- *x* can't be used in a with statement

▶ **See** "Control Structures," **p. 45**, which explains that many of these errors have to do with incorrect use of control structures.

# LiveConnect Errors

Netscape's technology to connect JavaScript to Java is not without its risks. If you attempt to do something to a Java applet that doesn't make sense (such as accessing a Java field that doesn't exist), you'll get a JavaScript error.

If you get LiveConnect errors that you can't explain, try one of the simple applets that Netscape includes as examples. If none of your applets work, double-check that the Java classes are properly installed. (They're in a .zip file—don't unzip them!) You should be particularly careful to check your Java installation if you get errors like can't call Java from JavaScript or couldn't load class JavaScript.

> **N O T E**  Get a simple LiveConnect example from Netscape's Web site at **http://
> home.netscape.com/eng/mozilla/3.0/handbook/javascript/livecon.htm#996824** and
> use it to verify that your Java libraries are installed correctly. On this page, scroll down until you see
> "Example 2: Flashing color text applet." Below that header you should see "Hello, world" in large letters
> flashing different colors. Use the text field and button to change the text, verifying that LiveConnect is
> functioning correctly on your machine. ▦

Note that the error messages that mention uncaught Java exceptions aren't JavaScript errors at all. Java includes a powerful mechanism that enables the Java programmer to handle a variety of error conditions. If the Java program raises an exception (called "throwing" an exception) that the programmer *doesn't* handle (called "catching" the exception), the exception comes out to the end user. If you're not doing something obviously wrong with the applet, your best course is to contact the Java programmer who wrote the applet.

> **CAUTION**
>
> If a Java applet attempts to run a page's JavaScript, and you, as the HTML author, haven't set MAYSCRIPT in the <APPLET> tag, Java throws an exception. The Java programmer should catch this exception and put up an appropriate message to the user, but if they forget, you'll get an uncaught exception error. If you're expecting the applet to be able to control your HTML page through JavaScript, be sure to include MAYSCRIPT.

▶ **See** "JavaScript and Java Applets," **p. 392**, for more information on LiveConnect, including information about the MAYSCRIPT attribute.

- can't access field *x*
- can't access Java field *x*
- can't instantiate Java class
- illegal access to Java class
- Java slots have no properties
- no field with name "*x*"
- can't call Java from JavaScript
- couldn't load class JavaScript
- *x* doesn't refer to any Java value
- no Java *x* field found with name *y*
- can't convert Java object *x* to function
- can't convert Java array element to JavaScript datum
- Java array index *x* out of range
- can't set length of a Java array
- illegal assignment to Java array element
- Java array doesn't have a field named "*x*"
- can't convert Java object to JavaScript object

- unknown Java signature character '*x*'
- can't convert Java return value with signature *x*
- no Java *x.y* method matching JavaScript arguments (*z*)
- no Java method matching arguments
- illegal access to Java constructor
- uncaught Java exception *x* ("*y*")
- uncaught Java exception of class *x*
- can't load class *x* from JavaScript

# VRMLScript

**W**hen Netscape created JavaScript (originally LiveScript), it opened the door to a much broader range of interactivity on the client side of the Web. Static Web pages now have a lot more interactivity, as well as the capability to be customized to an individual's preferences.

Another breakthrough for the Web has been VRML, a language for specifying objects in a 3-D space. VRML was made to be accessed via the Internet—usually with a Web browser. Because of its basis on the Web, it is natural for VRML to take advantage of the browsers' scripting ability. With VRMLScript, 3-D objects not only can come alive with movement, but can also interact with the viewer in interesting ways.

VRMLScript was written by Chris Marrin and Jim Kent of SGI to meet the need of an easy-to-learn scripting language for VRML. Given that JavaScript already provides much of what they needed, they made VRML a subset of the JavaScript language by using built-in data types.

This appendix will give you a quick overview of VRMLScript. To get the most complete reference, you should visit **http://vrml.sgi.com/moving-worlds/spec/vrmlscript.html**. If you are not already familiar with VRML 2.0 (the current version as of this writing), you should visit **http://vrml.sgi.com/develop/**. This discussion assumes that you are at least somewhat familiar with VRML. ■

# VRMLScript Basics

VRMLScript performs a very similar role in VRML as JavaScript does in HTML. Objects in VRML consist of *nodes*. Each node consists of data that specifies some aspect of the VRML world. VRMLScript scripts are contained within nodes called *scripts*, which can contain fields that specify that script's behavior. Scripts can be contained within the VRML code (inline) or can be referenced via an URL. If you simply want to reference a VRMLScript script in your VRML code, you can write:

```
Script { url "http://foo.bar.com/theScript.vs"}
```

You also can use the equivalent of the javaScript: protocol, called vrmlscript:, to place VRMLScript functions directly in the URL. The URL field may also contain—like many other fields in VRML—multiple URLs. If the first URL fails to load, then the second is used, and so on. Here is an example:

```
Script {
url [
"http://www.script.com/foo.vs",
"vrmlscript: function thisfunct() { somecode here }"
]
}
```

If you create scripts that are separate files from the VRML, you must name them something like this:

```
someName.vs
```

where the file always ends in "vs" and you configure your server to serve this file with a MIME type of:

```
application/x-vrmlscript
```

Basically, VRMLScript contains the functionality of the first version of JavaScript released—which was implemented in Netscape 2.0 (and later in MSIE 3.0).

## Script Example:

Here is an example of a VRMLScript embedded in a VRML file:

```
Script {
    field    SFFloat aField  0
    field    SFVec3f aVector 0 0 0
    eventOut SFInt32 anEventOut
    eventIn  SFBool  event

    url "vrmlscript:
        function event(value, timestamp) {
            if (aField == 1.5) {
                a = true;       // 'a' contains a boolean
            }

            if (a) {            // this is NOT the same 'a' as above!
                value = 5;      // ERROR,
```

```
                                // can't assign to function parameter!
            }

            aField = anEventOut; // SFInt32 converted to SFFloat
            b = aField;          // 'b' contains a number
            b = anEventOut;      // 'b' now contains a different number
            aField = aVector;    // ERROR,
                                 //  can't assign SFVec3f to SFFloat!
            s = 'Two\nLines';    // 's' contains a String

        }"
}
```

As you can see from the example, VRMLScript enables you to fully access and manipulate other aspects of VRML.

# VRMLScript Objects:

VRMLScript uses the same statements and expressions as JavaScript. Where it differs from JavaScript is that it contains special objects and methods that enable you to directly reference special VRML variables. Following is a quick summary of the VRMLScript objects.

## *Browser* Object

This object enables scripts to get and set browser information, such as the version of the browser, the current URL, the current frame rate, and so on.

## *Math* Object

This object enables scripts to perform mathematical operations and is very similar to JavaScript 1.0 's Math object.

## *SFColor* Object

This object corresponds to the SFColor field in VRML. Colors are defined by their rgb values.

## *SFImage* Object

This corresponds to the SFImage field. It enables you to set the dimensions of the image, and to contain the actual image data.

## *SFNode* Object

This object corresponds to the *SFNode* object.

## *SFRotation* Object

This object enables you to create and set the attributes of a SFRotation field.

## *String* Object

This object is similar to the JavaScript `string` object. It contains methods of string manipulation such as `lastIndexOf()` and `toLowerCase()`.

## *SFVec2f* Object

This object pertains to the vector definition field of the same name. You can perform manipulations such as the dot product of two vectors, normalize it to a specific length, and more.

## *MFColor* Object

Corresponding to the `MFColor` field, this object enables you to store `SFColor` objects in a 1-D array.

## *MFFloat* Object

Similar to the `MFColor` object—it enables you to store `SFFloat` objects in an array.

## *MFInt32* Object

This object stores `SFInt32` objects in a 1-D array. Each element can be retrieved or replaced.

## *MFNode* Object

This object stores a set of `SFNode` objects in an array. You can get or set attributes of each element via the array.

## *MFRotation* Object

This object stores a series of `SFRotation` objects in an array.

## *MFString* Object

This object stores a series of `SFString` objects in an array.

## *MFVec2f* Object

As with most of the "MF" objects, this object stores `SFVec2f` objects into an accessible array.

## *MFVec3f* Object

Same as the previous object, but instead stores `SFVec3f` objects.

## *VrmlMatrix* Object

This object enables you to perform manipulations on 4×4 matrices.

# VRMLScript References

**http://vrml.sgi.com/moving-worlds/spec/vrmlscript.html**—to find the online specification for VRMLScript.

**http://vrml.sgi.com/develop/**—to find more information about VRML.

**http://webspace.sgi.com/cosmoplayer/**—Cosmo Player, a VRML plug-in for Netscape and MSIE that supports the VRMLScript specification.

**http://webspace.sgi.com/tools/**—more VRML authoring tools.

**http://reality.sgi.com/cmarrin/**—home page of Chris Marrin, one of the co-authors of the VRMLScript Reference.

**http://www.3dsite.com/3dsite/cgi/VRML-index.html**—more information about VRML and scripting.

App
E

# Index

## Symbols

# Complete and Return this Card
# for a *FREE* Computer Book Catalog

Thank you for purchasing this book! You have purchased a superior computer book written expressly for your needs. To continue to provide the kind of up-to-date, pertinent coverage you've come to expect from us, we need to hear from you. Please take a minute to complete and return this self-addressed, postage-paid form. In return, we'll send you a free catalog of all our computer books on topics ranging from word processing to programming and the internet.

Mrs. ☐   Ms. ☐   Dr. ☐

me (first) [ ][ ][ ][ ][ ][ ][ ][ ][ ][ ][ ]   (M.I.) [ ]   (last) [ ][ ][ ][ ][ ][ ][ ][ ][ ][ ][ ][ ][ ][ ][ ][ ]

dress [ ][ ][ ][ ][ ][ ][ ][ ][ ][ ][ ][ ][ ][ ][ ][ ][ ][ ][ ][ ][ ][ ][ ][ ][ ][ ][ ][ ]
[ ][ ][ ][ ][ ][ ][ ][ ][ ][ ][ ][ ][ ][ ][ ][ ][ ][ ][ ][ ][ ][ ][ ][ ][ ][ ][ ][ ]

y [ ][ ][ ][ ][ ][ ][ ][ ][ ][ ][ ][ ][ ][ ][ ]   State [ ][ ]   Zip [ ][ ][ ][ ][ ] [ ][ ][ ][ ]

one [ ][ ][ ]  [ ][ ][ ]  [ ][ ][ ][ ]   Fax [ ][ ][ ]  [ ][ ][ ][ ]

mpany Name [ ][ ][ ][ ][ ][ ][ ][ ][ ][ ][ ][ ][ ][ ][ ][ ][ ][ ][ ][ ][ ][ ][ ][ ][ ]

mail address [ ][ ][ ][ ][ ][ ][ ][ ][ ][ ][ ][ ][ ][ ][ ][ ][ ][ ][ ][ ][ ][ ][ ][ ][ ]

**Please check at least (3) influencing factors for purchasing this book.**

nt or back cover information on book ....................... ☐
ecial approach to the content ..................................... ☐
mpleteness of content ................................................ ☐
thor's reputation ....................................................... ☐
blisher's reputation ................................................... ☐
ok cover design or layout .......................................... ☐
lex or table of contents of book ................................. ☐
ce of book ................................................................. ☐
ecial effects, graphics, illustrations ........................... ☐
her (Please specify): _____ ☐

**How did you first learn about this book?**

w in Macmillan Computer Publishing catalog ........... ☐
commended by store personnel .................................. ☐
w the book on bookshelf at store ............................... ☐
commended by a friend .............................................. ☐
ceived advertisement in the mail ............................... ☐
w an advertisement in: _____ ☐
ad book review in: _____ ☐
her (Please specify): _____ ☐

**How many computer books have you purchased in the last six months?**

is book only ....... ☐   3 to 5 books ..................... ☐
ooks ................... ☐   More than 5 ..................... ☐

**4. Where did you purchase this book?**

Bookstore ....................................................... ☐
Computer Store ............................................... ☐
Consumer Electronics Store ............................. ☐
Department Store ............................................ ☐
Office Club ...................................................... ☐
Warehouse Club ............................................... ☐
Mail Order ...................................................... ☐
Direct from Publisher ...................................... ☐
Internet site .................................................... ☐
Other (Please specify): _____ ☐

**5. How long have you been using a computer?**

☐ Less than 6 months   ☐ 6 months to a year
☐ 1 to 3 years           ☐ More than 3 years

**6. What is your level of experience with personal computers and with the subject of this book?**

| | With PCs | With subject of book |
|---|---|---|
| New | ☐ | ☐ |
| Casual | ☐ | ☐ |
| Accomplished | ☐ | ☐ |
| Expert | ☐ | ☐ |

Source Code ISBN: 0-7897-0000-0

## 7. Which of the following best describes your job title?

Administrative Assistant ................................ ☐
Coordinator ................................................. ☐
Manager/Supervisor .................................... ☐
Director ...................................................... ☐
Vice President ............................................. ☐
President/CEO/COO .................................... ☐
Lawyer/Doctor/Medical Professional .......... ☐
Teacher/Educator/Trainer ............................ ☐
Engineer/Technician .................................... ☐
Consultant ................................................... ☐
Not employed/Student/Retired ..................... ☐
Other (Please specify): _____ ☐

## 8. Which of the following best describes the area of the company your job title falls under?

Accounting ................................................. ☐
Engineering ................................................. ☐
Manufacturing ............................................. ☐
Operations .................................................. ☐
Marketing ................................................... ☐
Sales ........................................................... ☐
Other (Please specify): _____ ☐

*Comments*: _____
_____
_____

## 9. What is your age?

Under 20 ..................................................... ☐
21-29 .......................................................... ☐
30-39 .......................................................... ☐
40-49 .......................................................... ☐
50-59 .......................................................... ☐
60-over ....................................................... ☐

## 10. Are you:

Male ........................................................... ☐
Female ........................................................ ☐

## 11. Which computer publications do you read regularly? (Please list)

_____
_____
_____
_____
_____
_____
_____

Fold here and scotch-tape to ma

NE8LIN
90